CW01376645

COMPUTER ARCHITECTURE AND VAX ASSEMBLY LANGUAGE PROGRAMMING

COMPUTER ARCHITECTURE AND VAX ASSEMBLY LANGUAGE PROGRAMMING

James E. Brink
Pacific Lutheran University

Richard J. Spillman
Pacific Lutheran University

The Benjamin/Cummings Publishing Company, Inc.
Menlo Park, California • Reading, Massachusetts • Don Mills, Ontario
Wokingham, U.K. • Amsterdam • Sydney • Singapore • Tokyo • Madrid
Bogota • Santiago • San Juan

Sponsoring Editor: Alan Apt
Production: Merry Finley, Kate St. Clair
Copy Editor: Russell Fuller
Cover and Consulting Designer: Hal Lockwood
Illustration and Composition: Graphic Typesetting Service

The basic text of this book was designed using the Modular Design System, as developed by Wendy Earl and Design Office Bruce Kortebein.

Cover photo © Michel Tcherevkoff/The Image Bank

Copyright © 1987 by The Benjamin/Cummings Publishing Company, Inc.

All rights reserved. No part of this publication may be reproduced, stored in a retrieval system, or transmitted, in any form or by any means, electronic, mechanical, photocopying, recording, or otherwise, without the prior written permission of the publisher. Printed in the United States of America. Published simultaneously in Canada.

The programs presented in this book have been included for their instructional value. They have been tested with care but are not guaranteed for any particular purpose. The publisher does not offer any warranties or representations, nor does it accept any liabilities with respect to the programs.

Benjamin/Cummings Publishing Company has made every attempt to supply trademark information about company names and products mentioned in this book. The trademarks listed at the end of the book were derived from various sources.

Library of Congress Cataloging in Publication Data

Brink, James E.
   Computer architecture and VAX assembly language programming.
   Includes index.
   1. Computer architecture. 2. VAX—11 (Computer)—
Programming. 3. Assembler language (Computer programming language) I. Spillman, Richard J. II. Title.
QA76.9.A73B75   1986   005.2'45   86-17205
ISBN 0-8053-8920-2

ABCDEFGHIJK-AL-89876

The Benjamin/Cummings Publishing Company, Inc.
2727 Sand Hill Road
Menlo Park, California 94025

CONTENTS

Preface for Instructors — xv

Preface for Students — xix

PART 1 — INTRODUCTION TO ASSEMBLY LANGUAGE — 1

CHAPTER 1
Basic Computer Architecture — 3

1.1 Introduction to Assembly Language and Computer Architecture — 4
1.2 Basic Building Blocks of Computer Design — 7
1.3 Bus Structures — 10
1.4 Integer Numbers — 15
    Representation of Integer in Various Bases — 16
    Conversion of Integers Between Different Bases — 17
    Conversions Between Binary and Either Octal or Hexadecimal — 19
    Binary Arithmetic — 20
    Representation of Negative Numbers — 22
    Two's Complement Calculations in Hexadecimal — 25
    Representation of Binary Integers on the VAX — 26
1.5 Introduction to Floating Point — 28
    Conversion of Numbers with Fractional Parts — 28
    Floating-Point Representations — 30
    Summary — 33
    Exercises — 33

CHAPTER 2
Essentials of Assembly Language — 39

- 2.1 Instruction Format — 41
  - Instruction Components — 41
  - Instruction Formats — 42
  - VAX Instruction Formats — 45
  - VAX Instructions — 45
    - Clear — 47
    - Move — 48
    - Add — 49
    - Subtract — 50
    - Multiplication — 51
    - Division — 51
  - Example — 52
- 2.2 Addressing Modes — 53
  - The General Register Modes — 54
    - Register Direct Mode — 54
    - Register Deferred Mode — 55
  - The Program Counter Modes — 58
    - Relative Mode — 58
    - Immediate Mode — 61
- 2.3 VAX Macro Instructions — 62
- 2.4 Example Programs — 65
  - Summary — 67
  - Exercises — 67

CHAPTER 3
VAX Assembly Language — 71

- 3.1 Addressing Modes Revisited — 71
  - Additional General Register Modes — 71
    - Autoincrement Mode — 72
    - Autoincrement Deferred Mode — 74
    - Autodecrement Mode — 76
    - Displacement Mode — 76
    - Displacement Deferred Mode — 79
    - Literal Mode — 80
  - Additional Program Counter Modes — 81
    - Relative Deferred Mode — 82
    - Absolute Mode — 83
  - Index Mode Addressing — 83
  - A Summary of Addressing Opcodes — 85
- 3.2 VAX Assembly Instructions Revisited — 87
  - Branching Instructions — 87

Processor Status Word (PSW)	88
Conditional Branch Instructions	88
Compare	90
Test	90
Conditional Branching Examples	91
Unconditional Branch	92
Example Program	93
Another Example	95
Summary	96
Exercises	97

PART 2
THE CENTRAL PROCESSING UNIT — 101

CHAPTER 4
CPU Software — 103

4.1 Basic CPU Architecture	104
4.2 CPU Operation	107
Example 4.1	109
Example 4.2	110
Example 4.3	111
Example 4.4	111
4.3 Implementing Complete Instructions	112
Example 4.5	114
Example 4.6	115
Example 4.7	116
Reducing Memory Access Time	118
Reduced Instruction Set Computers	118
Summary	119
Exercises	120

CHAPTER 5
The ALU's Structure and Operation — 127

5.1 Computer Addition and Subtraction	128
Some Boolean Algebra	128
Logic Gates	129
Binary Adders	131
Fast Adders	134

Addition of Signed Numbers	137
Subtraction and Negation	139
Multiple-Word Addition and Subtraction	141
5.2 Multiplication and Division	143
Multiplication of Unsigned Integers	143
Multiplication of Signed Integers and the Booth Algorithm	146
Division	151
The VAX's Extended Multiply and Divide Instructions	154
5.3 Shift Instructions	157
5.4 Bit Manipulation	160
5.5 Coding an Integer Multiplication Algorithm	165
5.6 Floating-Point Arithmetic	167
Review of Floating-Point Notations	168
Calculations in Floating Point	169
Summary	171
Exercises	172

CHAPTER 6
Microprogramming 179

6.1 What Is Microprogramming?	180
Nature of the Control Signals	183
Grouping of Control Signals	186
6.2 Microprogramming Examples	187
6.3 Microprogram Branching	197
Conditional Branch Implementation	203
Summary	207
Exercises	207

PART 3
ADVANCED ASSEMBLY LANGUAGE 213

CHAPTER 7
Stacks, Subroutines, and Procedures 215

7.1 Stacks	216
Processing Stacks with Autoincrement and Autodecrement	216
Special Stack Instructions	218
An Example Using a Stack	222
Assembly Time Calculations	222
The .PSECT Directive	222

7.2 Introduction to Subroutines and Procedures	224
7.3 Subroutines	227
7.4 Procedures	233
The Argument List	233
The Entry Mask	234
The Call Frame	235
Operation of the Procedure Call Instruction	236
An Example Using Procedure Calls	236
Some Comments	238
7.5 Functions	241
7.6 Separately Assembled Subprograms and the Linker	243
Writing Separate Program Units	244
An Example of a Separately Compiled Subprogram	246
The Linker	247
7.7 Linking High-Level Languages with Macro	250
VAX FORTRAN	252
VAX Pascal	253
VAX C	254
Some Comments	255
7.8 Recursive Subprograms	256
Summary	261
Exercises	262

CHAPTER 8

Macros 269

8.1 Introduction to Macros	270
8.2 Alternate Formats for Arguments	274
Local Labels	274
Default Values	275
Keyword Arguments	276
8.3 An Example Using Macros with Argument Lists	277
8.4 Some Advanced Features	283
Argument Concatenation	283
Passing Symbolic Constants for Numerical Values	283
Passing Character Strings	284
Determining the Number of Positional Arguments	285
Finding the Length of a Character String	286
8.5 Conditional Assembly and Repetition	286
Conditional Assembly	286
Repeat Blocks	288
An Example	290
Summary	290
Exercises	291

CHAPTER 9

Character Strings, Packed Decimal, and Introduction to I/O — 299

9.1 Character Strings	300
9.2 Introduction to Character String Instructions and I/O	303
Two Character String Instructions	303
Two Procedures for I/O	306
An Example	308
9.3 More Character String Instructions	311
9.4 A Program Using Character Strings and I/O	316
Variable-Length Input	317
An Example	318
9.5 Decimal Numbers	320
9.6 Packed Decimal Instructions	323
9.7 Numerical Conversions and I/O	325
Conversions Between Binary Data Types	326
Conversions Involving Packed Decimal	328
Output Procedures	329
Summary	337
Exercises	338

PART 4
ADVANCED COMPUTER ARCHITECTURE — 345

CHAPTER 10

Memory Structure — 347

10.1 Memory Devices	348
10.2 Memory Organization	350
10.3 Cache Memory	353
10.4 Mapping Functions	355
Direct Mapping	355
Associative Mapping	357
Block-Set Associative Mapping	358
10.5 Virtual Memory	359
VAX Virtual Memory Structure	362
Summary	364
Exercises	365

CHAPTER 11
The I/O System — 369

11.1 Addressing I/O Devices	371
11.2 Data Transfer	372
Program-Controlled I/O	374
Direct Memory Access	375
I/O Channel	376
11.3 Interrupt-Driven I/O	377
Device Identification	378
Polling Method	378
Vector Method	378
Simultaneous Interrupt Requests	379
Priority	380
Interrupt Acknowledge Daisy Chain	380
Priority Arbitration	380
Mixed Approach	381
11.4 Queue I/O	382
System Services	384
An Example Using Queue I/O	385
A More Sophisticated Queue I/O Request	392
11.5 I/O Using RMS	393
Defining Files and Records	394
Executable RMS Macros	397
An Example Using RMS Macros	401
11.6 Advanced I/O Devices	406
Summary	409
Exercises	410

CHAPTER 12
Computer Communications — 417

12.1 Remote I/O Communications	417
RS-232C Standard	422
12.2 Communication Network Architecture	423
Communication Topology	424
A Complete Interconnection Network	425
A Distributed Control Loop	425
A Global Bus Network	426
A Star Network	427
Ethernet	427
12.3 Communication Protocols	428
12.4 Packet Switching	430
DECnet Example	431

Contents

12.5 Error Control	432
Error Detection	432
Error Correction	433
Generalized Parity Check Code (Hamming Code)	434
Checksum Codes	436
Summary	436
Exercises	437

PART 5
ALTERNATIVE ARCHITECTURES   439

CHAPTER 13
Microprocessors   441

13.1 Microprocessor History	441
13.2 Microprocessor Characteristics	442
Microprocessor Construction	442
General Microprocessor Architecture	445
13.3 The Motorola Family	446
The M6800	446
The M68000	456
13.4 The Intel Family	460
The 8080	461
The 8086	466
Summary	468
Exercises	469

CHAPTER 14
Large System Architecture   473

14.1 Architecture Classification	474
14.2 Pipeline Structures	476
Pipeline Analysis	477
The TI ASC	481
14.3 Array Structures	482
Complete Interconnection Network	483
Permutation Networks	485
14.4 Multiprocessors	487
14.5 The CRAY-1	491
Summary	492
Exercises	493

CHAPTER 15
Fault-Tolerant Computer Architecture — 497
- 15.1 Reliability Measures — 498
- 15.2 Hardware Redundancy — 499
  - Static Redundancy — 500
  - Dynamic Redundancy — 505
  - Hybrid Redundancy — 505
  - Summary — 506
  - Exercises — 507

Appendixes
- A. Alphabetical List of VAX Instructions — 509
- B. VAX Instructions in Numerical Order — 524
- C. ASCII Table — 527
- D. Preparing and Running MACRO Programs Under VMS — 529
  - D.1 File Types — 529
  - D.2 Developing MACRO Programs on the VAX — 530
  - D.3 An Assembly Listing — 533
- E. Using the Symbolic Debugger — 536
  - E.1 Preparing to Use the Debugger — 537
  - E.2 Some Debugger Commands — 538
  - E.3 An Example Using the Symbolic Debugger — 543
  - E.4 The Screen Mode — 546
  - E.5 The Keypad on VT100 and VT220 Terminals — 554
- F. Input/Output Macros — 556

Index — 567

PREFACE FOR INSTRUCTORS

This book had its beginning in the frustration that both authors experienced while trying to teach a course in assembly language and computer architecture to sophomore and junior computer science majors. There were excellent texts available that covered assembly language for several different machines, but they covered the architecture of the machines in a single chapter or less. In addition, equally outstanding texts covered the details of the architecture of different computers but devoted only a single chapter, if that, to software issues.

From the nature of these textbooks, we felt that perhaps we were teaching two different subjects in one course and would either have to abandon the course or require the students to purchase two texts and try to weave them together in the lectures. Neither seemed an acceptable alternative. We realized that, in order to learn assembly language well, students had to understand the architectural features that interact directly with the assembly commands. On the other hand, a working knowledge of assembly language allows students to manipulate directly many of the features of an architecture, thereby providing a tool for in-depth analysis of computer architecture. Despite the nature of available texts, it seemed to us that no two subjects were more closely related than these two.

Consequently, we decided to write a text that covered both assembly language and computer architecture in enough detail so that both subjects could be taught from a single book. Our goal was to organize the topics in a flexible manner so that, by selecting among the 15 chapters, instructors could customize a computer architecture/assembly language course to meet their specific needs. To assist in the customizing process, we have suggested three possible courses at the end of this preface.

The level of the text assumes that students have taken at least one language course. While a course in data structures or digital logic would be helpful, neither is necessary for students to understand the material presented in this text.

There are several unique features of this text besides its complete coverage of assembly language and computer architecture.

1. The book includes dozens of example assembly language programs, all of which (except for the first few programs, which were intentionally left incomplete) have been tested on the VAX. As a result, you may want to encourage your students to try to run several of the examples as they begin to explore the structure of assembly language.
2. Even the chapters that are primarily concerned with computer architecture cover assembly language commands relevant to the architectural issues in the chapter. In addition, most computer architecture chapters have some assembly language exercises.
3. The book covers the architecture of all the major components of a computer system, including the CPU, the ALU, the memory unit, I/O units, and the special features of microprocessors, mainframes, and highly fault-tolerant systems.
4. The book provides significant coverage of the linkage of assembly language to high-level languages such as FORTRAN, Pascal, and C.
5. The book offers several options for I/O including the use of the symbolic debugger (Appendix E), special I/O macros (Appendix F), I/O procedures (Chapter 9), and calls from high-level language programs handling I/O (Chapter 7). When we teach this course, we use the symbolic debugger for I/O during the early part of the class, because it provides easy access to data values and, more importantly, because use of the debugger becomes a habit for the students even when better I/O procedures are made available.
6. Most of the text assumes that your VAX is running under VMS, but the *Instructor's Guide* contains a discussion of the UNIX operating system and the differences between VMS and UNIX assembly languages.

Possible Course Structures

This text could be used effectively in several related courses. For example, in a pure assembly language course in which the architectural concepts are not as important as providing a student with a working knowledge of the full power of the VAX assembly language, the following chapters might be used:

Chapter 1: Basic Computer Architecture
Chapter 2: Essentials of Assembly Language
Chapter 3: VAX Assembly Language
Chapter 5: The ALU's Structure and Operation (In chapter 5 you would only cover the bit manipulation instructions.)
Chapter 7: Stacks, Subroutines, and Procedures
Chapter 8: Macros
Chapter 9: Character Strings, Packed Decimal, and Introduction to I/O
Chapter 11: The I/O System

On the other hand, a pure computer architecture course, in which the study of the structure and operation of a computer system is more important than providing assembly language programming skills, could be organized around the following chapters:

Chapter 1: Basic Computer Architecture
Chapter 2: Essentials of Assembly Language (This chapter may be optional.)
Chapter 4: CPU Structure
Chapter 5: The ALU's Structure and Operation
Chapter 6: Microprogramming
Chapter 10: Memory Structure
Chapter 13: Microprocessors
Chapter 14: Large System Architecture
Selected topics from
Chapter 11: The I/O System
Chapter 12: Computer Communications
Chapter 15: Fault-Tolerant Computing

The course we teach at Pacific Lutheran University is more of a mixed assembly language/computer architecture course. It includes the following chapters:

Chapter 1: Basic Computer Architecture
Chapter 2: Essentials of Assembly Language
Chapter 3: VAX Assembly Language
Chapter 4: CPU Structure
Chapter 5: The ALU's Structure and Operation
Chapter 7: Stacks, Subroutines, and Procedures
Chapter 8: Macros
Chapter 10: Memory Structure
Selected topics in Chapters 6, 9, and 11 to 15.

Acknowledgments

Many people have helped us in the preparation of this text. Over a period of two years, Pacific Lutheran University students served as guinea pigs, using preliminary versions. Their suggestions, corrections, comments, and patience have been greatly appreciated. Ed Harter offered encouraging comments after teaching from a draft version of the text in one of his classes. We wish to thank our institution's Department of Mathematics and Computer Science (Larry Edison, chair) and Computer Center (particularly Paul Rothi, system manager) for their support and encouragement. Marty Falkner, Montana State University, G. W. Grosline, Virginia Polytechnical Institute, especially Jean-Loup Baer, University of Washington, and James McKim, University of Hartford, provided critical but helpful reviews that resulted in substantial improvements in the text. We want to thank Alan Apt and the staff of Benjamin/Cummings and Bookman Productions, who provided guidance and skillfully converted our manuscript into the finished book. Finally, we wish to thank our families for their patience and understanding during preparation of this text.

James E. Brink
Richard J. Spillman

PREFACE FOR STUDENTS

When starting a new course, students often have a number of questions. For example, what is the course about? What are they expected to know before taking the course? What things can they do to maximize their learning (or grade, as the case may be)? While we cannot answer these types of questions for your particular class, we would like to provide some general answers that will apply to many using this book.

If your class if typical, you will spend part of the time learning how to write assembly language programs for a VAX. Yet this text covers more than just a new programming language. Learning how computers really operate and discovering some of the issues in their design will be the most important goal in many classes. A knowledge of assembly language is an important component in a complete understanding of these topics but not an end in itself.

While the prerequisites of classes using this book will vary, we assume that you know a high-level language, such as Pascal or FORTRAN, and have learned good program development and documentation skills. You will find these skills to be extremely important. Although assembly language does not permit true structured programming, careful attention to your program's structure is required. Assembly language operates at the computer's architectural level and, hence, introduces an additional layer of complications to program design. We strongly urge that you follow good programming practices, even if they are not a required part of your course. We are confident that you will generally find that the more time you spend organizing, planning and documenting your programs, the less time it will take to get them running.

It may be helpful if you have had at least one other computer science class beyond your introduction to a high-level language. Courses such as data structures and digitial logic are helpful but are not required to understand the material in this text.

What can you do to maximize your learning? We encourage you to read the text and work several problems at the end of each chapter. Avoid the tendency to ignore nonprogramming problems, because such problems are often designed to help you clarify your thinking about the material in the text. If your class covers Chapter 3, we urge you to spend some time on Exercise 3.9, which asks you to write a summary of the addressing modes available on the VAX. We could have provided this synopsis for you, but the students who used preliminary copies of this text told us not to do so. They found that the hour or two they spend condensing all the information about addressing modes to one page helped them a lot more than scanning someone else's summary would have.

We encourage you to spend some time learning how to read computer manuals. Some exercises in this book are marked "Manual Search." They ask you to look up the details about certain instructions or topics. The VAX's machine language instructions are described in detail in the *VAX-11 Architecture Handbook* and in the *VAX MACRO and Instruction Set Reference Manual*. The second manual also describes the other components of MACRO, the assembler supplied with VAX/VMX. You might find the manuals for the editor, command language, and high-level languages helpful. For advanced topics, see the following references.*

VAX/VMS Symbolic Debugger Reference Manual
VAX/VMS Run-Time Library Routines Reference Manual
Introduction to VAX/VMS System Routines
VAX/VMS System Services Reference Manual
VAX/VMS I/O User's Reference Manual, Part I
VAX Record Management Services Reference Manual

Some students are surprised to find that input and output are significant challenges to assembly language programmers. This topic is covered in some detail in Chapter 11. Before you get to that point, your instructor may suggest one or more of the following alternatives to get output: the symbolic debugger (Appendix E), supplied I/O macros (Appendix F), procedures (Chapter 9), or calls to your assembly language procedures from high-level language programs that handle the I/O (Chapter 7). Because there are several ways to get I/O, programs in Chapters 2 through 8 do not contain any I/O statements. It is assumed that you will either use the debugger, which lets you examine the values of the variables, or add calls to the I/O macros listed in Appendix F.

We conclude with a few words about this book. It is somewhat unusual in that it attempts to give VAX assembly language and an introduc-

---

*All of these manuals are published by Digital Equipment Corp., Maynard, MA. The *VAX-11 Architecture Handbook* was published in 1981; the others were published in 1984.

tion to computer architecture equal weight in their presentations. Many classes using this text will be biased toward one or the other of these topics, depending on the curriculum of the particular school. Thus, this text allows choosing and reordering topics as needed. You may have a personal interest in some topics omitted in your class. We hope that you will find this book allows you to explore such subjects on your own.

COMPUTER ARCHITECTURE AND VAX ASSEMBLY LANGUAGE PROGRAMMING

PART 1

INTRODUCTION TO ASSEMBLY LANGUAGE

CHAPTER 1
Basic Computer Architecture

CHAPTER 2
Essentials of Assembly Language

CHAPTER 3
VAX Assembly Language

CHAPTER CONTENTS

1.1 INTRODUCTION TO ASSEMBLY LANGUAGE AND COMPUTER ARCHITECTURE

1.2 BASIC BUILDING BLOCKS OF COMPUTER DESIGN

1.3 BUS STRUCTURES

1.4 INTEGER NUMBERS

Representation of Integers in Various Bases
Conversion of Integers Between Different Bases
Conversions Between Binary and Either Octal or Hexadecimal
Binary Arithmetic
Representation of Negative Numbers
Two's Complement Calculations in Hexadecimal
Representation of Binary Integers on the VAX

1.5 INTRODUCTION TO FLOATING POINT

Conversion of Numbers with Fractional Parts
Floating-Point Representations

SUMMARY

EXERCISES

CHAPTER 1

Basic Computer Architecture

In recent years an ever increasing number of people have become computer users. In fact many people find it impossible to avoid computers as they carry out their daily routine. However, while computer usage is becoming a nearly universal requirement for living in the modern world, the level of understanding that people need for using computers varies greatly. The required knowledge level depends on the way the computer is used and the available support for the required applications. It will be useful to look at some of these levels of understanding in order to better appreciate the purpose of this book.

Many people regularly use equipment or appliances ranging from microwave ovens to automobiles to vending machines that contain built-in microprocessors. Users of such items may not even be aware that they contain microcomputers and probably do not really care.

Many others rely on a computer as a major tool in their work. The advent of the microcomputer has encouraged many people to learn how to use word processing or spreadsheet programs to increase their abilities and improve their efficiency. These persons fully realize that they are using a computer but depend upon others to design the equipment and provide the programs needed for their applications. Their goal is to carry out their normal work more effectively, not to become computer experts.

Some computer users have learned a high-level language and write programs to meet their needs. This level of use requires knowledge of the language, the understanding of algorithms, and the art of programming. But programmers may not need to understand exactly how a computer carries out the instructions they program into it. In fact one goal of a high-level language such as FORTRAN or Pascal is to achieve independence from the exact computer the program is run on. Ideally a FORTRAN 77 program that calculates the average of 50 numbers on an IBM

370 will run just as well on a PDP-11 or Data General computer. Most users in this group are aware that their source program must be translated from the high-level language in which it is written into the machine language of the particular computer they are using before the computer can execute it. However, they are not particularly interested in the details of the resulting machine language version.

Finally, there is a smaller group of users who are interested in the actual operation of computers. They may just be curious, or they may be trying to carry out operations that are difficult or impossible in the context of a particular high-level language. They may need to achieve efficiency in execution speed or memory usage beyond what is possible in a high-level language. They may be working on a new computer for which a high-level language is not yet available or may be writing a compiler for a high-level language. They may even be designing a computer system. In each of these cases their knowledge of the computer must be much deeper than that needed to design algorithms and write programs. They need to understand the computer's inner operation at a level far beyond that needed by the other groups.

This book is intended for readers who can already program and who need or want a thorough understanding of a computer's operation. They may need to know the assembly language and architecture of the VAX family of computers from Digital Equipment Corporation (DEC). They may want an overview of computer architecture in general so that they can effectively compare the advantages and disadvantages of various computers and be prepared for future changes in the computer industry.

1.1 Introduction to Assembly Language and Computer Architecture

In this section we will explore the concepts of assembly language and computer architecture and then outline the goals of this book.

You may already understand the relationship between machine and assembly languages. A computer's **machine language** consists of the number codes that can be interpreted as instructions by the computer's hardware. Before a program can be executed by a computer, it must be translated into the computer's machine language. This language is computer dependent and varies from model to model of computer. For example, on a VAX the sequence

```
0467 9F 0453 9F C0
```

means "add the integer at location 453 to the integer at location 467." (This number code is expressed in hexadecimal notation; the characters

C and F are the hexadecimal representations of the digits 12 and 15, respectively.) The same sequence may mean something entirely different or nothing at all on another computer.

Assembly language is a symbolic code that allows mnemonics for machine language instruction codes and symbolic names for memory locations. This language is closely related to machine language but allows the use of symbols instead of number codes for instructions. For example, an add instruction might be expressed as

```
ADD   Value, Sum
```

in an assembly language. While this code is still not as clear as the Pascal statement

```
Sum := Sum + Value
```

it is much easier to understand than the corresponding machine language version.

Just as a high-level language program must be translated into the computer's machine language, an assembly language program must be converted to machine language before it can be executed by the machine. This is done by a program called an assembler. In addition to translating the assembly language version of instructions directly into their machine language equivalent, it can recognize some commands (called **directives**) that guide the assembler in carrying out its task. The assembler supplied by Digital Equipment Corporation for the VAX as part of the VMS (Virtual Memory System) operating system is called **MACRO** (named after a special feature that will be discussed in Chapter 8). VAX computers using the UNIX operating system (originally developed by Bell Laboratories) use a different assembler called **as**. This assembler is also included as part of some of the UNIX-like operating systems and emulators available for the VAX. Unfortunately, MACRO and "as" are not completely compatible with each other, even though both languages are translated into the same machine language.

Because of their close relationship with machine languages, assembly languages are also machine dependent. It is normally necessary to learn a new assembly language when you want to use a new computer.

This book uses the MACRO assembly language for DEC's VAX computers. DEC has used this assembly language for a family of computers ranging from microcomputers to superminicomputers to newer higher-speed models that all share a common machine language. Additional models are expected to appear in the future. This allows you to apply your knowledge of the MACRO assembly language to a range of computers. However, you may someday need to use a different assembly language for the VAX or you may eventually be interested in other types of computers. Hence you should be careful to look for the generalities of assembly language as well as the details concerning MACRO.

While many readers already have a feeling for assembly languages, fewer will understand the term **computer architecture**. Part of the difficulty with this term is that different authors define it somewhat differently. On the first encounter with the term, a person will undoubtedly try to reconcile the expression with the more familiar architecture of homes and buildings. Fortunately, there are some good comparisons. A building's architect must consider such issues as function, usability, cost, and reliability in its design as well as the more obvious issues of size, shape, and appearance. While computer architects are seldom concerned with the physical appearance of a computer being designed, they must consider its function, usability, cost, and reliability as well as its "appearance" to assembly language programmers.

There are several different views of computer architecture. The hardware expert may look at the hardware relationships as computer architecture. For example, the type, speed, and interconnection of memory chips used may be an important issue. The software expert may be more interested in the machine's assembly language and the function of the registers in the central processing unit (CPU). DEC seems to understand the term in this context. While discussing the VAX family of computers, they give the following definition in the *VAX Architecture Handbook*: "Architecture is the collection of attributes common to all family members, attributes that guarantee that all software runs without change on all family members. Particularly pertinent are the instruction set, the memory management algorithms, and certain other aspects of the design that help define contexts and processes."*

Although this definition is helpful, a less machine-dependent one is desirable. We will assume that computer architecture is "the interface between the software and the hardware, the abstraction of the computer as seen by the assembly language programmer and the compiler-writer." This definition is consistent with DEC's idea of architecture, as the various VAX computers appear identical to the programmer despite being different in such areas as memory capacity, speed, and bus structure.

Though we will spend most of our time at the interface between hardware and software, we will sometimes move to either side of the boundary as required to discuss related issues.

What is the purpose of this book? Certainly an important goal is to introduce assembly language, in particular, the MACRO assembly language for the VAX. However, a more important goal is to introduce the concept of computer architecture. The VAX provides an example of traditional **von Neumann architecture**. In the last few chapters, however, we will look at other examples of computer architecture to provide comparisons and alternatives.

VAX Architecture Handbook. Maynard, Mass.: Digital Equipment Corporation, 1981, p. 2. Copyright, Digital Equipment Corporation, 1981. All rights reserved. Reprinted by permission.

In the remainder of this chapter we will look at some basic issues of computer architecture that must be understood before an assembly language can be introduced in the second chapter. These include the basic structural building blocks used in computer design, the interconnection of these components, and number representations used by computers. This is simply an overview. The topics will be studied in more detail later in the book.

1.2 Basic Building Blocks of Computer Design

High-level language programmers find it useful to have a simple model of an idealized computer even though high-level languages are designed to hide the structural differences between various computers. Assembly language programmers must have a more precise model of the particular computer they are using because the architectural features play an important role in their coding. The architectural details are so important that we will devote five chapters to a study of the basic computer building blocks introduced in this section.

In the mid-1940s John von Neumann suggested the concept of the stored program computer and the use of binary arithmetic. While there has been an increasing amount of experimentation with other designs, the von Neumann architecture is still the basis of the vast majority of modern computers. Thus far, most improvements in computers have been breakthroughs in hardware technology and in design variations rather than major revolutions in the basic architecture itself.

Our simplified model of a typical computer is composed of five basic blocks: input, output, memory, the arithmetic and logic unit (ALU), and the control unit. These are shown in Figure 1.1.

The **central processing unit (CPU)** contains the **arithmetic and logic unit (ALU)** and the **control unit**. The construction of this unit is the most important factor in both the computer's appearance to the assembly language programmer and the overall power of the computer.

The ALU carries out the arithmetic functions of the computer. It contains the hardware that processes such instructions as addition and subtraction, and it may contain special hardware for multiplication and division. Alternatively, repeated additions or subtractions may be used to carry out these operations. The trade-off between speed and cost determines the actual capabilities of this unit. Sophisticated hardware simplifies programming a particular computer. Simpler hardware cuts costs but increases the burden on the assembly language programmer. The ALU also carries out logical operations such as "and" and "or" and aids in the process of answering such questions as "Is $X < Y$?" or "Is $A = 8$?"

The control unit is the "brain" of the computer. Its job is to determine what instruction is to be processed, interpret the instruction, and then

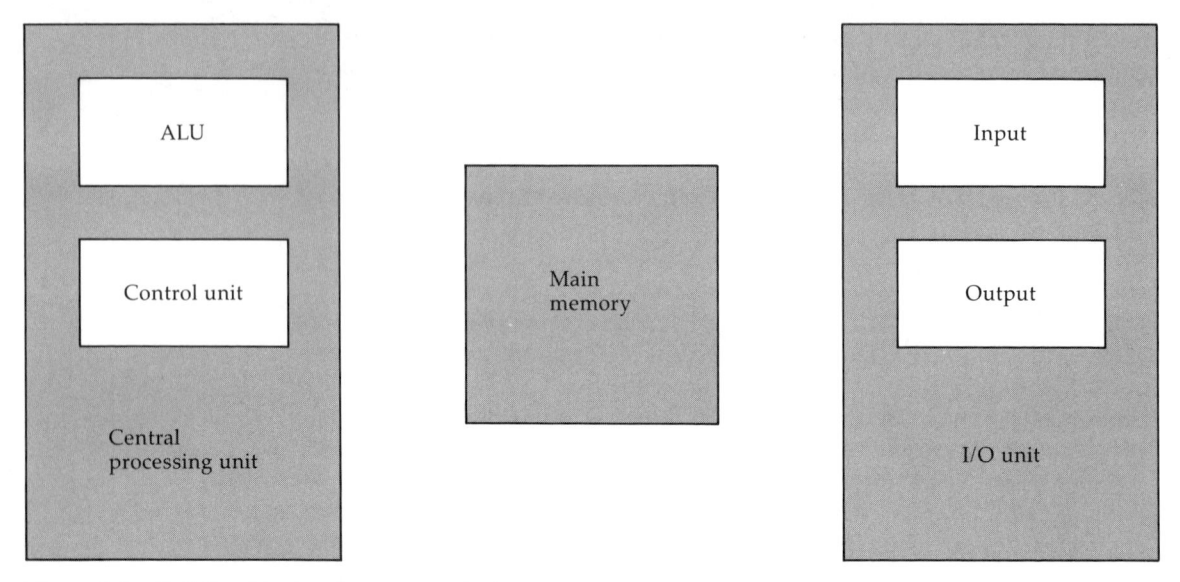

Figure 1.1 Building blocks of computer design

coordinate the various parts of the computer in order to carry out the instruction.

The computer, under the direction of the control unit, continually executes the following **instruction execution cycle**, which enables the computer to fulfill its duties.

1. Determine the address in memory of the next instruction to be processed.
2. Fetch the instruction from memory and then decode it to determine what is to be done.
3. Fetch any operands (that is, specified information or data) from main memory.
4. Carry out the instruction.
5. If required, store the results back in memory at the specified location.
6. Return to step 1.

In order to carry out its operations, the CPU contains some high-speed storage locations called **registers**. Some of these registers have a special purpose. For example, the **instruction register (IR)** holds the instruction being processed, and the **program counter (PC)** contains the address of the next instruction to be processed. Another special-purpose register, the **processor status register (PSR)**, contains the status of the current process. Some of the information stored in this register indicates if the result of the last calculation was 0 or negative. One or more registers, called **accumulators**, are used to store intermediate values generated by the ALU. Sometimes there are several registers called **general-purpose registers**, some of which may serve as accumulators. The advantage of having general-purpose registers is that information can be retrieved from or stored in them much faster than from main memory. Some CPUs have other types of registers that are designed to increase the computer's speed and simplify the job of writing assembly language programs and compilers. The CPU will usually have additional registers that are necessary to carry out its work but are hidden from the programmer. We have already mentioned one hidden register, the instruction register.

The **main** or **primary memory unit** is used to store information and instructions while they are being used by a program running on the computer. Many devices have been used for main memory over the years, but modern computers now use integrated circuit chips. Two general types of memory cells are used. Memory that can be both read from and written into is called **random access memory (RAM)**, which reflects the fact that all memory cells can be accessed in the same amount of time. Most semiconductor RAM forgets its contents whenever its electrical power supply is turned off. Another type of memory chip, called **read only memory (ROM)** is used for permanent program and data storage. ROM can be accessed randomly just like RAM, but its contents cannot be changed and it does not forget when the power is turned off. ROM is especially popular in microcomputers, where it is often used to hold parts of the operating system and possibly an interpreter for a language like BASIC so that these programs are immediately available when the computer is turned on.

Main memory is divided into cells numbered 0, 1, 2, . . . , . These numbers are called memory addresses. A cell's **address** is specified in machine language when information is stored into or retrieved from the cell.

The basic memory cell on many computers, including the VAX, holds one byte or 8 bits. Such machines are called **byte-addressable** or **byte-oriented machines**. Other computers have a larger storage unit, containing from 12 (PDP-8) to 60 (CDC 6600) bits per cell. Their storage unit is called a **word**, and such machines are called **word-addressable** or **word-oriented machines**.

The time that a computer needs to retrieve or fetch information from memory is called **memory access time**. This time is typically between 0.1 and 2 microseconds. Memory speed contributes significantly to the overall speed of a computer.

As shown in Figure 1.1, the input and output units are combined in the **input/output unit**, normally referred to as the **I/O unit**. This unit connects the computer with devices such as printers, terminals, magnetic disks, and magnetic tape drives that the computer uses to communicate with the external world. This information must be transmitted to and from the computer using some coding system that both the computer and the I/O devices understand.

In early computers it was often possible to make a distinction between the input and output units. The card reader was an input and the printer was an output unit. However, today devices such as terminals, disk drives, and tape drives serve dual roles. Consequently, the roles of input and output have tended to merge into a single unit.

Many computers have provisions for adding I/O components in piecemeal fashion. For example, a so-called DZ controller board is often used to connect up to eight terminals to a DEC PDP-11 or VAX-11 computer. Additional controller boards are needed if more terminals are used. Other controller boards are used to support other types of devices. This type of arrangement offers a great deal of flexibility in allowing a particular installation to meet the specific communication needs of its users.

We will now look briefly at how these concepts are implemented on the VAX. The VAX is a byte-addressable machine so that it is convenient to process individual characters while manipulating character strings. However, many instructions are designed to process larger units of information such as 16-bit **words** or 32-bit **longwords**. These longer information units are addressed by the location of the lowest number byte contained in that unit. Memory addresses are 32 bits long, sufficient for an extremely large number of memory cells. Since such a large memory would be overly expensive, the VAX uses a **virtual memory** concept, which allows the programmer to think that the computer has more main memory than is actually installed within the machine. The computer uses disk space to supplement main memory when users demand more memory space than is available.

The VAX CPU has 16 so-called general registers in addition to the instruction register and processor status register. The first 12 of these registers are simply numbered, R0, R1, . . . , R11. But the last 4 are reserved for special purposes. For example, the register numbered R15 serves as the program counter and is called the PC.

The VAX's design illustrates just one of the various ways the von Neumann architecture can be adapted to provide a particular set of features when it is implemented in a computer. Moreover, the different VAX models demonstrate that there are several ways to implement a particular architecture depending upon the cost/speed trade-off desired for a particular machine.

1.3 Bus Structures

In the previous section we looked at the building blocks of a basic computer. In this section we will look at the bus structure that interconnects the various blocks, allowing them to communicate with each other. This topic can be overlooked by many assembly language programmers, but it is important for those who get involved in designing low-level I/O routines called device drivers. In general, the smaller the computer and more primitive its operating system, the more likely that the assembly language programmer must consider its bus structure since the operating system is less apt to hide the computer's hardware features.

The different functional units of a computer are connected by communication lines called buses. In simplest form a **bus** is a set of wires used to carry information in the form of electrical signals between the different units of the computer. The information that must be moved between the various units includes the actual data, addresses for that data, and control signals sent between the control unit and the other units outside the CPU.

In order to move data quickly between the various units, the data bus is capable of transferring several bits at once. Many microcomputer chips, such as the 8080, 6800, and 6502, use a data bus that is designed to transmit 8 bits (one byte) at a time. Hence, on these computers, the bus uses eight wires for data transfer. The bus on more powerful computers may carry a larger number of bits. Popular data bus sizes include 12 (DEC's PDP-8), 16 (PDP-11), 32 (VAX 11/780, IBM 370/155), 36 (PDP-10), and 60 (CDC 6600) bits. Because computers must move a great deal of information between memory and the CPU, computers with wide buses are usually faster than similar computers with narrow buses. The bus width is important because it determines the **word length** of the computer. In general, a computer with an 8-bit bus is considered an 8-bit machine, a computer with a 16-bit bus is considered a 16-bit machine, and so on. The VAX 11/750 and 11/780 are considered 32-bit machines because of their bus design.

We should point out that this terminology is not universally accepted. Some people use the size of the accumulator registers in the CPU as the size of the machine, while others use the width of the data paths connecting the CPU registers. On the VAX 11/780 and many other computers, the bus size, the register size, and the width of the register interconnections are identical, so there is no problem. However, some microcomputers have wider registers than buses, which leads to some confusion. For example, Intel, which designed the 8088 microprocessor chip, refers to it as an 8-bit processor chip because it uses an 8-bit data bus to distinguish it from the otherwise nearly identical 8086 chip, which uses a 16-bit bus. However, many of the companies using the 8088 in their microcomputer refer to it as a 16-bit computer because the chip has a 16-bit internal architecture in the CPU and they want prospective customers to know that their computer is more powerful than microcomputers with chips having both an 8-bit bus and 8-bit registers. Still others refer to the chip as an 8/16-bit microprocessor to reflect both its bus size and the register size. Even DEC makes such hybrid machines. The MicroVAXes use 16-bit data buses even though their registers are 32 bits wide like the other VAX models. It will be interesting to see which terminology wins out.

We will discuss the portions of the bus that carry memory addresses and control signals later in the text as we discuss the various computer components in more detail.

A computer manufacturer can choose from among several different bus structures when designing a computer. Some computers have a single bus that is used to interconnect the various units as shown in Figure 1.2. This structure has several advantages compared to the double-bus structure that will be discussed next. It is relatively cheap because only a single bus needs to be included in the machine, so it is commonly used on microcomputers and minicomputers. This structure is relatively flexible because the various units can be modified and expanded without disturbing the other units. The CPU can transfer data between main memory and the I/O units using the same instructions that it uses to communicate with memory. Thus it is possible to add or replace I/O components, even unanticipated ones, by providing appropriate **device controllers** that are electronically compatible with the bus. If desired, intelligent controllers can be used to move data directly between main memory and the I/O units without disturbing the CPU. The primary disadvantage of this structure is that the bus often limits the speed of the whole computer. This single resource must be used for all data transfers between the various units, but only one piece of data can be moved at a time. For example, while the CPU is sending data to memory, the I/O unit cannot send data to the CPU. It must wait until the bus is available.

In order to solve this problem, some computers have a two-bus organization. Two possibilities for this structure are shown in Figure 1.3. These structures increase both the computer's speed and cost. Method A allows the simultaneous use of the memory and I/O buses. Special machine instructions are usually needed for I/O operations. This method makes it difficult to move data directly between main memory and the I/O unit. Such transfers are often highly desirable for moving large quantities of data quickly. Computers using this bus structure often need extra hardware to provide a direct link between the I/O units and memory. Thus this arrangement is rarely used in the simple form shown in the figure. While Method B provides for direct access between I/O and memory, it does not have a direct data path between the CPU and the I/O unit.

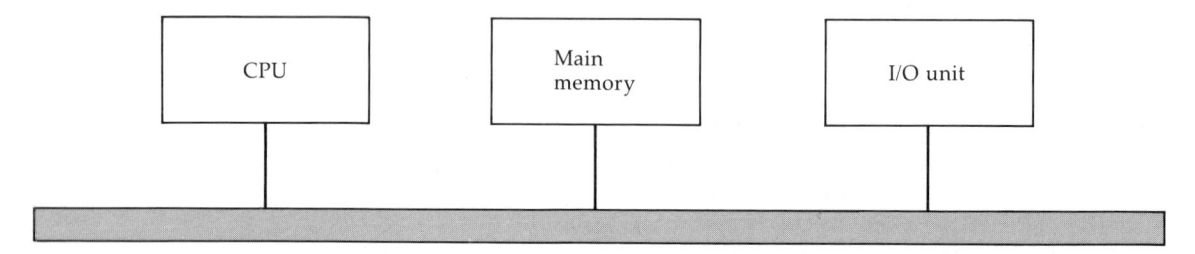

Figure 1.2 A single-bus computer

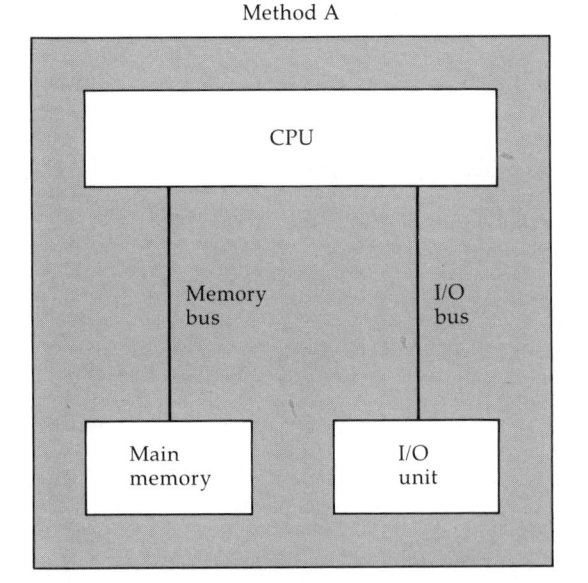

Figure 1.3 Two-bus computer structures

Consequently, it requires an I/O controller to manage the I/O. This controller, however, relieves the CPU of the task of handling routine I/O operations and increases overall computer speed.

Several variations of the basic bus structures can be found on real computers. For example, the bus structure of a VAX 11/780 and 11/785 is shown in Figure 1.4.

Logically, the 11/780 and 11/785 utilize a single-bus arrangement. The bus, called the **synchronous backplane interconnect (SBI)**, connects the CPU, main memory, and (via the adaptors) the I/O units. Instead of attaching the I/O units directly to the SBI, they are connected to one of two types of I/O buses. These I/O buses are only 16-bit buses because external devices rarely work with larger units of data. The **Massbus** is a high-speed bus typically used for disk or tape drives. Though the **Unibus** was originally designed as the primary bus of DEC's PDP-11 minicomputers, its use is normally restricted to slower devices such as terminals and printers on a VAX 11/780. It was included in the VAX to make it easy to attach many of the numerous PDP-11 I/O devices to the newer machine. In fact, because it can support disk and tape drives, it provides the only I/O connections on some VAX 11/750 configurations. It is interesting that although the VAX 11/750 allows the use of both the Massbus and Unibus, it does not have an SBI; instead it uses a **memory interface** to connect the CPU to main memory.

Graphically, the bus arrangement of the newer VAX 8200 is quite similar to that of the VAX 11/780 as shown in Figure 1.4. However, the

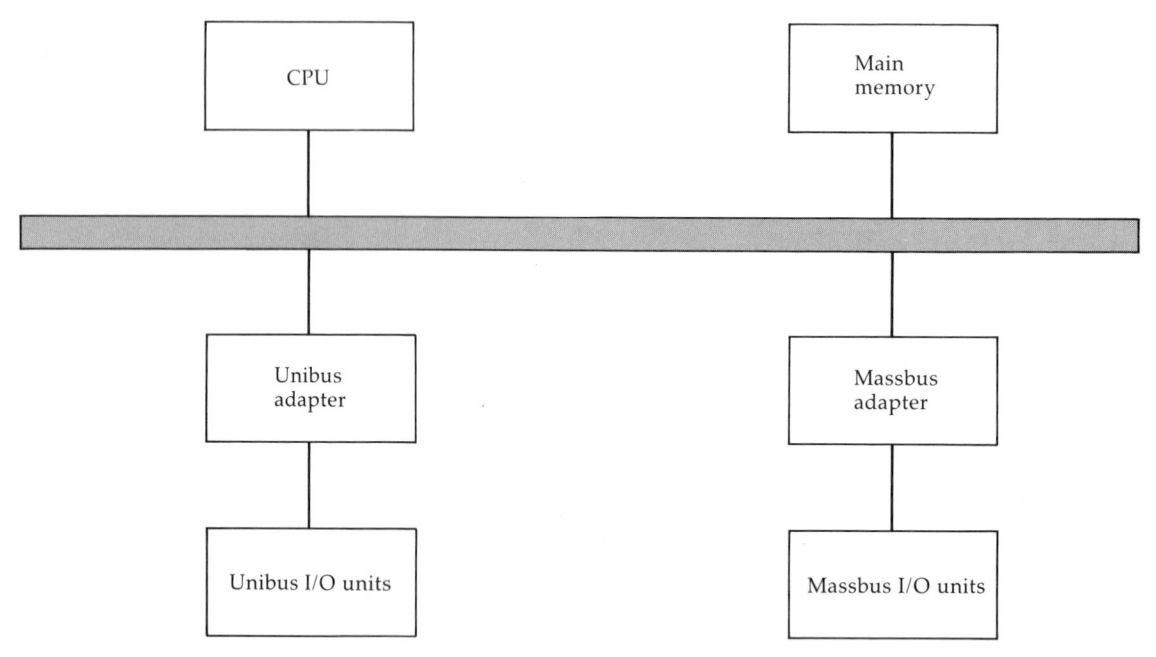

```
                    ┌─────────┐                      ┌─────────┐
                    │   CPU   │                      │  Main   │
                    │         │                      │ memory  │
                    └────┬────┘                      └────┬────┘
                         │                                │
    ═════════════════════╪════════════════════════════════╪═════════════════
                         │                                │
                    ┌────┴────┐                      ┌────┴────┐
                    │ Unibus  │                      │ Massbus │
                    │ adapter │                      │ adapter │
                    └────┬────┘                      └────┬────┘
                         │                                │
                    ┌────┴────┐                      ┌────┴────┐
                    │ Unibus  │                      │ Massbus │
                    │I/O units│                      │I/O units│
                    └─────────┘                      └─────────┘
```

Figure 1.4 Basic bus configuration of VAX 11/780 and 11/785

names and specifications of some of the buses and connections have changed. A new multipurpose bus called the **VAXBI** has replaced the synchronous backplane interconnect. Two CPUs are attached to this bus in the dual processor 8300. The much faster 8800 requires a faster memory bus but uses two or four VAXBIs as communication buses.

The VAX 8600 and 8650 use a bus structure that is a variation of that shown in Method A in Figure 1.3. Part of this machine's higher speed is obtained by providing two different bus structures. As shown in Figure 1.5, the Mbox is a distinct module that acts as interface and controller for memory and I/O. It connects these units to the other portions of the CPU that carry out the traditional functions of the control unit and ALU. This arrangement allows parallel memory and I/O operations as well as allowing the CPU to process instructions in parallel to the operation of the Mbox.

That the bus structure of the various VAX models differs considerably without affecting application software is one reason why the exact bus structure of a computer may not seem important to many users. However, the bus structure affects all users because it helps determine the overall speed of the computer. Consequently, hardware designers must pay a great deal of attention to the bus. Persons writing device drivers (discussed in Chapter 11) must have a good understanding of the bus structure in order to complete their task.

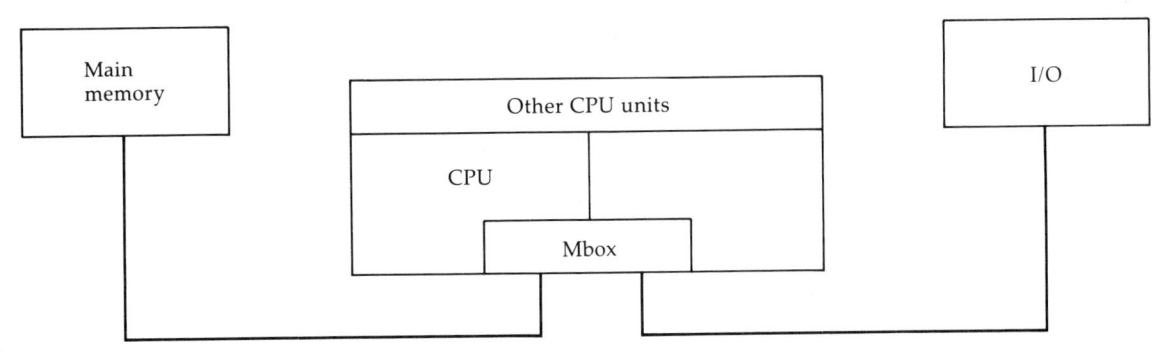

Figure 1.5 Bus configuration of a VAX 8600 and 8650

1.4 Integer Numbers

The way a computer represents numbers is an architectural feature that affects nearly every user. Even casual users may need to know the number of digits their computer's standard instructions use while processing their data. In this section we will look at some of the ways computers represent and calculate integer values. Floating-point numbers will be covered in the next section.

Computers often provide several different representations for integers. Two or more different lengths (number of bits used in the representation) are available on many computers. However, many operations on some 8-bit microcomputers are limited to 8-bit integers even though these short values are inadequate for many purposes. Integers may be assumed to be unsigned, nonnegative numbers. Alternatively, they may be considered signed numbers, that is, numbers with a plus or minus sign. While high-level programmers are typically forced to use the representation picked by the compiler writers, assembly language programmers may choose between the available representations.

Assembly language programmers often find it necessary to work with different bases for numbers. The value of an integer may be represented at various times in binary, octal, decimal, or hexadecimal. It may be essential to convert a number from decimal to binary or hexadecimal before coding it into a program. It may be helpful to convert numbers back to decimal while interpreting output from assembly programs. You may even need to write code that converts numbers between internal binary and external decimal formats.

In this section we will look at some number representations, the techniques for converting between them, and some methods for calculating with them. We will also look at some of the data types available on the VAX.

To distinguish between the different numbering systems used in this section, we must use a special notation to indicate what base a number is represented in. In this section numbers will often be written inside of parentheses followed by a subscript specifying the base. For example, $(1101)_2$ represents the binary number 1101, whose decimal value is 13. Numbers written normally (for example, 13) will represent decimal values unless context implies another base. In most other portions of this book, it is more convenient to assume that numbers are in hexadecimal or binary unless otherwise specified.

Representation of Integers in Various Bases

Before looking at the representation of numbers in various bases, it is useful to look at the meaning of a decimal number. Consider the number 6352. Its value is 6 thousands plus 3 hundreds plus 5 tens plus 2, or in mathematical notation

$$6352 = 6*1000 + 3*100 + 5*10 + 2$$
$$= 6*10^3 + 3*10^2 + 5*10^1 + 2*10^0$$

The number is said to be a **decimal number** because it is written in base 10.

We can use alternate bases if we like. In general, if $d_n, \ldots, d_1, d_0$ are digits for numbers in base b, then the number

$$(d_n \ldots d_1 d_0)_b = d_n * b^n + \ldots + d_1 * b^1 + d_0 * b^0$$

The digits $d_n, \ldots, d_1$, and d_0 will be at least 0 but less than the base b. Thus in binary, base 2, the digits can only be 0 or 1. The number $(100101)_2$ is

$$(100101)_2 = 1*2^5 + 0*2^4 + 0*2^3 + 1*2^2 + 0*2^1 + 1*2^0$$
$$= 1*32 + 1*4 + 1*1$$
$$= 32 + 4 + 1$$
$$= 37$$

We can use other bases just as easily. **Octal** (base 8) allows digits from 0 to 7. For example:

$$(217)_8 = 2*8^2 + 1*8^1 + 7*8^0$$
$$= 2*64 + 1*8 + 7*1$$
$$= 143$$

Hexadecimal (base 16) is used on many computers. It presents a notational problem because it requires digits from 0 to 15. The common solution is to represent the digits 10 to 15 with the letters A to F, as shown in Table 1.1. For example:

$$(3BF)_{16} = 3*16^2 + 11*16^1 + 15*16^0$$
$$= 3*256 + 11*16 + 15$$
$$= 959$$

Table 1.1 Hexadecimal Digits

Decimal	Binary	Hexadecimal	Decimal	Binary	Hexadecimal
0	0000	0	8	1000	8
1	0001	1	9	1001	9
2	0010	2	10	1010	A
3	0011	3	11	1011	B
4	0100	4	12	1100	C
5	0101	5	13	1101	D
6	0110	6	14	1110	E
7	0111	7	15	1111	F

Conversion of Integers Between Different Bases

It is frequently necessary to convert numbers between various bases. First, we will look at general conversion techniques. Except for some special cases, the methods for converting between arbitrary bases do not depend on the particular bases involved as much as they depend on whether we are converting to or from the base in which the calculations are being done. In the last subsection we illustrated converting from various bases into decimal. The method was convenient because we were doing the calculations in decimal. The same method could be used to convert decimal numbers into binary if we were calculating in binary. While that method works correctly, the following algorithm is more efficient. It is known as Horner's method or synthetic division and can be used to evaluate any polynomial.

Algorithm 1.1 *Conversion of integers* into *the base in which calculations are done.*

The value x of $(d_n \ldots d_1 d_0)_b$ can be calculated by
$x \leftarrow d_n$
For $i = n - 1, \ldots, 1, 0$ do
$\quad x \leftarrow x * b + d_i$

To illustrate this algorithm, we will convert $(3BF)_{16}$ to decimal again. In this case $n = 2$, $d_2 = 3$, $d_1 = $ B or 11, $d_0 = $ F or 15. The calculation would proceed as follows:

$\quad\quad\quad x \leftarrow 3$
$i = 1, \quad x \leftarrow 3 * 16 + 11 = 59$
$i = 0, \quad x \leftarrow 59 * 16 + 15 = 959$

Since computers customarily do their calculations in binary, this algorithm is often used in computers to convert decimal numbers input by the user into the internal binary used by the computer. In this case base b = 10 or $(1010)_2$. In the above example, the hexadecimal digits B and F had to be converted to decimal before we could carry out the calculations. Likewise when a computer converts a decimal number to binary, it must convert the decimal digits into their binary values before the algorithm can be used. On many computers, when decimal numbers are input from a terminal, the digits will be represented in American Standard Code for Information Interchange (ASCII). Inspection of the ASCII table in Appendix C shows that the binary value of a digit can be calculated by subtracting the ASCII value of the digit 0 from the representation of that digit. This is also true in most other character representations used by computers.

To convert an integer number from the base we are calculating into some other base b, it is convenient to use a process requiring repeated integer division by the base b while keeping track of the remainders. We will convert the decimal integer 37 to binary to illustrate this method.

Value	Quotient When Divided by 2	Remainder When Divided by 2
37	18	1
18	9	0
9	4	1
4	2	0
2	1	0
1	0	1

Observe that the first value is the number being converted and the remaining values are the previous quotients. The binary value can be found by writing the remainders in reverse order. That is,

37 = $(100101)_2$.

The same process can be used for other bases. For example, to convert decimal 959 to hexadecimal, the following calculations can be used.

Value	Quotient When Divided by 16	Remainder When Divided by 16
959	59	15 = F
59	3	11 = B
3	0	3

Thus, 959 = $(3BF)_{16}$.

The mathematical principle being used here is quite simple, and we can show that this representation is correct by using a process of repeated substitution. For example, by referring to the previous table, we find

$$959 = 59 * 16 + 15$$
$$= (3 * 16 + 11) * 16 + 15$$
$$= 3 * 16^2 + 11 * 16^1 + 15 * 16^0.$$

which justifies the hexadecimal representation for this value.

If we use the notation "div" to indicate integer division and "mod" to specify the remainder from integer division, we can formalize this method into the following algorithm.

Algorithm 1.2 *Conversion of integers* from *the base in which the calculations are done.*

The representation of x in the base b as the number $(d_n \ldots d_1 d_0)_b$ can be obtained as follows:

$y \leftarrow x$
For $i = 0, 1, \ldots, n$ do
　$d_i \leftarrow y$ mod b
　$y \leftarrow y$ div b

If the value of d_i is calculated using the formula $y - b * (y \text{ div } b)$, the value of y div b should be saved so that it can be assigned to y in the last step inside the loop without having to repeat the division.

This procedure, with base $b = 10$, is often used on computers for converting the internal binary integers into the decimal integers most easily understood by humans. When the decimal value is to be printed or sent to the user's terminal, the remainders must be converted to the required representation (normally ASCII) by some appropriate means, such as adding the digit's value to the representation of the character 0.

Conversions Between Binary and Either Octal or Hexadecimal

Because 8 and 16 are powers of 2, the process of converting between binary and octal or binary and hexadecimal is easy. The following decimal example will illustrate the process.

$$65{,}102{,}235 = 65 \text{ million} + 102 \text{ thousand} + 235 \text{ ones}$$
$$= 65 * 1000^2 + 102 * 1000^1 + 235 * 1000^0$$

Observe that we have effectively converted from base 10 to base 1000. The same process can be used to convert from binary to octal. Starting at the right-hand side of the number, we mark off groups of three binary digits. If the left-hand group has too few digits, we add zeros on the left as needed. Then we convert each group to octal using Table 1.2.

Table 1.2 Octal Digits

Octal	Binary	Octal	Binary
0	000	4	100
1	001	5	101
2	010	6	110
3	011	7	111

To convert $(10011010110)_2$ to octal, we can proceed as follows. First the binary number is broken into groups of three, and then each group is converted to octal.

$$\begin{array}{cccc} 010 & 011 & 010 & 110 \\ 2 & 3 & 2 & 6 \end{array} \quad \begin{array}{l}\text{(binary)}\\ \text{(octal)}\end{array}$$

Hence, $(10\ 011\ 010\ 110)_2 = (2326)_8$.

We can proceed in the same manner when converting binary numbers to hexadecimal except that we arrange the bits in groups of four. Using the same binary number as in the previous example, we observe

$$\begin{array}{ccc} 0100 & 1101 & 0110 \\ 4 & D & 6 \end{array} \quad \begin{array}{l}\text{(binary)}\\ \text{(hexadecimal)}\end{array}$$

Thus, $(100\ 1101\ 0110)_2 = (4D6)_{16}$. (If necessary, you can refer to the hexadecimal table presented earlier when converting binary patterns to hexadecimal.)

Converting from octal or hexadecimal back into binary just reverses the process. Each digit is expressed in binary.

$(1067)_8 = (1\ 000\ 110\ 111)_2$
$(2FA)_{16} = (10\ 1111\ 1010)_2$

To convert between hexadecimal and octal, we can first convert the given number into binary and then convert the binary number to the desired base.

Because of the ease with which numbers can be converted between binary, octal, and hexadecimal, it is common to represent binary numbers in octal or hexadecimal to achieve some compactness in notation. When it is necessary to write numbers in binary, we will often group the bits by threes or fours to simplify reading the numbers.

Binary Arithmetic

Binary numbers are commonly used on computers for two reasons. Computers are built with **bistable** components, that is, components with two possible states that conveniently can be used to represent 0 and 1. Moreover, arithmetic is particularly simple in that base. Addition and multiplication tables are elementary.

Binary addition

+	0	1
0	0	1
1	1	10

Binary multiplication

*	0	1
0	0	0
1	0	1

We can refer to the above tables to carry out calculations. When adding, we proceed in the normal fashion remembering that 1 plus 1 is 10. For example:

```
Binary              Decimal
  1110 1010           234
+  110 1001         + 105
1 0101 0011           339
```

Binary multiplication can be done exactly as it is done in decimal except that summing of the partial products is done in binary. For example:

```
Binary           Decimal
      1011          11
    * 1101        * 13
      1011          33
     0 000          11
    10 11          ___
   101 1           143
  1000 1111
```

Sometimes we must add octal or hexadecimal numbers. There are two possibilities. One may convert the given values to a more convenient base, do the calculation, and then convert the answer back to the original base. Alternatively, it may be easier to develop at least rudimentary abilities to do arithmetic in the required base. For example, we will repeat the addition problem but work in hexadecimal this time.

```
Hexadecimal    Decimal
     EA           234
   + 69         + 105
    153           339
```

The hexadecimal problem might be worked as follows:

$A + 9 = 10 + 9 = 19 = 16 + 3$ write the 3, carry 1 (for the 16)
$1 + E + 6 = 1 + 14 + 6 = 21 = 16 + 5$ write the 5 preceded by 1.

Representation of Negative Numbers

So far we have worked only with nonnegative numbers, but computers must also be able to use negative values. Inside the computer, the minus sign must be denoted by a 0 or 1. There are three common representations of signed numbers: (1) sign and magnitude, (2) one's complement, and (3) two's complement. In each case the left-hand bit will be used as a sign bit. Consequently, when signed arithmetic is used, the number of bits must be fixed at some agreed upon value so that we can recognize and operate with the leading sign bit. Positive values often must be padded with zeros to achieve this length.

The first method, **sign and magnitude**, simply uses the left-hand or most significant bit to represent the sign instead of contributing to the size of the number. Zero indicates a nonnegative value; 1 indicates a negative value. The remaining $n-1$ bits are used to represent the magnitude (or size) of the number. Using 8-bit values, we see

$$37 = (0010\ 0101)_2$$
$$-37 = (1010\ 0101)_2$$
$$\uparrow \text{sign bit}$$

While this method is easy to understand, implementation of addition of signed numbers is reasonably difficult and hence is rarely used in computers for integer arithmetic. The reasons for this are covered in Chapter 5 on the ALU.

Calculating with values represented in sign and magnitude notation is similar to calculating with our normal decimal numbers. When adding numbers with the same sign, the magnitudes are added. When adding numbers with different signs, the magnitude of the smaller is subtracted from the larger. In either case the proper sign bit is attached to the result. Likewise, if we need to multiply or divide signed numbers, we would carry out the required operation on the numbers' magnitudes and attach the proper sign to the result.

One's complement also uses the left-hand bit as the sign bit, but in this case the negative of a number is formed by complementing every bit; that is, all zeros are replaced by ones and ones are replaced by zeros. Positive numbers are represented in the same manner as sign magnitude. For example, using 8-bit integers:

$$37 = (0010\ 0101)_2$$
$$-37 = (1101\ 1010)_2 = \text{one's complement of } 37$$

The one's complement of a negative number can be found in the same manner. For example,

$$-37 = (1101\ 1010)_2$$
$$37 = -(-37) = (0010\ 0101)_2$$

The method for addition of numbers written in this notation is discussed in section 5.1. Because addition is easier to implement in one's complement than in sign and magnitude, one's complement is used on some computers (for example, the CDC 6600).

One unusual aspect of the first two negative representation methods is that both have two representations of 0. In addition to the usual all-zero format, $(1000\ 0000)_2$ is an 8-bit 0 in the sign and magnitude method and $(1111\ 1111)_2$ is a 0 in one's complement.

The most popular system for representing signed integers is **two's complement** because it is easiest to implement in computer hardware. A decimal example is useful. Suppose that you were using an old eight digit mechanical adding machine that did not have a subtraction key and you needed to calculate the following:

```
  14,596,187
-  2,532,172
```

An old trick to get some help with the subtraction from the adding machine was to subtract 2,532,172 from 100,000,000 mentally and then add the result to 14,596,187 using the adding machine.

```
   100,000,000 = 10^8
-    2,532,172
    97,467,828  =  -  2,532,172 + 100,000,000
+   14,596,187  =  + 14,596,187
   112,064,015  =    12,064,015 + 100,000,000
```

Since the mechanical adding machine only had eight digits, it would display the correct result, namely 12,064,015. The value 97,467,828 is called the ten's complement of 2,532,172.

Two's complement uses a similar concept. If we are using n bits for integers, the two's complement of a value is found by subtracting the number from 2^n. For example, to find the two's complement of 37 using 8-bit integers, we can calculate

```
    2^8  =    (1 0000 0000)_2
  -(37)  =  -  (0010 0101)_2
   -37   =    (1101 1011)_2  =  two's complement of 37
```

There are five important points to be made at this time.

1. The left-hand bit still acts as the sign bit; hence it is easy to tell if a number is negative or not.
2. In two's complement, there is only one way to write 0. Instead of having two representations of 0, there is one more negative number than there are positive numbers. In n-bit representations, the range of two's complement values is from -2^{n-1} to $(2^{n-1} - 1)$.

3. A number can be subtracted from another by calculating its two's complement and adding.

4. The two's complement of the two's complement of a number is the original number. For example, one can calculate the two's complement of

   $(1101\ 1011)_2 = -37$

   and find that it is

   $(0010\ 0101)_2 = 37$

5. Overflow may occur when adding two numbers having the same sign. It is easily detected because the sum will have the wrong sign bit. Overflow also occurs when trying to find the negative of -2^{n-1} since the result is one larger than the largest number that can be represented in this system.

There is a simple way to determine the two's complement of a value. First, determine the one's complement and then add 1. To illustrate this procedure, we will find the two's complement of 37 again.

$$
\begin{array}{rll}
37 = & (0010\ 0101)_2 & \\
 & (1101\ 1010)_2 & = \text{one's complement of 37} \\
+ & \underline{1} & \\
-37 = & (1101\ 1011)_2 & = \text{two's complement of 37}
\end{array}
$$

Because of the way these numbers are designed, addition can be carried out using normal binary addition without any special consideration for the signs of the numbers. For example, using eight-bit calculations,

$$
\begin{array}{rll}
37 = & (0010\ 0101)_2 \\
+\ (-20) = & +\ (1110\ 1100)_2 \\
\hline
17 = & (0001\ 0001)_2
\end{array}
$$

The carry from the most significant bit position is ignored.

Next we will look at a subtraction problem. Suppose that our computer uses two's complement to represent signed numbers. Consider

$(1101\ 1011)_2 - (1110\ 1100)_2$

Recalling that we can add numbers quite easily in this system, we will find the two's complement of the subtrahend, the number being subtracted, and then add.

$$
\begin{array}{rl}
(1110\ 1100)_2 & \text{the subtrahend} \\
(0001\ 0011)_2 & \text{its one's complement} \\
+\ \underline{1} & \\
(0001\ 0100)_2 & \text{its two's complement}
\end{array}
$$

Hence, we can solve the problem by adding as follows:

$$\begin{array}{rl} (1101\ 1011)_2 = & (1101\ 1011)_2 \\ -\ (1110\ 1100)_2 = & +\ (0001\ 0100)_2 \\ \hline & (1110\ 1111)_2 \end{array}$$

You may find it useful to verify that we just calculated

$(-37)_{10} - (-20)_{10} = -17_{10}$

Multiplication and division of numbers represented in two's complement notation are more difficult. Special methods are discussed in section 5.2. In the meantime, you should find the absolute value of any negative numbers, carry out the calculation, and then take the two's complement, if needed, to obtain the proper sign.

There are some extremely important concepts that must be understood.

1. Given a representation of a number, we must know what representation system is being used before we can determine its value. For example, the 8-bit pattern $(1101\ 1011)_2$ may represent 219 in an unsigned binary, -91 in sign and magnitude, -36 in one's complement, or -37 in two's complement.

2. We must distinguish between representing signed numbers in two's complement and finding the two's complement of a number. The two's complement representation of 37 (or the way a computer using two's complement represents 37) is $(0010\ 0101)_2$, exactly the same as it is in the other systems we discussed. The two's complement of 37 is $(1101\ 1011)_2$ or -37.

3. A general-purpose computer must have some means of representing signed integers as well as unsigned binary. Engineers must design its ALU so that it can operate in both systems. The program being run tells it how to interpret data and which calculating system to use. The computer is not confused by the different meanings of a data value even though we humans may be overwhelmed the first time we are confronted with them.

Two's Complement Calculations in Hexadecimal

While computers typically do calculations in binary, humans find writing and reading long binary numbers of 8 to 32 bits a problem. Hence binary numbers are often printed in hexadecimal. We have already found that it is easy to convert between binary and hex. However, we will often find it useful to calculate with two's complement numbers represented in hexadecimal.

First, we will look at the problem of determining the two's complement of a number expressed in hexadecimal. Consider the 8-bit representations of 37 and -37 again. If we add these values, we find

Decimal		Binary	Hexadecimal
37	=	(0010 0101)$_2$	(25)$_{16}$
+ (−37)	=	+ (1101 1011)$_2$	+ (DB)$_{16}$
0	=	(1 0000 0000)$_2$	(1 00)$_{16}$

↑———— ignore ————↑

Therefore, we can think of two's complement numbers written in hex as being sixteen's complement numbers. The two's complement of such numbers can be readily determined by subtracting each digit from 15 and adding 1 to the resulting number. For example, to find the two's complement of the 16-bit two's complement number (789A)$_{16}$, we might proceed as follows:

	Hexadecimal	Binary
Value	(789A)$_{16}$	(0111 1000 1001 1010)$_2$
One's complement	(8765)$_{16}$	(1000 0111 0110 0101)$_2$
Plus 1	+ 1	+ 1
Two's complement	(8766)$_{16}$	(1000 0111 0110 0110)$_2$

Since two's complements of numbers can be calculated in a fairly natural way, calculations with these numbers are straightforward. For example, suppose we want to add (789A)$_{16}$ and (FFE3)$_{16}$ or −(001D)$_{16}$. We can proceed as follows:

Hexadecimal	Binary
(7 8 9 A)$_{16}$	(0111 1000 1001 1010)$_2$
+ (F F E 3)$_{16}$	+ (1111 1111 1110 0011)$_2$
(7 8 7 D)$_{16}$	(0111 1000 0111 1101)$_2$

The carries generated by the high-order bits have been ignored.

Representation of Binary Integers on the VAX

The VAX allows several different representations of binary integers. First, there is the choice of signed or unsigned values. Second, different data lengths can be used, including 8, 16, 32, 64, or 128 bits. However, there are some restrictions because most integer arithmetic operations are only provided for the 8-bit **byte**, 16-bit **word**, and 32-bit **longword**. There are only a few operations for the 64-bit **quadword**, and operations on the 128-bit **octaword** are limited to instructions for moving data from one location to another. Accordingly, we will primarily be concerned with bytes, words, and longwords.

The terminology "word" and "longword" may be confusing to readers who know that the VAX is considered to be a 32-bit machine. Calling the 16-bit data length a "word" reflects the VAX's heritage. The VAX-11 name was designed to remind potential customers of the very successful

Table 1.3 Binary Integer Data Types

Data Type	Size in Bits	Range of values — Unsigned Integer	Range of values — Signed Integer
Byte	8	0 to 255	−128 to 127
Word	16	0 to 65,535	−32,768 to 32,767
Longword	32	0 to 4,294,967,295	−2,147,483,648 to 2,147,483,647
Quadword	64	0 to $2^{64}-1$	-2^{63} to $2^{63}-1$
Octaword	128	0 to $2^{128}-1$	-2^{127} to $2^{127}-1$

family of PDP-11 computers also made by DEC. In fact many of the VAX-11 computers have a compatibility mode that allows them to emulate the PDP-11; that is, some VAX computers can run software written for the PDP-11 computers, a feature designed to simplify the transition between the two families. The PDP-11 series has a 16-bit word length. DEC chose to continue to refer to 16-bit data as a "word" to avoid confusion on how many bits there are in a "word." Table 1.3 shows the range of values that can be represented by the various data lengths.

In each of the data lengths, the bits are numbered right to left. The least significant or right-hand bit is numbered 0. For signed arithmetic, the highest numbered bit (the one on the left) is used as the sign bit.

We will frequently represent these binary numbers in hexadecimal. Each 8-bit byte holds two hex digits, which means that a 2-byte word holds four hex digits, while a 4-byte longword holds eight hex digits.

The VAX is a byte-addressable machine; that is, each byte of data in main memory has its own address. Data types that use more than one byte are specified by the address of the first byte of data. The least significant byte of the number is stored first. On the VAX, that means we specify the address of a multibyte integer by the byte that contains the lowest-order bits, those numbered 0 to 7. For example, suppose the 16-bit binary number 1111 0000 1100 1010 is stored at location 510. The resulting word and its bit numbering are shown as follows.

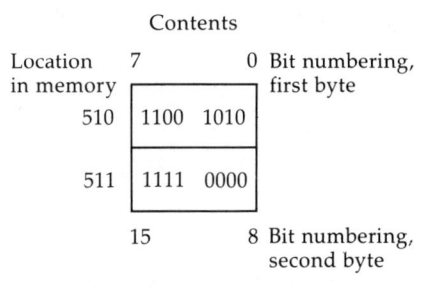

```
              Contents
Location    7         0  Bit numbering,
in memory  ┌─────────┐   first byte
    510    │1100 1010│
           ├─────────┤
    511    │1111 0000│
           └─────────┘
           15        8  Bit numbering,
                        second byte
```

To sum up our discussion of integer numbers, number representation is an architectural feature that is important to most computer users because it determines the range and precision of the data that can be processed. Signed numbers may be represented in sign and magnitude, one's complement, or two's complement. Techniques are available for converting between different bases and for adding and subtracting both signed and unsigned integers. Binary numbers are often represented in hexadecimal.

The VAX uses data lengths of 1, 2, 4, 8, or 16 bytes called bytes, words, longwords, quadwords, or octawords for binary integers. They can represent either unsigned integers or signed integers in two's complement notation.

1.5 Introduction to Floating Point

Integers are inadequate for many calculations, general-purpose computers provide representations of nonintegers. From your experience with high-level languages, you are aware that computers typically allow floating-point notation for reals. In this section we will look quickly at the representation of floating-point numbers on the VAX. This will allow us to consider both integer and floating-point instructions when we look at arithmetic operations in Chapters 2 and 3. However, we will delay a detailed look at how the VAX processes this data type until Chapter 5, when we look at the operation of the ALU.

Conversion of Numbers with Fractional Parts

Before we look at floating-point numbers, we will look at how to convert numbers with radix points ("decimal points") from various bases into decimal. We can do this in the same manner as we convert integers. Consider, for example:

$$\begin{aligned}(11011.0101)_2 &= 1*2^4 + 1*2^3 + 1*2^1 \\ &\quad + 1*2^0 + 1*2^{-2} + 1*2^{-4} \\ &= 16 + 8 + 2 + 1 + 0.25 + 0.0625 \\ &= 27.3125\end{aligned}$$

The technique is the same for other bases. In hexadecimal we would proceed as follows:

$$\begin{aligned}(1B.5)_{16} &= 1*16^1 + 11*16^0 + 5*16^{-1} \\ &= 16 + 11 + .3125 \\ &= 27.3125\end{aligned}$$

The same technique can be used on a computer to convert from decimal into binary because the computer works in binary. However, it may be better to convert the integer and fractional portions separately as if they were integers. The fractional portion would then be divided by the appropriate power of ten before summing to get the actual value. For example:

$$(4.25)_{10} = (4)_{10} + (25)_{10}/(100)_{10}$$
$$= (100)_2 + (11001)_2/(1100100)_2$$
$$= (100.01)_2$$

We can convert numbers with fractional parts from binary to hex in the same manner as we performed integer conversions. Binary digits are grouped in sets of four on either side of the "binary" point as shown and the value is converted group by group. For example:

$$(1\ 1011\ .\ 0101)_2 = (1B.5)_{16}$$

We reverse the process to convert from hex to binary.

In the last section we looked at how to convert decimal integers to another base. Converting a decimal fraction to another base requires a different process. The fraction is multiplied by the new base. The integer portion of the resulting number becomes the next digit in the fraction's expansion, and the process is repeated with the fraction portion replacing the old fraction. For example, to convert 0.3 into binary, we proceed as follows:

Calculation	Integer	Fraction
0.3 * 2 = 0.6	0	.6
0.6 * 2 = 1.2	1	.2
0.2 * 2 = 0.4	0	.4
0.4 * 2 = 0.8	0	.8
0.8 * 2 = 1.6	1	.6
0.6 * 2 = 1.2	1	.2
0.2 * 2 = 0.4	0	.4
0.4 * 2 = 0.8	0	.8
0.8 * 2 = 1.6	1	.6
0.6 * 2 = 1.2	1	.2
⋮	⋮	⋮

We see that the numbers will repeat every four calculations. The digits in the integer column give the binary expansion of 0.3.

$$0.3 = (0.0100\ 1100\ 1100\ \ldots)_2$$

The conversion of a number containing both integer and fraction parts is done in two parts, one for the real part and one for the decimal part. For example, to convert 37.3 to binary, we determine binary values of 37 and 0.3 separately. We find that $(37)_{10}$ equals $(10\ 0101)_2$. Combining this with the value of $(.3)_{10}$, we see

$37.3 = (10\ 0101.0100\ 1100\ 1100\ \dots)_2$

Computers would use this technique to convert from binary to decimal.

Floating-Point Representations

We can now turn our attention to the primary topic of this section. Scientific calculations often involve numbers of very large or very small magnitude. In many other situations the number of required decimal places varies greatly. Therefore the most common representation of such numbers uses the concept of **floating point**. That is, given a **base** b, numbers are represented in the form

$m * b^e$

where e is the **exponent**, and m is called the **mantissa** and has the representation

$m = (0.d_0 d_1 \dots d_k)_b$

assuming there are $k + 1$ digits available. Computers typically use base $b = 2$ or $b = 16$. The base b representation for the number is said to be *normalized* if the exponent has been adjusted so that the leading digit, d_0, is not a 0. Some computers, including the VAX, require that floating-point numbers are normalized. For example, the number

$27.3125 = (11011.0101)_2 = (1B.5)_{16}$

would be represented as $0.110110101 * 2^5$ in binary or $0.1B5 * 16^2$ in hexadecimal. Of course, inside the computer the exponent has to be expressed in an appropriate notation that will be discussed later.

The VAX allows 4 different formats for floating-point numbers, all of which use base 2. The most common is **F floating**. This format is stored in a longword (4 bytes) and uses 1 bit for the sign, 8 bits for the exponent, and 23 bits for the mantissa. Because the values must be normalized, the first digit of the mantissa cannot be 0 and must be a 1. Since this digit is always a 1, the VAX assumes it instead of storing it and achieves 24-bit accuracy while only storing 23 bits (d_2 to d_{24}) of the mantissa. Since the resulting accuracy of approximately 7 significant decimal figures is inadequate for many purposes, the VAX also has a double-precision floating-point representation called **D floating**. This quadword representation of a number is identical to the shorter version except the 8 bytes allow 55 bits to be used in the mantissa. It has 56-bit accuracy, which is equivalent to about 16 significant decimal digits of accuracy. The format of these data types and their bit numbering can be diagrammed as follows:

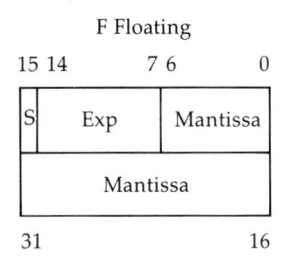

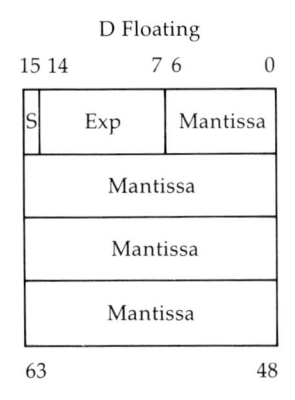

```
            F Floating                    D Floating
    15 14        7 6       0       15 14      7 6        0
   ┌──┬──────┬────────┐          ┌──┬──────┬────────┐
   │S │ Exp  │Mantissa│          │S │ Exp  │Mantissa│
   ├──┴──────┴────────┤          ├──┴──────┴────────┤
   │    Mantissa      │          │    Mantissa      │
   └──────────────────┘          ├──────────────────┤
   31                 16         │    Mantissa      │
                                 ├──────────────────┤
                                 │    Mantissa      │
                                 └──────────────────┘
                                 63                 48
```

As the leading digit d_0 is not stored, d_1 is stored in bit 6 of the first word of these representations. The remaining bits are stored consecutively in the locations marked mantissa. For example, bit d_7 is stored in bit 0 of the first word and bit d_8 is in bit 15 of the second word. (If the organization of these floating-point values seems peculiar, remember that VAX's relationship to the 16-bit PDP-11. It uses the same formats.)

The "s" in these representations denotes the sign bit. The VAX uses sign- and magnitude-type notation for floating point, so only the sign bit changes when negating a value. As usual, the sign bit is 0 for a positive value and 1 for a negative. Sign and magnitude representations are used for floating-point numbers in order to optimize multiplication. Recall that on the VAX, two's complement is used in integer arithmetic to optimize addition.

To simplify calculations, the exponent is stored in what is called **excess 128** notation. This means the exponent is stored as an 8-bit number, which is said to be **biased** because it is 128 larger than the true exponent.

For example, we will look at how

$$27.3125 = (0.110110101)_2 * 2^5$$

is stored. The sign bit is 0 because the number is positive. The 8-bit exponent field is 128 + 5, or 1000 0101 in binary. The leading bit of the mantissa is omitted. Thus the representation of this number is as follows:

```
        F Floating                     D Floating
   Sign  Exp.     Mantissa        Sign  Exp.     Mantissa         Bit numbering
   ↳ 0 1000 0101 1011010          ↳ 0 1000 0101 1011010           15 . . . 0
       1000 0000 0000 0000            1000 0000 0000 0000         31 . . . 16
                                      0000 0000 0000 0000         47 . . . 32
                                      0000 0000 0000 0000         63 . . . 48
```

The hexadecimal representations of these values can be found by converting four bits at a time.

F Floating				D Floating				Bytes
4	2	D	A	4	2	D	A	1 ... 0
8	0	0	0	8	0	0	0	3 ... 2
				0	0	0	0	5 ... 4
				0	0	0	0	7 ... 6

Hexadecimal representations of these numbers seem strange since the VAX stores them byte by byte starting with bits 0 to 7. Moreover, MACRO assembly listings show the high-order bytes on the left. This is helpful for integer values but produces strange results for floating-point numbers. The hexadecimal representation for 27.3125 would be written 80 00 42 DA as an F floating value and 00 00 00 00 80 00 42 DA in D floating. Fortunately, the computer comprehends this even though it looks strange to us.

Two other optional floating-point representations are used by the VAX. **G floating**, like D floating, uses 8 bytes but uses 11 bits for the exponent and 1 for the sign, leaving 52 bits for the mantissa. **H floating** uses 16 bytes, of which 15 bits are reserved for the exponent. These data types are available to provide a greater range in exponents and extended accuracy, which are often needed in scientific calculations (see Table 1.4).

The number 0 must be treated as a special case in floating point. On the VAX any floating-point number whose sign and biased exponent fields are both 0 is considered to denote the number 0. The floating-point 0 is normally represented by setting all the bits equal to 0.

There is a possible problem when calculations are done in floating point. We must be aware that the internal binary representation for these numbers can lead to rounding errors that cannot be explained in terms of the decimal format we are accustomed to.

In summary, floating-point numbers on the VAX are represented in binary. Standard floating types are F floating, which uses 4 bytes, and D floating, which uses 8 bytes. Bit 15 is the sign bit. The 8-bit exponent is expressed in an excess 128 notation (that is, it is 128 larger than its real value). Floating-point values are assumed to be normalized, and the

Table 1.4 Floating-Point Representations

Type	Size (bytes)	Approximate Range (magnitude)	Approximate Precision
F floating	4	$.29*10^{-38}$ to $1.7*10^{38}$	7 decimal digits
D floating	8	$.29*10^{-38}$ to $1.7*10^{38}$	16 decimal digits
G floating	8	$.56*10^{-308}$ to $.9*10^{308}$	15 decimal digits
H floating	16	$.84*10^{-4932}$ to $.59*10^{4932}$	33 decimal digits

most significant bit of the mantissa is not included because it must always be a 1. There are two optional floating types: the 8-byte G floating which uses 11 bits for the exponent, and the 16-byte H floating which uses 15 bits for the exponent.

Summary

This chapter has had two goals. The first was to introduce the concepts of computer architecture, the interface between the software and the hardware. While it is assumed that you have had experience writing high-level language programs, this may be your first experience with computer design issues. Consequently, several ideas have been presented in a simple fashion. They will be developed more completely later in the book.

The second goal was to acquaint you with some of the basic ideas and terminology that we will need to discuss computer architecture. In Section 1.2 we presented an elementary survey of the main building blocks of a computer. We followed this in Section 1.3 with a description of the bus that allows the various blocks to communicate with each other. Then in Section 1.4 we turned to another common architecture issue, the way numbers are represented in the computer. We discussed methods for converting between various bases and calculation in binary and hexadecimal. Finally, we introduced floating-point numbers and their representation on the VAX.

The discussion on most of these topics was limited to a brief introduction in preparation for more thorough coverage later. The discussion of number representations was more detailed, and you may want to refer back to Section 1.4 as you learn to use binary and hexadecimal numbers on a regular basis in the process of writing assembly language programs.

The next two chapters will introduce assembly language. In them you will not only learn how to write simple assembly language code but also begin to see how the assembly language for a particular machine relates to its architecture.

Exercises

1. Compare high-level languages, assembly language, and machine language in terms of use, readability, transportability, and capabilities.
2. What is meant by computer architecture?
3. Describe each of the main building blocks in a computer.
4. Distinguish between RAM and ROM.
5. What is meant by byte addressable?

6. What are some characteristics of a von Neumann architecture?
7. What is the purpose of a bus? Give some advantages and disadvantages of a single-bus system compared to a two-bus system.
8. What is meant when we say that a VAX-11 is a 32-bit machine? Are the MicroVAXes really 32-bit computers by your definition?
9. Convert the following unsigned numbers into the specified base.

   a. $(100)_{10}$ into binary
   b. $(259)_{10}$ into hexadecimal
   c. $(1001011)_2$ into decimal
   d. $(1011101010)_2$ into octal
   e. $(1011101010)_2$ into hexadecimal
   f. $(271)_8$ into decimal
   g. $(546)_8$ into binary
   h. $(ABC)_{16}$ into decimal
   i. $(FF)_{16}$ into binary
   j. $(1D36)_{16}$ to octal

10. Complete the following table by converting the given number in each row into the other bases.

	Decimal	Binary	Base 4	Octal	Hexadecimal
a.	79				
b.		1010111			
c.			231		
d.				256	
e.					3A2F

11. Express these signed numbers in the given representation system using the specified number of digits.

    a. $(-37)_{10}$, sign and magnitude, 8-bit binary
    b. $(-37)_{10}$, one's complement, 8-bit binary
    c. $(-37)_{10}$, two's complement, 8-bit binary
    d. $(37)_{10}$, two's complement, 8-bit binary
    e. $-(0010\ 1010\ 0111)_2$, two's complement, 12-bit binary
    f. $(-4)_{16}$, two's complement, 16-bit binary but express the result in hexadecimal
    g. $(-16)_{16}$, two's complement, 16-bit binary but express the result in hexadecimal

12. What is the decimal value of the given number assuming 8-bit binary notion and the given method of representing signed numbers?

    a. 0110 0101, unsigned
    b. 0110 0101, sign and magnitude

c. 0110 0101, one's complement
  d. 0110 0101, two's complement
  e. 1010 1010, unsigned
  f. 1010 1010, sign and magnitude
  g. 1010 1010, one's complement
  h. 1010 1010, two's complement

13. What is the smallest two's complement data representation available on the VAX that will hold the given decimal number? Convert the number to that representation expressing the result in hex.
    a. 181
    b. −81864
    c. −69
    d. 2048

14. What is the decimal value of the following two's complement numbers represented in hex?
    a. 64
    b. 7FFF
    c. 8000
    d. FC18
    e. EF
    f. ABCDEF00

15. Carry out the calculation leaving the answer in the given number system. (Indicate if the result is illegal because of overflow.)

    a.   1011 0101   sign and magnitude, 8-bit binary
         + 0011 1011

    b.   1011 0101   two's complement, 8-bit binary
         + 0011 1011

    c.   1011 0101   two's complement, 8-bit binary
         − 1111 1011

    d.   1011 0101   two's complement, 8-bit binary
         − 0011 1011

    e.   1110101   unsigned binary
         ×   11011

    f.   1111 0101   two's complement, 8-bit binary
         × 0000 1011

    g. 1101)1011011   unsigned binary

    h. 43 + 3F =   two's complement, 8-bit binary expressed in hexadecimal

    i. 48A3 + FF24 = two's complement, 16-bit binary expressed in hexadecimal

j.   253A   two's complement, 16-bit binary expressed
− 00A7   in hexadecimal

k.   12EA63   unsigned hexadecimal
+   E 365

16. a. Count from $(-17)_{10}$ to $(1)_{10}$ in 8-bit binary using two's complement representations of the values.
    b. Repeat part a but represent the numbers in hexadecimal.

17. Convert the following numbers to decimal.
    a. $(100101.110001)_2$
    b. $(0.01)_2$
    c. $(123.45)_8$
    d. $(100.77)_8$
    e. $(ABC.DEF)_{16}$
    f. $(0.002A)_{16}$

18. Convert the following decimal numbers into the given number system.
    a. 73.75 into binary
    b. 20.1 into binary
    c. 20.1 into octal
    d. 63.21875 into hex

19. Give the VAX's F floating notation for the following numbers, writing them in hexadecimal with the highest-order bytes first in the manner of the MACRO assembler.
    a. $(100101.110001)_2$
    b. $(1)_2$
    c. $(-0.01)_2$
    d. $(123.DEF)_{16}$ (Hint: convert to binary first.)
    e. $(-0.002A)_{16}$

20. What is the decimal value of the following F floating values assuming that the numbers appear in the same format as used by the MACRO assembler?
    a. 40004572
    b. 0000C080
    c. 00004100

CHAPTER CONTENTS

2.1 INSTRUCTION FORMAT

    Instruction Formats
    VAX Instruction Formats
    VAX Instructions
        Clear
        Move
        Add
        Subtract
        Multiplication
        Division
    Example

2.2 ADDRESSING MODES

    The General Register Modes
        Register Direct Mode
        Register Deferred Mode
    The Program Counter Modes
        Relative Mode
        Immediate Mode

2.3 VAX MACRO INSTRUCTIONS

2.4 EXAMPLE PROGRAMS

    SUMMARY

    EXERCISES

CHAPTER 2

Essentials of Assembly Language

In this chapter we introduce the underlying language of the VAX 11—the VAX assembly language. Most programs for the VAX or any other computer are written in a high-level language such as BASIC, Pascal, FORTRAN, or C. While these languages are easy for a human programmer to use, computers cannot use them directly. A computer simply manipulates electrical signals in the form of low and high voltages that we interpret as zeros and ones. So these high-level languages must be translated from their English-like statements to strings of zeros and ones. These zeros and ones are called machine language, and the program that translates the high-level language statements into machine language is called a **compiler**. In the early days of computers, before compilers and hence before high-level languages, programmers had to write their programs in machine language. This meant that their programs would consist of a sequence of zeros and ones such as

```
0010100010010010
1110101010111010
0001010101111000
```

Imagine trying to debug a program such as the one above. Beause of this problem, the first step on the road to high-level programming languages was the development of an assembly language that replaces the zeros and ones with mnemonics. An assembly language **mnemonic** is a code word for a basic machine operation. Thus a programmer could write a program in assembly language such as

```
ADD 100,200
MOV 200,300
```

which would add the contents of memory location 100 to those of memory location 200 and then move the contents of memory location 200 to memory location 300. This program is easy to both write and debug, and it can be translated directly into machine language using a program called an **assembler**.

Even though high-level languages are available today, many programmers still use assembly language because it allows them to write very efficient code. However, while high-level languages are portable (that is, with some care a program written in FORTRAN on an IBM could run on a VAX), assembly language is not portable. It is tied so closely to a computer's machine language (and hence to the architectural features of the system) that it is impossible to write an assembly language program for the VAX and run it on an IBM. However, since assembly language is related directly to a machine's architecture, a programmer can take full advantage of all the architectural features of a machine when writing a program in assembly language. The potential result is a program with the minimum execution time and the most efficient use of system resources. Because this text covers the assembly language for the VAX, it depends on the architecture of the VAX. For this chapter we will assume that the architecture looks something like that shown in Figure 2.1. In later chapters we will add several levels of detail to this basic architectural picture

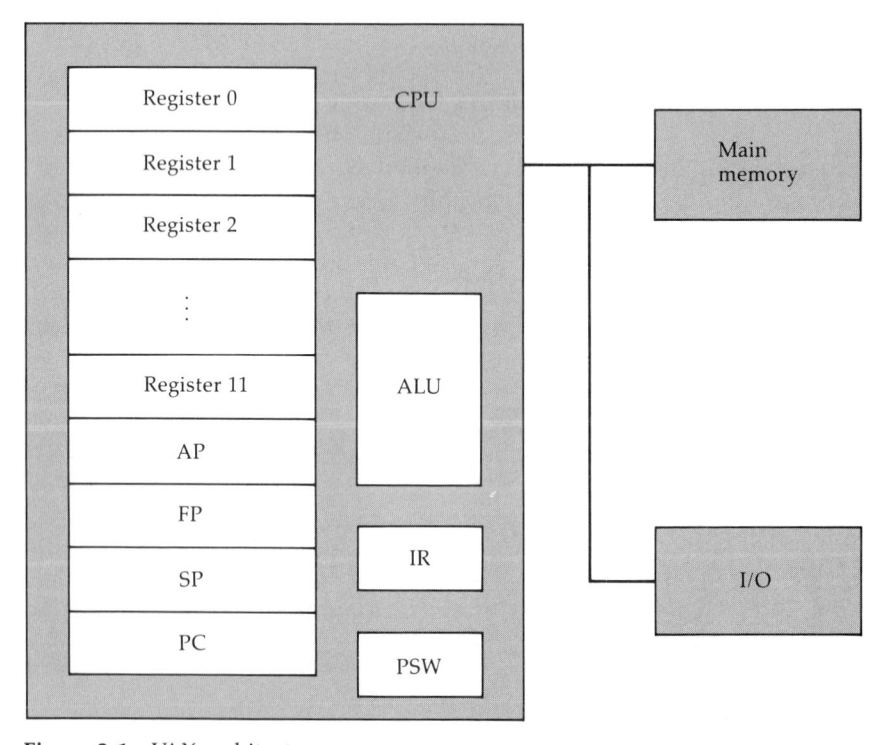

Figure 2.1 VAX architecture

of the VAX. The major components are a set of 16 registers, an ALU, a main memory module, and an I/O module. Each register can hold one longword (32 bits). Some instructions use only part of a register. For example, to save a word (16 bits), only the first (right-hand) 16 bits are used (bits 0 to 15), and to save a byte (8 bits), only the low-order 8 bits of the register are used.

In this chapter we will introduce the basic features of both the VAX assembly language and its machine language. At the conclusion of this chapter, you should be able to write simple programs in assembly language for VAX applications. In Chapter 3 we will continue the theme of this chapter and expand on both the addressing modes and the instruction set.

2.1 Instruction Format

The goal of this section is to explore the basic structure of assembly language statements in general and the specific format of VAX assembly language statements.

Instruction Components

There are four different types of assembly language instructions:

1. **Data transfers** are designed to move or copy data between main memory and the CPU. They include such actions as saving data in given memory locations, reading data from specified memory locations, and copying data from one register to another.
2. **Arithmetic and logic operations** on data perform the basic data manipulation tasks of the computer. They include addition, multiplication, subtraction, and division as well as the basic logic operations of AND, OR, and complement.
3. **Program sequencing and control** are instructions that modify the sequence of program instructions. They include branching-type instructions.
4. **Input/output (I/O) instructions** interface the computer with the outside world. They include instructions that send data to a terminal or receive data from some peripheral device.

Assembly languages are made up of sets of instructions from each of the four categories.

Each assembly language instruction may be divided into two major sections:

1. An operation code (opcode) that specifies the function to be performed, such as ADD, STORE, and so on.
2. One or more specifiers, called operands, that describe the location of the data on which the operation is performed.

The general format, then, of an assembly language statement is

Opcode A, B, C

where A, B, and C are operands and specify in some fashion the data to be operated on by the opcode. They could be symbols that have been assigned values or they could be specific values. A specific example of the development of an assembly language instruction is given in the next subsection.

Instruction Formats

In this section we will consider possible formats for specifying mnemonics for the machine operations and the data that will be used by the operations. The overall goal is to produce a mnemonic scheme that is clear enough to be easily read and understood by a programmer yet simple enough to be directly translated into machine language sequences of zeros and ones. Obviously there is a trade-off between these two subgoals, as will be illustrated in the continuing example of a set of mnemonics for an ADD instruction.

Consider the following operation:

1. Add the contents of memory location A to the contents of memory location B.
2. Store the result in memory location C.

This represents a basic ADD operation that all computers should be able to implement. In a high-level language such as BASIC, this operation would be expressed as

10 C = A + B

At the assembly language level, however, the programmer must specify both the operation (ADD) and the location of the data elements (A, B, C). To do this in one assembly instruction would require one opcode and three operand specifiers. The format would be

ADD A, B, C

This assembly language instruction is closely related to the machine language sequence of zeros and ones that the computer understands. For example, the machine language version of the above ADD instruction could consist of four fields:

2.1 Instruction Format

| Opcode | Source 1 address | Source 2 address | Destination address |

Each field would contain a 0 and 1 code such as the one below:

Opcode	Source 1	Source 2	Destination
1011	1010	1100	0100

The problem with this method is that given a fixed word size (fixed number of 0 and 1 bits per instruction), dividing it into four parts leaves only a few bits for each one (4 bits for the 16-bit word in the example). Even if an instruction allowed a word size of 32 bits, dividing it so that each field is the same size would allow only 8 bits per field. That would mean only 8 bits per address, thus limiting the total address space of the machine to 256 words of data. Of course, using 8 bits for the opcode would allow 256 different instructions for the machine. In order to increase the total address space for data using the same fixed-instruction word size, it is necessary to reduce the number of addresses per instruction. As a result, an ADD instruction could be implemented using only two addresses in the following way:

    ADD   A, B

where the action of the ADD instruction is to add the contents of A to those of B and save the result in location B. Though it is impossible to use three different addresses in one instruction in this system, the equivalent operation could be performed using two two-address instructions:

    MOVE   B, C   ;move the contents of B into C
    ADD   A, C   ;add A to C and store in C

Together these instructions produce the same result as the ADD A, B, C instruction. Now, using the two-address instruction, the number of bits in the fixed-instruction word could be distributed as

    Opcode   8 bits
    Address 1   12 bits
    Address 2   12 bits

The possible address space for the data is expanded to 4K (4096) words.

Another level of improvement could be achieved by moving to a single address instruction such as

    ADD   A

where the operation is to add the contents of A to those of a general-purpose register in the CPU called the **accumulator** and save the result in the accumulator. This of course requires that the new hardware register be added to the architecture of the CPU. This is just the first of many examples where the nature of the hardware architecture has a direct impact on the nature of the assembly language. Using this approach, the single three-address instruction could be implemented as three one-address instructions.

```
LOAD   A     ;put A into the accumulator
ADD    B     ;add B to the accumulator
STORE  C     ;save the accumulator in location C
```

Now, using the one-address mode, an instruction word could be divided into just two parts, allowing, for example:

Opcode 16 bits

Address 16 bits

so the effective addressable memory space is now 64K. Actually most computers have more than one general-purpose register or accumulator; in fact they usually have eight or more such registers. In this case some of the address or opcode bits must be put aside and used to indicate which general-purpose register is to be used for data storage. The one-address instructions become (assume that **Ri** is one of the general-purpose registers):

```
LOAD   A, Ri
ADD    B, Ai
STORE  Ri, C
```

If there are 8 general-purpose registers, only three bits are required to address each one. On the VAX there are 16 such general-purpose registers, so four bits are required to address them. Such instructions are sometimes called $1\frac{1}{2}$ operand instructions.

The end result of this analysis is that a definite trade-off exists between the number of operand specifiers in an assembly language instruction and the size of addressable memory. If we use more operand specifiers in a single instruction, we require fewer instructions, so the program runs faster; however, fewer bits are available for the memory addresses, so memory size is restricted. On the other hand, if only one operand specifier is used, the available memory space is quite large; however, we require more instructions to complete the operation, so the program may take longer to run. We can get around this trade-off by using some inventive addressing methods. Rather than assuming that each assembly language instruction carries with it the exact address of the data it requires, we will construct instructions that will use other means for determining the location of any required data in memory. Of course the requirement for a fixed-length instruction can be removed. Many computers allow instructions to have a variable length so that there can be plenty of room for the desired addresses.

VAX Instruction Formats

The specific assembly language instructions for the VAX are covered later in this chapter. However, in this section we present a brief picture of the format of general assembly language statements that may also be used for VAX assembly language programs.

A VAX instruction has four parts: (1) label (used for branching), (2) opcode (instruction specification), (3) operand specifier(s) (data or address[es] of data), and (4) comment (explain the operation of the instruction). The format appears as

```
Label:   Opcode   Operands    ;Comment
```

The column positions of these fields are optional and are suggested here only as a guideline for readability. The **Label** field begins in column 1 and is optional. It is used only if it is necessary to label a statement. For example, you may want to branch to a specific statement, so you need to label it. A label can consist of up to 31 characters, including both letters and digits as long as the first character is a letter. The **Opcode** field begins in column 9 and is made up of the instruction mnemonic. The **Operands** field begins in column 17 and consists of 0 to 6 addresses, which are used to specify the location of the data required by the specific instruction. Many common arithmetic instructions, such as ADD, allow the programmer to select between two or three operand formats. The **Comment** field begins with a semicolon in column 41. While comments are optional, in practice, assembly language programs are nearly impossible to read without comments on almost every line. Both the opcode and operands fields will be covered in detail in this chapter, starting with the nature of the opcode field.

VAX Instructions

The VAX has a rich instruction set, with more than 240 different assembly-level instructions. DEC also provides an optional extended instruction set that increases the number of instructions to more than 300. Don't worry, you needn't learn them all in order to write an efficient assembly language program. In fact, in this section we will look at only a small subset of the most commonly used instructions that serve as a starting point in the development of an assembly language program. We will

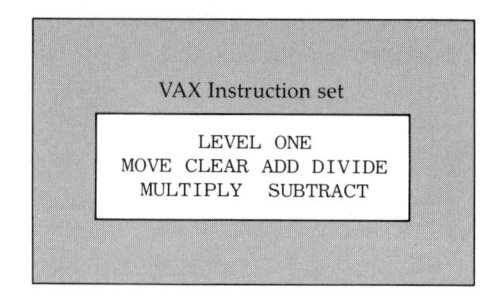

```
            VAX Instruction set
         ┌─────────────────────────┐
         │        LEVEL ONE        │
         │  MOVE  CLEAR  ADD  DIVIDE│
         │    MULTIPLY   SUBTRACT  │
         └─────────────────────────┘
```

Figure 2.2 VAX instruction set by levels

save the majority of the instruction set for study in later chapters. The initial set of instructions is shown in Figure 2.2.

Each instruction can be expressed in one of two ways:

1. Mnemonic form, which is the assembly language format.
2. Opcode form, which is the set of actual bits used by the machine.

The mnemonic form consists of an operation prefix, a data type suffix, and in some cases the number of operands. Some examples are shown in Table 2.1. These operation mnemonics and data types are mixed to form the basic assembly language instruction mnemonics such as

```
MOVW     move word data
CLRB     clear one byte of space
```

The mnemonics represent in a somewhat readable fashion the actual machine instructions. The assembler translates these mnemonics into a sequence of bits that the VAX can understand. The specific physical instruction format on the VAX is a variable-length format in which each instruction consists of a variable number of bytes. The format is shown in Figure 2.3, where byte 0 is always the opcode. Since there are eight

Table 2.1 Mnemonic Format for Instructions

Operation	Data Type	Number of Operands	Assembly Version
MOVe	Byte	2	MOVB
ADD	Word	2	ADDW2
CLeaR	Longword	1	CLRL
SUBtract	Floating	3	SUBF3
DIVide	Double	2	DIVD2

2.1 Instruction Format

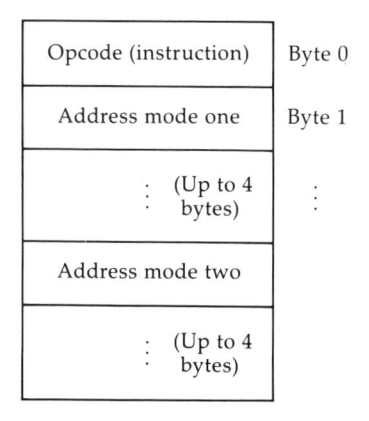

Opcode (instruction)	Byte 0
Address mode one	Byte 1
⋮ (Up to 4 bytes)	⋮
Address mode two	
⋮ (Up to 4 bytes)	

Figure 2.3 VAX instruction format in memory

bits in a byte, there are 256 possible instructions for the VAX, and DEC uses almost all of them. The optional extended instruction set uses 2 bytes for each additional opcode. The second byte is the first address mode, followed by up to 4 bytes that provide the data necessary for the address mode. This is followed, if needed, by a second address mode byte and up to another 4 bytes for its data. This may be repeated for additional address modes, each followed by up to 4 bytes of information. As a result, an instruction could consist of only 1 byte to as many as 31 bytes and in some cases even more.

The following discussion provides a detailed description of the first set of VAX instructions, including the mnemonics, the actual machine language opcodes, and examples that use the instructions.

Clear The clear instruction sets the contents of the destination address to 0. The assembly mnemonic is

```
CLRx    destination
```

where x = B, W, L, Q, F, D and *destination* is an addressing mode that specifies which register or memory location you want to clear. B, W, L, Q, F, and D are data types and stand for byte, word, longword, quadword, floating point, and double. They indicate the size of the register or memory location to be cleared. It should be noted that the optional instruction set also includes CLRG and CLRH for the G and H floating-point data types and CLRO for octawords. These types will not be covered in the text; however, you may refer to Appendix A for additional information on their use. Each clear instruction has an operation code as shown below:

Mnemonic	Opcode (hex)	Action
CLRB	94	Clear byte
CLRW	B4	Clear word
CLRL	D4	Clear longword
CLRF	D4	Clear floating
CLRQ	7C	Clear quadword
CLRD	7C	Clear double

Notice that CLRL and CLRF have the same opcode, as do CLRQ and CLRD. This is because both longwords and floating-point values are 32 bits long, and it makes no difference what the specific format of the 32 bits is when they are cleared. The same is true of the 64-bit quadword and double-precision data. An instruction that would clear, say, register 5 would be given by

```
CLRL    R5
```

If this instruction were stored in memory location 200, it would appear in machine language as

Address	Opcode (hex)	Opcode (binary)	
200	D4	1101 0100	CLRL
201	R5 addressing mode		

D4 is the hexadecimal version of the opcode (or machine language) for the CLRL instruction. The method of accessing or addressing register 5 will be covered in the next section on addressing modes. For the moment, it is important that you concentrate on the instructions.

Move The move instruction will replace the contents of the destination with the contents of the source. The source contents are unchanged. The mnemonic for this instruction is

```
MOVx    source, destination
```

where x is the data type and source and destination are addressing modes. The opcodes for the move instructions are

Mnemonic	Opcode (hex)	Action
MOVB	90	Move byte
MOVW	B0	Move word
MOVL	D0	Move longword
MOVQ	7D	Move quadword
MOVF	50	Move floating
MOVD	70	Move double

For example, to transfer the contents of register 1 to register 5, you would use the instruction

    MOVL   R1, R5

The assembler would translate this instruction into the following opcodes (we will assume that the instruction begins at memory location 200):

Address	Opcode (hex)	Opcode (binary)	
200	D0	1101 0000	MOVL
201	R1 addressing mode		
202	R5 addressing mode		

You may also use the move instruction to copy data from memory into a register or from a register into memory, or to load data directly into a register by selecting the proper addressing modes. For example, to move the number 70 directly into register 7, the correct instruction would be

    MOVL   #70, R7

which uses what is called the immediate addressing mode for the number 70.

Add Both two- and three-operand ADD instructions are available on the VAX. The two-operand instruction will add the source and destination and save the result in the destination. The three-operand instruction will add the contents of the two source locations and save the result in the destination location. The mnemonics for the two classes of ADD instructions are

    ADDx2   source, destination
    ADDx3   source 1, source 2, destination

where x is the data type. The opcodes for the ADD instruction are

Mnemonic	Opcode (hex)	Action
ADDB2	80	Two-operand, byte addition
ADDB3	81	Three-operand, byte addition
ADDW2	A0	Two-operand, word addition
ADDW3	A1	Three-operand, word addition
ADDL2	C0	Two-operation, longword
ADDL3	C1	Three-operand, longword
ADDF2	40	Two-operand, floating
ADDF3	41	Three-operand, floating
ADDD2	60	Two-operand, double
ADDD3	61	Three-operand, double

For example, to add the contents of register 4 to those of register 10 and save the result in register 10, you would use the instruction

```
ADDL2    R4, R10
```

The machine language version of this instruction is

Address	Opcode (hex)	Opcode (binary)
200	C0	1100 0000 ADDL2
201	R4 addressing mode	
202	R10 addressing mode	

Subtract The subtract instruction has the same two- and three-operand modes. The mnemonics are

```
SUBx2    source, destination
SUBx3    source 1, source 2, destination
```

The two-operand subtract instruction will subtract the contents of the source from the destination and save the result in the destination, while the three-operand instruction will subtract the contents of source 1 from those of source 2 and save the result in the destination. The opcodes for these instructions are

Mnemonic	Opcode (hex)	Action
SUBB2	82	Two-operand, byte subtraction
SUBB3	83	Three-operand, byte
SUBW2	A2	Two-operand, word
SUBW3	A3	Three-operand, word
SUBL2	C2	Two-operation, longword
SUBL3	C3	Three-operand, longword
SUBF2	42	Two-operand, floating
SUBF3	43	Three-operand, floating
SUBD2	62	Two-operand, double
SUBD3	63	Three-operand, double

For example, to subtract the contents of register 3 from those of register 5 and save the result in register 8, you would use the instruction

```
SUBL3    R3, R5, R8
```

The opcodes for this instruction are

Address	Opcode (hex)	Opcode (binary)
200	C3	1100 0011 SUBL3
201	R3 addressing mode	
202	R5 addressing mode	
203	R8 addressing mode	

Multiplication   The VAX also provides multiplication instructions in both the two- and three-operand modes. The mnemonic format is given as

```
MULx2     source, destination
MULx3     source 1, source 2, destination
```

The opcodes for the multiply instruction are

Mnemonic	Opcode (hex)	Action
MULB2	84	Two-operand, byte
MULB3	85	Three-operand, byte
MULW2	A4	Two-operand, word
MULW3	A5	Three-operand, word
MULL2	C4	Two-operand, longword
MULL3	C5	Three-operand, longword
MULF2	44	Two-operand, floating
MULF3	45	Three-operand, floating
MULD2	64	Two-operand, double
MULD3	65	Three-operand, double

For example, to multiply the contents of register 3 by those of register 5 and store the result in register 6, you would use the instruction

```
MULL3   R5, R3, R6
```

This instruction would be translated into the following opcodes:

Address	Opcode (hex)	Opcode (binary)
100	A5	1010 0101 MULL3 OPCODE
201	R5 addressing mode	
202	R3 addressing mode	
203	R6 addressing mode	

Division   The mnemonics for the two division instructions are

```
DIVx2     source, destination
DIVx3     source 1, source 2, destination
```

The two-operand division instruction will divide the destination by the source and save the result in the destination, while the three-operand instruction will divide source 2 by source 1 and save the result in the destination. For integer division, the quotient is truncated to an integer if necessary. The opcodes for these instructions are

Mnemonic	Opcode (hex)	Action
DIVB2	86	Two-operand, byte division
DIVB3	87	Three-operand, byte
DIVW2	A6	Two-operand, word
DIVW3	A7	Three-operand, word
DIVL2	C6	Two-operand, longword
DIVL3	C7	Three-operand, longword
DIVF2	46	Two-operand, floating
DIVF3	47	Three-operand, floating
DIVD2	66	Two-operand, double
DIVD3	67	Three-operand, double

For example, to divide the contents of register 2 by those of register 1 and save the answer in register 2, you would use the instruction

```
DIVL2   R1, R2
```

The VAX opcodes for this instruction are

Address	Opcode (hex)	Opcode (binary)
200	C6	1100 0110 DIVL2
201	R1 addressing mode	
202	R2 addressing mode	

Example

With just these instructions, we can actually write a simple assembly language program segment. The problem is to find the average of three-words of data currently stored in registers 2, 3, and 4 and store the average in register 6. A sequence of steps that will solve this problem is shown in Figure 2.4. The sequence of assembly language statements that implement the steps of Figure 2.4 are given in AVERAGE Version 1. Note that in the process of developing a set of assembly language statements to solve a problem, it is helpful to first think about the problem in terms of the elementary steps before writing the code. In other words, a flowchart or pseudocode for the logic of the algorithm you wish to implement is very important.

```
                Add                        Add                Divide the sum
              R2 + R3                    R5 + R4              in R5 by the
            and save the              and save the            number of
             result in                  result in             terms, 3, and
                R5                         R5                 save the result
                                                              in R5
```

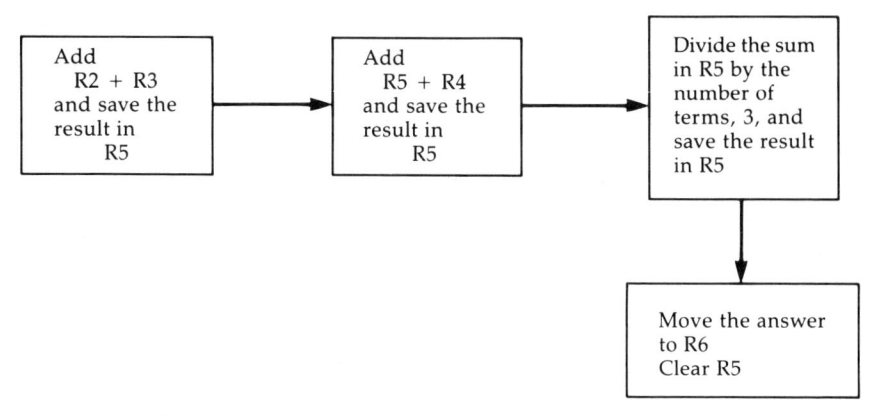

```
                                                              Move the answer
                                                              to R6
                                                              Clear R5
```

Figure 2.4 Elementary steps to find the average

```
                AVERAGE Version 1
Begin:  ADDW3   R2, R3, R5  ;R5 contains the sum of R2 and R3
        ADDW2   R4, R5      ;R5 contains the sum of R4 and R5
        DIVW2   #3, R5      ;R5 contains R5 divided by 3
        MOVW    R5, R6      ;R5 is moved to R6
        CLRW    R5          ;R5 is reset to 0
```

While this program segment is certainly not the most efficient one for calculating an average (it is not even a complete assembly language program), it gets the job done. The first two instructions add the three data items together and save the result in a temporary register, R5. The third instruction divides the contents of R5 by 3 (the number of data items) and saves the result in R5. The fourth instruction moves the average to the required location, R6. The final instruction resets the temporary register. There are, however, some problems with running this program. How did the data get from main memory into the three registers, R2, R3, and R4? What can be done to save the average in main memory in case we want to use the value at some later time? To answer these questions, we must know how to address data and memory locations. This forms the subject matter of the next section.

2.2 Addressing Modes

The operand specifiers in the basic VAX assembly language instruction supply the necessary data to the operation. They tell the system where the data it requires is located. In other words, they contain the value of the data, the address of a register that contains the data, or the memory address of the data. Remember that the VAX memory is byte-addressable, which means that even though the basic word size on the VAX is the 32-bit longword, memory still supplies data to the CPU in 8-bit or byte slices.

There are four general ways in which the "address" of the data may be supplied in an operand specifier. They are the (1) general register mode, (2) program counter mode, (3) index mode, and (4) branch mode. Each of these general modes has several submodes. Initially we will look at only a few of the addressing modes available on the VAX. They will allow us to solve the problems noted in the example that ended the last section. In Chapter 3 addressing modes will be studied in great detail.

The General Register Modes

The characteristic of the general register mode is that one of the general-purpose registers in the VAX is used to help locate the data. The register either will contain the data or will tell us where the data is located in main memory by giving us its memory address. The VAX has 16 general-purpose registers to work with, labeled R0 through R15. While all the registers could be used for data or address storage, some have a special purpose and should not be used unless it is absolutely necessary. The registers with special uses are R12 through R15: R12 is the argument pointer (AP); R13 is the frame pointer (FP); R14 is the stack pointer (SP); and R15 is the program counter (PC). These special-purpose applications will be explained later. For now it is enough to know that when it comes to truly general-purpose registers, the VAX has only 12, R0 through R11.

There are eight ways in which each of these 12 general-purpose registers can be used to locate or store data. The two most common methods will be covered in this section; the other six will be discussed in Chapter 3.

Register Direct Mode This mode is the most natural way to use the registers. You simply store the data in the registers. In fact this is so natural that it was used in the previous section without much discussion. This is noted in the operand field of an assembly language statement by Rn, where n is the register number. For example, the instruction

```
CLRL    R5
```

will clear the longword of data in register 5, that is, set the contents of register 5 to 0. Each general-purpose register is 32 bits long, so if we store double-precision data, which is 64 bits long, we must use two registers. The two registers are Rn and Rn + 1. The instruction to clear a 64-bit quadword stored in R6 and R7 is

```
CLRQ    R6
```

and the operation will be performed on both R6 and R7. If an instruction operates on fewer than 32 bits, only the rightmost part of the specified register is used and the remaining part of the register is unchanged. For example, to clear the lower 8 bits of register 3, the command is

    CLRB   R3

which will set bits 0 through 7 to 0 and leave the remaining 24 bits unchanged.

The machine language code for this addressing mode is stored in a single byte (eight bits), which consists of two parts. The high-order four bits contain the binary value of 5, while the low-order four bits contain the binary equivalent of the register number (0 to 15).

0101	Register ID

So the machine language version in hex of the CLRB R6 instruction would take up two bytes of memory and be given by

    94   CLRB
    56   Register 6

An assembly listing that gave the machine language code as well as the assembly mnemonics for this instruction would look like this:

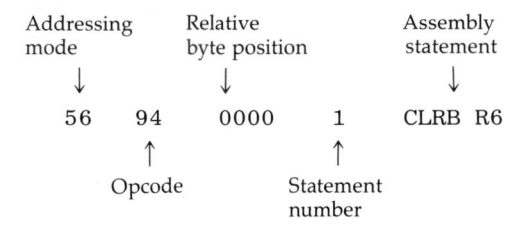

```
Addressing      Relative                Assembly
  mode         byte position            statement
    ↓              ↓                       ↓
    56    94     0000         1        CLRB  R6
          ↑                   ↑
        Opcode             Statement
                            number
```

This format is covered in more detail in Appendix D.

This mode is the best one to use for intermediate results, which will be needed soon since it is the fastest way to access data in the computer. In fact, in AVERAGE Version 1, this is the addressing mode that was used in every case but one.

Register Deferred Mode Instead of containing the data, in the register deferred mode the register contains the address of the data. That is, the data is in the main memory unit and the register simply points to its location. This addressing mode is closely related to the concept of pointers in Pascal and C. Sometimes this is called the indirect register mode. The assembly language format for this operand mode is

   (Rn)

For example, the instruction

   CLRB   (R5)

will clear the location in main memory pointed to by register 5. This instruction is demonstrated in Figure 2.5, assuming that location 2208 in the VAX main memory contained the number 68 before the instruction is executed.

The machine language code for this addressing mode is also stored in a single byte, where the high-order four bits are 0110 (binary 6) and the low-order four bits are the register ID.

| 0101 | Register ID |

In hex, this would be given by 6n, where n is the number of the register.

This addressing mode could be used to solve two of the problems with AVERAGE Version 1. First, if the three numbers that we want to find the average of were initially stored in main memory, then we could use this mode to move them into the three registers. For example, if the first number had been stored in a location in main memory pointed to by register 7, that number could have been moved into register 2 using the instruction

   MOVW   (R7), R2

So, let's change the specification of the example program to allow for this type of operation. Now we want to find the average of three numbers located in main memory where the addresses of the numbers are contained in R7, R8, and R9. The average is to be saved in main memory at the location pointed to by register 10. A flowchart of this set of assembly language statements is shown in Figure 2.6. Our sample code becomes

```
       AVERAGE Version 2
Begin:    MOVW    (R7), R2         ; Load R2
          MOVW    (R8), R3         ; Load R3
          MOVW    (R9), R4         ; Load R4
          ADDW3   R2, R3, R5       ; R5 contains R2 + R3
          ADDW2   R4, R5           ; R5 contains R5 + R4
          DIVW2   #3, R5           ; Find the average
          MOVW    R5, (R10)        ; Save the result in memory
          CLRW    R5               ; Reset R5 to 0
```

2.2 Addressing Modes

VAX Registers

CLRB (R5)

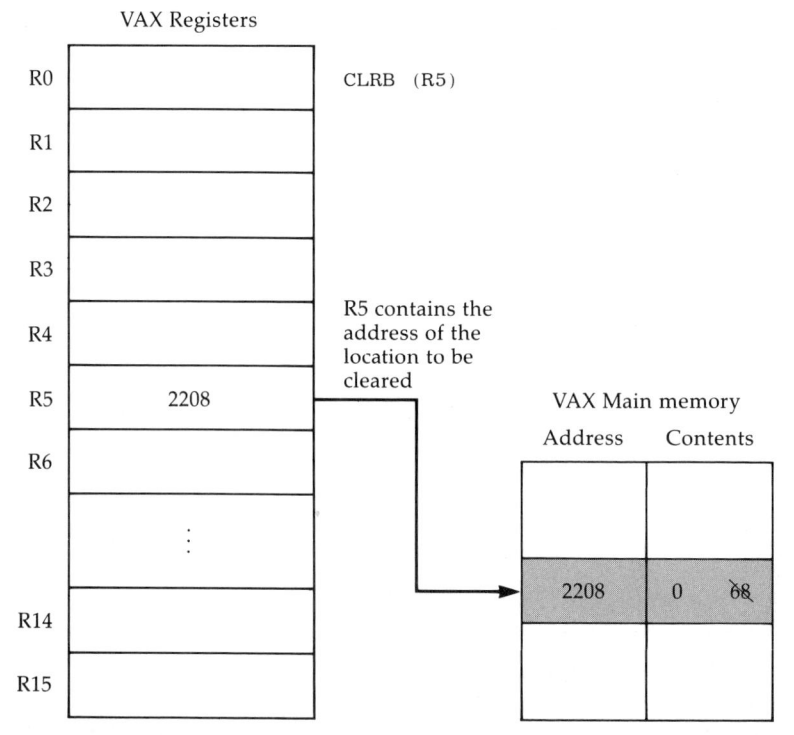

R5 contains the address of the location to be cleared

R5: 2208

VAX Main memory

Address	Contents
2208	0 68

Figure 2.5 Register deferred addressing

Move the data from memory to R2, R3, R4

↓

Add R2 + R3 Save the result in R5

↓

Add R5 + R4 Save the result in R5

→

Divide the contents of R5 by the number of data items, 3

↓

Move the answer to the memory location pointed to by register 10

↓

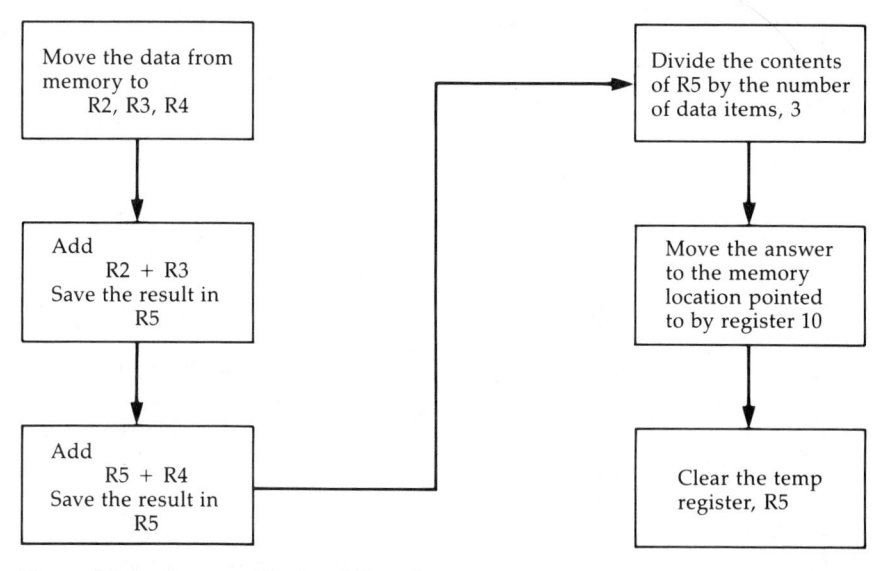

Clear the temp register, R5

Figured 2.6 Average Version 2 flowchart

This set of assembly language statements will still find the average but is even more inefficient than the original version. For one thing, we really do not need all the temporary registers. As a result, the example program may be reduced significantly as shown in AVERAGE Version 3.

```
    AVERAGE Version 3
Begin:   ADDW3   (R7),  (R8),  R5    ;Add the first two numbers
         ADDW2   (R9),  R5           ;Add the third number
         DIVW3   *3, R5,   (R10) ;Divide by 3 and save ave
```

The Program Counter Modes

On the VAX register 15 is the program counter (PC), which means that it always points to the location immediately following the location of the last fetch from main memory. You should understand that the PC is always incremented at the end of a fetch cycle, so each addressing mode is fetched in a different cycle. As a result, the PC always points to the next instruction or part of an instruction to be used in the next fetch cycle. For example, for the time being we will assume that the instruction ADDL2 R2, (R3) will be processed in three fetch cycles—one for ADDL2, one for R2, and one for (R3). The use of one of the general-purpose register addressing modes with the PC results in four special program counter addressing modes. Two of these modes will be covered in this section, the other two in Chapter 3.

Relative Mode In this mode the address of the data is given directly in the instruction. For example, if the label SPACE is used to represent a storage location in main memory, that location will be cleared by the instruction

```
CLRB  SPACE
```

This is a common addressing mode, but when translated to machine language and stored in main memory in the instruction stream, it takes on an unusual form. Instead of storing the absolute or **effective address** of the data in the instruction, the VAX will store an offset or **displacement** that, when added to the PC, will give the correct value of the address. The offset is stored as a two's complement number so that just by adding it to the PC, we can move forward and backward in memory. In an attempt to save memory space, there are three relative addressing modes: (1) byte relative addressing, (2) word relative addressing, and (3) longword relative addressing.

Byte relative addressing is used when the effective address is between +127 and −128 bytes from the current value of the PC. In this case only 1 byte is needed to store the displacement. The machine language code for the byte displacement mode is AF (the hex value A indicates that it is a byte relative addressing mode, and hex F identifies the PC or register 15), so the structure of an instruction using the byte relative addressing mode would be

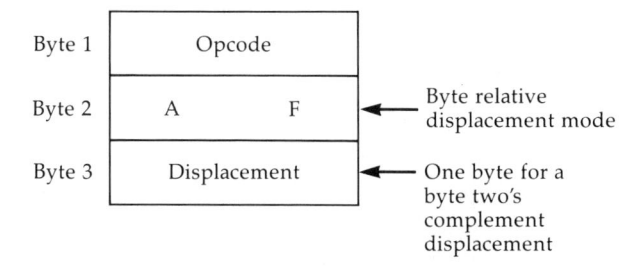

```
Byte 1  | Opcode       |
Byte 2  | A       F    | ← Byte relative displacement mode
Byte 3  | Displacement | ← One byte for a byte two's complement displacement
```

Word relative addressing is used when the effective address is between +32k and −32k bytes from the current instruction. This mode requires 2 bytes to store the displacement. Its code is CF, and its structure is given as

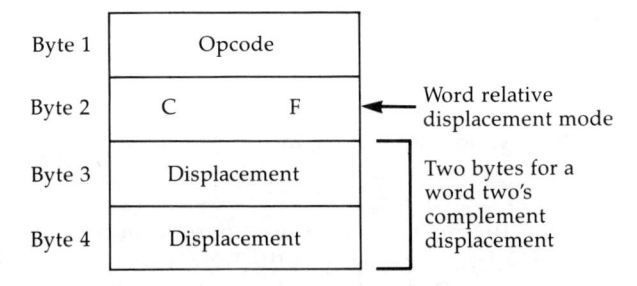

```
Byte 1  | Opcode       |
Byte 2  | C       F    | ← Word relative displacement mode
Byte 3  | Displacement | ⎫
Byte 4  | Displacement | ⎭ Two bytes for a word two's complement displacement
```

Longword relative addressing is used when the effective address is more than 32k bytes from the PC. Its machine language code is EF, and its structure is given by

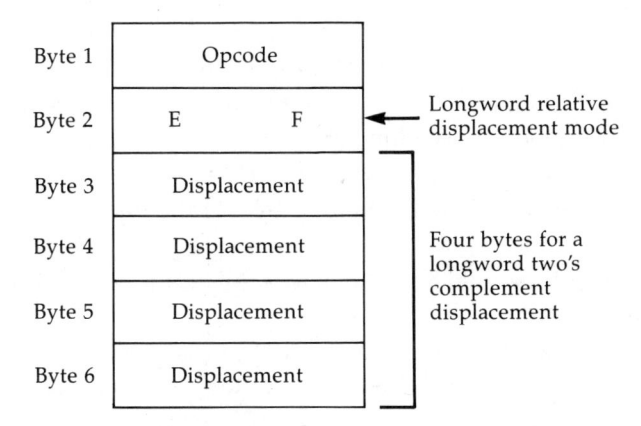

```
Byte 1  | Opcode       |
Byte 2  | E       F    | ← Longword relative displacement mode
Byte 3  | Displacement |
Byte 4  | Displacement | Four bytes for a longword two's complement displacement
Byte 5  | Displacement |
Byte 6  | Displacement |
```

The operation of this addressing mode is shown in Figure 2.7, where we want to clear the byte SPACE when it is located in memory at address

Chapter 2 Essentials of Assembly Language

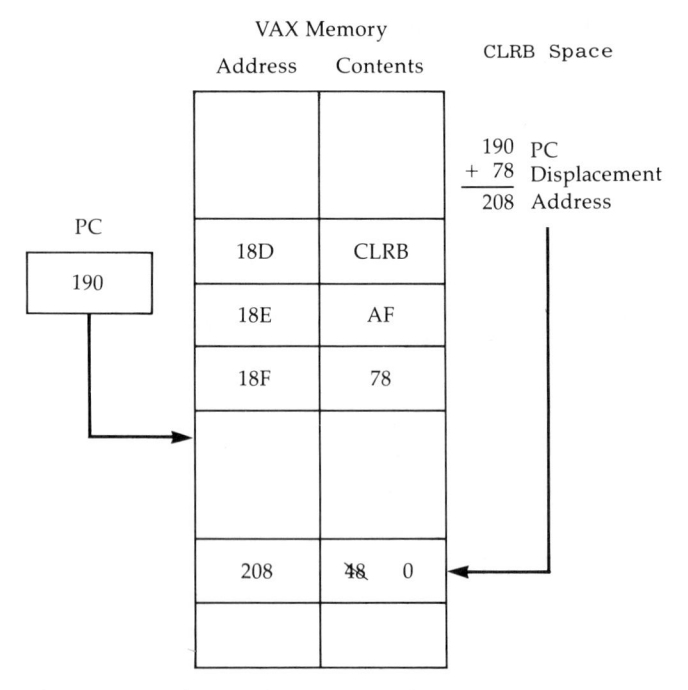

```
              VAX Memory
         Address    Contents         CLRB Space

                                     190   PC
                                   + 78    Displacement
                                     208   Address
     PC
              18D        CLRB
     190
              18E        AF

              18F        78




              208        4̶8̶   0
```

Figure 2.7 Relative addressing mode

208. Assuming that the instruction is stored at locations 18D, 18E, and 18F, the required displacement mode is the byte mode and the displacement value is 120 decimal or 78 hex. Remember that the PC is incremented after each fetch, so after the displacement byte has been fetched, the PC has the value 190 and thus the effective address is 208 = 190 + 78. The overall process of implementing this instruction from the standpoint of the PC is as follows:

1. The PC begins by pointing to location 18D.
2. The fetch operation brings in the opcode for CLRB and increments the PC to point to location 18E.
3. The machine now "knows" that it is being asked to clear some location, so it must fetch the next byte of the instruction (location 18E).
4. The fetch is completed—the byte is AF and the PC is updated to point to location 18F.
5. The machine "knows" that the location is given in terms of an offset, so it must fetch the next byte to determine the amount of the offset.
6. The fetch is completed—the byte is 78, and the PC is updated to point to location 190.

7. Now the offset of 78 is added to the current PC, which is 190, and the result is 208.
8. The byte at location 208 is cleared.

As a programmer, however, you do not have to enter these offsets. You simply write the program using the symbolic name for the memory location, and the assembler will calculate the displacements and set up the correct sequence of instructions.

The example program could also have used this addressing mode to get at the three numbers. If it were known that the three numbers were stored at locations given by X, Y, and Z, then version 4 of the example program would become

```
              AVERAGE Version 4
Begin:    ADDW3   X, Y, R5
          ADDW2   Z, R5
          DIVW3   #3, R5, (R10)
```

In the next section we will explain how to reserve room for X, Y, and Z.

Immediate Mode This is sometimes called the unlimited literal mode because the data can be any size. In this mode the data is stored directly in the instruction. The assembly format is

 I^#data

Where the I^ is optional. The code 8F is used to specify the immediate mode in machine language.

For example, Figure 2.8 illustrates the use of this addressing mode to move data directly into a register with the instruction

 MOVL   #376, R6

Note that 376 decimal is 178 hex.

This mode has been used in all four versions of the example program. In each case the number of data items (three) appeared in the divide instruction. It is assembled using a version of the immediate mode called the literal mode. In addition, if all three numbers are known, the immediate mode could have been used in several places in the example program. That is, if we want to find the average of 1560, 1432, and 2167 and store the result in the memory location pointed to by register 10, then

```
              AVERAGE Version 5
Begin:    ADDW3   #1560, #1432, R5
          ADDW2   #2167, R5
          DIVW3   #3, R5, (R10)
```

Note that while the assembler uses the immediate mode for its three numbers 1560, 1432, and 2167, it only allows the programmer to assume

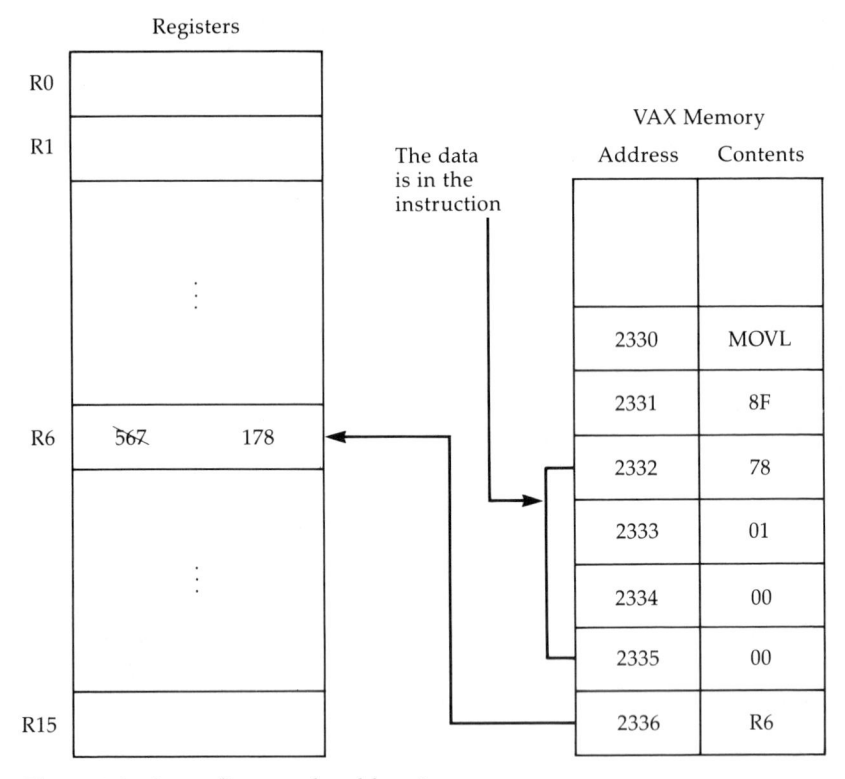

Figure 2.8 Immediate mode addressing

that the immediate mode is used for #3. In fact the assembler automatically selects another mode, called the short literal, for this small value. This mode, which will be discussed in Chapter 3, produces more compact code.

2.3 VAX Macro Instructions

Two languages actually form an assembly language program on the VAX:

1. The actual assembly language statements, which consist of executable instructions directed to the machine.
2. A MACRO language, which has been developed by DEC to help the assembler translate the assembly language program into machine code.

The assembly language instructions reviewed so far are all executable. However, it is sometimes necessary to "set up" your assembly language program with instructions to the assembler. This includes such tasks as program identification and reserving space for data storage. Such instructions are called directives and in MACRO are easily recognizable because they begin with a period. For example, to assign space to a longword called Cost and give it the initial value 1600, we would code

```
Cost:    .LONG   1600
```

To define and reserve space for data, the format of the MACRO instruction is

```
LABEL:   .TYPE   VALUE
```

LABEL may be any user-selected variable name. TYPE specifies the size of the data, that is, byte, word, long, quad, float, double, ASCII. VALUE is the data to be stored. The data may be supplied with a base designation of the following form:

^B for binary data
^O for octal data
^X for hex data
^D for decimal (this is the default mode)
^A for alphanumeric
^F for floating point

For example, suppose you want to reserve two memory locations to store data; one way would be to use the following code:

Address	Assembly Language Code
200	A: .LONG ^D55
204	B: .LONG ^D22

The addresses are for example purposes only and are determined by the assembler, not the programmer. These two instructions do not generate machine language instructions because they are directed to the assembler, not the machine. Instead, they tell the assembler to reserve two longwords in memory, one at 200 and the other at 204, and to store the number decimal 55 in the first and the number decimal 22 in the second. As a programmer, you could refer to these two memory locations in the following assembly language code as A and B. For example, you may want to add the data as follows:

```
ADDL2   A, B
```

This instruction would store the number 77 (the sum of A and B) in location B.

Other types of data are stored using similar statements. For example, to store data given in a hex format in a word slot (16 bits), you could use

```
NEW:     .WORD   ^XC12
```

which would store the hex value C12 in the memory location called NEW. You could then reference it in any following assembly language statement as NEW. Remember that while you may specify the format for the way data is given to the assembler, the assembler always stores data in binary. Strings may also be given as input data using

    NEXT: .LONG   ^A/STRG/

which would store the ASCII codes for STRG. Note that the four characters in STRG exactly fill the four bytes reserved by .LONG. The slash (/) is used in this example to delimit the string.

You can supply a set of values, for example,

    A: .WORD   ^D21, ^D31, ^D12

would store 21, 31, and 12 in three word locations where A references the first data item (in this case 21). In general we don't use the ^D because decimal is the default; hence, the code would normally appear as

    A: .WORD   21, 31, 12

You can use a similar method to define a block of storage. The general format for specifying such a block is

    LABEL: .BLKX   COUNT

where *X* gives the data type of the array (B, W, L, Q, F, or D) and *COUNT* indicates the size of the array. For example,

    ARRAY: .BLKW   50

defines a block of 50 words starting at the location ARRAY, all of which are initialized to 0.

An optional but very useful directive or MACRO statement is the .TITLE command, which should be the first line of every assembly language program. The format is given by

    .TITLE   name   comment

where the name is used by the debugger, and the combination of name and comment is printed on the top of each page of assembler output. The name can be up to 31 characters long without any blanks, and the comment can be up to 40 characters long.

Two important directives that must appear in every assembly program are the .ENTRY and .END. The .ENTRY is a MACRO directive that identifies the beginning of the executable code and assigns the program a name. The format of .ENTRY is

```
        . ENTRY    program_name, 0
```

The .END MACRO is used to mark the physical end of a program. The format is

```
        . END    program_name
```

2.4 Example Programs

Now, a working version of the AVERAGE program can be created. Version 6 of AVERAGE is a program that will run on the VAX in the form given. It will find the average of three numbers—1560, 1432, and 2167—and save the result in the memory location called AVE.

```
                  AVERAGE Version 6
                  . TITLE    Average    Version 6
            ; This program will calculate the average of
            ;    three numbers: X, Y, and Z. The result will be
            ;    saved in location Ave
   X:       . WORD      1560       ; Create storage for the
   Y:       . WORD      1432       ; data
   Z:       . WORD      2167
   Ave:     . BLKW      1          ; Save room for the answer
            . ENTRY Average, 0
   Begin:   ADDW3       X, Y, R5        ; R5 contains X + Y
            ADDW2       Z, R5           ; R5 contains X+Y+Z
            DIVW3       #3, R5, Ave     ; Ave contains R5/3
            $EXIT_S
            . END    Average
```

The $EXIT_S statement is a macro built into the VAX assembler to handle an exit from a program and will return control of the computer over to the operating system.

Another example of an assembly language program is the following, which will evaluate the function $f(x) = 2x + 512x^2$.

```
            . TITLE Function    Evaluate F(X)
            ; This program will calculate the value
            ;    of the function F(X) = 2X + 512X^2 for
            ;    integer inputs.
   X:       . LONG 15                   ; input is decimal 15
            . ENTRY Function, 0
            MULL3       #2, X, R2       ; R2 now has 2X
            MULL3       X, X, R3        ; R3 now has X^2
            MULL2       #512, R3        ; R3 now has 512X^2
            ADDL2       A2, A3          ; R3 has the value of F
            $EXIT_S
            . END Function
```

This program begins by defining the data X as a longword with the value decimal 15. The assembler would translate this program into the following machine language version given in hex. Note that some directives to the assembler, such as .END, are not translated into machine language because they are executed while the assembler is running.

	Machine Language Bytes	Comments
0	0F	Longword decimal value
1	00	15 in location of H
2	00	
3	00	
4	00	Stored by the .ENTRY
5	00	Directive
6	C5	MULL3 opcode
7	02	#2, Short literal mode
8	AF	Byte relative addressing
9	F6	2's complement of 10
A	52	R2 address mode
B	C5	MULL3 opcode
C	AF	Byte relative addressing
D	F2	2's complement of 14
E	AF	Byte relative addressing
F	F0	2's complement of 16
10	53	R3 addressing mode
11	C4	MULL2 opcode
12	8F	Immediate mode addressing
13	00	Data--value 512 in longword
14	02	(Decimal 512 = hex 200)
15	00	
16	00	
17	53	R3 addressing mode
18	C0	ADDL2 opcode
19	52	R2 addressing mode
1A	53	R3 addressing mode

The size of this program is easy to determine—counting the number of machine language bytes gives a size of 27 memory locations, not including the code for $EXIT_S. The above example is generated by replacing each assembly language mnemonic with its machine language code for the VAX. The only calculations required are those to determine the displacement values. For example, in location 8 the first byte relative addressing mode occurs (AF). The byte following this line (location 9) is the two's complement displacement from the PC, which, when added to the PC, gives the location of the data X. Because the PC points to location 10 after the displacement has been fetched, the byte in location 9 must be a −10 or, in two's complement, an F6 (hex).

A general framework that you could use for the moment to set up and run your own assembly language programs on the VAX would look like the following:

```
.TITLE name comment
; Comments
data assignments
.ENTRY program_name, 0
program statements
$EXIT_$
.END program name
```

In Appendix D we show how you can actually prepare and run your programs. In Appendix E we show how to use DEBUG to inspect the values of the registers and memory locations while the program is being run. This allows you to ignore code for I/O at this point. But if you desire, in Appendix F we discuss some I/O macros that could be added to the program to allow you to run it in a more realistic manner. Methods for I/O will be discussed in Chapters 9 and 11.

Summary

In Chapter 2 we have introduced some of the concepts of a simple assembly language for the VAX. The structure of assembly language statements and the methods of addressing data were combined to form a complete set of assembly commands. Even though the set of commands included only six operations (move, clear, add, subtract, divide, and multiply), they are enough to allow for the development of complete assembly language programs. The power of this small instruction set was further enhanced by the study of several VAX addressing modes. These addressing modes allow the instruction to access data anywhere in the computer. As a result, data could be stored in one of the registers—as part of the program—or anywhere in main memory. Both the size of the instruction set and the addressing modes will be discussed further in the next chapter.

Exercises

1. Rewrite AVERAGE Version 6 so that the program will find the average of five numbers.
   a. Use the immediate mode and the numbers 1227, 1345, 3456, 2280, and 4391
   b. Use any five numbers initialized as longwords.
2. Without using the multiply instruction, write an assembly language program that will multiply a number stored in a memory location by decimal 10 and save the result in another memory location. Do not use any more than seven executable instructions (you may use any number of MACRO directives, however).

3. Assume the following state of the VAX memory and its registers before each of the following instructions is executed (all values including addresses are in hex).

Registers	Memory Address	Memory Contents
R0 3010	3010–3011	3016
R1 3012	3012–3013	0
R2 3014	3014–3015	127
R3 455	3016–3017	322
R4 2276	3018–3019	0

   What changes occur in the registers and memory locations after each of the following instructions is executed (assuming that each instruction operates on the same initial data given above)? Give the register or memory locations that change and their new values.

   a. CLRW (R2)
   b. CLRB (R2)
   c. MOVW R2, (R0)
   d. ADDW3 R1, R3, (R1)
   e. MOVL R4, (R1)
   f. CLRB R2

4. Translate the following statements into machine language.

   a. DIVB3 R1, R3, (R5)
   b. MOVL (R4), R10
   c. CLRL (R7)
   d. ADDL2 #2105, R7

5. Translate the following machine language code into assembly mnemonics.

a. 80	b. C7	c. B4	d. A0
53	66	6B	8F
5A	54		0A
	68		17
			00
			00
			64

6. Write an assembly language program that will evaluate the function

   $$f(x, y) = 3x^2y + 4xy^2 + xy - 10$$

   and determine the value for $(x,y) = (1,0); (2,6);$ and $(3,1)$.

7. Write an assembly language program that will determine the area of a rectangle, given its length and width as inputs.

8. Write an assembly language program that will find the sum of squares of four numbers.

   a. Use word arithmetic
   b. Use floating-point arithmetic

9. State the purpose of the following directives.
   a. .BYTE
   b. .LONG
   c. .BLKL
   d. .TITLE
   e. .ENTRY
   f. .END

10. Write an assembly language program to find the value of the cubic polynomial

    $C3 * x^3 + C2 * x^2 + C1 * x + C0$

    given the coefficients C0, C1, C2, C3, and x as inputs.
    a. Use longword arithmetic
    b. Use floating-point arithmetic

11. Compile (translate) the following Pascal program into assembly language by hand. Use longwords to represent integer values. (Your code will be quite different from that generated by the Pascal compiler.)

    ```
    program Example;
    var A, B, C: integer;
    begin
      A: =0;
      B: =2;
      C: =B;
      A: =A * B + C - 5    (Use a register for intermediate results.)
    end;
    ```

12. Repeat Exercise 11 for the following FORTRAN program.

    ```
    integer  Cost, Quan, Value, Price
    Cost = 20
    Quan = 35
    Value = Cost * Quan
    Price = Value - Value/10
    end
    ```

13. Suppose that a computer allocated the bits of a 36-bit instruction as follows:

    bits 0–9:   opcode
    　 10–22: first operand address
    　 23–35: second operand address

    a. How many opcodes are possible?
    b. How many memory locations could be accessed directly?

14. Given an assembly language program that begins at location 200 with the following lines of code

    ```
         STUDENTS:     .BLKW 35
        AVE_GRADE:     .FLOAT 0
     TOTAL_POINTS:     .WORD 250
    ```

    What are the values of STUDENTS, AVE_GRADE, and TOTAL_POINTS? (Hint: the answers are not 35, 0, and 250.)

15. Write an assembly language program that will find the volume of a cube given the length of a side, s.

CHAPTER CONTENTS

3.1 ADDRESSING MODES REVISITED

    Additional General Register Modes
        Autoincrement Mode
        Autoincrement Deferred Mode
        Autodecrement Mode
        Displacement Mode
        Displacement Deferred Mode
        Literal Mode
    Additional Program Counter Modes
        Relative Deferred Mode
        Absolute Mode
    Index Mode Addressing
    A Summary of Addressing Opcodes

3.2 VAX ASSEMBLY INSTRUCTIONS REVISITED

    Branching Instructions
    Processor Status Word (PSW)
    Conditional Branch Instructions
        Compare
        Test
    Conditional Branching Examples
    Unconditional Branch
    Example Program
    Another Example

SUMMARY

EXERCISES

CHAPTER 3

VAX Assembly Language

In this chapter we continue the major themes of Chapter 2. Additional VAX assembly instructions and additional addressing modes will be introduced. The AVERAGE example program from Chapter 2 will be enhanced, and additional example programs will be developed. You should carefully study each example to ensure that you understand both the new instructions and the new addressing modes. By the time you complete this chapter, you should be able to write sophisticated assembly language programs.

3.1 Addressing Modes Revisited

In this section we will complete the discussion of VAX addressing modes. While the material in this section deals with the very specific approach to addressing developed for the VAX, you will see in Chapter 13 that some other computers have similar addressing modes. All four general classes of addressing that were mentioned in Chapter 2—the general register mode, the program counter mode, the indexed mode, and the branch mode—will be covered.

Additional General Register Modes

In Section 2.2 we introduced the two most common general register addressing modes: the register direct mode (the data is in one of the general-purpose registers) and the register deferred or indirect register mode (the address of the data is in one of the general-purpose registers). Six other modes also rely on the general-purpose registers.

Autoincrement Mode In this mode, as in the register deferred mode, the address of the data is contained in the identified register. However, once the data is located, the contents of the register are incremented. The amount of the increment depends on the nature of the instruction.

For a	Increment by
Byte instruction	1
Word instruction	2
Longword instruction	4
Quadword instruction	8

This is a very useful mode for working with an array of data when the data is stored in sequential memory locations. In such a case the register would initially point to the first data item, and each time the addressing mode is used, the register would automatically be incremented to point to the next data item. The assembly language format for this mode is

(Rn)+

An example instruction using this specifier is

CLRB   (R5)+

The operation of this instruction is demonstrated in Figure 3.1. The opcode for this mode is given by

1000	Reg ID

In hex the code appears as 8n where n is the register number. For the CLRB (R5)+ instruction, the machine language version is

Address	Opcode(hex)	
100	94	CLRB
101	85	(R5)+

This addressing mode could be useful in the AVERAGE program from Chapter 2. In this new version (Version 7) we will store the address of

3.1 Addressing Modes Revisited

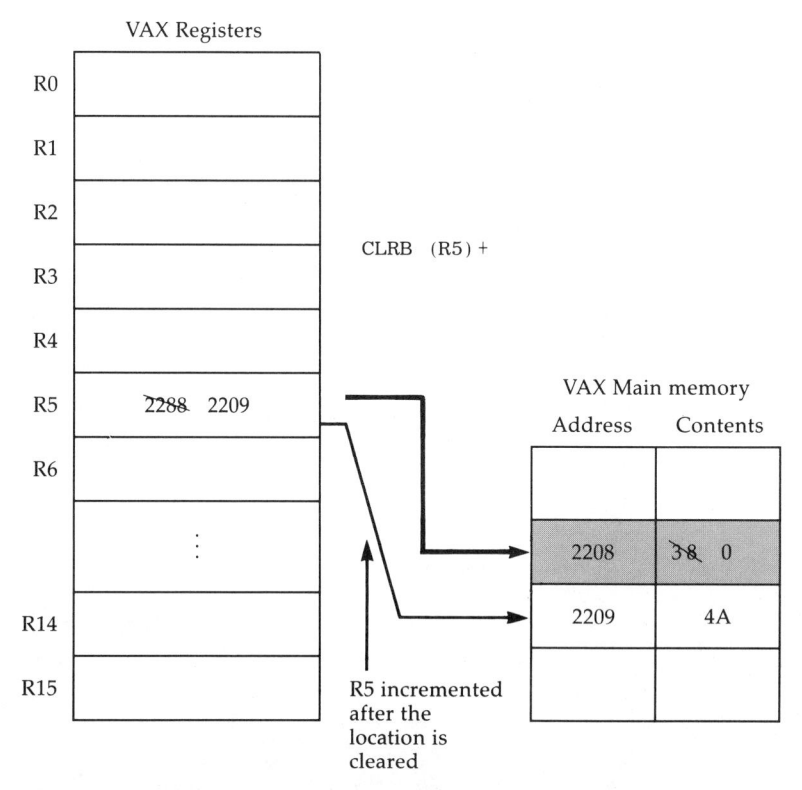

Figure 3.1 Autoincrement mode addressing

[Figure shows VAX Registers with R5 containing 2288 crossed out and replaced with 2209, CLRB (R5)+ instruction, VAX Main memory with address 2208 containing 38 crossed out to 0, and address 2209 containing 4A. Note: "R5 incremented after the location is cleared"]

the first of the three data words in register 6 and then, using the autoincrement addressing mode, automatically increment register 6 to point to the next data item after we use it to find the current one. This version uses a new instruction that we have not yet covered. The MOVAW instruction will move the *address* of the first data item listed to the location given by the second addressing mode. It does not, as does the MOV*x* instruction, move the data itself. The MOVA*x* will move a 32-bit address of byte, word, longword, floating-point, or quadword data. The opcodes are

Mnemonic	Opcode(hex)	Action
MOVAB	9E	Move the address of the byte
MOVAW	3E	Move the address of the word
MOVAL	DE	Move the address of the longword
MOVAF	DE	Move the address of the floating
MOVAQ	7E	Move the address of the quadword
MOVAD		or double

```
                         AVERAGE Version 7
                     .TITLE   Average  Version 7
           ;This program will calculate the average of
           ;  three numbers X, Y, and Z. The result will be
           ;  saved in location Ave.
    X:          .WORD     1560         ;Create storage for X(0)
                .WORD     1432         ;This word is X(1)
                .WORD     2167         ;This word is X(2)
    Ave:        .BLKW     1            ;Save room for the answer
                .ENTRY AVERAGE, 0
    Begin:      MOVAW     X, R6                    ;Move the address of
                                                   ;  X(0) into R6
                ADDW3     (R6)+, (R6)+, R5  ;R5 contains X(0) + X(1)
                ADDW2     (R6)+, R5         ;R5 contains final sum
                DIVW3     #3, R5, (R6)      ;Ave contains R5/3
                $EXIT_S
                .END   AVERAGE
```

The sequence of steps that AVERAGE Version 7 implements is shown in Figure 3.2. As you examine AVERAGE Version 7, note that the three data items are treated as if they were in an array rather than as separate data items as in Version 6. In addition, notice that the division operation does not refer to location AVE but relies on the fact that R6 points to location AVE after its final increment.

Autoincrement Deferred Mode With this somewhat complicated mode, the register contains the address of the address of the data; that is, the register points to a location in memory that contains the address of the data. It is simply one more level of indirection than the register deferred mode. After the data is located, the register is incremented by four. Note that in this case there is no variability in the increment size; it is always four because the register always points to an address and all addresses are four bytes long. The assembly language format for this mode is

   @(Rn)+

For example, the following instruction is demonstrated in Figure 3.3.

   CLRB   @   (R5)+

The opcode for this addressing mode is given by

1001	Reg ID

In hex the code is 9n where n is the register number. The machine language version of the example instruction is

3.1 Addressing Modes Revisited

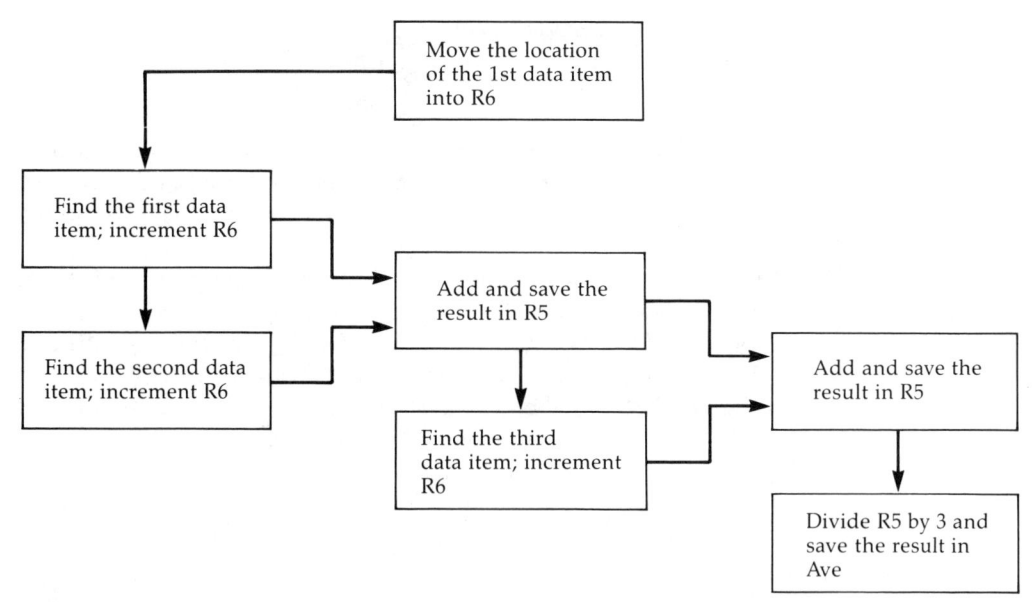

Figure 3.2 Flow sequence for AVERAGE version 7

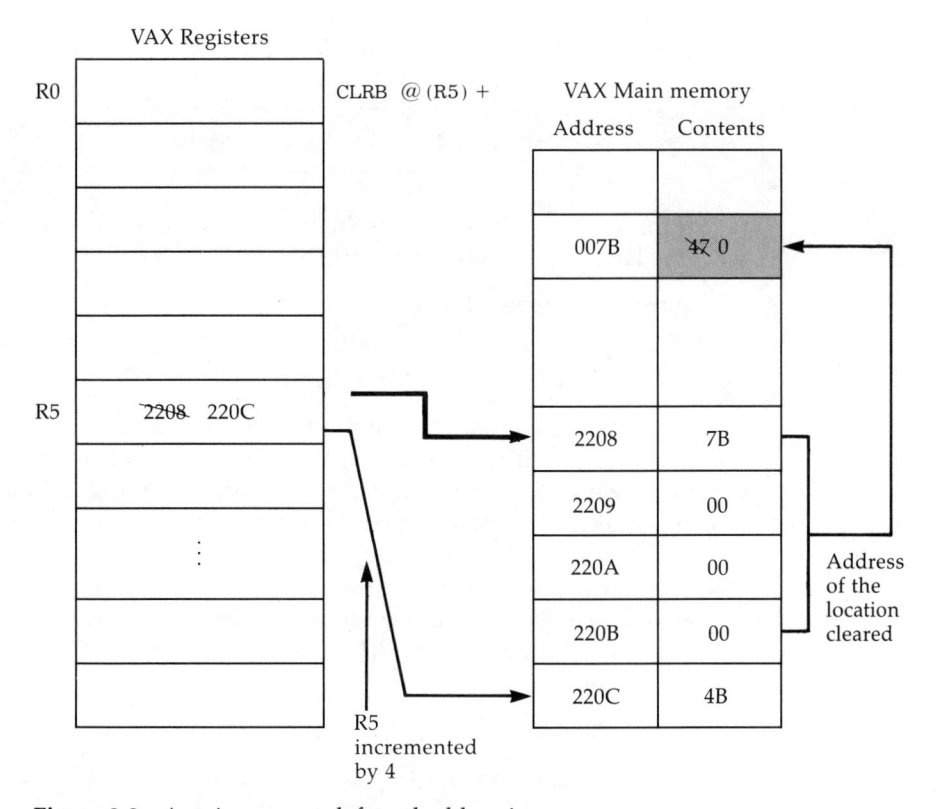

Figure 3.3 Autoincrement deferred addressing

Address	Opcode(hex)	
100	94	CLRB
101	95	@(R5)+

In Chapter 7 we will find that lists of addresses are often used to pass arguments to subroutines. Autoincrement deferred addressing can be used to access the values of the arguments pointed to by those addresses.

Autodecrement Mode This mode is not the exact opposite of the autoincrement mode, but it is close. In this mode the contents of the register are decremented by one, two, four, or eight (depending on the nature of the instruction), and the result is the address of the data. Note that for this mode the decrement is accomplished first, and then the data is found. The assembly language format for this mode is

    −(Rn)

An example of the use of this mode is found in Figure 3.4, which implements the instruction

    CLRB   −(R5)

The opcode for this addressing mode is given by

0111	Reg ID

In hex this code would appear as 7n where n is the register number. The machine language version of the CLRB −(R5) instruction is given by

Address	Opcode(hex)	
200	94	CLRB
201	75	−(R5)

This addressing mode is often used to access array elements in reverse order, starting with the last element and working toward the first. In Chapter 7 we will see how both the autodecrement and autoincrement modes are used to implement push and pop operations on a stack.

Displacement Mode This is another unusual addressing mode. The address of the data is found by adding a displacement value to the contents of the selected register. The assembly language format for this addressing mode is

    displacement(Rn)

where displacement has two parts:

    displacement = specifier^number

3.1 Addressing Modes Revisited

VAX Registers

CLRB -(R5)

Decrement R5 before the instruction is implemented

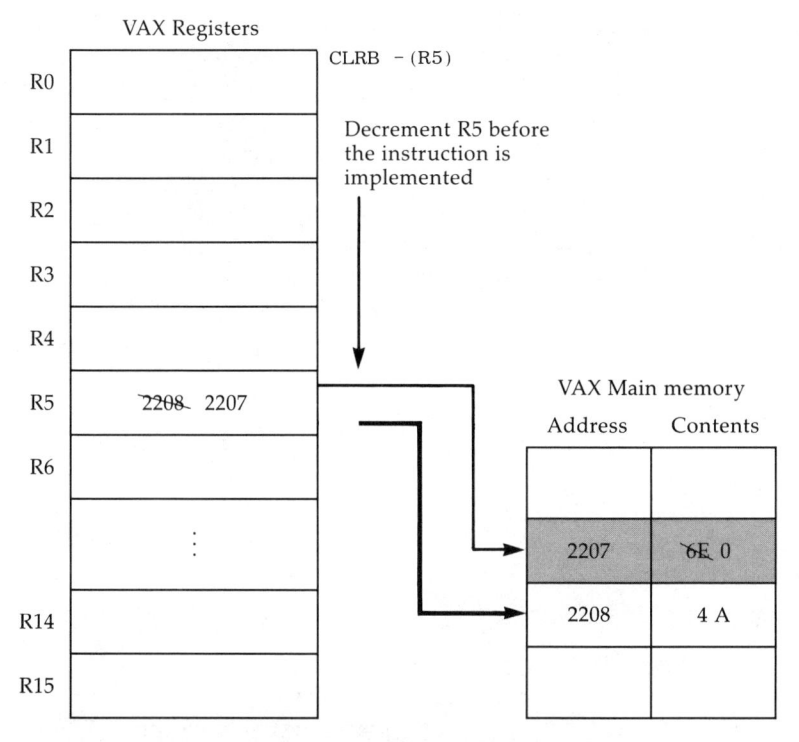

R5: ~~2208~~ 2207

VAX Main memory

Address	Contents
2207	6E 0
2208	4 A

Figure 3.4 Autodecrement addressing

The optional specifier indicates the size of the displacement value as given below.

B^ = byte displacement
W^ = word displacement
L^ = longword displacement

That is, B^ means store the displacement value in the byte following the opcode; W^ means store the value in the word following the opcode; and L^ means store the value in the longword following the opcode. The actual address of the data given in the displacement mode is determined by the CPU using the equation

address = (Rn) + displacement

The machine opcodes for this addressing mode are

Byte displacement: An   (n = register number)
Word displacement: Cn
Longword displacement: En

In each case the opcode for the mode is followed by a byte or bytes that give the value of the displacement. The displacement value may be given by an expression or as a positive or negative decimal integer. In either case it is stored in machine language as a two's complement integer. If you leave off the displacement size specifier (B^, W^, or L^), the assembler will determine the smallest size capable of storing the displacement value. For example, 12(R4) means move to the memory location that is 12 bytes beyond the one to which register 4 points. The hexadecimal equivalent of the displacement, 0C, is stored in the byte following the addressing mode specifier. If register 4 contains the hex value 1100, the memory location we want is 110C. Figure 3.5 illustrates the effect of the assembly language instruction

```
CLRB    B^18(R5)
```

The code for the displacement mode is the same as the code for the relative mode discussed in Chapter 2. The difference is that instead of identifying register 15 (hex F), which is the PC, one of the other registers is specified in the opcode. For example, the instruction CLRB B^18(R5) would be represented in machine language by

Address	Opcode(hex)	
200	94	CLRB
201	A5	Byte displacement with R5
202	12	Displacement value in hex

(Note: decimal 18 equals 12 in hex.)

The following example program illustrates the use of displacement mode addressing. Given two arrays of test scores for three students, you are asked to write a program that will store the sum of the two scores in another array.

```
                .TITLE  Test Scores
          ;This program will find the sum of two
          ;   test scores for a group of three students
Test_Ave:       .BLKW   3
Test_One:       .WORD   20, 22, 27      ;First test scores
Test_Two:       .WORD   32, 30, 35      ;Second test scores
                .ENTRY  TEST, 0
Begin:    MOVAW Test_One, R6            ;R6 points to the array
          MOVAW Test_Ave, R7            ;R7 points to the ave
          ADDW3   6(R6), (R6)+, (R7)+   ;Add the first two scores
          ADDW3   6(R6), (R6)+, (R7)+   ;Add the second scores
          ADDW3   6(R6), (R6), (R7)     ;Final addition
Done:     $EXIT_S
```

Each ADDW3 instruction in the above example takes advantage of the fact that the second test score for each student is located six bytes beyond the first test score, as shown in Figure 3.6.

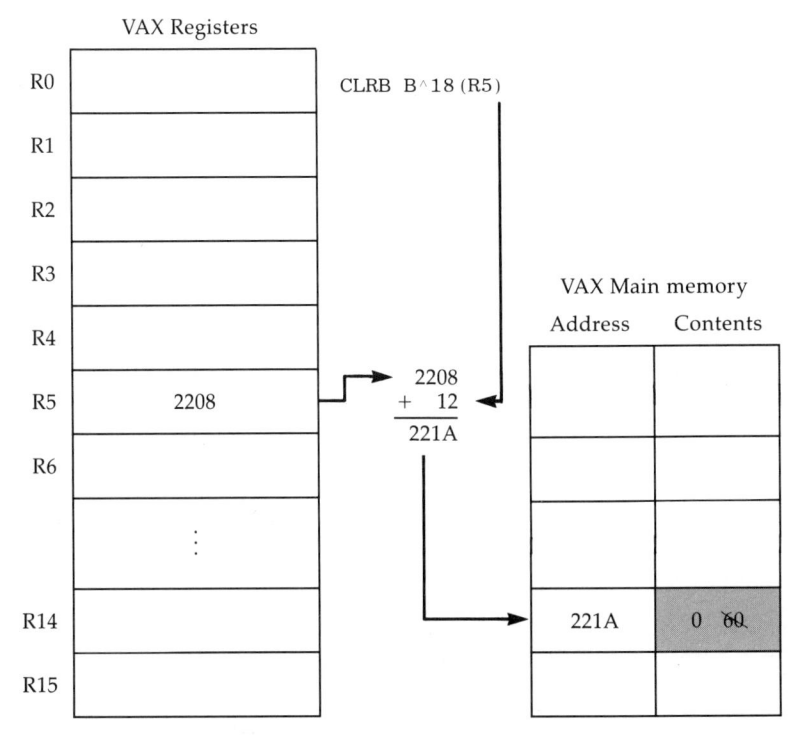

Figure 3.5 Displacement mode addressing

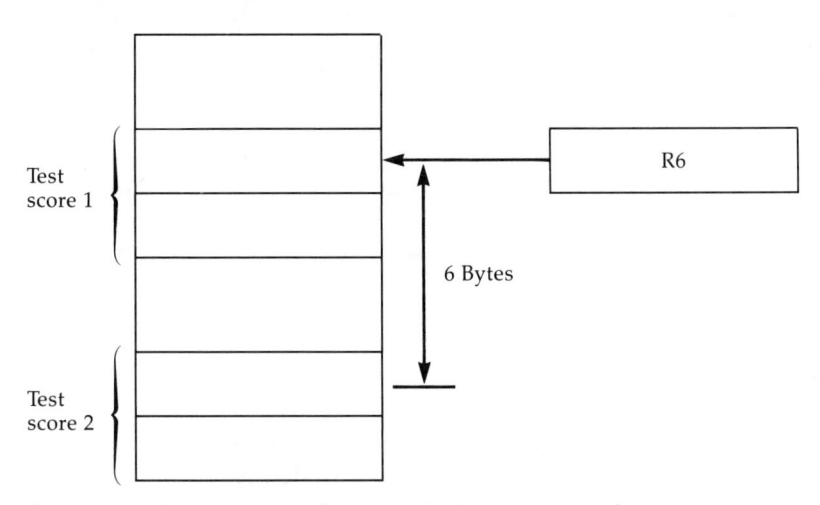

Figure 3.6 Displacement addressing in the sum example

Displacement Deferred Mode This mode combines the operation of the displacement mode and the deferred mode. The result is that the address of the data is determined by adding the contents of the identified register to the displacement and fetching the contents of that memory location. In other words, **the address of the address** is given by the sum of the register contents and the displacement value. The assembly format for this mode is

@displacement(Rn)

Figure 3.7 shows an example of the operation of the instruction

CLRB   @B^18(R5)

For the example shown in Figure 3.7, R5 contains 2208. When the displacement 12 is added (in hex), the result is the new address 221A. However, this is not the location to be cleared. Memory location 221A contains 31, which is the address of the memory location to be cleared. The machine language codes for this addressing mode are similar to the displacement mode codes. The actual machine codes are Bn for byte displacement, Dn for word displacement, or Fn for longword displacement, where n is the register ID. The addressing mode is followed by the displacement value. For the CLRB @B^12(R5) instruction, the opcodes are given by

Address	Opcode(hex)	
200	94	CLRB
201	B5	Byte displacement deferred, R5
202	0C	Displacement value in hex

In Chapter 7 we will see that this addressing mode is very useful for finding the value of a parameter whose address has been passed to a procedure.

Literal Mode The final register mode is the literal mode. In this mode the data is included directly in the instruction, and so an address is not needed. However, the size of the data is restricted in this mode because only the integers 0 to 63 may be used. As a result, this is usually called the *short literal mode*. To store larger values in the instruction, it is necessary to use the immediate mode (which was covered in Chapter 2). The assembly format for this addressing mode is

S^#value

For example, MOVB S^#5, R7 asks the computer to move the value 5 into register 7. The machine language opcode for this mode is denoted by two leading zero bits in the mode byte, followed by the literal value in the remaining six bits as shown.

00	Value

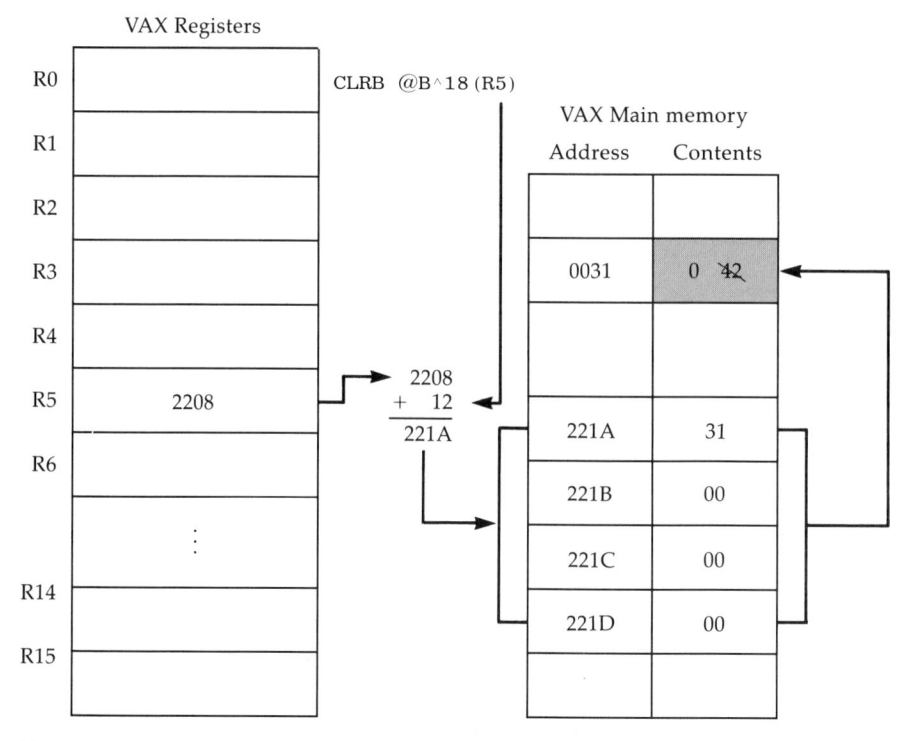

Figure 3.7 Displacement deferred addressing

Because only six bits are left for the value, it should be clear why this mode is restricted only to values from 0 to 63. For the example instruction, MOVB S^#5, R7, the machine language version would be

Address	Opcode(hex)	
200	90	MOVB
201	05	Literal value 5
202	57	Register direct mode with R7

Note that if we simply use the notation #value in our programs and do not directly specify either the literal or the immediate mode using S^ or I^, MACRO will automatically select the short literal mode if it can use the more compact form; otherwise MACRO will select the immediate mode. The VAX also allows 64 floating-point values to be represented in the short literal mode.

Additional Program Counter Modes

In Chapter 2 we introduced the two most common program counter addressing modes, the relative and immediate modes. The VAX provides two additional program counter addressing modes, which are reviewed in this section.

Relative Deferred Mode In this mode the address of the address is contained in the assembly language instruction. The assembly format for this mode is

@address

For example, Figure 3.8 illustrates the use of this addressing mode in the following clear instruction where we assume that SPACE has been assigned the value 130.

CLRB   @SPACE

As with the relative addressing mode, this mode stores an offset or displacement from the PC value rather than the absolute address of the

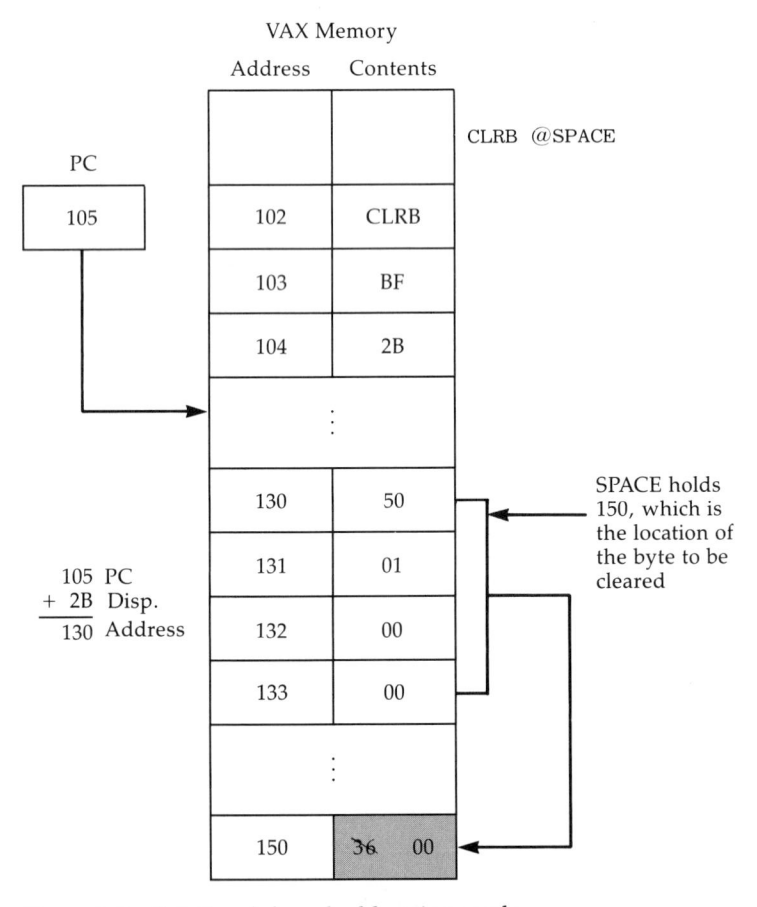

Figure 3.8 Relative deferred addressing mode

address. It also has the same three displacement modes: (1) byte with the machine language code BF; (2) word with the machine language code DF, and (3) longword with the machine language code FF. In the figure the contents of location 130 contain the address of the location to clear.

Absolute Mode In this mode the address of the data is given in assembly language and follows the addressing mode byte in the machine code. This mode is not recommended for general use because it does not allow for relocatable code. The assembly format for this mode is

@#address

Index Mode Addressing

In Chapter 2 we listed two other general addressing modes, the index and branch modes. While discussion of the branch mode will be deferred until the branching instructions have been covered, we will cover the index mode in this section.

Often data is arranged in the form of an array in main memory much like the structure shown in Figure 3.9 for storing the byte data A(0) to A(5). There are several ways to access the example data array. The first is by the address of the data items. In this case A(0) is at location 100, while A(1) is at location 101 and so on. A second method that we have already seen is to use the autoincrement or autodecrement mode. A third method is based on the use of displacement addressing. Suppose that

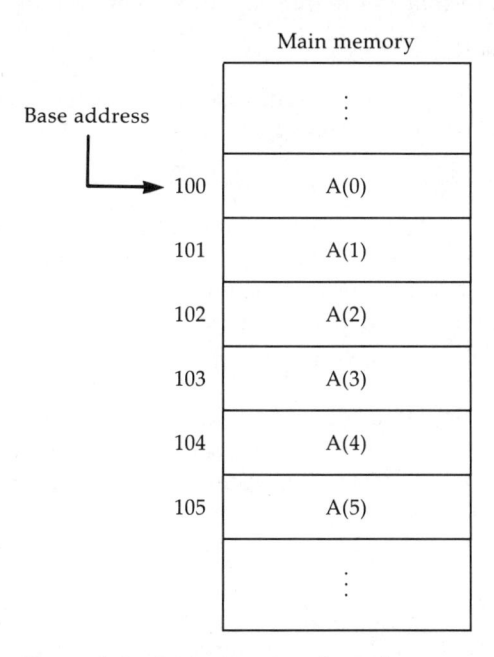

Figure 3.9 Array structure in main memory

the address of A(0) is in R4 and we want to move A(2) to R5. If each element of A is one byte, as in the figure, the instruction is

```
MOVB 2(R4),R5
```

A fourth method to access particular elements of A uses relative addressing. Suppose that we declare the array using the statement

```
A:    BLKB  6    ;Array elements A(0) to A(5)
```

Now, we can refer to A(0) as A, A(1) as A + 1, A(2) as A + 2, and so on. This may seem strange at first, but remember that the assembler treats the label A as an address, not as the value stored at A(0). To move A(2) into R3 using this addressing method, we could write MOVB A + 2, R3. In this example we were discussing an array of bytes. If B is an array of longwords and denotes the location of B(0), the location of B(1) is B + 4 and the location of B(2) is B + 8.

The fifth and final method introduces a new addressing mode called the indexed mode. The data in the array is referenced by the offset from the base address for the array. If the base address of the array is taken to be 100, then A(0) is zero units from the base address, A(1) is one unit from the base address, and so on. This offset from the base address is called the index. The VAX indexed addressing mode is based on the concept of an offset from the base address for an array.

The general format of the indexed addressing mode is given by

base address[Rx]

where Rx is one of the general-purpose registers. The actual address of the data is determined by the expression

data address = base address + (Rx) * size

where size is the number of bytes specified by the instruction. That is, for a byte instruction size equals 1, while for a word instruction size equals 2, and for a longword instruction it is 4. The base address can be specified using one of the other addressing modes. The most common addressing methods used for generating the base address are the register indirect and the relative modes. For example, using the register indirect mode and assuming that R4 contains the base address 100, while R7 contains the index value of 3, the instruction CLRB (R4)[R7] (if applied to the array of Figure 3.9) would clear A(3). This addressing mode is implemented in machine language in several bytes as shown below.

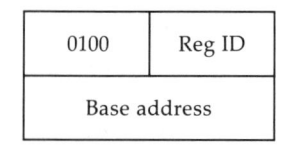

0100	Reg ID
Base address	

3.1 Addressing Modes Revisited

For the example instruction CLRB (R4)[R7], the opcode sequence would be

Address	Opcode(hex)	
200	94	CLRB
201	47	[R7]
202	64	(R4)

This addressing mode could be used in the AVERAGE program example resulting in Version 8. Version 8 uses the increment word (INCW) instruction to add 1 to the index register. The increment instruction opcodes are

Mnemonic	Opcode(hex)	Action
INCB	96	Increment a byte
INCW	B6	Increment a word
INCL	D6	Increment a longword

All three instructions represent a quick and easy way to add 1 to the data.

```
                  AVERAGE Version 8
                      .TITLE    Average    Version 8
          ;This program will calculate the average of
          ;   three numbers X(0), X(1), and X(2). The result will be
          ;   saved in location Ave.
X:                .WORD     1560           ;Create storage for the
                  .WORD     1432           ;  data
                  .WORD     2167
Ave:              .BLKW     1              ;Save room for the answer
                  .ENTRY AVERAGE,0
Begin:            MOVAW     X,R6           ;Move address of X into R6
                                           ;  this will serve as the base
                                           ;  address
                  CLRL      R4             ;R4 will contain the index
                  MOVW      (R6)[R4],R5    ;R5 now contains X(0)
                  INCL      R4             ;Increment the index
                  ADDW2     (R6)[R4],R5    ;R5 contains X(0) + X(1)
                  INCL      R4             ;Increment the index
                  ADDW2     (R6)[R4],R5    ;R5 contains the final sum
                  DIVW3     #3,R5,AVE      ;Ave contains R5/3
Done:             $EXIT_S
                  .END      AVERAGE
```

A Summary of Addressing Opcodes

The machine language codes for these addressing modes are summarized below. The general form of the machine language version of the operand specifier bytes is also shown for both addressing modes. See also Table 3.1 for addressing modes.

Operand Specifier Bytes

General register mode

| Mode | Register ID (4 bits) |

Program counter mode

| Mode | 1111 (PC Register ID) |

Table 3.1 Addressing Modes

Mode	Assembler	Machine Language
General Register Modes		
Register direct	Rn	5n
Register deferred	(Rn)	6n
Autoincrement	(Rn)+	8n
Autoincrement deferred	@(Rn)+	9n
Autodecrement	−(Rn)	7n
Displacement	dis(Rn)	An (byte)
		Cn (word)
		En (longword)
Displacement deferred	@dis(Rn)	Bn (byte)
		Dn (word)
		Fn (longword)
Literal	S^#value	00 - 3F
Program Counter Modes		
Relative	Address label	AF (byte)
		CF (word)
		EF (longword)
Relative deferred	@address	BF (byte)
		DF (word)
		FF (longword)
Immediate	#data	8F
Absolute	@#address	9F
Indexed mode		
Indexed mode	base[RN]	4N

3.2 VAX Assembly Instructions Revisited

In Chapter 2 we introduced several basic assembly language instructions for the VAX. Now we will expand the instruction set to include branching and branching support instructions. The new level of VAX instructions brings us to the set listed in Figure 3.10.

Branching Instructions

Another class of useful instructions is the branch instructions, which are designed to change the normal instruction sequence based on certain conditions in a program. For example, if a certain variable is positive, you may want to execute one set of instructions, and if the variable is 0, you may want to execute a different set. The VAX uses the processor status word (PSW) to keep track of possible branch conditions based on the last instruction executed. A branch instruction uses the PSW to decide if a branch should be executed.

Processor Status Word (PSW)

Internal to the CPU is a 32-bit processor status longword (PSL) register that contains information about the current state of the program being executed. The lower 16 bits of the PSL make up the PSW, while the upper 16 bits contain privileged processor information. The first 4 bits of the

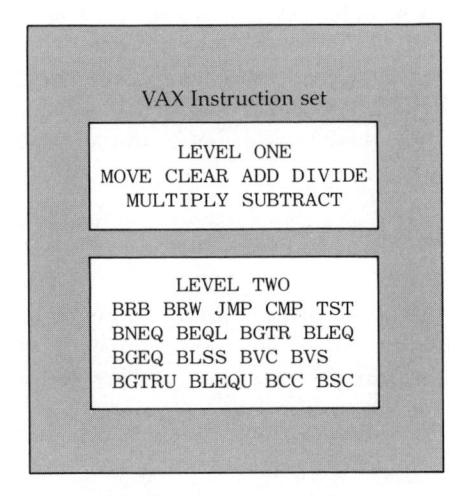

```
VAX Instruction set

    LEVEL ONE
MOVE CLEAR ADD DIVIDE
   MULTIPLY SUBTRACT


       LEVEL TWO
BRB BRW JMP CMP TST
BNEQ BEQL BGTR BLEQ
BGEQ BLSS BVC BVS
BGTRU BLEQU BCC BSC
```

Figure 3.10 VAX Instruction set—levels one and two

PSW are the condition flags used for branching decisions, as shown below.

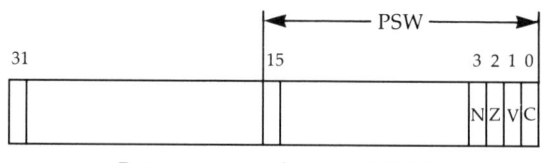

Processor status longword (PSL)

Bit 0: C—set to 1 if a carry occurred in the last operation; cleared otherwise.

Bit 1: V—set to 1 if an overflow occurred; cleared otherwise.

Bit 2: Z—set to 1 if the result of the last operation was 0; cleared otherwise.

Bit 3: N—set to 1 if the result of the last operation was negative; cleared otherwise.

These bits are checked whenever a conditional branch decision is required, and the branch is either executed or ignored based on their status.

Conditional Branch Instructions

There are 12 conditional branch instructions on the VAX, as shown in Table 3.2, some of which have two mnemonics. In the table the notation (N or Z) equals a 0 or a 1 implies a logical or Boolean OR on the values of N and Z. Each branch instruction requires that the CPU check the PSW. If the condition is satisfied, the program will jump to the location given in the branch instruction; if the condition is not satisfied, the program instruction following the conditional branch will be executed. Notice that there are two types of conditional branch instructions, one for unsigned integers and another for signed integers. This is necessary because the VAX must know if two integers are signed or unsigned before it can correctly evaluate their relative size. For example, given the two binary integers A and B

```
A   1000 1011
B   0011 0100
```

ask yourself which is larger. If they are unsigned integers, A is clearly larger than B. However, if they are signed integers, then A is negative because its most significant bit (MSB) is 1; so B is larger than A.

While the typical assembly language format for these conditional branch instructions is

```
Bxxx     destination
```

Table 3.2 Conditional Branch Instructions

Instruction	Code	Condition for Branch	Branch Operation
BNEQ, BNEQU	12	Z = 0	BRANCH ON NOT EQUAL
BEQL, BEQLU	13	Z = 1	BRANCH ON EQUAL
BGTR	14	N = 0 and Z = 0	BRANCH ON GREATER THAN
BLEQ	15	N = 1 or Z = 1	BRANCH ON LESS THAN OR =
BGEQ, BGEQU	18	N = 0	BRANCH ON GREATER OR =
BLSS, BLSSU	19	N = 1	BRANCH ON LESS THAN
BGTRU	1A	C = 0 and Z = 0	BRANCH ON GREATER THAN UNSIGNED
BLEQU	1B	C = 1 or Z = 1	BRANCH ON LESS THAN OR EQUAL TO UNSIGNED
BVC	1C	V = 0	BRANCH ON NO OVERFLOW
BVS	1D	V = 1	BRANCH ON OVERFLOW
BCC	1E	C = 0	BRANCH ON CARRY CLEAR
BCS	1F	C = 1	BRANCH ON CARRY SET

(where *destination* must be a label in your program), they appear in machine language as two bytes, as shown below.

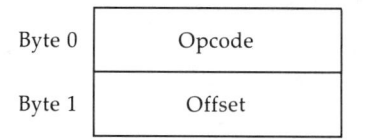

Byte 0	Opcode
Byte 1	Offset

The offset is calculated by the assembler and replaces the absolute destination supplied by the programmer. This offset is an eight-bit two's complement number that is added to the current value of the PC to determine the branch destination. Because only eight bits are allowed for the offset, a conditional branch instruction is limited in its choice of destinations. That is, a conditional branch may be used only if the destination address is within 127 bytes of the branch instruction (more precisely, from −128 to 127 bytes away from the branch instruction). The VAX provides a set of branch instructions not subject to this limitation called unconditional branch instructions. We will examine those later in this chapter.

Before looking at an example of a conditional branch instruction, let's consider how the PSW condition codes are set. There are two ways that the branch conditions may be determined prior to execution of the conditional branch instruction. One way is based on the use of standard operations. For example, you may execute a subtract instruction and follow it with a BLEQ. If the result of the subtract instruction was less than or equal to 0, it would have automatically set either the N or Z bit of the PSW to 1, and the branch would be executed. Otherwise, both bits would have been cleared and the branch would be skipped. Thus a conditional branch instruction uses the PSW to determine if a branch is necessary. As shown in Appendix A, many instructions (including all the arithmetic instructions) set the condition codes in the PSW. Consult that table whenever you need to determine what effect a certain instruction may have on the condition bits of the PSW. The other mechanism for changing bits of the PSW involves two special instructions, the compare and test instructions.

Compare This instruction allows the programmer to determine the relative size of two numbers using the basic addressing modes. The mnemonic for this operation is given by

```
CMPx    source 1, source 2
```

The instruction does not change the value of either source but will change the condition codes in the PSW based on the size of the source elements. Specifically,

1. If source 1 < source 2, N = 1; otherwise N = 0.
2. If source 1 = source 2, Z = 1; otherwise Z = 0.
3. The V bit is cleared.

The opcodes for the five compare instructions are

Mnemonic	Opcode(hex)	Action
CMPB	91	Compare two bytes
CMPW	B1	Compare two words
CMPL	D1	Compare two longwords
CMPF	51	Compare two floating-point values
CMPD	71	Compare two double

Test If you simply want to compare a number to 0 and branch based on the result of that comparison, you can use the instruction

```
CMPL source, #0
```

However, the same result can be achieved using the test instruction, which automatically compares a source to 0 and executes much faster than the compare instruction (and requires fewer bytes to store the instruction). The mnemonic for the test instruction is

```
TSTx    source
```

This does not affect the value of the source but will change the condition codes as follows:

1. If the source < 0, $N = 1$; otherwise $N = 0$.
2. If the source $= 0$, $Z = 1$; otherwise $Z = 0$.
3. C and V are cleared.

The opcodes for this instruction are

Mnemonic	Opcode(hex)	Action
TSTB	95	Test two bytes
TSTW	B5	Test two words
TSTL	D5	Test two longwords
TSTF	53	Test two floating-point values
TSTD	73	Test two double

Conditional Branching Examples

If you want to repeat a segment of code as long as a counter stored in register 3 is greater than 0, the following assembly language statements can achieve the desired effect:

```
LOOP:   xxxxxxx
        xxxxxx
        xxxxxxx
        TSTL    R3
        BNEQ    LOOP
```

Use of the compare instruction will allow more complicated forms of branching decisions, such as

```
LOOP:   xxxxxx
        xxxxxx
        xxxxxx
        CMPL    R3, R2
        BGTR    LOOP
```

The above set of instructions will execute the statements in the loop as long as the contents of register 3 are larger than those of register 2.

Unconditional Branch

There are three branch statements that do not check the PSW before the branch operation. These statements, like the high-level language GOTO, will always result in a branch. They are

Mnemonic	Opcode(hex)	Action
BRB	11	Branch with byte displacement
BRW	31	Branch with word displacement
JMP	17	Jump

Format: BRB *destination* Destination is a program label

The branch with byte displacement is used for short unconditional branches because it allows only 1 byte for storing the displacement data (offset to the branch destination). The branch with word displacement is used for longer branches because it stores the displacement data in a word. This will allow the program to branch up to 32K bytes from the current PC location. The jump instruction is unique among the branching options because it does not necessarily use a displacement from the PC mode to keep track of the branch destination. Instead, it allows any of the general or program counter address mode selections to specify an absolute destination address. For example:

```
JMP     (R1)
```

will jump to the location pointed to by register 1.

The unconditional branches can be used to overcome the 127-byte offset limitation of the conditional branch instructions. For example, say we want to branch to the label GREATER if X if greater than 5. We might try the following code:

```
CMPL    X,#5          ; is X > 5?
BGTR    GREATER       ; if so, branch to location GREATER
```

This code will work fine as long as the location GREATER is within 127 bytes of the branch statement. However, if it turns out that GREATER is 276 bytes away from the branch statement, the conditional branch will not work. But a combination of a conditional and an unconditional branch will work. In this case 276 bytes can be represented by a word displacement. As a result, the code would become

```
        CMPL    X,#5          ; is X > 5?
        BLEQ    Cont          ; if not, go to Cont
        BRW     GREATER       ; if so, go to GREATER
CONT:   xxxxxxxxxxxxxxx
```

Because the conditional test is used to skip around the unconditional branch, it looks for the condition under which we do not want to branch. This construct is common in unstructured languages such as assembly.

Example Program

The branching statements will allow us to write a more general version of the program AVERAGE. Version 9 of AVERAGE will find the average of any number of data items. This version introduces another instruction, decrement word (DECW). Decrement will subtract 1 from the data given by the address mode, and like the increment instruction, it will work with byte, word, and longword data types. The opcodes for the decrement instruction are

Mnemonic	Opcode(hex)	Action
DECB	97	Decrement byte
DECW	B7	Decrement word
DECL	D7	Decrement longword

The flowchart that illustrates the operation of AVERAGE Version 9 is shown in Figure 3.11.

```
                        AVERAGE Version 9
                      .TITLE    Average    Version 9
             ;This program will calculate the average of a set of
             ;numbers and store the result in the location Ave.
             ;The first data item must be the size of the set
             ;followed by the data values to average over.
Size:                   .WORD     5            ;Number of data points
Data:                   .WORD     2776         ;First data point
                        .WORD     2167         ;Second data point
                        .WORD     133          ;Third data point
                        .WORD     512          ;Fourth data point
                        .WORD     24           ;Fifth data point
Ave:                    .BLKW     1            ;Save room for the answer
                        .ENTRY AVERAGE, 0
             MOVW       Size, R3              ;Initialize R3 to data set size
             CLRW       R5                    ;Initialize sum in R5 to 0
             CLRL       R4                    ;Initialize index register to 0
             MOVAW      Data, R6              ;Initialize R6 to data base
                                              ;   address
             TSTW       R3                    ;Any data left?
             BEQL       Done                  ;If R3=3 go to Done
             ADDW2      (R6)[R4],R5           ;R5 contains current sum
             INCL       R4                    ;Add one to the index
             DECW       R3                    ;Decrease count by one
             BRB        Next                  ;Add next data item on list
Done:        DIVW3      Size, R5, Ave         ;Ave contains R5/Size
             $EXIT_S
                        .END    AVERAGE
```

An assembly listing of Version 9 of AVERAGE will include the machine language codes. The codes should appear as in Table 3.3. Note that the

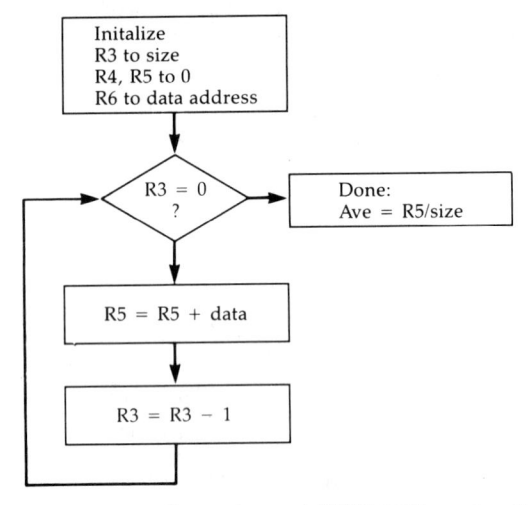

```
                    ┌─────────────────┐
                    │ Initalize       │
                    │ R3 to size      │
                    │ R4, R5 to 0     │
                    │ R6 to data address │
                    └─────────────────┘
                            │
                            ▼
                         ╱R3 = 0╲        ┌──────────────┐
                    ────◁   ?   ▷──────▶ │ Done:        │
                   │     ╲     ╱         │ Ave = R5/size│
                   │        │            └──────────────┘
                   │        ▼
                   │  ┌──────────────┐
                   │  │ R5 = R5 + data│
                   │  └──────────────┘
                   │        │
                   │        ▼
                   │  ┌──────────────┐
                   │  │ R3 = R3 - 1  │
                   │  └──────────────┘
                   │        │
                    ────────┘
```

Figure 3.11 Flow chart of AVERAGE version 9

Table 3.3 Machine Language Codes for AVERAGE Version 9

Byte	Hex	Comments
1	05	Value 5 stored in location SIZE
2	00	
3	D8	Value 2776 stored in hex
4	0A	
5	77	Value 2167 stored in hex
6	08	
7	85	Value 133 stored in hex
8	00	
9	00	Value 512 stored in hex
10	02	
11	18	Value 24 stored in hex
12	00	
13	00	Location saved for AVE
14	00	
15	00	.ENTRY location
16	00	
17	B0	MOVW
18	AF	Byte relative addressing to location SIZE (to byte 1)
19	ED	−19 in two's complement
20	53	R3 addressing mode
21	B4	CLRW
22	55	R5 addressing mode
23	D4	CLRL
24	54	R4 addressing mode
25	3E	MOVAW

program requires 48 bytes of storage plus some additional bytes for the $EXIT_S routine. It is not the best approach to writing an assembly language program for finding the average of a list of numbers, but it does illustrate a number of the instructions and addressing modes that have been covered in this chapter. Exercise 1 suggests some ways to shorten the code and make it run faster.

Another Example

The branching instructions presented in this chapter are useful for decision making. We will look at a simple example that illustrates this type of application. Suppose we want to write a program that will calculate the weekly pay for an employee. The employee gets time and one half for any hours beyond 40. The only variables that we need are Hours, PayRate, and Pay (the weekly pay). We can use **symbolic constants** for the hours in a normal work week and for the value $\frac{1}{2}$. The format for a

Table 3.3 *(continued)*

Byte	Hex	Comments
26	AF	Byte relative addressing to location DATA (to byte 3)
27	E7	−25 in two's complement
28	56	R6 addressing mode
29	B5	TSTW
30	53	R3 addressing mode
31	13	BEQL
32	0B	Add decimal 10 to PC to move to byte 43
33	A0	ADDW2
34	44	Indexed mode on register 4
35	66	(R6) addressing on indexed mode
36	55	R5 addressing mode
37	D6	INCL
38	54	R4 addressing mode
39	B7	DECW
40	53	R3 addressing mode
41	11	BRB
42	F2	−14 in two's complement (back to byte 29)
43	A7	DIVW3
44	AF	Byte relative addressing to SIZE
45	D3	−45 in two's complement (back to byte 1)
46	55	R5 addressing mode
47	AF	Byte relative addressing to AVE
48	DC	−36 in two's complement (back to byte 13)
$EXIT_S		

symbolic constant is symbol = constant. We will use floating-point numbers, although some programmers may want to use integer arithmetic in pennies. There are several different ways the calculation can be carried out, but we have chosen to do it as follows:

If hours ≤ 40 then
    Pay := Hours * PayRate
else
    Pay := (0.5 * (Hours − 40) + Hours) * PayRate

The program shown below does not include any I/O. You could use the symbolic debugger to test the program, or you could add the calls to the input and output macros of Appendix F.

```
            .TITLE Payroll
;Calculate Pay given Hours and PayRate. Use time and
;  a half for any hours beyond 40
NormalHours = ^F40
Half = ^F0.5
Hours:      .FLOAT    42.0      ;Assign value for Hours
PayRate:    .Float    9.5       ;Assign hourly pay rate
Pay:        .BLKF     1         ;Reserve room for pay earned
            .ENTRY CalculatePay,0
; *******Determine if employee worked overtime******
Begin:  CMPF    Hours,#NormalHours    ;IfHours>40
        BGTR    Overtime              ;branch to Overtime
; **********Calculate normal pay***********
        MULF3   PayRate,Hours,Pay
        BRB     Done        ;Skip over alternative calculation
;**********Calculate pay if there is overtime********
Overtime:
        SUBF3   #NormalHours,Hours,R3   ;R3 gets overtime hours
        MULF2   #Half,R3                ;R3 gets adjusted overtime
                                        ; hours
        ADDF2   Hours,R3       ;R3 gets adjusted total hours
        MULF3   PayRate,R3,Pay
Done:   $EXIT_S
        .END CalculatePay
```

Summary

In this chapter we have continued the theme of Chapter 2 covering the basic assembly language of the VAX. Additional addressing modes and instructions were examined, including the move address, increment, decrement, and branching instructions. The new addressing modes increase the flexibility of the new instructions. The autoincrement, autodecrement, and displacement addressing modes, for example, allow the system to access an array of data efficiently, eliminating the need for special instructions to increment or decrement an array address pointer. Since each instruction can utilize any of the addressing modes, we have defined—using only a few instructions—a very powerful set of operations. As a result, using only the information contained in Chapters 2 and 3, you should be able to write some very sophisticated assembly language programs. Additional VAX assembly language instructions will be provided in subsequent chapters. These new instructions will also work with the addressing modes specified in Chapters 2 and 3 and will add to your programming options.

Exercises

1. Fix Version 9 of AVERAGE so that it requires fewer than 48 bytes of memory to store the program. Some possibilities, not all of which can be used in the same program, include: observe TSTW is not really needed; add values in the reverse order, eliminating the need for R4; use autoincrement addressing.

2. Translate the following to their hex code.
   a. SUBW2   (R2), R1
   b. MULL3   #14, (R4), (R2)+
   c. MOVL   @(R2)+, -(R3)
   d. DIVB3   16(R2), #^B11, 1028(R3)
   e. MOVL   (R11)[R10], R2
   f. TSTL   (R2)   ;all 4 lines form one code segment
      BEQL Cont
      INCL (R3)+
      Cont: DECL @130(R3)

3. Translate the following assembly language program into machine language and determine the amount of memory required to store it.

```
A:          .WORD    23
B:          .LONG    ^XAB11
            .ENTRY   EXAMPLE, 0
            MOVW     A, R3
            MOVAW    A, R4
            MULW3    #5, R3, (R4)
            MOVL     #0, R6
            CLRL     R5
NEXT:       ADDL2    #1, R6
            ADDL2    B, R5
            CMPL     B, R6
            BLEQ     NEXT
            $EXIT_S
            .END     EXAMPLE
```

4. Repeat Exercise 3 using the following assembly language program:

```
X:      . LONG  D^10
Y:      . LONG  20
SUM:    . LONG  0
AVG:    . LONG  0
        . ENTRY  EXAMPLE2, 0
        MOVL     X, R5
        ADDL3    Y, R5, SUM
        DIVL3    #2, SUM, AVG
        . END    EXAMPLE2
```

5. Translate the following machine language code into assembly language mnemonics. There are 19 bytes in this program segment going down column 1, then down column 2.

```
D0      0C
03      55
55      84
D0      D1
8F      55
82      64
16      18
00      F7
00
64
C1
```

6. Draw a flowchart (or write the pseudocode) and then write an assembly language program that will find the largest element in a list of five numbers.

7. Repeat Exercise 6 but allow the list length to be a variable.

8. Draw a flowchart for a program that will calculate n factorial. Then write an assembly language program that will calculate n factorial.

9. Write a one-page summary of the VAX address modes. This will be a very helpful reference. Include the four columns:

Addressing Mode   Assembler Notation   Machine Code   Purpose

10. Draw a flowchart and write an assembly language program that finds the component-by-component product of two five-element vectors and stores the result in a new five-element vector.

11. Draw a flowchart and write an assembly language program that will search for a given number in a block of data and return the index of the number in the block or a -1 if the number is not in the block (if the first element matches the given number, then set index = 1; if the second matches, set index = 2; and so on).

12. Draw a flowchart and write an assembly language program that will take a block DATA of ten integers and replace each element in the block by the sum of all elements up to and including that element.

13. Write an assembly language program that determines the absolute value of a data item.

14. Write a program that finds the average of a list of ten floating-point numbers. Include the number of values in the list as one variable in the program.

    a. Use autoincrement addressing to process the elements in the list.
    b. Use indexed addressing.

15. "Compile" the following Pascal program into assembly language. Use floating-point values for reals, longwords for integers.

    ```
    Program PROBLEM;
    var Price, Tax, TotalCost: real;
        Taxable: integer;
    begin
       if Taxable = 1 then
          Tax:=0.05*Price
       else
          Tax:=0;
       TotalCost:=Price + Tax;
    end.
    ```

16. Consider the following record describing a student's grades:

    ```
    Student:   .WORD    6123     ; Student ID
               .FLOAT   72.0     ; Hours
               .FLOAT   256.0    ; Quality points
               .BLKF    1        ; GPA
               .BLKB    1        ; Class year
    ```

    Without adding any labels to the above record, write a program segment that will:

    a. Calculate and store the GPA for the student (one instruction is sufficient).
    b. Determine and store the student's class code according to the following table:

Class	Code	Required hours
Freshman	1	Hours ≤ 28
Sophomore	2	28 < Hours ≤ 60
Junior	3	60 < Hours ≤ 94
Senior	4	94 < Hours

17. Suppose you borrow $50 from a friend at 1 percent per month interest on the outstanding balance (not much of a friend). If you pay your friend only $2 a month on the loan, write an assembly language program that will determine how much you owe at the end of the year.

18. The first two integers in the Fibonacci series are 1 and 1, and all the subsequent integers are formed by adding the preceding two elements of the series. That is, element 3 is 1 + 1 or 2, element 4 is 1 + 2 or 3, element 5 is 2 + 3 or 5, and so on. Write an assembly language program that will calculate the first 100 integers in the Fibonacci series.

19. The harmonic mean of three numbers A, B, C is given by

$$HM = [(1/A) + (1/B) + (1/C)]^{-1}$$

Write an assembly language program that will find the harmonic mean of a list of five integers.

PART 2

INTRODUCTION TO COMPUTER ARCHITECTURE

CHAPTER 4
CPU Structure

CHAPTER 5
The ALU's Structure and Operation

CHAPTER 6
Microprogramming

CHAPTER CONTENTS

4.1 BASIC CPU ARCHITECTURE

4.2 CPU OPERATION

    Example 4.1
    Example 4.2
    Example 4.3
    Example 4.4

4.3 IMPLEMENTING COMPLETE INSTRUCTIONS

    Example 4.5
    Example 4.6
    Example 4.7
    Reducing Memory Access Time
    Reduced Instruction Set Computers

SUMMARY

EXERCISES

CHAPTER 4

CPU Structure

After considering some of the instructions available on the VAX in the previous two chapters, we will look at the CPU and how it carries out those instructions. There are several different levels at which this study can be conducted. For example, consider the instruction

    ADDL3   R1, R2, (R3)

We can simply say that the CPU adds the contents of R1 and R2 in the ALU and stores the result in memory at the location pointed to by R3 (that is, at the location whose address is in R3). However, that leaves many unanswered questions. How is data moved around in the CPU? How does the CPU interpret the instruction code? How does the CPU signal the memory unit that data is to be stored? How are calculations carried out? You should be able to answer such questions after studying Chapters 4 through 6. They are some of the questions that must be answered before a CPU can be designed.

A thorough understanding of the CPU is valuable even if you do not plan to design one. Understanding the nature of the CPU will help reveal the reasons behind many of the seeming idiosyncrasies of a CPU's instruction set as well as its different addressing modes. It will help make learning another machine's assembly language easier. But most important, knowledge of the CPU will enable you to write more efficient assembly language code.

As you study these three chapters, you will learn that it is useful to consider the CPU as a computer inside a computer. Implementing a machine language within a CPU can be compared to writing code for this internal computer. In fact, in Chapter 6 we will discuss writing microcode, which is used to implement machine language instructions in many computers.

In this chapter we will begin the discussion of the CPU by presenting a simple model of a processing unit and illustrating how it can be used to implement portions of a machine language. We will introduce many of the concepts without presenting all the detail that is needed for a real computer. We will discover that the machine language of a particular computer could be implemented in several different CPU designs. In fact the VAX machine language has been implemented differently in each of the VAX models to achieve various cost/performance objectives. The different implementations reflect both design and technological changes.

Additional information about the operation of a CPU will be presented in the following two chapters as the ALU and control unit are studied in more detail. This introduction to the CPU is much like the top-down approach used by the program designers who look at the overall picture of the program being designed before adding layers of detail as they devise the final product. Just as studying the various layers of a top-down program design can aid in understanding the program, so looking at the general principles of a CPU before covering the details will help us achieve a thorough understanding of it.

4.1 Basic CPU Architecture

Before we could write assembly language code for the VAX, we needed a simple model of the CPU showing the registers that can be used by the assembly language programmer. In this section we will discuss a refined model that reveals additional details of the CPU structure, including the interconnections between the registers. The model shown in Figure 4.1 represents a simple, hypothetical central processing unit, which we will call the **single-bus-1 (SB-1)**. In the next section we will demonstrate how the model could process some machine language instructions from two different instruction sets. We will consider both a machine language using a fixed-length instruction set and the VAX's variable-length instruction set. The organization of an actual VAX would present many complications that are not necessary for this introduction. As you become more familiar with CPU operation, you may be able to suggest changes in the model that would enable it to operate more efficiently. After completing Chapters 4, 5, and 6, you should be able to understand models of some actual computers.

You are already familiar with some components in the SB-1's CPU. The **program counter (PC)** holds the memory address of the next instruction to be processed. R15 serves as the PC in a VAX. The SB-1, like the

4.1 Basic CPU Architecture

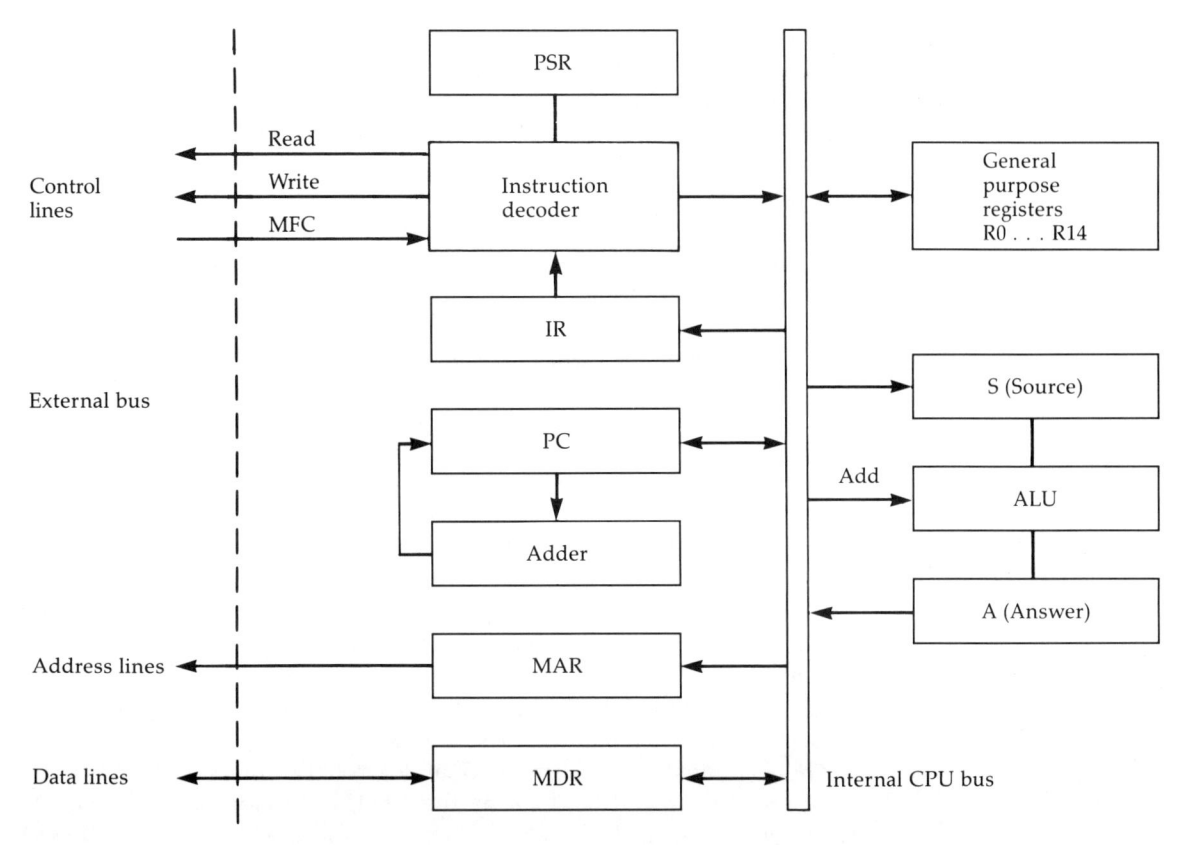

Figure 4.1 SB-1 Central processing unit

VAX, has 15 general-purpose registers in addition to the program counter. If we used this model to implement some other computer, the general-purpose registers might be replaced by such things as accumulators, index registers, and so on. Another register, called the **instruction register (IR)**, holds the current instruction while it is being processed. The **processor status register (PSR)** holds information about the status of the current process. On a VAX, this 32-bit register is called the **processor status longword (PSL)** and contains the PSW.

The **internal CPU bus** is used to transmit information between the different registers in the CPU, just as the external bus (discussed in Section 1.3) is used to transmit information between the various units of the computer. For simplicity, our model has a single internal bus. To increase their speed, some computers have two or more internal CPU buses, allowing simultaneous data transfers within the CPU. For example, the VAX 8600 has six internal buses to help it obtain its higher speed.

The ALU carries out the arithmetic and logic operations for the computer. In most computers it is capable of addition, subtraction, and such logic operations as "and" and "or." In some computers it is capable of multiplication and division, although in others these calculations are simulated by repeated addition and subtraction. It may have floating-point operations. These topics will be covered in more detail in Chapter 5, which focuses on the ALU. The ALU's ability to carry out subtraction is also used to compare the magnitude of two values before a conditional branch instruction is executed. Thus the ALU must have direct connections to the PSR so that it can read and set the status flags (these connections are omitted from Figure 4.1 for simplicity). The ALU has no internal storage, although in a normal arithmetic operation such as addition, it needs two operands (for addition, they are the numbers to be added), and generates a third number (for addition, the sum). This poses a problem for a single-bus CPU because it can only transmit one number at a time. Only one source operand will be available on the bus when the ALU is told to carry out an operation, so additional registers are required to store the other source operand and the answer. In the SB-1 the **source register (S)** is used to hold one of the source operands for arithmetic operations. Because the result of the calculation cannot be handled immediately by the bus, which is already transmitting a source operand to the ALU, another register, the **answer register (A)**, holds the result until it can be placed on the bus and moved to the required location. As an alternative to source and answer registers, some computers use a single **accumulator**, which stores one of the operands before the calculation and the result after the calculation is completed.

The PC must be incremented at least once for each instruction processed. This could be done by the ALU, but that requires repeated movements of the PC's contents to and from the ALU. Our model shows an alternative. A simple adder is connected to the PC and used to increment that register. This will simplify instruction processing and increase the CPU's speed at a small extra cost.

Implementing a machine language in a CPU requires several extra registers that the assembly language programmer does not actually see. They are needed to carry out important functions while executing code. We have already introduced three such registers—IR, S, and A. The SB-1 has two other hidden registers that are used to communicate with the external memory bus. When a memory function is initiated by a signal on either the "read" or "write" line, the address of the desired memory cell must be readily available. This is the purpose of the **memory address register (MAR)**. In memory read and write operations, the CPU needs a register to serve as the communication link for data being passed between the external and internal buses. The **memory data register (MDR)** is designed to provide the special storage needed for these two functions. Together the MAR and MDR serve as the link between the internal CPU bus and the external memory bus.

The **instruction decoder** interprets the command held in the IR and directs the various segments of the computer to carry out their functions.

To do this, it must be connected to all the other components in the computer. Only four of these connections are shown in the figure. The **read line** is used to instruct memory to copy the value stored at the location pointed to by the MAR into the MDR. The **write line** is used to instruct memory to store the data currently in the MDR at the location pointed to by the MAR. The **memory function complete (MFC)** line allows memory to inform the instruction decoder that the memory operation has been completed and the CPU can proceed. The instruction decoder must also be connected to the PSR so that it can both access the status register's contents to determine the computer's response to conditional branch instructions and adjust the PSR's contents as required by other instructions. Additional control lines are required but were suppressed in the figure to avoid cluttering the model with unnecessary detail. The instruction decoder must have lines to the ALU so that it can select the ALU operation. Links to the various registers inform them when they are to write their contents onto the bus or to read and store the information they find on the bus. The instruction decoder is the heart of the control unit. In Chapter 6 we discuss one common way of implementing an instruction decoder using what is called microcode.

The CPU model shown in Figure 4.1 could be modified in many ways. For example, there could be two, three, or even more internal buses to allow parallel transmission of data within the CPU. The ALU could have been shown with an extra source register instead of the answer register. In a different computer architecture, the ALU might be directly connected to an accumulator, which replaces both the source and answer registers. A CPU may have additional components designed to increase its speed in response to certain instructions. In Chapters 13 and 14 we will look at some alternatives.

In the next section we will begin looking at the operation of the CPU. In particular we will observe how the CPU breaks a single machine language instruction down into several sequential steps in order to execute it.

4.2 CPU Operation

In this section we will look at the steps that the instruction decoder must generate in order to carry out some common operations. In many respects it will seem that we are writing an algorithm to carry out the steps on a simple computer embedded within the CPU. After we are familiar with the CPU's operation, we will be able to carry out some VAX machine language instructions in the next section.

Expressing the simple operations that can be executed by the CPU will be easier if we have some appropriate notation.

[R0]	The contents of R0
R1 ← [R0]	Copy the contents of R0 into R1
[[R0]]	The contents of the memory location pointed to by R0, that is, the contents of the memory location whose address is in R0
R1 ← [[R0]]	Copy the contents of the memory location pointed to by R0 to R1
[R1] ← [R0]	Copy the contents of R0 to the location pointed to by R1

Though many people would like to see a simpler notation come into standard use, the notation given above is widely used, and you may find it helpful to become familiar with it. In this section we will express computer operations both in words and in this notation to help you become comfortable with it.

Just as a statement in a high-level language may need to be broken down into several steps before it can be expressed in assembly language, the CPU must break an assembly language instruction down into more basic operations in order to execute it. The basic operations that can be carried out by the SB-1 CPU are shown below. An example of each operation is shown to illustrate our notation.

Move data between registers	MDR ← [R1]
Move constants generated by the instruction decoder to a register	R0 ← 7 (that is, move the number 7 to R0)
Begin a read operation	Read byte, word, or longword
Begin a write operation	Write byte, word, or longword
Wait for memory function complete	Wait for MFC
Increment the PC	Increment the PC by 1, 2, or 4
Arithmetic	Add, subtract, multiply, divide
Clear the source register	Clear S
Set the carry flag	Set carry

When determining the basic operations needed to carry out some function, we must remember that only one value can be transmitted on a particular bus at one time. If an operation requires placing two values on the bus, it will take at least two CPU steps or cycles. We assume that during any cycle, in addition to moving one value on its bus, the CPU can carry out a number of the other operations not requiring the use of the bus.

Remember that because memory is much slower than the CPU, it often takes several CPU cycles to obtain or store a value in main memory. If the CPU finishes all its internal operations before the memory operation is completed, the CPU must wait until the memory function complete (MFC) signal is issued by the memory. Consequently, the instruction decoder must include a "wait for the memory function complete" operation after a read or write signal is issued. This allows the memory unit to complete its operation before the CPU continues its work.

Next to correctness, speed is the most important goal in designing the CPU steps used to carry out a particular operation. Sometimes we can find one sequence of steps that will perform the required operation in less time than another. For example, consider the following steps that add the contents of the memory location pointed to by R0 to the value stored in R1.

1. MAR ← [R0], Read longword, Wait for MFC   ; Read value pointed to by R0
   ;   into MDR
2. S ← [R1]   ; Load source register with R1
3. ALU ← [MDR], Add   ; Put the value in MDR on the bus
   ;   and add

Just as in MACRO, we will use a semicolon to indicate that the remainder of the line is a comment.

A computer's speed depends both on the speed of the electrical circuits and on the number of operations that can be carried out in parallel (that is, at the same time). For example, the memory value requested above in step 1 is not actually used until step 3. Therefore, the time needed to execute the operation can be reduced by delaying the "Wait for MFC" signal until step 2, thus allowing the CPU to carry out another internal operation while the memory fetch is taking place. This change is shown in the following steps:

1. MAR ← [R0], Read longword   ; Start read operation
2. S ← [R1], Wait for MFC   ; Load source with R1 and
   ;   wait for MFC
3. ALU ← [MDR], Add   ; Put the value in MDR
   ;   on the bus and add

The revised steps execute faster than the previous ones because they transfer the value in R1 to S while the read operation is taking place rather than waiting until after the memory operation has been completed. The CPU's effective speed is increased without modifying the hardware.

Example 4.1 Implement an instruction fetch cycle.

Before the CPU can execute an instruction, the instruction must be fetched from memory. This is done during the **instruction fetch cycle**, when the instruction pointed to by the PC is copied into the instruction register.

Then the PC is incremented by the length of the instruction. Because most opcodes on the VAX are one byte long, its PC would normally be incremented by 1. The operation can be represented symbolically as

```
IR ← [[PC]]         ; Put the opcode pointed to
                    ;   by the PC into the IR
PC ← [PC] + 1       ; Increment the PC by 1
```

This operation requires three CPU steps:

1. Copy the value in the PC to the MAR and start the read operation to get the next opcode.
2. Increment the PC by 1 because the opcode is one byte long. (This is done by the PC's own adder in the SB-1.) Then wait for the memory function complete signal, which signals that the data is in the MDR.
3. Copy the value in the MDR into the IR.

Using our standard notation, we can write the steps as follows:

```
1. MAR ← [PC], Read byte            ; Fetch opcode and
2. Increment PC by 1, Wait for MFC  ;   increment PC
3. IR ← [MDR]                       ; Move opcode to IR
```

Observe that we have increased the computer's effective speed by incrementing the PC while the memory operation is in progress.

Example 4.2 Copy the word in main memory whose address is in R0 to the location whose address is in R1.

[R1] ← [[R0]]

In MACRO we would write this operation as

```
MOVW    (R0), (R1)
```

Because the data is in main memory, we have to move the value pointed to by R0 to the MDR register in the CPU and then store it back in main memory. The steps are as follows:

```
1. MAR ← [R0], Read word,     ; Fetch data whose
     Wait for MFC             ;   address is in R0
2. MAR ← [R1], Write word,    ; Store data at
     Wait for MFC             ;   address in R1
```

The first instruction tells main memory to copy the word pointed to by R0 into the MAR, while the second copies the word into the location pointed to by R1. Though the operation takes only two steps, it may take some time if the memory cycle time is slow compared to the CPU cycle time.

Example 4.3 Increment the contents of R3 by 1.

R3 ← [R3] + 1

We could implement this operation as a typical addition problem, but a little cleverness with the carry flag simplifies the operation. The ALU always adds the value in the S register to the value on the bus; if the carry flag in the PSR is set, it also adds 1 to that sum. (The way the ALU uses the carry flag resembles the way humans carry while adding two numbers like 527 and 638. When adding the middle digits, 2 and 3, we would add in the 1 that was carried after adding the right-hand digits because we had "set our carry bit." On the other hand, we would not add 1 when adding the left-hand digits because we had "cleared our carry bit" after processing the middle column. Of course, the computer does not normally add one digit at a time, but we will see that similar actions may be needed when we study Section 5.1.) The steps are as follows:

1. ALU ← [R3], Set carry, Clear S, Add   ; Add 1 to R3
2. R3 ← [A]   ; Store the result

The first step tells the ALU to add the value stored in R3 to the 0 forced into S and then add 1 because the carry bit is set. Thus this instruction causes the value [R3] + 1 to be placed in the A register. The second step stores the result back in R3 to complete the operation.

Example 4.4 Fetch a longword operand with autoincrement mode addressing, (R0)+.

R1 ← [[R0]]
R0 ← [R0] + 4

The autoincrement mode means that we must first fetch the data whose address is in R0 and then increment that register by 4, the length of the value. Because we need to use the contents of R0 as both the address in memory and as a source operand for the addition, we can reduce execution time by taking advantage of the bus operation. When a value is put on the bus, it can be stored in more than one register during the same CPU cycle. Thus, when the value of R0 is placed on the bus, it can be stored in the MAR and the S register at the same time.

1. MAR, S ← [R0], Read longword   ; Read value pointed
2. ALU ← 4, Add   ;   to by R0 and
3. R0 ← [A], Wait for MFC   ;   increment R0 by 4
4. R1 ← [MDR]   ; Store data in R1

The first step moves the value in R0 to both S and the MAR, and the read operation is initiated. The second statement adds 4 to the copy of R0 stored in S. In this step the instruction decoder generates the value 4 and places it on the bus to send it to the ALU for the addition operation. The new address can be stored back in R0 before we need to wait for the read operation to be completed.

This section illustrated how the SB-1, the model CPU of Figure 4.1, could carry out some simple but common operations. Unfortunately, executing a complete machine language instruction is more difficult since it must be fetched from memory before it can be processed. We will look at the process of executing an instruction in the next section.

4.3 Implementing Complete Instructions

In the previous section we looked at implementing standard operations on our model CPU. Implementing a complete machine language instruction is more difficult because the instruction must be fetched from memory before it can be carried out. The extra difficulties involved depend on the nature of the machine language itself.

Many early computers had fixed-length instructions. In the case of a multiple general register machine like the VAX, the typical instruction had a memory operand specifying a memory location and a register operand specifying a register to be used while carrying out the instruction. The complete instruction, including both operands, was packed in one of the computer's standard words that typically was 16 to 60 bits long. Most instructions for the PDP-11 computers are packed into exactly 16 bits. This is possible since these machines have a smaller instruction set, only eight general-purpose registers (including the PC), and fewer addressing modes. However, addressing modes specifying 16-bit offsets or immediate values clearly require additional words to hold those values. (Many VAX computers can run this instruction set in what is called **compatibility mode**, showing that we can use more than one instruction set with a given CPU design.)

Implementing a machine language with a fixed-length instruction set is not too difficult because it is only necessary to fetch the instruction, increment the PC by the length of the instruction, and then execute the specified operation in the manner suggested previously. Unfortunately, this simplicity has some costs. A machine language using a fixed-length instruction set typically has relatively few addressing modes and few sophisticated instructions because only a limited amount of information can be packed into the fixed number of bits available for one instruction. Consequently, several such instructions may be required to perform the same operation that can be carried out with a single VAX instruction.

Implementing machine language on computers with a sophisticated, variable-length instruction set like that used by the VAX—and many other modern computers—is more difficult. When a computer processes a variable-length instruction, it is necessary to fetch the opcode and interpret it before the number of operands can be determined. These operands must then be fetched before the instruction's execution can be completed. Moreover, if the computer allows variable-length operands, the addressing mode for each operand must be determined before any addresses, offsets, and displacements used by that mode can be processed. For example, consider the VAX instruction

ADDL3   A, B, C

Recall that the relative mode used by this instruction uses one byte to specify the addressing mode followed by a one-, two-, or four-byte displacement. This displacement is added to the value in the PC to determine the address of the operand.

To process this instruction, the machine must first fetch the opcode and update the PC. After discovering that the current instruction is ADDL3, it will fetch the first operand's mode specifier and update the PC again. After determining that relative mode is being used, the displacement for A is read and the PC updated. The displacement is added to the value of the PC, and the first operand (A) can be fetched from the resulting address. The process is repeated for the second operand (B). The sum of A and B can then be determined, but before it can be stored, several steps must be taken. The destination's addressing mode must be read and the PC updated, after which the displacement for C must be read and added to the updated value of the PC to obtain the required address. This seems quite complicated, but remember that this one instruction may take the place of three on some machines with simpler, fixed-length instructions. (In fact, at least two instructions would be required on computers that use variable-length instruction sets but do not allow three-operand instructions.)

To illustrate how the CPU carries out commands, we will look at some examples and show the steps that might be used to process some instructions on the SB-1 model CPU shown in Figure 4.1 for two different instruction sets: first, a fixed-length, 16-bit instruction set, and second, the VAX's variable-length instruction set. It may be useful to review VAX instructions and addressing modes while looking at these examples.

Example 4.5

```
CLRL   X                    ; Clear longword X
```

This instruction uses relative mode to clear the longword memory location labeled X. Figure 4.2 illustrates a possible format for this instruction in both of the instruction sets. First, we will use the fixed-length, 16-bit (2-byte) instruction set. The instruction, including the displacement, must be fetched, and then we can clear location X after we calculate its address.

1. MAR ← [PC], Read word   ; Fetch the 2-byte
2. Increment PC by 2, Wait for MFC ;   instruction and update
3. IR ← [MDR]   ;   the PC
4. S ← [PC]   ; Calculate address of X
5. ALU ← [IR$_{displacement}$], Add
6. MAR ← [A]   ; Store the 0 in X
7. MDR ← 0, Write longword,
      Wait for MFC

Steps 1–3 are the standard steps to fetch an instruction, and steps 4–7 implement that instruction. In steps 4 and 5 the displacement portion of the instruction is added to the value of the program counter and temporarily stored in register A. In step 6 the address of X is moved to the memory address register. Finally, in step 7 the instruction decoder generates a 0 and sends it to the memory data register. The memory location is cleared by writing 0 in the proper location.

In contrast, look at the steps needed if the VAX's instruction set is used. We assume a longword displacement is needed for X. The instruction format is shown in Figure 4.2.

1. MAR ← [PC], Read byte   ; Fetch a 1-byte opcode
2. Increment PC by 1, Wait for MFC   ;   and update PC
3. IR ← [MDR]
4. MAR ← [PC], Read byte   ; Fetch operand mode
5. Increment PC by 1, Wait for MFC   ;   specifier and increment
6. IR ← [MDR]   ;   PC
7. MAR ← [PC], Read longword   ; Fetch the displacement of
8. Increment PC by 4   ;   X, increment the PC, and
9. S ← [PC], Wait for MFC   ;   add them to get the
10. ALU ← [MDR], Add   ;   address of X into A
11. MAR ← [A]   ; Store 0 in X
12. MDR ← 0, Write longword,
       Wait for MFC

The first six steps are needed no matter what addressing mode is used for the operand. The last six steps are used to process the relative addressing mode.

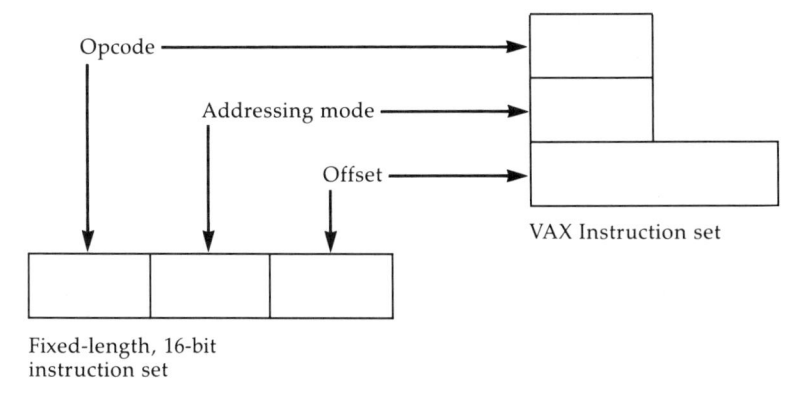

Figure 4.2 Formats of CLRL X

In this case we see that the sophisticated instruction set complicates processing. The VAX requires going to memory and incrementing the PC three times instead of just once. Simpler instructions, such as this, may take longer to execute on a variable-length instruction computer than on a similar machine with a fixed-length instruction set. This strongly suggests the need to provide special means for rapid memory access. Some techniques for doing so will be discussed later in this section and in Chapter 10.

You may have observed that our comparison of the instructions sets is not really valid. Our fixed-length instruction packs the opcode for the instruction, the addressing mode, and the displacement all into 16 bits. Though we have not specified exactly how the bits in the instruction are used, it is clear that not many could be used for the displacement. However, the VAX instruction allowed 32-bit offsets. Moreover, the VAX would allow us to use 8- or 16-bit offsets if the displacement was small enough. You may be wondering how the PDP-11 provides reasonable-size offsets. The answer is that it does not store the displacement in the 16-bit instruction. Instead, the displacement is found in the word following the instruction. If we were to model the PDP-11 instruction set on the SB-1, we would have to use steps much like those used for the VAX except that steps 4–6 would be omitted because there is no addressing mode byte.

Example 4.6

```
BRB LOOP      ; An unconditional branch to LOOP
```

Again we will first look at the steps needed to implement this instruction using the fixed-length instruction set. We assume that the displacement that must be added to the program counter to produce the address of the next instruction is part of the instruction.

1. MAR ← [PC], Read word   ; Fetch instruction
2. Increment PC by 2, Wait for MFC   ;   and increment the PC
3. IR ← [MDR]
4. S ← [PC]   ; Add displacement to the
5. ALU ← [IR$_{displacement}$], Add   ;   PC
6. PC ← [A]

This instruction is very straightforward when a fixed-length instruction set is assumed. On the SB-1 the ALU is used to find the new value of the program counter because the PC's adder is restricted to incrementing the PC by 1, 2, or 4. The implementation on the VAX is a little more complicated because the displacement must be read separately. Recall that in the VAX assembly language, the branch opcodes are immediately followed by a one-byte displacement.

1. [MAR] ← [PC], Read byte   ; Fetch opcode and
2. Increment PC by 1, Wait for MFC   ;   increment the PC
3. IR ← [MDR]
4. MAR ← [PC], Read byte   ; Fetch displacement
5. Increment PC by 1
6. S ← [PC], Wait for MFC   ; Add displacement to the
7. ALU ← [MDR], Add   ;   PC
8. PC ← [A]

After these two examples, you might ask why we don't automatically fetch two bytes when we get the opcode. The answer is that a few instructions, such as NOP (no operation, do not do anything) and RET (return from a procedure), have no operands and are exactly one byte long. Clearly it would be helpful to find a clever way to fetch more than one byte at a time and save any extra bytes until they are needed.

Example 4.7

    ADDL3 R1, (R2), (R3)+   ; Three-operand add

This example illustrates three of the addressing modes available on the VAX. This instruction would usually not be included in the fixed-length instruction set because three-operand instructions are difficult to pack into a few bits. Moreover, autoincrement addressing is less likely to exist on machines with shorter, fixed-length instructions. Such machines usually offer a smaller selection of addressing modes in order to reduce the number of bits that must be assigned to distinguish between the modes. Fixed-length machines would need two or three instructions to accomplish the same result. In such cases one may need to (1) add the memory value pointed to by R2 to R1, (2) write R1 in the location pointed to by R3, and (3) increment R3 by 4 in separate instructions. Accordingly, we will only implement this instruction on the VAX instruction set.

4.3 Implementing Complete Instructions

The register direct, register deferred, and autoincrement addressing modes used by this instruction all use a single byte for the addressing mode specifier. The steps needed by our model CPU using the VAX variable-length format would be as follows:

```
                    ;      {{ Fetch opcode }}
1.  MAR ← [PC], Read byte            ; Fetch opcode and
2.  Increment PC by 1, Wait for MFC  ;   increment PC
3.  IR ← [MDR]
                    ;      {{ Fetch first operand }}
4.  MAR ← [PC], Read byte            ; Fetch first operand mode
5.  Increment PC by 1, Wait for MFC  ;   specifier and increment
6.  IR ← [MDR]                       ;   PC
                    ;      {{ ... and process 'R1' }}
7.  S ← [R1]                         ; Copy first operand to S
                    ;      {{ Fetch second operand }}
8.  MAR ← [PC], Read byte            ; Fetch second operand mode
9.  Increment PC by 1, Wait for MFC  ;   specifier and increment
10. IR ← [MDR]                       ;   PC
                  ; {{ ... and process '(R2)' }}
11. MAR ← [R2], Read longword,       ; Fetch second operand from
      Wait for MFC                   ;   memory and add it
12. ALU ← [MDR], Add                 ;   to the value in S
                    ;  {{ Fetch third operand }}
14. MAR ← [PC], Read byte            ; Fetch third operand mode
15. Increment PC by 1, Wait for MFC  :   specifier and increment
16. IR ← [MDR]                       ;   PC
                  ; {{ ... and process (R3)+ }}
17. MAR, S ← [R3]                    ; Store result in location
18. MDR ← [A], Write longword        ;   pointed to by R3 and
19. ALU ← 4, Add                     ;   increment R3 by 4
20. R3 ← [A], Wait for MFC
```

Despite the length, most of the steps are routine. Possibly the last four steps should be explained. By this time the control unit has learned that the addressing mode is autoincrement, so it must store the result at the address pointed to by R3 and then increment that register. Thus R3 is copied to both MAR and the S register. The sum is moved from the A register to the MDR, and the write operation is started. While this write operation is being carried out, the number 4 is generated by the instruction decoder and added to the contents of R3.

The comments have been designed to help distinguish between the steps that must be taken any time the ADDL3 instruction is processed (namely 1–3, 4–6, 8–10, and 14–16) and those that are taken in response to a given mode specifier (namely 7, 11 and 12, and 17–20).

It is an interesting exercise to try to replace the given mode specifiers with some of the other available modes. In some cases this turns out to be nearly impossible on the SB-1. For example, suppose that the register mode (R2) of the second operand was replaced by the autodecrement mode −(R2). There is a problem. R2 must be decremented using the ALU and the S register, but the first operand is already in the S register, and there is nowhere else to put it while R2 is being decremented. If we are implementing the VAX instruction set on the SB-1, it would be illegal to use one of the other general registers, because the rules for the VAX require that they remain unchanged during this particular instruction. The solution is to add additional registers to the CPU that are hidden from the assembly language programmer. They can be used for temporary storage in situations like this while the CPU processes the assembly language instructions. In fact actual VAX processors have several such registers (see Exercises 24 and 25).

Reducing Memory Access Time

Our examples indicate that the flexibility provided by variable-length instruction sets increases the number of memory accesses. This tends to decrease computer speed. As a result, computer designers have developed several ways to decrease the effective memory access time in order to speed up the processing of variable-length instructions.

One method for doing this is to prefetch instructions. A special set of registers called an **instruction queue** or **instruction buffer** is included in the CPU. Control circuitry is provided to fetch instructions from memory in sequential order whenever the instruction queue is not full and the memory bus is not busy. Except after a branch instruction, when the queue must be emptied and refilled with code from the new location pointed to by the PC, the CPU rarely has to wait for portions of instructions to be read from memory. The bytes of code in the instruction queue are immediately available. Several VAX models include instruction buffers.

Another technique to reduce memory accesses (used by the VAX 11/780 and some other models) is to fetch eight consecutive bytes of instruction code at a time whenever it must go to memory. This is usually helpful because the computer typically processes code in sequential order. The extra code is then saved until it is requested by the CPU, at which time it is immediately available to the CPU. The 11/780 and 11/785 are designed so that reading eight bytes at once is much faster than reading the same eight bytes in smaller units. (In Chapter 10 we will discuss other techniques to reduce memory access time.)

Reduced Instruction Set Computers

Because rich, sophisticated instruction sets like those used on the VAX may slow instruction execution, there has been increasing research recently into what is called a **reduced instruction set computer (RISC)**. This type of machine features simple, fixed-length instructions and few addressing modes. A machine like a VAX, which offers a large selection of instructions and addressing modes, is sometimes called a **complex instruction set computer (CISC)**. Though it may take several simple instructions on a RISC machine to replace one of the more complicated instructions found on the VAX, it is possible to process the simpler instructions more rapidly. A simpler instruction set leads to a simpler CPU design, permitting the use of fewer but faster components. Some designers believe that it will be possible to build RISC machines that will actually be faster than a similar machine using a typical variable-length instruction set. Additional motivation for such machines comes from some compiler writers, who find it difficult to design compilers that can take full advantage of some of the more exotic instructions found in some variable-length instruction sets. They feel that it will be simpler to write compilers that produce highly efficient (optimized) code for reduced instruction set computers.

Example 4.7 illustrates one problem with RISC instruction sets. While the VAX instruction set used four bytes for the ADDL3 instruction, a RISC machine that needed three instructions to process the same operation would require six bytes, even if the machine used a short 16-bit instruction. It has been established that a RISC machine usually requires more machine code for a given program than a CISC like the VAX.

In this section, we have looked at the way a CPU executes an instruction by breaking it up into several simple steps determined by its internal structure. In addition, fixed length and variable length instruction sets were compared. More complex instruction sets may actually degrade machine performance unless the CPU is given elegant ways of fetching the instructions. As a result, some researchers are looking at reduced instruction sets as a means of increasing computer speed.

Summary

In this chapter we have learned how the different registers in the CPU could be interconnected and how machine language instructions must be broken down into several steps in order to be processed. We have looked at the steps that would be needed to carry out a few instructions on our simple CPU model, the SB-1. We have observed some advantages and disadvantages of the VAX's sophisticated instruction set as compared to a simple, more traditional one. In the next chapter we will look more closely at the ALU, and in Chapter 6 we will investigate the control unit and look at one of the methods used to make the CPU execute the correct sequence of steps necessary to process a machine language instruction.

The hypothetical SB-1 CPU model was introduced for two reasons. Real CPUs have design considerations that would tend to unnecessarily complicate our initial discussion of this unit. Moreover, several different VAX CPUs are on the market. Picking one for detailed study would have unnecessarily biased our viewpoint. Each of these CPUs was designed to meet a particular performance goal and reflect the technology and engineering concepts available when it was first introduced. For example, the VAX 8600 has six CPU buses to provide parallel data transfers within the CPU. It also uses a concept called **pipelining**. As implemented on the 8600, the CPU can be concurrently processing different parts of up to four different instructions at the same time. (This concept will be discussed in Chapter 14.) While studying this chapter, you may have detected ways in which our simple CPU model could be modified to increase its speed, recognizing that such improvements may also increase its cost.

Some of the exercises at the end of this chapter will ask you to determine the steps needed to implement several of the instructions and addressing modes available on the VAX. There are two purposes to such exercises. They provide a valuable opportunity to become better acquainted with the CPU's operation. Moreover, they will help you achieve a better understanding of the VAX machine language because you must fully comprehend an instruction's operation before you can generate the steps the CPU would need to carry it out.

Exercises

1. Describe the use of the following types of CPU registers:
    a. Instruction register
    b. Program counter
    c. Program status register
    d. General-purpose register
    e. Memory address register
    f. Memory data register
    g. Accumulator
2. a. Explain the purpose of control lines.
   b. Explain the use of the read, write, and memory function control lines on the SB-1.
3. Define:
    a. ALU
    b. Instruction decoder
    c. CPU bus
4. State the advantages and disadvantages of having multiple CPU buses.
5. a. Give some advantages of a variable-length machine language instruction set.
   b. Give some advantages of a fixed-length machine language instruction set.

6. What is a RISC machine? What are some hoped-for advantages of such a machine? What are some disadvantages of this type of computer?

7. Provide comments explaining the purpose of the following steps for the SB-1 CPU. Then determine the assembly language instruction that would use these steps. Assume the variable-length VAX instruction set.
   1. MAR ← [PC], Read byte
   2. Increment PC by 1, Wait for MFC
   3. IR ← [MDR]
   4. MAR ← [PC], Read byte
   5. Increment PC by 1, Wait for MFC
   6. IR ← [MDR]
   7. MAR ← [R6], Read longword, Wait for MFC
   8. S ← [MDR]
   9. MAR ← [PC], Read byte
   10. Increment PC by 1, Wait for MFC
   11. IR ← [MDR]
   12. ALU ← [R3], Add
   13. R3 ← [A]

8. Provide comments explaining the purpose of the following steps for the SB-1 CPU. Then determine the assembly language instruction that would use these steps. Assume the fixed-length instruction set.
   1. MAR ← [PC], Read word
   2. Increment PC by 2, Wait for MFC
   3. IR ← [MDR]
   4. S ← [R1]
   5. ALU ← [IR$_{displacement}$], Add
   6. MAR ← [A], Read longword, Wait for MFC
   7. S ← [MDR]
   8. ALU ← [R4], Multiply
   9. R4 ← [A]

In Exercises 9–17, write the steps needed to implement the given instruction on the hypothetical SB-1 CPU shown in Figure 4.1, using the

    a. Fixed-length, 16-bit instruction set.
    b. VAX instruction set.

Some instructions require 16 bits of displacement or data that obviously will not fit in the fixed-length instruction set's two-byte instruction. In those cases the exercise suggests a possible method of encoding the extra information. Assume that the other instructions can somehow be packed into the 16-bit format.

9. Write the CPU steps needed to carry out the instruction
   MOVW   R2, (R4)

10. Assuming that the subtrahend (the number to be subtracted) must be in the S register when the ALU is given the command to subtract, write the CPU steps needed to carry out the instruction

    SUBL2   -(R1), R7

11. Write the CPU steps needed to carry out the instruction

    JMP   @(R6)+

12. Write the CPU steps needed to carry out the instruction

    CLRW   @B^d(R2)

    for byte-length displacement "d."

13. Assuming that the easiest way to set the PSR's zero and negative flags for a TSTB instruction is to add 0 to the value being tested, write efficient CPU steps to carry out the instruction

    TSTB   W^d(R8)

    where "d" is a word-length displacement. (Recall that in the VAX's word displacement mode, the displacement is part of the instruction code and immediately follows the mode specifier byte. In the fixed-length instruction set, it is clear that we cannot store a word-length displacement in the same 16-bit instruction that also must hold the opcode and addressing mode. Consequently, we will assume that the displacement is stored in the word immediately following the instruction. The PC will have to be incremented by 2 after the displacement is fetched.)

14. Assuming that a short literal value can be moved from the IR onto the bus, write the CPU steps needed to carry out the instruction

    MULL2   S^#value, R0

    (Recall that in the VAX machine language, the short literal value is in the mode specifier byte.)

15. Assuming that the divisor (the number to be divided by) must be in the S register when the ALU is given the command to divide, write the CPU steps needed to carry out the instruction

    DIVW2   I^#value, R6

    (Recall that in the VAX machine language, the immediate value is in the instruction code following the operand mode specifier byte. Since a 16-bit instruction cannot hold both the opcode and a 16-bit data value, we will assume that the data value is stored in the word following the instruction in the fixed-length instruction set. See Exercise 13.)

16. Write the CPU steps needed to carry out the instruction

    ADDB2   @#address

    where the absolute address is given in the instruction code. (In the fixed-length instruction set, we assume that the address is small enough to fit in the instruction.)

Exercises

17. Write the CPU steps needed to carry out the instruction

    CLRL   B^address

    which uses byte relative mode addressing. (Recall that the VAX stores the relative mode specifier followed by the displacement.)

18. Referring to Example 4.7, find and rewrite the steps that must be changed in order to implement the instruction

    ADDL3   -(R1), #value, R3

    where we assume that the value requires the immediate mode. (It may be necessary to renumber the steps.)

19. Referring to Example 4.7, find and rewrite the steps that must be changed in order to implement the instruction

    ADDL3   A, #value, (R8)

    where the byte relative mode is used for A and the short literal mode can be used for the value. (It may be necessary to renumber the steps.)

20. Referring to Example 4.7, assume that the following instruction sequence is needed to carry the same addition in the fixed-length, 16-bit instruction set that the VAX can carry out in one instruction:

    ADDL2   (R2), R1
    MOVL   R1, (R3)
    ADDL2   #4, R3

    a. Write the CPU steps needed to carry out these three instructions.
    b. In what way does the above instruction sequence affect the registers differently than the original VAX instruction?

In Exercises 21 and 22 you will be asked to compare the time required to execute a given instruction in the fixed-length, 16-bit instruction set to that required by the VAX instruction set based on the three different timing situations given below. State your conclusions based on SB-1 as shown in Figure 4.1, realizing that the relative advantages of a particular instruction set depend on the structure of the CPU it is implemented on.

    a. Each memory access requires five CPU cycles from the time the read command is issued to the time MFC is signaled. For example, we assume that the step

    R1 ← [R0]

    takes only one CPU cycle while the step

    MAR ← [R0], Read Word, Wait for MFC

    and the sequence

    S, MAR ← [R0], Read Word
    ALU ← 4, Add
    R0 ← [A], Wait for MFC

    both take five CPU cycles. The second and third steps in the last sequence are executed while memory is fetching the value being read into the MDR.

b. Assume that an instruction queue is added to the SB-1 that eliminates the need to wait for instructions. However, the machine still takes five CPU cycles to fetch data values. That is, the instruction fetch

MAR ← [PC], Read byte, Wait for MFC

takes only one CPU cycle, while the data read step

MAR ← [R1], Read byte, Wait for MFC

takes the full five cycles.

c. Assume that the computer's internal CPU cycle and the external read and write times are equal so that no waiting is needed. Each CPU step takes exactly one CPU cycle.

21. Count the number of CPU cycles needed to carry out the CLRL X instruction in Example 4.5 for both instructions sets under all three timing assumptions given above.

22. For each of the three timing assumptions given before Exercise 21, calculate:

a. The number of CPU cycles needed to carry out the ADDL3 instruction in Example 4.7 using the VAX's instruction set.

b. The number of cycles needed to simulate that instruction in the fixed-length instruction set using the sequence of instructions found in Exercise 20.

23. Based on your answers for Exercises 21 and 22 and the SB-1 CPU, what conclusions can you draw about the relative speed at which instructions in the two instruction sets can be executed on the SB-1? Pay attention to both the complexity of the instruction and the timing assumptions used.

24. Suppose that a new hidden register called TEMP (for temporary storage of values) is added to the SB-1. Can you implement

ADDL3   R1, (R2), -(R3)

in the VAX's variable-length instruction set? (See Example 4.7.)

25. Using the extra TEMP register of Exercise 24, write the CPU steps needed to carry out the instruction

CMPL   R1, -(R2)

(Assume that the appropriate flags will be set if the values are subtracted. Also recall that in Exercise 10, we adopted the convention that the subtrahend is put in the S register before subtracting.)

CHAPTER CONTENTS

5.1 COMPUTER ADDITION AND SUBTRACTION
   Some Boolean Algebra
   Logic Gates
   Binary Adders
   Fast Adders
   Addition of Signed Numbers
   Subtraction and Negation
   Multiple-Word Addition and Subtraction

5.2 MULTIPLICATION AND DIVISION
   Multiplication of Unsigned Integers
   Multiplication of Signed Integers and the Booth Algorithm
   Division
   The VAX's Extended Multiply and Divide Instructions

5.3 SHIFT INSTRUCTIONS

5.4 BIT MANIPULATION

5.5 CODING AN INTEGER MULTIPLICATION ALGORITHM

5.6 FLOATING-POINT ARITHMETIC
   Review of Floating-Point Notations
   Calculations in Floating Point

SUMMARY

EXERCISES

CHAPTER 5

The ALU's Structure and Operation

In this chapter we will investigate the operation of the **arithmetic and logic unit (ALU)**. We begin by looking at how an ALU performs standard arithmetic functions such as integer addition and multiplication. We will be working at a level of system architecture that will allow us to see how the interaction between software and hardware determines some major performance characteristics, such as the speed and efficiency of arithmetic operations. This will lead to discussions of other ALU functions such as shifting, logic operations, and bit manipulation. After covering the basic operations for processing integers, we will conclude the chapter by looking at floating-point operations.

In addition, we will introduce some assembly language instructions which use the ALU. Section 5.5 develops a program to implement one of the multiplication algorithms. Though such a program is hardly needed on a VAX, it demonstrates the use of several instructions introduced in this chapter.

If your assembly language experience has been limited to machines having numerous instructions for arithmetic operations, you may question the need for the detailed algorithms presented in this chapter. It is easy to assume that all standard operations, such as addition and multiplication, are built into the ALU's hardware. While this is true in many larger machines, the situation is much more complicated in many micro- and minicomputers. For example, on many 8-bit microprocessors it is necessary to implement standard arithmetic operations with sequences of assembly language instructions, because their built-in arithmetic capabilities are limited to 8-bit numbers that are inadequate for many purposes. In fact some of these chips lack any kind of built-in multiplication or division. Even on minicomputers, hardware for floating-point operations may be an optional extra feature. Consequently, floating-point operations are frequently carried out with software instructions instead of expensive hardware on minicomputers as well as microcomputers. Even the VAX, with its extensive selection of arithmetic instructions, has limitations. Though its assembly language has instructions for moving quadword and octaword binary integers, it lacks any instructions capable of calculating with these data types.

Determining the capabilities of the ALU and CPU is one problem faced by the hardware designer. For example, it is possible to include the special hardware required for binary multiplication within the ALU. But it is less expensive to implement multiplication by having the instruction decoder issue a sequence of add and shift commands to the ALU. It is even cheaper to use software to implement multiplication as a sequence of machine language instructions. However, the trade-offs are clear. Reducing the ALU's and CPU's power reduces the computer's overall speed. Designing a successful computer requires finding the balance that best satisfies the design goals of that computer.

5.1 Computer Addition and Subtraction

We begin the study of the ALU's operation with addition and subtraction of integer numbers. Some form of binary addition must be implemented in hardware because this operation is essential to almost any computer application. Thus it is helpful to study elementary addition circuits and then look at methods that may be used to increase their speed. We will then look at signed numbers and subtraction. The advantages of two's complement arithmetic are apparent when we look at the hardware needed for addition and subtraction. Moreover, these operations form the basis of multiplication and division. Consequently, any real understanding of the ALU's operation requires some comprehension of basic addition circuits.

While discussing addition and subtraction, we will introduce the move negative instructions available in the VAX instruction set. The add with carry and subtract with borrow instructions are also presented to illustrate the type of instructions required to implement multiword addition and subtraction used on computers with a short word length.

Short introductions to Boolean algebra and to the logic gates used in digital circuit design will prepare us for the discussion on circuits for unsigned binary addition.

Some Boolean Algebra

Circuit designers use **Boolean algebra** as one of the tools that enable them to transform a truth table (such as the one shown in Figure 5.3) into the actual electrical circuits needed to implement the table in hardware. You have probably used some Boolean algebra while writing high-level language programs. People who use it regularly have developed a notation for this algebra: "$x + y$" means "x OR y"; "xy" or "$x \cdot y$" means "x AND y"; "$x \oplus y$" indicates "x EXCLUSIVE-OR y"; "$\bar{x}$" signifies "NOT x". This notation seems strange at first, but it allows about half the formulas used in Boolean algebra to be written in a form that looks like standard algebra. For example,

$$x(y + z) = xy + xz \quad (1)$$

says that x AND (y OR z) is the same as (x AND y) OR (x AND z). You can prove this formula using an eight-line truth table that determines the value of each side of the rule for each possible input. Alternatively, you can derive this rule from Boolean algebra's axioms in much the same manner that rules of standard algebra can be derived from its axioms.

Be aware that not all the rules of Boolean algebra are as obvious as the distributive law (1). For example, there is a second distributive rule

$$x + yz = (x + y)(x + z)$$

which looks extremely strange to those accustomed to standard algebra. If this topic is new to you, do not be overly concerned. The familiar-looking factorization or **distributive rule** (1) is the only Boolean algebra formula that we will need.

Logic Gates

Figure 5.1 shows the standard graphical representations for some of the **logic gates** used to implement the Boolean operations in digital logic circuits together with their truth tables. The logic gates are fairly simple electrical circuits that carry out elementary logic functions. They are the

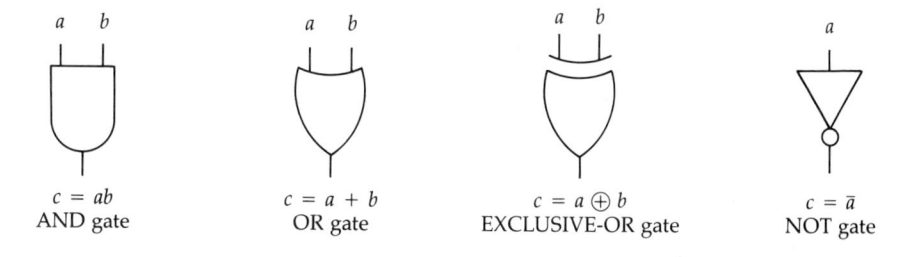

$c = ab$
AND gate

$c = a + b$
OR gate

$c = a \oplus b$
EXCLUSIVE-OR gate

$c = \bar{a}$
NOT gate

| Inputs | | Output | | | Input | Output |
a	b	ab	$a+b$	$a \oplus b$	a	$\bar{a}$
0	0	0	0	0	0	1
0	1	0	1	1	1	0
1	0	0	1	1		
1	1	1	1	0		

Figure 5.1 Symbols for logic gates and their truth tables

building blocks of basic digital circuit design. The AND and OR gates are shown with two inputs, but more inputs can be included when necessary. The EXCLUSIVE-OR gate always has two inputs, while the NOT or INVERTER gate has one input.

Given an appropriate logic formula, it is not too difficult to construct a logic circuit to implement the formula. For example, consider the formula

$$k = (y + x)c + xy$$

which is a simplified version of a look-ahead carry formula presented later in this section. The formula has three inputs (x, y, and c) and one output (k). To build the circuit from logic gates, we can determine y OR x (or, using the notation, $y + x$) and x AND y (xy) immediately. The output of $y + x$ can then be ANDed with c. Finally, the output of the two AND gates can be ORed to generate our final output. The circuit shown in Figure 5.2 follows these steps exactly. By using some Boolean algebra and standard design principles, a digital logic expert may be able to suggest an alternate circuit minimizing the number of gates needed. Actual circuits are commonly built using NAND (Not AND) and/or NOR (Not OR) gates. These gates are logically equivalent to normal AND and OR gates whose output is inverted by a NOT gate. They are widely used because current semiconductor technology makes it cheaper to construct NAND and NOR gates than AND and OR gates. However, the circuit shown is adequate for the purposes of this book.

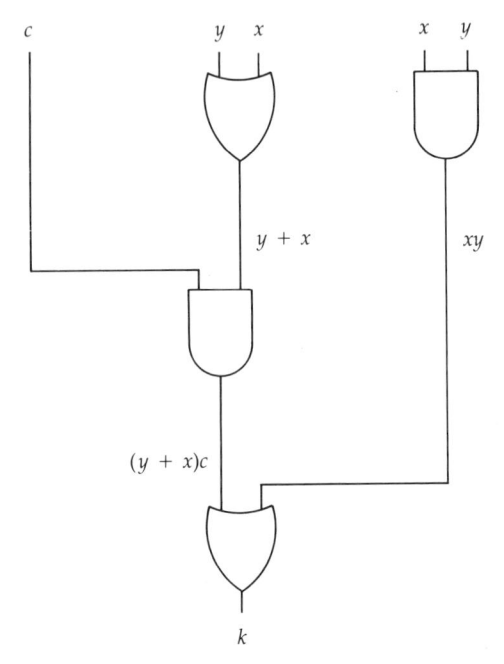

Figure 5.2 Logic circuit for $k = (y + x)c + xy$

Binary Adders

In a computer's ALU addition is based on the ability to add two numbers digit by digit in the same way that decimal numbers are added. The binary addition table below shows the possibilities.

+	0	1
0	0	1
1	1	10

The calculation of 1 plus 1 demands that any circuit for adding binary digits must allow for a carry to the next digit pair and, consequently, for a carry from the previous digit pair. Thus a circuit used for adding the ith binary digits in two multibit numbers must have three inputs: two, say x_i and y_i, are for the binary digits to be added, and another (c_i) is for the carry input from the previous digit. There must be two outputs, the sum (s_i) and the carry to the next digit (c_{i+1}). The binary adder can be illustrated as a black box as shown in Figure 5.3. Its operation is characterized by its truth table. The truth table lists the eight different binary inputs and shows the corresponding outputs.

If you are familiar with digital logic, you can use the truth table in Figure 5.3 to write the following **Boolean expressions** for the output variables.

$$c_{i+1} = x_i c_i + y_i c_i + x_i y_i \tag{2}$$

$$s_i = \bar{x}_i \bar{y}_i c_i + \bar{x}_i y_i \bar{c}_i + x_i \bar{y}_i \bar{c}_i + x_i y_i c_i \tag{3}$$

The expression in formula (2) is read

(x_i AND c_i) OR (y_i AND c_i) OR (x_i AND y_i)

while the expression in formula (3) is read

(NOT x_i AND NOT y_i AND c_i) OR (NOT x_i AND y_i AND NOT c_i)
OR (x_i AND NOT y_i AND NOT c_i) OR (x_i AND y_i AND c_i)

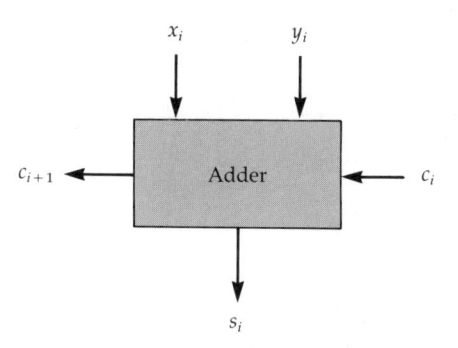

Inputs			Outputs	
x_i	y_i	c_i	c_{i+1}	s_i
0	0	0	0	0
0	0	1	0	1
0	1	0	0	1
0	1	1	1	0
1	0	0	0	1
1	0	1	1	0
1	1	0	1	0
1	1	1	1	1

Figure 5.3 Single-bit adder and its truth table

If you are unfamiliar with digital logic, you can verify these formulas by substituting the input values for each line of the truth table into the expressions, simplifying, and observing that the correct output values are obtained.

A possible logic circuit for a **single-bit binary adder** is shown in Figure 5.4. In practice the design used may vary somewhat from that shown because of constraints imposed by the technology used to build the circuit. In any case the design shown is the most straightforward implementation of formulas (2) and (3) and is sufficiently representative of the possible implementations to be useful in the timing considerations that follow.

Observe that after the signals are placed on the inputs of the single-bit adder, they must be processed by two layers of logic gates before the value of c_{i+1} is ready and three layers of logic gates before s_i is formed. Although logic gates used in modern computers are extremely fast, each gate requires about 2–20 nanoseconds to complete its function, depending on the technology used (a nanosecond is 10^{-9} seconds and is abbreviated ns). That doesn't seem very long at this point, but it becomes critical when one considers the process of adding two multibit numbers.

Suppose that the binary numbers to be added have n bits where n could be 8, 16, or 32 on a VAX and even longer on some other computers. This can be done by connecting n single-bit binary adders as shown in Figure 5.5.

Though it may not seem necessary at first glance, the right-hand carry input (c_0) is useful. For example, in Chapter 4 we found that a convenient way to increment a number by 1 was to set the carry and add the number to 0. While normally c_0 is set to 0 so that it has no effect on the calculation,

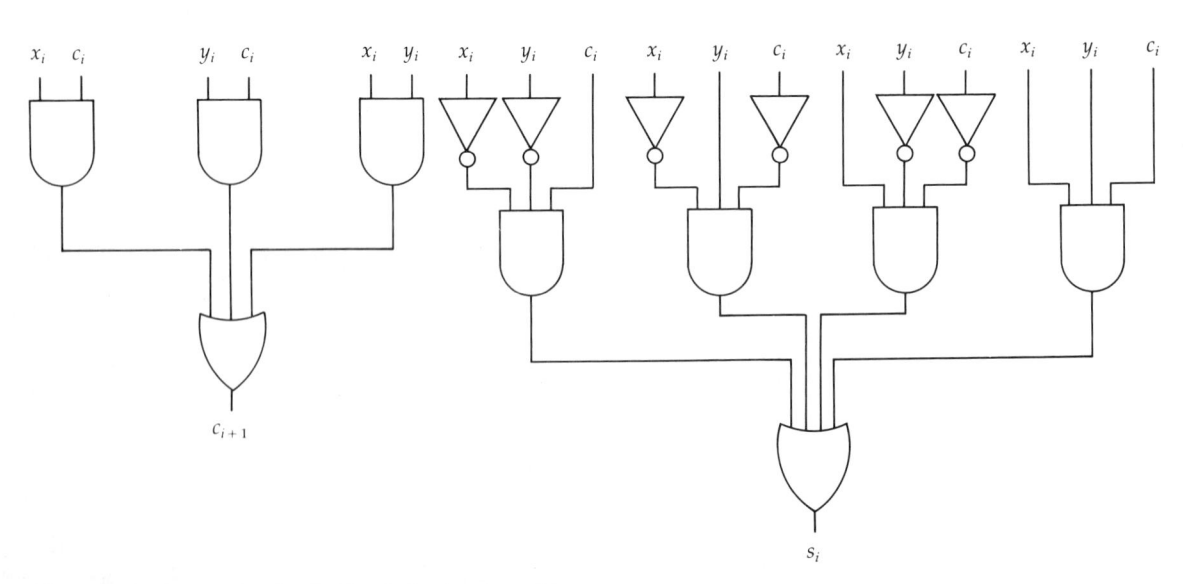

Figure 5.4 Logic circuit of a single-bit binary adder

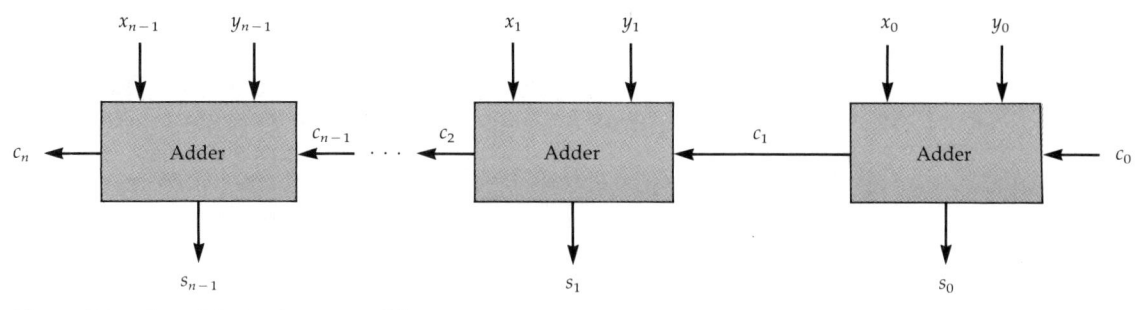

Figure 5.5 An n-bit ripple carry adder

we will find that this carry input is essential when one adds (or subtracts) numbers longer than the register size of a given machine. When adding unsigned numbers, the left-hand carry (c_n) indicates overflow; that is, the sum is too large to be represented in the available number of bits. In some applications the carry bit in a process status register is set equal to c_n. Depending on the situation, c_n equal to 1 may signal an error, provide helpful information, or be irrelevant.

To add two numbers, the n bits of one number are placed on the x inputs of the adder, the other number is placed on the y inputs, and the initial carry is set to 0. The result will eventually appear on the sum outputs. How long does it take to add two 32-bit longwords? For simplicity we will assume that in our hypothetical computer a simple gate needs 10 ns to determine its output. So the right-hand adder has its carry output ready 20 ns after the inputs were set because the signal must pass through the two layers of logic gates shown in Figure 5.4. The sum is ready 10 ns later because the sum requires an additional layer of gates. However, the next adder cannot begin its work until the carry from the first adder is ready. Then there is an additional 20-ns delay as it determines its carry (c_2). Consequently, this bit is not ready until 40 ns after the add operation was initiated. The addition continues in this manner, with each successive carry delayed by two logic gates (or 20 ns later than the previous carry) as the carries ripple through the adder from right to left. Each successive bit of the sum is also delayed 20 ns. That means that the adder requires 32 times 20 ns (or 640 ns) before the final carry is completed. Then it takes an additional 10 ns to compute the final sum bit, which uses one more gate level than the carry circuit. Consequently, the adder will take 650 ns to complete a 32-bit addition if its logic circuits need 10 ns per gate. The hypothetical ALU would be able to add about 1.5 million numbers per second. However, an actual CPU would be considerably slower. As discussed in Chapter 4, carrying out a machine language add instruction requires several internal operations to set up the addition before the ALU can be requested to carry out the operation.

Because of the way the carry signal moves through our n-bit adder, the adder is called a **ripple carry adder**.

Fast Adders

What can be done to impove the speed of the ripple carry adder? One answer is obvious—use a faster technology for the logic circuits in the adder. We could certainly find logic gates that operate twice as fast as those used in our example. Doing so would decrease the time needed for the add operation by one half but could also increase the cost, possibly in a very significant way. Moreover, the faster technology may not have all the desired traits of the original one.

In this section we will explore an alternate way to increase the speed of a multibit adder. We will modify the method for treating carries because the ripple carry operation is responsible for the slow addition time. The improved method will provide a significant increase in speed at the expense of a few extra logic gates.

The derivation of a faster carry algorithm uses the Boolean algebra distributive rule (1) to rewrite equation (2) for c_{i+1}.

$$c_{i+1} = y_i c_i + x_i c_i + x_i y_i$$
$$= (y_i + x_i)c_i + x_i y_i$$

If one defines the **propagate** function

$$P_i = y_i + x_i \tag{4}$$

and the **generate** function

$$G_i = x_i y_i \tag{5}$$

then the carry function can be written

$$c_{i+1} = P_i c_i + G_i \tag{6}$$

Because the propagate and generate functions depend only on the two input bits (x_i and y_i), they can be calculated immediately with only one logic gate delay after the adder is instructed to carry out the addition. The determination of c_{i+1}, however, must wait until the carry bit (c_i) is available. But fortunately, some additional algebra will show that this carry bit can be found sooner than previously anticipated.

If i in formula (6) is set first to 0 and then to 1, it is found that

$$c_1 = P_0 c_0 + G_0 \tag{7}$$

and

$$c_2 = P_1 c_1 + G_1 \tag{8}$$

Substituting (7) into (8), we find that

$$c_2 = P_1(P_0 c_0 + G_0) + G_1$$

or

$$c_2 = P_1 P_0 c_0 + P_1 G_0 + G_1 \tag{9}$$

Formula (9) expresses a direct relationship between the carry out from the second stage of the n-bit adder and some bits that are readily available—namely, the initial carry and the propagate and generate values. Hence this formula shows that by adding some extra logic gates, we can determine c_2 with only three gate delays—one to calculate the P and G functions, one for the AND operations, and one for the OR operation. This means that it is possible to start calculating c_2 before c_1 is known. Figure 5.6 shows a two-bit adding circuit using look-ahead carry formulas (7) and (9).

But we can do even better. Setting i in formula (6) to 2 and substituting formula (9) into the result gives

$$c_3 = P_2 c_2 + G_2$$
$$= P_2(P_1 P_0 c_0 + P_1 G_0 + G_1) + G_2$$
$$c_3 = P_2 P_1 P_0 c_0 + P_2 P_1 G_0 + P_2 G_1 + G_2 \qquad (10)$$

This formula is even more impressive. It shows that it is also possible to determine c_3 at the same time that c_2 is found. In fact we can determine

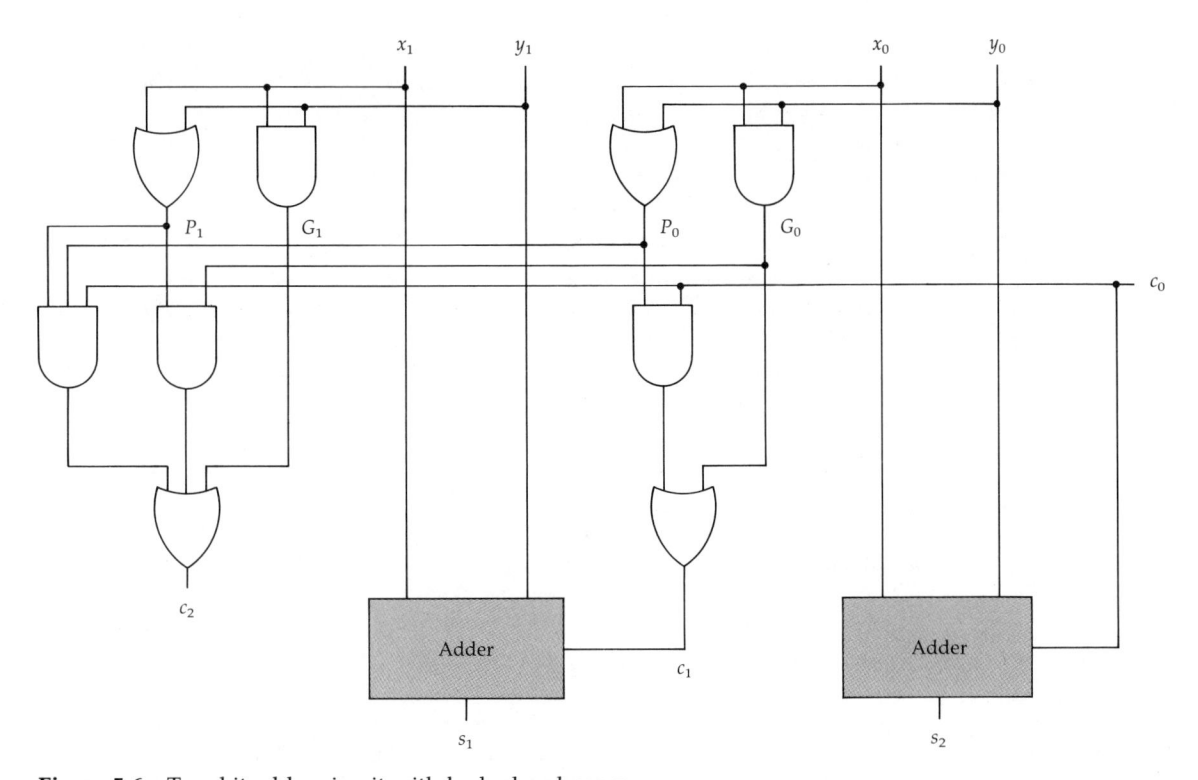

Figure 5.6 Two-bit adder circuit with look-ahead carry

all the carries at the same time using this type of "look-ahead" algorithm. For example,

$$c_4 = P_3P_2P_1P_0c_0 + P_3P_2P_1G_0 + P_3P_2G_1 + P_3G_2 + G_3 \tag{11}$$

and in general

$$c_{i+1} = P_i \ldots P_1P_0c_0 + P_i \ldots P_1G_0 + \ldots + P_iG_{i-1} + G_i \tag{12}$$

Formula (12) shows that it is possible to complete all the carry operations in two gate delays after forming the P and G functions. The sums, which need three more gate delays after the carry operations are completed, can be ready in six gate delays after the beginning of the add operation. Thus it is mathematically possible to complete an addition of two n-bit numbers in 60 ns using our hypothetical 10-ns gate logic.

Unfortunately, the technology used to produce the gates may prevent implementation of formula (12) for large i because of the large number of interconnections needed. Just as we can blow a fuse by running too many appliances on the same electrical circuit in our homes, connecting a large number of inputs to the output of one logic gate can cause the circuit to malfunction. (Logic designers use the term **fan-out** to specify the maximum number of logic gate inputs that can be connected to the output of one gate. The fan-out capabilities of a gate depend on the technology used to build that gate. In one common technology, the 74xx logic family, a standard output has a fan-out of 10; that is, one output can provide power to drive up to 10 gate inputs. **Fan-in** is the number of input gates connected together in a logic circuit and represents the load that the circuit places on the line that is providing the power to those inputs. For example, the single-bit adder shown in Figure 5.4 places a fan-in of 6 on all the input lines, x_i, y_i, and c_i. Alternate designs for the circuit may change that figure.)

Electronic circuits that use the look-ahead carry formulas to add 4-bit numbers have been available for several years. Our design requires one gate delay to calculate the P and G functions, two gate delays to determine all four carries, and then three more gate delays to complete the addition. To add longer numbers, several of these circuits can be connected. For example, eight of these circuits can be used to sum 32-bit values. Figure 5.7 shows an 8-bit version using two of these circuits. In its simplest form, carries ripple through the resulting circuit 4 bits at a time. Consequently, after the one gate delay to form the P and G function values, all the carries can be completed in a sequence of eight carry operations, each needing two gate delays. The last circuit on the chain of adders needs another three gate delays to complete its additions. Consequently, a 32-bit addition can be completed in 20 gate delays, or 200 ns if each gate requires 10 ns. This corresponds to five million additions per second, which is more than three times faster than our ripple carry adder, even though the technology is unchanged. If this time is still unacceptable, we can reduce it further by using an additional layer of look-ahead

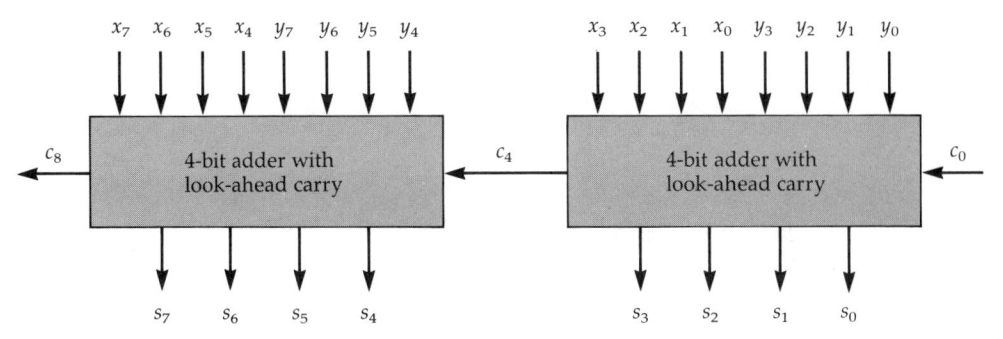

Figure 5.7 An 8-bit adder using two 4-bit look-ahead carry adder circuits

carry gates or combining the bits in larger groups. Look-ahead carry circuits for up to 16 bits were available in the mid-1980s. Using the same rationale used above, the use of 16-bit look-ahead circuits would reduce the add time for 32-bit operands to only eight logic gates or 80 ns.

While the exact timing calculations for an adder depend on the technology used to make it, we have shown that appropriate algorithms can make a significant difference in hardware speed.

Addition of Signed Numbers

Thus far our discussion of addition has been limited to unsigned numbers. What changes are needed for processing signed numbers? The answer depends on the method of representing them. Three methods were presented in Chapter 1. After investigating them in more detail, the reasons why most modern computers use two's complement arithmetic for signed integers will become obvious.

First we will consider the sign and magnitude method, which is used for floating-point numbers on many computers, including the VAX. If we want to add two signed numbers in this notation, we must first determine if both values have the same sign. If so, we add the numbers in the normal fashion except that we must use special care in handling the sign bits. However, if the numbers have different signs, the magnitude of the smaller number must be subtracted from that of the larger and the result is then given the proper sign. Consequently, addition with sign and magnitude representations requires that the signs of the numbers be compared before it is possible to determine whether the magnitudes must be added or subtracted. Clearly, as far as addition is concerned, use of sign and magnitude representation will decrease computer speed and require extra hardware.

The situation is much simpler for one's complement. Numbers using this representation can be added using normal logic for addition, with one modification called **end-around carry**. Assuming that the sum can be represented in this notation, we need only add the high-order carry

Dec	Binary	Dec	Binary	Dec	Binary	Dec	Binary
+3 =	00011	+3 =	00011	−3 =	11100	−3 =	11100
+6 =	+00110	−6 =	+11001	+6 =	+00110	−6 =	+11001
	001001		011100		100010		110101
	↳+0		↳+0		↳+1		↳+1
+9 =	01001	−3 =	11100	+3 =	00011	−9 =	10110

Figure 5.8 Examples of addition using end-around carry with one's complement arithmetic

bit back into the sum. This concept is illustrated in Figure 5.8, which shows examples of four different cases using 5-bit numbers. You may find it useful to try other examples to verify that this rule works correctly.

One's complement can be implemented by just adding end-around carry circuitry to a standard adder. However, unless a number of extra logic gates are used for a complete look-ahead carry system, the time needed to perform addition is increased because it is necessary to determine the carry from the highest order bit before it can be added to the sum, if needed. This is a serious problem because the carry bits already slow addition considerably.

The advantage of two's complement arithmetic now becomes obvious. In Chapter 1 it was shown that if signed numbers are represented in two's complement notation, any two of them can be added in the same manner as unsigned numbers regardless of their signs. Consequently, any computer capable of adding unsigned numbers can add two's complement integers without modifying the hardware or increasing the operation's time.

We must now face two related problems. One is the requirement of being able to find the negative of any given number (which we will discuss shortly). The other issue is the matter of interpreting the results of the calculation to provide warnings when overflow occurs. This was easy for unsigned values because a carry out of the highest-order bits indicates overflow. With signed numbers, the problem is slightly more complicated. A couple of examples illustrate the problem and the solution. Five-bit integers are used in the example so that legal values range from $(-16)_{10}$ = 10000 in two's complement to $(15)_{10}$ = 01111.

Decimal	Two's Complement	Decimal	Two's Complement
$(+10)_{10}$ =	01010	$(-10)_{10}$ =	10110
$(+8)_{10}$ =	+01000	$(-8)_{10}$ =	+11000
$(+18)_{10} \neq$	10010 = $(-14)_{10}$	$(-18)_{10} \neq$	01110 = $(14)_{10}$

The presence of overflow is obvious because the results have the wrong sign. The overflow bit in the process status register can be set whenever the two numbers being added have the same sign but the result has a different sign in s_{n-1}. EXCLUSIVE-OR gates can be used to determine if the values have the same signs and if the sign of one of the numbers being added agrees with the sign of the sum. (Some texts recommend detecting overflow by checking $c_n \oplus s_{n-1}$ when both numbers being added have the same sign. This method is equivalent to the one we suggested because if the two numbers being added have the same sign, c_n will always equal the sign bit of those numbers.)

You may wonder why the VAX, like many other computers, uses sign and magnitude representations for floating-point numbers when two's complement is clearly much more efficient for handling addition. The answer is that the choice of floating-point representation was made to optimize multiplication and division instead of addition and subtraction. Multiplication of floating-point numbers in sign and magnitude notation is conceptually much simpler than in the other representations.

Subtraction and Negation

Subtraction is a standard arithmetic operation required by most computers. The close relationship between subtraction and addition of signed numbers indicates that an addition circuit can be used for subtraction if it is possible to change the sign of the **subtrahend** (the number to be subtracted) and then add it to the **minuend** (the number subtracted from). Thus it is useful to incorporate the ability to negate a number into an adder. Most computers not only have instructions for subtraction but also provide machine language instructions for negating values. The VAX assembly language move negated instructions will be introduced after we study the modifications needed to incorporate subtraction into an adder.

The key to subtraction is to find the negative of the subtrahend so that it can be added to the minuend. We can use a modified adder for both addition and subtraction. Clearly, negating a number is easiest in the sign and magnitude representation. All that is needed is to complement the sign bit whenever we wish to subtract. This can be done with the circuit shown in Figure 5.9. The sign bit of the number being subtracted or added is input on the S input. The add/subtract (A/S) line is 0 when we want to add. In this case the left AND gate has a 0 input, so the output must be 0. However, the right AND gate has one input equal to 1, so its output will equal the S input. When we want to subtract, the A/S line is set to 1. This time the output of the right-hand AND gate is always 0, and the left-hand gate outputs the complement of S. Thus the output from this circuit's OR gate is S when we are adding and NOT S when we subtract. The truth table is included in the figure and is identical to the one for an EXCLUSIVE-OR gate shown in Figure 5.1. Consequently, we will refer to this circuit as an EXCLUSIVE-OR gate in the remainder of this section. Knowing that the circuit carries out the function of an EXCLUSIVE-OR gate is helpful because we can replace the circuit in the figure by any other EXCLUSIVE-OR circuit, and the adder

Figure 5.9 Circuit for conditionally inverting sign bit S of a number to be added or subtracted

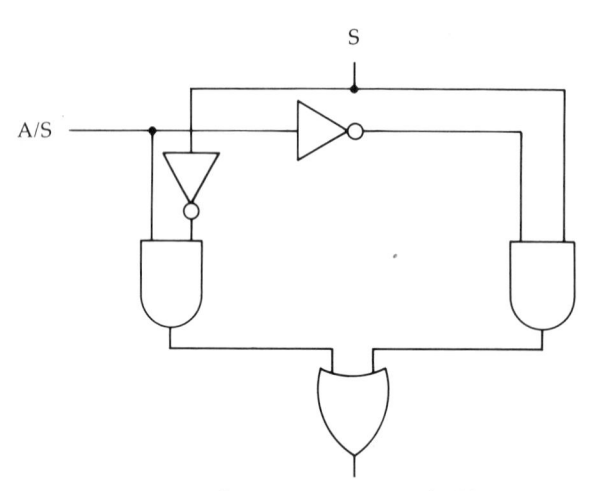

Truth Table

A/S	S	Output	
0	0	0	
0	1	1	Add
1	0	1	
1	1	0	Subtract

still can be used for both addition and subtraction. We see that we can also use the adder for subtraction in a sign and magnitude machine by simply inserting the EXCLUSIVE-OR gate on the sign bit input of the number to be subtracted.

If the machine uses one's complement, it is necessary to complement every bit of the number, not just the sign bit. This is not a serious problem because n-bit numbers can be complemented by a series of n EXCLUSIVE-OR gates. One input of each gate is connected to the add/subtract line and the other to one of the bits of the subtrahend. (In actual circuits a different circuit may be used to avoid fan-in problems.)

The situation in a two's complement machine would seem more complicated because it is necessary to complement each bit of the subtrahend and then add 1 to find the negative of an integer. Fortunately, that is not as difficult as it seems. Figure 5.10 shows a modification to the n-bit adder that satisfies this requirement. The diagram supposes that when we want to subtract, the subtrahend is placed on the y inputs. The add/subtract line is connected to the carry input of the adder as well as one of the inputs in each gate of the EXCLUSIVE-OR array. When the add/subtract line is set to 0, the number on the y inputs is passed through the EXCLUSIVE-OR array without modification and added to the number on the x inputs. When the add/subtract line is set to 1, the number on the y inputs is inverted, and the result is added to the 1 on the carry input as well as the minuend on the x inputs. That performs a two's complement subtraction. Note that at this level of detail, the hardware cost of using two's complement instead of one's complement is only a single connection between the add/subtract line and the carry input to the adder.

In a machine using two's complement arithmetic, we have shown that it is useful to employ the adder itself as part of the hardware used to

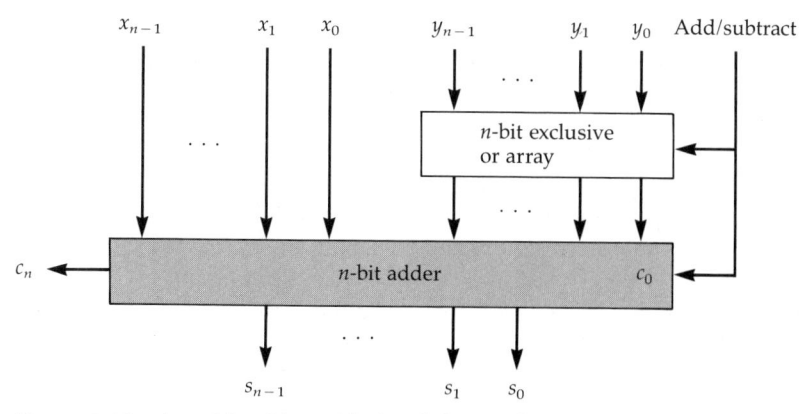

Figure 5.10 An n-bit adder with the ability to do two's complement subtraction

negate numbers for subtraction. But the instruction set of many computers includes special instructions to find the negatives of numbers. How can the ALU carry them out? The answer is to subtract the number from 0. The number to be negated is placed on the y inputs of our adder, 0 is placed on the x inputs, the add/subtract line is set to 1, and the adder is commanded to add.

The VAX uses "move negated" instructions to find the negatives of values. These instructions are similar to the move instructions and have the two-operand format

    MNEGx   source, destination

where x is the data type. The instructions and their opcodes are

Mnemonic	Opcode	Mnemonic	Opcode
MNEGB	8E	MNEGF	52
MNEGW	AE	MNEGD	72
MNEGL	CE		

For example, to put the negative of the longword in R2 into the memory location whose address is in R5, the instruction

    MNEGL   R2, (R5)

would be used. In keeping with the policy of not providing arithmetic capabilities for quadwords, there is no MNEGQ instruction.

Multiple-Word Addition and Subtraction

There is an additional problem concerning addition and subtraction when the computer's registers have fewer bits than are needed for some calculations. This is a common problem on 8-bit microcomputers because many operations require using integers outside the small range allowed by a single byte. Unusual problems may even make the 32-bit longwords on the VAX inadequate. Consequently, its designers (like those of the 8-bit microprocessors) included special machine language addition and subtraction instructions that simplify calculation with multiword integers.

When adding two numbers by hand, we must account for carries from one digit to the next because we can only add one digit pair at a time. When implementing multiword addition on a computer, the same problem arises, except that the computer can operate with several bits at a time. Similar problems occur with subtraction because borrowing may be needed. Consequently, special machine language instructions commonly handle carries or borrows from the previous section of the number. The VAX instructions needed for multiword calculations and their opcodes are

Mnemonic	Operands	Opcode
ADWC	source, destination	D8
SBWC	source, destination	D9

The operation of ADWC (ADd With Carry) can be represented as

destination ← destination + source + C

where C is the carry bit in the process status word. Likewise, SBWC (SuBtract With Carry, which might be better understood as subtract with borrow) performs the operation

destination ← destination − source − C

In both cases the operation is carried out with longwords.

For example, suppose that we need to add a 64-bit quadword integer stored at X to another quadword stored in Y. In accordance with standard policy on the VAX, assume that the low-order bits are stored first. The following assembly language code can be used to add the numbers.

```
ADDL2   X, Y            ; add low-order part of values
ADWC    X + 4, Y + 4    ; add high-order part of values
```

The first instruction adds the least significant halves of the values and stores the result in the least significant part of Y. The carry bit in the PSW is set to 0 if there is no carry out of high-order bits and to 1 if a carry is necessary. The second command adds the carry bit to the most significant halves of the values and stores the result in the most significant part of Y. (X + 4 tells the assembler to use relative addressing and to add 4 to the address of X to find the most significant half of the variable X.) If 64-bit arithmetic is insufficient, the ADWC commands also set the carry flag so that additional ADWC commands can be used to process additional 32-bit portions of the value. The SBWC command is used in a similar manner.

5.2 Multiplication and Division

Our study of the ALU's operation now turns to multiplication and division, which are more complicated and time-consuming than addition or subtraction. Their special hardware circuits are quite expensive. Fortunately, computer designers can choose between several algorithms and can implement these operations in several ways, depending on the speed/cost ratio goal for the particular computer. If speed is the most important consideration, the algorithms can be implemented using hardware circuits; if reducing hardware cost is the chief goal, the algorithms can be implemented in software. Between these two choices, there is a third option—the algorithm can be coded in microcode. (This concept will be introduced in Chapter 6.) No matter what technique is used, it is essential that an appropriate algorithm be selected to ensure correctness and speed.

We will also introduce the extended multiply and divide commands included in the VAX instruction set. These commands represent natural implementations of the algorithms for these two operations.

In this section we will assume that numbers are stored in binary as either unsigned integers or signed integers expressed in two's complement notation unless otherwise noted.

Multiplication of Unsigned Integers

Before considering multiplication algorithms, it is useful to review the method humans normally use for multiplying nonnegative binary integers as illustrated in Figure 5.11. There are two observations to be made.

First, multiplication of the two 5-bit values yielded a 10-bit result. In general, the product of two n-bit values could have as many as $2n$ digits. The VAX's usual multiplication instructions, described in Chapter 2, do not allow for this. The product they generate has the same length as the numbers being multiplied. If the actual product requires more bits than can be used, these instructions store the lower half of the result, ignore the high-order bits, and set the overflow bit to provide a warning. Later in this section we will cover an extended multiplication instruction that allows a double-length product. The advantages and disadvantages of double-length products will be discussed at that time.

If a machine does not provide for double-length products (or if the program ignores the high-order portion of the product), overflow is a possibility. In fact in certain situations, such as the calculation of random numbers, this type of overflow is used to advantage. Consequently, machines may not consider overflow from integer multiplication an error; instead, they often provide some means of allowing the program to determine if overflow occurred. On the VAX integer overflow sets the V bit in the processor status word (PSW). In assembly language the programmer may include code to test this bit to determine if there is a problem. Some high-level language compilers allow the programmer to request that overflow from integer calculations be treated as an error.

The second observation that can be made while studying Figure 5.11 is that it would be awkward for a computer to use this technique. As shown in the figure, most humans will calculate the various products of the multiplicand by a digit of the multiplier, align them appropriately, and then find their sum by adding one column at a time. Not only would this method be slow for a computer, there is the added complication of possible double carries as illustrated in the fifth column from the right, whose sum (including a carry) is binary 100, forcing a carry of a binary 10. It is much easier for a machine to carry out multiplications as shown in Figure 5.12, where partial products are calculated row by row. The technique is relatively simple to implement. The multiplicand is multiplied by the appropriate digit from the multiplier and added to the previous partial product using standard addition principles.

Conceptually, building a straightforward hardware multiplier is relatively simple. The AND gate's truth table shows that it can serve as a single-bit multiplier. Suppose that we need to build a multiplier for five-bit numbers such as shown in Figure 5.12. We could use 25 AND gates, one at each location where a digit of the multiplicand was multiplied by a digit of the multiplier. Single-bit adder circuits could be installed at each of the 20 locations where an addition was carried out. The resulting multiplier would operate correctly but become increasingly complex as the length of the numbers being multiplied increased. Fortunately, more efficient multiplying circuits have been designed. Jean-Loup Baer's book contains examples.*

The resulting high cost of this type of hardware multiplier might be justifiable on fast, expensive machines. But what can be done in less costly computers? Fortunately, certain algorithms allow the machine to multiply using its adder. Figure 5.12 suggests a possible algorithm for multiplication of n-bit unsigned binary integers. However, because the result can have up to $2n$ bits, implementation takes some care on a machine designed with n-bit registers and accumulators. Careful observation of the calculation shows that even though the result can have up to $2n$ digits, only n of them together with a carry bit are ever actually involved in an addition at any one time. Consequently, we can carry out a multiplication with an n-bit adder. The idea is to look at individual digits of the multiplier one at a time in a right-to-left order, adding the multiplicand whenever the digit is a 1. To ensure that the multiplicand is aligned properly with the partial sum before adding, it is convenient to shift the partial sums to the right as the digits of the multiplier are inspected.

---

*Jean-Loup Baer, *Computer Systems Architecture*. Rockville, Maryland: Computer Science Press, 1980.

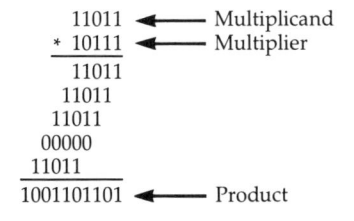

```
    11011    ←──── Multiplicand
  * 10111    ←──── Multiplier
    11011
    11011
    11011
    00000
    11011
 1001101101  ←──── Product
```

Figure 5.11 Multiplication of binary numbers

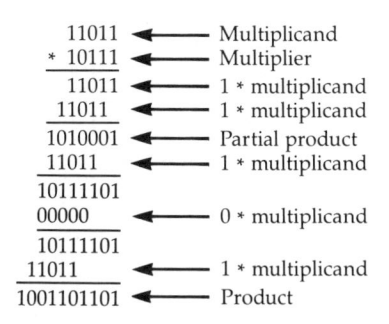

```
    11011    ←──── Multiplicand
  * 10111    ←──── Multiplier
    11011    ←──── 1 * multiplicand
    11011    ←──── 1 * multiplicand
   1010001   ←──── Partial product
    11011    ←──── 1 * multiplicand
   10111101
    00000    ←──── 0 * multiplicand
   10111101
    11011    ←──── 1 * multiplicand
 1001101101  ←──── Product
```

Figure 5.12 Multiplication of binary numbers using partial sums

The algorithm uses two registers referred to as M and Q, the accumulator, denoted by A, and the carry bit, referred to as C. It is convenient to imagine that the registers are arranged in the following manner:

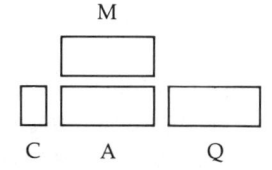

```
           M
          ┌─┐
          └─┘
         ┌─┐┌─┐
         └─┘└─┘
        ┌─┐
        └─┘
         C  A  Q
```

M holds the multiplicand and Q initially holds the multiplier. When finished, the high-order portion of the result is in the accumulator (A), and the Q register holds the low-order part of the result. It is convenient to refer to the combination of the accumulator and Q register as the AQ register. Bit C holds the carry bit, which results when M is added to the accumulator.

It is helpful to think of it as an extension of the accumulator and, hence, of the AQ register. CAQ refers to the $2n + 1$ bits of this combination. The exact steps are shown in the following algorithm.

Algorithm 5.1 *Multiplication of unsigned n-bit integers.*

1. Initialize:
   a. Load A and C with zeros.
   b. Load the multiplicand into M.
   c. Load the multiplier into Q.
2. Repeat *n* times:
   a. If the least significant bit of Q is 1, add M to A.
   b. Shift the combined CAQ register one bit to the right, putting a 0 in C.

The result is in the AQ register.

The calculations shown in Figure 5.13 illustrate this technique by calculating the product of multiplicand $M = (1101)_2$ and multiplier

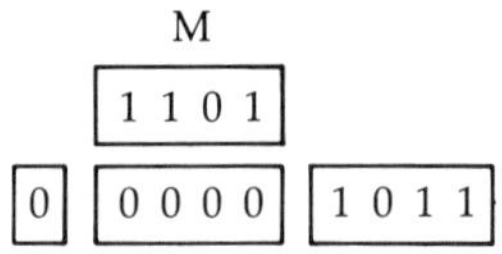

```
                        M
                      1 1 0 1

                   0  0 0 0 0   1 0 1 1

       Cycle   C      A         Q              Operation
               0   0 0 0 0 : 1 0 1 1
         1     0   1 1 0 1 : 1 0 1 1            Add M to A
               0   0 1 1 0   1:1 0 1            Shift right

         2     1   0 0 1 1   1:1 0 1            Add M to A
               0   1 0 0 1   1 1:1 0            Shift right

         3     0   0 1 0 0   1 1 1:1            Shift right

         4     1   0 0 0 1   1 1 1:1            Add M to A
               0   1 0 0 0   1 1 1 1:           Shift right
```

Answer: 1000 1111

Figure 5.13 Example of unsigned integer multiplication using Algorithm 5.1

$Q = (1011)_2$. The colon is used to illustrate the boundary between the product and the multiplier. The arrows point to the least significant digit of register Q that is inspected in step 2a and determines the action taken in the next cycle.

While this algorithm is straightforward once we understand the shift operation, some improvements are possible. We need a multiplication algorithm that works with signed integers. A faster algorithm would be desirable. Methods to achieve these goals are discussed next.

Multiplication of Signed Integers and the Booth Algorithm

Previously, we looked at a simple way to implement multiplication of unsigned numbers. What can be done if the numbers are signed? We will study this question now. All numbers will be binary signed integers represented in two's complement unless otherwise stated.

One possible answer is to use the same method used by humans, who multiply the absolute values of the numbers and then determine the correct sign of the product. The computer could test the multiplier and multiplicand to see if either is negative. Negative values can be replaced by their absolute values, and then the multiplication can proceed as if the values were unsigned. Finally, the correct sign could be determined, and if necessary, the result would be replaced by its negative. However, we can find a simpler solution by modifying the technique used in Figure 5.12 so that it works even when the multiplicand is a negative number.

This algorithm uses a concept called **sign extension**. We use it when we are increasing the number of bits in the representation of a two's complement integer. When we convert a nonnegative number from n bits to $2n$ bits, we need only add n zeros on the left of the number. Clearly, this will not change the number's value. But to convert a negative number, we must add n ones on the left. To see that this will not change the number's value, consider what would happen if we find the two's complement of the negative number, extend it with zeros, and then find the two's complement of the result. This roundabout process would result in adding the same ones. Observe that in either case, we extend the number by adding more bits equal to the sign bit to the left-hand side of the value's representation. For example, consider extending the binary values of 27 and -27 from 6 bits to 12 bits:

Decimal	6-Bit Binary	12-Bit Binary
27	011011	000000 011011
-27	100101	111111 100101

We can verify that both representations of -27 are valid by taking their two's complement. This conversion can be understood as extending the sign of the original number by propagating the left-hand sign bit through the new high-order bits.

Consider the calculation of $-27 * 23$.

```
 (-27)₁₀  =        -011011  =  111111 100101
* (23)₁₀  =        * 010111  =         010111
  - 81                          111111 100101
  - 54                          111111 00101
                                111110 0101
                                000000 000
                                111001 01
                                000000 0
─────────     ─────────────     ─────────────
(-621)₁₀  =  -001001 101101  =  110110 010011
```

This is the same problem as in Figure 5.11 except that the multiplicand has been replaced by its negative. Notice that the multiplicand and each of the intermediate products has been sign extended to 12 digits. Because the product of any two 6-bit values can be expressed in 12 bits, exactly 12 bits are summed. Any carries beyond the twelfth bit are ignored.

We can modify Algorithm 5.1 to multiply signed numbers when the multiplier (Q) is nonnegative by replacing the carry flag (C) with a sign bit (S). S is initially set to 0 but replaced by the sign of the multiplicand (M) when the multiplicand is added to the accumulator (A). Because S is shifted right when SAQ is shifted, S provides sign extension for the partial product in the accumulator. When finding the sum, carries out of the left-hand digits are ignored as usual in two's complement addition.

This change makes the algorithm independent of the sign of the multiplicand. If the multiplier is negative, one solution would be to negate both the multiplier and multiplicand and then multiply them. This leads to the following algorithm for multiplication of signed integers.

Algorithm 5.2 *Multiplication of signed n-bit integers assuming two's complement arithmetic.*

1. Initialize:
   a. Load A and S with zeros.
   b. Load the multiplicand into M.
   c. Load the multiplier into Q.
   d. If Q < 0, replace M and Q by their negatives.
2. Repeat *n* times:
   a. If the least significant bit of Q is 1, add M to A and set S to the sign of M.
   b. Shift the combined SAQ register one bit to the right without changing S.

The result is in the AQ register.

Figure 5.14 shows the results of calculating decimal $(-13) * 11$ using 5-bit numbers that include a sign bit. Observe that the value of S changes only once, the first time the negative multiplier is added to the accumulator.

Although this algorithm will work with any two signed integers, a faster method would be desirable. The Booth algorithm can be used to speed up multiplication in some situations. The motivation underlying this technique is as follows. Suppose that we wish to multiply the binary number 001011 by 001111. If algorithm 5.2 is used, the multiplicand would need to be added four times, once for each 1 in the multiplier. The amount

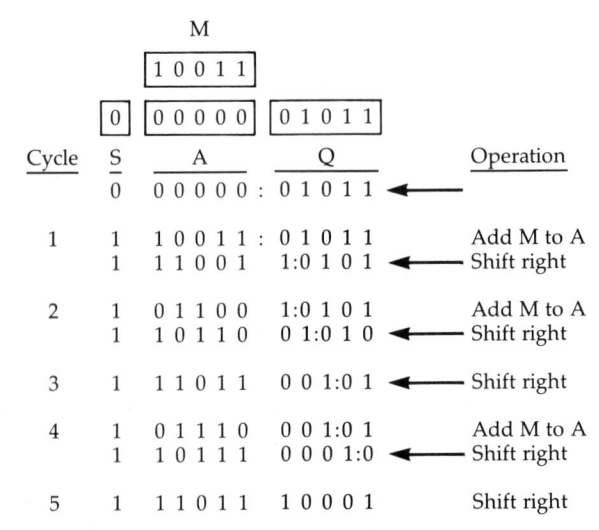

```
                          M
                       1 0 0 1 1
                  0  0 0 0 0 0   0 1 0 1 1
       Cycle      S       A           Q            Operation
                  0    0 0 0 0 0 : 0 1 0 1 1

         1        1    1 0 0 1 1 : 0 1 0 1 1      Add M to A
                  1    1 1 0 0 1   1:0 1 0 1      Shift right

         2        1    0 1 1 0 0   1:0 1 0 1      Add M to A
                  1    1 0 1 1 0   0 1:0 1 0      Shift right

         3        1    1 1 0 1 1   0 0 1:0 1      Shift right

         4        1    0 1 1 1 0   0 0 1:0 1      Add M to A
                  1    1 0 1 1 1   0 0 0 1:0      Shift right

         5        1    1 1 0 1 1   1 0 0 0 1      Shift right
```

Figure 5.14 Example of signed integer multiplication using Algorithm 5.2

of effort could be reduced if we observe that the multiplier 001111 could also be written 010000 − 1. The original problem can be solved with only two additions, as follows:

$$001011 * 001111 = 001011 * (010000 - 000001)$$
$$= 001011 * 010000 - 001011 * 000001$$
$$= 000010\ 110000 - 000000\ 001011$$
$$= 000010\ 100101$$

This system could be helpful for more general multipliers. For example, if the multiplier (Q) is the signed number

0111 1110 1111

(2031 in decimal), Q could be rewritten as

0111 1110 1111 = 1000 0000 0000 − 10 0000 + 1 0000 − 1

before multiplying. We can verify that the value of the right side is still decimal 2031. Moreover, multiplying a value by the right-hand side requires adding or subtracting only four values, while the original form required ten additions. The Booth algorithm is based on this scheme. For hand calculations, it is helpful to allow "+1" and "−1" values for "bits" and transform the multiplier according to the following scheme:

Original		Transformed
Bit i	Bit $i - 1$	Bit i
0	0	0
0	1	+1
1	0	−1
1	1	0

To determine the value of "transformed bit 0," we assume that "original bit −1" equals 0. For example, to transform the number 0111 1110 1111, we proceed in this manner:

Original value   0 1 1 1   1 1 1 0   1 1 1 1   0 ← assumed b_{-1}
Transformed   +1 0 0 0   0 0 −1 +1   0 0 0 −1

which can be interpreted as

1000 0000 0000 − 10 0000 + 1 0000 − 1

Sign extended multiplication is needed so that any value multiplied by −1 (in practice, the two's complement of the multiplicand is added during hand calculations) will sum as a negative number. Figure 5.15 shows the calculation of decimal 100 * (−31). We can verify that the result is −3100 by evaluating its two's complement.

For machine calculations, it is inconvenient to actually carry out the bit transformation. Instead, during each step of the process, bits i and

Figure 5.15

$$M = (100)_{10} = 0110\ 0100$$
$$(-100)_{10} = 1001\ 1100$$

$$(31)_{10} = 0\ 0\ 0\ 1\ 1\ 1\ 1\ 1$$
$$Q = (-31)_{10} = 1\ 1\ 1\ 0\ 0\ 0\ 0\ 1$$
$$\text{Transformed:} \quad 0\ 0\text{-}1\ 0\ 0\ 0\text{+}1\text{-}1$$

```
(M)                              0 1 1 0   0 1 0 0 =              (-0110 0100)
                               * 0 0-1 0   0 0+1-1 =            * (-0001 1111)
                              ─────────────────────          ──────────────────
(-M)  1 1 1 1   1 1 1 1        1 0 0 1     1 1 0 0                 0110 0100
(M)   0 0 0 0   0 0 0 0        1 1 0 0     1 0 0                 0 1100 100
                                             0                   01 1001 00
                                                                011 0010 0
                                          0                     0110 0100
(-M)  1 1 1 1   0 0 1 1        1 0 0                                   0
                                 0                                     0
                               0                                       0
                              ─────────────────────          ──────────────────
      1 1 1 1   0 0 1 1        1 1 1 0     0 1 0 0 =         -0000 1100 0001 1100
```

Figure 5.15 Comparing the Booth algorithm with normal multiplication

$i - 1$ are checked to determine if it is necessary to add the multiplicand or its two's complement. Consequently, this algorithm requires an extra bit (B) on the right-hand side of the Q register to hold bit "b_{-1}." We will store it in a one-bit register called B. It is helpful to arrange the registers as follows:

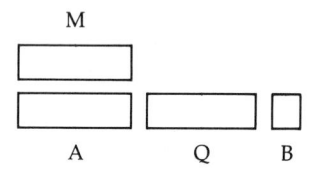

```
           M
         ┌────┐
         └────┘
    ┌────┐┌────┐┌─┐
    └────┘└────┘└─┘
      A     Q    B
```

AQB is treated as one register for some operations.

Algorithm 5.3 *The **Booth algorithm** for multiplying two n-bit two's complement integers.*

1. Initialize:
   a. Load A and B with zeros.
   b. Load M with the multiplicand.
   c. Load Q with the multiplier.
2. Repeat *n* times:
   a. If the least significant bit of Q = 1 and B = 0, subtract M from A. Else, if the least significant bit of Q = 0 and B = 1, add M to A.
   b. Shift AQB one bit right using sign extension.

The result is in the AQ register.

For hand calculations, adding the two's complement of M is a convenient way to subtract M from A. The calculation of 13 * 11 is repeated in Figure 5.16, using 5-bit numbers to allow for the sign bit. Again, the

```
                     M                  (−M = 10011)
                  0 1 1 0 1

              0 0 0 0 0   0 1 0 1 1             0

     Cycle        A           Q             B      Operation
              0 0 0 0 0 : 0 1 0 1 1  ←——— 0 ←———

       1    1 0 0 1 1 : 0 1 0 1 1        0      Subtract M from A
            1 1 0 0 1   1:0 1 0 1  ←——— 1 ←——— Shift right

       2    1 1 1 0 0   1 1:0 1 0  ←——— 1 ←——— Shift right

       3    0 1 0 0 1   1 1:0 1 0        1      Add M to A
            0 0 1 0 0   1 1 1:0 1  ←——— 0 ←——— Shift right

       4    1 0 1 1 1   1 1 1:0 1        0      Subtract M from A
            1 1 0 1 1   1 1 1 1:0  ←——— 1 ←——— Shift right

       5    0 1 0 0 0   1 1 1 1:0        1      Add M to A
            0 0 1 0 0   0 1 1 1 1        0      Shift right
```

Answer: 00100 01111

Figure 5.16 Example of multiplication using the Booth algorithm

colon is used to separate the partial product and the multiplier, while the arrows point to the two digits that are inspected to determine the next operation. Observe that the algorithm does not make any restrictions on the sign of either the multiplier or multiplicand.

Although the Booth algorithm can significantly speed up multiplications when the multiplier has strings of ones or zeros, it has some disadvantages. The number of additions can actually increase when such strings do not exist. This happened in the example where the number of additions increased from three to four. In some computer designs all multiplications are allotted the same amount of time. In this case every multiplication would have to be allotted the amount of time needed for the slowest multiplication, so the Booth algorithm would not help at all. More sophisticated algorithms are available for multiplication. For example, see Hamacher, Vranesic, and Zaky for an algorithm similar to the Booth algorithm that processes two bits at a time and hence is guaranteed to reduce the number of additions and subtractions to n over 2 or less.*

Division

In this subsection we will consider only signed numbers represented in two's complement. If negative values are processed, they must be replaced by their two's complements and the correct sign attached to the result.

*V. Carl Hamacher, Zvonko G. Vranesic, and Safwat G. Zaky, *Computer Organization*, 2nd ed. New York: McGraw-Hill, 1984.

Consider the division of decimal 113 by 11.

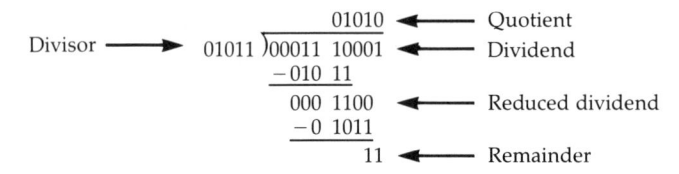

```
                            01010      ←——— Quotient
        Divisor ——→ 01011 )00011 10001 ←——— Dividend
                          - 010 11
                            000 1100   ←——— Reduced dividend
                          -   0 1011
                                  11   ←——— Remainder
```

In this example observe that when the 10-bit dividend is divided by a 5-bit divisor, a 5-bit quotient is found. Generalizing, we will assume that the quotient of a $2n$-bit dividend by a n-bit divisor has at most n bits. However, this assumption is not always true, so there is a possibility that overflow may result and the overflow bit in the process status register must be set. (For example, consider dividing the double-length number 01111 11111 by 00001 or even the 4-digit decimal number 1246 by the 2-digit decimal number 10.) However, it nicely complements our multiplication algorithms where the product of two n-bit numbers is assumed to have $2n$ bits.

Though binary division is simpler than decimal division, this operation is more difficult than multiplication because it is necessary to test to see if the divisor will go into the reduced dividend before we can decide whether to place a 0 or 1 in the quotient. While humans can do this "rapidly," machines must subtract in order to make the test. Algorithm 5.4 makes use of this subtraction by assuming that the reduced dividend is larger than the divisor. If the assumption is false, the divisor must be added back in to correct for this "error." The abbreviations msb and lsb stand for most and least significant bit.

Algorithm 5.4 *Restoring division of positive two's complement integers. Assumes that quotients can be stored in a single n-bit word.*

1. Initialization:
   a. Load divisor into M.
   b. Load double-length dividend into AQ (or zero into A and single-length dividend into Q).
2. Shift and check for overflow:
   a. Shift AQ one bit left.
   b. If A is greater than or equal to M as an unsigned integer, signal overflow and stop. Otherwise, set lsb of Q to 0.
3. Repeat $n - 1$ times:
   a. Shift AQ one bit left.
   b. Subtract M from A (or add the two's complement of M to A).
   c. If A is nonnegative, set lsb of Q to 1. Otherwise, set it to 0 and add M back onto A.

The quotient is in Q and the remainder is in A.

Figure 5.17 shows an example of restoring division of 00011 10001 (decimal 113) by 01011 (decimal 11). The arrows point to the most sig-

5.2 Multiplication and Division

```
                    M
                 ┌─────────┐
                 │ 0 1 0 1 1│         (−M = 10101)
                 └─────────┘
                 ┌─────────┐ ┌─────────┐
                 │ 0 0 0 1 1│ │ 1 0 0 0 1│
                 └─────────┘ └─────────┘
     Cycle          A           Q            Operation
                 0 0 0 1 1   1 0 0 0 1

                 0 0 1 1 1   0 0 0 1:?      Shift left
                 0 0 1 1 1   0 0 0 1:0      No overflow, insert 0

       1         0 1 1 1 0   0 0 1:0 ?      Shift left
               → 0 0 0 1 1                  Subtract M from A
                 0 0 0 1 1   0 0 1:0 1      Insert 1

       2         0 0 1 1 0   0 1:0 1 ?      Shift left
               → 1 1 0 1 1                  Subtract M from A
                 0 0 1 1 0   0 1:0 1 0      Add back and insert 0

       3         0 1 1 0 0   1:0 1 0 ?      Shift left
               → 0 0 0 0 1                  Subtract M from A
                 0 0 0 0 1   1:0 1 0 1      Insert 1

       4         0 0 0 1 1 : 0 1 0 1 ?      Shift left
               → 1 1 0 0 0                  Subtract M from A
                 0 0 0 1 1 : 0 1 0 1 0      Add back and insert 0
```

Quotient is 01010 and remainder is 00011.

Figure 5.17 Example of restoring division

nificant bit of A, which is tested to determine the next operation, and the question mark denotes a digit that is not yet determined.

Unfortunately, Algorithm 5.4 often wastes considerable time restoring the reduced quotient when it becomes negative. Consequently, an alternate procedure that does not require the restoration is often used.

Algorithm 5.5 *Nonrestoring division of positive two's complement integers. Assumes that the quotient can be stored in a single n-bit word.*

1. Initialization:
   a. Load divisor into M.
   b. Load double-length dividend into AQ (or zero into A and dividend into Q).
2. Shift and check for overflow:
   a. Shift AQ one bit left.
   b. If A is greater than or equal to M as an unsigned integer, signal overflow and stop. Otherwise, set lsb of Q to 0.
3. Repeat $n - 1$ times:
   a. Shift AQ one bit left.
   b. If A is nonnegative, subtract M from A. Otherwise, add M to A.
   c. If A is nonnegative, set lsb of Q to 1. Otherwise, set it to 0.
4. If A is negative, add M to A.

The quotient is in Q and the remainder is in A.

```
            1                          1000 − 100 + 10 − 1 = 909
       ─────────                       ─────────────────────────
    31) 28177                       31) 28177
      − 31                             −31000
      ─────                            ──────
        −3                             −2823
                                      −(−3100)
                                      ───────
                                          277
                                         −310
                                         ────
                                          −33
                                         −(−31)
                                         ──────
                                           −2
```

$28177 = 909 * 31 - 2$
$ = 908 * 31 + 31 - 2$
$ = 908 * 31 + 29$

Quotient = 908
Remainder = 29

a. Must we start over?   b. Not necessarily

Figure 5.18 Nonrestoring decimal division

We will look at a decimal example to get some idea why this algorithm works. We need to divide 28,177 by 31. Suppose that we mistakenly thought that the first digit of the quotient should be 1, as shown in Figure 5.18a. We discover this error when we determine that the reduced dividend is negative. Normally we would start over and erase our "invalid" digit. However, this is unnecessary. Figure 5.18b shows how we can continue. We just follow the normal rules of division except that we use signed arithmetic and insert zeros as place holders. When we finish, we observe that the remainder is negative, so we reduce the initial quotient by 1 and add the divisor to the remainder.

Working in binary simplifies the computation because there are only two possible digits, 0 and 1. Consequently, in step 3c we can just insert the appropriate digit into the quotient and avoid having to carry out the subtraction needed in Figure 5.18b. In step 4 we add the divisor to a negative remainder, just as we did in the extra calculations in the figure to get the standard form of the remainder. However, unlike the calculations in the figure, there is no need to reduce the value of the quotient because step 3c already reduced the last digit by one when it inserted the 0 into the quotient.

Figure 5.19 repeats the problem of Figure 5.17 using nonrestoring division. Again, the arrows point to the most significant bit of A, which helps determine the next operation.

Similar algorithms are available for unsigned integers.

The VAX's Extended Multiply and Divide Instructions

The result of the standard VAX multiplication instructions is a product having the same length as the multiplier and multiplicand, but the algorithms in this section generate a double-length product. Some computers, such as the IBM 370 and its equivalents, always produce double-length products. Why did the VAX's designers choose to provide single-

5.2 Multiplication and Division

```
                    M                (-M = 10101)
                  0 1 0 1 1
                  0 0 0 1 1    1 0 0 0 1
    Cycle            A             Q          Operation
                   0 0 0 1 1    1 0 0 0 1
                   0 0 1 1 1    0 0 0 1:?    Shift left
                   0 0 1 1 1    0 0 0 1:0    No overflow, insert 0
      1     →    0 1 1 1 0    0 0 1:0 ?    Shift left
            →    0 0 0 1 1                  Subtract M from A
                   0 0 0 1 1    0 0 1:0 1    Insert 1
      2     →    0 0 1 1 0    0 1:0 1 ?    Shift left
            →    1 1 0 1 1                  Subtract M from A
                   1 1 0 1 1    0 1:0 1 0    Insert 0
      3     →    1 0 1 1 0    1:0 1 0 ?    Shift left
            →    0 0 0 0 1                  Add M to A
                   0 0 0 0 1    1:0 1 0 1    Insert 1
      4     →    0 0 0 1 1 :  0 1 0 1 ?    Shift left
            →    1 1 0 0 0                  Subtract M from A
            →    1 1 0 0 0 :  0 1 0 1 0    Insert 0
                   0 0 0 1 1 :  0 1 0 1 0    Add M to A
```

Quotient is 01010 and remainder is 00011.

Figure 5.19 Example of nonrestoring division

length products? In practice double-length products are often unusable and inconvenient. High-level languages rarely provide for double-length products. Thus, if a machine calculates them, compiler writers must provide extra storage for the longer product and then ignore the high-order half of the result. Moreover the same multiplication instruction can be used for both unsigned and two's complement arithmetic if single-length products are used but not if double-length products are provided.

If a computer's designers decide not to use double-length products in the common multiply and divide commands, they can use the same algorithms that we have studied with simple modifications to meet the single-length requirements. For example, the ALU can calculate a double-length product, but the instruction decoder can be designed so that only the low-order bits of a product are stored and the overflow bit is set as required.

Though double-length products and dividends are often more a nuisance than a help, sometimes they are needed, so the VAX offers optional extended multiplication and division instructions for two's complement arithmetic. Both are more powerful than the standard instructions and have an extra operand. The opcodes and formats are as follows:

Opcode	Assembly Format
7A	EMUL multiplicand, multiplier, add, product
7B	EDIV divisor, dividend, quotient, remainder

The operands of these instructions are all longwords except for the product and dividend, which are quadwords. The extended multiply instruction calculates the quadword product of the multiplicand and multiplier and then adds the "add" operand to it (after extending the sign of "add" to form a quadword). The result is stored in the "product." The low-order 32 bits are stored at the product's address, and the high-order 32 bits are stored 4 bytes later. When the product is stored in the registers, the low-order bits are in the specified register (say, R_n) and the high-order bits are in the next register (R_{n+1}). This storage policy is consistent with the VAX's standard rule that the least significant part is stored first. It applies to all quadword integers. The extended divide instruction differs from DIVL3 in two ways. The dividend is a quadword. The fourth argument is the remainder, which is calculated in such a way that it always has the same sign as the dividend.

For example, suppose that given longwords A, B, and C, it is necessary to calculate

$X \leftarrow A * B / C$

allowing for a quadword product. The operation might be coded as follows:

```
EMUL  A, B, #0, R0      ; Product in R0 and R1
EDIV  C, R0, X, R0      ; Result stored in X
```

The EMUL instruction adds 0 to the product of A and B. The low-order bits of the product are stored in R0, and the high-order bits are stored in R1. This format is exactly that needed by EDIV. The unneeded remainder can be stored in R0 (because the product is no longer required) and then ignored.

The EDIV instruction can be very useful for evaluating the "Mod" operation (remainder from integer division) in Pascal. For example, suppose that it is necessary to compile the statement

```
K := I mod J;
```

Pascal requires that J have a positive value. If the program allows I to be negative, some extra care must be used to obtain the correct results. The VAX Pascal compiler translates the statement in the following manner:

```
       EMUL   #0, #0, I, R2      ; R2, R3 <-- I
       EDIV   J, R2, R0, R2      ; R2 <-- remainder
       TSTL   R2                 ; If remainder is negative
       BGEQ   Store              ;    then
       ADDL2  J, R2              ;    add J to it.
Store: MOVL   R2, K              ; Store result in K
```

The EMUL command is used to extend I into a quadword and put it into the R2 and R3 registers to be ready for the EDIV instruction. This time the quotient calculated by EDIV is unneeded, so it can be dumped into any available register. The standard mathematical definition and Pascal both specify that I mod J is positive even when I is negative, while EDIV gives the remainder the same sign as the dividend. To resolve this problem, the computer is told to check the sign of the remainder. If it is negative, J is added to the remainder to get the correct value of the mod operand. The value is stored by the statement at Store. The code could be reduced to just two instructions if we know that I is positive.

5.3 Shift Instructions

Unless the ALU includes both hardware multiplication and division circuits, we must implement these operations with algorithms that require shifting data to the right or left. Shift instructions are useful in several other applications, including quick methods of multiplying and dividing by powers of 2. These operations are the subject of this section.

Shifting may be done by the ALU circuitry or by special hardware. For example, the VAX 11/750 has a device called the **super rotator** that carries out the shift operations.

The VAX machine language provides special instructions for many of the operations, such as multiplication and division, whose algorithms require that data be shifted. While the VAX has only a few shift instructions in its machine language, they provide most of the needed shifting operations. Computers that rely on software for multiplication and division often have a greater variety of shift instructions to simplify the task of coding those operations.

There are two types of shift instructions on the VAX. The two ASHx instructions provide **arithmetic shifts**, while the ROTL instruction provides what is called **rotation**. The opcodes and formats of these instructions are as follows:

Opcode	Assembly Format
78	ASHL count, source, destination
79	ASHQ count, source, destination
9C	ROTL count, source, destination

Before explaining these commands in detail, it may be useful to explain some common features. The last two operands determine the location of the item to be shifted and the location where the result will be stored. The count operand serves a dual purpose: the data is shifted by the number of bits specified by the magnitude of the count, and the sign of the count determines the direction of the shift. A positive count value indicates that a left shift is desired, while a negative count value specifies a shift to the right.

The arithmetic shift ASHL shifts longwords, while the ASHQ instruction is for quadwords. The data is taken from the source, shifted by the amount specified by the count, and stored at the location specified by the destination. The source is unchanged. If the count is positive, bits are shifted out the left end of the data and replaced by zeros on the right. If the count is negative, bits are lost as they are shifted out the right end. They are replaced on the left by the sign bit of the original data. The ASHQ instruction assumes the normal quadword integer order. The high-order bits are in the second longword of storage or in the next register and are treated as being on the left side of the number during a shift operation. Figure 5.20 illustrates the operation of the shift instructions and shows bits being lost into the "bit bucket" as they are shifted out of the data.

The ROTL instruction rotates bits out one end of the data and into the other. Bits are never lost during a rotation. If the count is positive, the bits are inserted into the right end of the data item as they are shifted out the left. If the count is negative, the bits are inserted into the left end of the data as they are pushed out the right end.

Recall, for example, that the VAX uses two's complement for signed numbers. Suppose that R0 holds decimal −14. What are the contents of R0–R6 after the following instructions are executed?

```
ASHL    #4, R0, R1      ; 4-bit left arithmetic shift
ASHL    #-2, R0, R2     ; 2-bit right arithmetic shift
ROTL    #4, R0, R3      ; 4-bit left rotation
ROTL    #-2, R0, R4     ; 2-bit right rotation
ASHQ    #1, R0, R5      ; 1-bit left arithmetic shift
                        ;   of a quadword
```

The answers are:

Register	Binary	Decimal
R0	1111 . . . 1111 1111 0010	−14
R1	1111 . . . 1111 0010 0000	−224
R2	1111 . . . 1111 1111 1100	−4
R3	1111 . . . 1111 0010 1111	
R4	1011 . . . 1111 1111 1100	
R5	1111 . . . 1111 1110 0100	
R6	1111 . . . 1110 0100 0001	

The decimal values of R0, R1, and R2 are included in this example because of an interesting application of the arithmetic shift instructions. These instructions can be used for quick multiplication and division of signed integers by powers of 2. Just as multiplication by a power of 10 in decimal can be accomplished by moving the decimal point (or shifting the digits),

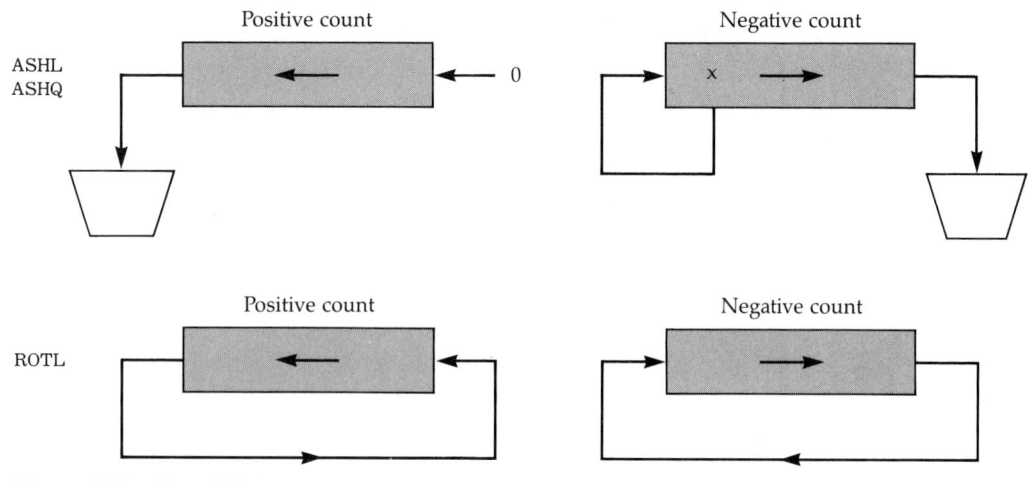

Figure 5.20 The shift instructions

multiplication by a power of 2 in binary can also be accomplished by shifting the bits the appropriate number of times. The count determines the power of 2 used by the operation. For example, when the count is 4, the value of the data is multiplied by the fourth power of 2 (that is, 16), as illustrated in the example by the contents of R1. When the count is negative, the situation is slightly more complicated. If the division is even, there is no problem. If not, the result must be rounded or truncated as significant bits are shifted out the right end.

Because the VAX uses two's complement arithmetic for integers, the following interpretation is possible. If the value is positive, any fractional part of the result is truncated. If the value is negative, the value is rounded down, away from 0. These rules can be summarized by the statement "Arithmetic shifts result in multiplying the data by 2 to the power specified by the count; if the count is negative, the result is then reduced to the largest integer less than or equal to the true quotient." In the example, -14 shifted right two places yields -3.5, which is reduced to -4 and is stored in R2. On the other hand, $+14$ shifted two places to the right yields $+3$. (You may recognize that the rounding operation works the same way as the greatest integer function, or INT, in BASIC.)

The way the shift instructions affect the condition codes may have a significant effect on code using them. On a VAX the negative and zero bits are determined only by the value of the result of the shift or rotation. Neither disturb the carry condition code. The overflow bit is set to 0 except in one case. On a left-hand arithmetic shift, the overflow bit is set to 1 if the sign bit ever changes sign during the shifting operation. This interpretation is consistent with the instruction's arithmetic interpretation. On some other computers certain condition codes may be changed by the bits being shifted out of the value. For example, some computers include the carry bit in a rotation.

5.4 Bit Manipulation

The ability to manipulate individual bits is required by multiplication and division algorithms and is useful for several other applications. In this section we look at several VAX instructions that allow us to set, clear, complement, and test individual bits. We will also study instructions that allow setting or clearing status bits in the PSW. The types of instructions described in this section exist in most computers but often have different names.

We begin with instructions that test bits specified by a mask supplied with the instruction. The bit test instructions are

Opcode	Mnemonic	Operands
93	BITB	mask, source
B3	BITW	mask, source
D3	BITL	mask, source

These instructions do not change either the mask or the source. Instead, in the manner of the CMPx instructions, corresponding bits of the mask and source are logically ANDed, and the condition codes in the PSW are set appropriately. A bit test instruction is normally followed by a conditional branch instruction. If temp = mask AND source, the condition codes are evaluated as follows:

Condition Code	Action
Negative	N ← sign bit of temp
Zero	Z ← 1 if temp is 0, otherwise Z is set to 0
Overflow	V ← 0
Carry	C ← C (unchanged by these instructions)

Consequently, the BITx instructions are particularly helpful for determining if a certain set of bits are all 0. For example, suppose that we want to jump to AllZero if bits 1, 2, 3, and 7 of a byte stored in R4 are 0. The mask for the BITB instruction has a 1 in the specified bit positions, and the rest of the bits are 0. The instructions are

```
BITB    #^B10001110, R4      ; Test the bits
BEQLU   AllZero              ; Branch if all are zero
```

If R4 = ^B10110101, the computer would calculate as follows:

The mask	1000 1110
R4	1011 0101
Temp = mask AND R4	1000 0100

Because temp's sign bit is a 1, the condition code bit N is set to 1, while Z is set to 0 because temp is not 0. The branch would not be taken.

The VAX has two instructions that cause a conditional branch to a specified location depending on the value of bit 0 of the source operand. The instructions are

Opcode	Mnemonic	Operands
E9	BLBC	source, location
E8	BLBS	source, location

BLBC branches if the low bit is clear; BLBS branches if it is set. The operands are assumed to be longwords, but only the low bit is actually processed. These instructions provide an easy way to check if the source is an odd or even number.

We now turn to instructions that manipulate the bits in one of the operands in addition to setting the condition codes. These instruction are

Mnemonic	Operands	Purpose
BISx2	mask, destination	Set bits to 1
BISx3	mask, source, destination	Set bits to 1
BICx2	mask, destination	Clear bits to 0
BICx3	mask, source, destination	Clear bits to 0
XORx2	mask, destination	Exclusive-or
XORx3	mask, source, destination	Exclusive-or

These instructions can process bytes, words, or longwords, so "x" can be B, W, or L. Just as in the BITx instructions, the mask indicates which bits will be processed. However, unlike the BITX instructions, they store the result of the operation in the destination. In the two-operand format, the destination doubles as the source, just as in the two-operand arithmetic instructions.

The BISx (Bit Set) instructions set the bits specified by the ones in the mask, leaving the remaining bits unchanged. The operation performed is a logical "inclusive-or" because the mask and the source are ORed bit by bit to form the destination. In fact this operation is called OR on some computers.

The BICx (Bit Clear) instructions clear the bits corresponding to ones in the mask. The bits corresponding to zeros in the mask are not disturbed. The operation can be defined as

destination ← (NOT mask) AND source.

That is, the mask is complemented and ANDed with the source. These instructions substitute for the AND instructions found on many computers.

The XORx (eXclusive-OR) instructions complement the bits specified by ones in the mask. That is,

destination ← mask EXCLUSIVE-OR source.

All three of these bit-manipulating instructions set the N and Z condition codes according to the value of the calculated destination; V is cleared and C is left unchanged.

For example, suppose that

Mask = ˆB00001111 and Data = ˆB01010101

Consider the instructions

```
BISB   Mask, Data, R4
BICB3  Mask, Data, R5
XORB2  Mask, Data
```

The calculations performed are:

Mask	0000 1111	Mask	0000 1111
Data	0101 0101	NOT Mask	1111 0000
Mask OR Data	0101 1111	Data	0101 0101
		(NOT Mask) AND Data	0101 0000

Mask	0000 1111
Data	0101 0101
Mask EXCLUSIVE-OR Data	0101 1010

The following values would be stored:

R4 = 0101 1111,   R5 = 0101 0000,   Data = 0101 1010

Because of the particular mask used, the last four bits are set, cleared, and complemented by the instructions.

Sometimes it is necessary to adjust the values of the condition codes before processing the next instruction. The VAX has two instructions for this purpose. They are

Mnemonic	**Operands**	**Purpose**
BISPSW	wordmask	Set bits in PSW
BICPSW	wordmask	Clear bits in PSW

These instructions set or clear the bits in the PSW as specified by the ones in the word-length mask. The bit assignments are as follows:

Condition	Code	Bit Position	Trap Enable	Code	Bit Position
Carry	C	0	Trace	T	4
Overflow	V	1	Integer oVerflow	IV	5
Zero	Z	2	Floating Underflow	FU	6
Negative	N	3	Decimal oVerflow	DV	7

Bits 4 to 7 in the PSW are for trap enables; that is, the computer will jump to some special code when the associated condition occurs. For

5.4 Bit Manipulation 163

example, the computer usually ignores integer overflow; that is, if a calculated integer number is too large to fit in the destination, the computer simply sets the V bit in the PSW and continues with an incorrect result. This can be prevented by setting the IV flag, bit 5, to 1. Then program execution will be terminated, and an error trap procedure will be processed if integer overflow occurs. Setting the trace flag (T) causes the computer to jump to the trace trap code after the next instruction. The VAX/VMS Symbolic Debugger uses this facility to allow you to single step through your program. Bits 8 to 15 are not used in the PSW; the corresponding bits of the mask must be 0.

For example, suppose that the carry bit of the PSW must be cleared. The appropriate instruction is

```
BICPSW     #^B00000001     ; Clear carry flag
```

The opcodes for the bit-manipulating instructions follow:

Opcode	Instruction	Opcode	Instruction	Opcode	Instruction
88	BISB2	8A	BICB2	8C	XORB2
89	BISB3	8B	BICB3	8D	XORB3
A8	BISW2	AA	BICW2	AC	XORW2
A9	BISW3	AB	BICW3	AD	XORW3
C8	BISL2	CA	BICL2	CC	XORL2
C9	BISL3	CB	BICL3	CD	XORL3
B8	BISPSW	B9	BICPSW		

The move complement instructions may be useful when manipulating bits. These instructions, which move the one's complement of the source into the destination are

Opcode	Mnemonic	Operands
92	MCOMB	source, destination
B2	MCOMW	source, destination
D2	MCOML	source, destination

For example, if X = 1100 1010 and we issue the instruction

```
MCOMB      X, Y            ; Move one's complement of X to Y
```

then Y = 0011 0101.

The bit-manipulating instructions are clearly useful for processing Boolean operations. It might not be as evident that they are useful for finite set operations. For example, suppose that we are working with a set containing the elements $X_0, X_1, \ldots, X_7$. We can represent subsets of this set with eight-bit bytes where the ith bit is 1 if X_i is in the subset, 0 otherwise. For example, if SetA = 0100 0011, then X_6, X_1, and X_0 are in the set. Some standard set operations can be processed in the following manner:

```
MOVB    #^B00000110, SetB      ; SetB <-- {X_1, X_2}

BISB3   SetA, SetB, SetC       ; SetC <-- SetA union SetB

MCOMB   SetA, R1               ; SetC <--   SetA intersection SetB
BICB3   R1, SetB, SetC         ;

MCOMB   SetA, SetC             ; SetC <-- complement of SetA

BITB    #^B00001000, SetB      ; If X_3 is in SetB
BNEQU   Next                   ;    then branch to Next
```

If the universal set had fewer than eight elements, not all the bits in the data bytes would be used. The MCOMB instruction would be replaced by XORB2, so only the bits actually used would be complemented.

In the next section we show how the shifting and bit-manipulating instructions are used when coding an arithmetic algorithm.

We have looked at some of the VAX instructions that manipulate individual bits in the standard data types. The VAX also has a so-called data type called a **bit string**, which allows us to specify a string of bits by a base address, a bit offset to the string, and the number of bits in the string. Several instructions manipulate or test bit strings. For example, the instruction

```
BBS     #17, (R2), ItsSet      ; Branch if 17th bit set
```

would cause a branch to ItsSet if the seventeenth bit past the location pointed to by R2 is set. To extract a bit pattern from another string, we could use the EXTZV. For example, to find the value of the ninth four-bit nibble past InputString, we could code

```
EXTZV   #36, #4, InputString, R0  ; R0 <-- 9th nibble past
                                              InputString
```

The EXTZV (EXTract with Zero extension of a Variable-length field) instruction would copy four bits, starting with the thirty-sixth bit past bit 0 of InputString, and then extend the result to a full longword with zero bits. Although these operations could be carried out with simpler instructions, they may allow a significant reduction in the amount of code needed, especially if the bit offset or the field width is a variable. (Interested readers can refer to the manuals to learn about the BBx, BBxx, FFx, INSV, EXTV, EXTZV, CMPV, and CMPZV instructions.)

5.5 Coding an Integer Multiplication Algorithm

Because the VAX has a rich selection of multiplication and division instructions, it is unnecessary to write software to implement the algorithms of Section 5.2 on a VAX. Despite this, we will show how to code Algorithm 5.1. There are several reasons for doing so. While the VAX has built-in instructions for multiplication and division, they are not available on many smaller computers. Consequently, this example may be helpful if you ever program such machines. Implementation of a multiplication algorithm provides an excellent demonstration of the techniques used in writing assembly language programs. Moreover, it illustrates the use of some of the shifting and bit-manipulating instructions introduced in the previous two sections.

Programmers often find that the particular computer or language used forces small modifications of the algorithm being programmed. This is the case when implementing Algorithm 5.1 on a VAX. When comparing the algorithm's requirements to the VAX instruction set, we discover that the VAX is missing instructions that include the carry flag in a shifting operation. Its designers felt that such instructions were unneeded because the machine does not depend on software for common calculations. Designers of machines lacking some common arithmetic instructions often include such shift commands to simplify coding these operations. Another problem is that the VAX's shift instructions clear the carry flag. Consequently, this condition code bit must be tested before the shift instruction is used.

We must arrange the control variable for the loop. R6 is used as the loop's counter. The required number of loop iterations is obtained by initializing the iteration count to 32 and counting down to 1.

Listing 5.1 gives the code for the algorithm. Direct assignment statements are used to define two constants, MostSigBit and ClearCarry, which are used as masks in bit instructions.

During the initialization step, the multiplier and multiplicand are moved into registers, and another register is initialized to serve as the accumulator to reduce time-consuming memory accesses. R2 initially holds the multiplier (Q); R3 serves as the accumulator. The order of these registers was carefully picked so that AQ (actually R3 and R2) can be shifted as one register with ASHQ. The multiplicand (M) is stored in R5.

It is natural to use the carry flag in the PSW for C. However, we must use some care. Many instructions change the value of the carry flag. In this program it must be cleared just before it is needed and tested immediately after the add instruction before its value is changed by another instruction.

Listing 5.1 A program for multiplying unsigned integers

```
;       Multiplication of unsigned integers using Algorithm 5.1

;       Register usage:
; R2:   Q (multiplier)
; R3:   A (accumulator)
; R5:   M (multiplicand)
; R6:   Count

;       Constants:
MostSigBit = ^X80000000         ; Selects highest-order bit
ClearCarry = 1                  ; Selects carry bit

;       Variables:
Multiplier:     .LONG   25      ; (Value Can be changed)
Multiplicand:   .LONG   1000    ; (Value can be changed)
Product:        .BLKQ   1       ; Reserve room for result

                .ENTRY  Mult, 0

;       1.      Initialize:
Init:           CLRL    R3                      ; Clear A
                MOVL    Multiplicand, R5        ; M <-- Multiplicand
                MOVL    Multiplier, R2          ; Q <-- Multiplier

;       2.      Loop:
                MOVL    #32, R6                 ; Count <-- 32
Repeat:         BICPSW  #ClearCarry             ; Make sure carry is clear
                BLBC    R2, CheckCarry          ; If lsb. of Q = 1 then
                ADDL2   R5, R3                  ;   A <-- A + M
CheckCarry:
                BCS     CarrySet                ; If C = 0 then
                ASHQ    #-1, R2, R2             ;   Shift AQ right
                BICL2   #MostSigBit, R3         ;   and put 0 in left bit
                BRB     Decrement
CarrySet:       ASHQ    #-1, R2, R2             ; Else shift AQ right
                BISL2   #MostSigBit, R3         ;   and put 1 in left bit

Decrement:
                DECL    R6                      ; Decrement Count
                BGTR    Repeat                  ; Repeat if needed

;       3.      Store product:
Store:          MOVQ    R2, Product             ; Product <-- AC
                $EXIT_S
                .END    Mult
```

The program is written without any input or output, assuming that it will be run with the VAX/VMS Symbolic Debugger, which would allow depositing values for the multiplier and multiplicand and examining the product. If this is done, we must carefully specify the proper data length for these variables. Alternatively, we can add appropriate I/O routines.

This program restricts itself to instructions that have already been introduced in the text. If you want to become proficient in VAX assembler and are willing to research a new instruction, you will want to work Exercise 15 at the end of the chapter that suggests an advanced instruction that can shorten the code.

Algorithm 5.1 *(Revised to run on the VAX.) Calculate the quadword product of unsigned longwords.*

1. Initialize:
   a. Load A with zeros.
   b. Load the multiplicand into M.
   c. Load the multiplier into Q.
2. Loop:
   a. Load 32 into Count.
   b. Clear carry bit (C).
   c. If the lsb of Q is 1, add M to A.
   d. Shift the combined CAQ register one bit right. (If C is 0, shift AQ and clear most significant bit of A. Otherwise, shift AQ and set the most significant bit of A.)
   e. Decrement Count and repeat at step 2b if Count is greater than 0.
3. Store product.

5.6 Floating-Point Arithmetic

In Section 1.5 we looked at the representation of floating-point numbers on the VAX. In this section we will look at how computers can carry out the basic operations of addition and multiplication with this type of representation. Computer designers have the same type of choices for implementing floating-point calculations as they have in implementing integer multiplication. That is, these operations can be implemented in hardware circuits, in microcode, or in software—the implications are the same. Hardware implementations are faster but more expensive; software implementations are slower but cheaper. Designers of microprocessors have often elected to omit built-in floating-point operations from their CPU chip. However, they sometimes provide an optional chip for floating-point arithmetic. For example, computers using Intel's 8088 (such as the IBM PC) may add the 8087 "numerics processor extension." The resulting combination is claimed to achieve approximately one hundred times the throughput of the 8088 alone for some applications. Even the VAX 11/780 and 11/785 have an option called a floating-point accelerator. If this unit is installed, the CPU gathers floating-point data and then lets the optional unit carry out the calculations. The CPU can continue carrying out other operations in parallel while the floating-point unit carries out its duties. This unit greatly increases throughput and is a highly desirable option on busy computers processing a significant amount of floating-point arithmetic. (In fact the accelerator even speeds up 32-bit integer multiplications.) However, these machines can process the same programs without the optional hardware if the unit's cost is a problem.

Before we look at algorithms for floating-point multiplication and addition, we will briefly review floating-point representations.

Review of Floating-Point Notations

As discussed in Section 1.5, numbers are said to be written in floating point if the number is in the form $0.m * b^e$ for some base b. The m represents the mantissa; e is the exponent. The number is said to be normalized if the first digit in the mantissa is nonzero. For example,

$37.375 = (10\ 0101.011)_2$
$ = (0.10\ 0101\ 011)_2 * 2^6$

Computers usually use 2 or 16 for the base. Base 2 provides greater accuracy for a given number of bits in the mantissa, but the range of values is smaller for a fixed number of bits in the exponent. Many computers use a biased representation of the exponent. That is, if n is the number of bits available to store the exponent, 2^{n-1} is added to the true exponent to obtain the biased exponent. This representation is designed to simplify calculations.

The VAX uses base 2 for floating point. The most common representation on a VAX is F floating; it uses 1 bit for the sign, 8 for the exponent, and 23 for the mantissa. The exponent is biased by 128. Because numbers are assumed normalized, the first bit of the binary mantissa is always a 1, and does not need to be stored. Floating values use the sign magnitude representation for the sign and mantissa bits. The various fields are packed as follows:

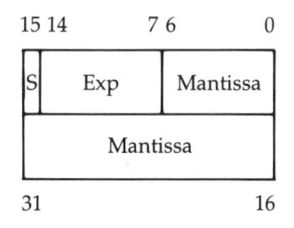

15 14	7 6	0
S	Exp	Mantissa

Mantissa
31 ... 16

where s represents the sign bit and exp the exponent field. Any number with a 0 sign and 0 exponent is considered to be 0. For example, the representation of 37.375 would be

0 1000 0110 001 0101
1000 0000 0000 0000

Writing this in hexadecimal with the most significant word (second row), first, we would have 80 00 43 15.

The representations of floating-point numbers can be quite different on other computers. For example, the IBM 370 and its successors use base 16 for floating-point values. The CDC 6600 represents negative floating-point values in one's complement and treats the mantissa as an integer instead of as a fraction (that is, the assumed binary point is on the right side of the mantissa instead of the left).

Calculations in Floating Point

Calculations with floating-point numbers are more complicated than with integer numbers. However, even when values are expressed in the methods used by computers, they can be manipulated using standard algebraic techniques as long as the notation is correctly interpreted. You may find it helpful to practice using the algorithms in this section on numbers written in scientific notation. For example, you could multiply

$(0.3 * 10^3) * (0.2 * 10^2) = 0.06 * 10^5 = 0.6 * 10^4$

or add

$(0.3 * 10^3) + (0.2 * 10^2) = (0.3 * 10^3) + (0.02 * 10^3) = .32 * 10^3$

in order to get the flavor of the procedure to be used.

Multiplication of floating-point numbers can be carried out in the following manner:

Algorithm 5.6 *Multiplication of two floating-point numbers.*

1. If either of the numbers is 0, set the result to 0 and terminate the calculation.
2. Multiply the mantissas and determine the sign of the result.
3. Add the exponents.
4. Normalize the resulting value if needed and then truncate or, preferably, round the result's mantissa to the correct number of digits. If rounding caused the number to be unnormalized, repeat this step.

If an excess notation is being used for the exponent, we must be careful to express the result correctly. One technique is to add the exponents still stored in the excess notation and then subtract the amount of the bias to get the result in correct excess notation. Because of the way the bias was chosen, we can accomplish the subtraction by just complementing the first bit of the exponent field. We can easily verify this procedure by just observing that each biased exponent must be too large by the amount of the bias. So after adding, the biased exponent for the result is larger than the actual exponent by twice the amount of the bias. Subtracting the bias leaves the result inflated by one bias, as required by the notation.

For example, let's square $(27.3125)_{10}$ or $(1\ 1011.0101)_2$. That is, we will calculate

$$[(0.1\ 1011\ 0101)_2 * 2^5] * [(0.1\ 1011\ 0101)_2 * 2^5]$$

The biased exponent would be $128 + 5 = 133$ in excess 128 notation.

Because the numbers are not 0, we square the mantissa (0.1 1011 0101) and get (0.1 0111 0100 1111 1100 1). We add the biased exponents $133 + 133 = 266$ and then subtract the bias (128) to get 138, which is 128 larger than the true result of 10. In this problem the product's mantissa is already normalized because the bit just right of the "radix" point is a 1. The number of bits needed to represent the result's mantissa is less than the 24 bits allowed by the F floating notation, so rounding is not needed. The binary result would be represented by the following on the VAX.

0 1000 1010 011 1010
0111 1110 0100 0000

Addition is somewhat more complicated because it is necessary to adjust the exponents of the two values to make them equal before adding the mantissa. The following algorithm describes the process.

Algorithm 5.7 *Addition of two floating-point numbers*

1. Adjust the number with the smaller exponent so that its exponent equals the larger exponent. This would require moving the "radix" point to the left.
2. Set the exponent of the result to the larger exponent.
3. Add the signed mantissas.
4. Normalize the result if needed and then truncate or round the result's mantissa to the correct number of bits. If rounding caused the number to be unnormalized, repeat this step.

For example, to add $0.11101 * 2^5 + 0.10101 * 2^2$, we might proceed as follows if we assume five-significant-figure mantissas. The second value has a smaller exponent, so it must be rewritten as $0.00010101 * 2^5$. Steps 2 and 3 can be carried out in a straightforward manner.

$$\begin{aligned} 0.11101 * 2^5 &= 0.11101 * 2^5 \\ + \ 0.10101 * 2^2 &= \underline{0.00010101 * 2^5} \\ & 0.11111101 * 2^5 \end{aligned}$$

If the computer truncates to five significant figures, the answer would be $0.11111 * 2^5$. However, if the computer rounds the result off, we would get $1.0000 * 2^5$, but this must be normalized, and the final answer would be $0.10000 * 2^6$. The IBM 370 and some other computers truncate numbers when carrying out this step, but it is more accurate to round, as is done by the VAX.

Subtraction is performed in a manner nearly identical to addition, and division can be carried out in a manner similar to multiplication. However, some computers (including some large ones) do not actually divide. Instead of calculating x/y directly, they use an iterative technique to find the reciprocal y (that is, $1/y$) and then multiply that value by x.

Writing software to implement the algorithms suggested in this section would take some effort. The code would depend on the available integer arithmetic and the exact representation used. Before calculation, it may be necessary to separate each number's exponent from its sign and mantissa and then regroup the three parts in the result after the calculation. We might do this with a combination of shifting and bit manipulation. We would also use shifting to adjust the radix point's location as needed before adding mantissas and during normalization. Integer arithmetic would be used to carry out the indicated arithmetic operations on the mantissas and exponents. Some of the operations suggested here could be simplified if the floating-point representation had been designed to be particularly convenient for the given machine.

Summary

When designing an ALU, a computer engineer has many choices of how to implement common arithmetic operations. Even such simple operations as integer addition must be carefully considered because the total cost and speed of the computer depend heavily on the choices made. Some form of addition is built into the ALU using logic circuits. Because ripple carry slows their operation, computers often have look-ahead carry circuits that decrease the time needed to carry out an addition. Two's complement arithmetic is a popular way to handle signed integers and subtraction because it simplifies hardware design. Computers with a small word size present special difficulties. Special machine language add instructions, which process the carry flag properly, are required for the software addition routines.

Multiplication and division can be time-consuming operations. The computer engineer has several ways to implement these operations, ranging from fast but expensive hardware to slow but cheap software. Between these two extremes, microcode provides a convenient way to implement algorithms for these operations. The Booth algorithm is representative of algorithms that have been developed to increase speed and simplify handling of signed numbers during the multiplication operation.

Multiplication and division algorithms include shift and bit-manipulation steps. A variety of shift instructions may appear in machines depending on software for multiplication because they simplify the required coding and decrease execution time. Bit-manipulation instructions are used in various applications, including Boolean algebra and set operations.

Floating-point operations are missing from many cheaper CPUs because their cost cannot be justified in some applications. Floating-point hardware may be an optional extra on some machines. The algorithms that we looked at could be implemented in hardware, microcode, or software depending on the speed and cost requirements.

We introduced a number of VAX instructions in this chapter. Some represent hardware implementations of the concepts studied in this chapter, while others represent the type of instructions needed on machines that depend on software for arithmetic operations. While the VAX provides all the common arithmetic operations, these instructions are included in its instruction set to meet other needs. For example, they are needed for the low-level I/O routines discussed in Chapter 11.

Exercises

1. Find the 8-bit one's complement representations of 97, 43, and -43. Then calculate $97 - 43$ by adding $97 + (-43)$ using end-around carry.

2. Repeat Exercise 1 but use appropriate methods for two's complement arithmetic.

3. Determine the value of R0 after each of the following instructions is executed. Assume that the contents of R0, R1, and the condition code (C) are exactly as shown before each instruction is executed.

    R0 = ^X0000AB12

    R1 = ^X00002C20

    C = 1

    a. MNEGB   R1, R0
    b. ADWC   R1, R0
    c. SBWC   R1, R0

4. Write and test a program that carries out quadword subtraction of integers, $C \leftarrow A - B$.

5. Write and test a program that carries out octaword addition of integers, $C \leftarrow A + B$.

6. a. Design (draw) a logic circuit that implements formula (10) of Section 5.1. The inputs are $P_2, P_1, P_0, G_2, G_1, G_0, c_0$. The output is c_3.

    b. Determine the fan-in of each input to this circuit.

7. A half-adder is a logic circuit with just two inputs, a and b, that calculates the sum and carry for those inputs. It does not allow for a carry input. (The addition circuit allowing a carry input that we described in Section 5.1 is sometimes called a full adder.)

    a. Design (draw) a logic circuit having two inputs and two outputs that implements the formulas for a half-adder written in the following form:

$s = a \oplus b$

$c = ab$

b. EXCLUSIVE-OR gates are not common in some logic families. One formula that can be used to replace the EXCLUSIVE-OR gate with simpler gates is

$s = (\overline{ab})(a + b)$

That is, $s = $ (NOT(a AND b)) AND (a OR b). Use a four-row truth table with inputs a and b to prove that the two formulas for s are equivalent.

c. Redesign the logic circuit for a half-adder using the formula given in part b.

8. a. Calculate the product of the unsigned eight-bit binary integers 0001 0111 and 1001 0011 using Algorithm 5.1.
   b. Calculate the product of the signed eight-bit integers 0001 0111 and 1001 0011 using Algorithm 5.2.
   c. Repeat part b but use the Booth Algorithm.
   d. Calculate the 8-bit quotient and remainder when the signed 16-bit integer 0011 0000 0101 0111 is divided by 0101 1011 using Algorithm 5.4.
   e. Repeat part d but use Algorithm 5.5.

9. Determine the value of R0 and R1 after each of the following instructions is executed. Assume that the contents of R2 through R4 are exactly as shown before each instruction is executed.

   R2 = ^X0000A100

   R3 = ^X00000123

   R4 = ^X00001000

   a. EMUL   R4, R2, R3, R0
   b. EDIV   R4, R2, R0, R1

10. Write and test a program that calculates $(ab + cd)/e$ where each of the values a, b, c, d, and e are longwords, but the products *and sum* are calculated as quadwords. Use EMUL and EDIV.

11. Given the initial values

    R0 = 1111 1000 1000 1000 1000 1000 1010 0011

    R1 = 0000 1111 0000 1111 0000 1111 0000 1111

    R2 = ^XABCDEF89

    Determine the contents of R4 – R9 after the following instructions are processed.

    a. ASHL   #3, R0, R4
    b. ASHL   #-5, R2, R5

c. ASHQ   #2, R0, R6
d. ROTL   #1, R0, R8
e. ROTL   #-8, R2, R9

12. Determine the values of R1 and the condition codes N, Z, and V after each of the following instructions is executed. Assume that the contents of R0 and R1 are exactly as shown before each instruction is executed.

    R0 = 1010 1100

    R1 = 0000 1111

    a. BISB2   R0, R1
    b. BISB3   #6, R0, R1
    c. BICB2   R0, R1
    d. BICB3   #^X0F, R0, R1
    e. XORB2   R0, R1
    f. XORB3   #^B10101100, R0, R1
    g. BITB   R0, R1
    h. MCOMB   R0, R1

13. What will the condition codes be after execution of the given instructions if the codes are initially N = 1, Z = 0, V = 1, and C = 0 before each instruction is processed?

    a. BICPSW   #^B0110
    b. BISPSW   #3

14. Will the branch be taken if the contents of the registers and memory locations are as shown?

Register	Contents	Location	Contents
R3	00 00 34 2B	34 2B	24
		34 2C	F2
		34 2D	AF
		34 2E	32

    a. BLBS   R3, Next
    b. BLBC   (R3), Next

15. (Manual search.) Look up the operation of the SOBGEQ instruction and show how it could be used to replace the DECL and BGTR sequence in the program shown in Listing 5.1. The *VAX Architecture Handbook* and the *VAX MACRO and Language Reference Volume* are good references.

16. Write and test a program to find the quadword product of two signed longword integers using Algorithm 5.2.

17. Write and test a program to find the quadword product of two signed longword integers using the Booth Algorithm.

18. Write and test a program to find the longword quotient and remainder when a quadword is divided by a longword using Algorithm 5.4.

Exercises

19. Write and test a program to find the longword quotient and remainder when a quadword is divided by a longword using Algorithm 5.5.

20. Hand compile the following segments of a Pascal program. (Hint: use the value 1 or bit 0 for ComSci, 2 or bit 1 for History, 4 or bit 2 for Math, and so on.)

    type ClassType = (ComSci, History, Math, English, Art);

    var Class: ClassType;
        ClassSet1, ClassSet2, ClassSet3: set of ClassType;

    begin
    a. Class := History;
    b. ClassSet1 := [ComSci, Math];
    c. ClassSet2 := ClassSet1;
    d. ClassSet3 := ClassSet1 + [ComSci, English];
    e. ClassSet3 := ClassSet1 * ClassSet2;
    f. ClassSet3 := ClassSet1 - ClassSet2;
    g. ClassSet3 := [];
    h. if History in ClassSet2 then Class := Math;
    i. if ClassSet1 = ClassSet2 then
         ClassSet3 := [Math]
       else if ClassSet2 >= ClassSet1 then
         ClassSet3 := [History];

21. In VAX Pascal a set of char has 256 elements.
    a. How many bytes are needed to represent this set?
    b. Which bits would be nonzero in the representation of the set ['A', 'B', 'C']?
    c. If Letters and Words are sets of char, compile the statement
       Letters := Words;

22. Write and test a program that converts a longword integer into its printable hexadecimal form consisting of eight ASCII characters.
    a. Use instructions like BICB3 and ROTL. (Hint: the lowest order digit in Value can be found using the following code.)

    ```
    ASCIIDigits:  .ASCII  "0123456789ABCDEF"
    Mask = ^XF0                           ; Mask high-order nibble
        ...
        CLRL    R3                        ; Clear high-order bits in R3
        BICB3   #Mask, Value, R3          ; Get low-order nibble
        MOVB    ASCIIDigits[R3], Output
    ```

    If Value is then rotated to the right four bits, the next digit can be found in the same manner.

    b. (Manual search.) Use the EXTV or EXTZV instruction. (There is no need to rotate the value.)

b. (Manual search.) Use the EXTV or EXTZV instruction. (There is no need to rotate the value.)

23. Express the following numbers in the F floating-point notation used by the VAX.
    a. 25
    b. 1
    c. .375
    d. 25.375
    e. .1

24. Consider a 16-bit hexadecimal floating-point notation with the following specifications.

    | S | Exp | Mantissa |

    The s is the sign bit (sign and magnitude representations are used), exp is a 7-bit exponent of 16 expressed in excess 64 notation, and the 8-bit mantissa is the hexadecimal fraction expressed in binary. For example, the value 0 100 0001 0001 0000 represents

    $+(0.10)_{16} * 16^{(65-64)} = +(0.10)_{16} * 16^1 = (1/16) * 16 = 1.0$

    Any value with a 0 sign bit and exponent will be treated as a 0.

    a. Express 28, -7.5, and 0.03 in this notation.
    b. What is the smallest positive number that can be represented in this notation?
    c. What is the largest number that can be represented in this notation?
    d. Calculate

       (1 100 0010 1100 1000) + (0 011 1111 1100 0000)

       (Express the answer in the same notation.)
    e. Calculate

       (1 100 0010 1010 1010) * (0 100 0001 1000 0000)

25. Repeat Exercise 24, but this time assume that the numbers represent base 2 binary values. Assume that, in the same manner as is done on the VAX, the leading bit of the mantissa is not stored, so the mantissa has nine-bit accuracy. In this notation 1 would be written as

    0 100 0001 0000 0000

26. Repeat Exercise 24, but this time assume that the numbers represent base 2 binary values. Assume that, unlike the custom of the VAX, the leading bit of the mantissa is stored by the notation, so the mantissa has only eight-bit accuracy. In this notation 1 would be written as

    0 100 0001 1000 0000

27. Write an algorithm for
    a. Floating-point division
    b. Floating-point subtraction
28. (Challenging.) It is common that micro- and minicomputers lack built-in floating-point operations. Write and test a program that carries out floating-point multiplication using the specified format of a normalized floating-point number. Use Algorithm 5.6 and specify if your procedures round or truncate the product. Be sure to test carefully, including problems like

    .1111 . . . 1 * .11 and 111.1 . . . 1 * 1.111 . . . 1 (base 2).

    a. Assume six-byte floating-point numbers consisting of one word for the exponent of 2, written in excess 32,768 notation, followed by a longword signed integer for the value's sign and mantissa with an assumed decimal point right after the sign bit. For simplicity, assume that the values are normalized and the leading 1 bit is *not* suppressed. Assume any number with a 0 mantissa is a 0.
    b. Assume the VAX's F floating-point notation. A 16-bit rotation may be useful to put the value in more convenient order before processing it. Shifts and/or bit manipulation can be used to separate the various parts of the value and reinsert the leading one that the VAX assumes but does not include in its floating-point notation.

CHAPTER CONTENTS

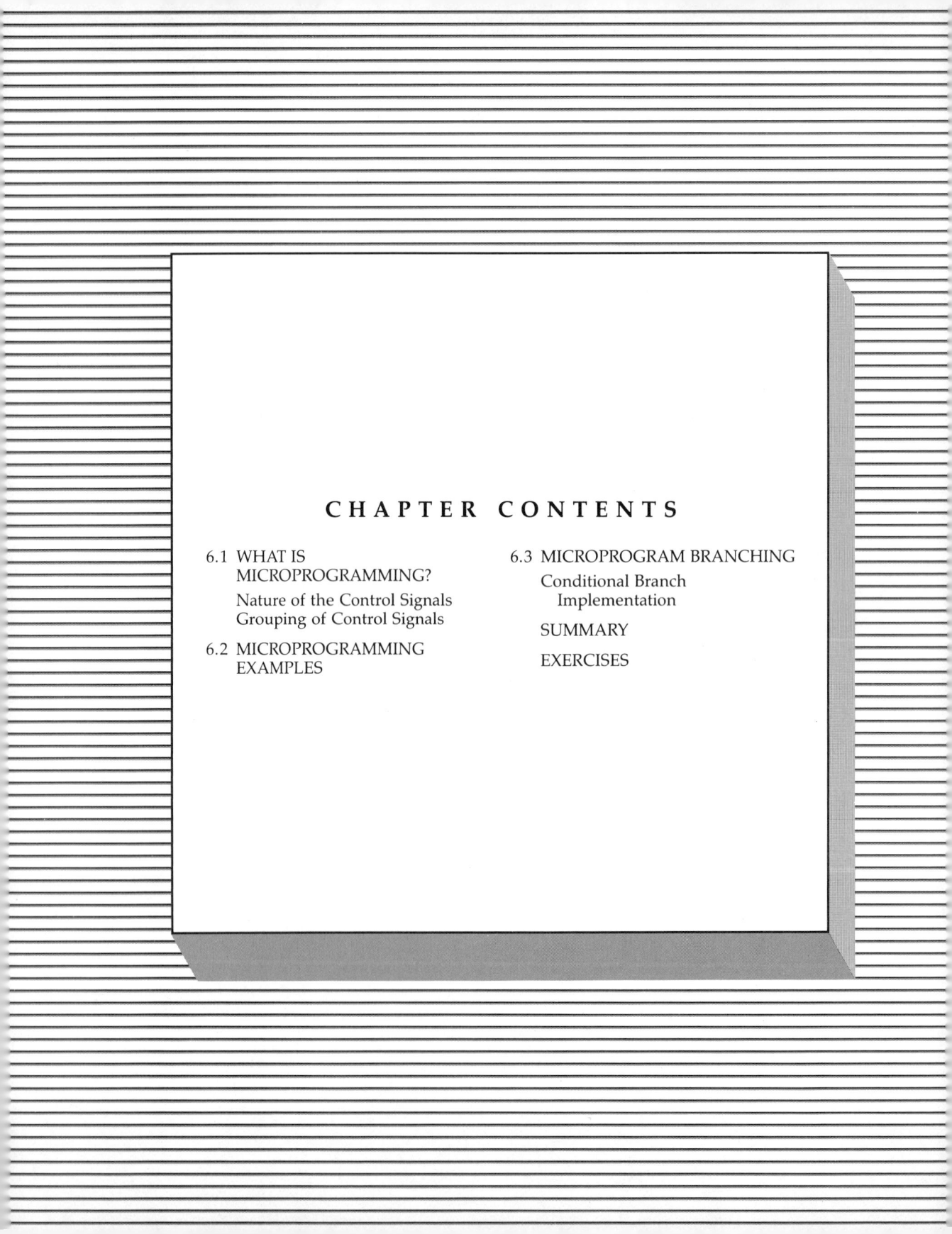

6.1 WHAT IS MICROPROGRAMMING?
   Nature of the Control Signals
   Grouping of Control Signals

6.2 MICROPROGRAMMING EXAMPLES

6.3 MICROPROGRAM BRANCHING
   Conditional Branch Implementation

SUMMARY

EXERCISES

CHAPTER 6

Microprogramming

As developed in Chapter 4, each assembly language instruction actually represents a series of elementary steps that must be implemented in the computer. For example, the basic move instruction, which transfers data from a register to a specified location in memory, is implemented in the typical single-bus CPU system by following these steps: (1) place the address in the MAR, (2) move the data from the register to the MDR, and (3) send a write instruction to memory. These instructions cannot be implemented all at once (in parallel) in a single-bus processor because both the address and the data cannot be on the bus at the same time. (In Chapter 4 we saw that a memory operation can occur at the same time as data is moved onto the internal CPU bus because these operations do not require the same bus lines.) As a result, the simple data move from a register to a memory location instruction requires at least two and maybe three sequential instructions at the internal CPU level.

Recall that in Chapter 4 we broke down machine language instructions into sequences of operations consisting of signals directing various parts of the CPU, ALU, and other components of the computer. The control of these sequential operations may be implemented in several ways. It is possible to design logic circuits that directly implement those operations. Computers built in this way are said to be hard-wired. Such computers would usually be very fast but expensive to design and difficult to modify. In this chapter we deal with another common method called **microprogramming**. We will introduce the concept of microprogramming and examine its effect on the CPU's architecture.

6.1 What Is Microprogramming?

Microprogramming provides a flexible method for generating the correct sequence of control signals required to implement assembly language instructions. This technique was first suggested by M. V. Wilkes and J. B. Stringer in the early 1950s. The basic structure of a microprogrammed CPU is shown in Figure 6.1. In many ways it looks much like the architecture we have already seen for a simple single-bus CPU. The signals that control the sequence of operations, called the **microinstructions** or control signals, are stored in the **control memory**, which is addressed by the **microprogram counter (μPC)**.

The instruction implementation process begins when the CPU fetches a machine language instruction from main memory and loads it into the instruction register (IR), as shown in Figure 6.2. Now microprogramming takes over. Its job is to generate the correct sequence of elementary steps needed to execute the assembly instruction. The control memory

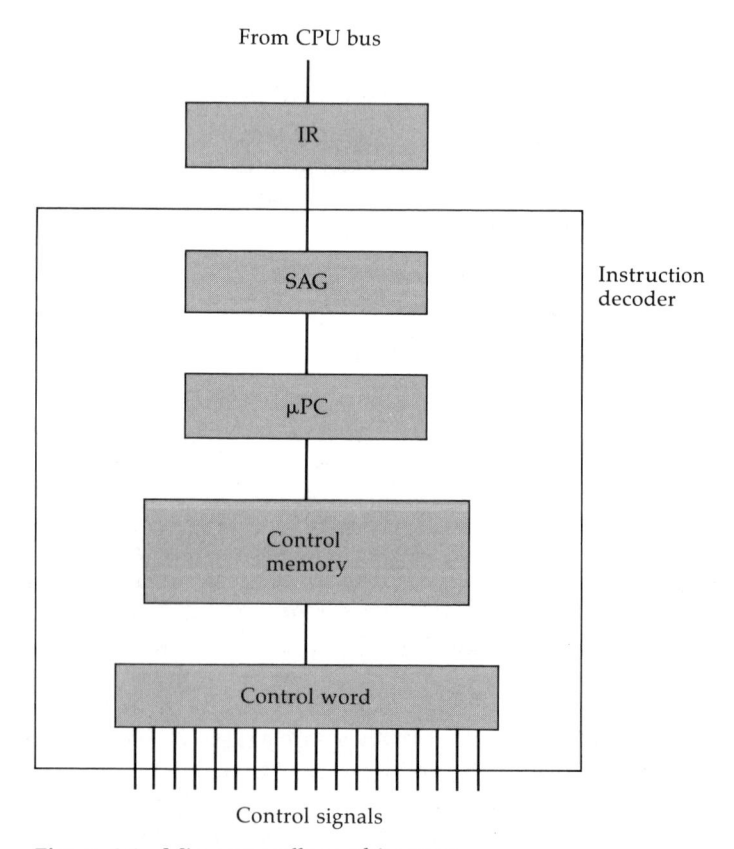

Figure 6.1 Microcontroller architecture

6.1 What is Microprogramming? 181

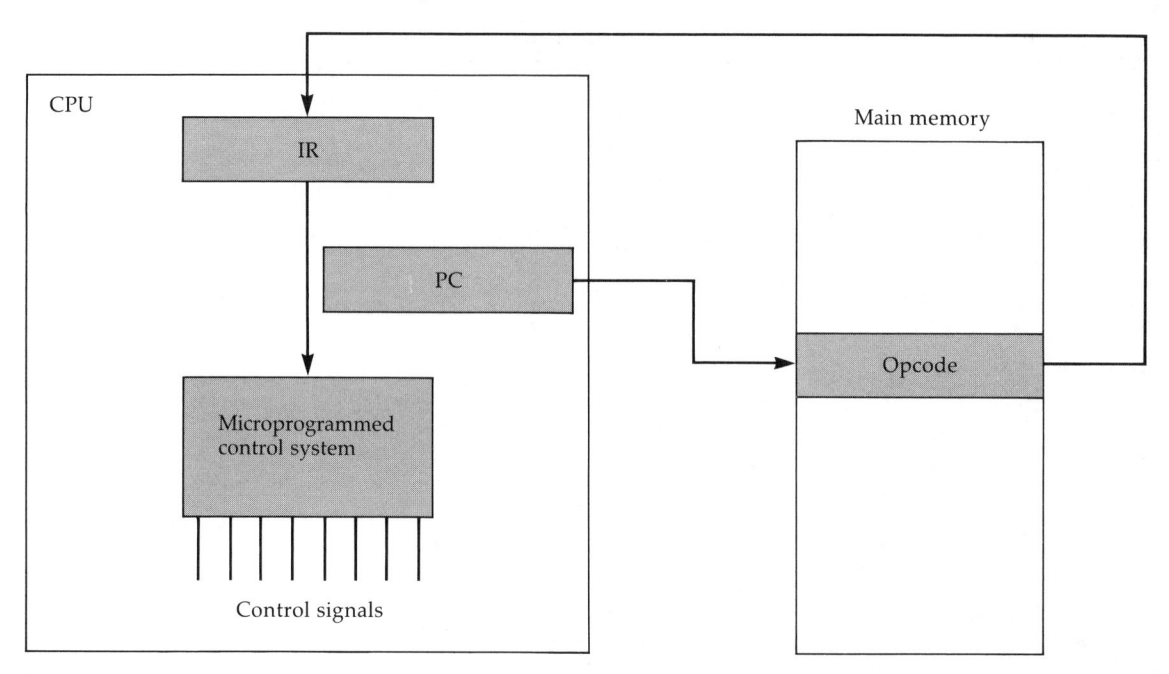

Figure 6.2 Opcode fetch sequence

contains all the elementary steps because the system designer programmed them into the control memory when the machine was first constructed. The instruction register, which contains the machine language version of the assembly level instruction, is decoded by the **starting address generator (SAG)**. The SAG "knows" where in the control memory to find the set of elementary steps corresponding to each assembly language instruction. As shown in Figure 6.3, the starting address generator outputs the address of the first microinstruction in control memory needed to implement the machine language instruction. This address is then loaded in the microprogram counter.

Now the process looks just like the CPU fetch cycle, but it takes place at a lower level. The contents of the control memory pointed to by the microprogram counter are fetched and loaded into the control word register, and the microprogram counter is updated to point to the next microinstruction in the sequence required to implement the machine language instruction. Figure 6.4 illustrates this portion of the control unit assuming that the location of the first elementary step in the sequence of operations for a CLRB instruction is at address D5 of the control memory. Each bit of the control word register is designed to control some part of the computer. Consequently, each bit of the control word register is connected to a destination point somewhere in the computer. The resulting control signal may be used to open or close a data path at that point or to signal an operation that must be performed.

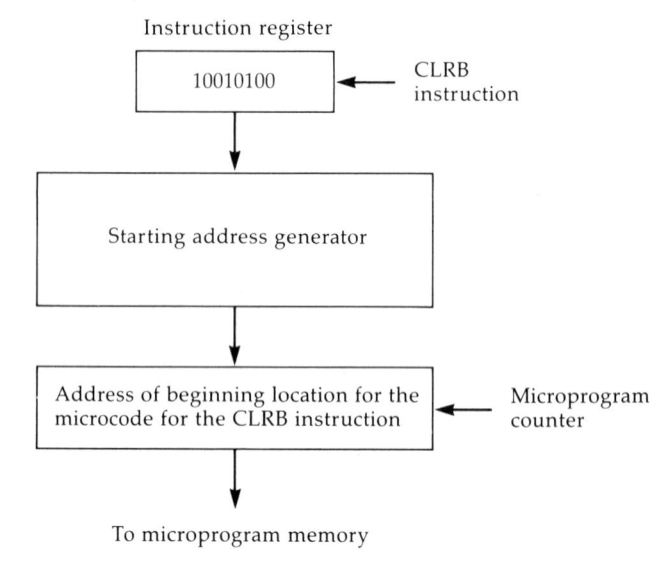

Figure 6.3 Starting address generator function

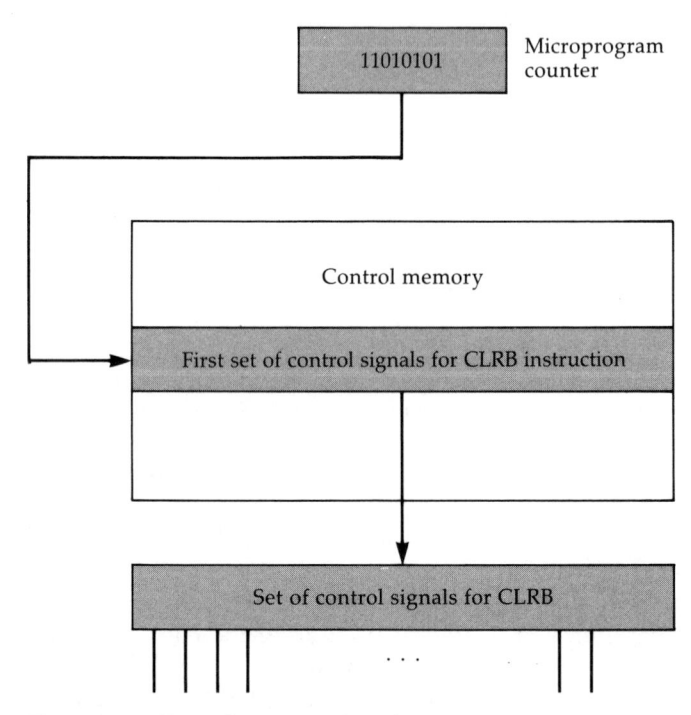

Figure 6.4 Control memory function

If some of the control memory is read/write memory (often called RAM), the control system and hence the computer is said to be "microprogrammable." This kind of control memory allows a programmer to write a sequence of control signals and store them in the RAM portion of the control memory. In this way programmers can create their own instruction set. The VAX 11/780 is microprogrammable; however, only programmers with very special privileges are allowed to write to the microprogram control memory. Imagine the havoc users could cause if they mistakenly replaced the sequence of control words for the CLRB instruction with a new sequence that would increment register 2. From that time on, any program that tried to clear a byte would instead increment register 2. In fact, most microprogram control memories are made up of read-only memory (called ROM). In this case the manufacturer writes the microcode and stores it in read-only memory, so it is impossible to change the microcode.

The main advantage of a microprogrammed control system is that it is very flexible. As noted, we can easily change the way in which a given microprogrammed machine responds to a machine language instruction by changing the contents of the control memory. In a sense this is "reprogramming" the machine. An expert programmer can even create custom instructions by adding new microinstruction sequences to the control memory if the machine allows general access to the microprogrammed memory. Even if the computer has only ROM in its control memory, so that it cannot be used to create custom code, the control system is still easier to design then a hard-wired system. However, note that a microprogrammed control system is typically slower than a hard-wired one because it requires several microfetch and micromemory cycles for each instruction.

Nature of the Control Signals

The control signals are sent along direct wire connections between the control word register and the various devices in the computer. The result is that information stored in the control memory is used to control the transfer of information in the system. For example, transferring data between registers requires a control signal instructing the source register to place its data on the bus and a control signal allowing the destination register to read the data on the bus. In effect these signals are used to control switches that connect and disconnect registers from the data bus, as shown in Figure 6.5. For example, to implement an instruction such as MOVL R1, R2, the system must tell register 1 to place its contents on the bus and also tell register 2 to read the bus. In other words, the "switches" must be set as shown in Figure 6.6, with $R1_{out}$ and $R2_{in}$ both on and all the other switches off. These switches in a computer system are actually "electronic" switches that are turned on and off by the register load and register out signals from the control word.

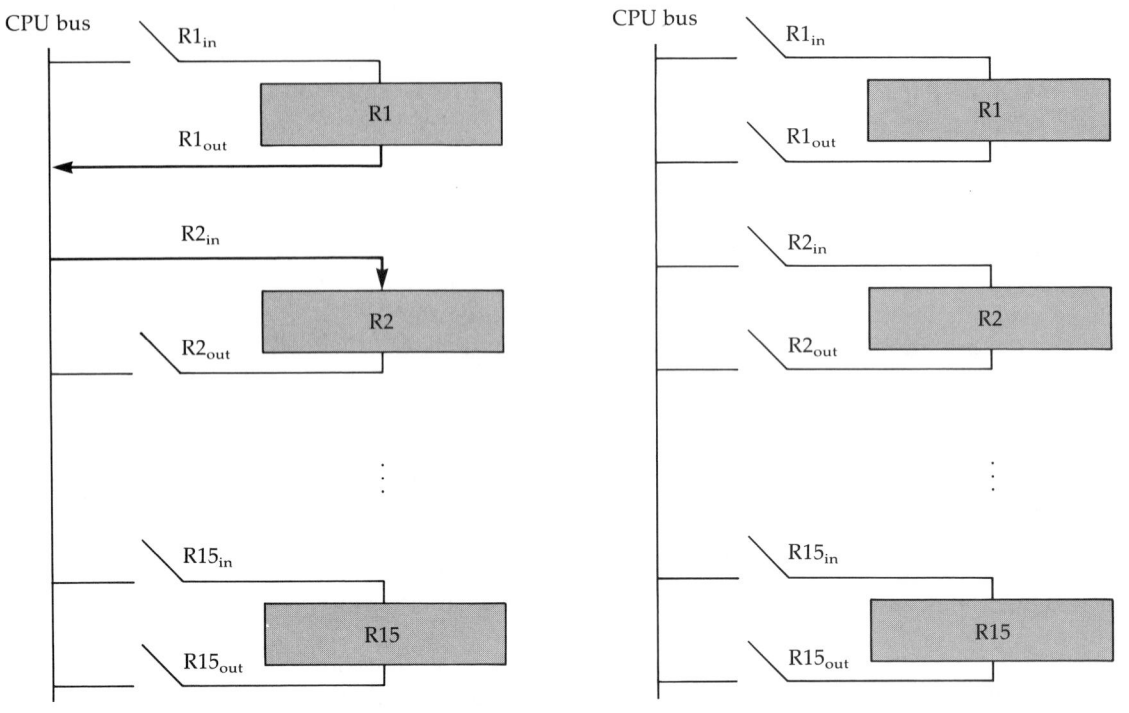

Figure 6.5 Switch structure

Figure 6.6 Switch settings for a MOVE operation

The register load signal from the control word instructs the register to replace its current contents with whatever appears on the input lines. Because registers are medium-scale integrated (MSI) circuits designed to store data, they have been designed to directly respond to load commands. A typical eight-bit register has a load input as shown below.

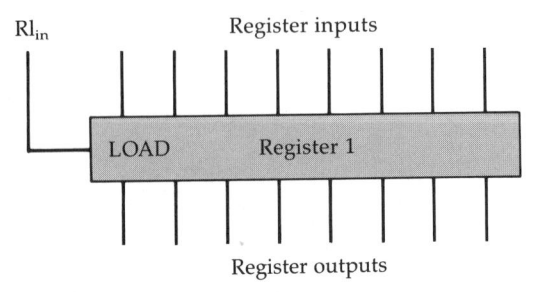

Because registers do not have a built-in register out command and we only want one register at a time using the bus for output, another device (typically called a tri-state gate) must be placed between the register output and the bus. This is a special type of logic gate, which has three output values (0, 1, and electronically disconnected) rather than the standard two logic levels (0 and 1). A special control signal will place the device in the disconnected state. In this state regardless of what appears on the standard inputs, the outputs cannot affect the bus. In the connected state, however, the inputs pass through the device to the bus as shown in Figure 6.7. Therefore, to place the contents of a register (say, register R1) on the bus, the microcontrol system must generate the signal $R1_{out}$. This closes the electronic switch (or activates the tri-state logic gate) to connect the output of register R1 to the bus. To load the value on the bus into register R2, then, the signal R_{in} must be generated to activate the load feature of the register.

Overall, to "run" the computer, the microcontrol system must be able to generate in and out signals for all the registers; generate control signals to the ALU telling it to add, subtract, and so on; generate control signals to memory telling it to read or write; and generate special control signals to the I/O devices. All these control signals must be provided along wires connecting the microcontrol system to each component in the computer. In addition, all these signals must be stored in the microprogram memory and accessed in the correct sequence in order to implement assembly language instructions. This could result in a very large memory unit for the microcontrol system. One way to reduce the size requirements but still maintain the control capabilities of the microcontrol system is covered next.

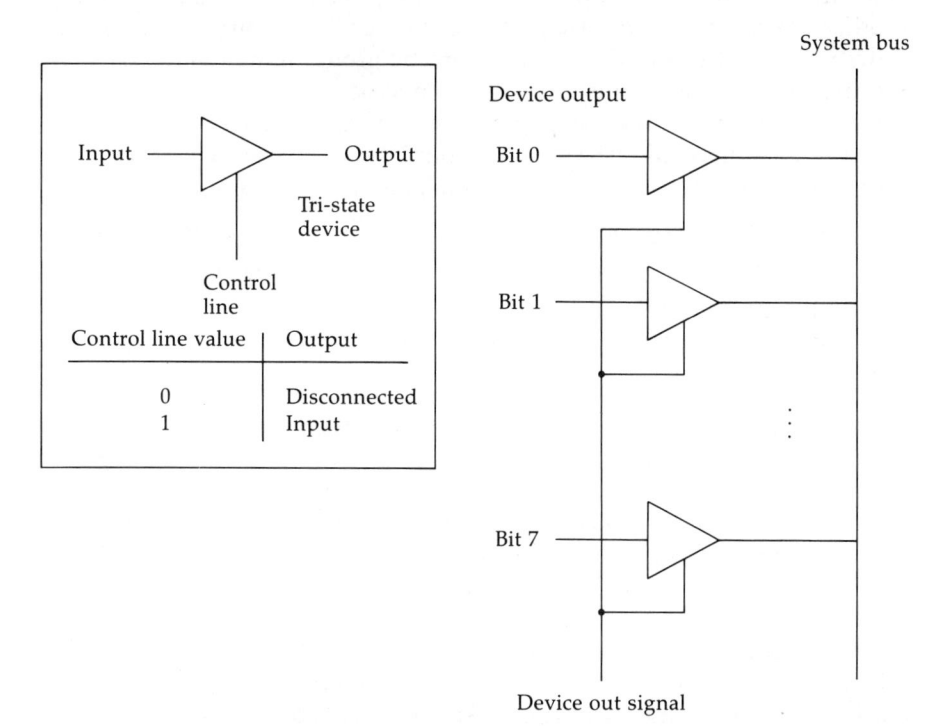

Figure 6.7 Tri-state logic devices

Grouping of Control Signals

One potential disadvantage of microprogramming is that the control word must be long enough so that there is 1 bit for each microoperation. Suppose that we really did use a separate bit for each operation. How many would we need? Each general-purpose register would require 1 bit for the microinstruction input and 1 for the microinstruction output. A system with 16 general-purpose registers would require 32 control bits in the control word just to generate the 16 register in and register out signals. Memory actions could require 3 bits to control the two memory interface registers, the MAR and MDR (2 bits for the MDR and only 1 for the MAR because the MAR is never read by the CPU), as well as 2 bits for the memory read and write instructions. If the ALU performs 16 operations (such as add, subtract, AND, OR, and so on), it would require 16 bits in the control word. Additional bits in the control word are required for the IR, the PC, I/O operations, and anything else that the CPU needs to control in the computer. The resulting control word may have to be as wide as 200 bits, which means that the control store memory would also have to be 200 bits wide. This is just too large for most systems to handle, and it is unnecessary because most bits of any microinstruction are 0.

For example, if you just want to load data into register 1, the control word would have a 1 in the bit slot for register 1 load and zeros in the other 199 control word bits. To overcome this limitation, we can reduce the number of bits in the control word by grouping mutually exclusive signals in the microcontrol word into microoperations in binary code. For example, instead of using one bit for each ALU operation, 16 different ALU operations could be coded into four bits because we will never want to add and subtract at the same time. A possible encoding might be

0000	No Operation	0100	AND
0001	ADD	0101	OR
0010	SUBTRACT		. . .
0011	COMPARE	1111	MULTIPLY

The general-purpose registers of a machine with 16 registers (like the VAX) could also be encoded using four bits for the register read operation (0000 for reg 0 out, 0001 for reg 1 out, and so on) and four bits for the register load operation (0000 for reg 0 load, 0001 for reg 1 load, and so on). The result is a significant reduction in the number of bits required in the control word and the control memory. However, the individual bits will still eventually be required to run the system. We recover the individual control bits by decoding the output of the control word using a special medium-scale integrated (MSI) circuit called a decoder, shown in Figure 6.8. A decoder takes a binary coded input signal and produces a 1 on the output line, which corresponds to the binary number on the input. The truth table for a 3-input, 8-output decoder is shown in Figure 6.9. Decoders with 2 inputs and 4 outputs as well as 4 inputs and 16

Figure 6.8 Three-to-eight MSI Decoder

Figure 6.9 Three-to-eight decoder truth table

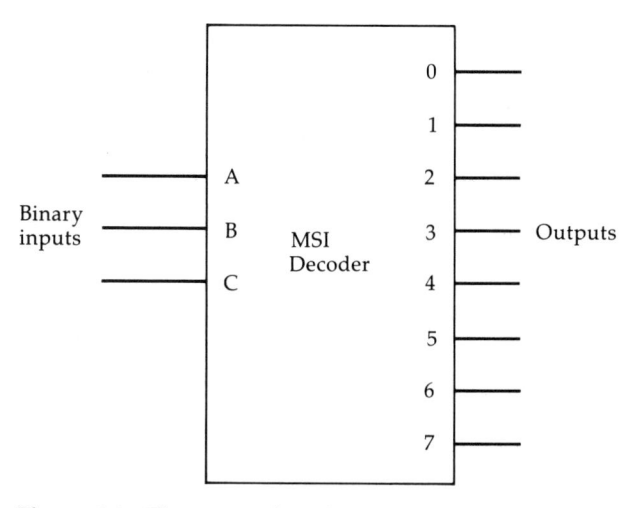

Inputs	Outputs
A B C	0 1 2 3 4 5 6 7
0 0 0	1 0 0 0 0 0 0 0
0 0 1	0 1 0 0 0 0 0 0
0 1 0	0 0 1 0 0 0 0 0
0 1 1	0 0 0 1 0 0 0 0
1 0 0	0 0 0 0 1 0 0 0
1 0 1	0 0 0 0 0 1 0 0
1 1 0	0 0 0 0 0 0 1 0
1 1 1	0 0 0 0 0 0 0 1

outputs are also available. The 4-input, 16-output decoder could be used to decode the 16 ALU operations discussed earlier.

A microprogrammed control system using this coding procedure has an architecture like that shown in Figure 6.10. Machines with highly encoded microprogramming schemes such as the one shown are called **vertical microprogrammed machines**. Systems with little or no encoding are called **horizontal microprogrammed machines**. Most systems use a mix of vertical and horizontal microprogramming where some signals are grouped together and others are not. The average minicomputer has a control word size of 40–100 bits. The VAX 11/780, for example, is a microprogrammed machine with a 96-bit control word.

A horizontal architecture results in a higher operating speed for the computer because it means that the control signals have one less logic level to pass through. In addition, because each elementary operation is represented by its own control word bit, the horizontal architecture may allow for parallel usage of resources. The price of the horizontal scheme is a larger microprogrammed memory word size. The vertical architecture may require more microinstructions to implement a given assembly language instruction.

6.2 Microprogramming Examples

Because the VAXs have large control words, it would not be very practical or instructive to illustrate microprogramming using one of their formats. Instead, we will construct a simple microprogrammable machine in this

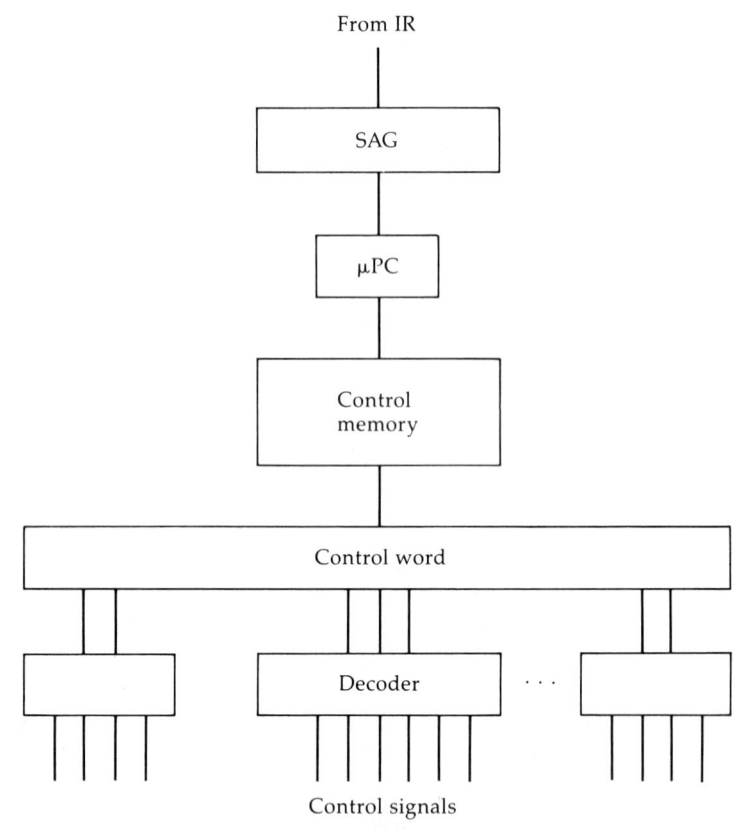

Figure 6.10 Decoders in the microcontroller architecture

section called the Microprogrammable-1 (MP-1). The MP-1 is a single-bus structure machine. It has four general-purpose registers, an IR, a PC, an MDR, an MAR, a PSW, and a 16-function ALU with a temporary storage register called the accumulator (ACC). For simplicity, it uses a fixed-length instruction set. Instructions are one (generic) word long. Note that to illustrate an alternative architecture, the MP-1 has only one ALU storage register (ACC) rather than the two registers (the S and R) used in the SB-1 of Chapter 4. The ACC holds both the input to and output from the ALU. The basic architecture of the MP-1 is shown in Figure 6.11. You may wonder why another architecture is being introduced. There are two reasons: (1) to illustrate the varied approaches to computer architecture, and (2), while the SB-1 proved useful for the discussion of the CPU architecture, it is more complex than needed to introduce the concepts of microprogramming.

Initially, the control word for the MP-1 has 21 bits and is organized as follows:

Bits	Function
1–2	GP register identification
3	GP register read
4	GP register load
5	IR load
6	IR read
7	PC load
8	PC read
9	MDR load
10	MDR read
11	MAR load
12	Wait for Memory Function Complete
13–16	ALU operations
17	Memory read
18	Memory write
19	Increment the PC
20	ACC read
21	ACC load

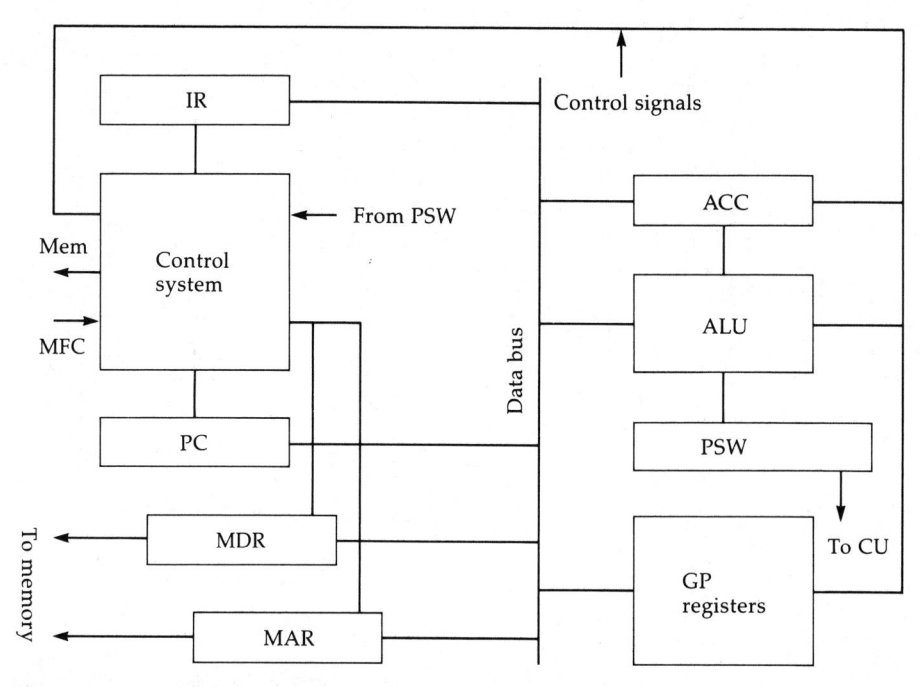

Figure 6.11 MP-1 CPU Architecture

Chapter 6 Microprogramming

The structure of the control system for the MP-1 is shown in Figure 6.12. Though it consists of a mixture of vertical and horizontal architectures, it is primarily vertical in nature. The process called microprogramming is simply one of determining the contents of the microprogram control store. Those contents are in turn determined by the sequence of elementary steps, or microsteps, necessary for the task. For example, the fetch cycle for the MP-1 is similar to that of most machines in that it involves the following microsteps:

1. Place the PC on the bus (read the PC) and load the MAR with the bus contents.

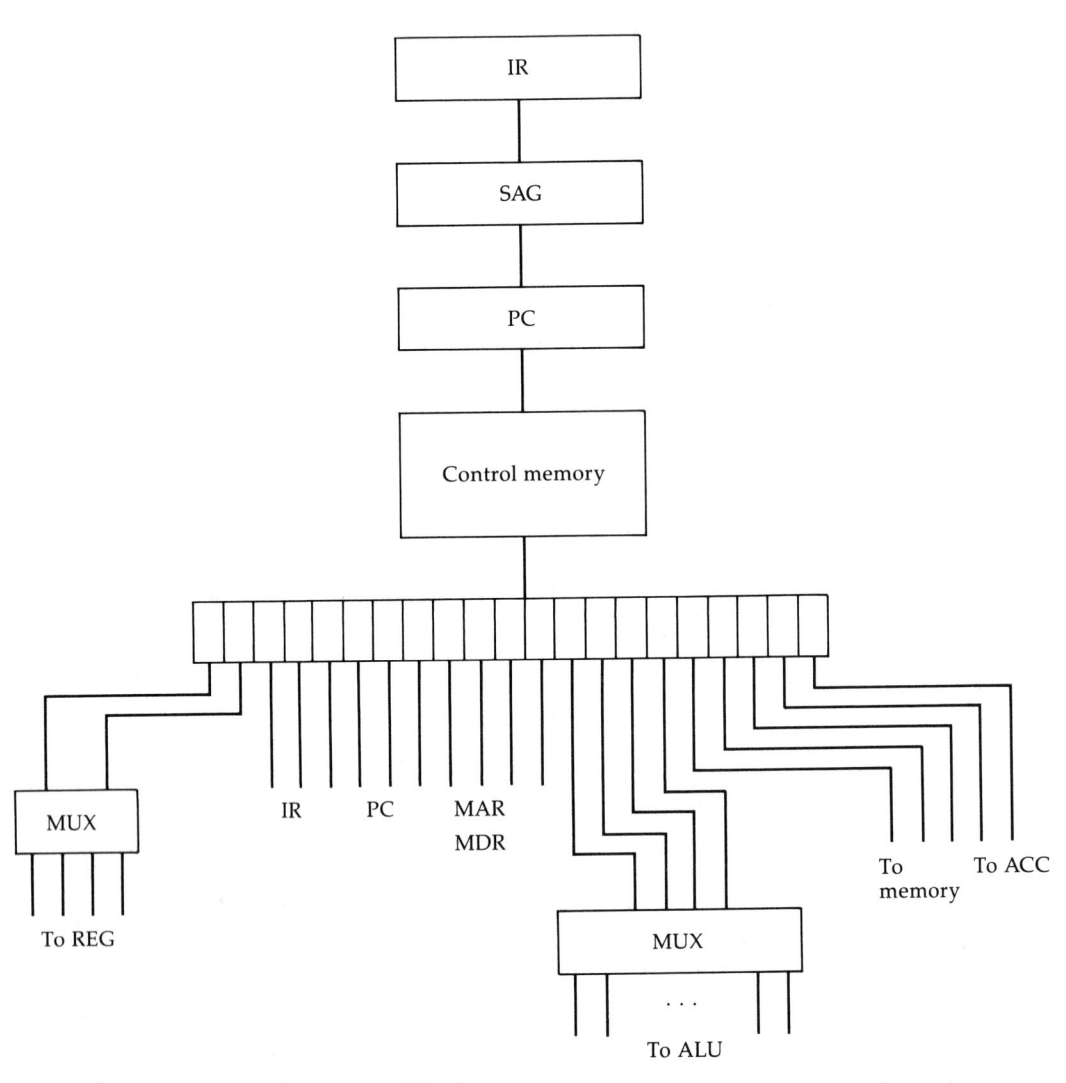

Figure 6.12 MP-1 control system architecture

2. Tell main memory to read.
3. Increment the PC.
4. Wait for Memory Function Complete.
5. Place the MDR on the bus (read the MDR) and load the IR with the bus contents.

As a result, the top of the MP-1 control store memory should contain the following bits to implement the fetch cycle:

1	5	9	13	17 21	
0000	0001	0010	0000	00000	PC to MAR
0000	0000	0000	0000	10000	Memory read
0000	0000	0000	0000	00100	Inc the PC
0000	0000	0001	0000	00000	Wait on mem
0000	1000	0100	0000	00000	MDR to IR

Note that in some cases more than one microstep may be encoded in the microprogrammed control word to reduce the size requirements on the control memory. For the above example of the fetch cycle, the five microinstructions could be reduced to three as shown below:

1	5	9	13	17	
0000	0001	0010	0000	10000	PC to MAR
					Memory read
0000	0000	0001	0000	00100	Inc the PC
					Wait on mem
0000	1000	0100	0000	00000	MDR to IR

In terms of the CPU architecture, the three microinstructions would produce the sequence of operations shown in Figure 6.13.

Now let's consider a simple ADD instruction such as ADD the contents of R1 to R2 and save the result in R3. We will assume that the MP-1 ALU will add the number on the bus to the contents of the ACC and save the result in the ACC when it receives an ADD command. This will require the following microsteps:

1. Place the contents of R1 on the bus and load the ACC with the bus contents.
2. Place the contents of R2 on the bus and send the ADD command to the ALU.
3. Place the contents of the ACC on the bus and load R3 with the contents of the bus.

The microcode that would be stored in the microprogrammed control store for this operation would consist of the following sets of words,

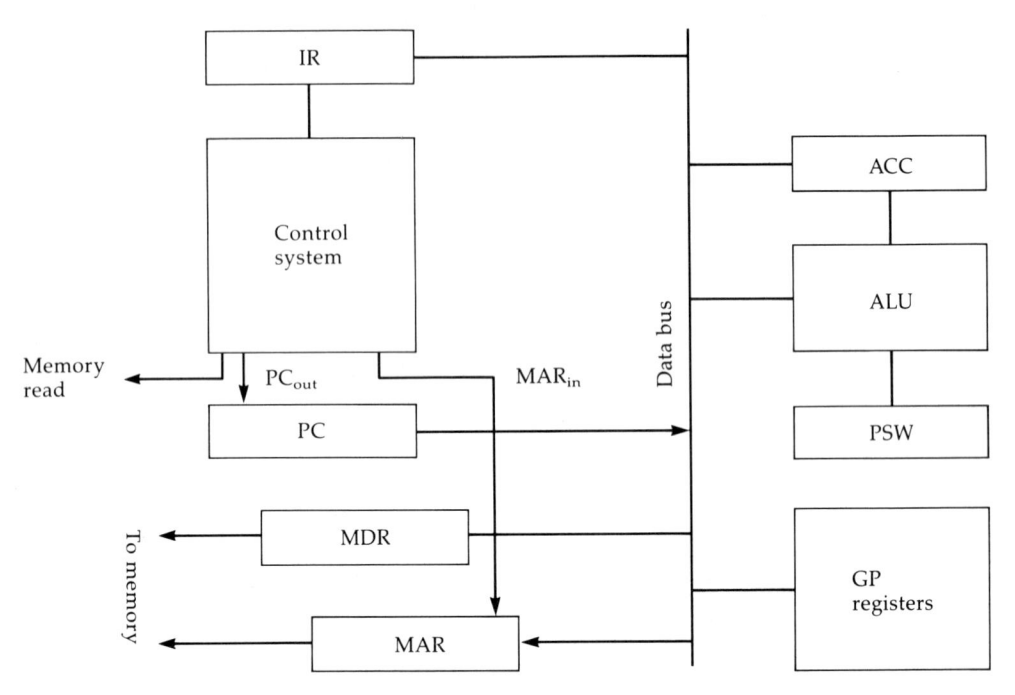

(a) Step one

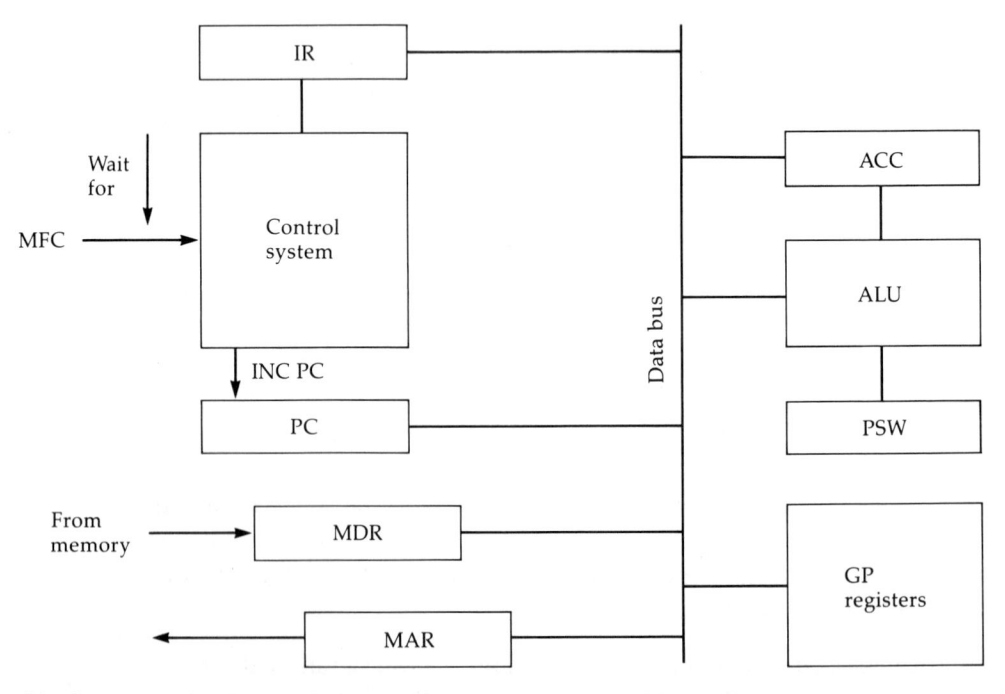

(b) Step two

6.2 Microprogramming Examples

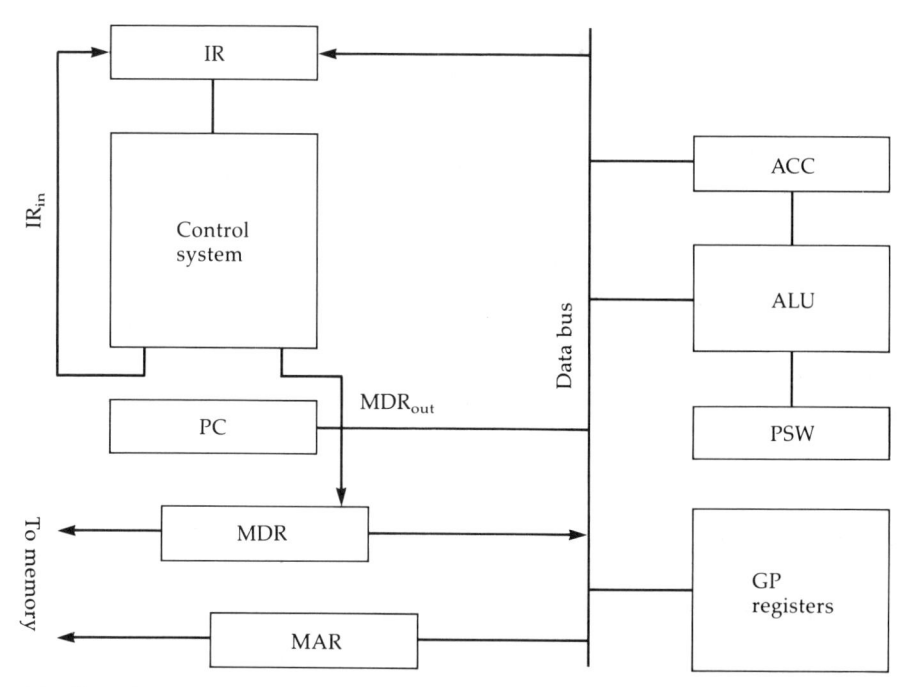

(c) Step three

Figure 6.13 The Fetch Cycle

assuming that the code that instructs the ALU to perform an ADD is 0001.

1	5	9	13	17 21	
0110	0000	0000	0000	00001	R1 to ACC
1010	0000	0000	0001	00000	R2 to bus, ALU ADD
1101	0000	0000	0000	00010	ACC to R3

These three operations are implemented on the MP-1 architecture as shown in Figure 6.14.

If we want to complete this operation by saving the result that is now in register 3 in the memory location pointed to by R0, the microsteps are

1. Read the contents of R0 and load the MAR with the contents of the bus.
2. Place the contents of R3 on the bus, load the MDR with the contents of the bus, instruct memory to write, and wait for memory to complete.

Step 1 tells the memory unit where the data is to be stored, and step 2 supplies the memory unit with the data and sends the write command

194   Chapter 6   Microprogramming

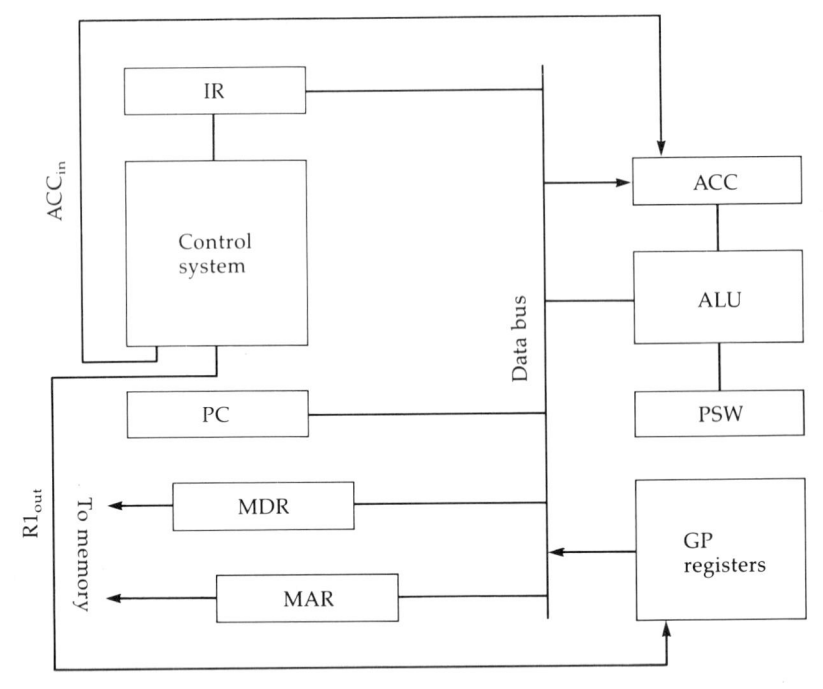

(a) Step one

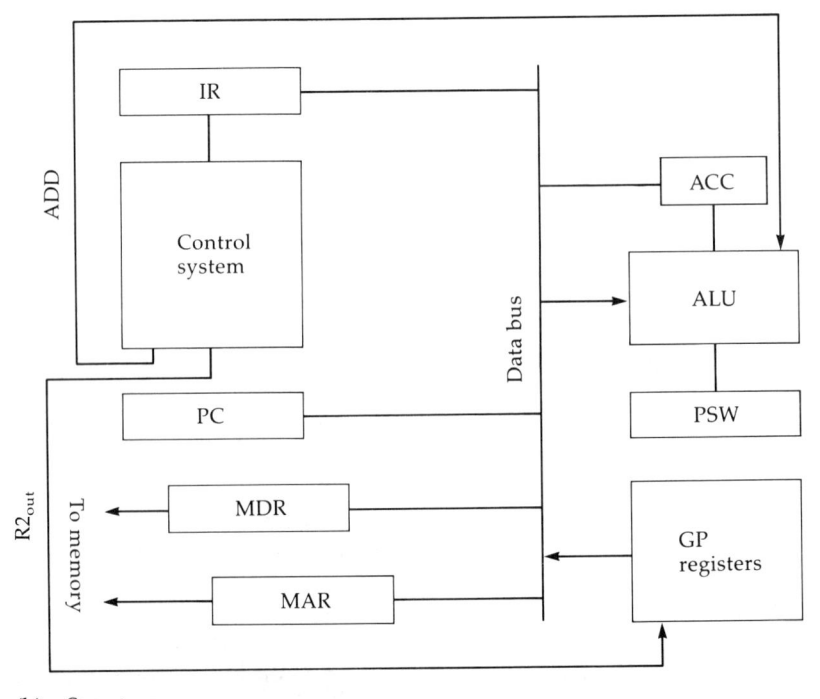

(b) Step two

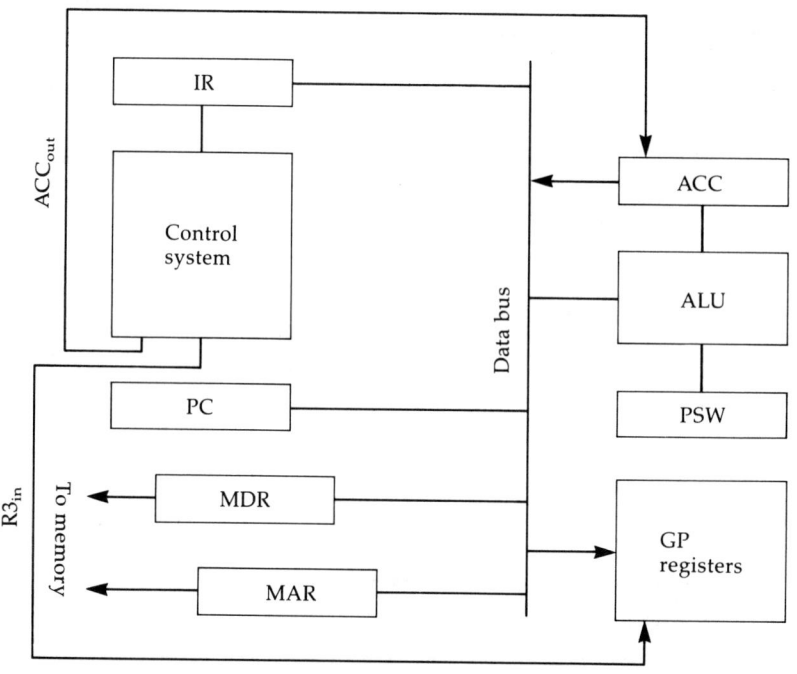

(c) Step three

Figure 6.14 ADD operation microsteps

to memory. The contents of the microcontrol store that would implement these microsteps are

```
1       5       9       13      17 21
0010    0000    0010    0000    00000   R0 to the MAR
1110    0000    1001    0000    01000   R3 to the MDR
                                        memory write
```

These two microinstructions are illustrated in Figure 6.15.

The steps involved in microprogramming a machine such as the MP-1 are to first identify the basic steps required to implement the instruction and then to translate those steps into a binary word corresponding to the requirements of the control word. This information is stored in the microprogram control memory. The actual process of executing a typical assembly language instruction requires that the microprogrammed machine sequence through the correct set of microcontrol words that are stored in the microprogram control store. A problem that we still must consider is how the microprogram control unit finds the correct starting location in the control store for a given assembly language instruction and sequences through the set of microinstructions. We will examine this problem in the next section.

(a) Step one

(b) Step two

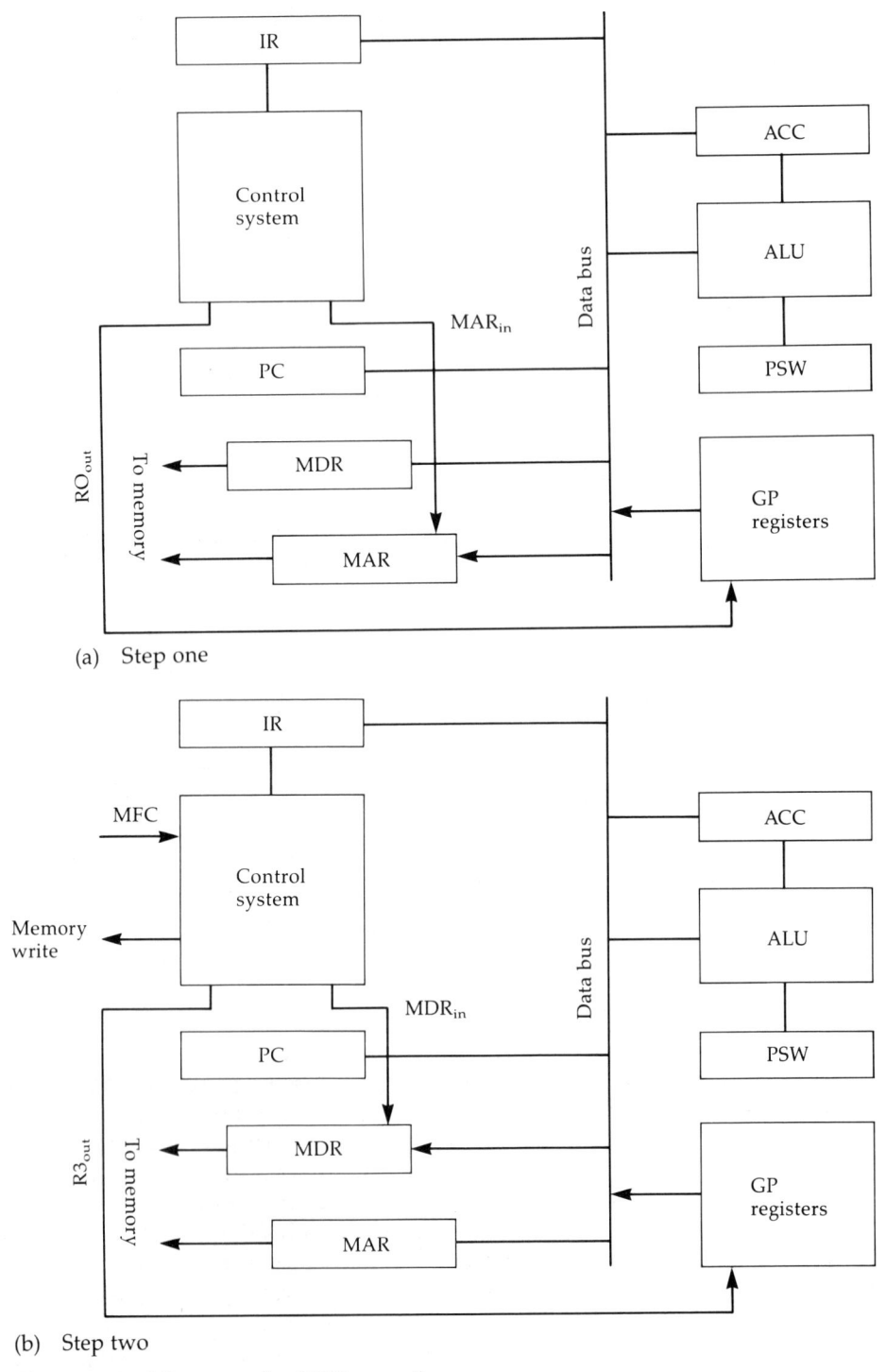

Figure 6.15 Microsteps for SAVE operation

6.3 Microprogram Branching

To save memory in the control store, it would be desirable to store just one copy of the instruction fetch cycle. This means that after completing an instruction fetch, we need to branch to the correct microcode for the instruction, and then, when the instruction is completed, we need to branch back to the instruction fetch cycle. This process is illustrated in Figure 6.16 for an add instruction. There are two problems associated with finding the correct location in the microprogram control memory for a given assembly language instruction: (1) selecting the initial address in the microprogram memory, and (2) determining the correct next addresses for the sequence of microprogram control words.

The starting address in the microprogram control store for any given machine language instruction is produced by the starting address generator, which could be a simple memory unit that contains all the initial addresses for each assembly language instruction. During the fetch cycle, it decodes the contents of the IR, looks up the correct starting address in its own memory, and places the address in the microprogram counter. Consequently, the microprogram counter (μPC) always has the correct starting address for the microcode at the beginning of the instruction execution cycle.

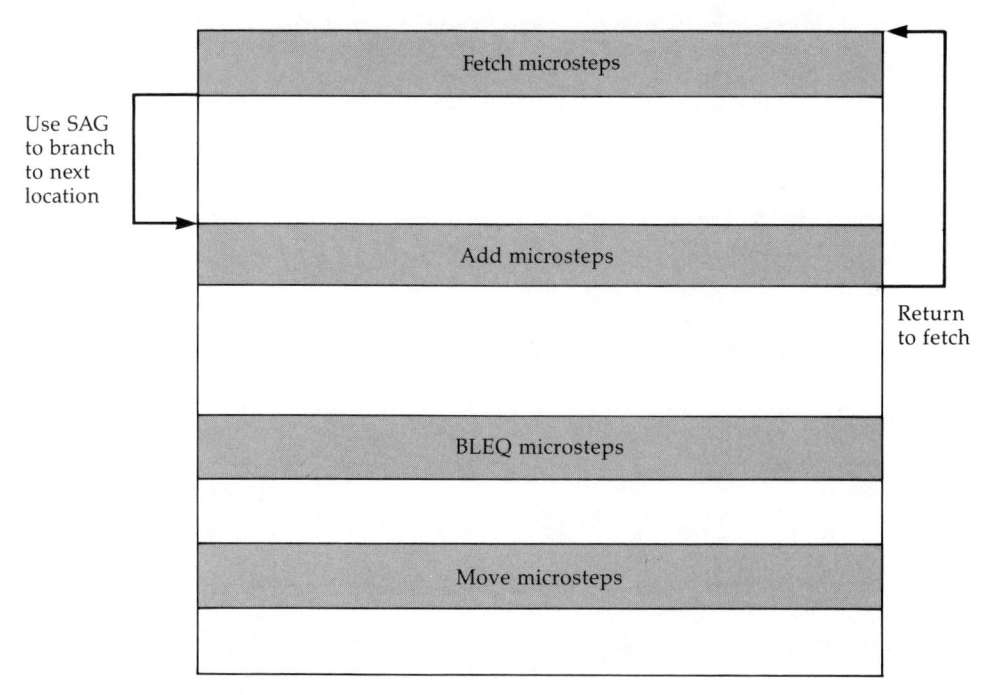

Figure 6.16 Example control memory organization

However, it is more difficult to determine the correct sequence of microinstructions to complete the instruction execution cycle. For some assembly language instructions, the microprogram code may be in a set of contiguous locations in the microprogram memory, in which case the correct sequence is found by just incrementing the microPC. However, even for these simple assembly language instructions, after the final microinstruction, the microPC must branch back to the fetch cycle code in the control store. Also, during the implementation of a microinstruction, it may be necessary to branch to other locations in the microprogram memory. This is illustrated in Figure 6.17, which shows add and subtract instructions that store their results in a memory location. The steps that move the result in the ACC to memory can be shared by these two instructions as well as several others requiring the same operation. This reduces the number of microcoded instructions needed in the control memory. Another example would be a microinstruction in the form "if <some condition is true> then <these microinstructions> else <these microinstructions>."

So how do we implement a microbranch in the hardware and software associated with the microprogram architecture? Such branching may be accomplished by adding two extra fields to the control word. One field, called the **condition select field**, consists of only two bits, S_0 and S_1, which could be encoded as follows:

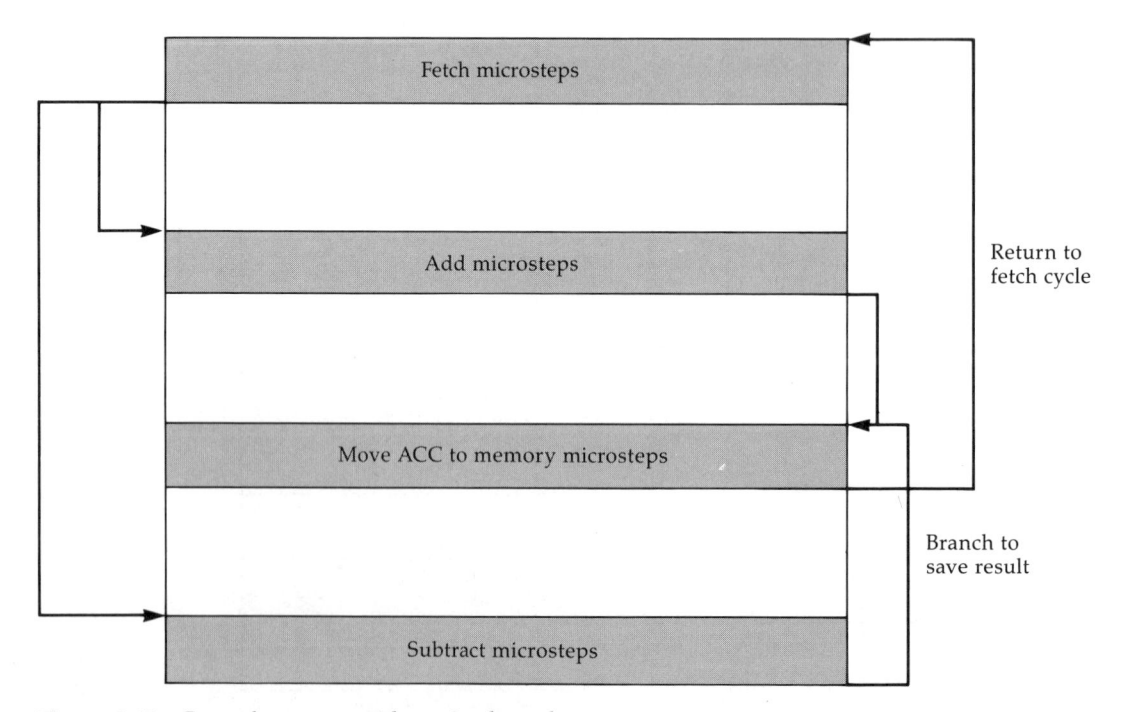

Figure 6.17 Control memory with a microbranch

s_0s_1	Action
0 0	Increment microPC
0 1	Branch to next address on condition true
1 0	Branch to external address supplied by the SAG
1 1	Unconditional branch to next address

For example, consider those assembly language commands in which the required sequence of microinstructions is stored in order in the microprogram memory. It would simply be necessary to increment the μPC to get to the next microinstruction. In this case the condition select field in each microinstruction would contain a 0 0. The only expectation in this case would be for the final microinstruction, which would have an unconditional branch (code 11) back to the fetch cycle.

The second field is called the **next address field**, which, as the name implies, contains the branch address. So, if the condition select field contains a 01 or 11, which indicates a possible branch, the address of the next microinstruction to be executed, providing the branch condition is satisfied, is located in the next address field.

The final condition in the condition select field is the 10 condition. This is used at the final step of the fetch cycle to force the contents of the SAG into the μPC. At this point, the μPC would point to the first microinstruction necessary to initiate the execution of the current machine language instruction. The architecture of such a system is shown in Figure 6.18.

An examination of Figure 6.18 illustrates the effect of each of the four possible values for s_0 and s_1. Note that the μPC register will increment when the signal on the load/inc input is low and will load when the signal is high. This architecture relies on another MSI device called a multiplexer (MUX), which in some ways is the opposite of a decoder. It selects one of many inputs to pass on to the output. The selected input is determined by the address lines. Its operation can be invisioned as a switch that moves to the selected input line in order to connect it to the output, as shown in Figure 6.19.

Consider each of the four possible values of s_0 and s_1:

1. $s_0s_1 = 00$. The condition select field bits address location 0 on MUX B. The 0 input on MUX B is tied to low, so the increment feature on the μPC is activated. As a result, the μPC now points to the next microinstruction in sequence.

2. $s_0s_1 = 01$. The condition select field bits address location 1 on MUX B, which allows the condition value (C) to pass through the MUX to the μPC. Because $s_1 = 1$, the next address field is selected on MUX A. As a result, if $C = 1$, the μPC will load the next address field; if $C = 0$, the μPC will increment. The relevant lines are highlighted in Figure 6.20 to illustrate the data flow when $C = 1$ and the next address field is selected.

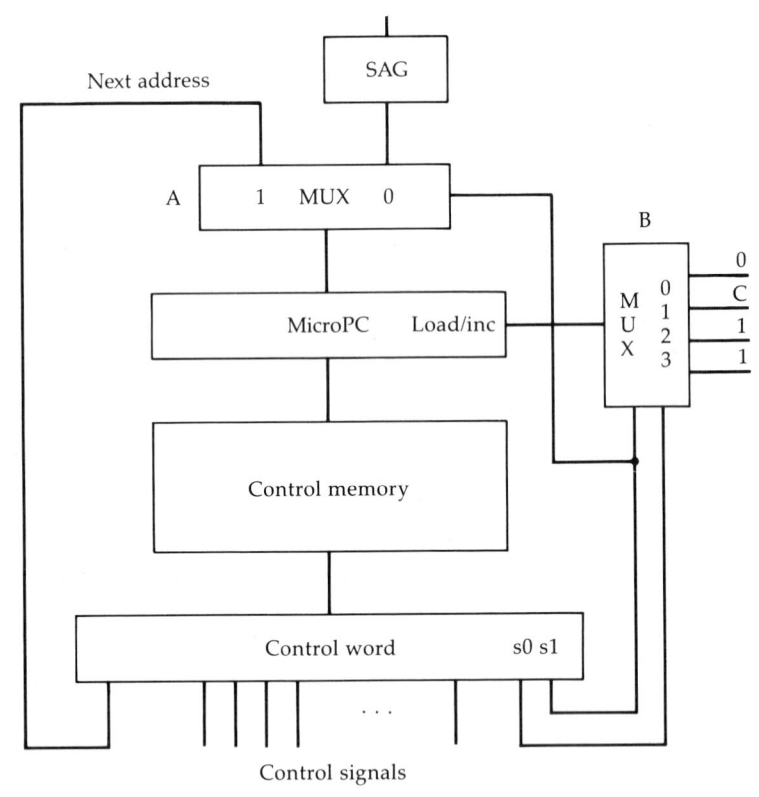

Figure 6.18 Microcontrol system architecture with next address feature

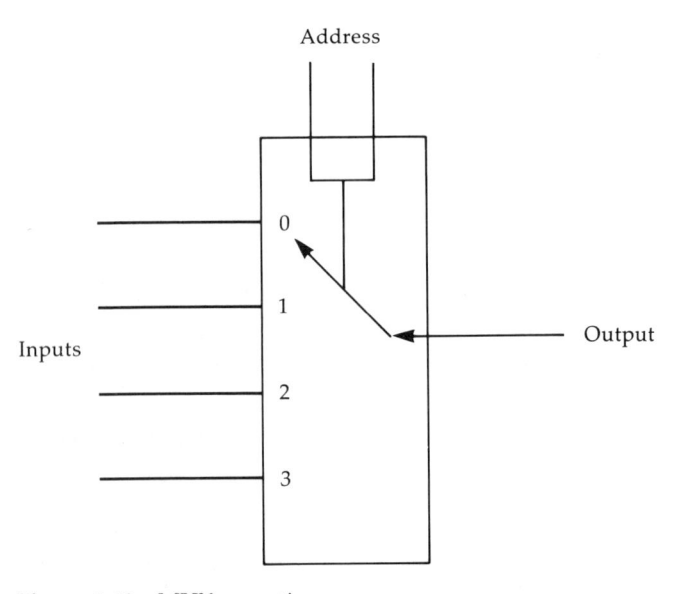

Figure 6.19 MUX operation

6.3 Microprogram Branching

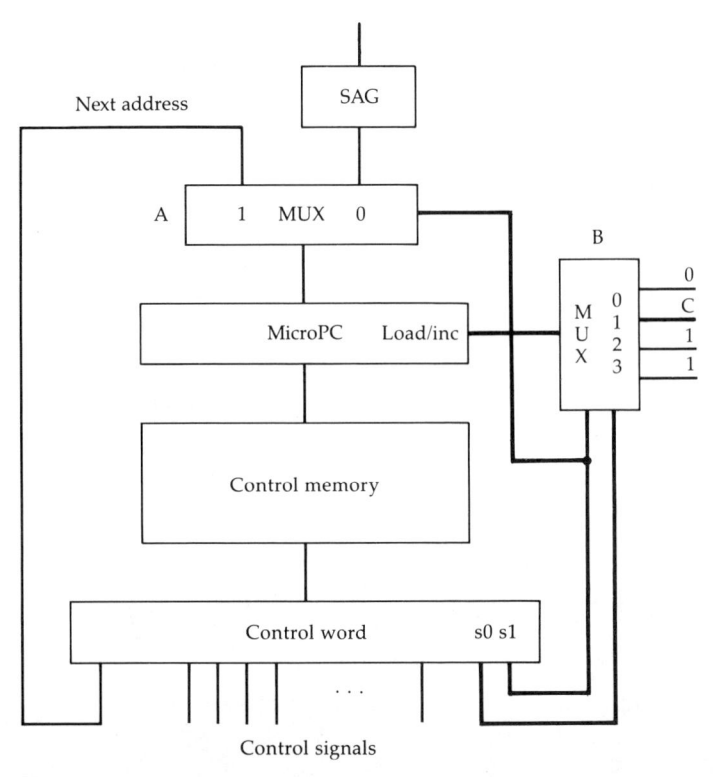

Figure 6.20 Conditional next address selection

3. $s_0s_1 = 10$. In this case the condition select fields address location 2 on MUX B, which selects a 1 to send to the load/inc inputs on the μPC, thus forcing the μPC to load. Because $s_1 = 0$, MUX A sends the output of the SAG into the μPC. The result is that the system branches to the address supplied by the SAG, as illustrated in Figure 6.21.

4. $s_0s_1 = 11$. Now the condition select fields address location 3 on MUX B, which is also tied to 1. The μPC is then forced into another load condition. However, because $s_1 = 1$, MUX A supplies the next address field to the μPC. The result is an unconditional branch to the next address, as shown in Figure 6.22.

For example, assume that the MP-1 has a 1K control store. That would mean that the next address field would require 10 bits. This increases the size of the control word to 33 bits (21 control bits + 10 next address bits + 2 condition select bits). If the next address field occurred in bit positions 22–31, and the condition select field bits were in positions 32 and 33, the control word for placing the contents of R3 on the bus with the required next microinstruction at location 251 (in binary 0 0 1 1 1 1 1 0 1 1) is

202   Chapter 6   Microprogramming

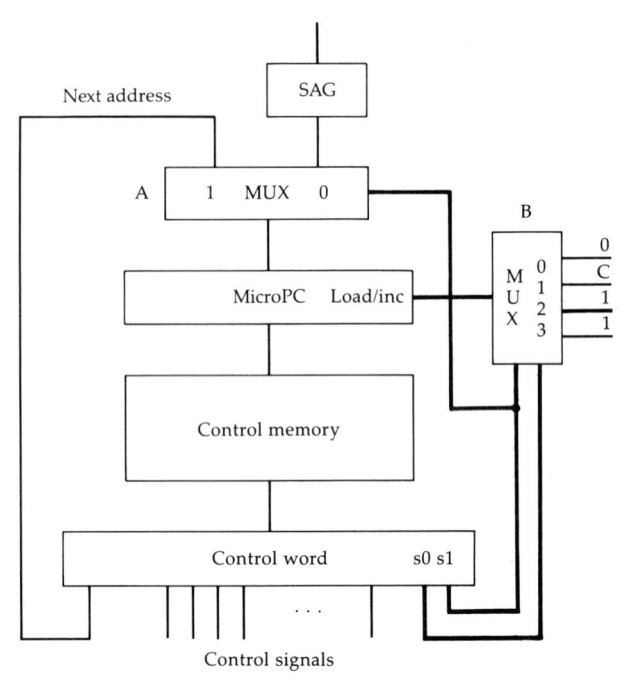

Figure 6.21 External address branch selection

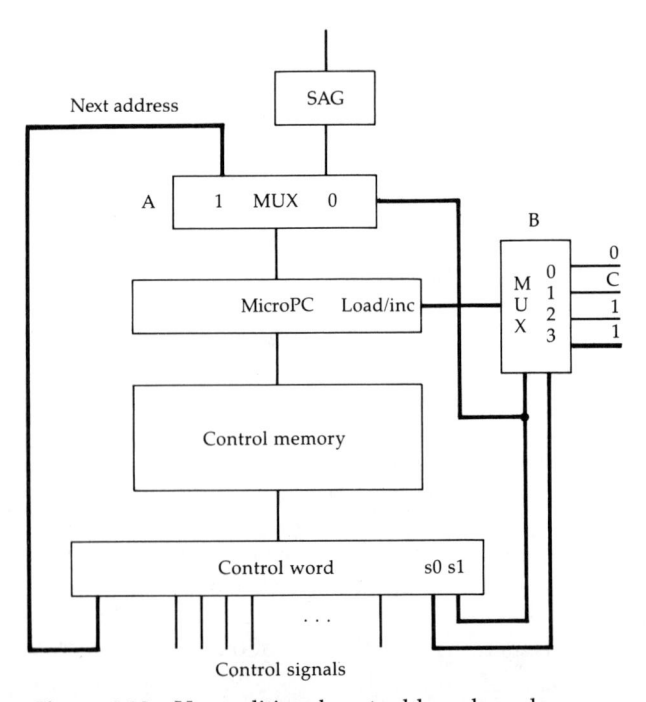

Figure 6.22 Unconditional next address branch

6.3 Microprogram Branching

Next address

| 1110 0000 0000 0000 00000 | 0011111011 | 11 |

↑
Condition
select

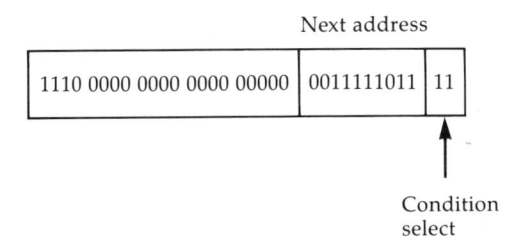

The condition select field in the last two bit positions indicates an unconditional branch to the next address (location 251).

Assume that in the MP-1, the following move instruction starts in location 562 of the microprogram memory and the fetch cycle code starts in location 5

```
MOV    (R2), R3
```

The output of the SAG at the end of the fetch cycle would be

1000110010

which is binary for 562. It would be stored in the μPC. Notice that because the microprogram memory for the MP-1 is 1K words long, both the μPC and the output of the SAG consists of ten bits.

Starting in location 562 of the microprogram memory would be the following code:

1010 0000 0011 0000 10000 0000000000 00

```
(load R2 into the MAR, tell memory to read, wait for memory,
and increment the microPC)
```

1101 0000 0100 0000 00000 0000000101 11

```
(load the MDR into R3, load #5 into the microPC)
```

Conditional Branch Implementation

The execution of a conditional branch instruction at the machine language level depends on the value of the condition codes in the PSW. The MP-1 has four flags in its PSW: N (negative), Z (zero), V (overflow), and CO (carry out). The microprogrammable architecture of Figure 6.18 assumed only one conditional value connected to input 1 of MUX B. This is all that is needed because only one condition is used to control a conditional branch. Therefore, it is necessary to introduce another MUX, MUX S, and another two-bit control word field, the **flag select field**, to select the correct flag value to pass on to MUX B. Such a circuit is shown

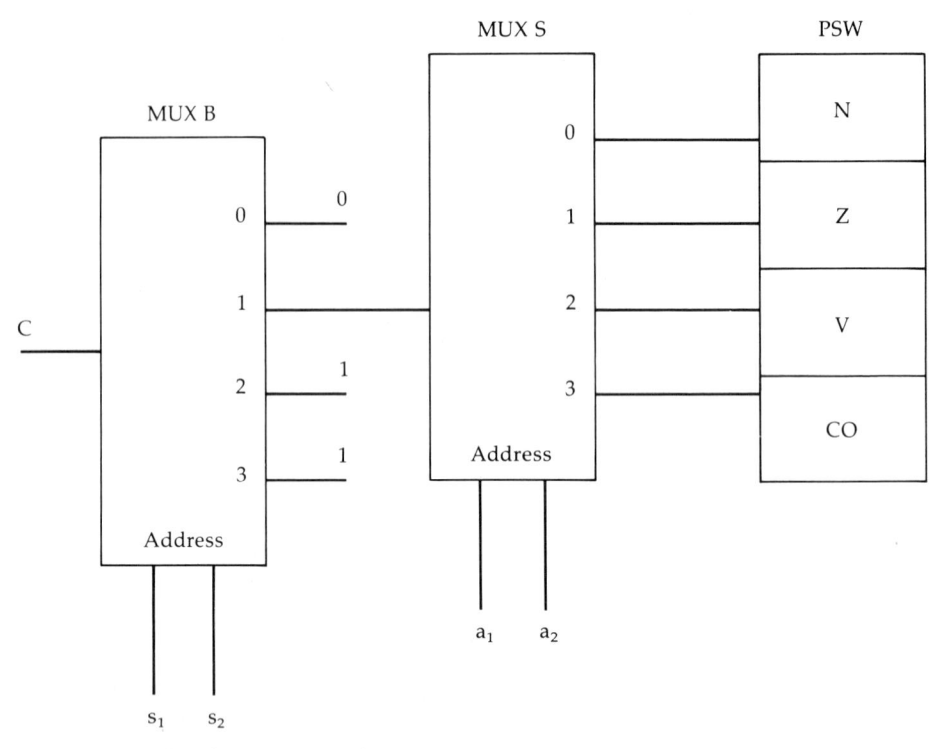

Figure 6.23 Conditional select feature

in Figure 6.23. The flag select field bits (a_1, a_2) in the figure address the PSW bits as shown below.

a_1	a_2	Flag
0	0	N
0	1	Z
1	0	V
1	1	CO

Now the MP-1 control word has 35 bits (21 control bits + 10 next address bits + 2 condition select bits + 2 flag select bits).

With the addition of the flag select field and MUX S, the MP-1 can implement an assembly language conditional branch instruction. For example, assume that the format for a branch on zero (BZ) instruction is

6.3 Microprogram Branching

Further, assume that the fetch cycle microcode begins at location 0 of the control store, the BZ microcode begins at location 562, and the fetch offset microcode begins at location 592. A map of the control store is shown in Figure 6.24.

The microsteps for the BZ operation are

1. Check the Z bit of the PSW. If it is 1, branch to the fetch offset microcode; if it is 0, increment the μPC.
2. Branch back to the fetch cycle microcode.

To check the Z bit of the PSW, the flag select field must contain a 01, and the condition select field must contain a 01. The resulting signal paths are shown in Figure 6.25. The microinstructions at locations 562 and 563 are given by:

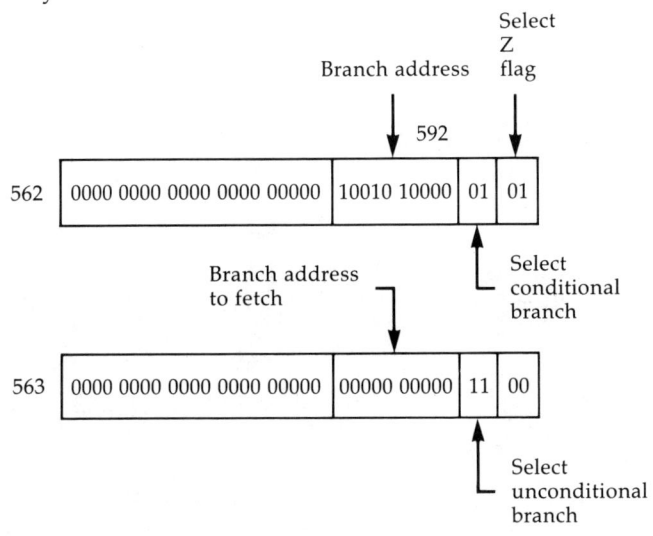

```
                          Select
                          Z
          Branch address  flag
                ↓          ↓
               592
562 | 0000 0000 0000 0000 00000 | 10010 10000 | 01 | 01 |
                                                    ↑
          Branch address                        Select
          to fetch                              conditional
                                                branch
563 | 0000 0000 0000 0000 00000 | 00000 00000 | 11 | 00 |
                                                ↑
                                            Select
                                            unconditional
                                            branch
```

If the condition is satisfied so that the μPC is loaded with the address 592, the system begins the fetch offset operation, which involves the following steps:

1. Move the PC to the MAR, read memory, and increment the PC.
2. Move the PC to the ACC and wait for memory.
3. Add the contents of the MDR to the ACC (the ACC has the current value of the PC; the MDR has the offset).
4. Move the ACC to the PC and return to the instruction fetch cycle.

The microcode for this operation looks like

```
592   0000 0001 0010 0000 10100 00000 00000 00 00
593   0000 0001 0001 0000 00001 00000 00000 00 00
594   0000 0000 0100 0001 00000 00000 00000 00 00
595   0000 0010 0000 0000 00010 00000 00000 11 00
```

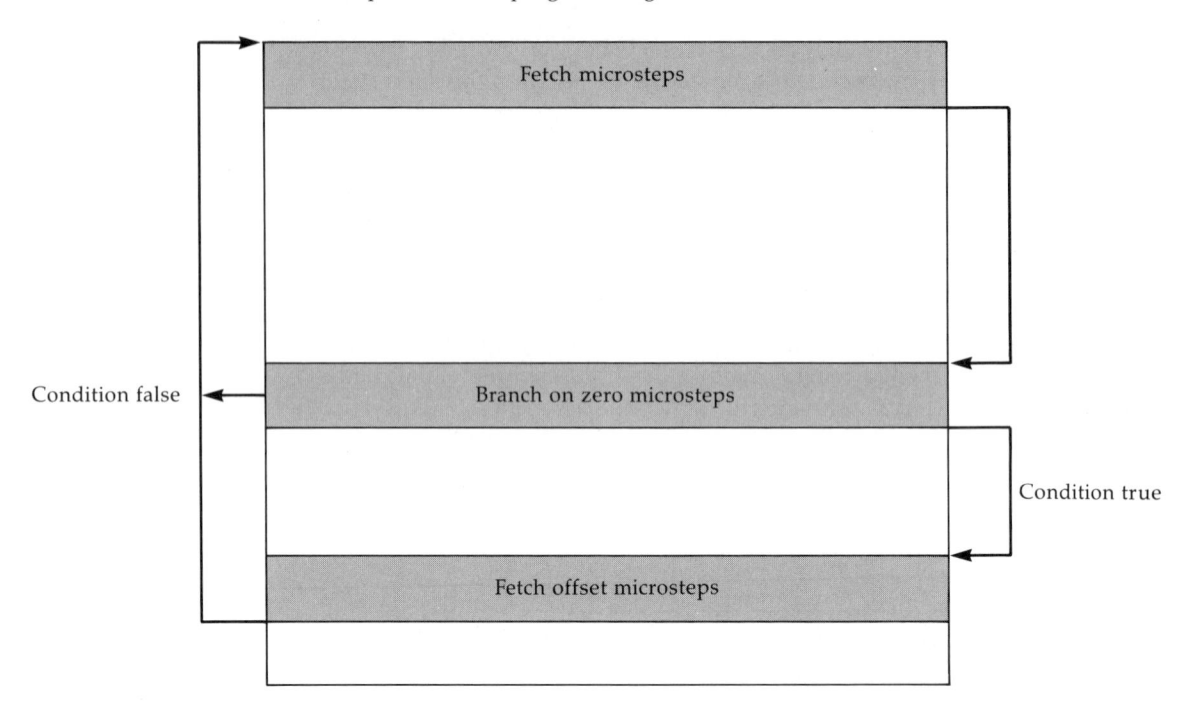

Figure 6.24 Control store memory map

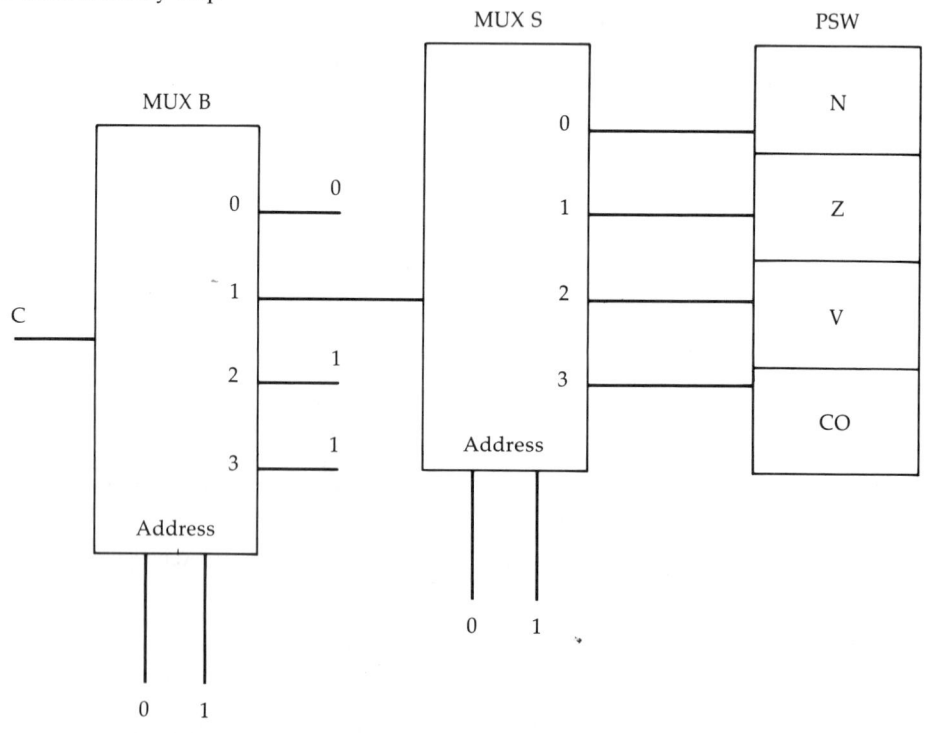

Figure 6.25 Zero condition signal paths

Note that the microcode shown above can be used by any assembly language branch command when the conditions for the branch have been satisfied. For example, a branch on negative command for the MP-1 would also execute the microcode in locations 592 to 595 if the N flag is set.

Summary

In this chapter we have studied the problem of how a typical CPU actually implements assembly language instructions. The process is a flexible combination of hardware and software features. The overall process of executing a single assembly language instruction involves the following steps:

1. You write the assembly language code.
2. The assembler translates your mnemonics into machine language.
3. The machine language bits are loaded into the instruction register (IR).
4. The IR is translated into a starting address.
5. The starting address is loaded into the microprogram counter.
6. The control words required to execute your original instruction are fetched in sequence from the control memory and loaded into the control word register.
7. The control word register is wired to all the devices in the computer, so 0 and 1 signals are sent to those devices to complete the instruction execution one step at a time.

Exercises

All of the following problems use the MP-1 with the full 35-bit control word. Assume that a two-address instruction stores the result in the second address, like the VAX. Use the 4-bit ALU codes given in the first section of the chapter. Assume that the instruction and the operands are all received on the first fetch of an instruction. Assume that the instruction fetch cycle microinstructions requested in Exercise 1 are stored beginning in location 5 of the control memory. In addition, for each exercise that involves microcode, illustrate your basic steps on the following general MP-1 architecture diagram (make photocopies for your work).

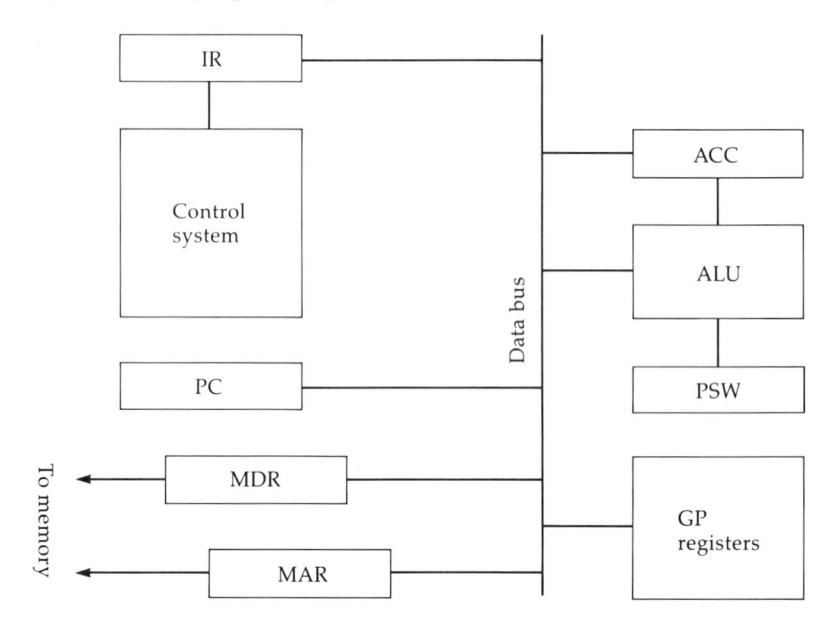

1. Rewrite the microcode for the fetch cycle, including the three new fields (the condition select field, the flag select field, and the next address field).
2. Write the basic steps, the microcode, and the sequence of diagrams for ADD R2, R3.
3. Write the basic steps, the microcode, and the sequence of diagrams for SUBT (R0), R3 (subtract the item pointed to by R0 from R3). Assume that the number being subtracted must be in the accumulator when the ALU is told to subtract.
4. Write the basic steps, the microcode, and the sequence of diagrams for MULT (R1), (R2).
5. It is possible to make the MP-1 more of a vertical microprogrammed machine by combining some of the current 21 control word signals. Suggest some possible combinations and assign codes to them. (Hint: think about operations that are mutually exclusive.)
6. Rewrite the fetch cycle with the new set of control words you generated in Exercise 5.
7. Write the microcode only for the combined set of instructions:
   ```
   Fetch cycle
   ADD R0, R1
   ADD R1, R2
   ADD R2, R3
   ```
8. Figure 6.26 shows a new architecture for the MP-1 in which the register ID is made from the bits in the IR, so the control word bits 1 and 2 are no longer used. In this case a specific register is identified

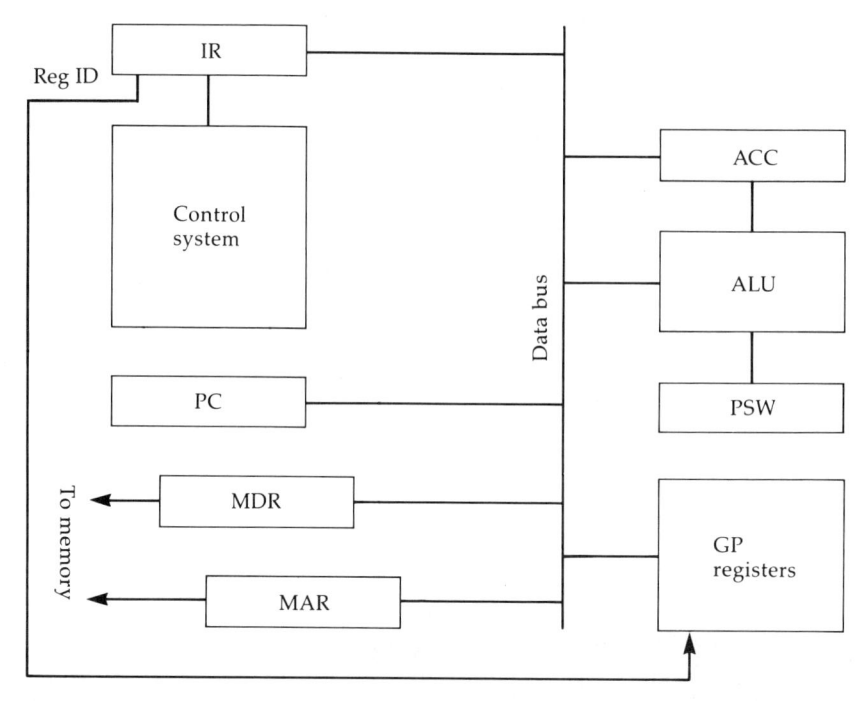

Figure 6.26 MP-1 with register ID from the IR

for a register out or register in signal using a decoder and the IR. For example, Figure 6.27 shows how the R3 read signal could be generated. That is, the two bits from the assembly language instruction stored in the IR are used to identify the register rather than the control word. The advantage is that the code for ADD Rn, Rm only has to be included in the control store once instead of being repeated for each possible combination of Rn and Rm as suggested in Exercise 7. Redo Exercise 7 with this architecture assuming that both a source and a destination register ID are available from the IR. How many lines of microcode are saved between Exercises 7 and 8?

9. Given the following control signal on the MP-1 without the next address field and the condition select field, what instruction does it implement?

   0110 0000 0000 0000 00001
   1010 0000 0011 0000 10000
   0000 0000 0100 0011 00000

10. Design a micro control word format for the SB-1. Include two bits to define the data length where

    00—byte
    01—word

Chapter 6 Microprogramming

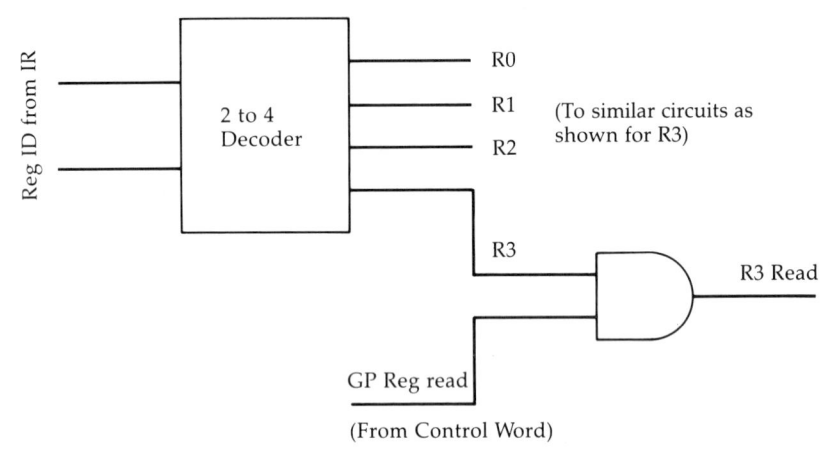

Figure 6.27 Read signal for Exercise 8

10—longword

11—quadword

11. Assume that the machine language for the MP-1 architecture handles the displacement addressing mode in the following manner. The displacement is stored in the machine code in the word following the instruction. For example, ADD 128(R2), R3 would be stored as follows:

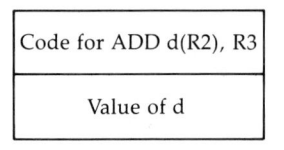

Code for ADD d(R2), R3
Value of d

Write microcode for ADD d(R2), R3.

12. Assume that the machine language for the MP-1 architecture handles the relative addressing mode in the same manner as the displacement mode (see Exercise 11) except that the PC is referenced instead of one of the general-purpose registers. Write microcode for SUB d(PC), R2.

13. Write the microcode to implement the instruction branch on negative (BN) assuming that the displacement is stored in the word following the opcode.

14. Advanced Programming Exercise. Write an assembly language program that will simulate the MP-1 interactively with the user serving as the main memory unit. To fit the control word into one longword, eliminate the wait for memory function complete bit (bit 12) and the flag select bits and renumber bits 13–35 to 12–32. Reserve four longwords for registers R0 to R3, a longword each for the ACC,

the MDR, the MAR, and the PC. In addition, the bus status will be represented by a longword containing the value on the bus. Create an array of longwords for the microprogram memory. Any memory interactions will require that the MP-1 load the MAR (and if necessary the MDR), show you the value(s), and request a read or write from the user. The starting address generator can be modeled by a series of if-then-else statements or by a case statement. Remember that the ALU always adds what is on the bus to what is in the ACC and saves the result in the ACC. Write the microinstructions for the following commands and store them in the microprogram memory.

```
MOV R0,R1     MOV R0,R2     MOV R0,R3
MOV R1,R0     MOV R1,R2     MOV R1,R3
MOV R2,R0     MOV R2,R1     MOV R2,R3
MOV R3,R0     MOV R3,R1     MOV R3,R2
MOV (R0),R1   MOV R1,(R0)
ADD R1,R2     ADD R0,R3     INC R0
AND R2,R3     OR R0,R1
```

Assume that the ALU input commands are

1010 MOV   0001 ADD   0100 AND   0101 OR   1100 INC
0000 No operation

Also assume that when the ALU receives an INC command, it automatically adds 1 to the contents of the ACC. Run the simulation on the following program, printing out in some easily read fashion the values in all the registers after each instruction has been executed assuming that the PC starts with 0 and R0 contains 1224.

```
MOV (R0),R1
MOV R1,R2
   INC R0
MOV (R0),R1
ADD R1,R2
    MOV R2,R1
MOV R1,(R0)
```

PART 3

ADVANCED ASSEMBLY LANGUAGE

CHAPTER 7
Stacks, Subroutines, and Procedures

CHAPTER 8
Macros

CHAPTER 9
Character Strings, Packed Decimal, and Introduction to I/O

CHAPTER CONTENTS

7.1 STACKS

Processing Stacks with Autoincrement and Autodecrement
Special Stack Instructions
An Example Using a Stack
Assembly Time Calculations
The .PSECT Directive

7.2 INTRODUCTION TO SUBROUTINES AND PROCEDURES

7.3 SUBROUTINES

7.4 PROCEDURES

The Argument List
The Entry Mask
The Call Frame
Operation of the Procedure Call Instructions
An Example Using Procedure Calls
Some Comments

7.5 FUNCTIONS

7.6 SEPARATELY ASSEMBLED SUBPROGRAMS AND THE LINKER

Writing Separate Program Units
An Example of a Separately Compiled Subprogram
The Linker

7.7 LINKING HIGH-LEVEL LANGUAGES WITH MACRO

VAX FORTRAN
VAX Pascal
VAX C
Some Comments

7.8 RECURSIVE SUBPROGRAMS

SUMMARY

EXERCISES

CHAPTER 7

Stacks, Subroutines, and Procedures

The goal of this chapter is to develop some of the programming tools necessary for writing good modular code in assembly language. We will also look at combining assembly language code with high-level language programs.

In Section 7.1 we will discuss how stacks can be processed in VAX assembly language. The VAX has several instructions that are designed to simplify stack operations. In Section 7.2 we introduce the concept of subroutines and procedures. We will learn how subprograms on many computers use a stack to provide the communication link needed between the calling program and the called routine. The VAX's architects provided two distinct methods for calling subprograms. A subroutine call is a simple, quick method that is useful when minimal communication is required, while a procedure call provides a powerful and standardized way of calling subprograms. The two types of subprograms are discussed in detail in their own sections.

In Section 7.5 we discuss the type of subprogram usually called a function in high-level languages. Functions are very similar to other subprograms except that they calculate a single result, which is normally returned in a register.

We can divide a program's source code into segments stored in different files to simplify coding and debugging long programs. The main program and the subprograms are partitioned into different segments as appropriate. All the segments may be written in assembly language or different segments can be written in different languages. The linker combines the object modules from the different segments into one executable image.

Finally, in Section 7.8 we will discuss recursive subprograms—subprograms that call themselves. They provide a convenient way to implement certain algorithms.

7.1 Stacks

Before we can understand how most modern computers (including the VAX) process subroutines and procedures, we must understand the concept of a stack. The program that we will use to illustrate the use of stacks will also introduce the directive .PSECT, which is an aid in modularizing MACRO assembly language code.

A **stack** is a storage structure in which data items are added or removed from one end, called its top; that is, items in a stack are processed in a **last-in, first-out (LIFO)** manner. On the VAX, when a block of memory is set aside for storing a stack, it is customary to place the bottom of the stack at the location with the largest address. In this scheme the stack "grows" toward smaller addresses. The stack structure includes a pointer to the top of the stack, that is, to the last item that was added. When a new item is added or **pushed** onto the stack, the stack pointer is first reduced by the length of the data and then the item is stored at the resulting address. After an item is removed or **popped** from the top of the stack, the address in the stack pointer is increased by the length of the data item so that it again points to the new top of the stack. In the format used on the VAX, the value of the stack pointer decreases as new items are added to the stack and increases as items are removed from the stack. Figure 7.1 illustrates the operation of a stack.

Processing Stacks with Autoincrement and Autodecrement

It is relatively easy to create and process a stack in assembly language on a VAX. First the program must declare a block of storage to hold the stack, possibly with a .BLKx directive. A register is selected to act as the stack pointer and is set to the address of the memory location just below the stack, that is, the address of the item that follows the stack in memory. The autodecrement and autoincrement addressing modes then make pushing or popping values easy. For example, if R6 is used for the stack pointer, the following instructions may be convenient:

```
MOVx     source, -(R6)          ; push source on stack
MOVx     (R6)+, destination     ; pop stack into destination
```

Additional coding may be required to ensure that the size of the stack never exceeds the allocated storage block and that the program does not attempt to pop items from an empty stack.

Suppose that we want to take a number of characters stored in one string and put them in another in reverse order. We can use the following algorithm to carry out this task.

1. Establish a pointer to the beginning of the old string.
2. Establish a pointer to the end of the new string.

7.1 Stacks

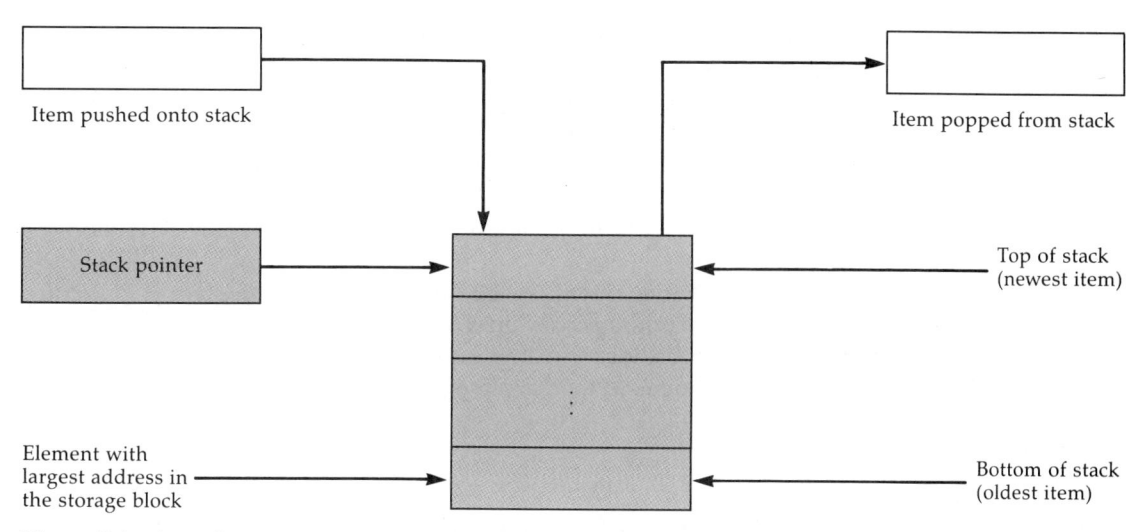

Figure 7.1 A stack

3. Until we get to the end of the old string do:
   Pop character off the old stack (old string)
   Push it onto the new stack (new string)

The following program segment implements the algorithm. It treats both the old and new strings as stacks. The autoincrement and autodecrement addressing modes greatly simplify the processing. The storage areas for both strings are reserved in the data section of the program. The initial steps of the code section are used to initialize the pointers to each of the stacks (strings). Because the old stack is full, its pointer is initialized to the first character in the string, the top of the stack. The new string is empty. Consequently, its pointer must be set to the address following the end of the string, which is the constant EndNewString.

```
        StringSize = 50
        OldString:    .LONG      StringSize
        EndOldString = .
        NewString:    .LONG      StringSize
        EndNewString = .
            . . .
              MOVAB    OldString, R2         ; R2 points to old stack
              MOVL     #EndNewString, R3     ; R3 points to new stack
Loop:         MOVB     (R2)+, -(R3)          ; Move byte from old to new string
              CMPB     R2, #EndOldString     ; If we are not at the end of the
              BLSSU    Loop                  ;   old string, repeat
```

The loop to copy the characters from the old string to the new one is simple because the VAX allows freedom in selecting the addressing modes. The values can be popped off the old stack with autoincrement addressing and pushed onto the new stack with autodecrement addressing all in one move instruction. While we have talked about "popping values" from the old string, we realize that the old string remains unchanged; only its stack pointer in R2 is actually changed as we pop values off the stack.

The program segment uses a new predefined constant ("."), which means "the current address" in VAX/VMS MACRO and is a convenient way to find the address of the end of an array. In this example, End-OldString happens to be the same as the address of NewString.

Special Stack Instructions

Because the VAX uses a stack for procedure calls and error detection, its operating system provides every program with a large block of memory called the **user stack**, and general register R14 is dedicated to act as the stack pointer for this stack. Because of this use, the assembler requires that we refer to this register as **SP (stack pointer)**. Before the operating system turns control over to the program, the stack is empty and SP is pointing to a memory location just beyond the bottom end of the stack.

To simplify use of the user stack, the VAX instruction set includes several instructions designed to push longwords onto this stack or pop them off it. They are

Opcode	Mnemonic	Operands	Operation
DD	PUSHL	Source	$-(SP) \leftarrow$ source
—	POPL	Destination	Destination $\leftarrow (SP)+$
9F	PUSHAB		
3F	PUSHAW		
DF	PUSHAL	Source	$-(SP) \leftarrow$ address of source
7F	PUSHAQ		
DF	PUSHAF		
7F	PUSHAD		
BB	PUSHR	Register mask	Push specified registers onto stack
BA	POPR	Register mask	Pop values from stack into specified registers

The notation "$-(SP) \leftarrow$" means that the stack pointer is decremented first, and then the data is pushed onto the stack at the resulting address. Likewise, "$\leftarrow (SP)+$" means that the stack pointer is incremented after the data it points to is copied into the destination.

7.1 Stacks

The push longword instruction, PUSHL, copies the longword stored in the source onto the stack after decrementing the stack pointer register (SP). The operation of this instruction is equivalent to the operation of

```
MOVL source, -(SP)
```

but uses less code. The pop longword instruction, POPL, pops longwords off this stack and then increments SP. Actually there isn't any machine language instruction that exactly corresponds to POPL. Instead the assembler translates

```
POPL destination
```

into

```
MOVL (SP)+, destination
```

during the assembly process.

Consider the instruction PUSHL X, which pushes the value of X onto the stack. Suppose that SP is equal to 00020A48 and X contains 12345678 when the instruction is processed. Figure 7.2 shows the result.

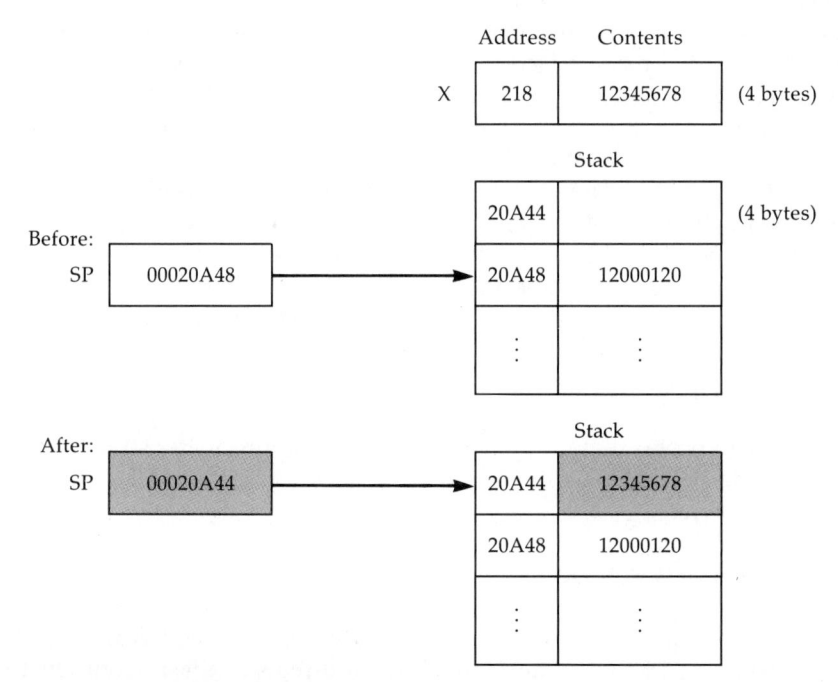

Figure 7.2 Processing PUSHL X

The push address instructions, PUSHAx, push the four-byte address of the specified source onto the stack instead of the value of the source. This instruction is equivalent to

```
MOVAx      source, -(SP)
```

The data type *x* may be byte, word, longword, quadword, floating, or double. (Actually, PUSHAL and PUSHAF represent the same machine instruction because the data lengths are identical; likewise, PUSHAQ and PUSHAD represent the same instruction.) Later in this chapter we will find that pushing addresses on the stack is a useful way to pass arguments to subprograms. Figure 7.3 illustrates the use of PUSHAL X to save the address of X on the stack. POPL or POPR can be used to pop addresses back off the stack.

The instructions PUSHR and POPR are designed to allow pushing or popping several registers on or off the stack at once. The operand is a 16-bit **register mask** that indicates which registers are to be processed, and each bit corresponds to one of the 16 general-purpose registers. If the bit corresponding to a particular register is a 1, that register will be processed by the instruction. A 0 indicates that the register is not to be included among those processed. For example, if the binary value

0000 0010 1000 0001

was used as the mask for a PUSHR instruction, registers R9, R7, and R0 would be pushed on the stack. There are several ways to write this mask. It could be converted into decimal 641; it could be expressed in hexadecimal as ^X0281 or written in binary as ^B1010000001. However, to simplify the task of writing a mask, the MACRO assembler provides a special notation. The mask in our example could be written ^M<R0, R7, R9>. The registers that are to be processed are simply included within the "^M<...>" symbol. The order of the registers is not important because the assembler just creates the corresponding binary number by setting the specified bits to 1, leaving the other bits as zeros. To push these registers, we would normally write

```
PUSHR      #^M<R0, R7, R9>
```

where # indicates that immediate mode (or, if appropriate, short literal) addressing is used. To pop data off the stack into registers R2 and R4, we could write

```
POPR       #^M<R2, R4>
```

We must make two technical comments about how PUSHR and POPR operate. First, PUSHR scans the bits in the register mask from left to right to determine which registers are to be pushed. Consequently, the

7.1 Stacks

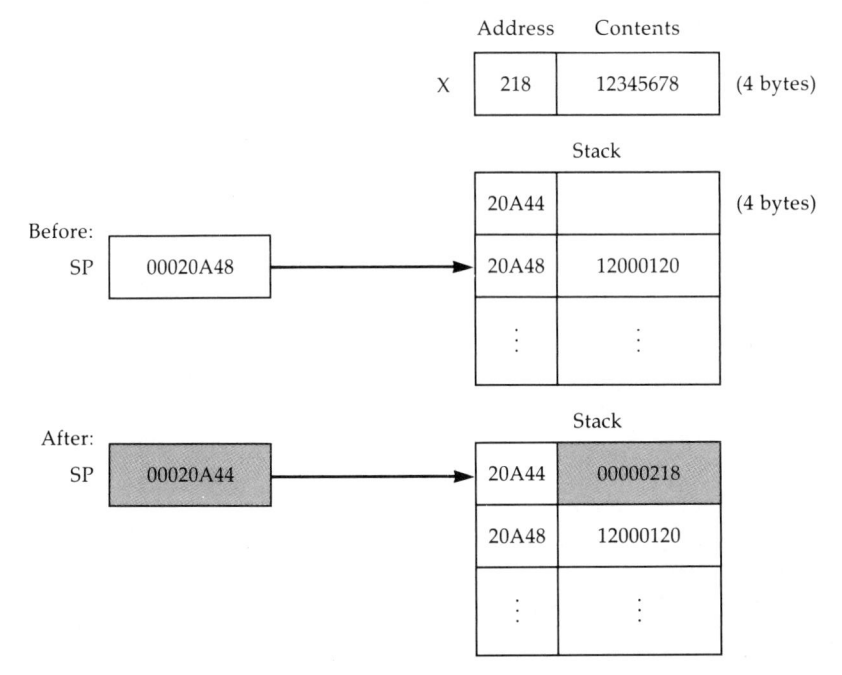

Before:

```
        Address  Contents
X       218      12345678    (4 bytes)

        Stack
        20A44               (4 bytes)
SP  00020A48 →  20A48    12000120
                  ⋮         ⋮
```

After:

```
        Stack
SP  00020A44 →  20A44    00000218
                20A48    12000120
                  ⋮         ⋮
```

Figure 7.3 Processing PUSHAL X

highest numbered registers are pushed onto the stack first. POPR reverses this procedure and pops the lowest numbered registers off the stack first as it scans the register mask from right to left. This means that if we follow a

    PUSHR   #^M<R2, R3, R4>

instruction with

    POPR   #^M<R2, R3, R4>

we can be assured that R2, R3, and R4 will be restored to their original values.

Second, bit 15 (the PC) is ignored by these instructions. It is impossible to use them to push or pop the program counter.

Although the VAX has special instructions for processing the user stacks, the autoincrement and autodecrement addressing modes and standard instructions are also useful when working with the user stack. In fact, their use is sometimes more efficient than the use of the special stack commands. For example the code sequence

    ADDL3   R1, R2, R3
    PUSHL   R3

can be replaced by the single instruction

```
ADDL3    R1, R2, -(SP)
```

if the sum is not actually needed in R3 for other purposes.

An Example Using a Stack

Listing 7.1 shows a program that uses a stack to reverse a list and stores the reversed list back in the original storage locations. This program is slightly more complicated than the one used for our earlier code segment that stored the reversed string in a different array. The entire list is pushed onto the user stack and then popped off. The double processing reverses the list because the last item in the original list will be the first item popped off the stack and will be stored in the first array element. The length of the list will be a variable.

This program has two new features that will be discussed in the following subsections. One, the .PSECT directive, can be ignored during your initial reading of the program. Exercise 3 at the end of this chapter suggests an improvement that will shorten the code.

Assembly Time Calculations

Observe that we want to reserve ArraySize elements for List and also want to assign six of them for quick testing with the symbolic debugger. That means that ArraySize-6 additional elements must be reserved with the .BLKL directive. MACRO will calculate constant, integer valued expressions for us while assembling the program. However, there is one point to be careful about. Calculations are done strictly in left-to-right order. Consequently, an expression such as 6 − 2 * 5 would evaluate as (6 − 2) * 5 not 6 − (2 * 5) as it would in most languages. If necessary, corner brackets can be used as parentheses. For example, we could write 6 − <2 * 5> for 6 − (2 * 5).

The .PSECT Directive

The program in Listing 7.1 introduced a new VAX MACRO directive. **.PSECT**, which divides the program into **program sections**. It has several purposes, including protecting read-only code sections from modification and separating the data from the instructions. The use of program sections encourages the development of modular programs. The format of this directive is

```
.PSECT    program section name, attribute list
```

The .PSECT can be used to identify parts of the object code to the linker and restrict their use to a given purpose. There are several attributes that

Listing 7.1 Reversing a list

```
        .TITLE ReverseList
; Program to reverse the order of items in a list

; Algorithm:

;   1. Initialize:
;         Put the address of the list and the count each into
;         two registers (one copy for pushing, one for popping).
;   2. Push list onto user stack:
;         Push next item onto the stack and decrement counter
;         until finished.
;   3. Pop list from user stack:
;         Pop next item from the stack and decrement counter
;         until finished.

; Register usage:
;    R2, R3    address of current item
;    R4, R5    counter (decreases)

        .PSECT Variables,  NOEXE, WRT

ArraySize = 20
Number:  .WORD 6                      ; Number of items in list
List:    .LONG 16, 1, 14, 18, 2, 10   ; Items in list
         .BLKL ArraySize - 6          ; Leave room for unused elements

        .PSECT   Code, EXE, NOWRT

        .ENTRY ReverseList, 0

; Initialize

Begin:     MOVAL   List, R2         ; Put address of List in R2
           MOVL    R2, R3           ;   and R3
           MOVW    Number, R4       ; Put number of items in R4
           MOVW    R4, R5           ;   and R5

; Push items onto user stack

PushLoop:  PUSHL   (R2)+            ; Push items onto stack
           DECW    R4               ; Decrement counter and
           BGTR    PushLoop         ;   repeat, if needed

; Pop items off user stack back into original list

PopLoop:   POPL    (R3)+            ; Pop items off stack
           DECW    R5               ; Decrement counter and
           BGTR    PopLoop          ;   repeat, if needed

Finished:  $EXIT_S
           .END    ReverseList
```

can be assigned to a program section, of which we will mention only a few. EXE and NOEXE are used to indicate if the program segment contains executable code. A branch to a program segment marked NOEXE will result in an error, and the operating system will indicate the problem after it halts the program's execution. WRT and NOWRT indicate if the program section can be altered during program execution. Trying to change the value of a location in a section marked NOWRT causes immediate program termination. Appropriate attributes for the various segments of the program can simplify the debugging process. For example, suppose that we need to store some constant values that are never modified by the program. It is wise to group them together in their own program section preceded by a directive like the following:

```
.PSECT    Constants,    NOWRT, NOEXE
```

Any program errors that would cause the computer to try to change values or execute code in this section would cause an immediate program termination with a message identifying the coding error for us.

7.2 Introduction to Subroutines and Procedures

We now turn our attention to subprograms. The term **subprogram** includes various types of program segments that may be called subroutines, procedures, or functions in different languages. Programmers have learned that program segmentation is essential for producing good code whether it is written in a high-level language or assembly language. Subprograms are useful for many reasons, including the following:

1. A subprogram can be used more than once by the calling program, thus reducing the amount of code needed.
2. Subprogram usage encourages top-down coding techniques because programmers find it convenient to place distinct code segments into separate subprograms.
3. A subprogram can be tested and debugged separately from the calling program, thus simplifying the development and maintenance of long, complicated programs.
4. It may be possible to use a subprogram in more than one program. The cost of writing new programs can be greatly reduced if large portions can be borrowed from previously written and tested programs or from subprogram libraries.

5. We can combine programs written in one language with subprograms written in another if we take care to provide a common means of linking subprograms. In fact it is common for commercial programs to be written primarily in a high-level language like FORTRAN or COBOL, which occasionally call assembly language subprograms for tasks that are impossible or inefficient in the high-level language.

Although the use of subprograms has many advantages, programmers must deal with two problems when using them. First, computer languages must include instructions that call (or cause a branch to) a subprogram and return from the subprogram to the calling program. The call statement must save the address of the instruction that follows it so that the return statement can branch back to the proper place. Many modern computers store this address on a stack.

A second problem associated with subprograms is the matter of argument passing. For high-level languages, the parameter list mechanics are worked out by language designers and compiler writers. Consequently, this is normally a minor issue for programmers in such languages. However, computer designers, compiler writers, and assembly language programmers find that parameter lists are a major concern. They need a method for passing the argument list from the calling program to the subprogram. There are at least two issues in designing this mechanism. First, what format will be used for passing the arguments? Second, where will this information be stored when the subprogram is invoked?

There are three common formats used for passing arguments. **Call by value** is the simplest. When this technique is used, the calling program makes a copy of the data and passes the copy to the subprogram. Because the subprogram operates with only a copy, it cannot destroy or modify the original data. Unfortunately, the process of making a copy of the data may be very time-consuming if large records or arrays are being passed. Moreover, in many situations it is impossible for the subprogram to return a value when call by value is used. **Call by reference** is another method. The calling program passes the address of the data to the subprogram instead of the data itself. The subprogram uses the address to access the original data. This technique is more complicated in some respects but is quicker when large quantities of information are passed. It allows the subprogram to modify the original data, which is sometimes desirable. **Call by descriptor** is primarily used for more complicated data structures such as character strings. A descriptor is a block of storage describing the data. For example, a character string might be described by its length and the location of the first character. In this method the address of the data's descriptor is passed to the subprogram.

Where should the subprogram linkage information, such as the argument list and the return address, be stored? One possibility is to store the arguments (or their addresses) in the computer's general registers.

This is convenient and fast but is impossible if the amount of information to be passed exceeds the capacity of the available registers. Another method, used on many modern computers, involves pushing the subprogram linkage information onto the stack. The called subprogram can then pop the information off the stack when it is needed. Sometimes the linkage information is stored in a block of memory, and then the address of that block is passed to the subprogram, possibly by pushing the address onto the stack.

The contents of the general registers present another problem to the assembly language programmer. Ideally, a subprogram call would not disturb the registers, but it is normally impractical to write a subprogram without using one or more of the registers. Yet changes in register values may cause problems when control returns to the calling program. So, to allow a subprogram to use the registers as needed, it may be desirable to save their contents before invoking the subprogram and to restore them upon the completion of the subprogram.

Some computers offer only a very simple instruction for calling subprograms. They leave it up to the programmer to determine what is the best way to pass information to the subprogram and save information stored in the registers. Although this instruction executes rapidly, the programmer must spend some time determining which argument-passing and register-preserving techniques are most appropriate for the individual situation. This linkage may require a number of lines of assembly code. Other computers offer a powerful instruction for calling subprograms that provides a built-in means for storing the argument list and saving the contents of the registers. The instruction uses very general techniques, so it can be used for various situations. However, it may require quite a long time to carry out the required processing. It may actually complicate coding and slow execution in situations not requiring an argument list or register saves.

The VAX's machine language recognizes both situations and provides two types of subprogram calls. One type of instruction is called a **subroutine call**. It is ideal for simple situations and executes quickly. Programmers must make provision for argument lists and register saves on their own. The second type is called a **procedure call**. It provides a universal means of handling these problems. It imposes a standardized structure on the programmer, that is helpful in many situations but may slow execution when the extra power is unneeded.

It is important to understand that the term *subroutine call* and *procedure call* as used in VAX assembly language are arbitrary and may not correspond to their usage in a high-level language. In fact, because compiler writers must be concerned with standardization and generality in high-level languages, subprograms (whether they are called procedures, subroutines, or functions) are most often implemented as assembly language procedures on the VAX.

When a subprogram is included with a program's code, the subprogram's code may be placed before the entry point to the main program or at the end of the main program after the $EXIT_S. Subprograms may also be placed in separate files and assembled separately. In this case the linker, which is invoked by the system command LINK in VAX/VMS, is responsible for joining the different object files together into one executable program.

Because of their simpler structure, we will discuss subroutines first and then cover procedures.

7.3 Subroutines

The VAX machine language interpretation of a subroutine call provides for branching to the subroutine and saving the return address. It does not provide any assistance in saving registers or passing arguments.

The VAX instruction set provides three different instructions that can be used to call a subroutine and one instruction to return from a subroutine. These instructions are

Opcodes	Mnemonic	Operand	Purpose
10	BSBB	Address	Branch to subroutine with byte offset
30	BSBW	Address	Branch to subroutine with word offset
16	JSB	Address	Jump to subroutine with general addressing
05	RSB		Return from subroutine

The instructions for calling subroutines are patterned after the unconditional branch instructions. The first two instructions use branch addressing, and the offset is stored immediately after the opcode. When the instruction is executed, the PC is first updated to point to the next instruction and then pushed on the stack. The offset is added to the PC to determine the location of the first instruction in the subroutine. The jump instruction allows general addressing, so branches can be made anywhere in memory and all the standard addressing modes are allowed. The return from subroutine instruction does not need any operands. Consider the following subroutine calls together with the machine code they generate. The offsets are arbitrary.

BSBB	DoIt	BSBW	DoIt	JSB	DoIt
10	BSBB	30	BSBW	16	JSB
29	Byte offset	25	Word offset	FF	Longword rel. mode
		45		12	
				AC	Longword offset
				0E	
				00	

The action of the three subroutine call statements can be summarized as follows:

Push the updated PC onto the user stack

PC ← address of subroutine

The return from subroutine statement simply pops the return address off the stack and places it in the PC. Figure 7.4 illustrates the action of a

```
Assembly code:
      BSBW    Sub           ; Call Sub
      CLRB    R2            ; Next instruction
      ...
Sub:  MOVB    R3, R2        ; Beginning of subroutine Sub
      ...
      RSB                   ; Return from Sub

Machine code:
   Address  code
     220    30     BSBW
     221    40     word offset = 363 - 223
     222    01                  = 140
     223    94     beginning of next instruction, CLRB
     ...
     363    90     beginning of Sub
     ...
     38B    05     RSB
```

Execution:

	Before BSBW		After BSBW		After RSB
SP	67008		67004		67008
PC	220		363		223

User stack:

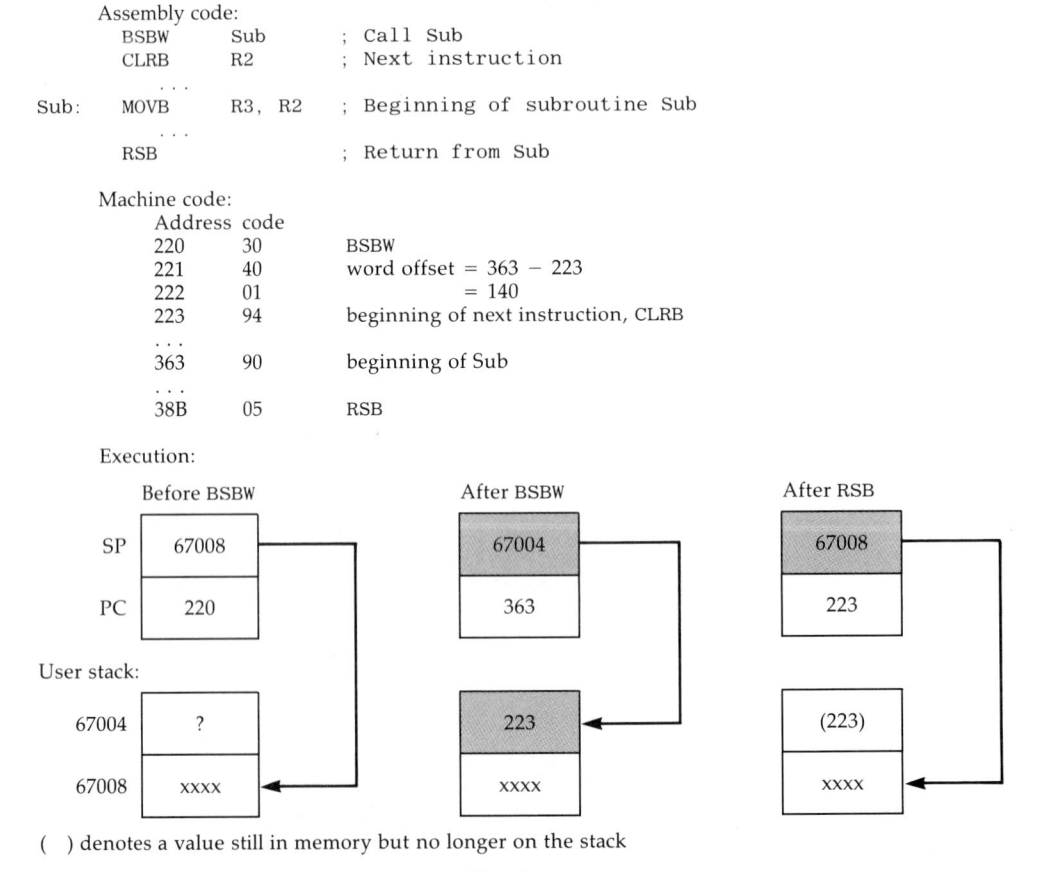

67004	?		223		(223)
67008	xxxx		xxxx		xxxx

( ) denotes a value still in memory but no longer on the stack

Figure 7.4 Execution of a subroutine call and return

subroutine call and return. The addresses shown are arbitrary. The simplicity of the subroutine call is apparent in the figure. The programmer must make arrangements for passing arguments or saving registers. The figure shows values that have been popped off the stack in parentheses because the action of popping a value from the stack only changes the stack pointer, not the values stored in memory. (Of course, reusing a value already popped from the stack is discouraged.)

An easy way to preserve registers is to push them on the stack before the subroutine call and pop them back immediately after the return. For example:

```
PUSHR    #^M<R2, R3, R4>    ; Push registers onto stack
```

(Push arguments on stack, if needed.)

```
BSBB     Sub                ; Call subroutine
POPR     #^M<R2, R3, R4>    ; Restore registers
```

Alternatively, if the stack is not used for parameter passing, it is possible to push the registers onto the stack in the first step of the subroutine and restore them just before the return.

There are several ways to pass an argument list to a subroutine, and we will illustrate a few in the following examples. For simplicity, in these examples we will assume that it is unnecessary to save and restore registers. In each case we will use the subroutine to calculate the sum of two longwords that are passed to the routine. The sum is returned to the program.

The simplest way to provide for the argument list is to use call by value with the arguments stored in registers as illustrated in Listing 7.2. The main program loads R0 and R1 with the argument's actual values before the subroutine call and assumes that the result is in R2 after the subroutine has been processed.

Alternatively, we can use call by reference. We would place the addresses of A, B, and S in the registers before the subroutine call and use register deferred addressing in the subroutine.

(Symbolic debugger users may find it convenient to add labels to the statement following the entry point and to the $EXIT_S statement. When stepping through the program, the entire subroutine will execute when the BSBB instruction is processed unless there is a breakpoint within the subroutine Add or the SET STEP INTO instruction is given to the debugger before instructing the computer to GO or STEP.)

Listing 7.3 shows a second way to implement an argument list. The addresses of the arguments are pushed on the stack by the PUSHAL instructions in reverse order before the subroutine call. The subroutine pops the return address and then the addresses of the parameters off the stack and stores them in registers. After completing its work, the

Listing 7.2 Sample program using call by value with values in registers.

```
                .TITLE    AddVersion1
;       Program to calculate the expression S = A + B
A:              .LONG     3               ; Initialize A
B:              .LONG     7               ; Initialize B
S:              .BLKL     1               ; Save room for S

;       Subroutine Add(X, Y, Sum) for calculating Sum = X + Y
;           Input:    X in R0, Y in R1
;           Output:   Sum in R2

Add:            ADDL3     R0, R1, R2      ; Sum <-- X + Y
                RSB                       ; Return from subroutine

;       The main program:

                .ENTRY    ByValueInRegisters, 0
;           Call Add (A, B, S)
                MOVL      A, R0           ; R0 <-- A
                MOVL      B, R1           ; R1 <-- B
                BSBB      Add             ; Call the subroutine
                MOVL      R2, S           ; Save S
                $EXIT_S
                .END      ByValueInRegisters
```

subroutine pushes the return address back on the stack just before the return from subroutine. Variables are accessed with register deferred addressing. The program in the figure uses call by reference. If desired, call by value can be used instead if there are no values to be returned. You are urged to determine the contents of the stack after each instruction is processed.

If it is necessary to save some registers when passing arguments in the stack, it would be most convenient to have the main program save them with PUSHR before pushing the parameters onto the stack and restore them with POPR in the instruction following the subroutine call.

The third method simplifies the call when there are several arguments. Either the values or the addresses of the arguments are placed in an argument list, which is stored with the variables or constants in the main program. The address of the list is then passed to the subroutine. The program shown in Listing 7.4 uses this technique. It uses call by reference, although it could use call by value for the input parameters.

The **.ADDRESS** directive is used to store the addresses of the various parameters in the argument list. The method for retrieving information from the argument list is interesting and makes the subroutine easier to

Listing 7.3 Sample program using call by reference with addresses in stack.

```
        .TITLE    AddVersion2
;   Program to calculate the expression S = A + B
A:      .LONG     3                  ; Initialize A
B:      .LONG     7                  ; Initialize B
S:      .BLKL     1                  ; Save room for S

;   Subroutine Add(X, Y, Sum) for calculating Sum = X + Y
;     Input:   X, Y;   Passed by reference on stack
;     Output:  Sum;    Passed by reference on stack
;     Destroys contents of R0, R1, R2, and R3

Add:    POPL      R3                 ; Pop return address into R3
        POPL      R0                 ; Move address of X into R0
        POPL      R1                 ; Move address of Y into R1
        POPL      R2                 ; Move address of Sum into R2
        ADDL3     (R0), (R1), (R2)   ; Sum <-- X + Y
        PUSHL     R3                 ; Push return address
        RSB                          ; Return from subroutine

;   The main program:

        .ENTRY    ByReferenceInStack, 0
;       Call Add (A, B, S)
        PUSHAL    S                  ; Push address of S
        PUSHAL    B                  ; Push address of B
        PUSHAL    A                  ; Push address of A
        BSBB      Add                ; Call the subroutine
        $EXIT_S
        .END      ByReferenceInStack
```

read. The names of the arguments are equated to their displacement in bytes from the top of the argument list and act as symbolic constants. The values of the parameters are then accessed using displacement deferred addressing. The argument names are used as the offset. (Displacement addressing would be used for arguments passed by value.) Because the displacement of X is 0, register deferred addressing would be sufficient for this value.

Once again, if register saving is required, it is recommended that the registers be saved before pushing the address of the argument list on the stack and that they be restored in the instruction following the subroutine call.

To sum up, VAX subroutine calls are fairly typical of subroutine calls on many simpler machines. The VAX provides three different subroutine call instructions that are modeled after the unconditional branches. Sub-

Listing 7.4 Sample program using call by reference with addresses in an argument list.

```
            .TITLE    AddVersion3
;   Program to calculate the expression S = A + B
A:          .LONG     3                 ; Initialize A
B:          .LONG     7                 ; Initialize B
S:          .BLKL     1                 ; Save room for S

ArgList:    .ADDRESS  A                 ; Argument list passing
            .ADDRESS  B                 ;   A, B, and S
            .ADDRESS  S                 ;   by reference

;   Subroutine Add(X, Y, Sum) for calculating Sum = X + Y
;   Assumes an argument list
;   Parameter  Displacement    Use      Passed by
;       X      = 0           ; Input    Reference
;       Y      = 4           ; Input    Reference
;       Sum    = 8           ; Output   Reference
;   Destroys R2 and R3

Add:        POPL      R3                ; Pop return address
            POPL      R2                ; Pop address of argument list into R2
            ADDL3     @X(R2), @Y(R2), @Sum(R2)
                                        ; Sum <-- X + Y
            PUSHL     R3                ; Push return address
            RSB                         ; Return from subroutine

;   The main program:

            .ENTRY    ByReferenceInMemory, 0
;       Call Add (A, B, S)
            PUSHAL    ArgList           ; Push address of the argument
                                        ;   list onto stack
            BSBB      Add               ; Call the subroutine
            $EXIT_S
            .END      ByReferenceInMemory
```

routines are a convenient method for handling subprograms if an argument list is unnecessary. If arguments are needed, three different methods for handling argument lists can be adopted. Argument passing is typically performed using call by value or call by reference procedures.

Though subroutines provide a great deal of flexibility, the programmer must provide for parameter passing and must ensure that important register contents are not destroyed. In the next section we will discuss procedure calls. They perform much more work but they also reduce flexibility.

7.4 Procedures

As implemented in VAX assembly language, procedures have two important advantages compared to subroutines. The procedure call and return statements do a great deal of work for the programmer by simplifying the passing of the argument list and saving registers. Their fixed format makes it easier to have compatibility between different programmers and even different languages. Consequently, high-level languages normally use procedure calls for their subroutines, procedures, and functions. However, when these features are not needed, procedure calls require more machine overhead than subroutine calls. The rigid structure they impose may place unnecessary restrictions on particular applications.

There are two procedure call instructions and one corresponding return statement. They are

Opcode	Mnemonic	Operands	Purpose
FB	CALLS	Number of arguments, procedure name	Call with argument list in stack
FA	CALLG	Address of argument list, procedure name	Call with argument list in memory
04	RET		Return from procedure

CALLS and CALLG use general addressing for their operands. RET has no operands.

Before we can appreciate the operation of these instructions, we must understand how they handle arguments and register saves.

The Argument List

Procedure calls use a formal **argument list** whose format is shown in Figure 7.5. The first longword contains the argument count, n, in its low-order byte; the rest is filled with zeros. The arguments can be passed either by value, reference, or descriptor, depending on which is most useful for the application.

The primary difference between the CALLS and CALLG instruction is the location of the argument list. With CALLS (CALL Stack), the argument list is pushed on the user stack. CALLG (CALL General) allows it to be stored anywhere in memory—normally in the data definition or constant section. In both cases R12 serves as a pointer to the argument list. Consequently, it is normally referred to as the **argument pointer (AP)**. When we call a procedure with either CALLS or CALLG, the computer automatically puts the address of the argument list into AP for us.

```
     AP                          31                            7        0
   ┌─────┐──────────────→    ┌─────────────────────────────┬─────────┐
   │     │                   │            0                │    n    │
   └─────┘                   ├─────────────────────────────┴─────────┤
                             │           Argument 1                  │
                             ├───────────────────────────────────────┤
                             │           Argument 2                  │
                             ├───────────────────────────────────────┤
                             │               ⋮                       │
                             ├───────────────────────────────────────┤
                             │           Argument n                  │
                             └───────────────────────────────────────┘
```

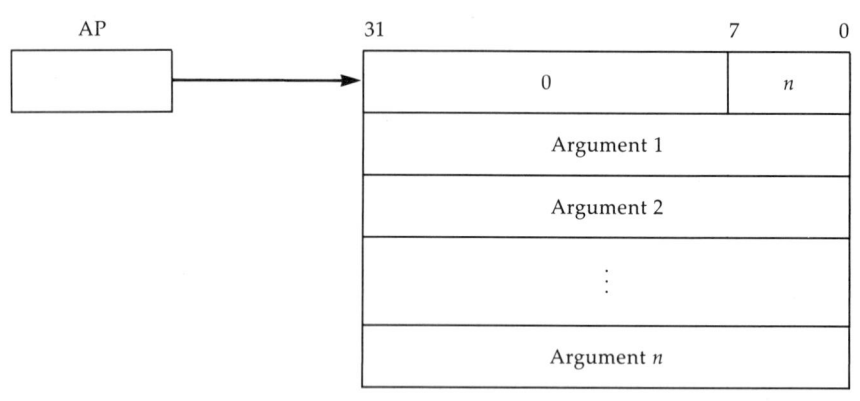

Figure 7.5 The argument list

(We can use this register for other purposes, and MACRO recognizes the symbol "R12," but such use is discouraged in any program segment that calls a procedure.)

The Entry Mask

Procedure calls automatically save the registers specified by a one-word **entry mask** that must be specified in the .ENTRY directive for every procedure. The assembler stores the entry mask in the resulting machine code. The general format of a procedure is as follows:

(data definitions, if any)
.ENTRY   procedure name, register mask
(instruction code)
RET

The machine code generated by the procedure has the following format:

(storage for data, if any)
(one word for entry mask stored at the address of the procedure)
(machine code for instructions)
(machine code for RET)

The register ask can specify any or all of the registers R2 to R11. By convention, a procedure is free to modify R0 and R1 without restoring them. However, the same convention requires saving any register in the range R2–R11 that is modified by the procedure so that it can be restored by the RET instruction. If none of these registers needs to be saved, ^M< > or 0 can be used for the register mask. The registers AP, FP, and PC are automatically saved in the call frame, which will be discussed next. It is unnecessary to save SP because its value can be determined from the other information that is preserved.

The Call Frame

A procedure call has a second standardized data structure, called the **call frame**, which is used for saving the registers and other information about the status of the process when the procedure is called. It is automatically pushed on the stack by both procedure call instructions. Figure 7.6 shows the format of the call frame. The second longword includes bits 5–15 of the PSW, bits 0–11 of the procedure's register mask, a bit that indicates whether the procedure was called by CALLS or CALLG, and two bits of alignment information (the number of bytes that were skipped to ensure that the call frame was longword aligned). The information stored in this longword allows the return instruction to reconstruct the calling program's status. For example, the portion of the register mask that is saved tells which registers are to be restored by the return instruction. The saved portion of the PSW can be copied back into that register. The first longword of the call frame is set to 0. It is reserved to allow procedures to specify the address of an optional code segment that is to be used to process run-time errors.

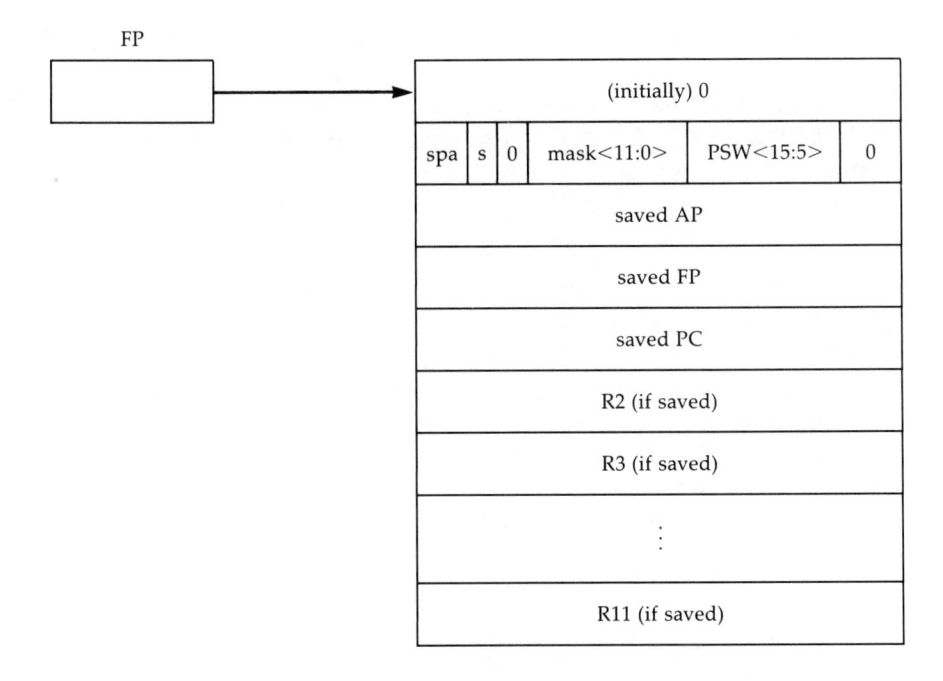

```
        FP
     ┌──────┐                 ┌────────────────────────────────────────┐
     │      │────────────────▶│            (initially) 0               │
     └──────┘                 ├─────┬───┬──────────┬────────────┬──────┤
                              │ spa │s│0│mask<11:0>│ PSW<15:5>  │  0   │
                              ├─────┴───┴──────────┴────────────┴──────┤
                              │               saved AP                 │
                              ├────────────────────────────────────────┤
                              │               saved FP                 │
                              ├────────────────────────────────────────┤
                              │               saved PC                 │
                              ├────────────────────────────────────────┤
                              │             R2 (if saved)              │
                              ├────────────────────────────────────────┤
                              │             R3 (if saved)              │
                              ├────────────────────────────────────────┤
                              │                   ⋮                    │
                              ├────────────────────────────────────────┤
                              │            R11 (if saved)              │
                              └────────────────────────────────────────┘
```

1. spa = 0 to 3 indicating number of bytes added for alignment.
2. s = 1 if CALLS, s = 0 if CALLG.
3. Bit 28 of the 2nd longword is unused and set to zero.
4. The condition codes and integer overflow trap bit in bits 0 to 4 of the PSW are cleared before being saved.

Figure 7.6 The call frame

After a procedure completes its processing, the RET instruction uses the information stored in the call frame to restore the registers and portions of the PSW to their original status. To do so, it must be able to determine where the call frame is stored. R13 is reserved exclusively to point to the call frame and is called the **frame pointer (FP)**. This is the only name recognized by the assembler for this register. CALLS and CALLG instructions push the call frame onto the stack and then put its address in FP.

Operation of the Procedure Call Instruction

We now know enough about the related issues to describe the action of call instructions. We begin with CALLS. It assumes that the arguments have already been pushed on the stack. First it pushes the argument count completing the argument list. The call frame is added to the stack. Because the stack grows upward toward smaller addresses, this process begins by pushing the registers specified by the procedure's register mask on the stack. Then the updated PC, which already contains the return address, is pushed on the stack, followed by the FP and AP. The condition codes are cleared. Finally, the longword for the status information and a longword of zeros are added to the stack. The argument pointer is assigned the address of the argument list, and the FP and SP receive the address of the call frame, which is also the top of the stack. The address of the first instruction after the procedure's entry mask is put in the PC. Then execution of the procedure can begin. CALLG works the same way except that it is unnecessary to push the number of arguments onto the stack because the complete call frame is stored in memory.

The return statement (RET) in effect reverses the process. The PSW is restored using the second longword in the call frame (clearing the condition codes). The required contents of AP, FP, and PC are taken directly from the call frame. The registers specified by the entry mask are popped from the stack. The stack pointer is restored by deleting any information that the procedure left on the stack, the call frame and, in the case of CALLS, the argument list. Instruction execution continues at the instruction following the call statement whose address was saved as the return address in the call frame. Except for bits 0–4 of the PSW, R0, R1, and any changes in memory, everything is restored to the state that existed before the procedure call.

An Example Using Procedure Calls

Listing 7.5 shows a program using a procedure that carries out the same operation as the subroutines in the previous section. It simply finds the sum of its first two arguments and stores it in the third argument. It uses call by reference, although it could use call by value for the input parameters. The procedure is called twice, to illustrate both CALLS and CALLG. Before CALLS, you must push the actual arguments onto the stack in reverse order to form part of the argument list structure. The .ADDRESS directive is used to store the addresses of the specified variables in the argument list required by the CALLG instruction. The procedure was placed after the main program, but the order could be reversed.

To make the procedure easy to read, the names of the arguments are equated to their displacement in bytes from the top of the argument list and act as symbolic constants. In the same manner as shown previously in Listing 7.4, parameters are accessed by displacement deferred addressing using the argument names as the displacements from the AP. (Displacement addressing would be used for arguments called by value.) The .PSECT statements are optional. If the procedure stored data or constants, the appropriate .PSECTs can be repeated as needed.

The operation of the program is illustrated in Figure 7.7. It shows the contents of some of the memory cells and registers at various points in the program. Each memory location represents four bytes. The initial contents of some of the registers are represented symbolically because the exact value is irrelevant to us. Because the value of the PC depends on the location of the code in the computer's memory, the PC's actual value is replaced by the instruction or macro to which the PC is pointing. All the memory addresses shown have been selected arbitrarily and may differ in an actual run.

We assume that the stack pointer was pointing to location 102C before the addresses of the three arguments were pushed on the stack by the PUSHAL instructions. The CALLS instruction completes the argument list by pushing the number of arguments on the stack. The procedure's entry mask asks that R2 be saved in the call frame. The contents of the updated PC, the current values of FP and AP, the status information, and the longword of zeros complete that data structure. The special-purpose registers are assigned their values, and control is passed to the procedure starting at the first MOVL instruction. The procedure uses R0, R1, and R2 in its calculations. During the return operation, the stack is cleaned up by resetting the SP. (The information stored on the stack normally remains in memory but is ignored.) R2, AP, FP, and PC are restored, and execution continues with the CALLG instruction. Its operation is nearly the same except that the AP points to ArgList instead of into the stack.

Some Comments

There are several reasons why procedures are not expected to save and restore R0 and R1. This policy encourages using these two registers for temporary storage and avoids wasting the time needed to push and pop their contents onto the stack with every procedure call. System proce-

Chapter 7 Stacks, Subroutines, and Procedures

Listing 7.5 Sample program with procedure calls

```
;           .TITLE    AddVersion4    Calculate sums

            .PSECT    Data,          NOEXE, WRT

A:          .LONG     2              ; Initialize A
B:          .LONG     7              ; Initialize B
S:          .BLKL     1              ; Save room for S

C:          .LONG     ^X10           ; Initialize C to 16
D:          .LONG     ^X20           ; Initialize D to 32
T:          .BLKL     1              ; Save room for T

            .PSECT    Constants,     NOEXE, NOWRT

ArgList:    .LONG     3              ; Start arg. list with length
            .ADDRESS  C              ;     Address of C (ArgList+4)
            .ADDRESS  D              ;     Address of D (ArgList+8)
            .ADDRESS  T              ;     Address of T (ArgList+12)

            .PSECT    Code,          EXE, NOWRT

;   The main program:

            .ENTRY    ProcedureCall, 0
;       Call Add (A, B, S) using CALLS
;       (Push arguments in reverse order)
            PUSHAL    S              ; Push address of S
            PUSHAL    B              ; Push address of B
            PUSHAL    A              ; Push address of A
            CALLS     #3, Add        ; Call the procedure
;       Call Add (C, D, T) using CALLG
            CALLG     ArgList, Add   ; Call the procedure again
            $EXIT_S

;   Procedure Add(X, Y, Sum) for calculating Sum = X + Y

;   Parameter  Displacement  Use       Purpose             Passed by
        X =         4;       Input     Value to be summed  Reference
        Y =         8;       Input     Value to be summed  Reference
        Sum =      12;       Output    Their sum           Reference

            .Entry    Add, ^M<R2>    ; Procedure entry point
            MOVL      @X(AP), R0     ; Get value of X
            MOVL      @Y(AP), R1     ; Get value of Y
            ADDL3     R0, R1, R2     ; Z <-- X + Y
            MOVL      R2, @Sum(AP)   ; Store sum
            RET                      ; Return from procedure

            .END      ProcedureCall
```

7.4 Procedures

Label	Address	Before CALLS	After CALLS	After RET, Before CALLG	After CALLG	After RET
A	200	2	*	*	*	*
B	204	7	*	*	*	*
S	208	?	?	9	*	*
C	20C	10	*	*	*	*
D	210	20	*	*	*	*
T	214	?	?	?	?	30
ArgList	218	3	*	*	3	*
	21C	20C	*	*	20C Arg.	*
	220	210	*	*	210 List	*
	224	214	*	*	214	*
R0		?	?	2	*	10
R1		?	?	7	*	20
R2		R.2.	*	*	*	*
AP		A.P.	─101C	A.P.	─218	A.P.
FP		F.P.	F.P.	F.P.	1014─┐	F.P.
SP		1020 ─	1004 ─	102C ─	1014─┘	102C ─
PC		CALLS	MOVL	CALLF	MOVL	$EXIT_S
User	1004	?	0	(*)	(*)	(*)
stack	1008	?	stat Call	(*)	(*)	(*)
space	100C	?	A.P. frame	(*)	(*)	(*)
	1010	?	F.P.	(*)	(*)	(*)
	1014	?	CALLG	(*)	0	(*)
	1018	?	R.2.	(*)	stat Call	(*)
	101C	?	3	(*)	A.P. frame	(*)
	1020	200	200 Arg.	(*)	F.P.	(*)
	1024	204	204 List	(*)	$EXIT_S	(*)
	1028	208	208	(*)	R.2.	(*)
	102C	?	?	?	?	?

? —Unknown and irrelevant
* —Same as before
(*) —Same as before but no longer on stack
stat—Status information, second longword in call frame

Figure 7.7 Execution of program in Listing 7.5

dures usually leave an error code in R0 indicating whether the procedure was able to complete its duties and, if not, an indication of the problem. Functions normally leave their result in R0 and possibly R1.

You may have observed a similarity between a procedure and the original program—both begin with an entry directive. This similarity occurs because the operating system treats the user's program as a procedure that is called by the operating system. The program's entry mask can be specified as 0 because the operating system does not trust the user to save the registers correctly; it preserves any important registers itself. The $EXIT_S macro is used to leave the program because it informs the operating system that the program completed its work and requests that the operating system clean up after the program. RET would normally work just as well except that the operating system may print an unneeded error message depending on the contents of R0. The sequence

```
MOVL    #1, R0
RET
```

solves this problem. In fact, if you use RET instead of $EXIT_S, the operating system calls the same procedure used by $EXIT_S.

Because procedures provide a standardized way of handling subprograms and argument lists as well as preserving registers, complicated subprogram calls are best handled by procedures. The two different procedure call instructions have different ways of handling the argument list but are compatible in the sense that many procedures can be called by either instruction. CALLG is somewhat faster as less information is pushed on the stack and may be preferred when the argument list is static. CALLS may be a better choice when the arguments are changing. Despite CALLG's name, CALLS is more general because it is easier to use in recursive subprograms.

We have finally discovered the purpose of all the VAX's general registers. Figure 7.8 provides a quick reference to their use.

Because of the extra detail needed in assembly language, it is very easy to lose track of the overall structure of a program when writing assembly language subprograms. It is important to use all the good coding techniques you have learned while writing high-level language programs. In addition, we strongly recommend that you carefully record such information as the purpose, variable type, and passing mechanism

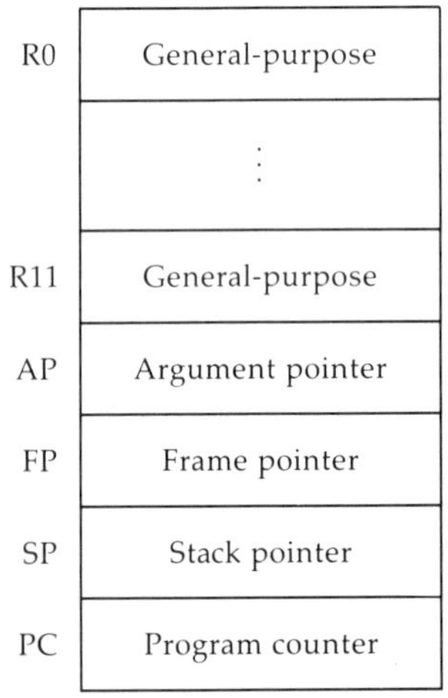

R0	General-purpose
	⋮
R11	General-purpose
AP	Argument pointer
FP	Frame pointer
SP	Stack pointer
PC	Program counter

Figure 7.8 The 16 general registers

for each parameter. Carefully follow the rules for saving registers because failure to do so may cause seemingly random errors that are very hard to locate.

7.5 Functions

In high-level languages the method for invoking a function differs considerably from that used for a procedure (subroutine), but the way these subprograms are coded normally is quite similar. The assembly language version of a function is normally programmed exactly like any other subprogram except that the function's value must be stored at some designated location where it can be found by the calling program. On many computers the result is put in one of the registers (assuming that it will fit). The language C recognizes the similarity between these two types of subprograms, and both types are called functions. In this language it is optional for a function to return a value. On the VAX the function's result is left in R0 or the R0, R1 register pair if the result is a quadword. If the result is a character string or a value requiring more than eight bytes of storage, it is treated as a phantom first argument of the subprogram. The *Introduction to VAX/VMS System Routines* manual details the calling conventions.

For example, suppose that we must calculate the quantity

$$(x_1 + x_1 + \ldots x_n) * (y_1 + y_2 + \ldots y_n)$$

for some arbitrary value of n and lists of floating-point numbers $x_1, x_2, \ldots, x_n$ and $y_1, y_2, \ldots, y_n$. Calculation of this quantity can be simplified by using a function that finds the sum of n numbers for us. The program ProductOfSums uses a function Sum for this purpose. Sum has two arguments: N is the number of values and is passed by value. List is passed by reference; that is, the address of the first number in the list is passed. The use of the function makes the algorithms for both the main program and the function quite straightforward.

The program uses both CALLG and CALLS to illustrate the use of both instructions. This normally would not be done unless there were good reasons for treating one call differently from another.

The symbolic debugger's CALL command can be used to test procedures or functions. For example, while testing this program with the debugger, we could issue the command

```
CALL Sum(6, List1)
```

Listing 7.6 A program using a function

```
                .TITLE      ProductOfSums
;   Calculates the product of the sums of two lists

;   Algorithm:
;       1.  Calculate sum of List1
;       2.  Calculate sum of List2
;       3.  Find Result, the product of the sums

Length = 5                              ; Number of elements in List

;   Variables:
Result: .BLKF       1
List1:  .FLOAT      2.5,    2.113,  2.3,    1.23,   7.213
List2:  .FLOAT      1.34,   12.32,  12.35,  4.26,   3.12

;   Argument list:
ArgList2:
            .LONG       2               ; Number of arguments
            .LONG       Length          ; First argument, by value
            .ADDRESS    List2           ; Address of second argument

            .ENTRY      ProductofSums, 0

;   R3 <-- Sum(Length1, List)
Start:      PUSHAF      List1           ; Push argument list in
            PUSHL       #Length         ;    reverse order
            CALLS       #2, Sum         ; Call function
            MOVF        R0, R3          ; Save result in R3

;   R0 <-- Sum(Length2, List2)
            CALLG       ArgList2, Sum   ; Call function

;   Result <-- R3 * R0
            MULF3       R3, R0, Result

Done:       $EXIT_S

;   * * * * * * * * * * * * * * * * * * * * * * * * * * *

;   Function Sum (N, List)

;   Returns the sum of N values stored in List.

;   Argument list:
;   Variable    Offset      Purpose             Type        Passed by
    N           = 4;        Number of values    Longword    Value
    List        = 8;        List of values      Float       Reference
```

Listing 7.6 (continued)

```
;   Register use:
;   R0          Sum
;   R1          Counter
;   R2          Address of next item in List

;   Algorithm:
;       1.  Initialize the sum to 0, set up the counter and
;           address of first element.
;       2.  While counter > 0 do
;               Add element to sum.
;               Decrement the counter.

        .ENTRY      Sum, ^M<R2>

;   Initialize:
        CLRF        R0                  ; Set Sum to zero
        MOVL        N(AP), R1           ; Copy value of N to R1
        MOVL        List(AP), R2        ; Copy address of List to R2

;   Calculate the sum:
Loop:   ADDF2       (R2)+, R0           ; Add value to Sum,
                                        ;   incrementing the address
        DECL        R1                  ; Decrement counter by 1
        BGTR        Loop                ; Repeat if not finished

        RET                             ; Finished, leave sum in R0

        .END        ProductOfSums
```

The function would be executed and the result returned in R0. It is important to pass the exact information required by the procedure. Sum requires the value of N and the address of a list.

7.6 Separately Assembled Subprograms and the Linker

A major advantage of using subprograms is that they can be written, assembled, and tested separately from the remainder of the program. This is particularly helpful when the coding for a long task is divided between several programmers who are responsible for distinct coding segments. When this is done, the program and subprograms are in different source files, which are assembled separately into different object files. The linker is used to combine these object files into one executable file that can be run. In this section we will look at how programs can be broken into separate units. There are three issues that we should discuss before attempting to take advantage of distinct assembly units. We will discuss local and global labels first, then the structure of the various units, and finally the required VAX/VMS system commands. After an example, we will look at the operation of the linker.

Writing Separate Program Units

When a program is broken into distinct assembly units, the labels or symbol names in a particular unit are not usually known to other segments because the code is assembled at different times. This can be an advantage when several people write different parts of the program because it is possible to pick labels for one segment without having to verify that they are not being used in another. However, this introduces some new problems. For example, how does the main program know where the subprogram's entry point is located? The answer is that the different segments must specify which labels are to be known globally instead of just locally within the particular code segment. The assembler passes this information on to the linker, which makes the necessary connections between the various segments.

A program can notify the assembler that a certain label is located in a different code segment by use of the .EXTERNAL directive. For example, if Sub is a separately assembled subprogram, the calling program could include the statement

.EXTERNAL   Sub

(The use of .EXTERNAL is optional in MACRO, which, unlike many other assemblers, assumes that any undefined labels are external unless it has been instructed otherwise. This assumption is not always wise because the assembler cannot provide warnings about incorrectly typed or omitted labels. Instead the linker produces error messages when it cannot find the invalid and missing labels in any of the code segments it has been supplied. If desired, you can use the directive

.DISABLE GLOBAL

which tells MACRO that undefined labels are to be considered errors unless they are specified as external.)

There are several ways that a subprogram can tell the assembler that one of its labels or symbols can be used externally. Many assemblers use a directive like .GLOBAL, which is available on the VAX. However, MACRO suggests the use of some alternatives. Recommended methods of declaring names as being global include using a double colon (::) when assigning labels or using a double equal sign (= =) when defining a constant in a direct assignment statement. The .ENTRY directive declares that a procedure's entry point can be used externally. For example, consider the statements

```
Value == 60
        .ENTRY    Proc,  ^M<R3>
Sub::   MOVW      A, B
```

Value, Proc, and Sub are globally defined.

While assembly language programmers have a great deal of freedom in arranging program segments, the simplest format for separately assembled programs and subprograms is shown in Figure 7.9.

There are several observations that we should make about the format of the various code segments. The code for programs begins with the .ENTRY directive because the operating system treats them as procedures. Subroutines cannot use the .ENTRY directive because it stores the entry mask, which would be misinterpreted by a subroutine call. The program terminates execution with $EXIT_S to inform the operating system that it has completed its work, while subroutines and procedures

```
Main program
        .TITLE ProgName   (optional)
;  remarks
(direct assignments)
(variable storage)
(internal subprograms, if desired)
        .ENTRY ProgramName, 0
(program code)
        $EXIT_S           ;terminate program
(internal subprograms, if desired)
        .END    ProgramName
```

```
Separate subroutine                    Separate procedure
        .TITLE ModuleName                      .TITLE ModuleName
;  remarks                             ;  remarks
(direct assignments)                   (direct assignments)
(variable storage)                     (variable storage)
Subname:: ...                                  .ENTRY ProcName, mask
(code)                                 (code)
        RSB    ; return                        RET      ; return
(other subprograms)                    (other subprograms)
        .END                                   .END
```

Figure 7.9 Format of code segments

return control to the calling program with RSB and RET, respectively. While all three types of segments use .END to tell the assembler that it has come to the physical end of the segment, only the .END statement of the segment containing the main program includes the name of the entry point where program execution is to begin. It is perfectly legal to include several subprograms in one code segment, and a subprogram may call other subprograms in the same or different segments.

The VMS commands needed to assemble and link programs and subprograms stored in different files are rather simple. For example, suppose that we have a main program stored in MAIN.MAR and a subprogram stored in SUB.MAR. The following commands could be used.

```
$ MACRO /DEBUG MAIN
$ MACRO /DEBUG SUB
$ LINK /DEBUG MAIN, SUB
$ RUN MAIN
```

Clearly /DEBUG is not always required and should be used only when appropriate. Several object modules can be combined by one link command if the program has been broken into several pieces. The name for the .EXE file is determined by the first object file mentioned in the LINK statement.

If you use the Symbolic Debugger, you may find that using the optional .TITLE directive in a subprogram file is particularly helpful. The linker considers each programming unit as a separate module and uses the titles for the names of those modules. The debugger command

```
SET MODULE   ModuleName
```

tells the debugger that it should recognize the names of the symbols in that module.

An Example of a Separately Compiled Subprogram

As an example, we will write a Function Factorial(K) and then a program that calls the function. The quantity K! (K factorial) can be calculated using the formulas

$$K! = 1 * 2 * \ldots * K \quad \text{if } K \geq 1$$
$$0! = 1$$

Factorials are defined only for nonnegative integers. The parameter K will be passed by reference.

If K is positive, a loop is needed to carry out the multiplication. We have already seen that it is often more efficient to count down from K to

1 than to count up from 1 to K. That way we can exit the loop when the counter reaches 0. Before entering the loop, we will have to set the product to 1 and then multiply it by the value of the counter within the loop. With some care, we can devise an algorithm that does not need an extra test for the special case K = 0. We have designed the algorithm shown in Listing 7.7 with those ideas in mind. When K = 0, the MOVL @K(AP), R2 sets the zero (Z) bit in the PSW so that the BLEQ instruction causes a branch to Done. For other values of K, the DECL instruction sets the zero flag when the counter is decremented to 0. This causes the BLEQ instruction to branch out of the loop. In either case R0 will have the desired functional value when execution reaches Done and the function returns control to the calling program.

The code in Listing 7.7 is only one solution to our problem. You can easily find others.

The value of K! increases rapidly as K increases. Because the value of the function is returned as a longword, the largest factorial that can be calculated as 12! = 479,001,600. 13! exceeds the largest signed integer the VAX can hold in a longword.

The main program found in Listing 7.8 tests our function by calculating the number of permutations of N things taken R at a time. This quantity, which is sometimes denoted $P(N,R)$, can be calculated as $N!/(N - R)!$. The program uses the function to calculate both of the factorials and then divides to obtain the desired result. CALLS has been used to call the function, though CALLG could be used instead. The labels Start and Finish have been added for convenience when using the debugger.

Although this program provides a nice illustration of using functions, you may have observed that they could be calculated more efficiently using the formula

$$P(N,R) = N * (N - 1) * \ldots * (N - R + 1)$$

In the next two sections we will discover how to call the function from a high-level main program and then demonstrate how the function could be calculated using recursive techniques. But first we will look at the linker.

The Linker

A **linker** is a program that accepts the object files produced by an assembler or compiler and produces an executable file that can be run. The role of a linker depends on the computer and operating system. Some assemblers and compilers carry out the function of a linker and produce code that is ready to run. This is more common on smaller computers or with assemblers or compilers that have been designed for speed rather

Listing 7.7 The function Factorial

```
            .TITLE      Factorial
;   Function Factorial (K)     Calculates K! for 0 <= K <= 12
;
;   Argument List:
;   Parameter   Offset   Purpose                Type       Passed by
;   K           =   4    ; Function argument    Longword   Reference
;
;   Result:
;   K!   returned as a longword in R0
;
;   Algorithm:
;      1.  Initialize Factorial = 1, Counter = K
;      2.  While Counter > 0 do
;              Multiply Factorial by Counter
;              Decrement Counter

            .DISABLE    GLOBAL

            .ENTRY      Factorial,      ^M<R2>

Begin:      MOVL        #1, R0          ; Initialize K Factorial
            MOVL        @K(AP), R2      ; Get K for Counter

Loop:       BLEQ        Done            ; Branch if Counter <= 0
            MULL2       R2, R0          ; Multiply R0 by Counter
            DECL        R2              ; Decrement Counter
            BRB         Loop            ; Repeat at loop

Done:       RET                         ; Return from subroutine

            .END
```

than versatility. Some systems link the program automatically every time it is run. Moreover, the amount of work the linker is required to carry out depends on the nature of the machine language and the operating system.

We know that the object files produced by an assembler (or compiler) contain executable machine language instructions. But additional code is often needed before the program can be run. Perhaps the program specifies external labels or symbols. The assembler can seldom supply these items. Instead the names of the symbols together with a list of locations where they are used in the program is added to the object file. For example, the Permutations program in Listing 7.8 uses the external entry point Factorial twice. The object file would include its name and

Listing 7.8 The program Permutations

```
        .TITLE    Permutation
; Calculation of P(N,R) - the number of permutations
; of N things taken R at a time using a function for
; evaluation of Factorials

; Method:  Calculate P(N,R) using N!/(N - R)!

        .DISABLE GLOBAL

; Uses external function Factorial
        .EXTERNAL Factorial

; Program Variables:
N:          .LONG   5
R:          .LONG   2
PNR:        .BLKL   1               ; P(N,R)
NMinusR:    .BLKL   1               ; N - R

; The main program:
        .ENTRY    Permutations, 0

;       R3 <-- N!
Start:  PUSHAL    N                 ; Push address of N
        CALLS     #1, Factorial     ; Calculate N!
        MOVL      R0, R3            ; Save N!

;       R0 <-- (N - R)!
        SUBL3     R, N, NMinusR     ; Calculate N - R
        PUSHAL    NMinusR           ; Push address N - R
        CALLS     #1, Factorial     ; Calculate (N - R)!

;       P(N,R) <-- quotient
        DIVL3     R0, R3, PNR

Finish: $EXIT_S

        .END      Permutations
```

pointers to where it is used. (MACRO marks external symbols with an X in the symbol table at the end of its listings.)

Other symbols may be specified as global. This can happen because the name is specified in a .GLOBAL or .ENTRY directive, or the symbol is followed by a "::" or "= =" in the assembly code. The names of these symbols must also be included in the object file so that the linker can match up external and global symbols.

Programs may directly or indirectly call system subprograms stored in a library of subprograms. For example, in Chapter 8 we will learn that the $EXIT_S macro calls the procedure SYS$EXIT. When the LINK instruction is sent to the operating system, it is unnecessary to specify the file holding this procedure. Instead the linker automatically searches a system-supplied library and adds any required code to our program. In fact many operating systems allow users to create and maintain their own object file libraries. This is done with the $ LIBRARY system command in VAX/VMS.

The linker's job is to create a single executable file out of the various object files supplied to it. This may mean placing the value of an external symbol at each place it is needed. If a subprogram was called with relative addressing, the linker must calculate the proper displacements and insert them into the code.

The linker's job may be complicated by certain features of a language. For example, if we use .PSECT to create program sections in our MACRO program, the exact order in which the linker will put the segments is unknown to the assembler. Consequently, it cannot determine offsets from one section to another. The linker must calculate these displacements after it arranges the program sections. You can tell which values must be determined by the linker when you look at a MACRO assembly listing because the assembler marks them with an apostrophe.

Unlike the VAX, some computers use absolute addressing extensively. This is fine if the assembler or compiler knows where the code will be located in the computer's memory when it is run. However, this is often very difficult. Again the linker comes to the rescue. The assembler typically supplies relative addresses that the linker converts to absolute addresses when it determines where the code is to be located. Note that sometimes even the linker does not know exactly where the code will be placed during a run. This is especially true on some multiuser computers where the code's location depends on available memory at run time. In this case the loader, which loads the executable image of the program, must determine the actual addresses. Clearly this increases the time needed to load a program. Avoiding this problem is one reason absolute addressing is little used on a VAX.

7.7 Linking High-Level Languages with MACRO

Writing and debugging assembly language programs is often a time-consuming and difficult task. The resulting programs cannot be transferred to different types of computers. Consequently, many programmers try to avoid assembly language whenever possible. However, this

7.7 Linking High-Level Languages with MACRO

is not always feasible. Certain tasks may be impossible or too difficult in a given high-level language. Sometimes programs in high-level languages execute too slowly. (This is a common problem when using interpreted BASIC.) In these cases is it necessary to write long, complicated assembly language programs? Fortunately, the answer is often no. It is common to write most of a program in a high-level language and call simple assembly language subprograms to carry out tasks that are impossible, impractical, or inefficient in the high-level language. This may be an effective way to produce quality code at a reasonable cost. It may even be useful to have libraries of assembly language subprograms that can be called from high-level languages. In this section we will look at the process of linking high-level language main programs with assembly language subprograms.

You might be asking "Is this really possible?" The answer depends on the language and its particular compiler. Some languages handle subprograms as **external subprograms**. The compiler treats them as being separate compilation units even if they are physically in the same file. A linker is used to connect the various object modules into an executable image. Most FORTRAN compilers allow separately compiled subprograms, and the programmer can substitute subprograms written in assembler for ones written in FORTRAN without making any changes in the FORTRAN main program.

Some other languages, such as standard Pascal, treat routines as **internal subprograms**; that is, subprograms are written and compiled as part of the program. Though standard Pascal makes no provisions for separately compiled routines, many compilers for this language provide special, nonstandard features that make separately compiled subprograms possible. This is true for VAX Pascal. In fact the VMS operating system has its own standards, which ensure that the compilers for various languages have a common set of subprogram-calling methods that make it possible to mix high-level language programs not only with assembler subprograms but also with subprograms written in other high-level languages.

Is mixing languages easy? It depends. If an assembly language subprogram is called from a high-level language, the subprogram must meticulously match the subroutine linkage methods used by the high-level language. Rules for saving and restoring registers must be followed carefully. One must be sure that the data types of the parameters are matched properly.

The rigid structure imposed by the CALLS and CALLG instructions helps solve many of the potential compatibility problems on the VAX. However, these procedure calls do not restrict the choice of passing mechanisms. Consequently, the operating system's designers have provided standards that tend to provide some uniformity in this area.

Except for C, most languages on the VAX use pass by reference to pass simple numerical data and either pass by reference or pass by descriptor for character strings. For those cases where the convention is not appropriate, high-level languages on the VAX usually provide some nonstandard features that allow the programmer to specify an alternate passing mechanism.

In this section we will look at three popular languages—FORTRAN, Pascal, and C—that are available in VAX/VMS and at main programs in those languages that use the Factorial function of the previous section. We will also discuss the methods for specifying optional argument-passing mechanisms in each language.

The command language needed to compile, link, and run programs that combine languages is straightforward. The following steps assume a Pascal main program. The command PASCAL would be replaced by the appropriate word for the other languages. Suppose that the main program is stored in Main.Pas, and the subprogram is in Sub.Mar.

```
$ PASCAL Main
$ MACRO Sub
$ LINK Main, Sub
$ RUN Main
```

C users must specify the appropriate libraries that must be searched for standard functions.

/DEBUG was not specified in these commands because the main program provides the I/O. If there are difficulties, the symbolic debugger can be specified in the compile, assemble, and link steps. The debugger instructions SET MODULE and SET LANGUAGE may be required to use it effectively.

VAX FORTRAN

FORTRAN programmers have few problems calling assembler subprograms. VAX FORTRAN normally passes numbers by reference; numerical arrays are passed by referencing the address of the first element of the array. Character strings are passed by descriptor. If the subprogram agrees with these conventions, the main program is identical to one calling a subprogram written in that language. For example, see Listing 7.9, which uses the Function Factorial of the previous section to inefficiently calculate P(N,R), the permutation of N things taken R at a time.

When necessary, nonstandard passing mechanisms may be specified to match the requirements of a particular subprogram. This information is included in the call statement or function use. The passing mechanism is specified in the format of a function: %**Val( )** is used for pass by value, %**Ref( )** for pass by reference, and %**Descr( )** for pass by descriptor. %Descr is the default for character strings; %Ref is the default for the other types of arguments. For example, consider the subroutine call

```
call Proc (%Val(N), %Ref(X), %Descr(Name))
```

Listing 7.9 FORTRAN program using function Factorial

```
*      FORTRAN main program using assembly language
*      function Factorial to calculate P(N,R).

       integer  N, R, NPR, Factorial

       print *, 'Enter values for N and R'
       read *, N, R
       NPR = Factorial(N)/Factorial(N - R)
       print *, 'Number of permutations =', NPR
       end
```

N is passed by value, X is passed by reference, and Name is passed by descriptor. Assuming X is real and name is declared as a character string, only the %Val for integer N is actually required in this call statement. The defaults for X and Name are sufficient.

VAX Pascal

Standard Pascal uses internal subprograms. Procedures and functions are written and compiled as part of the program. Because this poses severe restrictions on programs written in this language, VAX Pascal (Version 2.0 and above) has several nonstandard features that allow external routines and permit the programmer to specify the passing mechanism to be used with each parameter, if needed.

External subprograms are declared in the program in much the same way as standard procedures with a function or procedure statement giving the subprogram's argument list. The word **external** replaces the rest of the subprogram's definition.

Pascal defines two kinds of subprogram arguments, value parameters and variable parameters. But VAX Pascal passes all variables by reference. Pascal assumes that the subprogram will make a copy of any value argument and then use the copy in its processing. However, if the parameter is marked "var" in the subprogram's declaration, the procedure will use the original storage location in all calculations. It is very important to mark any parameter in the subprogram's declaration with "var" if the value of the variable is to be changed. Failure to do so may cause unpredictable results, especially if the compiler optimizes the code.

The parameter K of the Factorial routine of Listing 7.7 satisfies the requirements for a value parameter because the code copies the value of the parameter into a register in its initializing steps. The original value is never used again. Listing 7.10 gives a VAX Pascal program that uses the function.

Listing 7.10 Pascal program using function Factorial

```
program Permutations (input, output);

{ Pascal main program using assembly language
  function Factorial to calculate P(N,R) }

var  N, R, NPR:  integer;

function Factorial (K:  integer):  integer;  external;

begin
  writeln ('Enter values of N and R');
  readln (N, R);
  NPR := Factorial(N) div Factorial(N - R);
  writeln ('Number of permutations = ', NPR);
end.
```

If it is necessary to pass parameters by some means other than by reference, it is possible to specify the passing mechanism in the subprogram declaration. VAX Pascal provides four argument-passing declaration symbols: **%Immed** is used for pass by value; **%Ref** forces call by reference and implies that the subprogram might change the parameter's value; **%StDescr** is used to specify that a fixed-length string will be passed by descriptor; and **%Descr** is used to indicate call by descriptor for variable-length strings and other data needing descriptors.

For example, suppose that the external procedure Sum is being called. Assume that it has three parameters: the first is an integer passed by value; the second is a real passed by reference; and the third is a fixed-length string (packed array of char) passed by descriptor. The following declaration can be used.

```
procedure Sum (%Immed N:  integer;  %Ref X:  real;
               %StDescr Name:  String);  external;
```

The %Ref is optional if the procedure does not change the value of X. In most cases %Ref can be replaced by var, if desired. %Immed and %StDescr are required because the variables would be passed by reference otherwise.

VAX C

C is designed to encourage the use of external subprograms. Further, it is somewhat unusual in that the standard language definition allows for the programmer to select the passing mechanism of each argument. Most parameters are passed by value. Arrays (including strings) are passed

Listing 7.11 A C program using function Factorial

```
/*      C main program using assembly language
        function Factorial to calculate P(N,R)      */

main ()
{
    int     N, R, NPR, NMinusR, Factorial();

    printf ("Enter values for N and R\n");
    scanf ("%d%d", &N, &R);
    NMinusR = N - R;
    NPR = Factorial (&N) / Factorial (&NMinusR);
    printf ("Number of permutations = %d\n", NPR);
}
```

by reference to the first element in the array. If a variable must be passed by reference, the address operator "&" can be used to specify that the address of the variable is to be passed. Programmers can create structures to pass items by descriptor if necessary.

Listing 7.11 shows a VAX C program using the function Factorial. Observe that the function name is declared as an integer. The programmer must explicitly calculate and store N − R so that the address of the resulting variable can be passed.

The above program was tested with the VAX C compiler version 2.0–003 under versions 4.1 and 4.2 of VAX/VMS. The following command sequence was used.

```
$ DEFINE LNK$LIBRARY SYS$LIBRARY:VAXCRTL
$ CC ProgramFile
$ MACRO SubprogramFile
$ LINK ProgramFile,SubprogramFile
$ RUN ProgramFile
```

Somewhat different ways of taking care of the required library would be needed with earlier versions of VAX C. Different libraries might be needed with other programs.

Some Comments

It is fairly common for compilers and interpreters to provide some kind of support for calling assembly language subprograms from high-level language programs. Coding portions of a program in a high-level language may improve programmer efficiency, program readability and transportability while allowing critical portions of the program to be written in assembly language. Sometimes it is convenient to test assembly language subprograms with high-level language main programs that handle I/O.

As we have seen many languages running on a VAX under VMS provide excellent support for calling subprograms written in different languages. This is accomplished by standardizing the calling sequences as much as allowed by the particular language and adding nonstandard features as necessary.

For further information about calling subprograms, consult the language manuals for the particular language involved. The *Introduction to VAX/VMS System Routines* manual includes a lengthy section specifying the standards for parameter passing.

7.8 Recursive Subprograms

Sometimes it is useful to state an algorithm for a particular task in a recursive manner. That is, the algorithm is defined in terms of itself. For example, we could calculate K factorial using the following formulas:

$$K! = K * (K - 1)! \quad \text{for } K = 2, 3, 4, \ldots$$
$$K! = 1 \quad \text{for } K = 0, 1$$

To calculate 4! using this formulation, we observe that

$$\begin{aligned} 4! &= 4 * 3! \\ &= 4 * (3 * 2!) \\ &= 4 * 3 * (2 * 1!) \\ &= 4 * 3 * 2 * 1 \end{aligned}$$

This concept is frequently useful in computer science. A subprogram that calls itself is called a **recursive subprogram**. Some languages, such as FORTRAN, do not allow recursive subprograms, but many new languages, such as Pascal and C, do. Recursive programming on some computers is quite difficult because their architecture does not assist the programmer in writing recursive code. However, recursive programming is convenient on machines that have stacks.

We must solve three problems before a routine can call itself. Actually it is not particularly difficult for a subprogram to call itself—the problem occurs when trying to return after the call. For example, suppose that the computer was designed so that a call statement would automatically store the return address in the first word of the routine's code. Such a computer is useful if recursion is forbidden. The return statement would simply be a branch to the address stored in the first word of the routine. However, if the procedure called itself, the address for the second call would be stored in exactly the same location as the original return address. It would be impossible to return to the original calling program. The existence of a stack greatly simplifies this type of coding. Each time the procedure is called, the return address is pushed onto the stack. Each time there is a return instruction, the last return address is popped off the stack and used.

The argument list poses another problem. In general, a new argument list is needed each time the procedure calls itself because the parameters passed to the routine may be different. The stack provides a convenient place to find room for these structures. The CALLS instruction on the VAX is particularly convenient in recursive coding.

There is a third problem. What if the procedure needs storage space for a new set of variables each time it is called? While there is more than one way to solve this problem, it is convenient to store the new set of variables on the stack. Each time the procedure is called, the routine can reserve the necessary room on the top of stack. The frame pointer provides a convenient way to reference this space on the VAX.

We will demonstrate recursive coding with the Factorial function. The initial algorithm is straightforward if we assume that K is nonnegative.

```
If the current K ≤ 1 then
    K! = 1
else
    K! = K * (K − 1)!
```

Observe that when K is positive, the quantity K − 1 is actually needed twice—to carry out the comparison K ≤ 1 and to calculate (K − 1)!. As it is passed by reference, it must be stored somewhere in memory. There are several methods for handling this storage, but we will take the same approach that the VAX Pascal compiler uses. The technique will satisfy a broad variety of situations. Each time we enter the procedure, we immediately reserve room for this variable on the stack with

```
SUBL2    #SpaceNeeded, SP
```

where SpaceNeeded is a constant representing the total storage requirements of the procedure. (We subtract because the stack grows in the negative direction.) SpaceNeeded equals four bytes in our example because only one longword must be stored. How do we access this space? Recall that the stack pointer and frame pointer are equal when the procedure

Listing 7.12 A recursive version of function Factorial

```
            .TITLE      Factorial
;   Function Factorial (K)

;   Calculates K!  for 0 <= K <= 12 using recursion.

;   Argument List:
;   Parameter   Offset   Purpose               Type       Passed by
;   K           = 4      ; Function argument   Longword   Reference

;   Result:
;   K!  returned as a longword in R0

;   Algorithm (Assumes K is nonnegative):
;     1.  Find room on stack for local variable
;     2.  Get K and calculate K - 1
;     3.  If K - 1 <= 0 then
;             Factorial <-- 1
;         else
;             Factorial <-- Factorial(K - 1) * K

;   Register usage:
;   R0          Returns K factorial
;   R2          Holds K

;   Local Storage:
KMinus1        = -4       ; K - 1
LocalStorage   =  4       ; Number of bytes of local storage needed

            .ENTRY      Factorial,   ^M<R2>

Begin:      SUBL2       #LocalStorage, SP    ; Make room on stack for
                                             ;    local variable

            MOVL        @K(AP), R2           ; Put K in R2
            SUBL3       #1, R2, KMinus1(FP)  ; Calculate K - 1

            BGTR        Bigger               ; If K - 1 <= 0 then
            MOVL        #1, R0               ;     Factorial <-- 1
            BRB         Done                 ; else
Bigger:     PUSHAL      KMinus1(FP)          ;     Factorial <--
            CALLS       #1, Factorial        ;         Factorial(K - 1)
            MULL2       R2, R0               ;         * K

Done:       RET                              ; Return from procedure

            .END
```

7.8 Recursive Subprograms

is entered. Moreover, the FP remains constant during the procedure's execution. We can use negative offsets from the FP to locate variables in the space reserved on the stack. We define these offsets as symbolic constants and use them in much the same way as offsets into the argument list.

The resulting code is shown in Listing 7.12. It contains the final algorithm. CALLS is used to calculate $(K - 1)!$ because a new argument list will be needed each time the procedure calls itself.

This version of the function can be called by any variant of the main program that we looked at in the previous two sections. The initial call can be done with either CALLG or CALLS even though CALLS is preferred when the procedure calls itself.

To see how the stack is used by this procedure, suppose that it is called using a CALLS in the main program when $K = 3$. The main program pushes its argument list and the call frame on the stack, so we would see the following arrangement before executing the first instruction in the procedure.

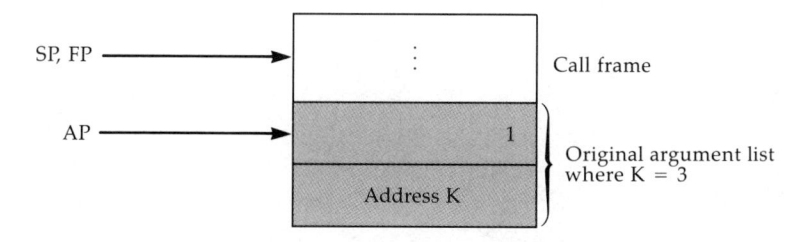

The function immediately requests room for four bytes on the stack and stores $K - 1$. At this point the stack looks like this.

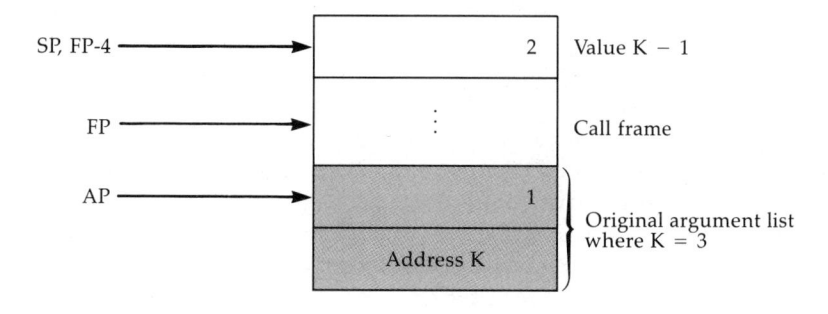

The function adds to the stack as it calls itself for $K = 1$ and $K = 2$. When $K = 1$, the stack looks like the diagram at the top of the next page.

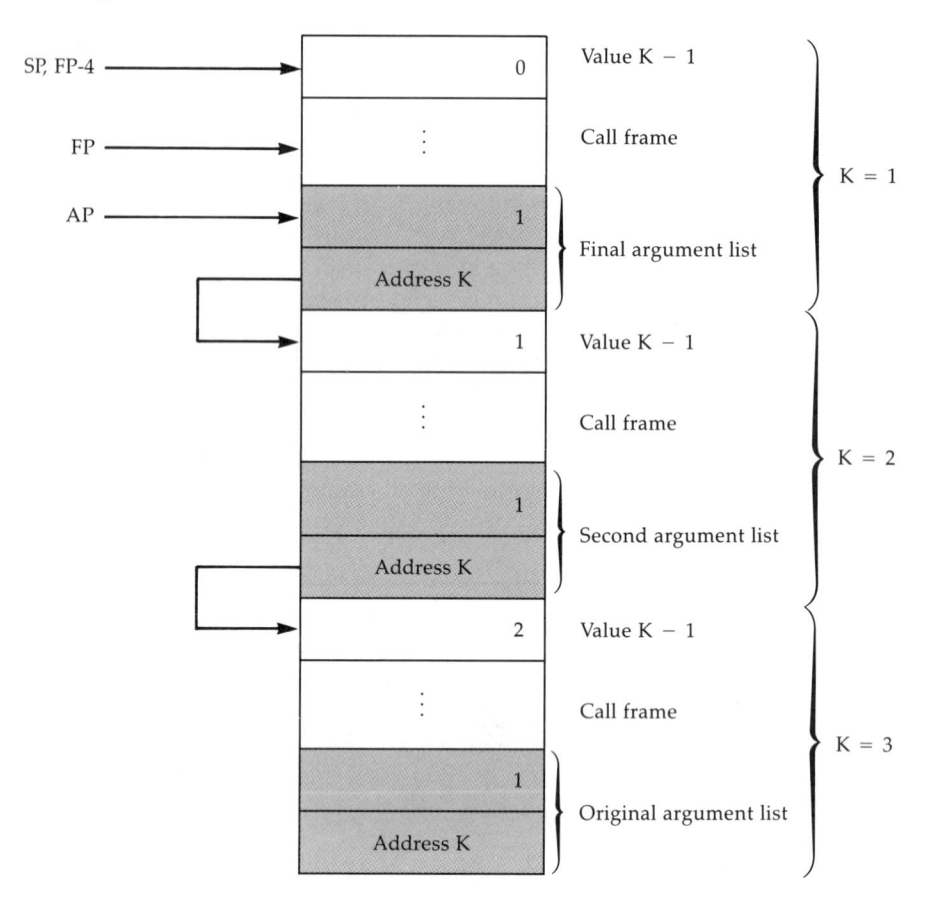

```
SP, FP-4 ──────────►  ┌─────────────┐
                      │      0      │  Value K − 1        ⎫
       FP ──────────► ├─────────────┤                     ⎪
                      │      ⋮      │  Call frame         ⎬ K = 1
       AP ──────────► ├─────────────┤                     ⎪
                      │      1      │ ⎫                   ⎪
                      ├─────────────┤ ⎬ Final argument list
                 ┌──► │  Address K  │ ⎭                   ⎭
                 │    ├─────────────┤
                 │    │      1      │  Value K − 1        ⎫
                 │    ├─────────────┤                     ⎪
                 │    │      ⋮      │  Call frame         ⎬ K = 2
                 │    ├─────────────┤                     ⎪
                 │    │      1      │ ⎫                   ⎪
                 │    ├─────────────┤ ⎬ Second argument list
            ┌────┼──► │  Address K  │ ⎭                   ⎭
            │    │    ├─────────────┤
            │    └────│      2      │  Value K − 1        ⎫
            │         ├─────────────┤                     ⎪
            │         │      ⋮      │  Call frame         ⎬ K = 3
            │         ├─────────────┤                     ⎪
            │         │      1      │ ⎫                   ⎪
            │         ├─────────────┤ ⎬ Original argument list
            └────────►│  Address K  │ ⎭                   ⎭
                      └─────────────┘
```

The procedure stores the value of K − 1 on the stack each time it is called. It then passes this address as the address of K when it calls itself. Consequently, the value for K − 1 at one level serves as the value of K at the next level of recursion.

You may have observed that using recursive subprogramming in this problem is actually quite inefficient because the computer must do a fair amount of work to push all the required information onto the stack. Part of the difficulty in this program is that the value K was passed by reference. The program would have been simpler and more efficient if call by value were used. Recursive subprograms may make inefficient use of computer time and/or memory for simple tasks such as calculating factorials. However, in more complicated situations recursive procedures may be much easier to program than equivalent nonrecursive procedures and may represent efficient use of programmer time. It may be best to use other techniques when they are obvious and use recursion when the most natural algorithm is recursive.

Summary

In this chapter we have introduced some concepts that can help improve program modularity and simplify coding.

Stacks are an important data structure in their own right. They are also an essential part of the calling mechanism used for subprograms on many computers, including the VAX. The autoincrement and autodecrement addressing modes simplify stack operations. The operating system provides every program with a large block of storage for the user's stack and some convenient instructions that simplify its use.

Two types of subprogram calls are available on the VAX. The subroutine calls (BSBB, BSBW, and JSB) execute rapidly because they do not provide any automatic way of saving registers or passing arguments. Programmers must take care of these matters with extra coding. The procedure calls (CALLS and CALLG) have a very formal way of saving registers and passing arguments. Consequently, they provide convenience and standardization but waste some run time if their extra features are unneeded. The argument list and call frame are used to pass parameters and save the status of the process when procedures are called.

Three different ways to pass arguments were discussed. Call by value and call by reference were used in sample programs. We will cover call by descriptor in Chapter 9 when it is used to pass character strings.

Subprograms can be referred to as subroutines, procedures, or functions in high-level languages. At the machine level, functions differ from other subprograms only in that a function returns a value (normally in R0).

It is often convenient to assemble subprograms separately from the programs that use them because it aids in debugging, simplifies group coding projects, and makes it easier to reuse routines in different programs. Calling assembly language subprograms from high-level languages permits coding much of the program at a higher level but allows the power of an assembly language when needed.

Recursive coding can be a productive coding technique in some difficult problems. Stacks simplify writing this type of code.

We introduced some new assembler directives that aid in modularizing subprograms. The .PSECT directive allows breaking a program into sections having distinct purposes and then specifying those uses. For example, the programmer can specify that the section for variable storage can be written into but not executed. Other new directives include .DISABLE GLOBAL and .EXTERNAL. The symbols "::" and "= =" as well as .ENTRY can be used to specify that symbols are to be known globally.

Four of the so-called general-purpose registers have special uses. In addition to the program counter, they include the argument pointer, which points to the argument list, the frame pointer, which points to the call frame, and the stack pointer, which holds the address of the top of the user stack.

Exercises

1. What are the contents of the user stack and the stack pointer after the following instructions are processed? Assume that X is stored at location (21A)$_{16}$ and the initial contents of the registers and variable X are as shown.

MOVL	#5, -(SP)	R2 = 00000385
PUSHL	X	R3 = 01234567
PUSHAL	X	SP = 00034230
PUSHR	#^M<R2, R3>	
		X = AAAABBBB

2. What are the contents of the variable Y and the registers R2, R4, R7, and SP after the following instructions are processed? Assume that the initial contents of the program counter and memory are as shown.

POPR	#^M<R2, R4>	SP = 0004 431C
POPL	R7	
MOVL	(SP)+, Y	0004 431C = 00000481
		0004 4320 = 12345678
		0004 4324 = 00001253
		0004 4328 = AAAABBBB

3. (Manual search.) Show how the SOBGTR instruction can be used to replace

   a. The DECW, BGTR sequences in Listing 7.1. (Hint: Number must be changed to a longword and MOVW to MOVL. Why?)

   b. The DECL, BGTR sequence in Listing 7.6.

4. (Manual search.) Rewrite the Factorial function of Listing 7.7 with either SOBGEQ or SOBGTR. Does the use of one of these instructions simplify the code?

5. The autoincrement and autodecrement addressing modes are unavailable on many computers. Show how stacks can be handled on such computers by writing a MACRO code segment that will push an item onto a program-defined stack and another to pop this stack without using these addressing modes.

6. a. Stacks on the VAX normally grow from high memory to low memory. Explain how stacks that grow from low memory to high memory could be coded on the VAX.

   b. Rewrite and test the program in Listing 7.1 so that instead of

using the user stack, it uses a program-defined stack area in which the stack grows from lower memory addresses to larger ones.

7. a. Explain the terms *call by value, call by reference* and *call by descriptor.*
   b. Explain the difference between subroutines and procedures in VAX assembly language.

8. Suppose that variables A, B, and S are stored at memory locations 200, 204, and 208. Also assume that the instruction following the BSBB is at location 382. Fill in the chart showing the contents of any registers or memory locations that are changed during the execution of the specified program.

Memory or Register	Initial Value	Before BSBB	After BSBB	Before ADDL3	Before RSB	After RSB
S	0					
R0	2BCD					
R1	A1					
R2	378					
SP	2014					
User Stack						
2008	0					
200C	24A					
2010	0					
2014	16					

a. Execute the program in Listing 7.2.
b. Execute the program in Listing 7.3.
c. Execute the program in Listing 7.4.

9. Write a program that uses a subroutine call to implement a function $F(x,y)$ that calculates the expression
$$x^2 + 3xy - y^2 - 3$$
To demonstrate the different ways to pass values, pass x by value and y by reference and return the result in R0. The program should evaluate $4 * F(x,y)$. Assume that all values are in floating point.

a. Pass the arguments in registers.
b. Pass the arguments in the stack.
c. Use an argument list.

10. Hand assemble the following code segments. Start each program code segment at location 240, argument lists at location 210, and code segments for subroutines and procedures at location 820. Assume that X is stored at location 21A.

   a.
   ```
           PUSHL   R5
           BSBW    Sub
           POPL    R5
   ```

b.
```
        .ENTRY   Proc, ^M<R3, R7, R9>
        MOVL     @4(AP), R3          ; Passed by reference
        MOVL     8(AP), R7           ; Passed by value
        DIVL3    R3, R7, R9
        ADDL3    #2, R9, @4(AP)
        RET
c. AList: .LONG   2
        .ADDRESS X                    ; Pass by reference
        .LONG    25                   ; Pass by value
d.      CALLG    AList, Proc
e.      PUSHAW   X
        CALLS    #1, Proc
```

11. Consider the following code:

```
X:      .LONG    10
Y:      .BLKL    1

Arg:    .LONG    2
        .ADDRESS X
        .ADDRESS Y

A = 4
B = 8
        .ENTRY   Proc, ^M<R3>
        ADDL3    #16, @A(AP), R3
        MULL3    #2, R3, @B(AP)
        RET

        .ENTRY   Main, 0
        CALLG    Arg, Proc
        PUSHAL   Y
        PUSHAL   X
        CALLS    #2, Proc
        $EXIT_S
        .END     Main
```

Supply the values of any memory locations or registers that are changed. Assume that X is stored at location 200, Y in 204, and Arg begins in 208. Use the given symbolic values and use the mnemonic of the next instruction instead of its address in the PC.

Memory or Register	Initial Value	After CALLG	Before RET	After RET	Before CALLS	Before RET	After RET
Y	0						
R3	65						
AP	A.P.						
FP	F.P.						
SP	2028						
PC	CALLG						

User Stack

2004	?
2008	?
200C	?
2010	?
2014	?
2018	?
201C	?
2020	?
2024	?

12. Rewrite the program in Listing 7.12 so that the parameter K is passed by value. Notice that it is no longer necessary to store K − 1 in memory.

Note: In Exercises 13–23 write and test an assembly language procedure called by a main program written in the manner specified below. Use appropriate I/O in high-level language main programs.

    a. Include the assembly code for the main program in the same file as the procedure.
    b. Store the assembly code for the main program in a different file than that in which the procedure is stored.
    c. Write the main program in Pascal.
    d. Write the main program in FORTRAN.
    e. Write the main program in C.
    f. (Manual search.) Write the main program in BASIC.
    g. (Manual search.) Write the main program in COBOL.
    h. Write the main program in the high-level language of your choice.

13. Write a function ITON(I,N) that calculates I to the N for integers I and nonnegative integers N using an appropriate loop. Use pass by reference and longwords. Write a main program that tests the function.

14. Repeat Exercise 13 but write the function in a recursive manner by observing that

    If N = 0 then ITON(I,N) = 1
        else ITON(I,N) = I * ITON(I,N − 1)

15. Write a function XTON(X,N) that calculates X to the N for floating-point numbers X and longword integers N (possibly negative or 0). Write a main program to test the function.

16. Write a function P(N,R) that calculates the number of permutations of N things taken R at a time efficiently as

$$P(N,R) = N * (N - 1) * \ldots * (N - R + 1)$$

Use longwords. Assume $0 \leq R \leq N$. Write a main program to test the function.

17. Write a procedure Sort(List, N) that sorts a list of N longwords stored in List. Assume that longword N is relatively small so that a bubble or insertion sort is appropriate. Write and test a main program using the procedure. Use pass by reference.

18. Write a procedure FindMax(List, N, Maximum) that returns the Maximum value in the List of N floating-point values. Write a main program to test the procedure.

19. If a language does not require declaring procedures in programs that call them, it may be possible to call an assembly language subprogram that has a variable-length list of arguments. Write a function MINIMUM(X, Y, . . ., Z) that finds the minimum of the arguments, X, Y, . . ., Z. Recall that the first number in an argument list is the number of arguments. Test the function with a program that calls it three times with one, two, and five arguments if the language permits this. Otherwise, test it in slightly different programs, using one, two, and five arguments in the different versions of the test program.

20. Write a function GCD(X,Y) that calculates the greatest common divisor of two positive longword integers X and Y using the following algorithm:

    While $X \neq Y$ do

    replace X by $|X-Y|$ and Y by the smaller of X and Y

    To test, write a program that finds the sum of two fractions given their numerators and denominators. (For example, given the fractions $\frac{4}{3}$ and $\frac{1}{6}$, calculate the sum $\frac{3}{2}$.)

21. Repeat Exercise 20 but use the following recursive algorithm:

    If X = Y then GCD(X,Y) = X

    else GCD(X,Y) = GCD($|X-Y|$, smaller of X and Y)

22. Write and test a function IRandom (Seed, Biggest) that calculates a uniformly distributed random integer in the range 1, 2, . . ., Biggest. Seed, Biggest, and the functional value are longwords. A typical random number generator is not really random but calculates a sequence of pseudorandom numbers based on the Seed. The user picks the initial value of the Seed, and the function updates the Seed each time it calculates a new random number. The following algorithm is suggested:

    1. Seed ← (69069 * Seed + 1) mod 2^{32}
    2. Temp ← Seed * Biggest
    3. IRandom ← (Temp div 2^{32}) + 1

    The calculation in the first step is the same as used in many of the random number generators (for example, RND in BASIC and MTH$RANDOM in the Runtime Library) supplied with VAX/VMS. Because 2^{32} is one larger than the largest unsigned, 32-bit integer on the VAX, coding is simpler than the algorithm suggested. Notice that if Seed is treated as an unsigned longword and longword calculations are used for 69069 * Seed + 1, the 32-bit result is exactly the new Seed because the high-order portion is ignored. In step 2 extended multiplication is needed to calculate quadword Temp. However EMUL treats Seed as a signed integer. If the product is negative, we must add Biggest to the most significant half of the product to correct for this. The integer division in step 3 can be accomplished by just using the high-order part of Temp. This step can be carried out by a simple addition.

One test of a random number generator is to calculate a large number of integers and count the number of times each possible integer appeared. If a Pascal main program is used, the Seed must be a variable parameter. When used in useful programs such as simulating games of chance or random events, the initial Seed should be different in each run.

23. Write the following procedures carrying out standard arithmetic with complex numbers. Represent complex numbers as a record or array of two floating-point values. The first represents the real part of the complex number, and the second represents the imaginary part. Pass complex numbers by reference to the address of the real part.
    a. Procedure ComplexAdd (A, B, C) where C ← B + A
    b. Procedure ComplexSub (A, B, C) where C ← B − A
    c. Procedure ComplexMult (A, B, C) where C ← B * A
    d. Procedure ComplexDiv (A, B, C) where C ← B/A
    e. Procedure ComplexConjugate (A, C) where C ← conjugate of A.
    f. Have the main program calculate the complex conjugate of the complex expression

    (A * B + C)/(D − E)

    for several values of complex numbers A, B, C, D, and E.

24. Write and test a main program that creates a list of up to 20 random integers and then sorts them using the procedures written for Exercises 17 and 22. Examine (print) the list of numbers before and after sorting. The main program can be written in any of the ways suggested in the note before Exercise 13.

CHAPTER CONTENTS

8.1 INTRODUCTION TO MACROS

8.2 ALTERNATE FORMATS FOR ARGUMENTS

　Local Labels
　Default Values
　Keyword Arguments

8.3 AN EXAMPLE USING MACROS WITH ARGUMENT LISTS

8.4 SOME ADVANCED FEATURES

　Argument Concatenation
　Passing Symbolic Constants
　　for Numerical Values
　Passing Character Strings
　Determining the Number
　　of Positional Arguments
　Finding the Length of a
　　Character String

8.5 CONDITIONAL ASSEMBLY AND REPETITION

　Conditional Assembly
　Repeat Blocks
　An Example

SUMMARY

EXERCISES

CHAPTER 8

Macros

Subprograms, commonly available in both high- and low-level languages, are one means of simplifying coding and improving program structure. Many advanced assembly languages provide another tool called macros. A **macro** is a named sequence of assembly language instructions that the assembler inserts into the code wherever its name appears in the opcode column of a program. As you may expect from its name, MACRO, the assembly language used with VAX/VMS, has been designed to allow very sophisticated uses of this programming tool.

The word *macro* has several uses in this chapter. We will try to avoid confusion by writing them in the following manner: MACRO will be used as the name of the VAX/VMS assembly language, while macro represents the assembly language tool discussed in this section. In addition, the directive **.MACRO** is used to define a macro in MACRO, and you will use $ MACRO to tell VMS that you want to run this assembler.

After introducing the fundamental concepts about macros, we will cover some additional argument types and follow the discussion with an example. In the fourth section we suggest some special techniques that are helpful when using macros. Then we will introduce the idea of conditional assembly and repetition, concepts often associated with macros but useful even when macros are not needed. The features covered in the first two sections are typical of those found in many assemblers and form a basic introduction to macros. The directives in sections 8.4 and 8.5 are representative of those in more advanced assemblers and are of interest to those wishing to become proficient in assembly language.

Chapter 8 Macros

8.1 Introduction to Macros

Suppose that it is necessary to clear registers R0–R3 several times in a program. This can be done by coding

```
CLRL      R0
CLRL      R1
CLRL      R2
CLRL      R3
```

each time this is required. If this had to be done 20 times in a program, 80 lines of code would have to be written. However, the program can be simplified and shortened by defining a macro that we will call ClearReg.

```
.MACRO    ClearReg
    CLRL      R0
    CLRL      R1
    CLRL      R2
    CLRL      R3
.ENDM     ClearReg
```

The .MACRO line names the macro and begins the macro definition. The .ENDM directive terminates it. The four lines between these directives are called the **body of the macro**. The macro's definition, which must appear before its use, is normally placed near the beginning of the program.

To **call** or **invoke** this macro when we need to clear the four registers, we can simply code

```
ClearReg                      ; Clear registers R0 to R3
```

The assembler would substitute the four lines in the body of the macro for ClearReg each time it is specified. The resulting machine code is exactly the same as if you had coded the four instructions in the body of the macro instead of simply mentioning the macro's name.

You should understand that an assembler does this substitution before it generates the machine language code for the program. As a result, using macros does not affect the amount of machine code generated or change the time required to run the resulting program. That is, the code segment

```
MOVL      R2, X
ClearReg
ADDL2     Y, R3
```

and the code segment

```
MOVL    R2, X
CLRL    R0
CLRL    R1
CLRL    R2
CLRL    R3
ADDL2   Y, R3
```

produce identical machine code.

There are several predefined macros included in various libraries supplied with the VMS operating system. Their names begin with a dollar sign ($). We have been using one of them already, the $EXIT_S macro. Perhaps you have already observed that the assembler substitutes the code

```
PUSHL   #1
CALLS   #1, G^SYS$EXIT
```

when we code

```
$EXIT_S
```

SYS$EXIT is a system-provided procedure that properly terminates the run of a program and returns control to the operating system.

There are some similarities between macros and subprograms. Both can be used to shorten a program's source code and improve its readability, and both can have argument lists. But there are important differences. The assembler does not generate any code when a macro is defined. Instead, the body of the macro is substituted into the program each time the macro's name appears in the program's opcode column. The resulting code is then assembled. The assembler generates code for subroutines and procedures when they are defined. The appropriate subprogram call instructions are used to transfer control to the subprogram during the run. Though both macros and subprograms can reduce source program length, use of a macro does not affect either the length of the machine code or the program's run time. On the other hand, use of a subprogram may increase run time because of the subprogram linkage that must be executed each time the routine is entered and exited. However, it may reduce the length of the program's machine code if the subprogram is used several times. Another distinction is that subprograms are useful only if they produce machine code, while macros can also be used for data definitions and symbolic constant definitions.

The complete format of a macro definition is as follows:

```
.MACRO      macroname    argumentlist
    .
    .
    .
body of macro
    .
    .
    .
.ENDM       macroname
```

Repeating the macro's name on the .ENDM line is optional but improves readability. Macros are called with statements of the following form:

```
label:      macroname    actual-argumentlist
```

The label is optional. The macro name and the formal or symbolic argument names have the same form as labels. In this book macro bodies will be indented to improve readability.

The argument list may have several formats. The simplest is just a list of symbolic names called **formal arguments** or, sometimes, dummy arguments. The symbolic names may represent labels, instructions, or operands. When we invoke the macro, the **actual arguments** specified in the call statement replace the formal arguments. For example, consider the macro AdjustR5, which allows various calculations with register R5.

```
            .MACRO      AdjustR5    Label, Inst, Arg1, Arg2
Label:      Inst        Arg1, R5
            Inst        Arg2, R5
            .ENDM       AdjustR5
```

If it is necessary to subtract X and R2 from R5, we could code

```
            AdjustR5    Reduce, SUBL2, X, R2
```

MACRO would substitute the code

```
Reduce:     SUBL2       X, R5
            SUBL2       R2, R5
```

The assembler replaces the symbolic names of the formal arguments in the body of the macro by the actual arguments used in the statement invoking the macro. It carries out this substitution by replacing the characters in the formal argument name by the characters in the corresponding actual argument.

As a more useful example, consider the following macro:

```
.MACRO      CallProc    Value, Kind
        ; Calls the procedure Proc using CALLS
    PUSHAL      Kind        ; Push address second argument
    PUSHL       Value       ; Push value first argument
    CALLS       #2, Proc    ; Call Proc
.ENDM       CallProc
```

If we call the macro with

```
    CallProc    #35, Sum
```

the assembler would generate code for

```
    PUSHAL      Sum
    PUSHL       #35
    CALLS       #2, Proc
```

The above examples illustrate the most common way of handling parameters for macros. The formal and actual arguments are matched strictly in the order determined by their position. We will discuss some alternate argument formats in the next section.

By default, MACRO does not print the expansion of macros in listings. Sometimes it may be useful to look at the expansions. This is particularly true when you are being introduced to this topic and need examples showing how they work. The expansions are also very helpful when debugging programs with errors in the macro calls. If you want to look at their expansion, you can use the directive

```
    .SHOW       ME
```

to tell the assembler to show the macro expansions and

```
    .NOSHOW     ME
```

to suppress these expansions.

The code in some of the system-supplied macros used later in this book is extremely long and normally should not be listed. If a listing is needed, you may prefer to use

```
    .SHOW       MEB
```

The resulting output shows only the lines in the macro that actually generate binary code. This can significantly reduce the length of the output and improve the readability of some macro expansions and is highly recommended for these situations. This option is also recommended when the I/O macros given in Appendix F are used. You can turn off this output by using

```
         .NOSHOW    MEB
```

If macro expansions are needed only occasionally, you may prefer to request the expansions with a qualifier on the $ MACRO command. You can do this by using

```
    $ MACRO /SHOW = MEB /LIST ProgramName
```

for example.

8.2 Alternate Formats for Arguments

Some assembly languages allow optional, more sophisticated methods of specifying arguments for macros. MACRO has three. These special formats help simplify the use of macros.

Local Labels

Sometimes we must generate statement labels in macro expansions. Writing a particular label in the body of a macro's definition will cause the duplicate label error if the macro is used more than once in a given program. For example, suppose that we wrote the macro

```
              .MACRO   Error
              BEQL     OK
              CLRL     R0
    OK:       .ENDM    Error
```

The macro would work perfectly the first time it is used. However, an error would occur the second time because the label OK would be repeated. We could make the label one of the regular arguments for the macro as we did previously in the AdjustR5 macro, but the user may tire of supplying seemingly meaningless parameters. In MACRO we can specify local labels in the macro's argument list. A **local label** is a label having the form n\$ where n is an integer. We can instruct the assembler to create a unique local label by including a symbolic name for the label preceded by a question mark in the argument list. The assembler will automatically generate a value for the label without forcing the programmer to supply the label's name.

Suppose that a "move absolute value" instruction would be convenient while writing a particular program. Although the VAX does not provide such an instruction, we can simulate it with the following macro:

```
        .MACRO    MoveAbs   X, Y, ?Neg, ?Cont
                          ; Move absolute value of X to Y
        TSTL      X                ; Test X
        BLSS      Neg
        MOVL      X, Y             ; Copy X to Y if X >= 0
        BRB       Cont
Neg:    MNEGL     X, Y             ; Copy -X to Y if X < 0
Cont:   .ENDM
```

Each time the assembler expands the macro, it will assign a new label of the form $n\$$ to the local labels Neg and Cont. The first local label will be assigned the value 30000$, and the numerical portion will be incremented by 1 each time a new local label is encountered. The MoveAbs macro could be used in the following manner:

```
        MoveAbs   A, R0      ; Move absolute value of A to R0
        MoveAbs   R2, B      ; Move absolute value of R2 to B
```

The following code would be generated

```
            TSTL      A
            BLSS      30000$
            MOVL      A, R0
            BRB       30001$
30000$:     MNEGL     A, R0
30001$:
            TSTL      R2
            BLSS      30002$
            MOVL      R2, B
            BRB       30003$
30002$:     MNEGL     R2, B
30003$:
```

Although it is not common, we can supply a value for a label argument when calling the macro.

Default Values

We often encounter another situation when we use macos. A macro may need parameters whose values are changed only rarely. MACRO provides a way to simplify the code for this situation by permitting us to assign defaults for parameters. A **default** is a value that will be assigned the symbolic name if no value is supplied by a formal parameter. We can specify defaults for a particular formal argument by coding

    ArgumentName = DefaultValue

in the argument list for the macro.

For example, consider this situation. A certain program must define records having a data structure consisting of a list of longwords, preceded by a longword specifying the length of the list and followed by a longword with an end-of-list mark. The list normally has 10 elements, and the end-of-list value is normally 0. The following macro will simplify defining the structure.

```
           .MACRO    MakeList    Name, Length=10, EndMark=0
Name:      .LONG     Length              ; Number of elements
           .BLKL     Length              ; Reserve room for list
           .LONG     EndMark             ; End-of-list mark
           .ENDM
```

The value of each parameter is shown for the following sample calls.

		Resulting Values		
Statement		Name	Length	Endmark
MakeList	A	A	10	0
MakeList	B, 20, -1	B	20	-1
MakeList	C, , -1	C	10	-1

In this application, the programmer wanted to use the default for the second argument even though a value was required for the third argument. The double comma informs MACRO that a value is not being provided for Length.

Keyword Arguments

Some macros need a lengthy list of parameters, but only a few are actually used in most calls to the macro. For this reason some assembly languages, like MACRO, allow keyword arguments when calling a macro. That is, instead of having to specify arguments in the same order as given in the macro definition, the macro call may list the arguments for which values are needed in any order using the format

    ArgumentName = Value

Coding and documentation are simplified because we need only specify those values whose default is inappropriate. For example, the following statements use the MakeList macro shown previously. We note that a value for name is required because it was not given a default.

		Resulting Values		
Statement		Name	Length	Endmark
`MakeList   Name=D, -`		D	30	10
`          EndMark=10, Length=30`				
`MakeList   EndMark=5, Name=E`		E	10	5

The dash in the first MakeList instruction means that the instruction on that line will be continued on the next line. (We will need to use this continuation mark frequently in Chapters 8, 9, and 11.)

We can specify actual arguments in several ways. If no value is supplied, the default value is used, if provided in the macro's definition. We can supply the actual values in positional order in the normal fashion or specify them in any order using the keyword format.

8.3 An Example Using Macros with Argument Lists

The following example illustrates the use of macros with argument lists. Suppose that we must write a procedure that processes an array of records containing information about the players on a baseball team. Each player's record will contain the following fields: ID, number of times at bat, number of singles, number of doubles, number of triples, number of home runs, and the batting average. We will store each field (item in the record) as a longword, with the batting average 1000 times its actual value. The records are to be sorted in descending order by batting average. The procedure will be called SortTeam and has two parameters: (1) the number of players that will be processed (20 or less) and (2) the name of the array holding the player records, called Team. Both parameters are passed by reference. The list of records, each consisting of seven longwords, will be stored consecutively, starting with the first record.

There are many ways to handle the problem. We selected one that is readable and moderately efficient. Perhaps you can think of some other solutions.

Although high-level language programs typically number arrays of items starting with 1, it will be easier to start counting at 0 in assembly language. Consequently, the first record in the list of players and the first field in the record will be numbered 0.

The choice of sorting method used in this procedure is not overly critical because there are at most 20 players. We have chosen to use an insertion sort because it is somewhat more efficient than a bubble sort. The algorithm, after adjusting the subscripts to start at record 0, is as follows:

For I going from 1 to (Number of players − 1) do
1. Copy the player record Team[I] into Temp
2. Set J = I − 1
3. While J ≥ 0 and the average in record Team[J] is less than the average in record Temp do
3a. Copy the record Team[J] into Team[J + 1]
3b. Decrement J by 1
4. Copy record Temp into Team[J + 1]

Two operations in this algorithm are complicated by the fact that we are working with a list of records instead of individual items: copying a record and determining if the average for the player in Team[J] is less than the average in Temp. In a high-level language we might implement the copy operation as a procedure. In assembler it is convenient to use macros for both steps.

A copy macro could be used for three different operations.
Temp ← Team[I]
Team[J + 1] ← Team[J]
Team[J + 1] ← Temp

At first these operations seem somewhat incompatible at the assembly language level because of the various ways that subscripts are used. To use one macro for all three operations, we conceptually replace the record Temp by an array having one record, Temp[0], which will have the same address as Temp. Such a tactic is common in assembly language, which does not impose artificial constraints such as those found in a high-level language such as Pascal.

The MoveRecord macro shown in Listing 8.1 carries out the copy operation for us. "From" is the address of the list we will copy from, and "FromSub" is the subscript of the desired record. If we want to copy the record containing Temp, the subscript will be 0. Consequently, we make 0 the default for FromSub. Likewise, "To" is the address of the list we will copy to and "ToSub" is the desired subscript. It is also defaulted to 0.

Selecting the addressing modes is another important consideration. Because the array of records is passed by reference to the address of the first record, Team[0], and because this address is used frequently, we will store it in a register (say, R3) to allow rapid access to the value it points to. Although the index addressing mode is convenient for processing one of the VAX's standard data lengths, it is not immediately helpful when we are processing records consisting of seven longwords. We must calculate the number of longwords in the list that precede the desired address and store this value in a register before we can use the index mode. For example, suppose that we want to look at the tenth record in the list. (Remember that this record will be numbered 9 because the first

8.3 An Example Using Macros with Argument Lists

Listing 8.1 Procedure to sort records by batting average

```
        .TITLE    SortProcedure

; Procedure to sort an array of records in descending order
; according to the contents of the average field

; Argument list:
; Parameter   offset    purpose                  data type         passed by
Number        = 4     ; Number of records        longword          reference
Team          = 8     ; Records for team         array of          reference
                      ;   members                  records
; Other constants:
Length = 7            ; Number of fields (longwords) in record
Ave = 6               ; The number of the field containing average

        .SHOW     MEB

;                   * * * * * * * * * * *

        .MACRO    MoveRecord    From, FromSub=#0, -
                                To, ToSub=#0, ?Loop

; Copies a record with Length bytes from
; From[FromSub] to To[ToSub].

                ; Get address of From[FromSub]
        MULL3     #Length, FromSub, R0    ; R0 <-- longwords before From[FromSub]
        MOVAL     From[R0], R1            ; R1 <-- address of From[FromSub]

                ; Get address of To[ToSub]
        MULL3     #Length, ToSub, R0      ; R0 <-- longwords before To[ToSub]
        MOVAL     To[R0], R2              ; R2 <-- base address To[ToSub]

                ; Move the longwords
        MOVL      #Length, R0             ; Put counter in R0
Loop:   MOVL      (R1)+, (R2)+            ; Move next longword
        SOBGTR    R0, Loop                ; Decrement counter and repeat
                                          ;   if needed
        .ENDM     MoveRecord

;                   * * * * * * * * * * *

        .MACRO    CompareField    AddressTeam = R3

; Compares the SortField in Team[J] to the corresponding field in Temp.
```

(continued)

Listing 8.1 (continued)

```
                ; Get address of field in Team
        MULL3   #Length, J, R0          ; R0 <-- longwords before Team[J]
                ; Compare fields
        CMPL    4*Ave(R3)[R0], 4*Ave+Temp
                                        ; Set condition flags
    .ENDM       CompareField

;                       * * * * * * * * * * * *

;   Local storage:
        .PSECT  LocalVar        NOEXE, WRT
I:      .BLKL   1                       ; Outer loop counter
J:      .BLKL   1                       ; Inner loop counter
JPlus1:
        .BLKL   1                       ; J + 1
Temp:                                   ; Save room for a record of
        .BLKL   Length                  ;   Length longwords

;   Register usage:
;       R0-R2       temporary storage in macros
;       R3          address of Team

;                       * * * * * * * * * * * *

        .PSECT  ProcCode        EXE, NOWRT
        .ENTRY  SortTeam  ^M<R2, R3>
Start:          ; Initialize
        MOVL    Team(AP), R3            ; R3 <-- address of Team
        MOVL    #1, I                   ; I <-- 1

OuterLoop:  ; Put record Team[I] in proper place
        CMPL    I, @Number(AP)          ; If I >= Number
        BLSS    L1                      ;   then
        BRW     Done                    ;     the list is in order
L1:     MoveRecord From=(R3), FromSub=I  - ; Temp <-- Team[I]
                To=Temp
        SUBL3   #1, I, J                ; J <-- I - 1

InnerLoop:  ; Find the correct place for Temp
        ADDL3   #1, J, JPlus1           ; JPlus1 <-- J + 1
        BEQL    Insert                  ; If JPlus1 = 0, insert Temp
        CompareField
        BGEQ    Insert                  ; Branch if location found
        MoveRecord From=(R3), FromSub=J, -; Team[J+1] <-- Team[J]
                To=(R3), ToSub=JPlus1
        DECL    J                       ; Decrement J
        BRB     InnerLoop               ; Repeat inner loop
```

Listing 8.1 (continued)

```
    Insert:       ; Insert Temp into proper place
        MoveRecord From=Temp, -           ; Team[J+1] <-- Temp
                   To=(R3), ToSub=JPlus1
        INCL       I                      ; Increment outer loop counter
        BRW        OuterLoop

    Done:                                 ; Return
        RET

        .END
```

record is numbered 0.) There are nine records or 9 * 7 = 63 longwords preceding this record. If we put 63 into register R0, the address of this record could be stored in R1 with

```
    MOVAL    (R3)[R0], R1
```

(Recall that we stored the address of Team in R3.)

To copy the record, we have used a loop and autoincrement addressing. One local label (Loop) is needed for this. If desired, we could have avoided the overhead of the loop. We could have processed the record more efficiently by using three MOVQ and one MOVL instructions to process the seven fields in the record.

The CompareField macro does not need any arguments because we use it only once to compare the average fields in Team[J] and Temp. We can write the address of the average field in Temp into the program because it is fixed. The number of bytes in the record that precede the average is given by 4 * Ave. We add this quantity to the address of Temp to determine the address of its average field. (Notice that the order of the calculations in the program ensures that multiplication precedes addition.) We handle the address of the proper field in Team[J] much as we did in MoveRecord except that we must again adjust for the fact that Ave is not the first field in the record. We will use indexed displacement addressing. The index will take care of the records that precede the desired record. The displacement is the number of bytes that precede the desired field and is added to the address of Team, which was stored in R3.

The use of macros allows us to code the main part of the procedure in a very straightforward manner. Observe that the code is quite general. Changing the size of the record or the field on which the sort is based would not affect the coding of the sort portion of the procedure, only the macros. The program's algorithm differs from the one stated earlier only in that J + 1 is calculated and stored at the beginning of the while loop so that it can be used as needed.

Listing 8.2 shows a simple Pascal program that can be used to test the sort program. If we were to use a FORTRAN main program instead, we could not declare a record. Instead, we would dimension Team using

```
Integer   Team(7, 20)
```

and use subscripts to pick the field and record. Because FORTRAN stores the array by columns, the first subscript is the number of fields, while the second is the number of records. Notice that in either language, the high-level main program subscripts the "records" 1 to 20 even though the procedure subscripts them 0 to 19. This is permitted because the programs do not communicate the value of the subscripts, only the address of the first record.

Listing 8.2 Pascal main program to call sort procedure.

```
program Sort (input, output);

type   PlayerType = record
             ID, AtBat, Single, Double, Triple, HR, Ave:   integer;
       end;
       TeamArray = Array [1 .. 20] of PlayerType;

var    N, I:   integer;
       Team:   TeamArray;

procedure SortTeam (N: integer; var Team: TeamArray); external;

begin
  writeln ('Enter number of players');
  readln (N);
  writeln ('For each player enter ID, at bats, singles, doubles, ');
  writeln ('triples and home runs in that order.');
  for I := 1 to N do
    with Team[I] do begin
        readln (ID, AtBat, Single, Double, Triple, HR);
        Ave := Round(1000 * (Single + Double + Triple + HR)/AtBat)
    end;   {with}
  SortTeam (N, Team);
  for I := 1 to N do
    with Team[I] do
        writeln (ID:3, AtBat:4, Single:4, Double:4, Triple:4,
                 HR:4, Ave/1000:10:3)
  end.
```

8.4 Some Advanced Features

In this section we will discuss some special features of the MACRO language. Consult the *VAX MACRO and Instruction Reference Volume* for additional detail and other directives.

Argument Concatenation

It is sometimes useful to use **argument concatenation**, that is, join an argument with other text. We can do that in MACRO by using an apostrophe as a **concatenation operator**. For example, suppose that we want a copy macro that can operate with more than one variable type. We can include the variable type as one of the parameters. Consider the macro Copy.

```
        .MACRO   Copy    Type, X, Y
           MOV'Type   X, Y
        .ENDM    Copy
```

We would include the standard instruction type suffix in the actual argument list to specify the desired variable type when invoking the macro. For example, the statement

```
        COPY    W, X, R0
```

would generate the code

```
        MOVW    X, R0
```

Also note that apostrophes should not be used to delimit character strings within macros because they might be interpreted as concatenation operators.

Passing Symbolic Constants for Numerical Values

If we pass a symbolic constant as an actual argument, MACRO normally substitutes the characters in the constant's name into the code. Sometimes we prefer to have it substitute the constant's value. To have it substitute the decimal value of an actual argument in the macro call, we precede the symbolic constant with a backslash (\). The backslash is especially helpful when the formal argument has been concatenated with other text. For example:

```
            .MACRO   Clear   Value
            CLRL     List'Value
            .ENDM    Clear
    Data = 6
            Clear Data
            Clear \Data
```

The resulting code is

```
            CLRL     ListData
            CLRL     List6
```

In the first call Data is not preceded by a backslash, and the characters in the symbol's name are used. In the second call the special character is used, so the value of Data is appended to the word List.

Passing Character Strings

Passing character strings containing separators such as blanks, tabs, commas, or semicolons as actual arguments for macros presents an interpretation problem to the assembler. To prevent ambiguous situations, enclose such character strings inside a pair of angle brackets (< >). For example, suppose that we write a macro to generate a message using the .ASCII directive.

```
            .MACRO   Message   Text=<His name is Fred>
            .ASCII   /Text/
            .ENDM    Message
```

Observe that if we omit the angle brackets around the character string, the assembler would assume that the default for Text is "His" while "name", "is", and "Fred" are three more arguments.

If we call this macro using

```
    FredName: Message
    MaryName: Message    <Her name is Mary>
```

the following code would be generated:

```
    FredName:   .ASCII   /His name is Fred/
    MaryName:   .ASCII   /Her name is Mary/
```

You may detect that there is still a potential problem. What if we need to pass a register mask including angle brackets? In this case we can designate a different symbol to act as the delimiter by preceding it with a circumflex. For example, consider the macro

```
.MACRO    PushReg    Mask=^"^M<R3, R4>"
  PUSHR   Mask
.ENDM     PushReg
```

The first circumflex says that quotation marks will serve as the delimiters for "^M<R3, R4>". If we invoke the macro with

```
PushReg                    ; Push registers R3 and R4
PushReg  ^/^M<R5>/         ; Push register R5
```

the resulting code would be

```
PUSHR    ^M<R3, R4>    ; Push registers R3 and R4
PUSHR    ^M<R5>        ; Push register R5
```

Here we have used a slash as the delimiter in the second call statement.

Determining the Number of Positional Arguments

The directive .NARG (Number of Argument) counts the number of positional arguments in the formal argument list. Only positional arguments actually used in the call statement are counted. This is particularly useful in macros designed to process a variable number of arguments. The format is

```
.NARG    symbol
```

MACRO assigns the number of actual positional arguments to symbol. For example, consider the macro ReserveRoom.

```
.MACRO   ReserveRoom A, B, C, D, Size=4
  .NARG  Count
  .WORD  Count
  .BLKQ  Size
.ENDM    ReserveRoom
```

Suppose that we invoke the macro with

```
ReserveRoom  Boy, Girl, D=6
ReserveRoom  C=4
```

The first call would result in Count = 2 because there are two positional arguments (Boy and Girl). The second call has no positional arguments, so Count = 0.

Finding the Length of a Character String

It is sometimes necessary to find the length of a character string. MACRO provides the .NCHR directive to offer a convenient way to do this. The format is

```
.NCHR    symbol, <string>
```

For example, suppose that we want to write a macro that stores a string preceded with a byte holding its length. We can do this in the following manner:

```
.MACRO   StoreString   Message
  .NCHR    NumChar, <Message>
  .BYTE    NumChar
  .ASCII   /Message/
.ENDM    StoreString
StoreString   <ice cream>
```

The resulting code would be

```
.BYTE    9
.ASCII   /ice cream/
```

While .NCHR is particularly helpful in macros, it can be used anywhere in a MACRO program. In the next section we discuss several other directives for which this is true.

8.5 Conditional Assembly and Repetition

The conditional assembly and repetition directives are often used in conjunction with macros but can also be useful in other portions of a program.

Conditional Assembly

Some assembly languages allow sections of code to be assembled or ignored depending on conditions detected during the assembly process. MACRO allows **conditional blocks** with the following format:

```
.IF condition argument(s)
   .
   .
   statements processed if condition is true
   .
   .
```

```
. IF_FALSE
    .
    .
    .
    statements processed if condition is false
    .
    .
    .
. ENDC
```

The conditional block begins with the directive .IF and ends with .ENDC. The .IF_FALSE directive and the block of statements following it are optional. Some conditions that can be processed include the following:

Long Form	Code	Meaning	Comments
EQUAL	EQ	Argument is $= 0$	
NOT_EQUAL	NE	Argument is $\neq 0$	
LESS_EQUAL	LE	Argument is ≤ 0	
LESS_THAN	LT	Argument is < 0	
GREATER_EQUAL	GE	Argument is ≥ 0	
GREATER	GT	Argument is > 0	
DEFINED	DF	Symbol is defined	
NOT_DEFINED	NDF	Symbol is not defined	
BLANK	B	Argument is blank	Only in macros
NOT_BLANK	NB	Argument is not blank	Only in macros
IDENTICAL	IDN	Arguments are identical	Only in macros
DIFFERENT	DIF	Arguments are different	Only in macros

Though conditional blocks using any of the first eight conditions can be used anywhere in a program, the last four are useful only within macros. The first six conditions test a numerical argument, DEFINED and NOT_DEFINED test whether the specified symbol has been previously defined, and the last four examine character strings. The last two conditions require two different arguments whose strings are compared.

The following examples illustrate the use of conditional blocks. In the first example, we save room for the list of longwords only if Length is positive.

```
        Length = 5
        .
        .
        .
                .IF  GT  Length          ; If Length > 0
        List:   .BLKL    Length          ;   save room for list
                .LONG    0               ;   and end of list mark
                .ENDC
```

The following example illustrates character string comparisons. Double adds X to X if only one argument is specified, but if the second argument is given in the macro call, the double of X is stored in Y.

```
            .MACRO    Double   X, Y
              .IF BLANK <Y>         ; If Y is blank
                ADDL2    X, X       ;     then double X
              .IF_FALSE              ;   else
                ADDL3    X, X, Y    ;     then Y gets double X
              .ENDC                  ; (End of conditional block)
            .ENDM     Double         ; (End of macro)
```

If a conditional needs only one line of code, the form

```
    .IF   condition argument(s)
    .
    .
    .
        statement
    .
    .
    .ENDC
```

can be replaced by

```
            .IIF condition, arguments(s), statement
```

The above macro could be rewritten using the .IIF (Immediate IF) as follows:

```
    .MACRO    Double   X, Y
      .IIF BLANK, <Y>,       ADDL2   X, X       ; X gets X + X
      .IIF NOT_BLANK, <Y>,   ADDL3   X, X, Y    ; Y gets X + X
    .ENDM     Double
```

Repeat Blocks

Sometimes a block of code must be repeated several times. We can use the .REPEAT macro to reduce the amount of code needed. The general format is

```
.REPEAT   NumberOfTimes
     .
     .
     .
     statements to be repeated
     .
     .
     .
.ENDR
```

The number of repetitions must be an expression that the assembler can evaluate. If it is less than or equal to 0, no code is generated. For example, macro Power calculates X to the P and stores the result in Y.

```
          .MACRO   Power    X, P, Y
              ; Calculates Y = X to the P for nonnegative P
              MOVF     #1, Y      ; Initialize Y to 1
          .REPEAT  P              ; Repeat P times
              MULF2    X, Y       ; Y <-- X * Y
          .ENDR
          .ENDM    Power
```

The statement

```
          Power    Value, 3, R2
```

would generate the following code:

```
          MOVF     #1, R2
          MULF2    Value, R2
          MULF2    Value, R2
          MULF2    Value, R2
```

The assembler must be able to determine the value of P so that it can determine the number of repetitions to be included in the code.

We can use an alternate repeat block called an **indefinite repeat** to instruct the assembler to repeat the block once for each argument used in an argument list. The arguments are substituted one at a time for a specified symbol. The directive is .IRP and its general format is

```
.IRP   symbol, <argument list>
     .
     .
     .
     statements to be repeated for each value in list
     .
     .
     .
.ENDR
```

For example, we might code

```
          .IRP   Value,   <A, B, C>   ; Sum A, B, and C
          ADDB2  Value,   Sum
          .ENDR
```

A, B, and C will be substituted one at a time for the symbol Value. The resulting code is

```
          ADDB2  A,  Sum
          ADDB2  B,  Sum
          ADDB2  C,  Sum
```

An Example

We can combine several directives to produce a very useful macro, which simplifies calling procedures with CALLS.

```
          .MACRO  CallProc  ProcName, Arg1, Arg2, Arg3, Arg4
                  ; Call ProcName with arguments specified

                  ; Determine number of formal arguments
          .NARG   Count
                  ; Push nonblank arguments
          .IRP    Arg,  <Arg4, Arg3, Arg2, Arg1>
          .IIF    NOT_BLANK, Arg,  PUSHL  Arg
          .ENDR
                  ; Call the procedure
          CALLS   #<Count-1>, ProcName
          .ENDM   CallProc
```

Notice that the arguments are pushed onto the stack in reverse order, as required by CALLS. We can use this macro to push up to four arguments onto the stack before doing a CALLS. For example, the call

```
          CallProc Evaluate, A, B
```

would generate the code

```
          PUSHL  B
          PUSHL  A
          CALLS  #2, Evaluate
```

Summary

We can use macros to shorten assembly code and improve its readability. The MACRO assembler substitutes the body of the macro for each occurrence of the macro's name. Parameters in the argument list in the macro's definition can have three formats: (1) simple arguments listing the symbolic name, (2) local labels preceded with a question mark, or (3) symbolic arguments with a default value. The actual values in the call statement's argument list can be listed in positional order or with a "name = value" format. The .SHOW and .NOSHOW directives, together with the options ME and MEB, control whether macros are expanded in assembly listings. MACRO has special facilities to handle certain problems such as concatenating an argument with other text, passing symbolic constants, and passing character strings containing blanks or semicolons. It can count arguments and characters in a character string. MACRO allows conditional assembly options using the .IF directive or the immediate form .IIF. The .REPEAT and .IRP directives provide different types of repeat blocks.

MACRO's name suggests that it provides powerful facilities for macros. This is certainly true. The macro facility in MACRO is sufficiently powerful to handle complicated coding situations. In fact, it is possible to simulate another assembly language or even a high-level language by using macro calls.

The I/O macros in Appendix F illustrate several of the concepts discussed in this chapter. They may be helpful in demonstrating the use of some of the various directives. You should be able to understand the coding after you complete Chapter 9, which introduces some of the instructions and procedures used in them.

VMS, like many operating systems, provides a means of storing macros in libraries. The assembler will automatically search libraries and add the required macros to your program. Appendix F includes the system commands needed to maintain the I/O macros in a library.

Exercises

1. Given the macro definition

   ```
           .MACRO    DefineRecord    Name, Days, Months, Years
   Name:   .BLKW         Days
           .BLKW         Months
           .BLKB         Years
           .ENDM         DefineRecord
   ```

   what code is produced by the following statements?

   a. DefineRecord LeapYear, 366, 12, 10
   b. DefineRecord Name=First, Days=5, Months=3, Years=10
   c. DefineRecord Months=3, Years=5, Days=4, Name=Last

2. Given the following definition

   ```
   .MACRO    Calculate    X = #2, Y = #3, Z
       ADDW3     X, Y, R0
       MULW3     X, X, R1
       SUBW3     R0, R1, Z
   .ENDM     Calculate
   ```

what code is produced by the following statements?

   a. Calculate   , , Answer
   b. Calculate   #4, #6, W
   c. Calculate   Z = Book, X = #32

3. Given the following definition

```
       .MACRO  Evaluate   Count, ?Label
       DECW    Count
       BGTR    Label
       ADDW2   #5, R3
Label: TSTW    R3
       .ENDM   Evaluate
```

what code is produced by the following statements? Assume that the statements are all part of the same program, the statement in part a is the first macro call, and the other statements appear in the order shown.

   a. Evaluate R6
   b. Evaluate Dale
   c. Evaluate R8, JumpHere

4. Given the following definition

```
.MACRO  AssignSpace  Message = <This is it>, Size = 20, -
                     Kind = W
    .ASCII      /Message/
    .LONG       Size
    .BLK'Kind   Size
.ENDM   AssignSpace
```

what code is produced by the following statements?

   a.   AssignSpace
   b. X: AssignSpace Kind = L
   c.   AssignSpace Message = <Fine work>
   d. Fix = 36
        AssignSpace Message = ^*^M<R2, R4>*, Size = \Fix

5. a. What code is generated by the following?

```
Error=5
    .IF GT Error
       MOVL    R2, X
    .ENDC
    .IF EQ Error
       MOVL    R3, X
    .ENDC
```

   b. Change the first statement in part a to

      Error = 0

     What code is generated?

6. Given the following macro definition
   ```
   .MACRO   FixIt   String, Value
     .NARG  ArgCount
     .IF NOT_BLANK <String>
       .NCHR CharCount   <String>
       .WORD CharCount
       .ASCII   /String/
     .IF_FALSE
       .WORD 3
       .ASCII   /ABC/
     .ENDC
     .IIF GT, ArgCount-1,   .LONG  Value
   .ENDM   FixIt
   ```
   what code is generated by the following macro calls?
   a. FixIt <Book>
   b. FixIt , 25
   c. FixIt <Terminal>, 24

7. What code is generated by the following repeat blocks?
   a. Count = 3
   ```
       .REPEAT   4
         .LONG    Count
         Count = Count + 1
       .ENDR
   ```
   b.
   ```
       .IRP  Data,   <A1, A2, A3, A4>
         ADDL2  Data, R3
         MULL2  Data, R4
       .ENDR
   ```

8. a. Write a macro

   XChange   A, B

   that interchanges two words (without checking to see if the words have the same label). State any assumptions or restrictions concerning the use of your macro.

   b. Rewrite the above macro so that it interchanges only if the two inputs have different symbols.

9. a. Write a macro

   DefineStudent

   that defines a record with the following fields about a student:

   Name   (24 bytes)
   Age   (word)
   GPA   (floating)
   Hours (byte)

   b. Write a macro

   CopyStudent   Source, Destination

that copies one of the above records from the source to the destination. Specify any registers whose contents are changed by the macro.

c. Write data definition statements using DefineStudent to reserve space for two records with the labels BestStudent and NextStudent.

d. Write instructions that copy the information in the record for NextStudent into the record for BestStudent if NextStudent's GPA is greater than the current value of BestStudent's GPA.

e. Given an array of five student records, write a complete program that copies the record of the student with the best GPA into a record called BestStudent. Use the macros suggested in parts a and b.

10. Write a macro

    JumpToSub   A, B, C

    that pushes the addresses of three floating-point arguments onto the stack and then causes a jump to subroutine Sub, which has three arguments (A, B, and C). (Sub requires the arguments in that order.) Also, write a statement that uses the macro to jump to Sub using the actual arguments Book, Pen, and Paper.

11. a. Write a macro

    ArgList   W, X, Y, Z

    that forms an argument list to be used by a CALLG instruction. Suppose that the arguments are called by reference. The procedure's parameters are the same as the macro's. Assume that all arguments are used.

    b. Same as part a, but the argument list is to include only those arguments actually specified in the macro call.

12. Write a macro

    CallFunct   A, B

    that pushes the two arguments for the procedure Funct onto the stack and then uses CALLS to call the procedure Funct. Funct has two longword arguments, A and B. The first argument (A) is passed by value, the second by reference. Also, write a macro call statement that passes the number 5 for A and the label Answer for B. Assume that the procedure requires both arguments.

13. Write a macro

    ADDQ3   Source1, Source2, Destination

    that adds the quadwords Source1 and Source2 and stores the result in Destination. Assume that all values are stored in memory. Also, use the macro to find the sum of the quadwords in Quad and Value; then put the sum in Result. What addressing modes can be used in the call statement for your macro?

14. Write a macro

    LogicalRightShift   Count, Source, Destination

    that logically shifts a longword to the right Count bits. (Recall that in right logical shifts, zeros are inserted on the left.) State any assumptions or restrictions concerning the use of your macro.

15. Rewrite the procedure in Listing 8.1 to make it more efficient and/or more useful by making one or more of these changes. (Not all parts can be done in one program.) Write a main program to test the procedure.

    a. Store I, J, and JPlus1 in registers to reduce memory accesses.
    b. Observe that the MoveRecord macro creates inefficient code when FromSub or ToSub are 0. Use conditional blocks to fix this problem.
    c. Replace the loop in MoveRecord with four move instructions.
    d. Add a third argument to the procedure that specifies the field number on which the list is to be sorted. If this argument is 1, we are to sort on ID; if it is 2, we are to sort on the number of at bats; and so on.
    e. Suppose that the procedure will be used to process all the players in the league (possibly as many as 300). Replace the insertion sort by a quick sort (or another faster sort).

16. Write a macro

    For   Counter, Start, End, BeginLoop, EndLoop

    that allows translating the Pascal statement

    ```
    For Count := 1 to 10 do
        Sum := Sum + Count
    ```

    in the following manner:

    ```
            For     Count, #1, #10, BeginForLoop, EndForLoop
            ADDL2   Count, Sum
            BRB     BeginForLoop
    EndForLoop:
    ```

    Be sure that your code will not execute the body loop if End < Start. Use the macro in a program that finds the sum of $3^2 + 4^2 + \ldots + N^2$.

17. Rewrite macro For ... in Exercise 16, giving it one additional parameter. The macro would now be

    For Counter, Start, Direction, End, BeginLoop, EndLoop

    Direction would have two possible values, TO and DOWNTO. A call to the macro might look like this

    For   Count, #1, TO, #10, BeginForLoop, EndForLoop

    Demonstrate your macro by calculating the sum given in Exercise 16 in both increasing and decreasing order.

18. Write a macro

    Until   Value1, Comparison, Value2, BeginLoop

    that allows compiling the Pascal program segment

    ```
    Repeat
       Sum   := Sum + Count
       Count := Count + 1.0
    Until Count = 10.0
    ```

    in the following manner:

    ```
    BeginRepeatLoop:
            ADDF2  Count, Sum
            ADDF2  #1.0, Count
            Until  Count, EQ, #10.0, BeginRepeatLoop
    ```

    Allow such comparisons as EQ for equals, NE for not equal, GT for greater than, and GE for greater than or equal. Assume that the two values specified are floating-point values. Use the macro in a program that finds the sum of $1 + 1/3^2 + 1/5^2 + \ldots + 1/(2N + 1)^2$.

19. (Group project.) HyPo is an elementary assembly language for an uncomplicated hypothetical computer used to demonstrate assembly language in beginning computer science classes. The computer features one accumulator for doing calculations, a process status register with two condition codes—Z (zero) and N (negative), a program counter, and an instruction register. The computer uses 16-bit, signed integer arithmetic and one-operand instructions. The instruction set and directives are as follows:

Opcode	Operand	Operation	Condition Codes
Instruction Set:			
LOAD	X	Loads X into the accumulator	*
STOR	X	Stores the accumulator in X	*
ADD	X	Adds X to the accumulator	*
SUB	X	Subtracts X from the accumulator	*
MUL	X	Multiplies the accumulator by X	*
DIV	X	Divides the accumulator by X	*
IN	X	Inputs value of X in decimal	—
OUT	X	Outputs value of X in decimal	—
BR	Label	Branches unconditionally to Label	—
BRNEG	Label	Branch on negative to Label	—
BRZER	Label	Branch on zero to Label	—
STOP		Terminates execution	—
Directives			
INIT	V	Reserves a word of storage and initializes it to the value V. (V is given in decimal.)	
RESERVE	N	Reserves N words of storage.	

BEGIN   Denotes the beginning of the
                 executable code.
END   Denotes the end of the program.

Notes:
1. A label of the form Label: can be placed before any opcode or directive except Begin and End. A comment can be added following an instruction or directive and is separated from it by a semicolon.
2. Under condition codes, "*" means that the instruction sets Z and N according to the result; "—" means that the instruction does not affect the condition codes.

The following program calculates N factorial (1 * 2 * . . . * N).

```
N:        RESERVE   1           ; Data storage
Product:  INIT      1
Counter:  INIT      1

One:      INIT      1           ; The constant 1

          BEGIN
          IN        N           ; Enter N
Loop:     LOAD      Product     ; Multiply by counter
          MUL       Counter
          STOR      Product
          LOAD      Counter     ; Increment counter
          ADD       One
          STOR      Counter
          SUB       N           ; Compare to N
          BRNEG     Loop        ; Branch in N greater
          BRZER     Loop        ;   or equal to Counter
          OUT       Product     ; Print Product
          STOP
          END
```

a. Write macros to implement each of the HyPo opcodes and directives so that HyPo programs can be assembled by MACRO and run on a VAX. (Hints: select one of the registers to serve as an accumulator and use some care to make sure that Z and N are not changed by the IN and OUT instructions. You may find the output macros of Appendix F useful in implementing the I/O opcodes. Test your macros with the above program and write another HyPo program that tests each macro.)
b. Provide instructions for assembling and running HyPo programs so that a beginner can do so. It may be helpful to store the macros in a library. See Appendix F.
c. Write a manual for HyPo suitable for beginners.
d. Add some additional useful instructions and/or directives to HyPo. Document and test them carefully.

CHAPTER CONTENTS

9.1 CHARACTER STRINGS

9.2 INTRODUCTION TO CHARACTER STRING INSTRUCTIONS AND I/O

   Two Character String Instructions
   Two Procedures for I/O
   An Example

9.3 MORE CHARACTER STRING INSTRUCTIONS

9.4 A PROGRAM USING CHARACTER STRINGS AND I/O

   Variable-Length Input
   An Example

9.5 DECIMAL NUMBERS

9.6 PACKED DECIMAL INSTRUCTIONS

9.7 NUMERICAL CONVERSIONS AND I/O

   Conversions Between Binary Data Types
   Conversions Involving Packed Decimal
   Output Procedures

SUMMARY

EXERCISES

CHAPTER 9

Character Strings, Packed Decimal, and Introduction to I/O

In this chapter we will introduce some new data types that will allow you to write sophisticated MACRO programs with input and output (I/O) capabilities. At the assembly language level, all terminal I/O must be done with character strings. Consequently, we begin with a section on that data type. In Section 9.2 we introduce two powerful instructions that make processing character strings much easier and two library procedures that allow you to enter and print strings. In the next section we discuss four more character string instructions, giving more detail about the operation of these instructions, and in Section 9.4 we introduce an input option and discuss an example that uses the topics introduced earlier.

In the following two sections we will look at representations of decimal numbers. It is possible to do calculations with one of these types, called packed decimal, which brings us to the questions of how do we convert between the various data types available on the VAX, and how do we do I/O with numbers? These questions are closely related because terminal I/O demands the use of character strings. Thus we must be able to convert between a number's internal representation and the ASCII characters needed for communication with a terminal. Finally, in Section 9.7 we introduce some of the conversion instructions available on the VAX and then suggest some procedures that convert numbers to ASCII and send them to the user's terminal. We also show a method of inputting a longword integer.

9.1 Character Strings

In this section we want to introduce some basic ideas about character strings and how they are handled on the VAX. We begin with the representation of a single character and move on to the representation of strings of characters. We will also discuss descriptors for character strings.

Outside the IBM mainframe world, most computers communicate with terminals using a seven-bit code called **ASCII (American Standard Code for Information Interchange)**, as shown in Appendix C. It provides for 128 characters, of which 95 are printable. The other 33 are designed for control functions. The interpretation of some control codes is fairly standardized. For example, the character whose numerical value is 7 means "bell," and most terminals will sound a bell or buzzer when they receive this character. However, some other control characters have quite different interpretations on different terminals and printers.

The VAX, like many other computers designed for interactive processing, uses an 8-bit variation of ASCII for representing characters internally. The VAX's internal representation for a character is normally obtained by prefixing the 7-bit character code with a 0 in the most significant bit, although occasionally the code is augmented with a 1 for some special purposes. Some computers, such as large IBM machines, use an 8-bit code called **EBCDIC (Extended Binary Coded Decimal Interchange Code)**, and a few use **BCD (Binary Coded Decimal)**, a six-bit code.

In the MACRO language character strings are represented by a sequence of characters enclosed inside matching delimiters. The delimiter can be any printable character not appearing in the string except a blank, tab, equal sign, semicolon, or the less than sign (<). Apostrophies are not recommended when working with macros. Common delimiters include quotation marks and the slash. For example, /Word/ and "This is an example" are delimited strings.

The operator ^A means to treat the following string as an integer. For example,

```
    MOVL    #^A"abc", R0
```

is equivalent to

```
    MOVL    #^X636261, R0
```

because 61, 62, and 63 are the hexadecimal representations for the ASCII characters "a", "b" and "c". The seeming reversal in the order between the character string and the hexadecimal numbers occurs because characters in a string are stored left-most character first, while numbers are stored with the least significant or right-most byte first. Because the instruction copies a four-byte data element and only three bytes are specified, the numerical value for the string is padded on the left by hexadecimal zeros.

MACRO provides some directives for storing character strings in memory. **.ASCII** simply stores the specified string in memory. However, in some cases further information about the string is needed so that the computer can determine its length or the end of the string. **.ASCIC** precedes the string with a byte that specifies the length of (or count of the characters in) the string. **.ASCIZ** adds a trailing hexadecimal zero byte to signal the end of the string. The following lists show three ways the string "MACRO" can be stored in memory.

.ASCII "MACRO"		.ASCIC "MACRO"		.ASCIZ "MACRO"	
Code	**Meaning**	**Code**	**Meaning**	**Code**	**Meaning**
4D	M	05	5 characters	4D	M
41	A	4D	M	41	A
43	C	41	A	43	C
52	R	43	C	52	R
4F	O	52	R	4F	O
		4F	O	00	Trailing 0

We can specify strings containing control characters by first using direct assignment statements to define symbols for the control characters and then enclosing the symbols in corner brackets when defining the string. For example:

```
BELL = 7
Alert:   .ASCII   <BELL>/Warning/<Bell>    ; Used to alert user
```

We now turn our attention to the issue of passing character strings to subprograms. In some special-purpose applications the number of characters is fixed, and both the calling program and the subprogram know exactly how many characters are in the string. In this case the string can be passed by reference. However, if the subprogram is a general-purpose routine that can operate on different length strings, it must be provided with the string's length as well as the string's address. There are various ways that this can be done. Some systems prefix character strings with a byte specifying their length in the format of the .ASCIC directive. Other systems (including UNIX) use a special code such as binary zero to mark the end of the string, as done by the .ASCIZ directive. For the most generality, the VMS operating system specifies that character strings are normally passed by descriptor (as was pointed out in Chapter 7).

A descriptor is a data structure used to describe the actual data type, address, and any other information about the argument needed by the subprogram. Though descriptors can be used for any type of data, one of their most common applications is to describe character strings. The

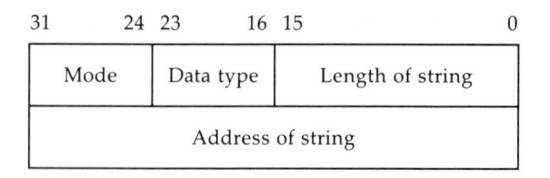

```
          31        24 23      16 15                    0
         +------------+----------+----------------------+
         |   Mode     | Data type|   Length of string   |
         +------------+----------+----------------------+
         |              Address of string               |
         +----------------------------------------------+
```

Mode = 1 for a static fixed-length string
Mode = 2 for a dynamic variable-length string
Data type = 14 (decimal) for a character string

Figure 9.1 Standard character string descriptor

format of the standard character string descriptor required by VMS is shown in Figure 9.1.

We will consider writing descriptors for known, fixed-length strings. This is mode 1 (we will discuss mode 2 later in the chapter). When using fixed-length strings, we must write code to set up both the descriptor and the string. This is not too difficult. If we want to pass a string called Sample, we can refer to Figure 9.1 and proceed as follows:

```
Descrpt:  .WORD     26          ; Length of string
          .BYTE     14          ; Data type is a character string
          .BYTE     1           ; Fixed-length character string
          .ADDRESS  Sample      ; Address of Sample

Sample:   .ASCII    "This is a character string"
```

However, MACRO provides a simpler method. The directive called .ASCID produces the descriptor as well as storing the string. All that is needed is

```
Descrpt:  .ASCID    "This is a character string"
```

.ASCID stores the same information as the original method. Only the label on the string is missing. The label Descrpt does multiple duties: it is both the address of the descriptor and the address of the length of the string. The address of the string is at "Descrpt+4," and the characters stored by the directive always follow immediately after the address at "Descrpt+8" when .ASCID is used.

The next section contains a sample program using descriptors to pass strings for input and output.

Part of the reason for discussing string descriptors is to allow you to pass strings between high-level language main programs and assembler subprograms. The techniques used to pass strings vary considerably from language to language. It is important to check the manuals for a particular language to determine the exact method used by that compiler. For example, VAX Pascal provides three different methods. Because standard Pascal assumes that character strings are fixed-length packed arrays of characters and that subprograms are internal, VAX Pascal passes strings by reference unless otherwise specified. We can use the mechanism %STDESCR with this data type if mode 1 descriptors are needed. VAX Pascal also defines a nonstandard, variable-length string called **varying of char**, which can be passed using the %DESCR mechanism.

For more information on passing character strings and descriptors, refer to the manuals for the particular language you are using and to the *Introduction to VAX/VMS Systems Routines* manual. This manual includes the symbolic names recommended by DEC for the various modes and data types. We have not used them because the names tend to be as difficult to remember as their values.

9.2 Introduction to Character String Instructions and I/O

The VAX machine language offers a number of convenient instructions for character strings processing. In this section we will introduce two of these instructions. One of them moves character strings, the other compares them. Some additional character string instructions are introduced in the next section. All these instructions simplify programs that use character data. Input and output also demand character processing, and in this section you will also learn how to use two I/O procedures provided as part of the VMS operating system. Later in this chapter, you will learn how numbers can be converted from the internal binary format to the external ASCII format needed by terminals and printers.

Two Character String Instructions

Before we discuss the special-purpose character string instructions, we will consider how characters can be processed using instructions covered in earlier chapters. Since characters are represented within a computer by unsigned integers, they can be processed by the same instructions that are used to process those integers. A string whose length equals the length of one of the VAX's standard integer data types can be processed rapidly in this manner. For example, MOVQ can move eight adjacent characters as easily as it can move one quadword number. However, if the character string's length is less convenient or is variable, it will have to be processed by a sequence of standard instructions including a loop. We could use the following code segment to copy Num characters from String1 to String2.

```
        MOVW    Num, R0           ; Put number of characters in R0
        BEQL    Finished          ; If Num = 0 then branch to Finished
        MOVAB   String1, R1       ; Move address of String1 to R1
        MOVAB   String2, R3       ; Move address of String2 to R3
Loop:   MOVB    (R1)+, (R3)+      ; Move next character and
        DECW    R0                ;   decrease R0 by 1
        BGTR    Loop              ; Repeat loop, if needed
Finished:
```

This code segment works fine if String1 and String2 do not share any memory locations. But editing operations often require that we shift characters a few bytes left or right to allow us to delete or add a few characters. The code segment could be used to delete some characters by shifting the remaining characters to the left, but it will not work when we want to shift characters to the right to make room for a few new characters. Suppose that we need to shift String1 one byte to the right. The address of String2 would be equal to the address of String1 + 1. This code would begin by moving the first character in String1 to the first location in String2, which is really the second location in String1. The second byte of the original string is destroyed before it is processed. To avoid this problem, we must process characters right to left in this situation.

Because character moving is an extremely common operation in nonnumerical processing, the VAX provides a single instruction that will carry out this task for us

```
        MOVC3   Num, String1, -   ; Move Num bytes from String1
                String2           ;   to String2
```

(The dash after "String1," tells MACRO that the instruction is continued on the next line.) The opcode and format of this move character instruction are

Opcode	Mnemonic	Operands
28	MOVC3	Length, source, destination

"Length" is the number of characters in the string.

The length operand is an unsigned word that specifies the number of bytes to be processed. This allows up to 64K bytes of data to be processed with one instruction. The instruction automatically picks out the appropriate order for processing the characters, so this instruction can be used for both right and left shifts.

The following example is a typical application. We want to move the ten characters in Name to Lady.

```
Name:    .ASCII   "Janelle   "
Lady:    .BLKB    10
```

.
.
.

```
         MOVC3    #10, Name, Lady    ; Copy Name to Lady
```

MOVC3 is clearly a much more sophisticated instruction than we have been using so far. Unfortunately, there are some side effects. Did you notice that our original character-moving code segment changed some registers while it moved the data? R0 was used as a counter; R1 and R3 held the addresses of the next characters to be processed. We must not be fooled by the fact that the MOVC3 instruction does not reference any registers. Actually, the VAX character string instructions use from two to six registers to help them carry out their function. MOVC3 uses R0–R5. R1 and R3 are used in just about the same way that our original code used them. After the instruction is processed, they hold the address of the bytes that immediately follow the end of the source and destination strings. R0, R2, R4, and R5 are all set to 0. In the next section we will discuss the use of these registers in more detail. In the meantime, remember the MOVC3 destroys R0–R5. Many programmers avoid using these registers in any code segment that uses character string functions, which helps them avoid unexpected bugs in their code.

Though MOVC3 is primarily designed for character processing, we can use it to move other types of data. For example, suppose that we have an array of 100 longwords that must be copied from Data to Result. Observing that 100 longwords is equivalent to 400 bytes, we could avoid writing a loop by just coding

```
   MOVC3    #400, Data, Result ; Copy array Data to Result
```

This extra capability of MOVC3 is actually quite natural if we remember that the computer stores characters as numbers.

The CMPC3 instruction compares character strings much as the CMPx instructions compare numerical data. It has the following format:

Opcode	Mnemonic	Operands
29	CMPC3	Length, source1, source2

The computer compares the two source operands character by character, starting at the left-most character, and continues until it reaches the end of the strings or finds corresponding characters that differ and then sets the condition codes accordingly. The Z bit is set to 1 if the strings are exactly equal; otherwise it is cleared. The N bit is cleared if the strings are equal; otherwise its value determines which source string operand would come first in dictionary order. If the first differing character in source1 comes before the corresponding character in source2, N is set. If this character comes after the corresponding character in the other string, N is cleared. Of course the instruction uses the ASCII alphabet, not the 26-character English alphabet. The C bit is processed in much the same way. The only difference in the two bits is that just as in integer comparisons, the N flag is determined considering the characters' codes as signed integers, while the C flag is evaluated considering them as unsigned integers. Normally a character's leading bit is set to 0, so these two flags will be equal. In summary the condition codes have the "same" meaning when CMPC3 is used to compare character strings as CMPL does when it compares integer longwords.

This instruction modifies registers R0–R3. If the strings are unequal, the registers contain values that allow us to determine which character caused the inequality. We will discuss this in more detail in the next section.

Suppose that we want to put the following eight-character words into alphabetical order. The code has the same structure as if we were comparing numbers.

```
        Count = 8
        First:  .ASCII    "computer"
        Last:   .ASCII    "complete"
        Temp:   .BLKB     Count
          .
          .
          .
                CMPC3     #Count, First, Last
                BLEQ      InOrder
                MOVC3     #Count, First, Temp
                MOVC3     #Count, Last, First
                MOVC3     #Count, Temp, Last
        InOrder:
```

The strings differ in their fifth bytes, so CMPC3 clears the Z bit. Lowercase "u" comes after "l" in the ASCII collating sequence, so the N and C condition codes are both cleared to 0. The branch is not taken, and the words are interchanged.

Two Procedures for I/O

VMS provides two library procedures called Lib$Get_Input and Lib$Put_Output for easy terminal I/O. They pass strings by descriptor. Lib$Put_Output has a single argument, the descriptor of the string to be sent to the terminal. It prints the string, followed by a carriage return and line feed. If the desired string is never changed by the program, it is easiest to declare it with a .ASCID directive. For example, consider the following:

9.2 Introduction to Character String Instructions and I/O

```
Greeting:
        .ASCID      "Hello, how are you?"
        .
        .
        .
        PUSHAW      Greeting
        CALLS       #1, G^Lib$Put_Output
```

The computer prints the message on the user's terminal. It makes little difference in this situation which of the PUSHAx instructions are used to push the address of the descriptor. The G^ before the procedure's name specifies general addressing. We use it because we are unsure whether we should use absolute or relative addressing for this procedure. The linker will select the correct mode for us.

If we want to print a string determined during run time, we have to work a little harder. Suppose that we want to print the string Name, which has Count = 7 characters. One technique is to set up a dummy descriptor for the output and then copy the desired variable into the proper location before requesting the output.

```
Out:    .ASCID      "        "              ; Reserve room for output
        .
        .
        .
        MOVC3       #Count, Name, Out+8     ; Copy Name to the blanks in Out
        PUSHAW      Out                     ; Push descriptor address
        CALLS       #1, G^Lib$Put_Output    ;    and print the string
```

The string is copied to Out+8 because the .ASCID directive stores the eight-byte descriptor before the specified characters. An alternative that executes faster but takes a little more coding is to write an appropriate descriptor that points to Name.

```
Out:    .WORD       Count                   ; The length of Name
        .BYTE       14                      ; Data type
        .BYTE       1                       ; Mode
        .ADDRESS    Name                    ; Address of string
        .
        .
        .
        PUSHAW      Out                     ; Print Name
        CALLS       #1, G^Lib$Put_Output
```

The input procedure works about the same way, but an option is available. We can include a prompt. Perhaps the easiest way to handle fixed-length input is to use the .ASCID descriptor with a dummy string that just allots room for the input. If the user types fewer than the specified number of characters, the right-most characters are filled with blanks. If the user types too many characters, the extra characters are ignored.

If desired, we can specify an optional prompt as the second parameter. As discussed in Chapter 7, the arguments are pushed in reverse order, so the address of the prompt is pushed on the stack first when it is used. Suppose that we want to input the value of Name, which has Count = 7 characters. We could code the following:

```
RequestInput:
        .ASCID    "Enter a name: "    ; The prompt
InBuf:  .ASCID    "       "           ; 7-character input buffer
        .
        .
        .
        PUSHAW    RequestInput        ; Push prompt descriptor
        PUSHAW    InBuf               ; Push input buffer
        CALLS     #2, G^Lib$Get_Input ; Call input procedure
        MOVC3     #Count, InBuf+8, Name ; Move input to Name
```

Only the descriptor's address would be pushed onto the stack if the prompt is not desired, and the parameter count in the CALLS instruction would be reduced to 1. We will discuss inputting variable-length strings in Section 9.4.

An Example

Suppose that we must write a demonstration program for a book store. A customer will input the name of an item, and the computer responds by saying whether the item is in the store's inventory. Though we will test the program with just a few items, the actual inventory list will be quite long. A binary search is an appropriate way to determine if the requested item is in the list, assuming that the list of items is arranged alphabetically. We will check the item midway in the list. If it happens to be the requested item, we are done. Otherwise we check to see if we are too far or not far enough through the list. Based on the answer to that question, we "discard" the last half or first half of the list and repeat this process with the remaining sublist. Eventually we either find the item or determine that it is not in the list.

The initial algorithm for this program is as follows:

1. Input the Target, the item to be searched for.
2. Carry out the binary search, branching to step 3 or 4 as appropriate.
    a. Initialize the search by giving Low the subscript of the first item in the list and High the subscript of the last item.

    b. If Low > Hi, then go to step 3.
    c. Calculate Mid = (Low + Hi)/2 (using integer division).
    d. If Item[Mid] = Target, go to step 4.
    e. If Item[Mid] > Target, go to step 2g.
    f. (The item must be in the last half of the list.) Set Low = Mid + 1 and go back to step 2b.
    g. (The item must be in the first half of the list.) Set Hi = Mid − 1 and go back to step 2b.
3. Print out a not found message and stop.
4. Print out a found message and stop.

We must resolve a few questions before coding the program. For example, where will the data base be located? We will just write the sample list of inventory items into our demonstration program. The final program would read it from a disk file. What is the format of the data? We will allow ten characters for the name of each item. How do we store the values Low, Hi, and Mid? Because speed seems to be important in this problem, we will use registers R6–R8 for these values to reduce memory accesses. In addition, we will move the address of the list into a register (R10) and use register deferred addressing instead of relative addressing because this can also slightly decrease search time. There would be some advantage of doing the same with Target, but we will avoid that for the sake of readability.

We can use index addressing in this program to determine the location of Item[Mid] but in a little different way than we might expect. CMPC3 is basically a byte-oriented instruction, so it assumes that each data item is one byte long when indexed addressing is used. However, Mid is the subscript of a data item having Length = 10 bytes. Accordingly, we will multiply Mid by Length to find the byte offset from the beginning of the array, which we can then use as the index in this instruction. The first few items are shown below:

Subscript	Byte offset	Item
0	0	Book
1	10	Computer
2	20	Notepad

Because we are using MOVC3 and CMPC3, R0 through R5 are reserved for their use. The program is shown in Listing 9.1.

Listing 9.1 A program using I/O and a binary search

```
        .TITLE   BinarySearch  Binary search of list

;   Inputs the name of an item and then does a binary search
;   of the inventory list called Items to see if the word is
;   included in the list.  It then prints an appropriate message.

;   Register usage:
;       R6:   Low       Lowest subscript currently being considered
;       R7:   High      Highest subscript currently being considered
;       R8:   Mid       Subscript of the middle item in the sublist
;       R9:             Offset for Items[Mid]
;       R10:            Address of Items

;   Constants:
NumItems = 10                   ; Number of items in the list
Length   = 10                   ; Number of characters in an item

;   Buffers and data:
InBuf:    .ASCID   "          "
Prompt:   .ASCID   "What item are you looking for?  (In caps) "
NotFoundMess:
          .ASCID   "We do not carry that item"
FoundMess:
          .ASCID   "That item is in stock"
Target:   .BLKB    10                    ; Save room for target
;   Inventory list:
Items:    .ASCII   "BOOK      "  "COMPUTER  "
          .ASCII   "NOTEBOOK  "  "NOTEPAD   "
          .ASCII   "PAPER     "  "PEN       "
          .ASCII   "PENCIL    "  "PROGRAM   "
          .ASCII   "RULER     "  "TERMINAL  "

          .ENTRY   Binary, 0
;                  ..... Input the Target  .....
Begin:    PUSHAW   Prompt                ; Prompt
          PUSHAW   InBuf                 ;    and input name of
          CALLS    #2, G^Lib$Get_Input-  ;    desired item
          MOVC3    #Length, InBuf+8,-
                   Target                ;    and move it to Target
;                  ..... Initialize binary search for Target  .....
          MOVL     #0, R6                ; Initialize Low
          MOVL     #NumItems-1, R7       ; Initialize High
          MOVAB    Items, R10            ; Init. address of Items
;                  ..... Main search loop  .....
Loop:     CMPL     R6, R7                ; If Low > High then
          BGTR     NotFound              ;    branch to NotFound
          ADDL3    R6, R7, R8            ; Mid gets average of Low
          DIVL2    #2, R8                ;    and High
```

Listing 9.1 (continued)

```
            MULL3       #Length, R8, R9         ; Calc. offset for Mid
            CMPC3       #Length, (R10)[R9], Target
                                                ; If found
            BEQL        Found                   ;     branch to Found
            BLSS        AboveMid                ; If Item[Mid] < Target
                                                ;     branch to AboveMid
            SUBL3       #1, R8, R7              ;   else update High
            BRB         Loop                    ;     and branch back to Loop
AboveMid:
            ADDL3       #1, R8, R6              ; Update Low
            BRB         Loop                    ;     and branch back to Loop
;           ..... Search failed - Output not found message  .....
NotFound:
            PUSHAW      NotFoundMess
            CALLS       #1, G^Lib$Put_Output;
            BRB         Done
;           ..... Success - Output found message  .....
Found:      PUSHAQ      FoundMess
            CALLS       #1, G^Lib$Put_Output

Done:       $EXIT_S
            .END        Binary
```

9.3 More Character String Instructions

Now we will look at four additional string instructions. Two will be more general versions of the move and compare instructions. The others are helpful when editing strings.

A characteristic of the string instructions is how they affect the general-purpose registers. While processing strings, the computer must keep track of the address of the current character and the number of characters left in each string. Consequently, two to six registers are reserved to hold this type of information. Figure 9.2 shows the standard register assignments used by some of these instructions. Depending on the number of strings processed, some instructions use only R0 and R1, while some others use just R0–R3. Programmers must be aware of the side effects of these instructions and avoid trying to save important quantities in these registers.

There are at least two reasons why general-purpose registers are used to hold these quantities during execution of character string instructions. First, some instructions leave useful information in some of the registers. For example, after comparing unequal strings with CMPC3, R1 and R3

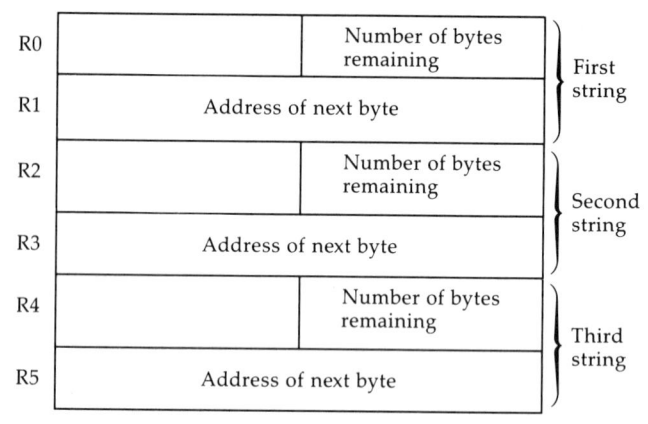

```
          ┌─────────────────────────────────────┐
    R0    │           Number of bytes remaining │ ┐
          ├─────────────────────────────────────┤ │ First
    R1    │         Address of next byte        │ ┘ string

    R2    │           Number of bytes remaining │ ┐
          ├─────────────────────────────────────┤ │ Second
    R3    │         Address of next byte        │ ┘ string

    R4    │           Number of bytes remaining │ ┐
          ├─────────────────────────────────────┤ │ Third
    R5    │         Address of next byte        │ ┘ string
          └─────────────────────────────────────┘
```

Some instructions process only one or two strings.

Figure 9.2 Register usage by character string instructions

hold the addresses of the first pair of characters that are unequal. Second, because these instructions can process as many as 64K bytes, they may need a fairly long time to complete their task. (In a ten-trial test run on a VAX 11/750, the CPU time needed to execute

```
MOVC3   #64000, A, B
```

ranged from 0.05 to 0.28 seconds depending on memory availability.) During execution of such an instruction, the computer may be faced with a higher-priority task that must be processed immediately. In Chapter 11 we will learn how the computer can interrupt the program it is processing, save the general-purpose registers and process status longword, and then carry out the high-priority task. When that task is completed, it can restore the registers and PSL and continue the original instruction sequence. Placing the important string-processing information in registers allows the character string instructions to be easily interrupted while they are being processed and then restarted when the computer can return to its original task.

The complete set of character-moving and comparing instructions is listed here.

Opcode	Mnemonic	Operands
28	MOVC3	Length, source, destination
2C	MOVC5	Length of source, source, fill character, — length of destination, destination
29	CMPC3	Length, source1, source2
2D	CMPC5	Length of source1, source1, fill character, — length of source2, source2

9.3 More Character String Instructions

Recall that MOVC3 copies the number of characters specified by "length" from the source to the destination. The MOVC5 is more general because it allows unequal string lengths. If the length of the destination is less than the source, only the first "length of destination" characters in the source are copied. If the source is shorter than the destination, the extra characters at the end of the destination are set equal to the "fill character". Both instructions allow the source and destination strings to overlap. As with all string instructions, length operands are treated as 16-bit words allowing up to 64K bytes to be processed by one instruction.

The following code segment illustrates the use of MOVC5.

```
Dot    =   ^A"."
Name:      .ASCII    /Mary/
Friend:    .ASCII    /^^^^^/
Initial:   .ASCII    /^/
           .
           .
           .
           MOVC5    #4, Name, #Dot, #6, Friend    ; Friend <-- "Mary.."
           MOVC5    #4, Name, #Dot, #1, Initial   ; Initial <-- "M"
```

The contents of R0–R5 after processing the MOVCn instructions are shown following Table 9.1. You can observe that the final values in registers R0 to R3 are consistent with the usage described in Figure 9.2. The usage of R4 and R5 is not as clear but we can speculate that they are used to help specify whether the strings are processed left to right or right to left.

The move character instructions are recommended for some not so obvious purposes. MOVC3 is suggested for copying blocks of storage of up to 64K in length, while MOVC5 is recommended for filling a block of storage with a single character. You can do this by setting the length of the source to 0 and using the desired character as the fill character. For example, you can clear a large block of storage by using the binary number 0 as the fill character.

Table 9.1 Registers After Executing MOVCn

Register	MOVC3	MOVC5
R0	0	Number of uncopied source bytes remaining when the destination is full; otherwise 0.
R1	Address of the byte following the last source byte copied.	
R2	0	0
R3	Address of the byte following the last character of the destination.	
R4	0	0
R5	0	0

The CMPCn instructions also come in two formats. When processing these instructions, the computer compares the two source operands character by character, starting at the left-most character, and continues until it reaches the end of the strings or finds corresponding characters that differ. In the case of the CMPC5 instruction, when the computer reaches the end of the shorter string, it continues the comparison using the fill character in place of the missing characters. The length operands are 16-bit words.

As discussed in the previous section, the condition codes are determined by the last character pair that is compared and are set as follows:

N ← 1 if the last byte compared in source1 LSS the last byte checked in source2.

Z ← 1 if the last byte compared in source1 EQL the last byte checked in source2.

V ← 0.

C ← 1 if the last byte compared in source1 LSSU the last byte checked in source2.

These instructions use registers R0–R3 as shown in Table 9.2. Consider the following example:

```
String1:   .ASCII    "The book"
String2:   .ASCII    "Their book"
              .
              .
              .
           CMPC5    #8, String1, #^A" ", #10, String2
           BNEQ     Unequal
```

Table 9.2 Registers After Executing CMPCn

Register	CMPC3	CMPC5
R0	Number of bytes remaining in source1, including the byte that caused the inequality. Zero if the strings are equal.	Number of bytes remaining in source1, including the byte that caused the inequality. Zero if the strings are equal or if string1 was exhausted before inequality found.
R1	Address of the byte in source1 that caused the inequality. If the strings are equal, it contains the address of the byte following source1.	Address of the byte in source1 that caused the inequality. If the comparison continued after source1 was exhausted, it contains the address of the byte following source1.
R2	Equals R0	Same as R0 except that it relates to source2.
R3	Same as R1 except that it relates to source2.	Same as R1 except that it relates to source2.

The comparison will terminate when the computer discovers that the fourth characters in these strings are different. The registers and conditions codes at this point will be set as follows:

- R0 = 5 (there are five characters remaining in String1)
- R1 = location of the blank in String1
- R2 = 7 (there are seven characters remaining in String2)
- R3 = location of the "i" in String2
- N = 1 (" " is LSS "i")
- Z = 0 (the strings are not the same)
- V = 0
- C = 1 (" " is LSSU "i")

The program will branch to the location called Unequal.

The last two instructions covered in this section are designed to locate or skip a specified character in a character string. They are as follows:

Opcode	Mnemonic	Operands
3A	LOCC	Search char, length of source, source
3B	SKPC	Skip char, length of source, source

For both instructions, characters in the source are compared with the specified character. For LOCC, the comparison continues until a matching character is found or all the characters have been tested. In the case of SKPC, the computer searches for the first character that does not match the skip character or for the end of the string if all the characters agree with the skip character. The Z condition code bit is set to 1 if the search is unsuccessful and the desired match or mismatch could not be found. It is cleared to 0 if the search terminated before exhausting the string. These instructions only use R0 and R1, and the final register values as shown in Table 9.3 are consistent with the general pattern for those registers as described earlier in Figure 9.2.

As an example of the use of these instructions, suppose it is necessary to locate a word enclosed by periods in the string labeled String and

Table 9.3 Registers After Executing LOCC and SKPC

Register	LOCC	SKPC
R0	Number of bytes remaining in the source, including the byte that caused the match. Zero if the search character was not found.	Number of bytes remaining in the source, including the byte that caused the mismatch. Zero if the whole string consisted of the skip character.
R1	Address of the first byte in the source that matched the search byte if there is one. Otherwise it contains the address of the byte following the source.	Address of the first byte in the source that does not match the skip byte if there is one. Otherwise it contains the address of the byte following the source.

move it to the beginning of that storage area, padding the extra spaces with dashes.

```
Period   = ^A"."
Dash     = ^A"-"
String:    .ASCII    "...MACRO..."
           .
           .
           .
           SKPC    #Period, #11, String   ; Find next non-period
           MOVW    R0, R6                 ; Save bytes remaining
           MOVL    R1, R7                 ; Save address
           LOCC    #Period, R0, (R1)      ; Find next period
           SUBW2   R0, R6                 ; Find length of word
           MOVC5   R6, (R7), #Dash, -     ; Move word found to the beginning
                   #11, String            ;   of String and pad with "-"
```

In this code segment the SKPC instruction is used to skip over the initial periods and locate the first letter of the word. The number of characters remaining in the string (eight in this example) and the address of the first letter in the word are saved in R6 and R7. The search in the remaining characters for the trailing periods begins at the address in R1. After locating the next period, the length of the word (8 − 3 = 5) can be calculated. The MOVC5 instruction moves the number of characters calculated in R6, starting at the address saved in R7, to the beginning of String, padding it with dashes. The final value of String is "MACRO------".

In this section we introduced some additional character string instructions available in the VAX assembly language. When using these instructions, remember that they may affect registers R0–R5. (The *VAX Architecture Handbook* and the *VAX MACRO and Instruction Set Volume* describe some of the other string instructions, including ones that can translate characters, find or skip a set of characters, find substrings, and edit character strings.) In the next section we will use some of the character string instructions in a program to demonstrate some useful I/O procedures.

9.4 A Program Using Character Strings and I/O

In this section we will look at a program that illustrates many of the concepts introduced in Chapters 7 to 9. The problem asks users to input their name, last name first. The computer is to reply with a friendly greeting, including the user's first name.

9.4 A Program Using Character Strings and I/O

In some languages inputting names poses a dilemma for programmers, who must set an arbitrary limit on the number of characters in the name. Fortunately, this is not the case in MACRO because Lib$Get_Input has an option that allows inputting a variable-length string whose length equals the number of characters typed by the user. We will look at this option before continuing the discussion of the problem.

Variable-Length Input

Lib$Get_Input provides for variable-length input by permitting a dynamic, variable-length string mode to be specified in a character string descriptor. We can specify this mode by writing a descriptor with the mode set equal to 2. When we input a dynamic string, it is unnecessary to reserve room for the string. Instead, Lib$Get_Input will find space for the exact number of characters typed by the user. It puts the address and the length of the string in the appropriate parts of the descriptor before returning control to the calling program. Unfortunately, MACRO does not provide a directive for a mode 2 descriptor. The following macro may be convenient.

```
       .MACRO    DynamicStringDesc
                 ; Define descriptor for variable string
       .BLKW     1               ; Reserve room for length
       .BYTE     14              ; Data type is character string
       .BYTE     2               ; Dynamic string allocation
       .BLKL     1               ; Reserve room for the address of
                                 ;   characters
       .ENDM     DynamicStringDesc
```

If we use this macro, a string can be input in the following way:

```
Input:    DynamicStringDesc            ; Descriptor for dynamic string
          .
          .
          .
          PUSHAL    Input              ; Push address of descriptor
          CALLS     #1, G^Lib$Get_Input
                                       ;   and input string
```

The procedure reserves the required number of memory bytes to hold the characters typed by the user. It places the number of those characters in the first word at Input, and their address is stored at Input+4. Relative deferred addressing may be a convenient way to access the data. Lib$Get_Input's ability to allocate the space required for the input can also be helpful in sophisticated programs that must input an unknown number of data items.

For output, Lib$Put_Output treats static, fixed-length, and dynamic variable-length strings as being equivalent. To echo input, we need only pass the descriptor when calling the output procedure.

An Example

We can now turn our attention to solving the problem stated earlier. We must write a program that can carry on the following type of conversation with the user.

```
Please enter your name, last name first:   Johnson, Mary
Hello, Mary
```

The underlined portion would be typed by the user.

If we use a top-down approach to the problem, the first draft of the algorithm is not too difficult.

1. Request user to input name, last name first.
2. Determine the user's first name.
3. Copy the first name to the output buffer.
4. Output the message.

Only step 2 needs serious consideration. To satisfy this step, we must find the memory location holding the first character of the user's first name and determine the number of characters in that name. Even if we ignore ways that users could fail to follow instructions properly, there are several manners in which users may type their names. They may type some initial blanks before the last name. We will assume that there must be at least one blank separating the last and first names, but some people might include several. A middle name following the first name is also possible. The following steps could be used to implement this portion of the algorithm. Observe that they operate correctly even if the user adds a comma immediately after the last name or includes a middle name.

2a. Skip any initial blanks
2b. Find the next blank, which marks the end of the first name.
2c. Skip any blanks separating the last and first name.
2d. Save the location of the first letter in the first name.
2e. Find the next blank or the end of the string, whichever marks the end of the first name.
2f. Calculate length of the first name.

The code in Listing 9.2 implements the resulting algorithm. The x's in Response will never be printed. Instead they act as a target for the user's first name. It simplifies our job of determining the exact location and the length of the field reserved for the name.

We assumed that the user types his or her name in the format

LastName,   FirstName

where the comma is optional. The input routine will store the length of the string in the first word of the descriptor and place its address at

9.4 A Program Using Character Strings and I/O

Listing 9.2 Sample program finding first names

```
            .TITLE    FirstName   Find first name and print message
;     Program to get and print a name using library I/O subroutines

;  ...... Define constant and declare external procedures ......
Blank       = ^A" "
            .EXTERNAL  Lib$Get_Input, Lib$Put_Output

;  ...... Define a macro ......
            .MACRO    DynamicStringDesc
              .BLKW   1                  ; Save room for length
              .BYTE   14                 ; Signifies character string
              .BYTE   2                  ; Dynamic, variable length string
              .BLKL   1                  ; Save room for address
            .ENDM     DynamicStringDesc

;  ...... Define descriptors ......
Question:   .ASCID    "Please enter your name, last name first: "
Name:       DynamicStringDesc            ; Descriptor for user's name
Response:   .ASCID    "Hello, xxxxxxxxxxxx"

;  ...... Set up argument list for CALLG ......
ArgList:    .LONG     1                  ; One argument
            .ADDRESS  Response           ; Points to argument

;  .......... Beginning of executable code ..........

            .ENTRY    NameIO, 0

;  ...... Use Lib$Get_Input to get user's name ......
GetName:    PUSHAL    Question           ; Prompt for name
            PUSHAL    Name               ; Input name
            CALLS     #2, G^Lib$Get_Input

;  ...... Find the user's first name ......
FindName:   SKPC      #Blank, Name, @Name+4  ; Find first nonblank
            LOCC      #Blank, R0, (R1)       ; Find end of last name
            SKPC      #Blank, R0, (R1)       ; Find beginning of first name
            MOVW      R0, R6                 ; Save remaining length
            MOVL      R1, R7                 ;   and address
            LOCC      #Blank, R0, (R1)       ; Find end of first name
            SUBW2     R0, R6                 ; Find length of name

;  ...... Move and output the user's first name ......
MoveName:   MOVC5     R6, (R7), #Blank, #12, Response+15
SayHello:   CALLG     ArgList, G^Lib$Put_Output

;  ...... Terminate run ......
            $EXIT_S
            .END      NameIO
```

Name+4. The FindName section first skips any initial blanks by using SKPC. After locating the first nonblank, R0 has the number of characters left in the string, and the address of that character is in R1. The first LOCC instruction finds the blank marking the end of the last name. The second SKPC instruction skips over the blanks and locates the beginning of the first name. This time the number of characters remaining and the address of the first character of the first name are saved in R6 and R7 for future use. Then we use LOCC once again to locate the end of the first name. After this instruction is processed, R0 contains the number of characters remaining in the string. It will be 0 if the end of the string was found. We can calculate the length of the first name with SUBW2.

We use a MOVC5 instruction to copy the first name into the "x"ed field in Response. This field has 12 characters and begins at 7 characters past the beginning of the string or 15 characters past the beginning of the descriptor.

CALLS and CALLG are both used to illustrate the possibilities. Normally we would use only one type of call unless there are good reasons to use both.

In this section we have demonstrated a convenient way of doing character string I/O. Although the program is a little too simple to be a useful application, it illustrates both types of procedure calls, a macro, character manipulation, and the I/O procedures. The power of the character string instructions will be obvious if you consider rewriting the program in a high-level language. You are very likely to find that the high-level program requires more executable statements to find the first name than are needed in MACRO.

9.5 Decimal Numbers

So far we have assumed that computers work exclusively with binary numbers. Binary numbers are desirable because they allow efficient storage and calculation. For this reason, computers usually use them for scientific and general-purpose calculations.

However, business programs often have different criteria for choosing a number base. Often there is relatively little arithmetic, so calculation speed is not an important consideration. Such programs often entail a large amount of input and output that must be readable to humans. Thus the use of binary numbers can require frequent conversions between bases. Business problems often require numbers that have more digits

9.5 Decimal Numbers

than are commonly available in the binary representations used on computers. (Consider the national debt, for example.) The use of floating-point binary numbers to represent amounts in dollars and cents can lead to unacceptable rounding errors. Consequently, many computers allow one or more decimal representations.

The VAX has four ways to store numbers in decimal. We will discuss two of them in some detail.

The simplest format for decimal numbers is called **leading separate** because each digit is stored as a separate byte using the ASCII code, and the sign byte is in the first or leading position. Numbers in this format can be written and printed on terminals and printers. Leading separate numeric strings are identified by two attributes: (1) the address of the leading sign and (2) the length, which is the number of digits (from 0 to 31) in the number. (The 0 length number has only a sign byte and always is interpreted as zero.) The total number of bytes in one of these numbers is length + 1, including the sign byte. The sign byte is a plus, a minus, or a blank. The blank is treated as a plus, but the computer uses the plus when it generates numbers of this type. The other characters in the string must be one of the digits from 0 to 9. The digits are stored with the most significant digit following the sign.

For example, suppose that we want to store 1234 in a leading separate format using five digits. We could code

```
Value:   .ASCII    "+1234"
```

If the value begins at location 208, the number would be stored as follows:

Location	ASCII	Hex
208	+	2B
209	0	30
20A	1	31
20B	2	32
20C	3	33
20D	4	34

The leading plus sign could be replaced with a blank if desired. Its negative would begin with an ASCII minus sign.

The primary use of leading separate is for input and output. The VAX does not provide any instructions that do calculations with this data type, but it does furnish instructions to convert it to and from the decimal format that we will discuss next.

Packed decimal is designed to store decimal numbers in a more compact format. Both calculation and conversion instructions are provided for this data type.

Like leading separate, packed decimal allows values whose lengths can vary from 0 to 31 digits. We also specify packed decimal numbers by giving their address and the number of digits in their representation. They are stored with the most significant digit first in the same manner as leading separate. However, each decimal digit is stored in a four-bit nibble instead of an eight-bit byte. Moreover, the sign nibble is stored after the least significant digit instead of before the most significant digit. The decimal digits are stored using the corresponding hex digits. The hex digit C is normally used for a plus sign, and D is normally used for a negative sign. However, A, E, and F are also interpreted as plus and B as minus.

If the length (the number of digits) of a packed decimal is L, the number of bytes used to store it is (L + 2)/2, rounded down when the fraction is not an integer. (Alternatively, the number of bytes could be written (L + 1)/2, rounded up.) If L is odd, an even number of nibbles are needed to store the number together with its sign, and the value fits its byte string exactly. If L is even, a leading 0 is added to pad the first byte. The 0 length string fits this pattern. It consists of one byte and has a sign nibble that is preceded by a hex 0 to fill up the byte. It is always considered to have the value 0.

The assembly language MACRO provides a directive called .PACKED to store integers in this format. For example, if we want to store the number 1234, we might code

```
PackedVal:    .PACKED   +1234
```

if the value begins at location 20E, the computer stores it as follows:

Location	Hex	Interpretation
20E	01	01
20F	23	23
210	4C	4+

In assembler listings the bytes appear in reverse order as usual, so it appears as the hard-to-read form 4C 23 01. PackedVal could be said to have either four or five digits.

The concept of packed decimal is not unique to the VAX; it is also used on the IBM 370 and compatible computers.

The VAX allows two other formats that store decimal numbers with the sign at the least significant end of the number. These forms are called **zoned numeric** and **overpunched** and collectively are referred to as **trailing numeric strings**. Both codes store all but the last digit in ASCII. Both encode the least significant digit and the sign into the last byte but do it in two different ways. For more details, consult an appropriate manual.

In the next section we will discuss the instructions for calculating with packed decimal.

9.6 Packed Decimal Instructions

The VAX provides several instructions for calculating with packed decimal strings. Although they require more processing time than the corresponding binary instructions, they can process up to 31 decimal digits at a time. By comparison, the largest signed integer that can be stored in a longword is a little more than 2,000,000,000. Packed decimal instructions need several operands because it is necessary to specify both the length and address of decimal strings.

The packed decimal instructions are as follows:

Opcode	Mnemonic	Operands
34	MOVP	Length, source, destination
35	CMPP3	Length, source1, source2
37	CMPP4	Length1, source1, length2, source2
20	ADDP4	⎱ Source length, source, −
22	SUBP4	⎰ destination length, destination
21	ADDP6	
23	SUBP6	⎧ Source1 length, source1, −
25	MULP	⎨ source2 length, source2, −
27	DIVP	⎩ destination length, destination

We must emphasize that the length of a packed decimal number is the number of digits in its representation, not the number of bytes. This number does not include the sign nibble. The VAX treats this length as a 16-bit word even though its value must be 31 or less.

The MOVP instruction copies the packed decimal string specified by the source into the destination. The compare instructions CMPP3 and CMPP4 are used to compare packed decimals and set condition codes. CMPP3 assumes that both decimal strings have the same length, CMPP4 allows different lengths. We can do addition with ADDP4 or ADDP6. Their operation is equivalent to the two- or three-operand additions used with other data types.

    ADDP4   destination ← destination + source
    ADDP6   Destination ← source2 + source1

The subtraction instructions operate in a similar manner.

    SUBP4   Destination ← destination − source
    SUBP6   destination ← source2 − source1

Multiplication and division come only in six-operand formats.

    MULP   Destination ← source2 * source1
    DIVP   Destination ← source2 / source1

These instructions are similar to the character string instructions in several ways. We have already mentioned that the length is treated as a word. In addition, instructions processing two strings use registers R0–R3 for temporary storage, while those processing three strings use registers R0–R5.

We must use special care with these instructions. Unlike most other instructions on the VAX, packed decimal instructions can give invalid results if the destination (or source2 in case of the compare instructions) overlaps one of the other operands.

The following program segment illustrates the use of some decimal instructions. It is designed to calculate the price of Quan items. If the quantity is less than PriceBreak, the Cost is calculated at the regular price; otherwise it is calculated at QuanPrice.

```
LenQuan = 4                               ; Number of digits in quantities
LenPrice = 2                              ; Number of digits in prices
LenCost = LenQuan + LenPrice              ; Number of digits in Cost

Quan:        .PACKED   0900               ; Quantity sold
PriceBreak:  .PACKED   1000               ; Minimum quan for low price
RegPrice:    .PACKED   14                 ; Regular price
QuanPrice:   .PACKED   11                 ; Reduced price for large quantities
Cost:        .BLKB     LenCost+2/2        ; Total cost
             .
             .
             .
             CMPP3     #LenQuan, Quan, -  ; If Quan is smaller
                       PriceBreak         ;     than PriceBreak
             BGEQ      BigAmount          ; then
             MULP      #LenQuan, Quan, -  ;     charge regular price
                       #LenPrice, RegPrice, -
                       #LenCost, Cost
             BRB       Done               ; else
BigAmount:   MULP      #LenQuan, Quan, -  ;     charge lower price
                       #LenPrice, QuanPrice, -
             ---       #LenCost, Cost
Done:
```

We could make a few observations about this program segment. Symbolic constants were used to specify the length of the variables to improve readability and simplify modification. The assembler would be satisfied with simple constants. For example:

```
CMPP3    #4, Quan, PriceBreak
```

Because Cost is the product of numbers whose lengths are LenQuan and LenPrice, its length is the sum of their lengths. The number of bytes in Cost is determined by the formula (LenCost+2)/2 rounded down.

Parentheses are unnecessary and indeed illegal in this MACRO constant definition because the assembler calculates constant expressions from left to right. (If desired, we could have written <LenCost+2>/2.) MACRO uses integer division when calculating constant expressions.

In the program Quan was assigned the value 900. However, the comparisons indicate that it might be 1000 or more in other situations. Thus the length of Quan was specified as four, which means that 900 must be written with a leading 0 to force a four-digit representation of this number.

In the next section we will learn that it is easy to convert packed decimal numbers to other formats, including leading separate, which can be used for input and output. In the meantime, we could use the debugger to check the operation of this program segment. The qualifier /Packed:n, where n is the number of digits, may be used for both examine and deposit instructions. It may be helpful to "set radix decimal" if packed decimal values will be deposited. Otherwise, we must enter their values in hex.

COBOL handles numerical values in interesting ways, as it allows the programmer to specify the number of digits needed for each variable. Moreover, unlike many other languages, VAX COBOL allows the programmer to specify almost any one of the VAX's data types by selecting the appropriate "USAGE clause" when declaring variables. As a result COBOL programmers need to be concerned about calculation and storage efficiency. As expected, ASCII formats like leading separate are discouraged for values used in arithmetic operations. Binary numbers are recommended for values used primarily in calculations, while packed decimal is recommended for values that are used in ASCII I/O operations as well as in computations. Mixing data types in the same calculation causes inefficient data conversions and should be avoided. To avoid round-off problems, programmers rarely use floating point. Instead, they can specify the number of decimal places for variables. The computer uses binary or packed decimal integers and scales the values as needed.

9.7 Numerical Conversions and I/O

The VAX has several numerical data types, and conversion between these types is frequently necessary. On some computers converting numbers between certain data types requires a lengthy set of instructions. Conversion between integer and floating point is particularly troublesome. However, the VAX provides many instructions that simplify this task; in fact, the conversion instructions are much more numerous than found on most computers. We will look first at conversions between standard numerical types and then at conversions involving packed decimal.

I/O presents a double conversion problem. Typically, outputting a value requires that we convert the value to decimal and then convert the resulting decimal digits to ASCII before we can send them to a terminal or printer. The process is reversed when inputting numbers from a terminal. High-level languages carry this process out automatically for the programmer. Assembly language programmers must include code to carry out these conversions.

Some of the conversion instructions can be used to simplify numerical I/O, but they cannot be expected to handle every situation because of the various formats that might be desired. For example, the number 10000 could be written 10,000, 10,000.00, or even 10E+4. The programmer must arrange for the particular format desired.

We conclude this section with a set of procedures that use Lib$Put_Output to provide simple output of some data types. The procedures illustrate the use of packed decimal and some of the conversion instructions.

Conversion Between Binary Data Types

The VAX provides instructions that convert numbers between the various binary integer and floating notations. The format of the CVT (ConVerT) instructions is

    CVTxy   Source, destination

where x is the code for the source's data type and y is the destination's type. The standard conversion instructions between various binary formats are shown in the following chart:

| | \multicolumn{5}{c}{To} |||||
From	Byte	Word	Longword	Floating	Double
Byte		CVTBW	CVTBL	CVTBF	CVTBD
Word	CVTWB		CVTWL	CVTWF	CVTWD
Longword	CVTLB	CVTLW		CVTLF	CVTLD
Floating	CVTFB	CVTFW	CVTFL		CVTFD
Double	CVTDB	CVTDW	CVTDL	CVTDF	

You can find the opcodes for the instructions presented in this section in Appendix A. The conversions involving G and H data can also be found there.

In general, conversion instructions act like special move instructions. However, they are subject to some conversion rules that depend on the data types and lengths involved.

1. Shorter integers to longer integers—sign extension is used to extend the number (that is, treat the values as signed numbers).
2. Longer integers to shorter integers—the most significant digits are deleted.
3. Longword to floating—integers are rounded, if needed.

4. Floating to integer—fractions are truncated.
5. Double to floating—values are rounded.

Overflow will occur in some conversions if the value is too large to be stored in the destination. You can check the overflow bit in the PSW to see if an error occurred.

Truncating fractions when converting floating point to integers as specified in rule 4 is undesirable in many situations. Consequently, the VAX offers the CVTR (ConVerT with Rounding) instructions.

	To:
From:	**Longword (rounded)**
Floating	CVTRFL
Double	CVTRDL

Suppose that we need to round the floating-point variable Payment off to the nearest penny. We could do it the following way:

```
MULF3    #100.0, Payment, R0  ; R0 <-- number of pennies
CVTRFL   R0, R0                ; Round to nearest integer
CVTLF    R0, R0                ; Convert back to floating
DIVF3    #100.0, R0, Payment   ; Convert back to dollars
```

The instructions considered so far are primarily for signed values. They do not always work correctly when unsigned integers are lengthened to a longer data type. MOVZxy instructions are designed to extend unsigned integers by adding zeros on the left. They include:

	To:	
From:	**Word**	**Longword**
Byte	MOVZBW	MOVZBL
Word		MOVZWL

For example, consider

```
B:   .BYTE ^B11111111
WS:  .BLKW 1
WU:  .BLKW 1
      .
      .
      .
     CVTBW   B, WS
     MOVZBW  B, WU
```

Observe that B equals -1 as a signed integer and 255 as an unsigned value. After the code is executed, we find that

$WS = (1111\ 1111\ 1111\ 1111)_2 = -1$ (in two's complement)

$WU = (0000\ 0000\ 1111\ 1111)_2 = 255$

Conversions Involving Packed Decimal

We now turn to the conversion instructions that make packed decimal useful even when we are not interested in doing decimal calculations. Conversions involving packed decimal include the following:

	To:		
From:	**Longword**	**Packed Decimal**	**Leading Separate**
Longword		CVTLP	
Packed decimal	CVTPL		CVTPS
Leading separate		CVTSP	

These instructions are more complex because decimal strings must be described by both their length and address. The operands for these instructions are as follows:

Mnemonic	**Operands**
CVTLP	Longword source, destination length, packed destination
CVTPL	Source length, packed source, longword destination
CVTPS	Source length, packed source, − Destination length, leading separate destination
CVTSP	Source length, leading separate source, − Destination length, packed destination

It is extremely important to remember that the lengths of both packed decimal and leading separate numbers represent the number of digits in those types of numbers. Except for trivial exceptions, the number of bytes needed to represent a packed decimal number will be smaller than the number of digits. The number of bytes needed to hold a leading separate number will always be one larger than the number of digits. Sixteen-bit words are used to represent the lengths of these strings.

These conversions use R0–R3 for temporary storage. The instructions involving longwords allow the destination to overlap the source; conversions involving leading separate do not. Illegal source data can cause the reserved operand fault, which causes the program to terminate immediately.

These instructions are helpful in conversions from ASCII to internal binary. Listing 9.3 shows one method of inputting a signed longword integer from your terminal. The value is inputted as a character string by Lib$Get_Input. The format must be acceptable as a leading separate string, and the code is designed to ignore leading and trailing blanks. To simplify the coding, the segment requires that positive numbers be preceded with a plus sign. (The input macro of Appendix F solves this problem.) It offers no protection if the value has too many digits or if it contains illegal characters. The exercises at the end of the chapter suggest some improvements.

Listing 9.3 Simple input of a longword

```
Blank    = ^A" "
StringDesc:  .ASCID "                    "   ; 20-character buffer
Temp:        .BLKB  6                        ; Packed decimal buffer
Value:       .BLKL  1                        ; Final value
             .
             .
             .
        PUSHAW  StringDesc                   ; Input a numerical string
        CALLS   #1, G^Lib$Get_Input
        SKPC    #Blank, #20, @StringDesc+4   ; Find leading sign
        MOVW    R0, R6                       ; Save remaining bytes
        MOVL    R1, R7                       ; Save address of sign
        LOCC    #Blank, R0, (R1)             ; Find end of number
        SUBW2   R0, R6                       ; Find number of bytes
        DECW    R6                           ; Find number of digits
        CVTSP   R6, (R7), R6, Temp           ; Convert to packed
        CVTPL   R6, Temp, Value              ; Convert to longword
```

After using Lib$Get_Input to input a character string containing an integer in leading separate notation, the program segment uses SKPC and LOCC to find the beginning and end of the value. The address of the sign byte is put in R7. The value's total length, including the sign byte, is calculated by SUBW2 and put in R6. Then DECW decreases the length by one to find the number of decimal digits. The conversion instructions first transform the number into packed decimal and then into the longword Value. The number of bytes in Temp was picked to allow the routine to process the largest value that can be stored in a longword.

The VAX has additional instructions that convert between the packed decimal and trailing numeric formats. There is also an EDITPC instruction that allows converting packed decimals into character strings according to a pattern specified by the programmer. Its output can be designed to be much more attractive that that produced by CVTPS.

Output Procedures

We now have the necessary background needed to look at general-purpose output procedures that can be used with our assembly language programs. Although the procedures are a little more difficult to use than the macros in Appendix F, they offer a great deal of flexibility in determining which values will be printed on each line of output.

Numbers can be converted to printable character strings in several ways. We can use Algorithm 1.2 to convert the binary values to decimal digits and then convert the decimal digits into ASCII characters. Alternatively, the VAX/VMS Run Time Library has several conversion routines. For example, OTS$CVT_L_TI converts longword integers to printable text. (The I/O macros in Appendix F use procedures of this type for floating-point values.) However, we will use the convert instructions discussed in this section to illustrate their use.

We would also like to illustrate how many high-level language compilers handle output. Many compilers use three basic steps for each line of output. First, a procedure is called to initialize the output. Next, the various values to be printed are processed one at a time by procedures designed especially for the values' data types. Finally, another procedure is called to signal that the output line is ready to be printed. This type of arrangement is popular because it allows any number of variables of various types to be printed on the same line.

The five procedures included in Listing 9.5 follow that outline. They use an output buffer that stores output until the program signals that it is ready to be printed. The following list gives their name, argument list, and purpose. The procedures are grouped by function.

Initialization:
  InitializeOutput   —Clear output buffer.

Process particular variable types:
  OutASCII (ASCII string, length of string)
      —Put an ASCII string in the buffer.
  OutLong (longword value) —Put a longword in the buffer.
  OutFloat (floating value, number of decimal places)
      —Put a floating value in the buffer.

Output completed line:
  TypeOutputLine   —Type contents of buffer.

The Outxxxx routines pass the value to be printed by reference. The string length and number of decimal places are passed by value.

To demonstrate how these procedures are used, suppose that we want to print a line something like the following:

```
+0000000005 books cost $ +00000023.95
```

We could write the program shown in Listing 9.4. First it initializes the output. Then procedure calls are used to put Number, Item, CostMsg, and Price into the buffer. After the complete message is put in the buffer, it is typed.

It is most convenient to keep the main program and the output procedures shown in Listing 9.5 in separate files and use the linker to connect the corresponding .OBJ files. This simplifies the use of the procedures in a new program because you do not need to get involved with the details of the coding used to print the values.

Listing 9.4 Program demonstrating use of the output package

```
        .TITLE    DemoOutputProcedures

        .EXTERNAL InitializeOutput, OutLong, OutASCII, -
                  OutFloat, TypeOutputLine

CostMsg:        .ASCII  " cost $"
LengthCostMsg = . - CostMsg            ; Length = current address
                                       ;      - address of CostMsg

Item:           .ASCII  "books"
LengthItem = . - Item
Number:         .LONG   5
Price:          .FLOAT  23.95

        .ENTRY  Demo,   0

;       Write (Number, Item, ' cost $', Price)
        CALLS   #0, InitializeOutput   ; Initialize output
        PUSHAL  Number                 ; Output Number
        CALLS   #1, OutLong
        PUSHL   #LengthItem            ; Output Item
        PUSHAB  Item
        CALLS   #2, OutASCII
        PUSHL   #LengthCostMsg         ; Output " cost $"
        PUSHAB  CostMsg
        CALLS   #2, OutASCII
        PUSHL   #2                     ; Output Price with
        PUSHAF  Price                  ;    2 decimal places
        CALLS   #2, OutFloat
        CALLS   #0, TypeOutputLine     ; Print Buffer
        $EXIT_S

        .END    Demo
```

The exercises at the end of the chapter suggest ways to improve the format of the output and some additional procedures that may be useful.

We will look at a few of the programming details that we considered while developing these routines. The output buffer Buf is required because Lib$Put_Output, like most low-level terminal I/O routines, processes a single character string and leaves it up to the program to collect the required information and format it properly. The assignment

```
BufDescrpt = .
```

assigns BufDescrpt the current memory location. Thus BufDescrpt and CurrentLength are two names for the same location and allow us to use

Listing 9.5 Output procedures

```
;                       O U T P U T   P R O C E D U R E S

        .TITLE    OutputRoutines

;    PURPOSE:
;        Provides output of several variable types to the standard
;        output device - normally the user's terminal.

        .EXTERNAL Lib$Put_Output

;    STANDARD CALLING SEQUENCE FOR EACH LINE OF OUTPUT:
;            CALLS    #0, InitializeOutput
;              call a procedure for each value to be printed
;            CALLS    #0, TypeOutputLine

;    Constants:

Blank = ^A" "
Dot   = ^A"."
LengthBuf = 80                      ; Length of output buffer
NumDigits = 10                      ; Number of decimal digits

;    Storage:

;    .... The output buffer, its descriptor, and argument list ....
Buf:               .BLKB    LengthBuf      ; Output buffer
BufDescrpt = .
CurrentLength:     .BLKW    1              ; Number of characters in buf
                   .BYTE    14             ; Data type
                   .BYTE    1              ; Fixed-length string
                   .ADDRESS Buf            ; Address of buffer
ArgList:           .LONG    1              ; Number of arguments
                   .ADDRESS BufDescrpt     ; Address of descriptor

;    .... Other data ....
NextLoc:           .BLKL    1              ; Address of next location in buf
PackedBuf:         .BLKB    NumDigits+2/2  ; Buffer for packed decimal
Stars:             .ASCII   '**********'   ; Used for error output


; * * * * * Macro CheckForRoom * * * * *

; Macro to check to see if there is enough room in the buffer for the
; next field.  If not, it prints the current buffer and reinitializes it.

;    Argument:  FieldLength:  Word, Length (number of characters) of the
;               field to be added to the buffer.
```

Listing 9.5 (continued)

```
            .MACRO   CheckForRoom,  FieldLength,  ?OK
            ADDW3    FieldLength, CurrentLength, R0
            CMPW     #LengthBuf, R0        ; Is there room in buf?
            BGEQ     OK                    ;   If not . . .
            CALLS    #0, TypeOutputLine    ;     output line,
            CALLS    #0, InitializeOutput  ;     initialize output,
            MOVW     FieldLength, R0       ;     set no. of char. in buffer
OK:         MOVW     R0, CurrentLength     ; Update number of characters
                                           ;     in the buffer
            .ENDM    CheckForRoom


; * * * * * Procedure InitializeOutput * * * * *

;   Purpose:  Called to clear out buffer and initialize a line of output.
;   Standard call:
;        CALLS    #0, InitializeOutput
;   Arguments:  None

            .ENTRY   InitializeOutput, ^M<R2, R3, R4, R5>

;   Initialize output by clearing output buffer
            MOVC5    #0, Buf, #Blank, #LengthBuf, Buf
                                           ; Store blanks in buffer
            CLRW     CurrentLength         ; No characters in buffer
            MOVAB    Buf, NextLoc          ; NextLoc = Beginning of buffer
            RET


; * * * * * Procedure OutASCII(ASCII string, Length) * * * * *

;   Purpose:  Puts an ASCII string in the output buffer.  Does not leave
;        any spaces around the string.
;   Standard call:
;        PUSHL    Length of string
;        PUSHAB   ASCII string
;        CALLS    #2, OutASCII
;   Arguments:
; Name    Offset   Use                    Type         Passed by
String  =   4      ; Character string     longword     reference
Length  =   8      ; Number of characters word         value

            .ENTRY   OutASCII, ^M<R2, R3, R4, R5>

            CheckForRoom   Length(AP)
            MOVC3    Length(AP), @String(AP), @NextLoc
            MOVL     R3, NextLoc           ; Save location of next field
            RET
```

(continued)

Listing 9.5 (continued)

```
;       * * * * * Procedure OutLong(Longword value) * * * * *

;       Purpose:  Puts a longword in the output buffer.  Leaves a blank
;               before and after value.  Prints 10 digits plus sign.
;       Standard call:
;               PUSHAL   Value
;               CALLS    #1, OutLong
;       Argument:
; Name   Offset    Use                    Type            Passed by
Value  = 4         ; Value to be printed   longword        reference

                .ENTRY   OutLong, ^M<R2, R3>

                CheckForRoom  #NumDigits+3
                INCL     NextLoc                       ; Leave leading blank
                CVTLP    @Value(AP), #NumDigits, PackedBuf
                CVTPS    #NumDigits, PackedBuf, #NumDigits, @NextLoc
                ADDL2    #NumDigits+2, NextLoc
                                              ; Leave room for digits, sign and
                                              ;      final blank
                RET


;       * * * Procedure OutFloat(Floating value, decimal places) * * *

;       Purpose:  Puts a floating-point number in the output buffer.  Leaves
;               blanks before and after value.  Prints 10 digits plus sign and
;               decimal point.  Call specifies number of decimal places.  If the
;               value is too large, it is replaced by stars.
;       Standard call:
;               PUSHL    Number of decimal places
;               PUSHAF   Value
;               CALLS    #2, OutFloat
;       Arguments:
; Name      Offset    Use                        Type        Passed by
Value     = 4         ; Value to be printed       floating    reference
NumPlaces = 8         ; Num. of decimal places    word        value

                .ENTRY   OutFloat, ^M<R2, R3, R4, R5, R6, R7>

                CheckForRoom  #NumDigits+4

;  .... Make sure the number of decimal places is legal ....
                MOVW     NumPlaces(AP), R2    ; Get decimal places
                CMPW     R2, #NumDigits       ; If decimal places > NumDigits
                BLEQU    OK2                  ;    then
                MOVW     #NumDigits, R2       ;        decimal places = NumDigits
OK2:            MOVZWL   R2, R6               ; R6 <-- decimal places
```

Listing 9.5 (continued)

```
;   .... Multiply by 10 to the number of decimal places ....
        MOVF    @Value(AP), R4      ; Get value
        TSTW    R2                  ; Check number of digits
Loop:   BLEQU   Done                ; Branch if done
        MULF2   #10.0, R4           ; Multiply value by 10
        DECW    R2                  ; Decrement counter
        BRB     Loop                ; Repeat

;   .... Convert the result to a longword, packed decimal, and ASCII ....
Done:   INCL    NextLoc                             ; Leave a leading blank
        CVTRFL  R4, R4                              ; Convert to integer
        BVS     TooBig                              ; Branch if too big
        CVTLP   R4, #NumDigits, PackedBuf
        CVTPS   #NumDigits, PackedBuf, #NumDigits, @NextLoc
        BRB     OK3
TooBig: MOVC3   #NumDigits+1, Stars, @NextLoc
OK3:    ADDL2   #NumDigits+3, NextLoc
                                                    ; Update NextLoc

;   .... Insert decimal point ....
        SUBL3   R6, NextLoc, R7     ; Find beginning of decimal
        SUBL2   #2, R7              ;    part
        MOVC3   R6, (R7), 1(R7)     ; Move decimal part right
        MOVB    #Dot, (R7)          ; Insert decimal point
        RET


;   * * * * * Procedure TypeOutputLine * * * * *

;   Purpose: Types the current contents in the buffer.
;   Standard call:
;       CALLS   #0, TypeOutputLine
;   Arguments: None

        .ENTRY  TypeOutputLine, ^M< >

        CALLG   ArgList, G^Lib$Put_Output
        RET

        .END
```

the most convenient one depending on whether we are discussing the descriptor or the length of the string. Arglist makes it convenient to call the library output routine with CALLG.

The macro CheckForRoom is designed to ensure that the output buffer is not filled beyond capacity. The Outxxxx procedures use it before a new value is put into the buffer. If the FieldLength required for the next value would cause the buffer to overflow, the current contents are printed and the buffer is reinitialized.

The procedure InitializeOutput clears out the buffer, zeros the current number of characters in the buffer, and initializes the location where the next character can be added to the buffer.

OutASCII is the simplest output routine and illustrates the steps needed to add a new character string of any type to the buffer. It simply checks to make sure that there is room in the buffer, copies the string into the buffer, and updates the location where the next field begins.

OutLong is also quite straightforward. After checking to make sure that the buffer has room for the value, it inserts a blank by incrementing the next location address and converts the value to packed decimal and then to leading separate. It then updates the location of the next field. The value of NumDigits was picked to ensure that the largest possible integer on the VAX can be processed.

OutFloat is the most complicated procedure in this package. You may require several readings of the code to understand it fully. (It is easy to see why the I/O macros in Appendix F use system conversion routines.) The general outline is as follows.

1. Make sure that there is room in the buffer for the field, which includes two blanks, a sign, and a decimal point in addition to the NumDigits characters for the value itself.

2. The number of decimal places specified in the call statement is checked to ensure that it does not exceed the number of digits actually printed. If so, it is replaced by the number of digits. Unsigned arithmetic is used because the number of digits is always nonnegative.

3. The procedure uses a traditional method of rounding a floating-point value to the correct number of decimal places—multiply by the correct power of 10, round off, and divide by the same power of 10. The first operation is to multiply the value by 10.0 the proper number of times within a loop. The repetition count is equal to the number of decimal places.

4. The resulting value is rounded to an integer and then converted to ASCII much as longwords are converted. If the value calculated in step 3 is too large to be converted to a longword, the field is filled with stars because the original value cannot be represented in the desired format.

5. All that remains is to divide by the correct power of 10. Because character strings cannot be used in calculations, we just move the decimal digits one character to the right and insert the decimal point in the correct spot.

The TypeOutputLine procedure seems simple because Lib$Put_Output does all the work. In Chapter 11 we will learn just how much effort is actually required when we look at I/O in a systematic way. The exercises at the end of the chapter suggest improvements and new procedures that would be helpful.

Summary

In this chapter we have looked at three related topics—character strings, decimal strings, and I/O. We began by looking at various representations for character strings, then at directives and descriptors for them. Particularly useful are the .ASCII directive and the .ASCID descriptor. Unfortunately, the .ASCID descriptor cannot be used in every situation where character strings are being passed to subprograms, so it is important to understand the format of a descriptor. The VAX provides some special instructions for processing character strings, including MOVC3, MOVC5, CMPC3, CMPC5, SKPC, and LOCC. Other character string instructions are described in reference manuals. These instructions use from two to six registers for temporary storage.

Input/output is a complicated topic, but the Run Time Library contains two useful procedures (Lib$Get_Input and Lib$Put_Output) that make printing character strings easy. Arguments are passed to these routines by descriptor.

Decimal numbers have important applications in computers for business data processing and for I/O. We looked at leading separate decimal strings, which use ASCII characters for the sign and decimal digits. The VAX also supports packed decimal, which reduces storage requirements because two decimal digits are stored per byte. The VAX provides arithmetic instructions for packed decimal strings. These instructions need both the lengths of the decimal strings (in digits) and their addresses. They use registers R0 through R3 or R5 for temporary storage.

The VAX has many instructions designed to convert numerical data from one type to another. They not only simplify calculations but also aid in the conversions between the various internal formats and the external ASCII format needed for human-readable I/O.

Because character string and packed decimal instructions use the first two to six registers for temporary storage, many programmers avoid the use of R0–R5 for other purposes in any coding using these instructions.

We must convert numerical values from their internal binary representations to ASCII strings before we can print them. It may be convenient to have some general-purpose procedures available for this purpose. High-level languages frequently use a three-step process in translating write statements. We introduced output procedures using this format in the last section. After a procedure call is used to initialize the output, each variable is processed in a separate call to a procedure especially designed for that variable's data type. Finally, the program signals that the line is ready to be printed with another procedure call. We can handle input in much the same manner.

Chapter 9 Character Strings, Packed Decimal, and Introduction to I/O

This chapter completes the introduction of new assembly language instructions in this book. You will get additional coding experience when more basic and versatile I/O techniques are introduced in Chapter 11.

Exercises

1. Hand assemble the following program segments.
   a. A: .QUAD   ^A"ABCDE"
   b. B: .ASCII   +ASSEMBLY+
   c. C: .ASCIZ   /Language/
   d. D: .ASCIC   "String"
   e. LF = 10
      E: .ASCID   *DO IT NOW*<LF>

2. Write assembler code that would define a descriptor for the following situations:
   a. You want to pass the expression "This book" to a procedure.
   b. You want to input a ten-character string.
   c. You want to input a string of unknown length.

3. Compile (rewrite in assembler) the following Pascal code segment:
   ```
   var Name:   packed array [1 .. 10] of char;
       X, Y:   array [1 .. 20] of integer;
       I:      integer;
   .
   .
   .
   Name := 'John Brown';
   Y := X;
   for I := 1 to 20 do X[I] := 0;
   ```
   Notes: translate the last statement in two ways: first literally and then give an optimized version that uses only one MACRO instruction and that does not need the counter I. Pascal uses longwords for integers.

4. Write and test a MACRO program that inputs a line of characters and then counts
   a. The number of blanks actually typed in the line.
   b. The number of uppercase letters on the line.
   c. The number of words on a line. Assume that any sequence of nonblank characters is a word. Words are separated by one or more blanks. Test your program on lines that begin and end with a word and on lines that begin and end in blanks.
   d. Count the occurrences of the word THE. (Convert all lowercase letters to uppercase before looking for matches.)

5. Repeat Exercise 4 but continue to read lines of input until you find one that begins with the character "%". Then print the count(s).

6. (Manual search.) Look up the character string instructions MOVTC and MATCHC. Then work part d of Exercise 4 using these instructions.

7. a. Write an assembly language procedure PackLine that has two arguments: String, which is a character string, and Count, which is a longword. String is passed by descriptor and Count by reference. The number of characters in String is found in its descriptor. PackLine moves any blanks that precede the last nonblank character to the end of the string. Count is set equal to the number of nonblank characters in String. For example, suppose that input to the procedure is

   String = "This Is A Message"

   Then the output returned to the calling program is

   String = "ThisIsAMessage   "

   Count = 14

   b. Write a main program for PackLine in assembler that uses the library I/O procedures for input and output.
   c. Write a main program for PackLine in a high-level language.

8. Write the given values in leading separate and packed decimal notation.
   a. 1776
   b. −26482

9. Can you give a justification for placing the sign in packed decimal notation after the least significant digit?

10. What are the contents of the memory locations 204–20C after the following code is executed? Assume that C is stored at location 204.

    ```
    A:      .PACKED    123
    B:      .PACKED    10
    C:      .BLKB      3
    D:      .BLKB      4
    E:      .BLKB      2
            .
            .
            .
    ADDP6   #3, A, #2, B, #3, E
    MULP    #3, A, #2, B, #6, D
    DIVP    #2, B, #3, A, #4, C
    ```

11. Work Exercise 16 in Chapter 7 but have the function P(N,R) calculate a floating-point result for integer inputs N and R.

12. a. Modify the program in Listing 9.3 so that nonnegative integers can be input with or without the leading plus sign.
    b. Modify the program in Listing 9.3 so that illegal input is rejected. Before attempting to convert the input, check each character to make sure that it is appropriate. The leading character should be a plus or minus character (or a digit if part a is also included). The value is rejected if it contains a nondigit or the number has more than nine digits. If the input is illegal, return the value ^X80000000.

13. Improve the output routines in Listing 9.5 by making the following changes.
    a. Observe that the program may destroy itself if a character string with more than LengthBuf characters is passed to OutASCII. If the Length of the String is longer than the output buffer, print only the first LengthBuf characters.
    b. Improve the output of OutLong and OutFloat by deleting plus signs and leading zeros and move a minus sign next to the first nonzero character. For example, instead of printing
    +0000001234 and -0000000567
    print
            1234 and   -567
    A macro that can be used with both variable types is suggested.
14. Add to the routines in Listing 9.5 by writing new output procedures as indicated.
    a. Procedure OutUnsignedByte (byte value)
        Puts a byte treated as an unsigned integer into the buffer. Use a field consisting of a leading blank, three digits, and a trailing blank. (Hint: extend Value to a longword.)
    b. Procedure OutWord (word value)
        Puts a word into the buffer. The field consists of a leading blank, a sign, five digits, and a trailing blank.
    c. Procedure OutVariableLong (longword value, number of digits)
        Puts a longword value into the buffer. It uses exactly "number of digits" in the field. If the value does not fit, replace it by stars. "Number of digits" is passed by value.
    d. Procedure OutLongBase (unsigned longword value, base)
        Use the method given in Algorithm 1.2 to convert the value into the given base, add each of the resulting digits to 0 or A to convert them to characters, and put the resulting characters into the buffer. If the base is larger than 10, use A to represent the digit 10, B to represent 11, and so on. Do not print leading zeros. You cannot use CheckForRoom until you know how many digits are needed to represent the number. Allow for up to 32 digits that might be needed when base 2 is used. Base is passed by value.
15. (Manual search.) Determine how the EDITPC instruction can be used to improve the format of the output. Then write
    Procedure OutEditLong (longword value)
    that outputs integers in a neat format, including commas placed at the normal three-digit intervals. For example, a line of output with four values might read
    1,234,567   32,000   65   0

16. Develop a set of general-purpose input routines that are used in the same way that the output routines are used. These routines could be called by a variety of programs for input of various data types. For example, the program in Listing 9.4 could be improved by inputting the variables Number, Item, and Price from the user's terminal. The following program segment shows the changes and additions to that program needed to allow it to use these routines.

```
            .EXTERNAL   InputLine, InASCII, InLong, InFloat, -
                        FinishedInputLine
LengthItem = 7
Item:       .BLKB       LengthItem
Number:     .BLKL       1
Price:      .BLKF       1

            .ENTRY Demo,      0
;           Input:      Number, Item, Price
            CALLS       #0, InputLine          ; User inputs values
            PUSHAL      Number                 ; Get Number
            CALLS       #1, InLong
            PUSHL       #LengthItem            ; Get Item
            PUSHAB      Item
            CALLS       #2, InASCII
            PUSHAF      Price                  ; Get Price
            CALLS       #1, InFloat
            CALLS       #0, FinishedInputLine  ; Terminate this input
            .
            .
            .
```

a. Procedure InputLine

Inputs a variable-length dynamic string from the user's terminal. It will be convenient to establish a next character pointer and variable holding the number of characters in the buffer.

b. Procedure InASCII (ASCII string, length of string)

Copies the next "length of string" characters in the input buffer to the address of a string supplied in the argument list. The string is filled with blanks if there are insufficient characters in the buffer. It also updates the next character pointer and the number of characters left in the buffer. The string is passed by reference; its length is passed by value.

c. Procedure InLong (longword value)

Converts the next nonblank character sequence into a longword that is returned to the location supplied by the parameter. It also updates the next character pointer and the number of characters left in the buffer. The value is passed by reference.

d. Procedure InFloat (floating value)

Converts the next nonblank character sequence into a floating-point number. It also updates the next character pointer and the number of characters left in the buffer. The value is passed by reference.

e. Procedure FinishedInputLine

Empties the input buffer by setting the number of characters remaining in it to 0. (Use of this procedure is optional for the time being; it is included for possible future extensions that might require its use.)

17. (Challenging.) Because of the rounding problems often found when binary floating-point arithmetic is used to calculate amounts of money in dollars and cents, it is common to use integer arithmetic for money calculations. The compiler (in the case of COBOL) or programmer (in most other languages) must keep track of the decimal point during the calculations. Values are adjusted after input or before output to ensure that decimal points are correctly represented for the users. In this problem assume that numbers with decimal points are represented in the following way: each "number" consists of one word specifying the current number of decimal places in the number followed by six bytes containing an 11-digit packed decimal number. For example, the number 123.45 could be stored in the following manner:

```
Number:    .WORD     2              ; number of decimal places
           .PACKED   +00000012345   ; the value, 123.45
```

In parts a–c, specify which registers are used by the macro.

a. Write a macro

MultNumWithDecimalPoint A, B, C

that finds the product of A and B and stores the result in C. A, B, and C are all of the type described above. (Both the number of decimal places and the product must be calculated.)

b. Write a macro

AddNumWithDecimalPoint A, B, C

that finds the sum of two numbers A and B and stores the result and the number of decimal places in C. Observe that the number with the fewer decimal places will have to be adjusted before the addition.

c. Write a macro

RoundNumWithDecimalPoint A, D, C

that rounds the number A off to D decimal places. The result is stored in C. Treat D as a word.

d. Write a program that inputs the principal amount, the annual interest rate, and the number of years and prints a table with the column headings Year, Interest Earned, and New Balance. The interest earned each year must be rounded to the nearest penny. You will have to work out the I/O for this program.

18. Write and test a program that inputs, sorts, and prints the given list as directed. Assume that the list has 15 or fewer elements, so a bubble sort or insertion sort would be appropriate.
    a. A list of reals. Sort in descending order.
    b. A list of names stored in 20-character strings. Sort in ascending order.
    c. A list of records consisting of a 20-character name, followed by a longword holding the person's pay. Sort in ascending order according to pay.

19. Hand assemble the following code segment.

```
Value:       .PACKED   1234
Sum:         .BLKL     1
Cost:        .ASCII    "2345"
Temp:        .BLKB     3
PackedSum:   .BLKB     3
             .ENTRY    Example, ^M<R2, R3, R4, R5>
             CVTSP     #4, Cost, #4, Temp
             ADDP6     #4, Value, #4, Temp, #5, PackedSum
             CVTPL     #5, PackedSum, Sum
```

20. Have you ever wondered how much time it takes your VAX to execute a certain instruction or sequence of instructions? The VAX/VMS Run Time Library provides several ways to find out. One of the simplest uses the procedures Lib$Init_Timer and Lib$Show_Timer. Lib$Show_Timer prints out timing and resource use information, including elapsed clock time, elapsed CPU time, counts of two types of I/O operations, and the number of page faults. Suppose that we want to know how much CPU time the MOVC3 instruction needs to move a string. Because the time needed to move a few bytes is smaller than we can measure, we will need to put the instruction in a loop that repeats many times.

    The following program is designed to determine the time needed to move Count characters from A to B. It calls the timing procedures twice. The first is designed to measure overhead (the time it takes to carry out the timing test and execute the loop). The second one adds the instruction we are interested in. We can find the time that the instruction needs by subtracting the overhead time from the time for the second loop and dividing by the repetition count (RepCount).

```
Count = 20                                ; Characters in string
RepCount = 10000                          ; Number of repetitions
A:       .BYTE    ^A"x" [Count]           ; A string of Count "x"'s
B:       .BLKB    Count

         .ENTRY   Timer, 0
; ..... Determine the time required to make the test .....
         CALLS    #0, G^Lib$Init_Timer
         MOVW     #RepCount, R6
```

```
Loop1:                                  ; This loop only counts
            DECW     R6
            BGTR     Loop1
            CALLS    #0, G^Lib$Show_Timer
;  .....  Find time to move Count bytes RepCount times .....
            CALLS    #0, G^Lib$Init_Timer
            MOVW     #RepCount, R6
Loop2:      MOVC3    #Count, A, B       ; Useful instruction added here
            DECW     R6
            BGTR     Loop2
            CALLS    #0, G^Lib$Show_Timer

            $EXIT_S
            .END     Timer
```

The following output was obtained from VAX 11/750.

```
ELAPSED: 00:00:00.06   CPU: 0:00:00.03   BUFIO: 0   DIRIO: 0   FAULTS: 0
ELAPSED: 00:00:00.41   CPU: 0:00:00.26   BUFIO: 0   DIRIO: 0   FAULTS: 0
```

The times are given in an hours:minutes:seconds format. Based on this run, the 20 characters can be moved in as little as $(.26 - .03)/10{,}000 = 0.000023$ CPU second or 23 microseconds, but the time can change depending on such considerations as addressing modes, other users, and model of the VAX.

a. Run the above program on your computer several times and determine the average CPU time needed.

b. Replace the MOVC3 instruction by a loop that moves the characters one at a time. Compare the CPU time needed with that found in part a.

c. Write and run a program that compares the time needed to add numbers with ADDL3 with the time needed to add nine-digit packed decimal numbers with ADDP6. What conclusions can you draw from your data?

PART 4

ADVANCED COMPUTER ARCHITECTURE

CHAPTER 10
Memory Structure

CHAPTER 11
The I/O System

CHAPTER 12
Computer Communications

CHAPTER CONTENTS

10.1 MEMORY DEVICES

10.2 MEMORY ORGANIZATION

10.3 CACHE MEMORY

10.4 MAPPING FUNCTIONS
    Direct Mapping
    Associative Mapping
    Block-Set Associative Mapping

10.5 VIRTUAL MEMORY
    VAX Virtual Memory Structure

SUMMARY

EXERCISES

CHAPTER 10

Memory Structure

The three major components of a computer system are the CPU, the memory unit, and the I/O unit. In Chapters 4, 5, and 6 we studied the operation and structure of the CPU and its subcomponents. In Chapter 11 we will look at the operation of the I/O unit. In this chapter we examine the structure and organization of the main memory unit of a computer system.

Because the memory address register (MAR) and memory data register (MDR) serve as the communication link between the CPU and main memory, they reflect the size of memory. If the MDR contains n bits, the basic word size of memory is n (memory contains n-bit words). The size of the MAR indicates the maximum possible number of words in main memory. If the MAR contains k bits, physical memory may be no larger than 2^k words. For example, if the MAR is only three bits wide, then only 2^3 or eight words can be stored in memory because the MAR can contain only eight possible addresses:

000
001
010
011
100
101
110
111

The VAX has a 32-bit MDR (so its basic word size is 32 bits) and a 32-bit MAR, so it can address up to 2^{32} or 4,294,961,296 bytes. Of course, most VAXs contain far less memory than the possible maximum. In fact, later in this chapter we will discover that not all 32 bits of the MAR are used for address information, which reduces the maximum allowable memory.

We will look first at the basic devices from which main memory is constructed. Then we will explore the hardware and software organization of these devices into a high-speed main memory unit. Special topics in memory organization and structure, such as virtual memory and cache memory, conclude this chapter.

10.1 Memory Devices

Various memory devices can be used to construct the main memory of a computer system. The most common is called **random access memory (RAM)**. The computer can write information into this type of memory and then read it back later. The name RAM is based on the fact that the memory access time (the average time required to read one word of memory) is independent of the memory address. That is, words with small memory addresses take just as much time to find as words with large memory addresses. In a **serial access memory (SAM)**, such as a tape, the memory access time depends on the address. Consider a tape drive. If the desired data is close to the read head, it can be found sooner than data far from the read head.

Other kinds of memory devices can also be used in a computer system for special-purpose applications. For example, some computers have a portion of their memory implemented as **read-only memory (ROM)**. A memory write operation is impossible on a ROM because the contents of the ROM are set when the device is manufactured. ROM is used to store boot routines (which are used to initialize the computer system when it is switched on), parts of the operating system, and sometimes application software. In fact, parts of the microprogram control store are often in ROM. Any software that the system manufacturer decides is important for running the machine and should not be modified by the user could be stored in ROM. The BASIC interpreter on some brands of home computers and cartridges sold for home computer games normally contain a ROM.

Rather than relying on the memory chip manufacturer to store your program on a ROM when it is constructed, you can purchase a programmable ROM (PROM) and store your program on it yourself. This device is manufactured with ones stored in all memory locations. The user places the chip in a special PROM programmer and forces zeros into the locations required by the software. This programming process may occur only once on a PROM; from then on it acts just like a pure ROM. In some situations even PROMs are too restrictive because they can be programmed only once. So some manufacturers produce special memory chips called EPROMs (erasable programmable read-only memories). These chips can be programmed, erased, and then reprogrammed. Of course, inside a computer system, both PROMs and EPROMs act like pure ROMs. PROMs and EPROMs can only be programmed or erased by special machines after they have been removed from the computer system.

While the contents of ROMs and PROMs are permanently stored even if power is lost, RAM memory is volatile. If the power is switched off, all information stored in a RAM memory is lost. RAMs, ROMs, and PROMs are constructed from transistor circuits laid on silicon called semiconductor memory. Such memory is fast, with cycle times on the order of 100 nanoseconds (1 nsec = 10^{-9} second). The cycle time for a memory unit is the time elapsed from the start of a read or write command until another memory command can be issued. Memory can run (return results to the CPU) no faster than its basic cycle time.

There are two types of semiconductor RAM, static memory and dynamic memory. Static memory chips store information indefinitely as long as the power is on, while dynamic memory chips save information for only a few milliseconds. If they must save data for longer periods of time, they must go through a **refresh** cycle. During a refresh operation, each memory cell is read and then the same data is written back into the cell. This may seem like a strange kind of memory to use in a computer, but there are strong economic reasons for its use. For one thing, dynamic memory chips are cheaper than static chips to design and manufacture. In addition, dynamic memory cells are smaller than static ones, so more memory can be packed into a single chip. Besides you must remember that a computer's concept of time is orders of magnitude different from our concept of time. (You must forgive the anthropomorphism but it is an occupational hazard that all computer scientists fall prey to at one time or another.) Consider this refresh limitation for a memory circuit with a cycle time of 10^{-7} seconds and a refresh requirement every 10^{-3} seconds. The number of memory read/write operations between refresh cycles is

$$\frac{10^{-3}}{10^{-7}} = 10^4 \text{ cycles/refresh}$$

or 10,000 memory operations between refresh operations. On our time scale this would be equivalent to being introduced to one new person every minute for a week and still being able to remember the first person's name at the end of the week.

10.2 Memory Organization

The basic physical structure of semiconductor memory is shown in Figure 10.1. It consists of an address decoder, an array of memory bits, and a data register. The nature of the device selected for main memory places a limit on the speed of memory operation. A large semiconductor main memory unit may have a 1-μsec (10^{-6} sec) cycle time, which equals 1,000,000-words-per-second transfer rate between main memory and the CPU. If the CPU works at a rate of 0.2 μsec per basic operation, even a 1,000,000-words-per-second transfer rate is too slow, and the CPU may be waiting for data up to 80 percent of the time. This is a waste of valuable CPU resources, so some method of speeding up the transfer of data between memory and the CPU is necessary. One approach is to change the memory organization or architecture so that more than one word may be located at a time. This requires constructing memory with a parallel structure. There are two fundamental parallel memory architectures. The first is called banked memory, and the second is called interleaved memory.

Banked memory involves dividing main memory into a set of independent blocks, each with its own MAR and MDR, as shown in Figure 10.2. With this architecture, while memory is responding to a CPU request

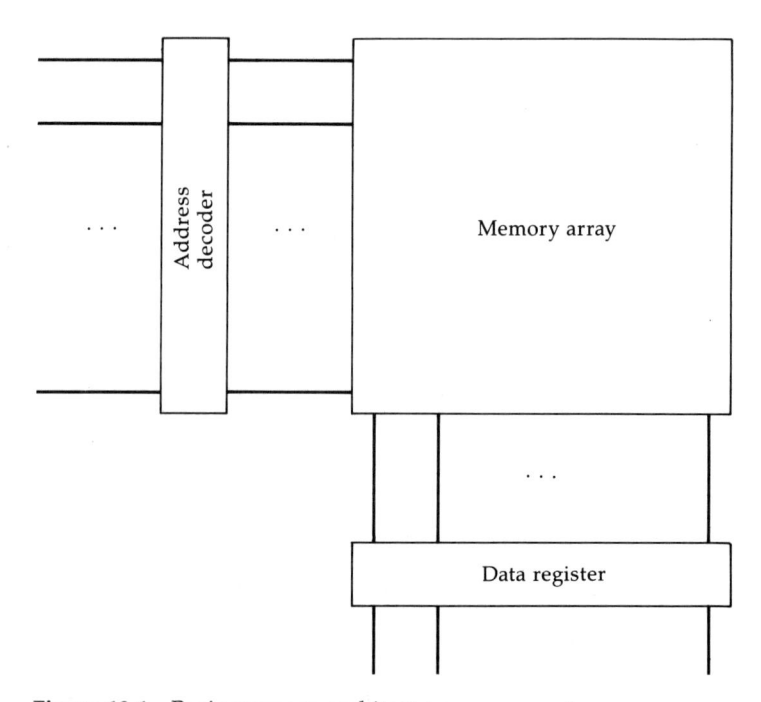

Figure 10.1 Basic memory architecture

10.2 Memory Organization

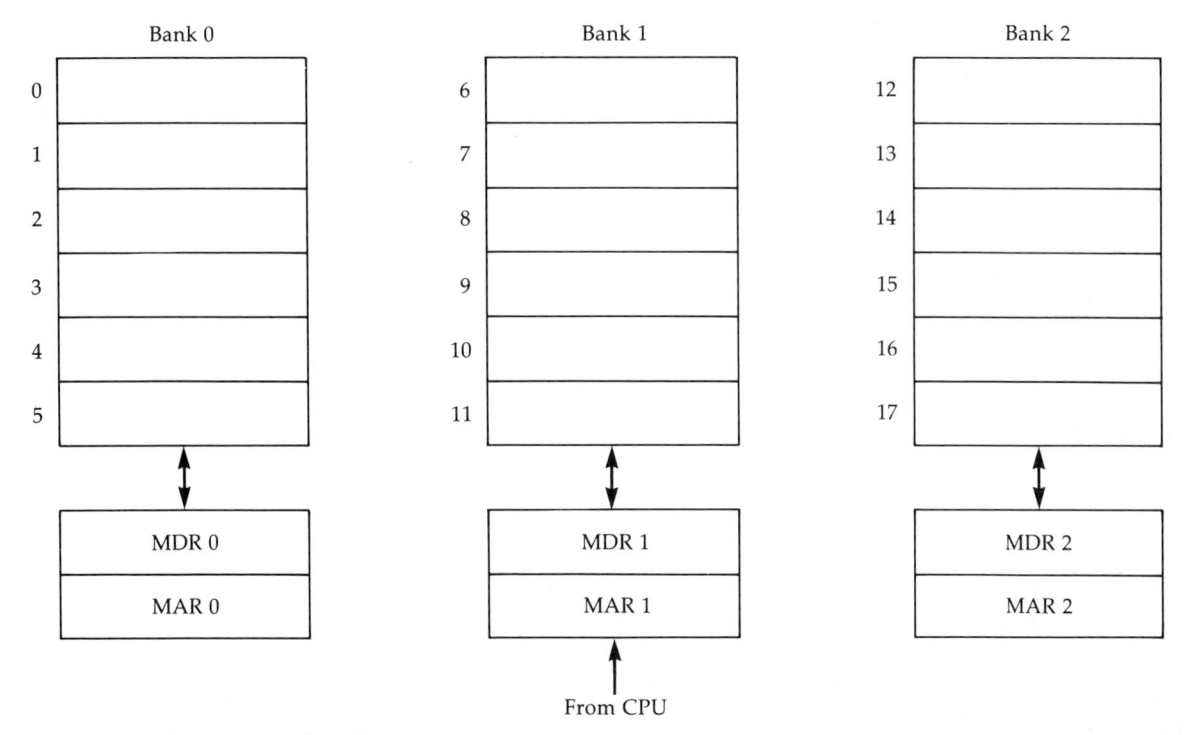

Figure 10.2 Memory bank architecture

```
Bank 0: 0, 1, 2, 3, 4, 5 — MDR 0 / MAR 0
Bank 1: 6, 7, 8, 9, 10, 11 — MDR 1 / MAR 1
Bank 2: 12, 13, 14, 15, 16, 17 — MDR 2 / MAR 2
From CPU
```

for data or instructions in bank 0, I/O devices with direct memory access can request data from another memory bank, say, bank 2 (we will cover direct memory access processes in Chapter 11). Memory can start the search in bank 2 without waiting for the bank 0 search to complete. The result is that data can be found and sent to the CPU and other devices at a faster rate than the memory cycle time might indicate. However, if the data required for a process all resides in the same bank, this architecture will not result in any net gain in speed because only one word at a time can be fetched from a single bank. Unfortunately, data and instructions are often stored in sequential locations and hence would be in a single bank.

Interleaved architecture can be used to overcome the problem noted above with memory banks, as shown in Figure 10.3. The only difference between this structure and the memory bank architecture is that sequential addresses jump bank boundaries. For example, a fetch of the three sequential words at locations 2, 3, and 4 requires only one memory cycle in the interleaved memory system of Figure 10.3. It would require three memory cycles in the banked architecture of Figure 10.2 to fetch the same three words.

For either method to work efficiently, when main memory receives the address in the MAR, it divides it into two parts: k bits, which identify

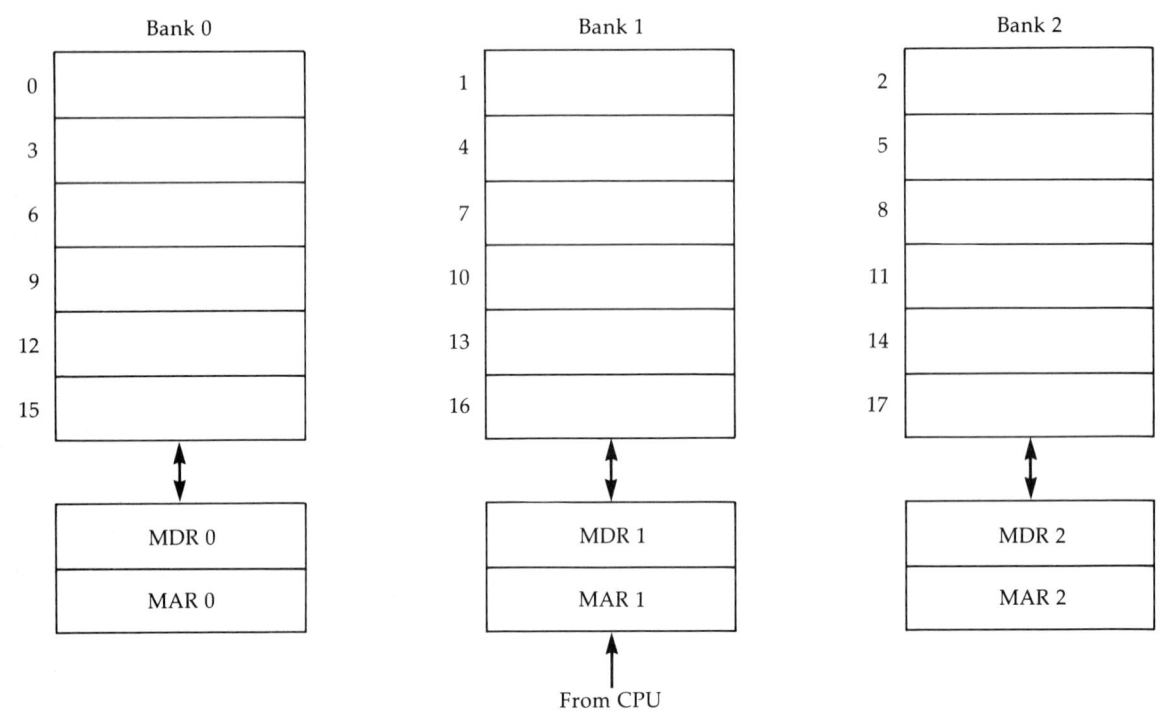

Figure 10.3 Interleaved memory architecture

the bank or memory module, and m bits, which identify the address within the module as shown in Figure 10.4. For example, given a 1K main memory system, a 10-bit MAR is needed. If the system is divided into eight banks with 128 words stored in each, the MAR for a banked memory system addressing location 308 (binary 0100110100) would look like the following:

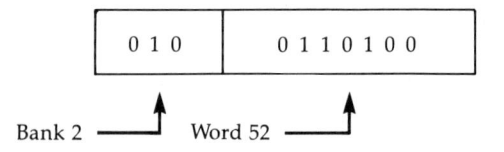

| 0 1 0 | 0 1 1 0 1 0 0 |

Bank 2 ⟶   Word 52 ⟶

That is, location 308 is the fifty-second word in bank 2. The next word in sequence is 309 (binary 010 0110101), which is also in bank 2. The last word in bank 2 is at the binary location 010 1111111, while the first word in bank 3 is at the binary location 011 0000000. The MAR for the same system with an interleaved memory architecture would look like (for location 308) the following:

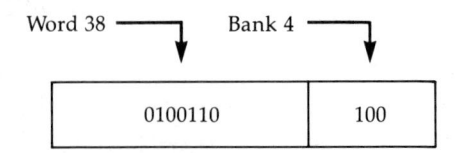

Word 38 ⟶   Bank 4 ⟶

| 0100110 | 100 |

K bits	M bits
Bank number	Address within the bank

MAR structure for bank architecture

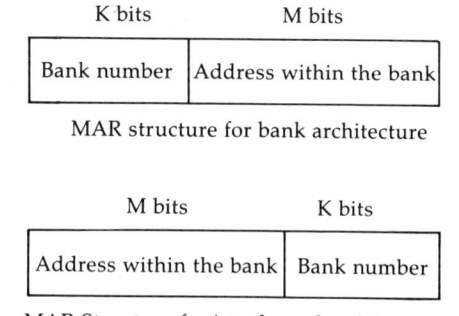

M bits	K bits
Address within the bank	Bank number

MAR Structure for interleaved architecture

Figure 10.4 MAR structure

The next address in sequence is 309 (binary 0100110 101), which is now word 38 of bank 5.

The basic distinction between these two approaches is that if the high-order bits are used to select the module, consecutive memory words are in the same module, whereas if the low-order bits are used to select the module, consecutive memory words are in different modules.

In addition to the interleaving approach, several other methods are commonly used to speed up the interaction between memory and the CPU. One commonly used method is a look-ahead approach. It is based on the observation that if data is requested from one memory location, there is a high probability that the next word of data required will be from a location nearby. The VAX 11/780, for example, will fetch a quad-word every time it reads data from memory even though the CPU may request only a single 16-bit word. When it does this, it increases the probability that for at least the next three data words requested by the CPU, it will not have to interact with main memory at all.

10.3 Cache Memory

In most programs the same data is used repeatedly, so it would be helpful to avoid using a complete main memory cycle every time the data is required. The use of main memory cycles could be avoided if the repeatedly used data were placed in general-purpose registers. This may require extra work for the programmer. Moreover, the general-purpose registers are often needed to store temporary results from other calculations. Further, the amount of data used repeatedly probably exceeds the capacity of these general-purpose registers. The best compromise is to design the computer so that it automatically stores the data in some intermediate memory unit called a **cache memory**. Note that while use of the general-purpose registers is at the option of the programmer, the machine takes

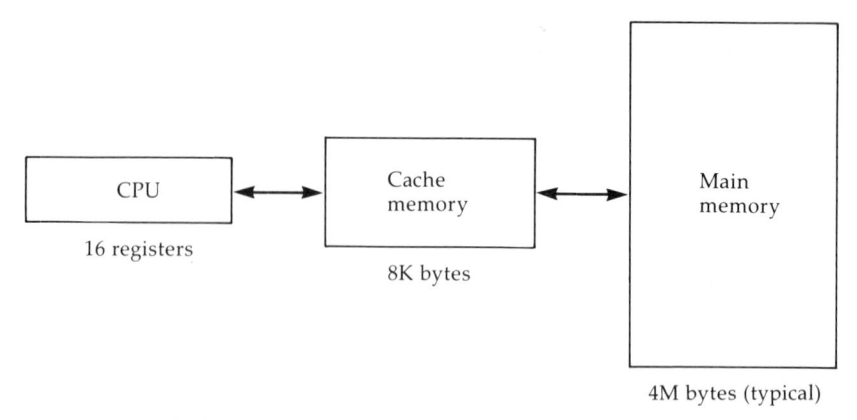

```
                                        ┌─────────────┐
                                        │             │
         ┌─────┐      ┌──────────┐      │    Main     │
         │ CPU │ ◄──► │  Cache   │ ◄──► │   memory    │
         └─────┘      │  memory  │      │             │
                      └──────────┘      │             │
        16 registers    8K bytes        └─────────────┘
                                          4M bytes (typical)
```

Figure 10.5 Cache memory organization on the VAX 11/780

care of all main memory–cache memory interactions so that they are transparent to the user. Cache memory is a small memory unit located between the main memory and the CPU, as shown in Figure 10.5. Because it is small compared to the main memory, faster, more expensive memory chips may be used. It is often five to ten times faster than main memory and hence matches the speed of the CPU. As a result, frequently used data may be stored in the cache memory unit to cut down on the memory access time by a factor of almost ten. The overall hierarchy of memory speed is as follows:

Memory Type	Typical Capacity	Typical Access Time
Registers	16 longwords	20 nsec
Cache memory	8 Kbytes	200 nsec
Main memory	8 Mbytes	1000 nsec
Disk	100 Mbytes	10,000 nsec
Tape	10 Mbytes	100,000 nsec

Because the CPU does not know about the cache, it simply places an address in the MAR and requests a read or write operation at that address. The memory unit must keep track of where data is located; that is, should it look for the data in main memory at the address that the CPU requests, or should it look in the cache memory? The system that performs this task for memory is called the **memory control circuit (MCC)**.

When the CPU requests a read operation, the MCC looks at the address in the MAR. If the data at that address has already been transferred to the cache memory, it is given to the CPU in about one-fifth the time that a main memory cycle would require. However, if the data has not been transferred to the cache, the MCC fetches the data from main memory and, at the same time, moves a block of several words around the requested data into the cache, because it is very likely that the next CPU request for data will be in the neighborhood of the current data. Moving the surrounding block into the cache increases the chances that the next word requested by the CPU will be in the cache. To accomplish these tasks, the MCC must keep track of the blocks of data in the cache, which it does by using a **mapping function**. If the cache is already full when a CPU read operation requires that a new block be loaded into the cache, the MCC must remove a block in the cache to make room for the new one. The method that the MCC uses to determine which block to remove is called the **replacement algorithm**. We consider possibilities for both mapping functions and the replacement algorithms in the next section.

A cache system's performance can be evaluated based on its efficiency. The efficiency is the cache **hit ratio (h)**, which is the percentage of total memory references for which the data is found in the cache.

$$h = \frac{\text{number of references found in the cache}}{\text{total number of references}} \times 100$$

The miss ratio is defined to be $1 - h$. The **average memory access time (t_a)** in a system with a cache is given by (assuming that the system always checks the cache first)

$$t_a = t_c + (1 - h)t_m$$

where t_c is the average cache access time and t_m is the average main memory access time. Experimental studies indicate that the miss ratio is minimized when the cache size is between 8 and 16K and the block size is between 64 and 128 bytes.

10.4 Mapping Functions

There are many possible mapping functions, but we will look at only three. The common assumption among all three is that the memory is divided into blocks of fixed size. On the VAX 11/780 the block size is eight bytes. This is not a physical division of main memory; it is imposed by the nature of the MCC operation.

Direct Mapping

Direct mapping is the simplest form of a mapping function. If n is the maximum number of blocks that the cache can hold, then block k in main memory is mapped into block $k \mod n$ of the cache. For example, if the VAX main memory contains 4 million bytes, there would be 500,000 8-byte blocks. The VAX 11/780 cache contains 8K bytes or 1024 8-byte blocks. (When DEC designed the VAX 11/785, an upgrade of the 11/780,

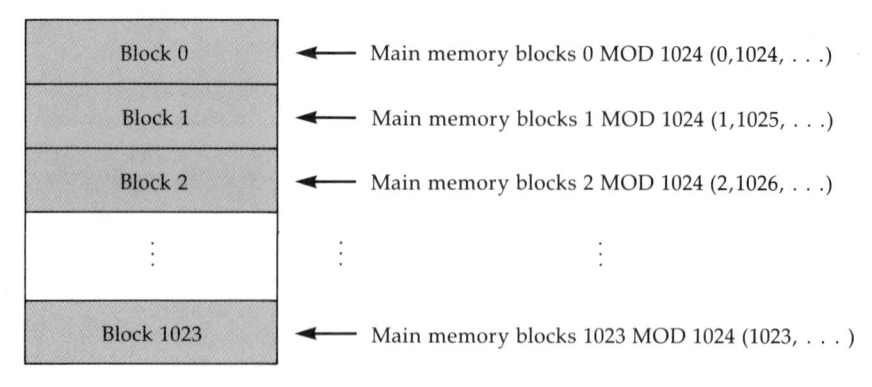

```
┌─────────────┐
│   Block 0   │ ◀── Main memory blocks 0 MOD 1024 (0,1024, . . .)
├─────────────┤
│   Block 1   │ ◀── Main memory blocks 1 MOD 1024 (1,1025, . . .)
├─────────────┤
│   Block 2   │ ◀── Main memory blocks 2 MOD 1024 (2,1026, . . .)
├─────────────┤
│     ⋮       │         ⋮                    ⋮
├─────────────┤
│  Block 1023 │ ◀── Main memory blocks 1023 MOD 1024 (1023, . . . )
└─────────────┘
```

Figure 10.6 Cache memory organization with direct mapping

they increased the cache memory size to 32K.) So a direct mapping function on the VAX could result in a cache organization as shown in Figure 10.6. The VAX 11/780 does not actually use direct mapping, so the following discussion outlines how direct mapping could be implemented on a machine like the VAX (the method used on the VAX will be discussed later in this section). The block number for a particular byte in main memory can be determined by dividing the memory address by 8 and ignoring any remainder. Now, if the CPU asked for a byte at location 22, the MCC would note that the byte is in block 2 (22 divided by 8 is 2 plus a remainder of 6), which contains bytes 16–23. So it would move block 2 of main memory into block 2 of the cache. If the CPU later asked for a byte at location 16405, the MCC would note that it is in block 2050 (because 16405 divided by 8 is 2050 plus a remainder that is ignored).

The cache block number is determined by dividing the main memory block number by 1024 and using the remainder. So block 2050 is also mapped by direct mapping into block 2 of the cache (because 2050 reduced mod 1024 is 2). The result is that the current contents of block 2 of the cache may have to be copied back into locations 16–23 of main memory before the new block is written into block 2 of the cache.

Fortunately, the computer does not need to perform all these calculations to determine the block in which a given byte is located; the MCC partitions the memory address passed to it by the CPU into three parts, as shown in Figure 10.7. Three bits in the byte field are used to identify which byte in a block of eight is the one actually addressed. The block field identifies one of the 1024 blocks in the cache. The tag field identifies the particular main memory block that was mapped into the cache memory block because there are 4K blocks that the main memory maps into each cache block.

For example, if the CPU is seeking the byte stored at location 00016575 (hex), the MCC is given the following binary address:

000 0000 0001 0110 0101 0111 0101

Tag	Block	Byte
14 bits	10 bits	3 bits

Figure 10.7 MAR Fields for direct mapping

which is subdivided into the following three parts:

00000000001011 TAG B (hex)
      0010101110 BLOCK AE (hex)
              101 BYTE 5 (hex)

So the MCC looks at the tag of block AE in the cache. If it is B, the MCC sends byte 5 of that cache block on to the CPU. If the tag field does not contain the value B, the MCC goes to block 2CAE (the combination of the tag and block fields) of main memory and loads the eight bytes of that block into block AE of the cache as well as sending byte 5 of that block on to the CPU. The major disadvantage of this method is that even if the cache is not full, there may be a contention for a given block "space," and the MCC may have to swap data between main memory and the cache. This operation requires that each block in the cache has a 14-bit tag register associated with it. The tag register will contain the current tag of the block in cache and will be compared to the tag field of any memory request to determine if the block is in the cache.

Associative Mapping

To overcome the inefficient use of cache memory by the direct mapping algorithm, **associative mapping** allows any block in main memory to be mapped into any block of the cache. In this case the MAR is subdivided into only two parts—a tag and a byte field, as shown below.

Tag field	Byte field

When the CPU requests a byte from memory, the MCC looks at all the tags of the blocks in the cache. If it finds a match between the requested block and one already in the cache, it fetches the requested byte from the matching block in the cache and sends it on to the CPU. If it does not find a match, it looks in main memory and moves the missing block into the cache while also sending the requested byte on to the CPU. If the cache is not full, it may place the new block in any empty slot. If the cache is full, however, the MCC must remove an existing cache block to make room for the new one. The disadvantage of associative mapping is that either it takes a long time for the MCC to search all the blocks of the cache to find a possible match, or some expensive circuitry must be included to make this searching faster. In addition, the replacement algorithms for the cache may be very complex. As a result, no existing system uses this method.

Block-Set Associative Mapping

Block-set associative mapping attempts to combine the best of both the associative and direct mapping methods. This algorithm requires that the cache be grouped into sets, each containing a collection of blocks. Blocks within a given set in main memory can be mapped into any block within the same set in the cache. Figure 10.8 illustrates the cache organization for the case of two blocks per set. In this case the MAR is subdivided into three fields—a tag field, a set field, and a byte field, as shown below.

| Tag field | Set field | Byte field |

Now when the CPU requests a byte from main memory, the MCC looks at the specified set in the cache. If any tag within that set matches the requested tag, the requested byte is fetched from the cache. However, if there is no match within the set, the MCC fetches the block from main memory and moves it into a slot in the designated set. For example, if the CPU requested the byte at location 003706B (hex), the binary contents of the MAR would be

000 0000 0011 0111 0000 0110 1011

Assuming that the byte field contains the first three bits, the set field contains the next nine bits, and the tag field contains the remaining bits, the MCC would interpret this address as byte 3 of set D, with a tag of 37.

In the latter two of these mapping schemes, the MCC requires a replacement algorithm to create space when the cache is full. The most common algorithm is the **least recently used (LRU)** algorithm. LRU requires that the MCC replace the block in cache that has been unused for the longest period of time. One way to implement the LRU replacement algorithm is to associate a counter with each block. Every time a byte within a block is accessed, the operating system increments the block counter. At fixed time intervals, the operating system decrements all the counters. In this way a block counter for a block that is never used is always decremented and never incremented. The LRU block, then, is the one with the smallest block register value. Another replacement policy involves selecting a block at random.

We should make one comment about the write operation. When the CPU writes data to a block in the cache, only the contents of the cache

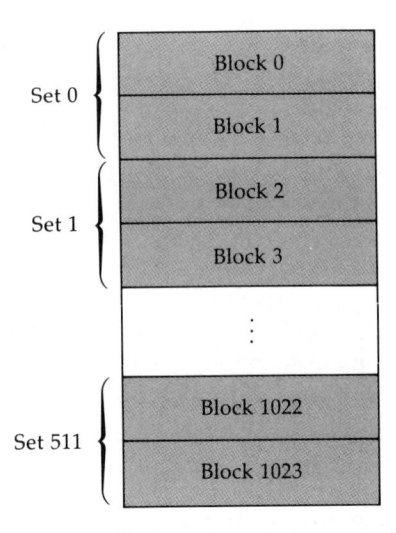

Figure 10.8 Block-set associative mapping

may be changed. In this case main memory is not updated until it is necessary to move the particular block out of the cache. Another possibility is to use a **write-through** approach, where both the cache and main memory are updated at the same time during a write operation. The write-through approach ensures that the main memory copy is always up to date. In addition, replacement is faster because it does not have to save the block that is bumped out of the cache.

The VAX 11/780 uses a set-associative write-through algorithm with two sets of 512 blocks in the cache. For its replacement algorithm, it uses a random selection system. The IBM 370/168 has eight sets of 128 blocks each in its cache, while the Amdahl 470v/8 has four sets of 512 blocks.

10.5 Virtual Memory

A cache memory architecture is designed to speed up the use of main memory. The other concern in terms of overall memory organization is the size of memory. To get around the limitations of a finite main memory, we can add a virtual memory organization to the system. **Virtual memory** is designed to provide almost unlimited memory space to a system by combining main memory and disk space into one large unit. Of course this is not done physically; instead the CPU only thinks that it has an infinitely sized main memory unit. Software and a limited amount of hardware are used to combine main memory and disk into a virtual memory system.

One approach to a virtual memory system is called a fixed-length paged system. All data and programs in such a system are organized into blocks called pages of fixed length (usually 512 to 4K bytes). These pages are initially stored on disk. When the CPU requests a data or instruction word from main memory, the system determines which page contains the requested word and where that page is located. If it is currently located in main memory, the word is fetched from either the cache or main memory. However, if the page is currently on disk, the entire page is brought into main memory in much the same way that a block is transferred from main memory to cache memory. If main memory is already full, some page in memory must be written back to disk before the required page can be transferred to main memory. Once the page is in main memory, the requested word is sent to the CPU. Several issues are raised by this memory utilization strategy, most of which are the concern of the operating system designer. The issue of most concern to the memory system architecture is "How does the system know the real location of the page?"

To translate between the memory address generated within a program (the virtual memory address) and the actual physical location of the data (the physical address), which may be somewhere in main memory or on disk, the memory address register contents must be divided into two parts: a page field and a displacement field. The page field is an index into a page table. The page table resides in main memory and keeps track of the real location of each page in the system. The page table could look like the structure shown in Figure 10.9a. This table serves as a map that allows the system to find the physical location of the page given its logical address used in the program. Such a map is illustrated in Figure 10.9b. The system uses the page table entry to construct the physical address of the data, as illustrated in Figure 10.10. The page table base register is a special register in the CPU that keeps track of the first entry in the page table for the current process. The page number field of the virtual address is added to this base to generate the address of the page table entry. The page table entry is fetched using the calculated address and examined to determine if the requested data is in main memory or on disk. If the data is on disk, a page fault occurs, and the page table entry contains the disk address for the entire page. The system will use the disk address to move the page from disk to main memory. If the data is in main memory, the page table entry contains the actual page location, which is combined with the byte offset from the original virtual address to form the real address of the data in main memory. Perhaps you have observed that the computer seemingly requires two memory accesses every time it wants a word of data—once to read the page table and once to access the data. Fortunately, this is not normally necessary because both the page table entry and the data will be in cache, so the operation can be processed rapidly.

10.5 Virtual Memory

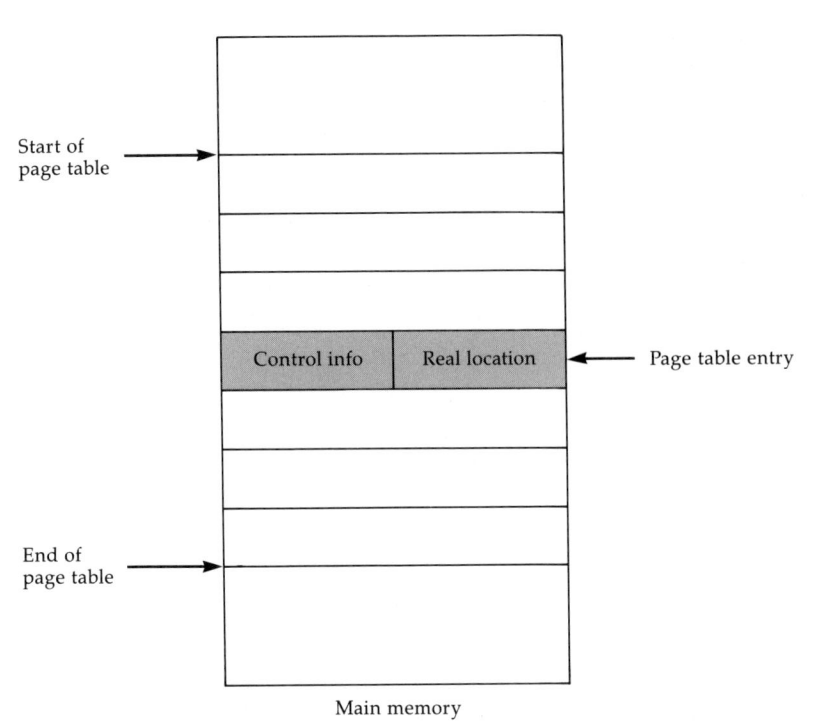

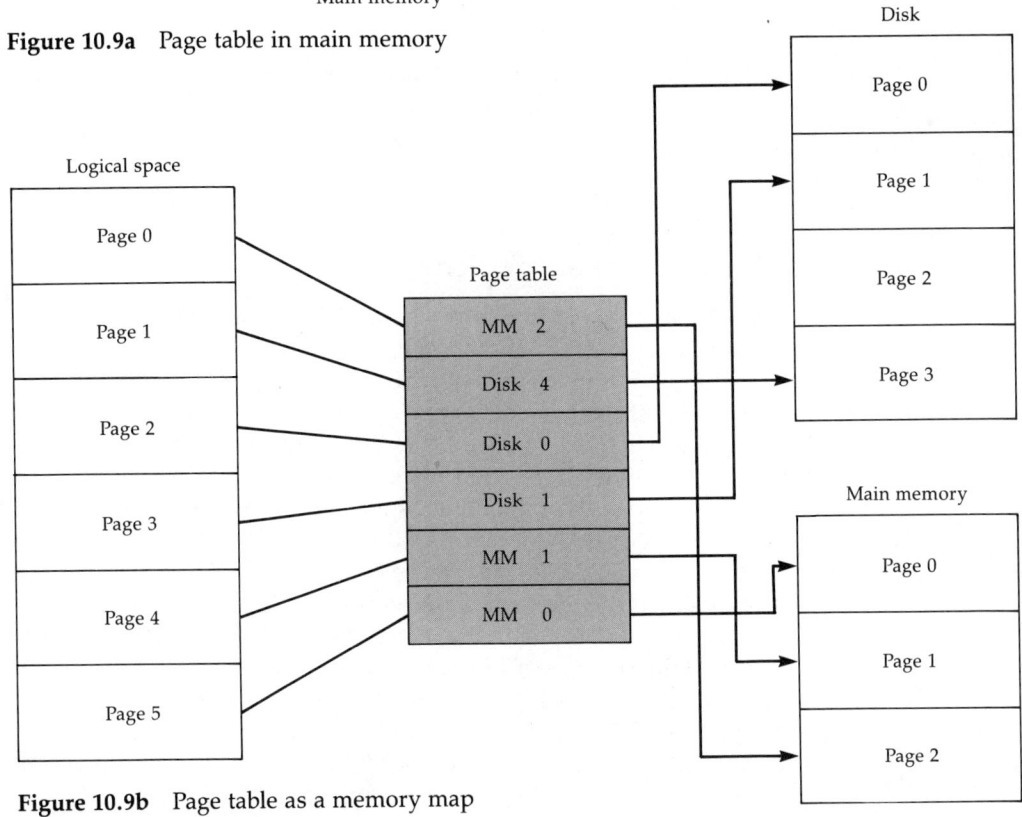

Figure 10.9a Page table in main memory

Figure 10.9b Page table as a memory map

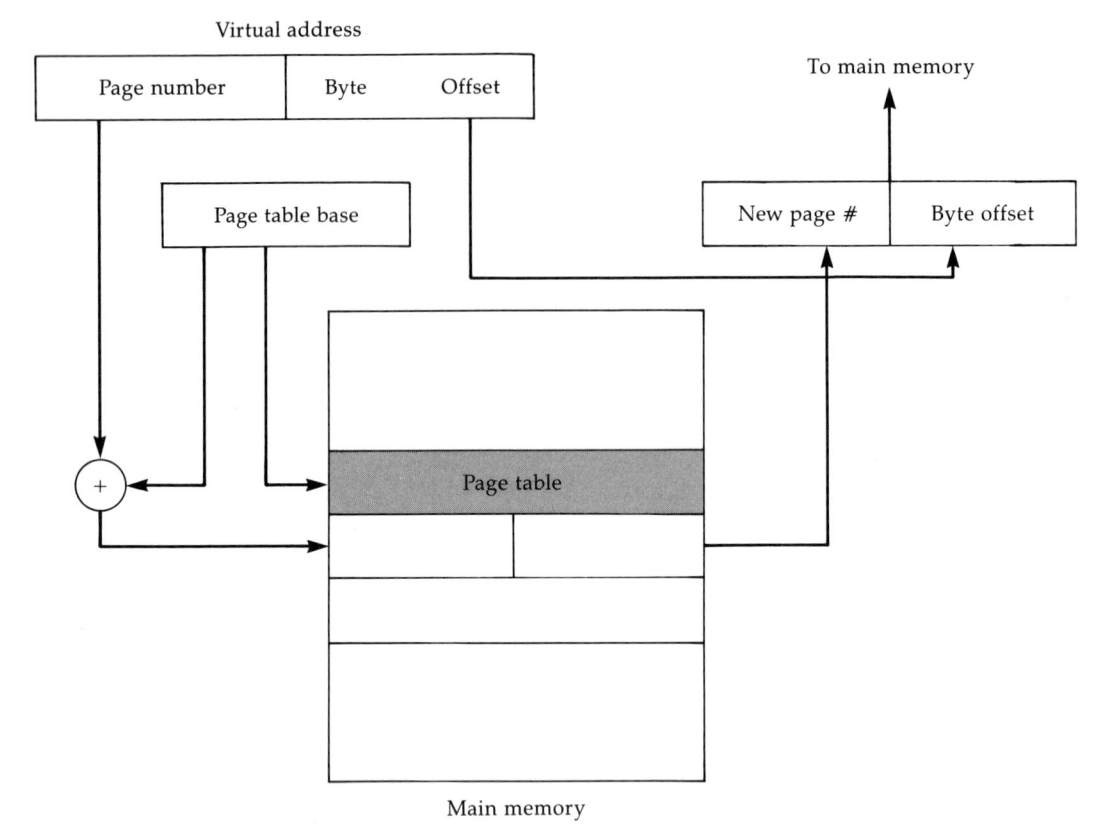

Figure 10.10 Virtual memory structure

VAX Virtual Memory Structure

On the VAX a 32-bit virtual address generated by the CPU is actually divided into two parts, as shown in Figure 10.11. Because a page on the VAX consists of 512 bytes, it requires nine bits to address a single byte within a page. Bits 0–8 of the virtual address are used to identify a byte within a page. The next 23 bits of the virtual address (bits 9–31) are not actual address bits but are used instead to find a specific entry in the page table. Because the page table is located in main memory, its base register keeps track of the location of the first entry in the page table. So bits 9–31 of the virtual address serve as an offset that, when added to the contents of the page table base register, points to the correct entry in the page table. The page table contains a set of longwords (32 bits) called **page table entries (PTE)**, as shown in Figure 10.12. The first 21 bits of each PTE (bits 0–20) form the page frame number, which, when combined with the byte offset, produce the physical address of the data if the data is located in main memory. Bits 21–25 are used only if the

```
  31                         9 8          0
  ┌─────────────────────────┬────────────┐
  │   Virtual page number   │ Byte offset│
  └─────────────────────────┴────────────┘
```

Figure 10.11 VAX virtual address

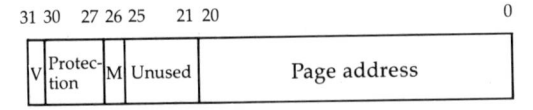

```
  31 30  27 26 25   21 20                    0
  ┌─┬─────┬─┬──────┬──────────────────────────┐
  │V│Protec-│M│Unused│      Page address      │
  │ │ tion │ │      │                         │
  └─┴─────┴─┴──────┴──────────────────────────┘
```

Figure 10.12 VAX page table entry

page is on disk. In that case bits 0–26 actually give the disk address. The remaining 6 bits of the PTE (bits 26–31) contain control information. Bit 31 indicates the location of the page (disk = 0, or main memory = 1). Bit 26 is the modify bit, which is set if the CPU has modified any data in the page while it has been in main memory. Bits 27–30 form the protection code. Using these bits, the operating system can control access to certain areas of memory. For example, a user is allowed read/write access to only those pages for which the protection code in the PTE is 0100. However, users may read pages in memory for which the protection code is any one of the following:

$b_{30}\ b_{29}\ b_{28}\ b_{27}$

1 1 0 0
1 1 0 1
1 1 1 0
1 1 1 1

Supervisor accounts, however, are allowed read/write capabilities to pages with protection bits.

0 1 0 0
1 0 0 0
1 1 0 0

This protection system is very helpful on a multiuser system because its prevents one user from accidentally changing memory locations that are being used by another program. Perhaps you have seen a "memory access error" while debugging a program. That indicates that the virtual memory system discovered that your program was trying to read or write on memory that was off limits to your program.

Summary

Our goal in this chapter has been to explore the structure and organization of memory systems. We considered the operation of several of the basic memory devices—RAM, ROM, PROM, and EPROM. Because memory operations tend to be slower than CPU operations, speed has always been a primary driving force behind memory organization. We explored memory interleaving and the use of high-speed cache memory as techniques to increase memory speed. Another consideration in the use of memory is the total size available to the CPU. We also reviewed the use of virtual memory techniques designed to increase the functional size of main memory.

The memory architectures introduced in this chapter indicate that the interaction between memory and the CPU consists of more than just setting up the MAR and MDR. A summary of the steps involved are shown in Figure 10.13.

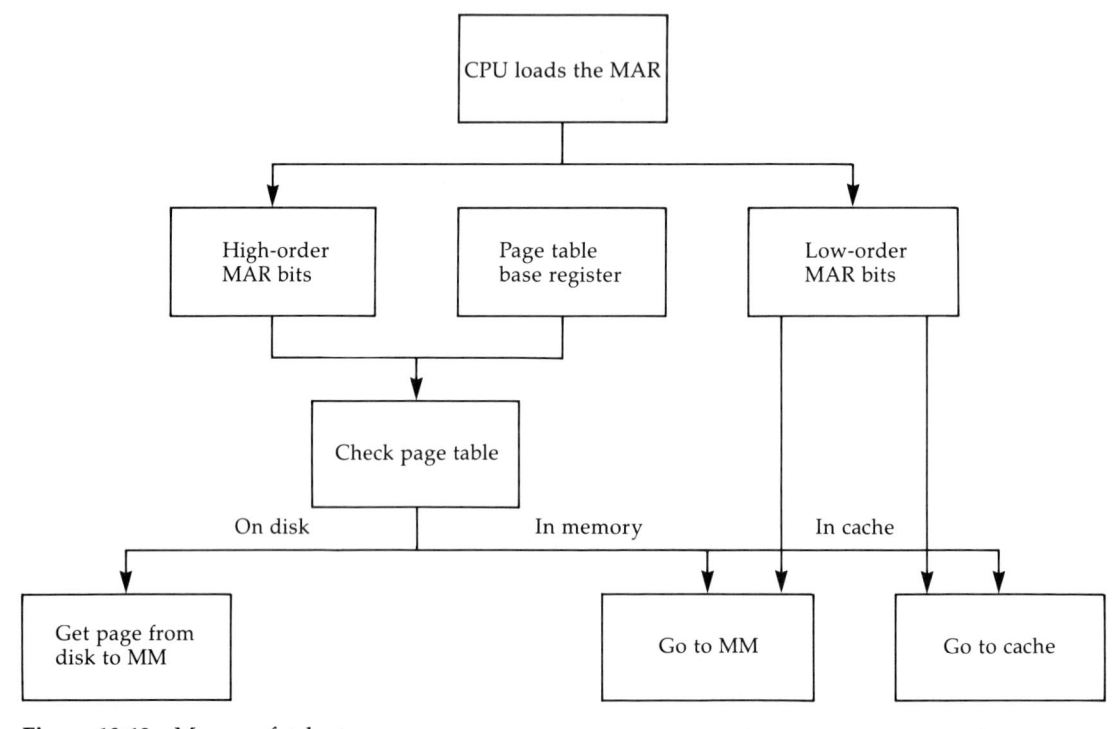

Figure 10.13 Memory fetch steps

Exercises

1. For each of the following memory sizes, determine the required size of the MAR.
   a. 16K memory
   b. 64K memory
   c. 1M memory

2. Given a memory unit that can store 32 words in a system divided into four banks, draw a diagram of each module showing all the bytes:
   a. When consecutive bytes are stored in consecutive banks (memory bank architecture).
   b. When consecutive bytes are stored in a single bank (interleaved memory architecture).
   c. If the memory unit has a cycle time of 100 nsec, how much time would it take to read locations 21–26 assuming part a?
   d. Repeat part c assuming the structure given in part b.

3. Given a 16K memory unit in a system with a block size of 512 bytes and a cache memory of 4K bytes:
   a. How many blocks are there in main memory?
   b. How many blocks will the cache hold?
   c. Using direct mapping, list all the blocks of main memory that are mapped into each block in the cache.

4. For the system described in Exercise 3, assume that main memory has a cycle of 10^{-6} sec and the cache has a cycle time of 10^{-7} sec. If the system were to execute a program with two nested loops where the instructions for the inner loop (which is executed ten times) are found in memory at locations 1026–1500 (decimal) and the instructions for the outer loop (which is executed twice) are found in memory locations 2112–2322:
   a. Find the total time required to fetch these instructions if the cache does not exist.
   b. Find the total time required to fetch these instructions using the cache.
   c. How much time does the cache save?

5. Given a main memory–cache system where the cycle time for the cache is 100 nsec and for main memory is 1μsec, you run an experiment and discover that of 1459 memory references, 1291 found the required data in the cache.
   a. What is the hit ratio?
   b. What is the overall average cycle time?

6. Given the memory unit from Exercise 3 organized using the block-set associative method with two blocks per set:
   a. Determine the number of bits in the tag, set, and word fields of the MAR.
   b. Given the following hex addresses, show the block and set into which they are mapped: (1) 1056, (2) 3456, and (3) A22.
7. Given a memory system consisting of 16 modules of 1K bytes per module:
   a. What is the total size of main memory?
   b. Assume a banked structure and determine the bank and the displacement within the bank for the following addresses:
      1. 00101100110011
      2. 01010100111010
      3. 11110101110001
   c. Repeat part b assuming an interleaved architecture.
8. For the structure of Exercise 7 and assuming a banked architecture, find
   a. The last memory address of bank 10.
   b. The address for word 12 (hex) in bank 5.
9. Repeat Exercise 8 assuming an interleaved structure.

   In Exercises 10 and 11 assume that a page table for a process starts at location 121 (hex) in main memory and a page size is 128 bytes. The format of the contents of the page table is as follows:

   ```
   7 6         0
   ┌─┬─────────┐
   │V│  Page   │
   │ │ address │
   └─┴─────────┘
   ```

   V = 0: Page is in main memory
   V = 1: Page is on disk

   The contents of the page table in hex are as follows:

121	AE	126	33
122	7F	127	80
123	45	128	93
124	B7	129	64
125	02	130	AC

10. How many pages are currently in main memory?
11. Determine if the following virtual addresses represent bytes that are on disk or in main memory. If they are in main memory, locate the real address.
    a. 00001011011100
    b. 00000000011001
    c. 00001000001010

12. Assume that a longword on the VAX is a virtual address where the first nine bits form a byte offset and the remaining bits specify the location within the page table. Given R3 as the page table base register, write the assembly language code for a virtual-to-real address translator. To run your program, define a page table array beginning at PTABLE with the following longwords in the VAX page table format.

11100100000010110100010111010000
01111010101000000000101011110101
01000101000001101011100000000000
01101010011100010001110001110101
11111010101000000001110110011001
01101010010101000011000110101111
00100101001010110011011010000100

Given the following sequence of virtual address requests:

User read from location 00000BAE (hex).
User write to location 00000567 (hex).
User read from location 000000C3 (hex).
User read from location 0000D72 (hex).

Your program should output the following:

Protection violation if it occurs.
Page fault if it occurs.
Or the real address if it can be found.

CHAPTER CONTENTS

11.1 ADDRESSING I/O DEVICES

11.2 DATA TRANSFER
   Program-Controlled I/O
   Direct Memory Access
      I/O Channel

11.3 INTERRUPT-DRIVEN I/O
   Device Identification
      Polling Method
      Vector Method
   Simultaneous Interrupt Requests
   Priority
      Interrupt Acknowledge
         Daisy Chain
      Priority Arbitration
      Mixed Approach

11.4 QUEUE I/O
   System Services
   An Example Using Queue I/O
   A More Sophisticated Queue I/O
      Request

11.5 I/O USING RMS
   Defining Files and Records
   Executable RMS Macros
   An Example Using RMS Macros

11.6 ADVANCED I/O DEVICES

SUMMARY

EXERCISES

CHAPTER 11

The I/O System

We have studied two of the major building blocks in a computer system—the CPU and the memory system. In this chapter we turn our attention to the remaining block—the I/O system—which can be investigated at many levels. The most elementary viewpoint is that taken by the designers of the I/O hardware and the device drivers. At this level communication is character by character. Both hardware and software must be designed so that the high-speed computer does not send output to slow devices such as printers and terminals faster than they can handle it. On the other hand, some high-speed disks and tape drives can supply data at speeds testing the computer's ability to accept it. On multiuser computers, care must be taken to ensure that the computer does not spend all its time waiting for a user to type the next input character. Solving these problems is complicated by the fact that the methods used to handle one type of device may be quite different from those used for another.

We will begin by surveying some of the factors that must be considered when I/O hardware is designed. Specifically, we will look at both the hardware and software characteristics of the interface between the CPU and the I/O devices. To support I/O operations, a computer's hardware designers must provide it with the following capabilities:

1. The ability to address different I/O devices
2. The ability to transfer data to and from selected devices
3. The ability to synchronize or coordinate the timing of I/O operations with the computer's internal operations

We will consider these requirements and their impact on the system architecture in the first three sections.

The operating system's designers face further problems. For example, how can users be allowed to select any one of the incompatible I/O devices without requiring a separate version of their high-level language program for each device?

To resolve this and similar issues, operating systems often break up the I/O system routines into several different levels with various abilities and limitations. For example, a VAX using the VMS operating system provides four levels of I/O routines to process input and output from a user's terminal.

I/O Level	Characteristics
High-level languages	Device independent, can format numbers and character strings, can handle files and records
RMS (Record Management Services)	Device independent, can handle character strings, can handle files and records
QIO (Queue I/O)	Device dependent, can handle character strings, can handle records
Device drivers	Device dependent, can handle characters one at a time; interface directly with I/O devices

The system is designed so that each level of I/O simplifies the I/O request enough so that it can be handed down to the next level until it finally reaches the device drivers that actually carry out the I/O operation.

We begin this chapter by looking at the hardware and device driver level. We then move up the I/O ladder to QIO and RMS. You will notice a major change in the presentation as we do so. The discussion at the hardware level will be quite general and will apply to most computers. The discussion of QIO and RMS applies to the VMS operating system running on a VAX.

There are several reasons for this. Writing and testing device drivers is a taxing job normally marked by frequent system crashes. On a multiuser system such testing is incompatible with other uses and is normally forbidden except on systems dedicated to system development. Device driver writing is a skill better practiced on mini- and microcomputers. However, VMS is designed to be highly tolerant of incorrect code at the higher I/O levels. Consequently, you are encouraged to try your hand at QIO and RMS programming.

At the hardware level, a number of general principles are machine independent, so a general introduction is feasible. Intermediate levels, however, are much more varied, and it would be hard to survey the field at this level. We will see how QIO and RMS provide a transition between high-level language and hardware I/O. They will also provide a good opportunity to improve your assembly language skills.

Although this chapter is primarily devoted to terminal communications, it includes a short section presenting some of the additional problems that must be faced when printer queues, tape units, and disk drives are included in a system. VMS provides one additional layer of I/O software for tape and disk drives. The programs at this level, called ACPs, fall between QIO and the device driver layers.

11.1 Addressing I/O Devices

There are two ways in which I/O devices are commonly connected to the CPU. The first uses a special I/O bus, as shown in Figure 11.1, which contains data, address, and control lines. Each device has a unique address, so the CPU selects a given device by placing the correct address on the I/O address lines. For example, if eight I/O devices are to be connected to a CPU, at least three address lines will be required. If the printer in such a system has the address 001, then to send data to the printer, the CPU must: (1) place 001 on the address lines, and (2) place the data on the data bus. Computers using this type of I/O require a special set of instructions to send data along the I/O bus.

The second method for selecting I/O devices operates in a single-bus architecture environment. The bus is divided into three sets of lines—control lines, address lines, and data lines—as shown in Figure 11.2. In

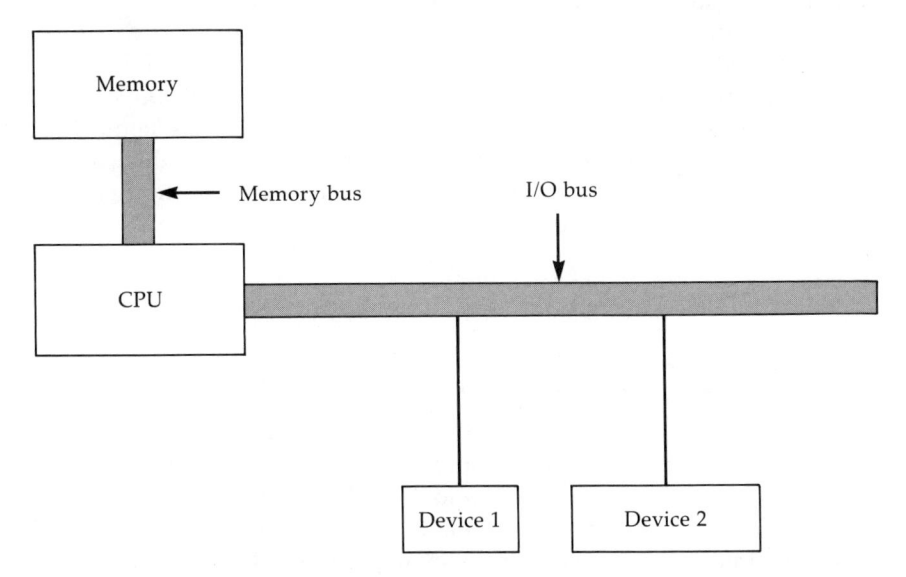

Figure 11.1 I/O bus architecture

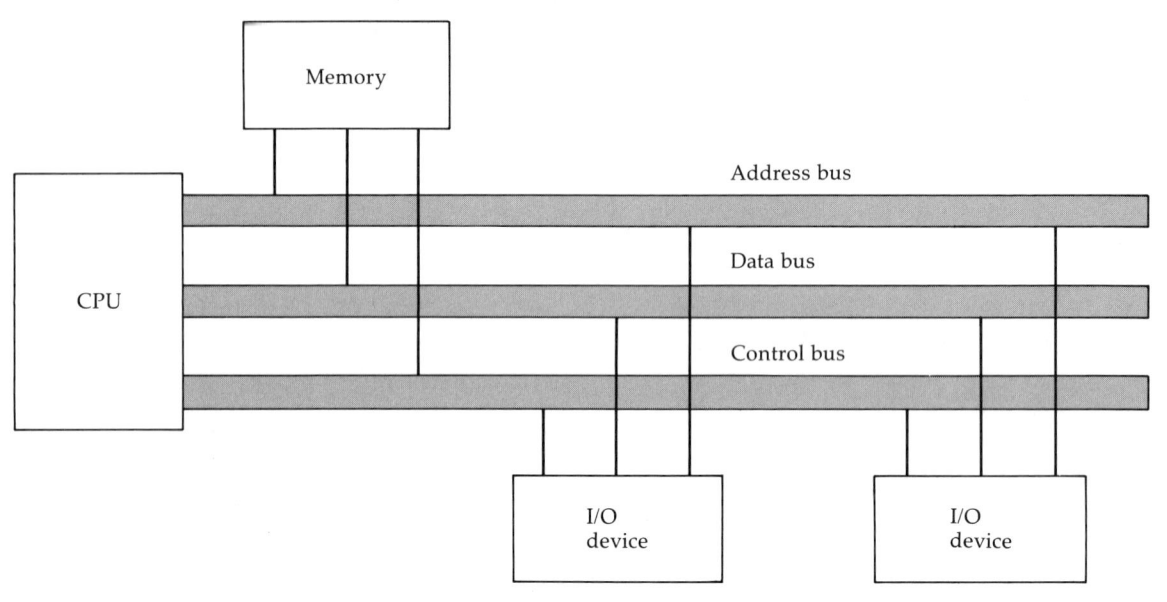

Figure 11.2 Memory-mapped structure

this case the I/O devices "look" like memory locations. This method is called **memory-mapped I/O** because devices are given addresses that look like memory addresses. This class of systems does not require any special I/O instructions because any instruction that will access memory could be used as an I/O instruction. In the rest of this chapter we will assume that all systems discussed are memory mapped.

Many devices are actually connected to the bus indirectly. An I/O interface board or controller board is connected to the bus, and the actual I/O device is connected to the interface board. This board converts the signals appearing on the computer's bus to signals that are compatible to the device. Consequently, use of the term *I/O device* in this chapter actually means the I/O interface controller because it is the unit that communicates directly with the computer.

11.2 Data Transfer

Each I/O device has at least two special registers used for data transfer: (1) a device data register (DDR), and (2) a device status register (DSR). The data register is used to transfer data, while the status register is used to control information. An I/O operation requires transferring data between a CPU register and an I/O device register. A possible system architecture

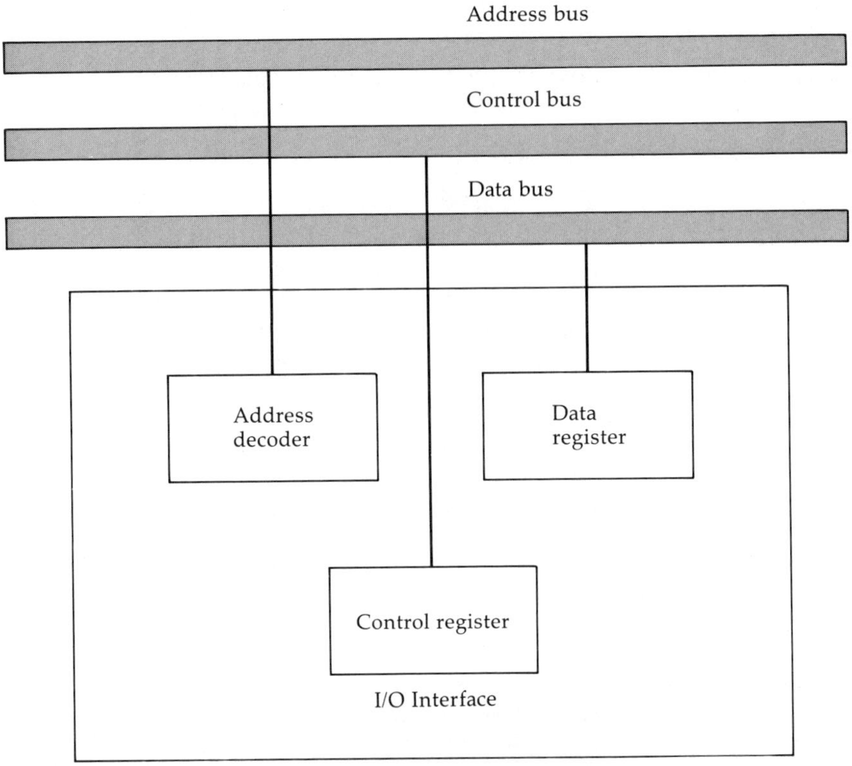

11.2 Data Transfer

Figure 11.3 I/O interface architecture

for an I/O device is shown in Figure 11.3. In memory-mapped I/O the I/O device register looks like a memory location. The main advantage of such an approach is that an I/O data transfer can be done using a memory move instruction, such as

```
MOVB Regin,Data
```

where Regin is the input data register for the I/O device.

I/O devices such as terminals may have up to four registers (two for input and two for output). In a memory-mapped architecture each register would have an address that looks like a memory location to the CPU. For example, a terminal may have the following four registers:

Register	Address
Input status	FFFF FFF0
Input data	FFFF FFF4
Output status	FFFF FFF8
Output data	FFFF FFFC

In this case there are three modes of data transfer: (1) program-controlled I/O, (2) direct memory access (DMA), and (3) interrupt-driven I/O. We will consider the first two in this section and the last later in the chapter.

Program-Controlled I/O

The status word in the I/O interface is necessary because I/O devices are usually slower than the CPU; so the CPU must wait until the device is ready before sending data, or the data may be lost in the transmission. The busy status of the I/O device can be determined by checking a single bit in the device status register. For example, bit 7 of the longword device status register (DSR) could be the done or ready bit. In this case the ready bit is the sign bit of the lowest byte of the DSR. We might have the following:

Bit 7 = 1   Device is ready   Status byte is negative
Bit 7 = 0   Device is not ready   Status byte is positive

With this information, we could write a short wait loop program to force the CPU to wait until the I/O device is ready for the next data transmission. For example:

```
Wait:   TSTB  DSR      ; Test device status register
        BGEQ  Wait     ; if not ready, go to wait
```

When the system leaves this wait loop, it can move data into the device data register. This procedure is referred to as **program-controlled I/O**.

A device driver is a subprogram that controls communication with a device. The following simple-minded subroutine sends one character in R0 to an output device:

```
;Output One Character:

Wait:   TSTB  DSR         ; test the DSR
        BGEQ  Wait        ; wait until device is ready
        MOVB  R0,RegOut   ; output character in R0
        RSB
```

The flowchart for this type of programmed I/O is shown in Figure 11.4.

Simple device drivers such as this are often used on small, single-user computers. However, they are usually unacceptable on larger, multiuser machines because the computer could end up in an infinite loop if the external device fails. If the input comes from a terminal, the computer might spend a great deal of time in the wait loop while the user is taking a coffee break. Hence the wait loop results in a long idle time for the CPU. Next we will look at a way to send data between the CPU and I/O devices that does not result in a wait loop for the CPU.

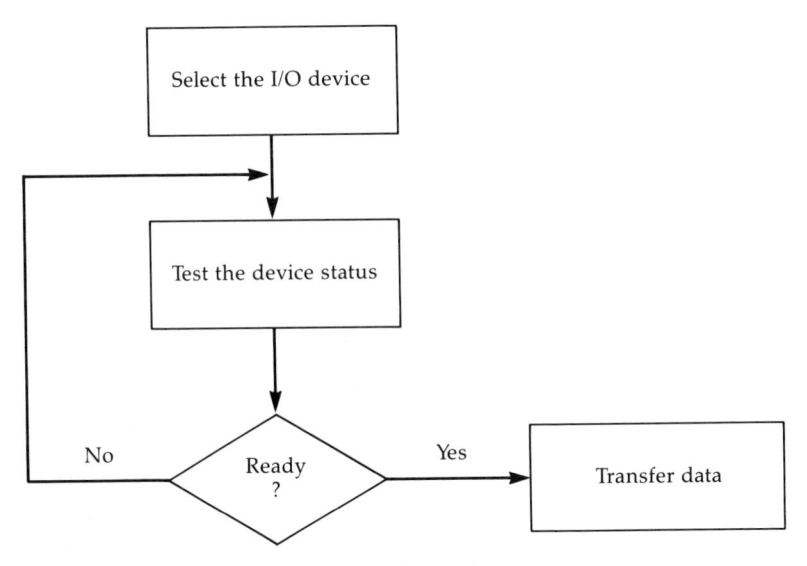

Figure 11.4 Program-controlled I/O wait loop

Direct Memory Access

Sometimes we want to transfer large blocks of data between the CPU and an I/O device. In such a case program-controlled I/O is inefficient because several program instructions may be required to transfer each character, and each program instruction may require several memory cycles. The result would be that the CPU would be tied up for a long time performing the relatively simple operation of transferring data blocks between an I/O device and memory. One way to overcome this potential problem is to construct a special hardware control device that can direct the transfer of large blocks of data between memory and I/O without using the CPU. Such a device is called a **direct memory access** controller. The device requires at least four registers, as shown in Figure 11.5.

A DMA block transfer is implemented in the following steps:

1. The DMA controller requests control of the bus from the CPU using the DMA request line.
2. When the CPU no longer needs the bus, it
    a. Acknowledges the DMA request using the DMA Ack line.
    b. Loads the word (or byte) count register.
    c. Loads the address register with the block's starting address.
3. The DMA directs the transfer of data between memory and the I/O device as long as the word (or byte) count register does not contain 0. After each transfer, the word (or byte) count register is decremented. When the word count register equals 0, the DMA returns control of the bus to the CPU.

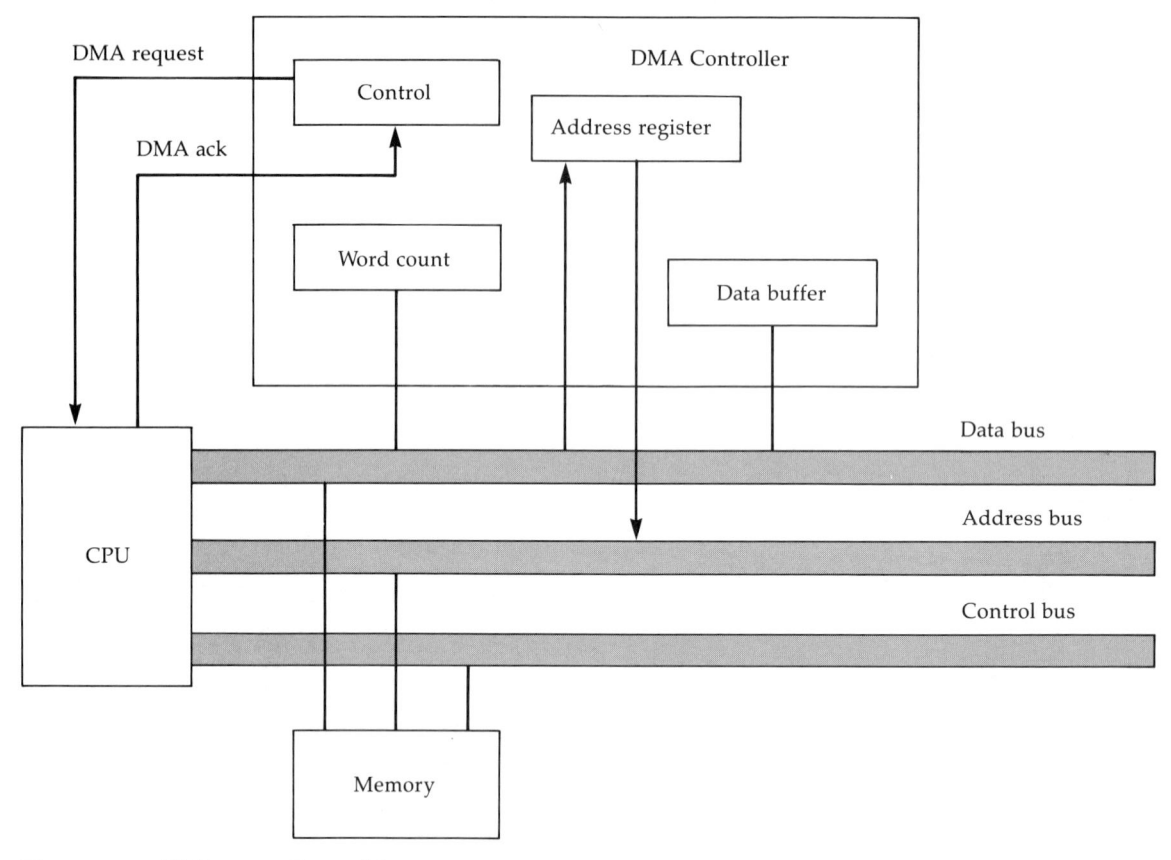

Figure 11.5 DMA controller architecture

While the above steps are being carried out, the CPU may process instructions that do not require memory access.

I/O Channel DMA is useful for transferring large blocks of data without having to rely on the continuous involvement of the CPU. In fact, it may be possible to allow the CPU to carry out other operations as long as they don't result in conflicts over the use of the bus. Requiring the CPU to control all I/O operations is inefficient in large computers. Consequently, such computers may use special I/O processors to carry out routine I/O operations without the active intervention of the main CPU. These special processors are sometimes called peripheral processors. IBM calls them I/O channels. An I/O channel is simply a processing unit whose operations and instruction set are limited to I/O operations. Though a separate DMA controller is usually needed for each device, a channel can typically process several I/O devices. The CPU tells the channel which I/O operation to initiate much as it might set up a DMA controller operation. The channel then takes over and carries out the I/O, leaving the CPU free to carry out other operations. This allows for parallel operations in the system and more efficient use of the CPU.

11.3 Interrupt-Driven I/O

So far we have considered the transfer of information between the CPU and an I/O device from the standpoint of the CPU. The CPU sets up the program-controlled I/O or the DMA and thus maintains control over the operation of these two systems. But what about an I/O device that would like to communicate infrequently with the CPU? We certainly do not want the CPU to have to repeatedly check the normally idle I/O device on the chance that it may require some processing. Instead, we would like the I/O device to signal the CPU whenever it wants service. We do this using an interrupt structure. An **interrupt** is an infrequent or unexpected request from an I/O device for CPU attention. The I/O device tells the CPU that it wants an interrupt by activating a special control line called the **interrupt request (INTR)** line. The INTR signal is stored in the CPU. At the end of each instruction cycle, the CPU checks the value of the INTR signal. If the INTR signal indicates that an I/O device requires attention, the CPU stops execution of the current program and branches to begin execution of a special program called the **interrupt servicing routine**. The task of this routine is to determine which I/O device generated the INTR signal and then branch to a program designed to handle that device. In many ways interrupts are like subroutines, but they can occur at any time.

Figure 11.6 illustrates an interrupt. Suppose that the interrupt occurs unexpectedly after instruction i in Program One has been completed.

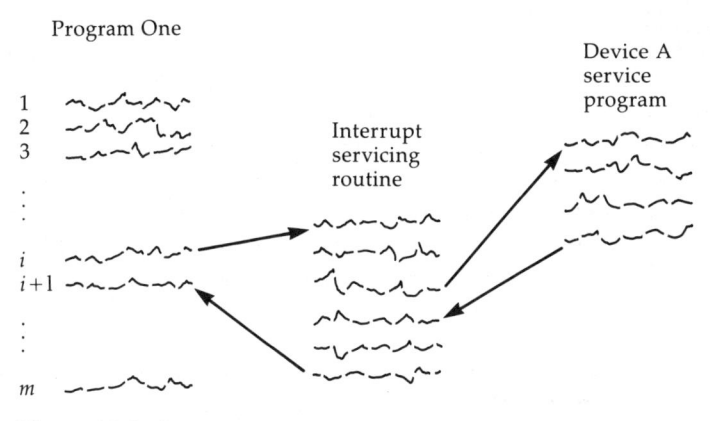

Figure 11.6 Interrupt process

Instead of fetching and executing instruction $i + 1$, the CPU branches to the interrupt servicing routine. Execution of the first few instructions of the interrupt servicing routine identifies device A as the source of the interrupt request, so the CPU branches to the program designed to service device A. When that program is completed, the CPU branches back to the last few statements in the interrupt servicing routine, which direct the CPU back to the interrupted Program One so that instruction $i + 1$ can be fetched and executed.

Each stage of this process involves some special considerations. For example, when the CPU completes an instruction in the current program and then notes that an interrupt has been requested, it must save the status of the current program before jumping to the interrupt servicing routine. This requires that the program counter (PC), process status register (PSR), and other register values be saved on the stack before moving to the servicing routine and then popped off the stack when leaving the servicing routine.

Although the CPU normally finishes the current instruction before acknowledging an interrupt, the VAX's string-processing instructions may take so long to execute that it is impossible to wait for their completion. In this case the microcode writers must allow the machine to process interrupts in the middle of the string instruction's execution.

Other considerations include the identification of the I/O device that generated the interrupt request and procedures for dealing with simultaneous interrupt requests.

Device Identification

The first major task of the interrupt servicing routine is to identify the device that generated the interrupt request. There are two approaches to device identification: polling and vector identification.

Polling Method When the CPU receives an interrupt request and reaches a point when it can respond, it can identify the device by polling all the I/O devices on the system. For example, it could check the status word of each I/O device in some predetermined order to find which one set the interrupt request line. This can all be done in software as the first set of instructions in the interrupt servicing routine. This is a simple method for device identification that does not require any additional hardware, but it is slow. For example, if the device requesting the interrupt is one of the last ones polled, it may take the CPU a long time to identify it.

Vector Method To speed up the device identification process, each I/O device is assigned a special code. When a device requests an interrupt, it also places its identification code on the system data bus. The CPU immediately identifies the interrupting device by reading the code. The

VAX, for example, uses vector interrupts where the code placed on the data bus is the starting memory address for the interrupt servicing routine for the specific device. So this system has a different interrupt servicing routine for each device, and the CPU immediately branches to the correct routine by jumping to the address given by the contents of the data bus.

Simultaneous Interrupt Requests

The CPU, using either the polling or vector method, can identify the I/O device that generated the interrupt request. But how should the CPU respond to simultaneous interrupt requests? We must consider two factors before we can answer this question.

First, the CPU may be busy when an interrupt request is made, so the device that generated the interrupt may have to wait before receiving any CPU resources. To coordinate the activities of both the CPU and the interrupting I/O device, the I/O device must know when it can stop waiting and begin to transfer data to the CPU. We accomplish this with a special line called the **interrupt acknowledge (INTA)** line. When the CPU is ready to service the I/O device that generated the interrupt request, it sets the interrupt acknowledge line to 1.

Second, it is sometimes important that the CPU complete its work without an interrupt. In this case the CPU may shut off the interrupt capabilities of all or some subset of the I/O devices using an **interrupt disable** signal. These considerations lead to the picture of CPU–I/O communications shown in Figure 11.7.

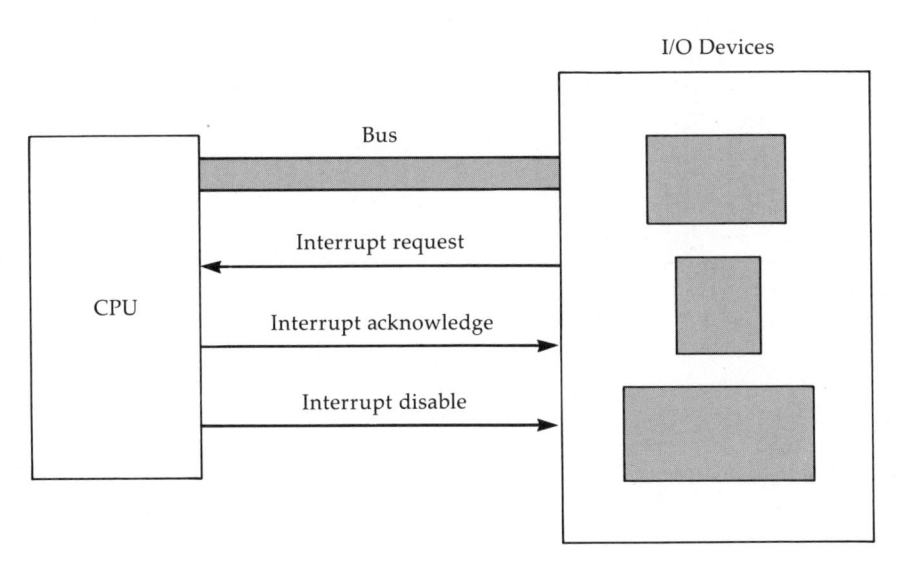

Figure 11.7 CPU–I/O interrupt signals

Priority

When two or more devices request an interrupt at the same time, the CPU must have some method for selecting the one device that it will service. It of course should select the highest priority device. If polling is used for device identification, priority is assigned automatically by the order in which the devices are polled. In this case, if several devices have requested an interrupt, the CPU selects the device that is polled first. However, if the vector method is used, there are several ways to build priority into the service process.

Interrupt Acknowledge Daisy Chain The CPU responds to the interrupt request signal when it is ready to service the interrupt by sending an interrupt acknowledge signal. This signal can be passed from one device to the next in a priority order as shown in Figure 11.8. When device 1 receives an INTA signal from the CPU after generating an interrupt request, it places its vector code on the data bus so that the CPU will select it for service. However, if device 1 did not generate the request, it sends the INTA signal on to device 2. The second device repeats this process. It either puts its vector on the bus or passes the INTA signal on to the next device. If more than one device requests an interrupt at the same time, only the first one in the daisy chain will receive the interrupt acknowledge signal, so only that device will identify itself to the CPU and receive service. Thus the priority is determined by the order of the devices in the daisy chain.

Priority Arbitration This method places the priority determination entirely within the hardware. A special **priority arbitration circuit (PAC)** receives interrupt requests from all I/O devices in the system and passes the vector identification code for the highest priority request on to the CPU. Such a system is shown in Figure 11.9. This system operates faster

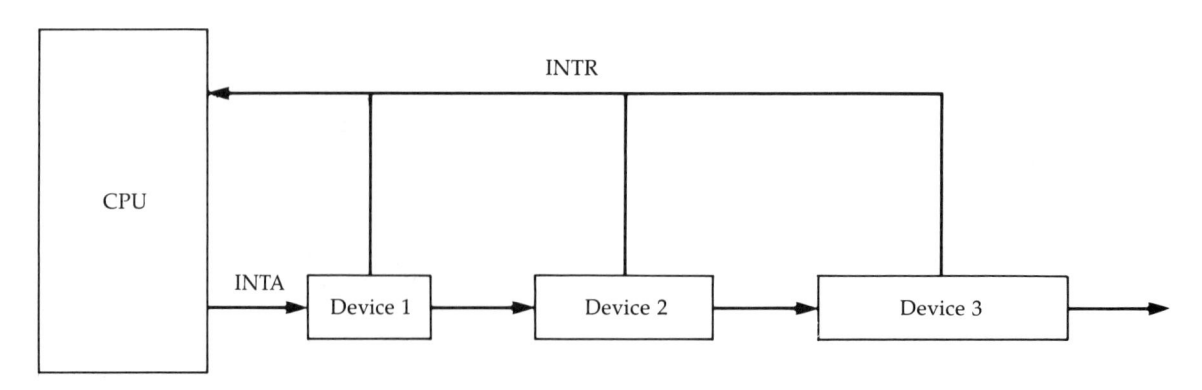

Figure 11.8 Daisy chain organization

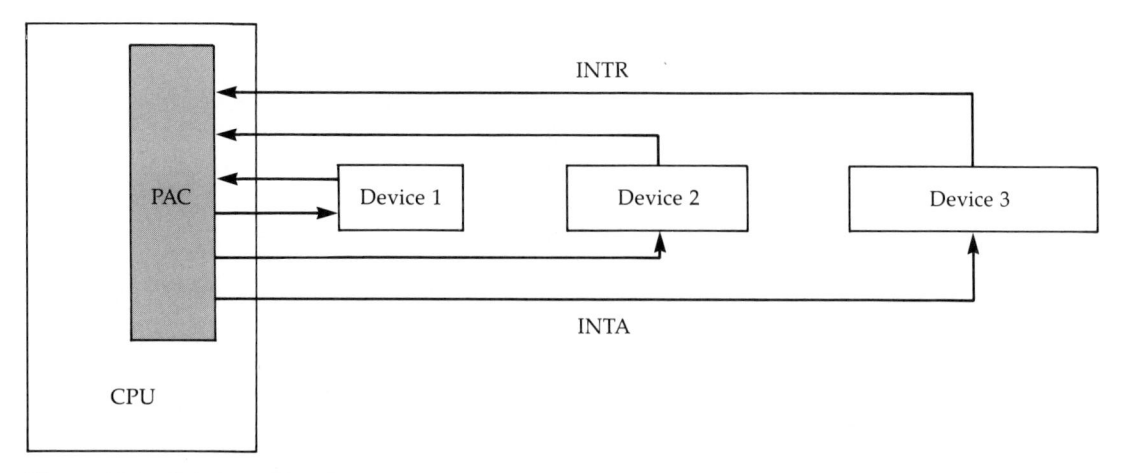

Figure 11.9 Priority arbitration

than the daisy chain approach; however, because the priorities are fixed in the hardware, it is difficult to add new I/O devices to the system.

Mixed Approach This approach attempts to gain the speed advantages of the priority encoder and the expansion flexibility of the daisy chain in one system. This can be done as shown in Figure 11.10 using a daisy chain for each PAC input.

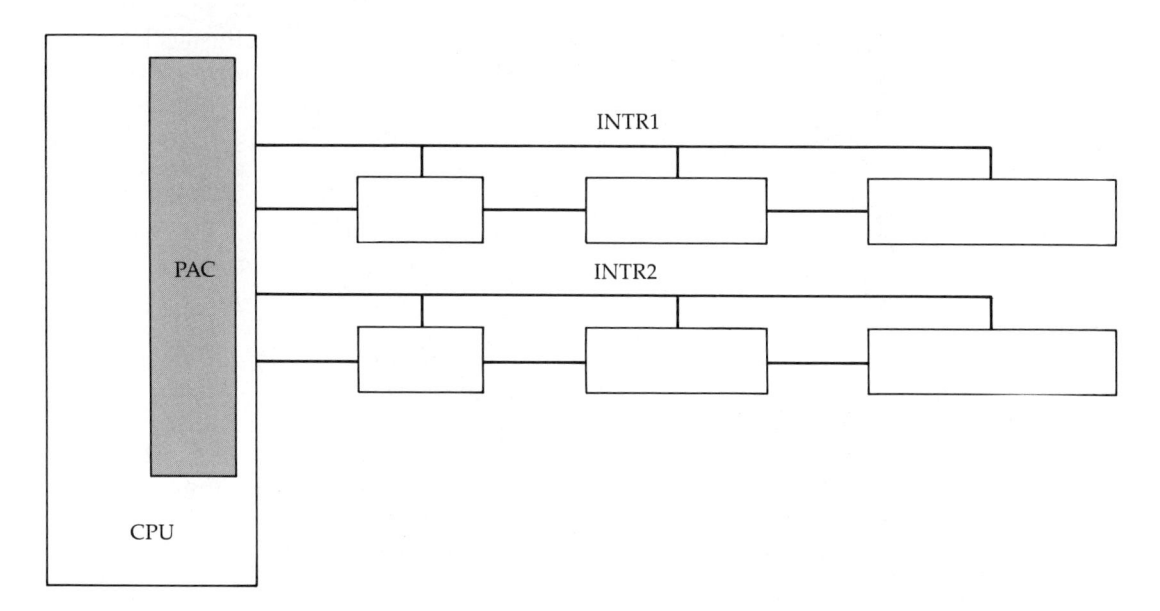

Figure 11.10 Mixed priority approach

The VAX has three levels of interrupts and 31 priority assignments. The assigned priority for a process is contained in bits 16–20 of the PSL. The first level consists of software-generated interrupts or traps. These interrupts are generated during the normal run of a program. Priorities 1–F are allocated to this level. The second level consists of I/O device interrupts, which are assigned priorities 10–17. As a result of these priority assignments, I/O devices have higher priorities than internal software processes. The third level consists of urgent interrupts, which are assigned priorities 18–1F. The two highest priority values assigned in the VAX are 1E and 1F. The priority 1E is reserved for a power failure event. That is, if the VAX detects a drop in its power supply, it will interrupt every process and start to save as much information as possible. It can do this because it takes a finite amount of time for the power level to drop to a point at which that VAX can no longer operate. In those few microseconds the VAX can save some memory contents. The highest priority level (1F) is reserved for "disasters" such as hardware failures. The initial system boot is also assigned priority 1F because it would not be useful to allow some I/O device to interrupt the system boot routines.

11.4 Queue I/O

So far we have examined I/O at the device level, looking at some considerations that hardware designers and device driver writers must take into account. Hardware-level I/O contrasts remarkably with the facilities provided by high-level languages. Many operating systems provide one or more layers of intermediate I/O routines between these levels. The VAX's VMS operating system has two layers: **Queue I/O (QIO)** and **Record Management Services (RMS)**. First we will look at the lower of these two levels, Queue I/O. While device drivers work with I/O one character at a time, QIO is designed to process complete records. Our discussion is primarily concerned with terminal communications. For further details, consult the *VAX/VMS System Services Reference Manual* and the *VAX/VMS I/O User's Reference Manual, Part I*.

The QIO procedures have two major purposes. First, they check all I/O requests to ensure that they are legal. Then valid requests are queued to the device drivers (or in the case of more complicated devices, such as disks and tapes, to control programs called ACPs). Both functions are vital for successful operation of the VAX. By verifying the validity of I/O requests, QIO protects the operating system and users from the consequences of improper or impossible requests to the device drivers. Because I/O requests can be generated much faster than most devices can process them, they are placed in a queue to wait their turn. In some cases it is possible to return control to the requesting program and allow it to continue processing while the I/O operation is waiting to be processed.

To protect the computer from illegal I/O requests, the device drivers are stored in system addressing space that is off limits to normal programs. This prevents a standard program from interfacing directly with the drivers. Only QIO routines have the required privileges of addressing the drivers. Consequently, user programs must use QIO directly or indirectly for all I/O processing. Moreover, many QIO functions require special privileges and are not available to most users. They must be called from the RMS routines discussed in the next section. These restrictions are also intended to protect the system from improper requests. We will limit our discussion of QIO to terminal operations because most users will have the necessary privileges for these operations. You may find it impossible to access other devices with these routines.

Because QIO deals closely with the device drivers, many of its operations are device dependent. The programmer must usually know what type of device will be used for input or output because it may be necessary to use different functions for different devices. For example, it is possible to request that a prompt be printed before a terminal read operation. A disk file user may need to specify a disk address for output to a disk file. Special procedures must be followed before information can be sent to a printer queue because the information is stored on disk until the printer is ready to print it.

When you use QIO directly for terminal I/O, you have considerably more control than when using a high-level procedure. For example, you can determine the following:

1. Whether the program must wait for a queued I/O operation to be completed before the program can continue processing.
2. The maximum number of characters the computer will accept on one line of input.
3. Which characters signal the end of a line.
4. Whether a prompt is given before input.
5. Whether certain special characters, such as control C, will be processed by the program or by the operating system.
6. Whether input should be echoed back to the terminal.
7. If lowercase letters should be converted to uppercase.
8. How long the program should wait for the user to input a string.

Because so many details are involved, it is beyond the scope of this book to explain how to use all the different options. We will illustrate three of them (the maximum characters accepted in one input, issuing prompts, and conversion of lowercase) to give you some feeling for the type of coding needed. You can refer to the references for further details.

There are several QIO macros. We will discuss only three because we will restrict our attention to terminals. The $ASSIGN_S macro opens an I/O channel to a device so that input or output operations can be performed on it. $DASSGN_S closes that channel when it is no longer needed. $QIOW_S is used to queue I/O requests to a channel and wait for their completion. It is used for both input and output operations.

Before showing how QIO is used, we will look briefly at the package of system services in which they are included.

System Services

The Queue I/O procedures are part of a package of **system services** supplied with VMS. These procedures were written to carry out many of the basic functions of the operating system. High-level language programs can take advantage of these procedures by calling them directly. For assembly language programmers, VMS provides a library of convenient macros that simplify their use. These macros begin with a dollar sign. Many come in two formats. The name of the macro may be suffixed with _S or _G, indicating whether the macro uses a CALLS or a CALLG instruction to call the procedure. We will use only the _S format to avoid having to set up argument lists.

In some cases it may be impossible for a system service to carry out its operation because of an error in the call or an unanticipated circumstance discovered during the run. For example, a program may try to input a string from a printer, or it may be impossible to create a new file because the user's disk quota is exceeded. Therefore, before system services return control to the calling program, they leave a number code in R0 indicating the status of the request. In general, odd numbers are used to indicate success, even numbers to indicate that the service failed to complete its task. The *System Service Reference Manual* describes symbolic constants, which represent the different return status codes that can be produced by the services. After calling a system service, a program should check the return status in R0 and take appropriate action if the operation failed. We will look at some techniques for doing this later in this section. We have used one system service throughout this book, the $EXIT_S macro. This macro carries out several functions that help terminate a program properly. If desired, we can provide a return status as an optional parameter. If the return status indicates an error, a short message explaining the error is printed in the user's output. This is done by terminating the program with

```
$EXIT_S    R0
```

immediately after the error is detected. This macro pushes the error code in R0 onto the stack before calling the exit procedure. This option provides a simple way of providing error messages when program termination is required. Successful completion is normally indicated by having the value 1 in R0 or by default by not including the parameter in the macro reference.

An Example Using Queue I/O

The simple program in Listing 11.1 illustrates the use of some QIO macros. The program inputs a character string of up to 80 characters and then echoes it back to the user's terminal. This process is repeated until the user types the four letters "STOP" or "stop". If an error occurs while using one of the QIO macros, the program is terminated and the operating system prints an appropriate error message. The algorithm consists of four steps:

1. Assign a channel to the user's terminal.
2. Print a prompt.
3. Until the user types "STOP" or "stop" do:
    Enter a line of input.
    Echo input back to the terminal.
4. Deassign the channel.

We will discuss the three QIO macros in the context of this program. It serves as an example of how the macros are used in a program and demonstrates the code needed to support their use. One of these macros, $QIOW_S, is used for both input and output and has a rather long list of arguments. Consequently, the program defines two macros called TerminalInput and TerminalOutput that simplify the use of this system macro.

Before performing any input or output, the program must request a channel number for the desired I/O device using the $ASSIGN_S macro. A **channel** is a logical communication path between the program and the device being used. The macro places some numbers describing the specified device in a **channel control block (CCB)** and then returns a channel number specifying the location of those values. After the program obtains a channel number for a device, it uses the number to specify that device in subsequent I/O requests. This macro has two parameters that are useful for terminal I/O. The program supplies a logical name for the device with the DevNam parameter. The device name is typically SYS$INPUT or TT: (the user's terminal) in this application. The device name is passed by descriptor, so the .ASCID directive provides a convenient way to code its value. The channel number is returned in the address of the 16-bit word supplied by the Chan parameter. The program in Listing 11.1 uses TTName as the device name and TTChan to hold the channel number. (In case you are wondering about the letters "TT," they stand for "teletype," a very common terminal in the early days of interactive programming.)

Listing 11.1 Example using QIO

```
        .TITLE    QIOExample

;   Purpose:   Illustrates simple QIO input and output by printing a
;              prompt and then inputting character strings and echoing
;              until STOP is entered.

;   Notes:
;     1. Only works on interactive runs connected to a terminal.
;     2. Adapted from VAX/VMS System Services Reference Manual.


;  .... Setup descriptions of the terminal for QIO ....
TTName:    .ASCID    "Sys$Input"     ; Descriptor for terminal name
TTChan:    .BLKW     1               ; Reserve room for channel number
TTIOSB:    .BLKW     1               ; I/O status block: status,
TTIOLen:   .BLKW     1               ;                  length,
           .BLKL     1               ;                  other info

;  .... Setup buffers for I/O ....
LenBuf = 81
IOLen:     .BLKL     1               ; Length of string in IOBuf
IOBuf:     .BLKB     LenBuf          ; I/O buffer
InstBuf:   .ASCII    "Enter a string: "  ; Instruction buffer
LenInst = . - InstBuf                ; Length of instruction buffer
                                     ;    = current loc - InstBuf loc


;  .... Input macro ....
;   Uses $QIOW_S to input from a terminal and checks for errors

           .MACRO    TerminalInput -   ; Input from terminal ...
                     Buffer, -         ;   input buffer
                     Length            ;   length of input buffer

           $QIOW_S   Chan = TTChan, -  ; Channel for I/O
                     Func = #IO$_ReadVBlk,-; function: Read a virtual block
                     IOSB = TTIOSB, -  ; put status in TTIOSB
                     P1 = Buffer, -    ; put input in Buffer
                     P2 = Length       ; maximum length of buffer
           BSBW      CheckQueueAndCompletionStatus
           .ENDM     TerminalInput


;  .... Output macro ....
;   Uses $QIOW_S to output to a terminal and checks for errors

           .MACRO    TerminalOutput -  ; Output to a terminal ...
                     Buffer, -         ;   output buffer
                     Length            ;   length of output buffer
```

Listing 11.1 (continued)

```
              $QIOW_S   Chan = TTChan, -         ; Channel for I/O
                        Func = #IO$_WriteVBlk, -
                        -                         ; function: Write a virtual block
                        IOSB = TTIOSB, -          ; put status in TTIOSB
                        P1 = Buffer, -            ; output buffer
                        P2 = Length, -            ; length of buffer
                        P4 = #^X8D010000          ; carriage control
              BSBW      CheckQueueAndCompletionStatus
           .ENDM        TerminalOutput


;    .... The program ....

           .ENTRY    QIOExample, 0

;    .... Assign channel to terminal ....
Start:     $ASSIGN_S -                          ; Assign channel
                     DevNam = TTName, -         ;   logical name of device
                     Chan = TTChan              ;   channel number returned
           BSBW      CheckEr

;    .... Issue the instruction (prompt) to the user ....
           TerminalOutput -                     ; Print instruction
                     Buffer = InstBuf, -        ;   address of instruction
                     Length = #LenInst          ;   length of instruction

;    .... Input and echo a string and repeat until 'stop' ....
Repeat:    TerminalInput -                      ; Input a string
                     Buffer = IOBuf, -          ;   put in IOBUF
                     Length = #LenBuf           ;   maximum length=#LenBuf

           MOVZWL    TTIOLen, IOLen             ; Get length from TTIOSB

           TerminalOutput -                     ; Output a string
                     Buffer = IOBuf, -          ;   location of string
                     Length = IOLen             ;   length of string

           CMPL      #^A'STOP', IOBuf           ; 'Stop' run?
           BEQL      Done
           CMPL      #^A'stop', IOBuf
           BEQL      Done
           BRW       Repeat                     ; Otherwise repeat

;    .... Terminate run ....
Done:      $DASSGN_S -                          ; First, deassign channel
                     Chan = TTChan
           BSBW      CheckEr
           $EXIT_S
```

(continued)

Listing 11.1 (continued)

```
;   .... Subroutines to check for errors ....
;   (errors are signaled by an even number)
CheckQueueAndCompletionStatus:
          BLBC     R0, ErStop           ; Branch if queue error
          MOVZWL   TTIOSB, R0           ; Move completion status to R0
CheckEr:  BLBC     R0, ErStop           ; Branch if error
          RSB                           ; Otherwise return

ErStop:   $EXIT_S  R0                   ; Finished

          .END     QIOExample
```

When the program no longer needs a particular channel (normally just before exiting from the program), it should be released using the $DASSGN_S macro. This macro needs only one parameter. Chan is used to specify which channel is to be deassigned.

The third QIO macro used by this program is $QIOW_S. Together with the almost identical macro $QIO_S, this macro can be used to queue a number of different types of requests to the channel associated with a particular device. Accordingly, their parameter lists are rather long. To improve the program's readability, input and output macros are defined to call $QIOW_S. TerminalInput inputs a character string from the user's terminal. These program-defined macros have just two parameters. Buffer is the address of the buffer used in the operation, and Length is a word containing the number of characters in the buffer. For TerminalOutput, it represents the number of characters to be printed, and for TerminalInput, it represents the maximum number of characters that can be put in the buffer. Normally, it should include one byte for the carriage return character typed by the user to mark the end of the input string.

We now turn our attention directly to the QIO macro used in the terminal input and output macros. VMS provides two macros that can be used for I/O operations. The only difference between $QIO_S and $QIOW_S is that $QIO_S returns control to the calling program immediately after the I/O request is placed in the queue, while $QIOW_S waits until the operation is complete before returning to the calling program. (The "W" in $QIOW_S stands for "wait.") Use of the $QIO_S macro can be efficient because the program can continue processing while the I/O operation is in progress. However, this can cause new problems for the programmer because it may be necessary to ensure that the I/O operation has been completed before processing can continue beyond some critical point in the program. For example, an input operation must be finished before the program can begin processing the data typed by the user. Thus extra coding is frequently required to check and wait for the I/O operation's completion. To avoid these problems, we have chosen to use $QIOW_S, which waits for the I/O operation to be completed before execution continues.

Both of these macros have 12 parameters to provide the required flexibility. Six of these arguments have particular fixed meanings and names. The other 6 depend on the function that is requested and are simply numbered P1, P2, . . ., P6. We will look at a few of these parameters. Several are not needed in simpler applications.

Chan is the channel number that was obtained with the $ASSIGN_S macro.

Func specifies the function or operation to be carried out. The *I/O User's Reference Manual* provides a long list of different functions that provide nearly every I/O operation that we can imagine (plus some beyond our imagination). The program uses two of them. IO$_ReadVBlk (Read a Virtual Block) can be used for input from several devices, including terminals. IO$_WriteVBlk (Write a Virtual Block) can handle output to several devices. Actually, these function names represent code numbers that the linker substitutes into the machine code. Thus they use the immediate addressing mode, and the "#" sign is required before the function name.

IOSB (I/O Status Block) is the address of an 8-byte status buffer supplied by the program. The $QIO procedures use it to store information concerning the data transferred by the procedure. In this program the status buffer begins at TTIOSB, whose address is specified in the macro call. As shown in Figure 11.11, the first word is reserved for status information, which indicates if the operation completed properly. After a call to one of the $QIO macros, the completion status should be checked for possible error codes. Even values indicate that the procedure was unable to complete its work. After an I/O operation, the second word will contain the number of characters actually transferred (not including the carriage return). The count could be represented as TTIOSB+2. However, it is convenient to give the second word a label, TTIOLen. This makes it easier to access the number of characters actually stored in the buffer. The final longword holds some device-dependent information that we do not need to be concerned with.

The meaning of the numbered parameters P1–P6 depends on the function specified by the Func parameter. In many cases not all of these

```
31                                              0
+-------------------------+---------------------+
|     character count     |  completion status  |
+-------------------------+---------------------+
|         device dependent information          |
+------------------------------------------------+
```

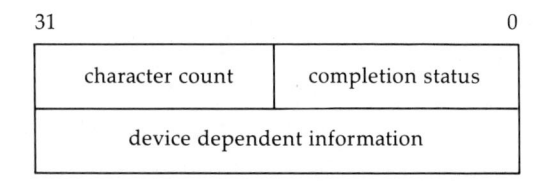

Figure 11.11 I/O Status Block

parameters are needed. P1 specifies the address of the I/O buffer for IO$_ReadVBlk, IO$_WriteVBlk, and several of the other functions. In these cases P2 is a longword specifying the number of characters in the buffer. For input, it represents the maximum number of characters that the buffer will hold. The length of the input buffer should normally be one larger than the longest input string allowed, because the character used to terminate the input (normally the carriage return) will be put in the buffer. For output, it represents the exact number of characters to be printed. P4 is commonly used for output. It uses a 32-bit numerical code to specify the desired carriage control. The programmer has many options, as described in the *I/O User's Reference Manual, Part I*. Some popular codes include the following:

Code	Meaning
^X8D010000	Go to the beginning of a new line, print the output, and then do a carriage return.
^X8D020000	Double space, print the output, and do a carriage return.
^X00 010000	Go to the beginning of a new line, print the output, but do not follow it with a carriage return.

The last format is useful when printing prompts. These options for P4 are representative of many of the options available to programs using QIO that may not be available in a high-level language that "simplifies" I/O by reducing the number of options.

We must use special consideration when assigning a value to the $QIOW_S parameter P2. Recall that this macro uses CALLS to call a procedure to carry out the required operation. To pass the P2 argument to the procedure, it pushes a longword on the stack using the equivalent of

```
    PUSHL    P2
```

If the buffer length is defined by a constant, the value of P2 must include a "#" sign. For example:

```
    P2=#LenBuf, -  ; Length of buffer is LenBuf
```

However, if the length of the buffer is variable, the value must be stored in a longword.

```
    IOLen:     .LONG    1              ; Length of the string
                 :
                 :
               P2=IOLen, -    ; Length stored in IOLen
```

The macros TerminalInput and TerminalOutput use their Length parameter for P2, so the same considerations apply to this parameter.

The IO$_ReadVBlk function does not blank out unused space in the input buffer, so it is important to use the count value stored in the I/O status block to determine the actual number of characters input. In the body of the program in Listing 11.1, MOVZWL copies the word at TTIOLen into the required longword at IOLen, extending the unsigned value with zeros.

As mentioned earlier, it is important to check the error code in R0 after using a system service. The subroutine call to CheckEr does this in the program. For simplicity, the program treats any even number as indicating an error and terminates the program with a branch to ErStop. The $EXIT_S R0 macro call treats the contents of R0 as the error code and instructs the operating system to print the appropriate error message as it cleans up after the program. After a call to $QIOW_S, the first word in TTIOSB should also be checked for the completion code. Again, even numbers usually mean an error. The subroutine CheckQueueAnd-CompletionStatus is used to check both items. It first checks R0 to see if the operation was queued correctly and then moves the word at TTIOSB to R0 for testing the completion status. In either case an error causes a jump to ErStop, and the program terminates. The operating system prints the pertinent message.

This program can be used only for terminal I/O for two reasons. First, the same channel is used for both input and output, severely restricting the type of device that can be used. Even if separate channels are used for input and output, it would still be impossible to send the output to a disk file unless the user has appropriate privileges and RMS macros are used to define and create the file with the appropriate name and characteristics. Because information queued to a printer is stored on disk until the printer is ready, similar requirements must be met before a printer queue can receive output.

You may be surprised by QIO's treatment of control characters during input. Unless otherwise instructed, CTRL/C, CTRL/O, CTRL/Q through CTRL/U, CTRL/X, and CTRL/Y are processed by the operating system in its normal manner and never reach the program. Depending on the computer's description of your terminal, other control characters may be treated as special editing characters and are not passed to your program either. If not intercepted by the operating system, the formatting characters BS, TAB, LF, VT, and FF (CTRL/H through CTRL/L) are passed to the calling program. All other control characters are treated as input line terminators in exactly the same way as the carriage return (CTRL/M) is treated. The terminator is stored in the input buffer following the other characters. In our program it would be the (TTIOLEN + 1)st character in the buffer whenever the number of characters input is less than the size of the buffer. The *I/O User's Reference Manual* explains how you can change the set of terminators, if desired.

What happens if the user fills the buffer to capacity before using return or another terminator? $QIO routines automatically terminate the input and return to the calling program immediately without waiting for a terminator. Accordingly, if the input buffer is specified as having a length of 1, the program will process characters one at a time. The EDT editor takes advantage of this feature so that the editor can respond to individual keystrokes during screen mode editing.

Because of the generality provided by the QIO macros, they are very long and complicated. If you are interested in seeing their expansion, we strongly recommend using .SHOW MEB instead of .SHOW ME. The MEB (macro expansion binary) modifier requests printing of only those instructions in the macro that actually produce binary code.

A More Sophisticated Queue I/O Request

The IO$_ReadVBlk and IO$_WriteVBlk functions are actually quite generic and can be used with a number of different devices, providing that the user has appropriate privileges. We will show one example of a device-dependent QIO application. It reads terminal input after issuing a prompt and converts all lowercase letters to uppercase. The code is shown in Listing 11.2.

Some explanation of this code is needed. Recall that the function names used with the Func argument are symbolic constants. The exclamation mark means to logically OR the two values on either side of it. This allows two carefully chosen values to be stored in one longword.

Listing 11.2 $QIOW_S input providing a prompt and lowercase conversion

```
LF = 10
TTName:   .ASCID    "Sys$Input"        ; Descriptor for terminal name
TTChan:   .BLKW     1                  ; Reserve room for channel number
TTIOSB:   .BLKW     1                  ; I/O status block: status
TTIOLen:  .BLKW     1                  ;                  length
          .BLKL     1                  ;                  other info
IOBUF:    .BLKB     81                 ; I/O buffer

Prompt:   .ASCII    <LF>"-->"
          . . .
          $QIOW_S   Chan = TTChan, -   ; Use $QIOW_S on TTChan
                    Func = #IO$_ReadPrompt!IO$M_CvtLow, -
                    -                  ;      read with prompt while
                    -                  ;      converting lowercase
                    IOSB = TTIOSB, -   ;      put status in TTIOSB
                    P1 = IOBuf, -      ;      put input in IOBUF
                    P2 = #81, -        ;      maximum length = 81
                    P5 = #Prompt, -    ;      address of prompt
                    P6 = #4            ;      length of prompt
```

The function IO$_ReadPrompt means issue a prompt before inputting. The modifier IO$M_CvtLow says to convert lowercase letters to uppercase. The combination

```
IO$_ReadPrompt!IO$M_CvtLow
```

says to read with a prompt and convert lowercase to uppercase. The function assumes that parameter P5 has the address of the prompt, and P6 has its length. Unfortunately, the general-purpose macro treats arguments P2–P6 as if they are passed by value and uses a PUSHL instruction to push the value on the stack. Therefore, Prompt is used as a symbolic constant whose value is the address of Prompt. It can be pushed onto the stack as an immediate value. The code generated by $QIOW_S,

```
PUSHL      #Prompt
```

is functionally the same as

```
PUSHAL     Prompt
```

The IO$_ReadPrompt function does not automatically issue a line feed before printing the prompt, so it must be supplied as part of the prompt string when desired. If you were to include this segment in a program, you might be surprised to see uppercase letters being echoed back to your screen as you type lowercase characters.

We have seen that QIO is designed to verify and queue all I/O requests as it handles I/O one record at a time. It provides programmers a great deal of flexibility and is highly efficient. Unfortunately it is very device dependent. Therefore, direct calls to this level are normally avoided. RMS macros, which are discussed in the next section, provide significant device independence making them more convenient to use. Direct use of $QIO macros is useful in situations where special operations are required or speed is essential.

11.5 I/O Using RMS

RMS (Record Management Services) is the subsystem of VAX-11 VMS that handles communication with files stored on external devices. It treats **files** as a collection of records. **Records** are a collection of one or more items or fields treated as a single block of data. For terminal and printer I/O, one line of input or output is considered to be a record. RMS provides ways to create and open files and then write and read them one record at a time. RMS allows various types of files, including sequential, relative, and indexed. A complete discussion of this system's capabilities would take a complete chapter, so we will limit our discussion to an introduction to sequential file processing. For more complete information, refer to the *VAX Record Management Services Reference Manual*.

RMS differs from QIO in two significant ways. First, RMS can recognize, create, and process files. Second, RMS achieves a great deal of device independence by treating physical devices such as terminals, card readers, and printers as sequential files. Consequently, high-level language I/O routines pass their I/O requests to RMS so that users are free to assign input and output to devices or files at run time. RMS passes these requests on to the appropriate QIO procedures discussed previously.

RMS is distinguished from high-level language I/O in that it can only process character strings. If input characters are to be interpreted as numbers, the programmer must arrange the appropriate conversions. For output, the programmer must arrange to have the required string passed to RMS exactly as it is to appear on the user's terminal, on the printer, or in the file.

RMS provides two general-purpose macros for I/O: $GET, which inputs a record, and $PUT, which outputs a record. These macro calls are completely device independent and are particularly easy to use because most applications require only one parameter, which identifies the record description and, indirectly, the file being used.

We will also discuss how you can open an existing file using $OPEN, create a new file using $CREATE, close files using $CLOSE, and relate a record description to a file description using $CONNECT. These macros also normally need only one parameter.

After reading about QIO, you may be asking "How can these macros be so general and yet need only one parameter?" The answer is that the parameter points to a table containing the information describing the file or record format. The table describing a file is called a **file access block (FAB)**, and the table defining a record is called a **record access block (RAB)**. Unfortunately, before we can describe how the executable macros mentioned earlier can be used, we must describe how we can set up these access blocks. (You were right! It is not quite as simple as we made it out to be.) To simplify the process of setting up these blocks, RMS supplies two macros, $FAB and $RAB, that format these tables for us.

Although the topics discussed in this section only apply directly to a VAX running under VMS, the same concepts are sometimes seen on other computers and operating systems.

Defining Files and Records

A file access block (FAB) must be defined for each file used by a program. (In this context remember that terminal input, terminal output, and printer output are considered files.) A FAB contains more than 20 fields that describe a file and its use. Because many of these fields are automatically supplied appropriate values or do not apply to sequential files, we will need only the fields summarized in Table 11.1. We will describe the fields more carefully as we show how they are used.

The $FAB macro provides an easy way to create a file access block. It is used in the data definition section of the program. The macro has the following format:

```
Label:   $FAB    FNM=<filename>, other options
```

It is only necessary to specify those fields without appropriate defaults. For example, the input file can often be declared using

```
InFAB:   $FAB    FNM=<Sys$Input>
```

This file access block will be referred to as InFAB in the rest of the program. The macro creates a storage location for the file's name (Sys$Input) and puts its address in the field FNA and its length in FNS. In this example input will come from the standard input device referred to as Sys$Input. Sys$Input is normally the user's terminal during interactive runs but can be reassigned to a file using the operating system command

```
$ ASSIGN  filename  Sys$Input
```

Alternatively, you may specify the name of an actual disk file inside the corner brackets following the FNM argument. In situations where the actual input device or file is unknown when you write the program, it may be convenient to use a logical name such as Input:. In this case the user must use the ASSIGN command to provide the actual filename for Input: before running the program.

What about all the other fields in the file access block? Some of the remaining fields are filled with default values supplied in the macro. RMS will fill some other fields with file directory information at run time when the file is opened.

Table 11.1 FAB Fields

Field Name	Symbolic Offset	Field Size	Description
FNA	FAB$L_FNA	Longword	Address of string holding filename
FNS	FAB$B_FNS	Byte	Size or length of filename
MRS	FAB$W_MRS	Word	Maximum record size
ORG	FAB$B_ORG	Byte	File organization (SEQ, REL, or IDX)
RAT	FAB$B_RAT	Byte	Record attributes (carriage control)
RFM	FAB$B_RFM	Byte	Record format

The output file is described in a similar manner except that it is often necessary to provide more detail because this file is normally created during the run. For example, consider the following file access blocks. The first is adequate for standard output, but it may be desirable to use some of the other fields when creating a data file as shown in the second example.

```
OutFAB:   $FAB    FNM=<Sys$Output>, RAT=CR, MRS=80
DataFAB:  $FAB    FNM=<DataFile.Dat>, ORG=SEQ, RFM=FIX, MRS=130
```

The file block called OutFAB is given a carriage return (CR) attribute in the record attribute field (RAT). RMS will add a carriage return and line feed after each record, making it possible to send the output to a terminal or printer. The maximum record size (MRS) is set to 80, limiting the size of the variable-length records in this file. Specifying MRS for variable-length files is good practice but not required. DataFAB defines a file called DataFile.Dat. The remaining arguments specify that the file is organized as a sequential file with fixed-length records 130 characters long. ORG=SEQ indicates that the file is to be treated as a sequential file. Actually this parameter is optional because SEQ is the default. RFM=FIX signifies that the file has fixed-length records, and MRS is used to specify the size of those records. The default for RFM, variable-length records, may conserve file space in many situations. Because DataFile.Dat is not given the record attribute CR, it is inconvenient to print it.

A record access block (RAB) describing a record also has more than 20 fields. Again, many are reserved for special purposes or have appropriate defaults. The fields that interest us are listed in Table 11.2.

The $RAB macro is used in the data declaration section of a program to declare a record's access block. The FAB field must be specified in every RAB. It indicates which file is to be associated with a particular record. Many of the fields are useful for input. Consider the following:

Table 11.2 RAB Fields

Field Name	Symbolic Offset	Field Size	Description
FAB	RAB$L_FAB	Longword	Address of the FAB for the file
PBF	RAB$L_PBF	Longword	Address of prompt for terminal input
PSZ	RAB$B_PSZ	Byte	Size or length of prompt buffer
RBF	RAB$L_RBF	Longword	Address of record buffer
ROP	RAB$L_ROP	Longword	Record options
RSZ	RAB$W_RSZ	Word	Size or length of record buffer
UBF	RAB$L_UBF	Longword	User buffer address for input
USZ	RAB$W_USZ	Word	Size or length of user buffer

```
InRAB:      $RAB    FAB=InFAB, UBF=InBuf, USZ=80, -
                    ROP=PMT, PBF=PromptMsg, PSZ=3
```

The record buffer called InRAB will be used with the file defined by InFAB. The characters input are to be put into InBuf, whose size allows a maximum of 80 characters. The last three arguments establish a standard prompt to be issued to a terminal before the input. They can be omitted if not needed. ROP allows several record options. For example, ROP=PMT indicates that a prompt will be used, ROP=CVT indicates that lowercase letters will be converted to uppercase, and ROP=<CVT,PMT> indicates that both options will be used. This field is omitted if no options are desired. PBF is used to specify that the prompt is stored at PromptMsg, and PSZ specifies its length as three characters. Prompts and case conversions are ignored if the input does not come from a terminal.

Generally, the RAB for sequential output files is simpler. The record buffer for the string to be written is described by RBF and RSZ. For example, if OutBuf is an 80-character buffer used for OutRAB, we would write

```
OutRAB:     $RAB    FAB=OutFAB, RBF=OutBuf, RSZ=80
```

We should make some comments. We can specify the buffers dynamically while the program is running. (We will discuss this when we discuss $GET and $PUT; it is particularly useful when the output does not have a fixed format.) Observe that the user buffer is used for input, and the record buffer is used for output. After a read operation, RMS puts the address of the input buffer into RBF and the actual number of characters input into RSZ. These quantities are useful in processing variable-length input.

Though it is common to include RAB and FAB in their labels, there are no special standards for naming either of the access blocks.

We should note one restriction in the use of the $FAB and $RAB macros. They must be **longword aligned**; that is, the address of an access block must be divisible by 4. The easiest way to accomplish this is to put these macros at the beginning of the program because the linker always starts a program at a longword boundary. (If this is impractical, it may be necessary to include LONG as an argument for the .PSECT and precede the $FAB and $RAB macros with the directive .ALIGN LONG.)

Executable RMS Macros

We will now turn our attention to the executable macros used to process files and carry out standard I/O operations. Because the necessary information has been stored in the file and record access blocks, these macros have a simple format. Macros that act on a file need only specify the label of the appropriate FAB. Macros that process a record use the name of the RAB. (We can also specify the addresses of two procedures: one would be called if the operation is a success; the other would be called if an error occurred. We will not need to use these options.)

The RMS macros leave completion codes in R0, just like system services. Again, odd values usually indicate success, while even numbers indicate that the macro was unable to complete its task. It is the programmer's responsibility to check R0 for possible errors after using an executable RMS macro. In this subsection we will use a macro called ErrorCheck for this task. We will present sample code for this macro later. Of course we could use other methods such as calling a subroutine.

We begin by looking at the ways to access a file. Before we can use an existing file, we must open it using the $OPEN macro. If we need a new file for output, we create it with the $CREATE macro. The format is as follows:

```
$OPEN     FAB=InFAB
ErrorCheck
$CREATE   FAB=OutFAB
ErrorCheck
```

When a file is opened, the open procedure copies a portion of the file's description from the user's directory into the FAB. Thus the $FAB statement for an existing file needs to do little more than name the file. On the other hand, a file being created must be described more completely in its FAB to give RMS an adequate description of its characteristics.

When we no longer need a file, we should close it using the $CLOSE macro. For example, we would use

```
$CLOSE    FAB=DataFAB
ErrorCheck
```

to terminate the program's use of a file whose FAB is called DataFAB.

Unless told otherwise in the FAB, RMS assumes that opened files will be used for input and created files will be used for output. There is an exception to this rule: a file opened for input from a terminal can also be used for output. In this case we should specify RAT=CR in the FAB. This dual use is recommended only for such simple applications as echoing the input or issuing prompts because it may prevent the resulting program from being device independent.

Before we can use a record access block, we must associate it with or connect it to the FAB for the appropriate file. We do this after the file is opened or created by using the $CONNECT macro. For example, we would use

```
$CONNECT  RAB=InRAB
ErrorCheck
```

to connect the RAB defined at InRAB to the file specified in its FAB field.

After opening or creating a file and connecting the RAB, we can read and write it using $GET and $PUT. For example:

```
$GET        RAB=InRAB
ErrorCheck
$PUT        RAB=OutRAB
ErrorCheck
```

The $GET macro gets the next record from the input file and stores it in the buffer specified by the UBF field in the record access block InRAB. The record is truncated (and a warning is issued) if it is longer than allowed by the USZ field. If the record is shorter than the buffer, the excess characters in the buffer are left unchanged. The address of the buffer is copied into RBF, and the number of characters actually input and written into the user buffer is placed in the RSZ field. The $PUT macro writes the characters stored in the record buffer specified by the RBF field into the file.

We can access the fields in an FAB or RAB during a run by adding the symbolic offset for the field to the block's address. For example, we can copy the number of characters input from the RSZ field in the input RAB to R0 using

```
MOVW        InRAB+RAB$W_RSZ, R0
```

In the same manner, we can modify the number of characters to be output.

```
MOVW        R0, OutRAB+RAB$W_RSZ
```

Suppose that we are writing a program that inputs the user's name and then prints "Hello (name of user)". Further suppose that the characters "Hello " are already in the output buffer OutBuf. The following code segment shows how to copy the name from the input buffer InBuf to six characters past the beginning of the output buffer and write the result into the output file.

```
$GET        RAB = InRAB                     ; Input name
ErrorCheck                                   ; Check for errors
MOVW        InRAB + RAB$W_RSZ, R0           ; Copy length to R0
ADDW3       #6, R0, OutRAB + RAB$W_RSZ      ; Find output length
MOVC3       R0, InBuf, OutBuf + 6           ; Copy characters
$PUT        RAB = OutRAB                    ; Write string
ErrorCheck                                   ; Check for errors
```

We can avoid having to copy a buffer's contents when just echoing input. We can just change the output buffer's address and length as shown in the following example:

```
        $GET        RAB = InRAB                     ; Input string
        ErrorCheck                                  ; Check for errors
        MOVW        InRAB + RAB$W_RSZ, -            ; Copy length to
                    OutRAB + RAB$W_RSZ              ;   output RAB
        MOVL        InRAB + RAB$L_RBF, -            ; Put buffer address
                    OutRAB + RAB$L_RBF              ;   in output RAB
        $PUT        RAB = OutRAB                    ; Write string
        ErrorCheck                                  ; Check for errors
```

When values in the access blocks are stored during the run, it is not necessary to specify them when defining the block.

The RMS macros can encounter many conditions that prevent them from completing their work. For example, a file specified by the FAB in an OPEN statement may not exist, or an end of file may prevent input. If the error code in R0 is even, the following macro transfers control to ErrorStop.

```
          .MACRO    ErrorCheck      ?Continue
          BLBS      R0, Continue           ; Continue if R0 is odd
          BRW       ErrorStop              ; Otherwise, terminate run
Continue:
          .ENDM     ErrorCheck
```

Conditional branches only allow byte displacement, which might be too short to jump to the program termination section. Thus the macro uses a word displacement branch to transfer control to that section when there is an error. Using a macro to carry out the error check lets us avoid having to create a new label for every error check and reduces the number of lines of repetitive coding. The sample program in the next subsection illustrates using a subroutine as an alternative error check mechanism.

We may want to inspect the error code that RMS leaves in R0 more carefully because some conditions that have even code numbers may not actually require us to terminate the program. In fact the VMS operating system provides for five levels of error messages indicated by the three least significant bits in the error code. They are as follows:

Low-Order Bits	Severity	Description
000	Warning:	Nonstandard condition, but the operation was at least partially successful.
001	Success:	Operation completed.
010	Error:	A problem exists; an alternate action should be taken.
011	Information:	Operation complete, but some comment is appropriate.

100	Severe error:	Unrecoverable error possibly caused by program logic; the program should be terminated.

RMS provides symbolic constants that can be used to help determine a particular error. The *VAX-11 Record Management Services Reference Manual* lists all the possible error codes. As a quick reference, we will list a few of them here.

Symbolic Value	Type	Description
RMS$_Normal	Success	Operation successful
RMS$_Supersede	Success	Created new version of file
RMS$_ACC	Error	ACP file access failed
RMS$_CRE	Error	ACP file creation failed
RMS$_EOF	Error	End of file reached
RMS$_EXT	Error	ACP file extend failed
RMS$_ISI	Severe	Invalid internal stream identifier (ISI) value
RMS$_RER	Severe	Read error
RMS$_RNF	Error	Record not found
RMS$_TNS	Warning	Terminator not seen (terminal input)

What might be considered an error requiring program termination in one situation may be corrected by an error recovery section in a different program and may even be ignored under certain conditions. Thus it may be necessary to check for certain error conditions and provide an alternative action. An end of file may indicate that the data is incomplete, or it may just signal that input has ended and processing is to begin. User-friendly programs should print a message explaining how to correct the error before program termination. Most of the error descriptions are reasonably self-explanatory, but the RMS$_ISI message may need some interpretation. It may mean that you are trying to connect a record that is already connected or trying to use a record access block that has not been connected. The latter error is unlikely if you always check for errors after connecting a $RAB.

An Example Using RMS Macros

The program in Listing 11.3 packs a file by removing multiple blanks between nonblank sequences of characters. This packing can conserve disk space if the extra blanks are unneeded.

Listing 11.3 Sample program using RMS

```
;   Program Pack

;       Deletes extra blanks in a file to conserve space:
;           Initial blanks are removed,
;           Consecutive blanks are replaced by just one blank,
;           At most one trailing blank will be output.

;       Before this program can be run, the user must assign the
;           actual file or device names to Input: and Output:.
;           For example:
;               $ ASSIGN Sys$Input INPUT:
;               $ ASSIGN Packed.Dat OUTPUT:
;               $ RUN PACK

;   .... Declare files ....
InFAB:      $FAB    FNM = <Input:>      ; FAB for input
OutFAB:     $FAB    FNM = <Output:>,-   ; FAB for output
                    RAT = CR            ;   use carriage return (and
                                        ;   line feed) after each line

;   .... Declare records ....
InRAB:      $RAB    FAB = InFAB, -      ; Associate InRAB with FAB
                    UBF = InBuf, -      ;   specify buffer
                    USZ = BufLen, -     ;   specify buffer length
                    ROP = PMT, -        ;   prompt terminal user
                    PBF = Prompt, -     ;   prompt buffer
                    PSZ = PromptLen     ;   prompt length
OutRAB:     $RAB    FAB = OutFAB, -     ; Associate OutRAB with FAB
                    RBF = OutBuf        ;   specify buffer

;   .... Declare buffers ....
BufLen = 80
InBuf:      .BLKB   BufLen              ; Input buffer
OutBuf:     .BLKB   BufLen              ; Output buffer
Prompt:     .ASCII  'Enter string: '    ; Input prompt
PromptLen = . - Prompt                  ; Calculate length of prompt


;   .... Begin main program ....

        .ENTRY  Pack, 0

;   .... Initialize files and records ....
        $OPEN       FAB = InFAB         ; Open input file
        BSBW        ErCheck
        $CREATE     FAB = OutFAB        ; Create output file
        BSBW        ErCheck
        $CONNECT    RAB = InRAB         ; Connect input record
        BSBW        ErCheck
```

Listing 11.3 (continued)

```
              $CONNECT  RAB = OutRAB       ; Connect output record
              BSBW      ErCheck

;  .... Begin loop by getting record ....
NextRecord:
              $GET      RAB = InRAB        ; Input a record
              CMPL      R0, #RMS$_EOF      ; Check for end of file
              BNEQ      Cont               ;    and
              BRW       Done               ;    branch if finished
Cont:         BSBW      ErCheck            ; Check for other errors

;  .... Use subroutine to pack record into OutBuf and put its
;          length into R3 ....
              BSBW      PackRecord

;  .... Output packed record ....
              MOVW      R3, OutRAB + RAB$W_RSZ
                                           ; Move length to RSZ field
              $PUT      RAB = OutRAB
              BSBW      ErCheck

;  .... Repeat ....
              BRB       NextRecord

;  .... Finished, terminate run ....

Done:         $CLOSE    FAB = InFAB        ; Close input file
              BSBW      ErCheck
              $CLOSE    FAB = OutFAB       ; Close output file
              BSBW      ErCheck
              $EXIT_S


;  .... Subroutine to pack InBuf into OutBuf ....
;          (uses R0 to R5)

Blank = ^A" "

;  .... Initialize  (and specify register usage) ....
PackRecord:
              MOVAB     InBuf, R0          ; R0: address next char. in InBuf
              MOVAB     OutBuf, R1         ; R1: address next char. in OutBuf
              MOVW      InRAB + RAB$W_RSZ, R2
                                           ; R2: number char. left in InBuf
              CLRW      R3                 ; R3: number char. in OutBuf
              MOVB      #Blank, R4         ; R4: last char. in OutBuf
                                           ;   (will skip initial blanks)
                                           ; R5: next char. in InBuf
```

(continued)

Listing 11.3 (continued)

```
        ;  .... Process next character in InBuf ....
        NextChar:
                TSTW    R2              ; Any characters left?
                BLEQ    Return          ;    if not, terminate loop
                MOVB    (R0)+, R5       ; Get next character
                CMPB    R5, #Blank      ; Is it a blank?
                BNEQ    MoveChar        ;    if not, move it
                CMPB    R4, #Blank      ; Was last character also a blank?
                BEQL    Count           ;    if so, don't move it
        MoveChar:
                MOVB    R5, (R1)+       ; Move character to OutBuf
                MOVB    R5, R4          ;    and save last character in R4
                INCW    R3              ; Increment count of char. in OutBuf

        ;  .... Get ready for next character ....
        Count:  DECW    R2              ; Decrement char. count in InBuf
                BRB     NextChar        ; Repeat

        ;  .... Return ....
        Return: RSB



        ;  .... Subroutine to check for errors ....

        ErCheck:
                BLBC    R0, Stop        ; Terminate if error
                RSB                     ;    otherwise return
        Stop:   $EXIT_S R0              ; Error termination

                .End    Pack
```

The algorithm for this program is as follows:

1. Initialize files and records.
2. Until there is an end-of-file error:
    Get next record from the input file.
    Pack the record.
    Write the record to the output file.
3. Close the files.

The algorithm must be modified slightly before it can be implemented. In MACRO the program must attempt to read the next record before it can check for end-of-file errors.

The main program is straightforward. The input file is opened, the output file is created, and the RABs are connected. In the main loop a record is read using $GET, packed using the subroutine PackRecord, and, finally, written with $PUT. This loop continues until the end-of-file condition is detected after a get operation. (The user would press "control Z" to simulate an end of file if the input comes from a terminal.) When that happens, the files are closed and the program is terminated.

The FAB blocks specify the logical filenames Input: and Output: because this is a general-purpose utility program that could be used with many different files. The user must use the operating system command ASSIGN to supply the appropriate filenames before the program is run. Because of the device independence provided by RMS, the input and/or output file can be the user's terminal. Consequently, a prompt is specified in InRAB. It is ignored when input comes from a disk file.

The length of the record buffer is not specified in OutRAB because the output record length is determined after packing the output record.

A subroutine called ErCheck is used for error checking.

PackRecord was implemented as a subprogram to simplify the main program's code. The following algorithm shows how it carries out this task.

1. Initialize:
    Address of next character in the input buffer
    Address of next character in the output buffer
    The number of characters remaining in the input buffer
    The number of characters already in the output buffer
    The last character processed
2. Where there are more characters in the input buffer:
    Move next character to a register.
    If either the next or last character is not a blank, then:
        Move next character to the output buffer and to the register holding the last character.
        Increment count of characters in the output buffer.
    Decrement count of characters in input buffer.

Because argument passing is limited to returning the length of the resulting record in R3, a subroutine was selected to avoid the overhead a procedure requires. The subroutine initializes several registers, including R4, the last character moved, which is set to a blank to prevent moving a leading blank into the output buffer. The loop gets a character from the input buffer. If it is not a blank or if it is a blank that does not follow another blank, it is moved into the output buffer, and the count of characters in the output buffer is incremented by 1. The loop continues until all the characters in the input buffer are exhausted.

11.6 Advanced I/O Devices

Many I/O devices require system programming beyond that needed for terminal operations. We will briefly discuss problems associated with some more sophisticated I/O devices.

On most larger systems printers operate from a queue using a technique called **spooling**. Output intended for a printer is not sent directly to it. Instead a program that "thinks" it is writing to the printer is actually writing to a disk file. The operating system sends the output to the printer when the printer is ready. There are two reasons for this arrangement. Printers are typically slow devices compared to CPUs and disk drives. Thus a program's run time is normally reduced if the output is stored on disk instead of being transmitted directly to a printer. Later, the information can be read from disk and printed at a rate that is convenient for the printer. This process greatly increases computer throughput because both the CPU and printer can operate at their maximum speed. Queuing printer output solves another problem on multiuser computers. Several users may try to use the same printer simultaneously. To keep the output from different programs from being intermixed, the output from each program is stored in its own disk file. The resulting output file is queued to the printer when the program finishes processing.

If a system has a card reader, input from this device is often handled indirectly for much the same reasons. When programs and data are placed on the card reader, the card images are copied into a disk file. The operating system then automatically submits the job to a batch queue. When the program is run, the data that the program assumes comes from the card reader actually comes from the disk file.

Though magnetic disk drives have replaced tape drives for many applications, tapes are widely used to back up disk drives, which has created a demand for fast tape drives. For example, some VAX computers use DEC's high-speed TU78 drive, which can read data from a tape encoded at 6250 bytes per inch (bpi) at 125 inches per second. That allows transmission of 781,250 bytes per second at the maximum transfer rate. This speed is equivalent to approximately 400 double-spaced typed pages per second, although we will discover that it is seldom possible to maintain that speed for more than a few milliseconds at a time.

Input/output with magnetic tape drives causes some special problems. High-level languages and RMS allow reading one record at a time from a tape drive. This means that the drive seemingly should be able to read a single record and then stop until the program requests that the next record be processed. This causes some difficulties. The drive is a mechanical device subject to the laws of physics. It cannot instantly start and stop a tape. Consequently, this mode of operation would require consecutive records to be separated by a blank section of tape long enough to allow the drive to stop and restart, if necessary. These **interrecord**

gaps are approximately $\frac{5}{8}$ of an inch long. Yet an 80-character record uses only $\frac{1}{20}$ of an inch of tape if it is recorded at 1600 bytes per inch, even less when the tape is encoded at 6250 bytes per inch. So most of the tape would be wasted and the effective transfer rate would be drastically reduced if the system placed an interrecord gap between every two records. Consequently, the operating system normally groups several records together in larger **blocks** of 1000–4000 characters. It writes entire blocks to the tape as a single unit. They are separated by **interblock gaps**. This greatly increases the tape's effective capacity and transfer rate, but it creates a new problem. How do we give a program the illusion that it is reading the tape one record at a time when several records must actually be read at the same time? The answer is to create a buffer in the computer's memory. The operating system transfers whole blocks of data between the drive and the buffer while moving records between the buffer and the program. To hide this extra processing from the user, the VAX uses an extra layer of I/O programs in between queue I/O and the device driver called an **ancillary control program (ACP)**. The tape ACP uses the tape's device driver to read or write the tape a block at a time and communicates with QIO one record at a time.

Because even interblock gaps greatly reduce the effective transfer rate, some newer drives can operate in a **streaming** or continuous mode, in which the computer attempts to transfer data at a constant speed without interruptions of any type. Interrecord or interblock gaps are not used. This is particularly useful during backup operations when large quantities of data must be processed.

Disk drives are now the most common form of mass storage. They come in several configurations and have a wide range of speeds and capacities. Figure 11.12 shows a typical multiplatter disk drive unit that might be used with a larger computer. The surfaces of the platters are coated with a magnetic material similar to that used on magnetic tapes. The read/write heads can be moved rapidly between the inside and outside of the disk. Data is stored on the surface of the disk in concentric circles called **tracks**, which may vary in number from less than 50 on a floppy disk drive to several hundred on a large-capacity, hard disk. On many computers each track is divided up into several sectors that contain a fixed amount of data, possibly 256 or 512 bytes. To read or write information to a particular sector, the heads are moved to the correct track, and the computer waits until the correct sector rotates over the head. The computer then reads or writes the information at the rate at which the information passes over the heads. The time required to move the heads to the desired track is called **seek time** and is typically about 30 ms on a high-speed drive, depending on how far the heads must move. On average the disk must rotate halfway around before the proper sector reaches the heads. This rotational delay, called **latency**, averages 8.3 ms on many high-speed drives. On such drives data may be transferred at roughly 1 million bytes per second once the desired sector is located. At

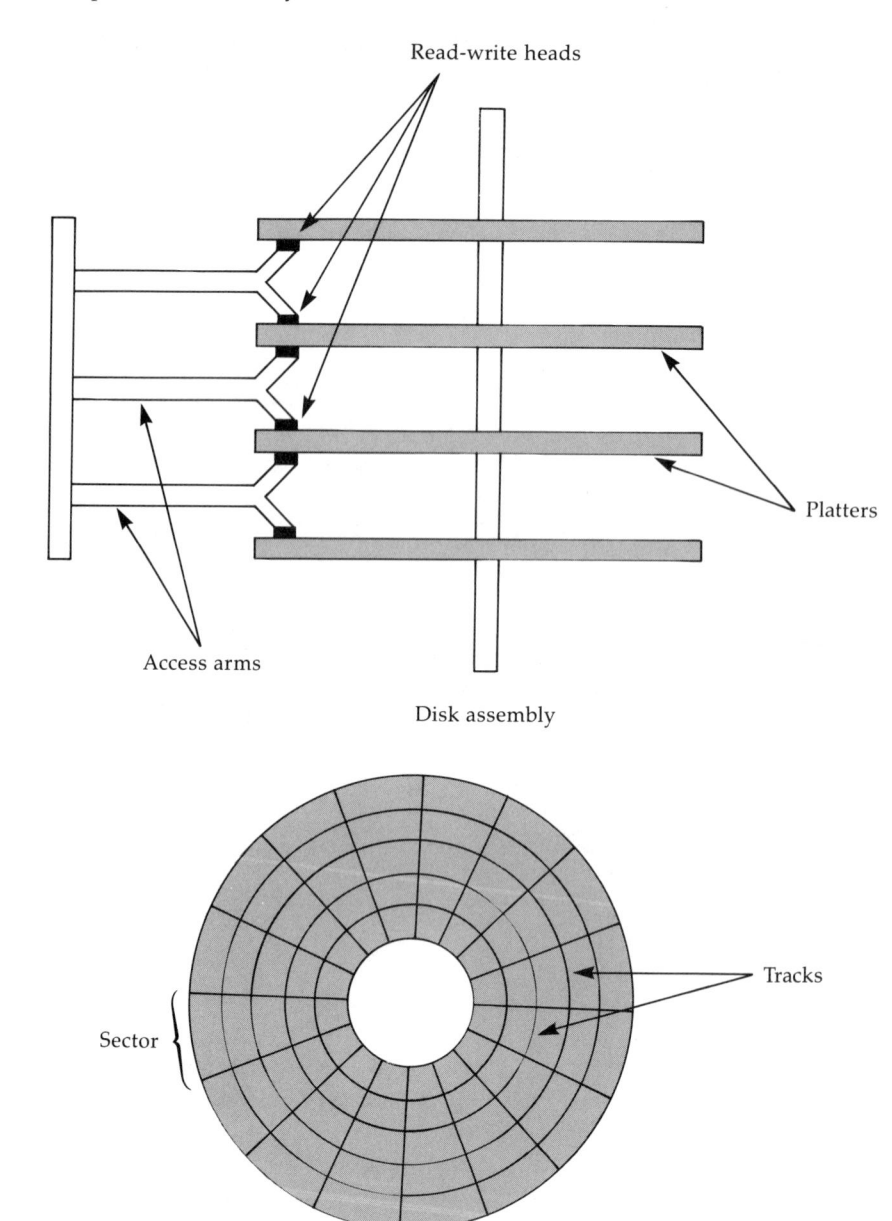

Figure 11.12 A multiplatter disk and its track and sector arrangement

that rate the **transfer time** to read a 512-byte sector would be only 0.5 ms. Of course it may be necessary to reposition the heads after reading one sector. Consequently, the average data transfer rate can be significantly slower.

Disk drives present the operating system with a number of problems. When a file is created on a disk, its name, location, and characteristics must be entered into the user's directory. When information is to be transferred, its location on the disk must first be determined by finding the data's relative position in the file and then looking in the disk directory to find the corresponding location on a disk. Because the storage area on a disk is divided into fixed-length sectors whose size is determined by the operating system and/or the disk's control unit, records may be divided between two different blocks. In most cases random use of a disk results in files that are separated into several noncontiguous segments that further complicate the process of locating a given record. On a VAX using VMS, the disk ACPs locate and transfer sectors of data to or from the disk while normally transferring one record at a time to the requesting program.

Consider some of the steps that must be carried out to create a new file on a disk. RMS must read the user's directory to find an appropriate location for the entry for the new file. It must then write the file's name, some of its characteristics from the FAB, and other information—such as the time of creation—into the directory. It then must read the disk's sector map table to determine which sectors are available for use. After writing information into the file, the sector map table must be updated to mark those sectors changed by the write operation as being in use. We can certainly be happy that RMS takes care of all these details for us.

Summary

In this chapter we looked at the I/O system from several viewpoints and discovered that this system is much more complex than most high-level programmers expect.

In the first three sections we looked at the hardware characteristics of simple devices. External devices usually operate at much slower speeds than the CPU. Consequently, special efforts must be made to ensure this system's proper operation. Computers may use program-controlled I/O, where the CPU enters a loop to wait for a particular device to become ready. However, because this is inefficient, interrupts may be used to allow the CPU to carry out normal processing until an I/O device signals that it is ready to be processed. Direct memory access (DMA) uses special hardware to transfer large blocks of data between an I/O device and memory without requiring active participation of the CPU. Computers normally have several I/O devices, so they need a priority system to determine which device should be handled first when two or more devices are ready to be serviced.

There is a large gap between users' desires for device-independent I/O and convenient formatting and the realities of the differing and limited capabilities of hardware devices. Operating systems often provide one or more layers of I/O routines between high-level languages and the drivers that service particular devices. VAX/VMS provides two such levels that are accessible to users. Queue I/O is device dependent but efficiently handles input and output one record at a time. It protects the system against illegal operations before it queues I/O requests to the device drivers. RMS allows file processing and provides a large degree of device independence. RMS passes I/O requests to the appropriate QIO procedures. The operating system provides assembly language macros for using these systems.

Sophisticated devices such as tape drives, disk drives, and even printers require special handling beyond that needed for terminals. Printer output is commonly stored on disks until the printer is available. Tape and disk drives often process data in different-sized units than required by the user's program. Consequently, special software is needed to account for these differences. This software must also keep track of disk files that may be divided into several nonconsecutive segments.

The I/O system provides interesting challenges to both hardware and software designers.

Exercises

1. Given a computer operating at 10^6 cycles/sec where the average instruction takes 6 machine cycles to complete and each memory read and write operation takes 1 machine cycle, find the maximum data transfer rate (words/sec) assuming that the computer uses
   a. Program-controlled I/O if it takes four CPU instructions to transfer each word.
   b. A DMA system.
2. Explain the advantages and any disadvantages of the interrupt method over program-controlled I/O.
3. What must be saved during interrupt processing?
4. What function does the interrupt acknowledge signal perform?
5. Consider the following alternatives for I/O systems:
   Program-controlled I/O with wait loops
   DMA
   Interrupts with polling
   Interrupts with vectors and daisy chain
   Interrupts with vectors and a PAC
   Interrupts with vectors and mixed priority approach
   Other methods
   a. Suppose that you are trying to build a cheap (about $50) microcomputer that uses a hard-copy terminal for input and output. Pick the most appropriate method for data transfer and justify your answer.

b. Suppose that you are trying to build a low-price (about $200) microcomputer whose purpose is to run arcade games with lots of fast, continuous action on the screen. The user will type on the keyboard occasionally to control the game. Pick the most appropriate method for data transfer *from the keyboard* and justify your answer.

6. We would like to have two VAX systems exchange messages assuming that each one views the other as an I/O device. Write the code for each system if a program-controlled I/O approach is used to accomplish this task. (You will probably not be able to test this code.)

7. Explain why assembly language programmers on many microcomputers can write their own devices drivers but most VAX assembly language programmers cannot.

8. Add to the output routines in Listing 9.5 by writing and testing new general-purpose procedures that will allow using QIO instead of Lib$Put_Output to print the buffer. A program using these routines would call AssignChannel at the beginning of the run, call WriteBuffer to output the values put in the buffer by the original Outxxx procedures, and use DeassignChannel at the end of the program. The complete package must be in one file for it to assemble and link correctly.

   a. Procedure AssignChannel

      Assigns a channel number to TT:.

   b. Procedure DeassignChannel

      Deassigns the channel for TT:.

   c. Procedure WriteBuffer

      Writes the contents of the buffer to TT: using queue I/O.

9. Add to the input routines suggested in Exercise 16 in Chapter 9 by writing and testing procedures that will allow using QIO. The complete package including output routines (if used) must be in one file for it to assemble and link correctly.

   a. Procedure AssignChannel:

      (Same procedure as in Exercise 8a). If both the input and output procedures are used, only one copy of this procedure is needed.

   b. Procedure DeassignChannel:

      (Same procedure as in Exercise 8b).

   c. Procedure ReadBuffer

      Uses QIO to read a line from the terminal into the input buffer.

10. Write the FAB and RAB control blocks needed for the following situations. Also include statements to define the buffers specified in the problem.

a. The sequential file Num.Dat will be used for input. Information will be put into the 60-character buffer NumBuf.
b. The sequential file with the logical name InFile will be used for input of records of up to 90 bytes. If the file is the user's terminal, the prompt "Enter value: " must be printed before each input. InFileBuf will be used as the input buffer.
c. The sequential file with the logical name Months, which may be printed, will be used for output. The variable-length records have 67 or fewer characters. The output buffer is called MonthsBuf.
d. Forty-byte, fixed-length records will be stored in the sequential file Values.Dat after it is created. The file will not be printable. ValuesBuf will be used as the buffer.

11. Add to the output routines in Listing 9.5 by writing and testing new procedures that will allow sending the information in the buffer to an arbitrary file using RMS. A program using these routines would call ReadyOutputFile and pass the name of the desired file at the beginning of the program. CloseOutputFile would typically be used at the end of the program. Calls to PutBuffer or PutBufferAndEcho would be used to write the buffer into the file in the same way that TypeOutputLine sends the buffer to the user's terminal. The file containing these procedures must include the FAB, the RAB, and the procedures of the original package if it is to assemble and link properly. Assume that the output may be printed and has 130 characters or less per record.

   a. Procedure ReadyOutputFile (FileName)

   Creates and connects the file whose name is passed by descriptor. Both the FAB$L_FNA and FAB$B_FNS fields must be filled before the file can be created.

   b. Procedure CloseOutputFile

   Closes the output file.

   c. Procedure PutBuffer

   Sends the completed buffer to the file.

   d. Procedure PutBufferAndEcho

   Sends the completed buffer to the file and also to the user's terminal using Lib$Put_Output. (This procedure allows you to send output to a printer file and the terminal at the same time. It may be a convenient way for you to get printed copies of your output.)

12. Add to the input routines suggested in Exercise 16 in Chapter 9 by writing and testing general-purpose input procedures that will allow using RMS to input from files. Procedures ReadyInputFile and CloseInputFile would be used at the beginning and end of the program to specify, open, and close the file. Calls to GetBuffer or GetBufferAndEcho would substitute for calls to InputLine. The com-

plete package, including the FAB and RAB, must be in the same file for it to assemble and link properly.

a. Procedure ReadyInputFile (FileName)

Opens and connects the file whose name is passed by descriptor. Both the FAB$L_FNA and FAB$B_FNS fields must be filled before the file can be opened.

b. Procedure CloseInputFile

Closes the input file.

c. Procedure GetBuffer

Inputs a variable-length record from the file.

d. Procedure GetBufferAndEcho

Inputs a variable-length record from the file and copies it to the output file using procedures from the output package suggested in Listing 9.5 and the previous exercise. (If you use your video terminal as the input file and send the output to a printer file, this procedure when used together with PutBufferAndEcho from the previous exercise will provide you with a transcript of your program runs.)

13. Write an assembly language program for encoding a string of capital letters. It should input a string of capital letters $I_1 I_2 \ldots I_n$ and output the encoded string $R_1 R_2 \ldots R_n$ formed according to the following rules:

For $i = 1, 2, \ldots, n$
$R_i \leftarrow I_i + (I_2 - I_1)$
If $R_i > $ "Z" then $R_i \leftarrow R_i - 26$
If $R_i < $ "A" then $R_i \leftarrow R_i + 26$
Switch R_1 and R_2

For example, the string EFABCXYZ would be encoded as GFBCDYZA. Observe that the first two characters, I_1 and I_2, form a key to the encoding process. They are normally added to the desired message, which begins in I_3. This coding scheme is self-decoding; that is, if an encoded message is input, the output is the original plain text.

a. Use QIO.
b. Use RMS. Use logical names for the input and output files. After ensuring that the program works correctly using the terminal for input and output, run the program two more times. First, input from a terminal and output to a disk file. Then input from the resulting disk file and output the decoded message to your terminal or printer.

14. Write an assembler program that inputs a list of real numbers and prints their sum and their average. The output should be neatly labeled.

a. Use QIO (and your solution to Exercises 8 and 9, if desired).
b. Use RMS (and your solution to Exercises 11 and 12, if desired).

15. Write an assembly language program that requests the number of records and then inputs those records from the user's terminal. The records contain a 24-character name and a 13-character phone number. The program sorts the records by name and writes them into a printable output file. Store the characters in uppercase even if they are typed in lowercase.

16. Write an assembly language program that uses the file described in the previous exercise. (If necessary, it can be created with a text editor.) When a name is input from the user's terminal, output the corresponding phone number or an error message, whichever is appropriate.
    a. After inputting a name, use a sequential search to find it in the file. Terminate the search when the name is found. If the name is not in the file, the search should terminate when a "larger" name is found.
    b. Input the complete file, storing the records in an array before inputting the first name. Then use a binary search to find the name that is input. Allow it to process names one after the other until the user types "STOP".

17. You can use RMS to transmit numbers in their internal binary form as well as their external ASCII character form. Given the number N, write a program that writes 8-byte records containing the two floating-point numbers X and X squared for $X = 1, 2, \ldots, N$. Also, write a program that reads the resulting file and prints its contents on the user's terminal. The file used in this exercise cannot be printed because it contains numbers in their internal binary form. The procedures presented in Listing 9.5, and suggested in Exercises 14 and 16 in Chapter 9, can be used for terminal I/O, if desired.

18. The output file produced by the program in Listing 11.3 does not allow us to re-create the original file because it does not contain any information telling how many blanks were removed.
    a. Modify the pack program so that it replaces any repeated character with a single copy of that character followed by a character representing the count of appearances. Use the formula

    count byte = number of repetitions + $(176)_{10}$

    to get its decimal value. This method sets the high-order bit on the count character so that it is possible to distinguish between a repetition count and a standard character. For example, abbcccdddde would be packed as ab2c3d4e, where the underlined characters are the special count bytes and have their high-order bits set but will usually appear as standard characters when printed. This technique will work as long as the number of repetitions does not exceed 79, although the resulting file will look strange when the number of repetitions is larger than 9.

b. Write a program to unpack the files produced by part a; that is, it should re-create the original files.

19. Rewrite the program previously written for one of the Exercises 6, 9, or 13–24 in Chapter 7 or 4, 7, 11, or 18 in Chapter 9, including a MACRO main program that uses

   a. QIO.
   b. RMS.

20. (Project.) Write a spelling-checking program that will input a text file and output any misspelled words (any words not in its dictionary). The dictionary is a file containing a list of correctly spelled words in alphabetical order, one word per record. The program should ignore differences in capitalization. The resulting program must be efficient. One reasonable scheme is to read the entire text file, alphabetizing all the unique words as it finds them, perhaps using a binary search and insertion sort. Then the dictionary file can be read and the words checked using a variation of the file merge algorithm. Other methods can be used, especially if you assume that the dictionary is small enough to be read into memory.

21. a. In theory, how many characters can be stored on a standard 2400-foot reel of magnetic tape if it is recorded at 1600 bpi?

   b. Suppose that the above tape is used to store individual 80-byte records separated by interrecord gaps. Calculate the number of characters that can be stored on the tape and the percentage of the tape that can actually be used to store information.

   c. Suppose that records of part b are combined into 2000-character blocks separated by an interrecord gaps. Calculate the number of characters that can be stored on the tape and the percentage of the tape that can actually be used to store information.

22. Same as Exercise 21, but assume that the tape is recorded at 6250 bpi.

CHAPTER CONTENTS

12.1 REMOTE I/O COMMUNICATIONS
    RS-232C Standard

12.2 COMMUNICATION NETWORK ARCHITECTURE
    Communication Topology
        A Complete Interconnection Network
        A Distributed Control Loop
        A Global Bus Network
        A Star Network
        Ethernet

12.3 COMMUNICATION PROTOCOLS

12.4 PACKET SWITCHING
    DECnet Example

12.5 ERROR CONTROL
    Error Detection
    Error Correction
    Generalized Parity Check Code (Hamming Code)
    Checksum Codes

SUMMARY

EXERCISES

CHAPTER 12

Computer Communications

A stand-alone computer system, no matter how powerful, is simply inadequate for many general-purpose computing needs. Such a system would require that the user be physically present to enter commands and data directly into the machine. Users once had little direct access to a computer; they just handed a deck of punched computer cards through a window to an operator, who later gave them their output (a system still in use at some computer centers). But it is more useful to send commands and data to the computer from our own homes or offices. Moreover, data transfer between two computers is more efficient if it can be done directly, without any human intervention. In each case some form of remote communication with a main computer system is required. We will review methods for achieving such communication links in this chapter.

Initially we will consider the problem of a remote terminal communicating with a computer system represented by the heavy links in Figure 12.1a. Issues associated with computer-remote terminal communication include parallel versus serial transmission, transmission hardware, and transmission standards. Then we will cover the problem of multiple computer systems sharing data and commands, as illustrated in Figure 12.1b. Issues associated with computer–computer communication include network topology, communication protocol, and error control methods.

12.1 Remote I/O Communications

Our primary goal in this section is to examine the problem of communicating with a main computer from some remote location. That is, we would like to send data to the CPU or memory unit and receive data

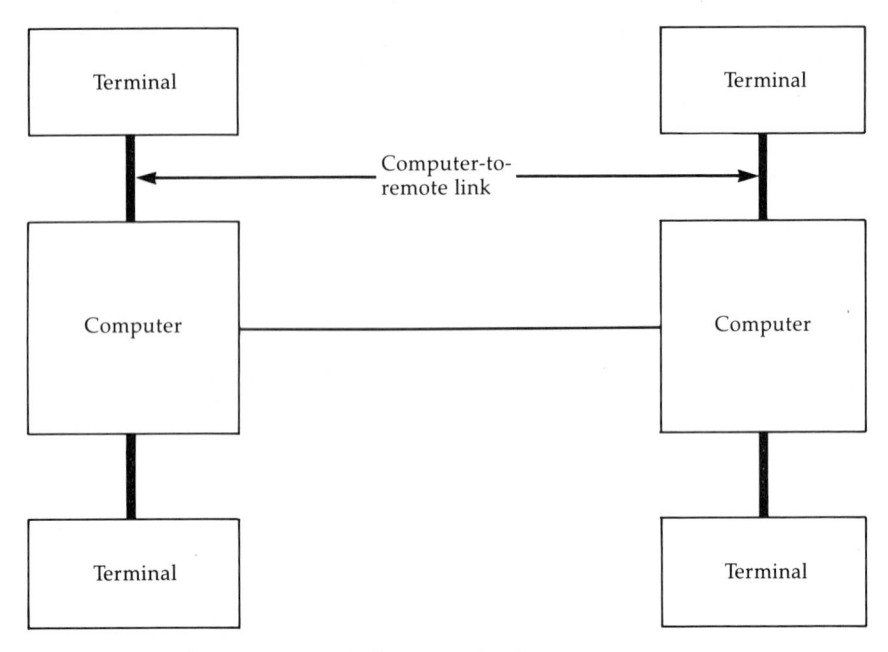

Figure 12.1a Computer-terminal communication

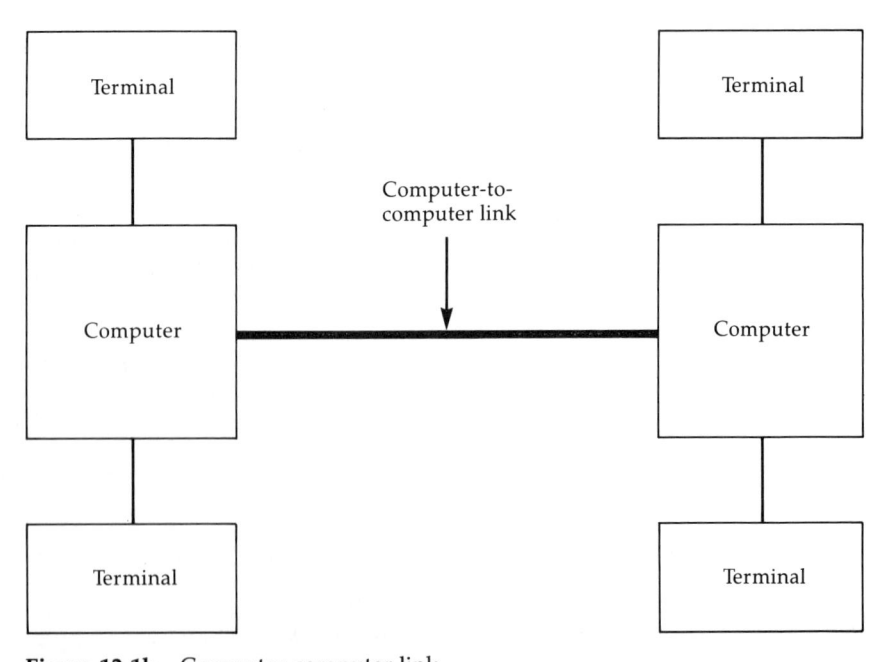

Figure 12.1b Computer-computer link

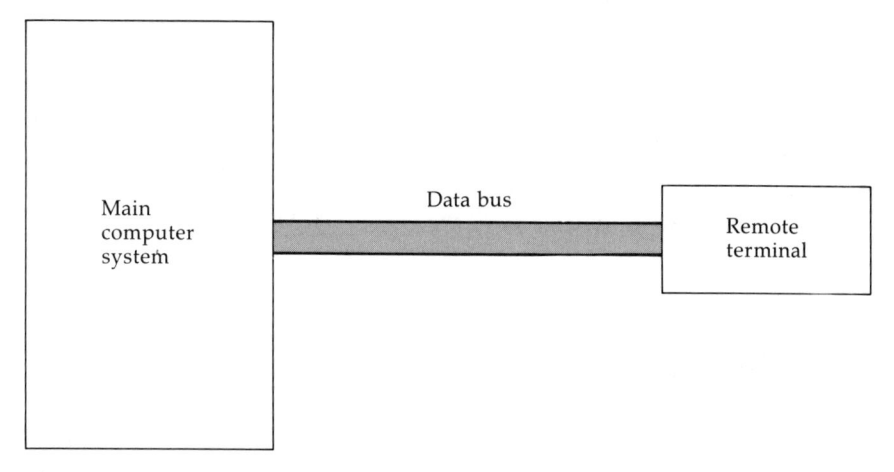

Figure 12.2 Basic communication system

from these units. The seemingly obvious approach would be to extend the data bus to the remote terminal as shown in Figure 12.2. However, connecting a 32-bit bus with extra control lines would result in lots of wires spread over potentially long distances. The cost of the wires and the potential for errors (because the long wires will pick up noise from external signals such as power lines) between the computer and the terminal make this an unacceptable alternative.

One way to reduce the number of wires is to convert the 32 parallel data lines into 1 line and transmit the data in a serial format. That is, both the computer and terminal have special communication registers, and as shown in Figure 12.3, these registers can convert between the parallel data format used internally and the external serial data format used along the transmission line. Now we need only extend 1 data wire between the computer and the terminal, which is certainly cheaper than 32 or more wires. However, communication will slow down because it will take 32 times longer to send data in the serial mode one bit at a time than in the parallel mode. In addition, serial transmission requires extra

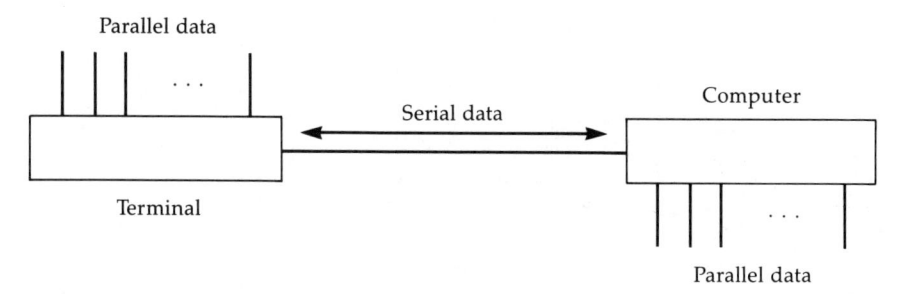

Figure 12.3 Serial transmission of data

overhead. For example, we must tell the receiving device when data is starting and ending. This means that we need a **message protocol**.

A commonly used protocol involves the transmission of ASCII characters. When transmitting a 7-bit ASCII code, three bits are typically added to the signal to mark the beginning and end of a character. A 0 is added to mark the beginning of a new character, and two trailing ones called stop bits are added to mark the end of the character. The resulting format is

0 7-bit ASCII code 11

For example, a 5 is represented in ASCII by 0110101, and it would be transmitted in this protocol as shown in Figure 12.4, with the least significant bit of the character being sent first.

A simple method of transmitting serial data, called a current loop, is shown in Figure 12.5. The twisted wires reduce noise problems. When the electronic switch on the transmitting side is closed, current flows through the wire and is sensed on the receiving end. Typically, a 1 is represented by a 20mA current, while a 0 is given by no current. This is the most common form of digital data transmission. For short distances (less than 100 meters), several million bits per second can be transmitted along a twisted pair link. For longer distances, however, the data transmission rate must be reduced.

In addition to wires, various other media, such as microwave links, have been used for transmitting data. Optical fibers are a new medium for data transmission that shows great promise. An **LED (light-emitting diode)** is used at the transmitting end to convert electrical signals into light, and a **photodiode** is used at the receiving end to convert the light back into electrical signals. There are several advantages to fiber optics, including the fact that light is not affected by electrical or magnetic fields, and optical fibers are more difficult to tap (that is, to intercept the signals illegally) than standard wires. In addition, optical fibers may operate at high data rates over long distances. Bell Labs has tested a 1112-kilometer optical fiber link that operated at a rate of 420 million bits per second.

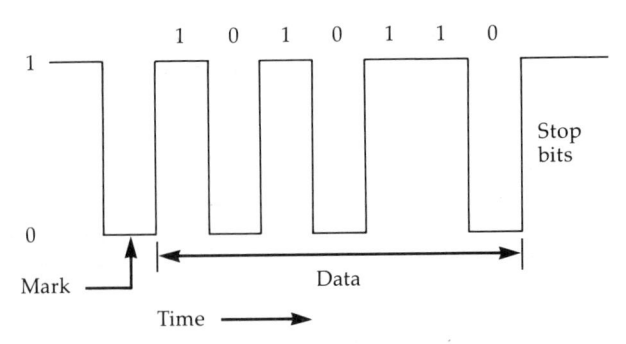

Figure 12.4 Transmission of an ASCII 5

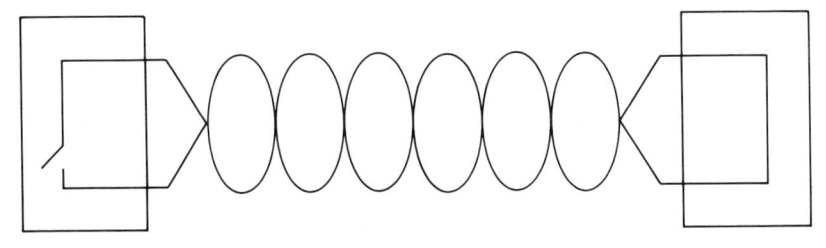

Figure 12.5 Current loop transmission

Phone lines can also be used for serial data transmission over long distances. After all, telephone companies have provided us with wire connections between almost any two locations in the world. The telephone system is a massive communication network. However, to transmit digital information along phone connections reliably, we must convert the information into frequencies compatible with the construction of the phone links. Then we must reconvert the frequencies into digital information at the receiving end of the transmission. We do this using a device called a **modem (MOdulator-DEModulator)**. The standard conversion is

0 is 1075 Hz

1 is 1275 Hz

There are three types of data communication links.

1. Simplex: transmission in one direction only
2. Half duplex: transmission in both directions but not simultaneously
3. Full duplex: transmission in both directions simultaneously

A full-duplex phone link would require four logic signal levels for two transmission channels, each carrying a 0 and a 1. The standards for this type of link are

Channel 1   0   1075 Hz   1 1275 Hz
Channel 2   0   2025 Hz   1 2225 Hz

So far we have assumed that only data is transmitted between the remote terminal and the computer. However, if we have only a single wire connecting the computer and the terminal, which is used for data transmission, how does the computer know that the terminal is prepared to receive any data? For example, a user may have switched a printing terminal offline to adjust the paper while the computer is trying to transmit the next page of data. For that matter, how does the terminal know that the computer is ready to receive its data? The mark and stop bits of the serially transmitted ASCII code only tell the system where the transmitted character begins and ends, not whether the system is ready to receive the character. Clearly, we send some control signals to indicate when a character is waiting to be transmitted from the source and when the destination is ready to receive the character. This, of course, adds a requirement of extra wires to the connection between the two systems. It also introduces a new problem. That is, if we want to plug one end of a cable into the transmitting system and the other end into the receiving system, we must be sure that the data wire and control wires are connected to the right location on both ends. In other words, we need a standard that specifies which wires will carry the data and which will carry each of the control signals. There are several standards for communication. (We know that the fact that there are several standards violates the concept of a standard, but that's life, isn't it?) Now we need only know what standard the two devices use, buy a cable for that standard, and then connect the two devices together. One commonly used standard is the RS-232C.

RS-232C Standard

The RS-232C standard was originally developed for data communication over telephone lines using modems. It is now widely used for serial data links between systems. The standard specifies the control and data lines for a 25-pin connector. However, in practice only 3–12 of the lines are actually used. By following the standard, manufacturers can provide external connections on their machines that match connections on other machines, allowing a communication link to be established. Some of the pins of the RS-232C standard are as follows:

Pin Number	Function
2	Transmitted signal
3	Received signal
4	Request to send
5	Clear to send
6	Data set ready
7	Signal ground
20	Data terminal ready

This structure allows for a handshaking procedure where the transmitting end requests permission to send data on line 4, the receiving end sends back a clear to send a message along line 5, and then data is sent along line 2. Pins 6 and 20 are often used in a similar manner. A terminal may put a signal on line 20 indicating that it is ready to send a message. This line is connected to pin 6 on the computer, so the computer knows that the terminal is ready to send data. The computer also uses pin 20 to send a signal to the terminal saying that it is ready to send a message. This is connected to the terminal's pin 6, so it knows that the computer is ready.

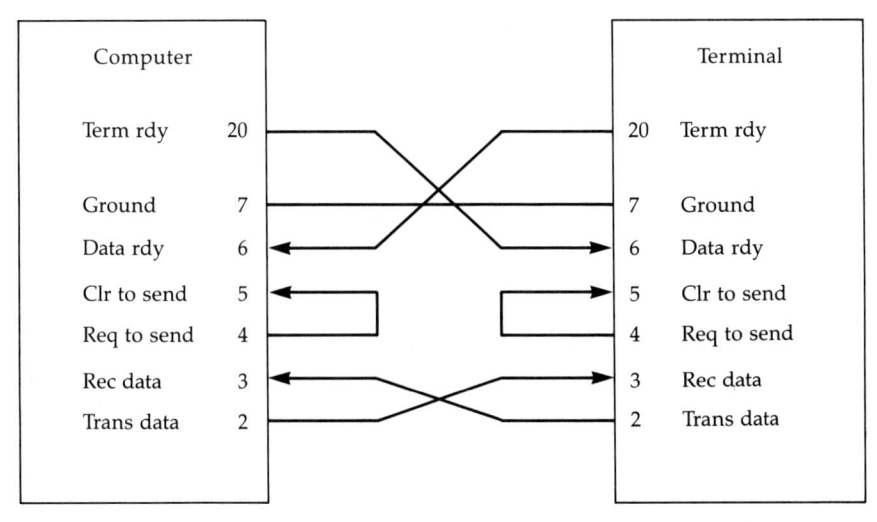

Figure 12.6 Typical RS-232C connection

In many applications it is unnecessary to use all the possible handshaking coventions provided by RS-232C. In the RS-232C connection shown in Figure 12.6, notice that the request-to-send pin is connected directly to the clear-to-send pin. This ensures that a transmission request is always granted and also reduces the number of wires that must be connected between the two devices. In this application pins 20 and 6 are interconnected so that each side can sense when the other is ready for a transmission.

Because the RS-232C standard only specifies which pins can be used but does not require their use, equipment from different manufacturers can vary. For example, DEC often uses the characters control Q and control S (commonly called XON and XOFF) to signal if a terminal is ready for data instead of using the extra wires provided by the standard. Such differences can cause us considerable grief when we try to connect equipment from different computers.

12.2 Communication Network Architecture

Rather than simply considering the communication link between a main computer system and its remote terminals, here we will look at communication links between networks of computers, each with their own terminals, disks, memory units, and I/O devices. Figure 12.7 illustrates a system in which we can have several different kinds of communication links between the different devices.

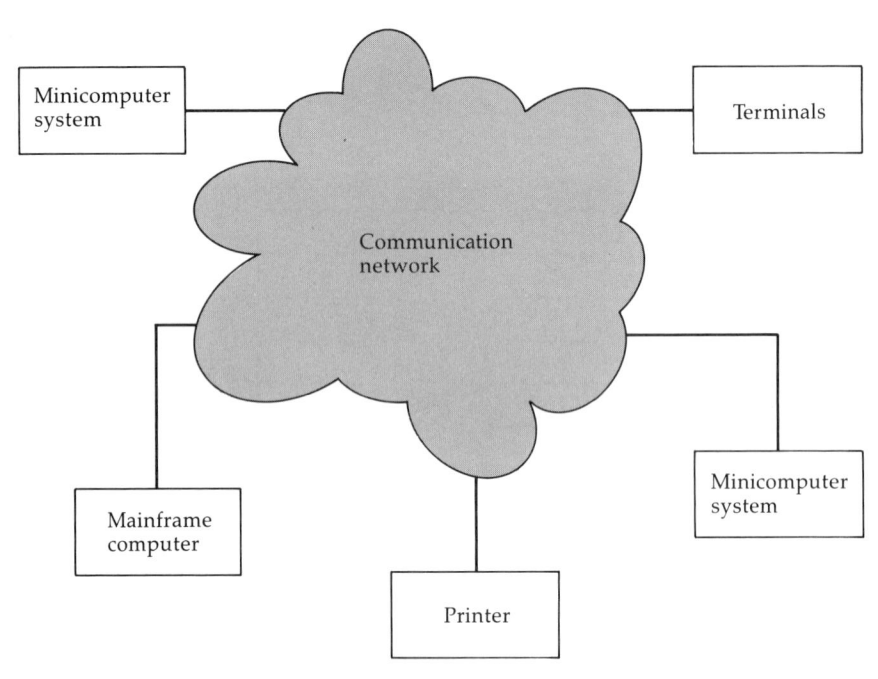

Figure 12.7 A general communication network

To produce a working system such as the one shown in Figure 12.7, it is of course not enough to just connect the different computers, printers, and terminals together. We must manage the data transfers between devices connected to the system in some coordinated fashion. This requires the specification of the network interconnection (the actual data paths), called the **network topology**; the specification of the structure of the data when it is shipped across the system, called the **protocol**; and the specification of the control mechanisms such as access control and error control. We will review the first two in this section and cover error control mechanisms in the next section. We will assume that communication from the standpoint of an individual computer in the network looks like I/O operations. That is, the transmitting computer formulates a message and sends it out along one of its outputs to the network. The network distributes the message to the destination computers, which receive the message on their inputs.

Communication Topology

The basic architecture of a network, its system topology, refers to the general interconnection structure of network's components. It determines the path of a message between components. We can send messages directly through a connection path or indirectly through a switch mechanism. We will discuss several structures that illustrate both approaches in this subsection.

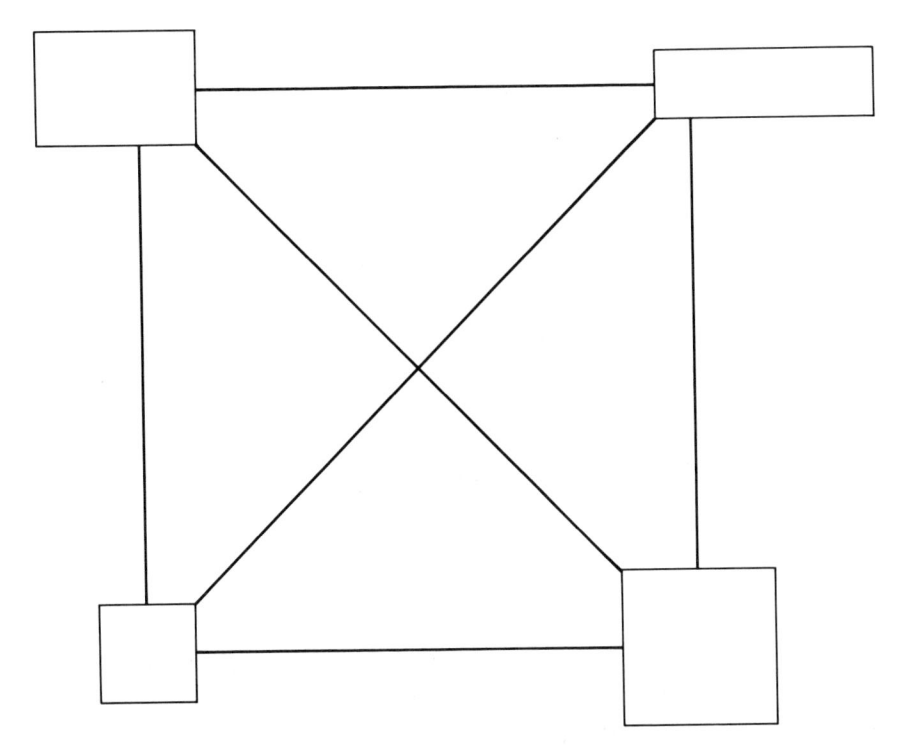

Figure 12.8 Complete interconnection network

A Complete Interconnection Network The simplest topology is the complete interconnection network, as shown in Figure 12.8 for a system with four nodes. Each component or **node** is directly connected to every other component. This is sometimes called a **direct dedicated complete network (DDC)**. It features fast data transfer because messages do not have to pass through any intermediate stages. It also allows for multiple data transfers at one time. However, it does require that each element have enough I/O ports so that a direct connection between elements can be made. For example, if there are n elements in the network, each element must have $(n-1)$ I/O ports. In addition, the network would require $n(n-1)/2$ bidirectional links. The cost of such a network makes it a poor choice for any large system.

A Distributed Control Loop The **distributed control loop (DCL)** or ring is used for components connected in a circular fashion, as shown in Figure 12.9. Each component is connected to its two nearest neighbors, and messages for a given system flow in either a clockwise or counterclockwise direction. The operation of a DCL is characterized by a source component that transmits a message; the message is passed along the loop until it reaches its destination component. The intermediate components simply act as buffer or relay units. This system requires only

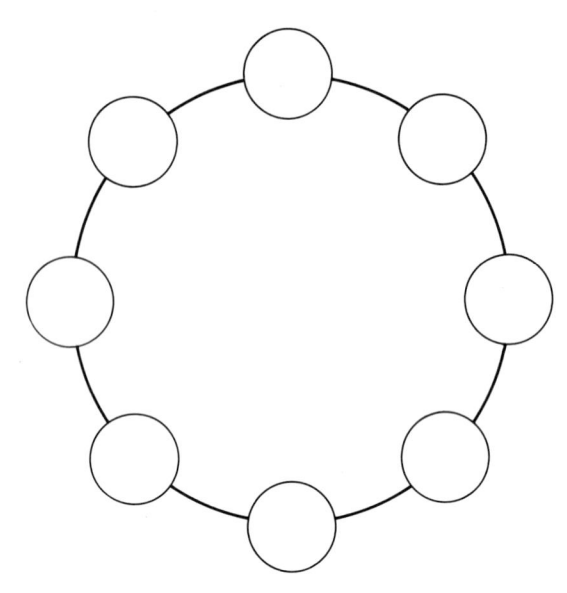

Figure 12.9 DCL Network

two I/O ports per component, and for n components there are only n links. However, this method is slower than a complete interconnection network. For example, if it takes one time unit to pass a message between neighboring components, some messages in an n-component network would require up to $(n - 1)$ time units to reach their destination.

A Global Bus Network This is similar to the internal bus architecture of most computer systems, as shown in Figure 12.10. It is sometimes called a **direct shared bus (DSB)** network. Data is placed on the bus by

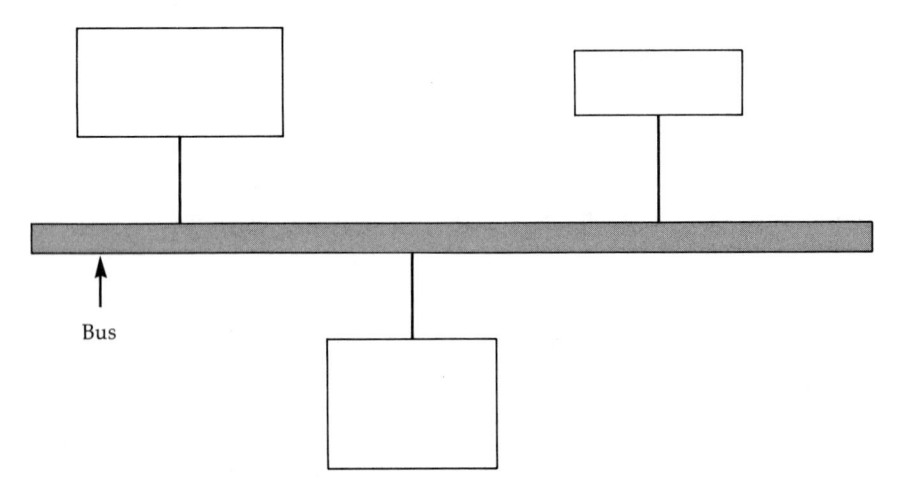

Figure 12.10 Global bus network

the source and then recognized and accepted by the destination. Of course, the bus is a major bottleneck in this network because only one message can be transmitted at a time. This system requires only one I/O port per component.

A Star Network The name **star network** is very descriptive of the architecture illustrated in Figure 12.11. This is sometimes called an *indirect centralized routine dedicated path*. Obviously, star is the preferred title. In this network the switch is the destination or source of all messages; that is, every terminal communicates with the switch. A message contains destination information that the switch decodes in order to send the message on to the correct source. Most time-sharing systems use this architecture. For these systems, the central switch is often the main computer system.

Ethernet One commercial approach to computer networks based on a buslike architecture is **Ethernet**, which is basically a coaxial-cable interconnection scheme for computer-to-computer communications. It provides a standard communication link, much as RS-232C has become a standard for computer-terminal communication. The Ethernet bus consists of a single line of coaxial cable with a terminator at both ends.

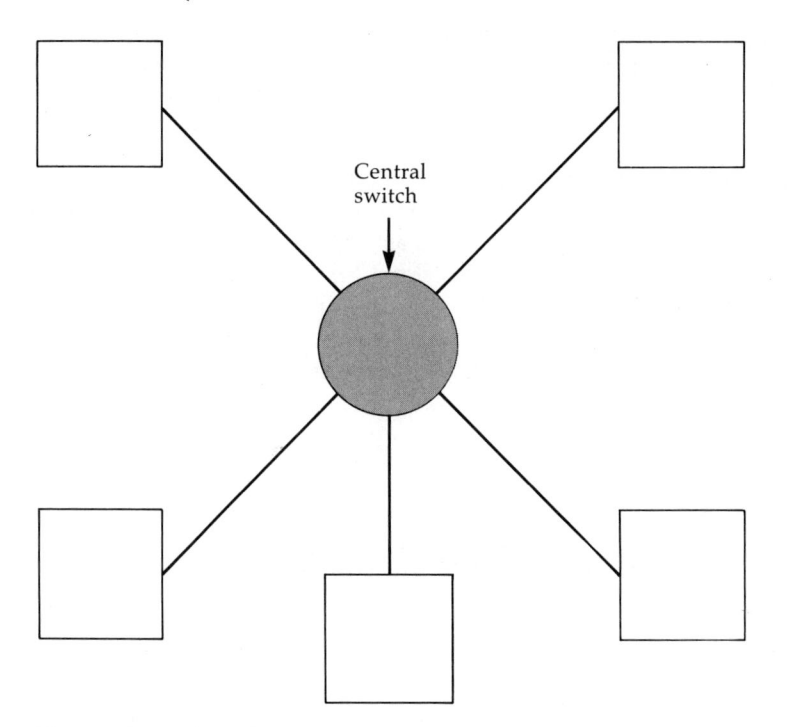

Figure 12.11 Star Network

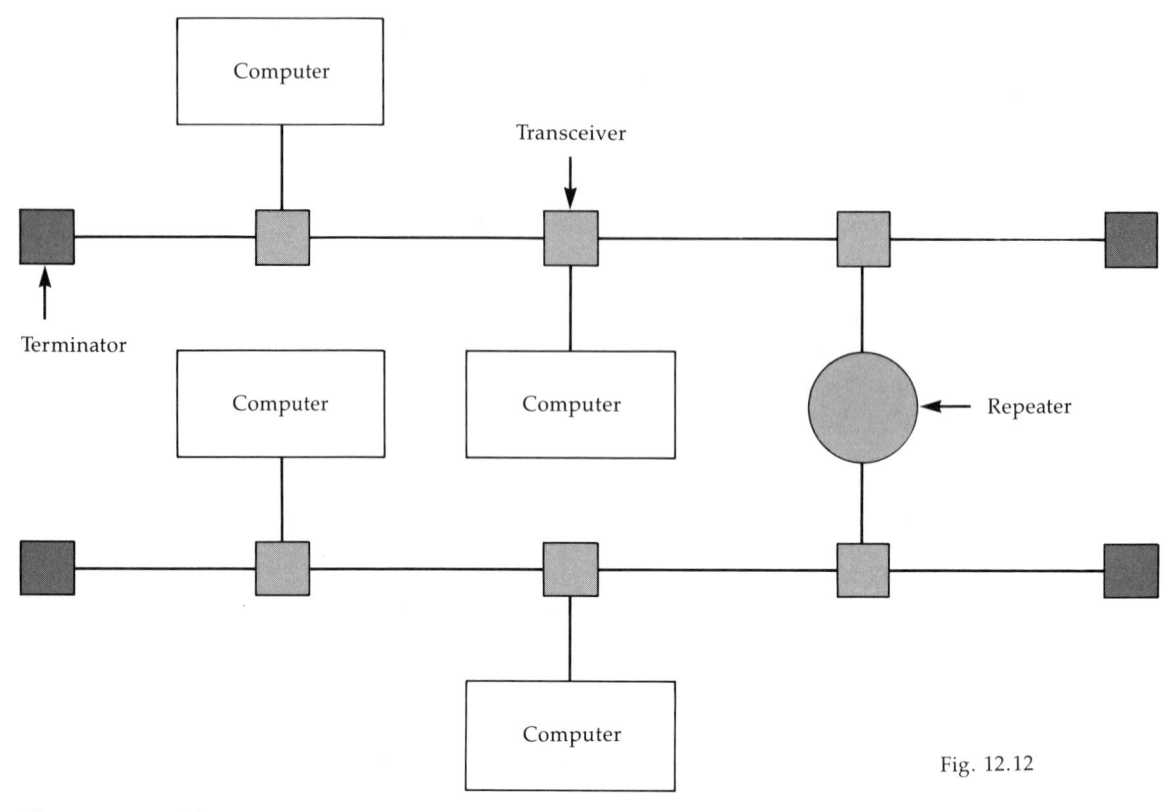

Figure 12.12 Ethernet system

Computer systems plug into the cable through transceivers. Ethernet is limited to a length of 1 km, with about 100 stations connected to the cable. It can transmit data at rates as high as 10 million bits per second. For a larger Ethernet system, several buses can be connected together through repeaters. A repeater consists of two transceivers and allows signals to pass between the two connecting cables. A 2.5 km Ethernet system could be constructed using repeaters. A diagram of a typical Ethernet system is shown in Figure 12.12.

12.3 Communication Protocols

While the architecture specifies the physical nature of the interconnection of several computer systems, an equally important feature of the communication link is the set of rules that specify how two or more

12.3 Communication Protocols

systems establish a connection. These rules form the system protocol. The protocol defines the **access path**, which is the sequence of functions that makes it possible for one network component to communicate with the other components to which it is physically connected.

The access path initially requires that a physical transmission connection exist between the components that will communicate. This is the system topology covered in the previous section. The access path also provides a way to generate addressing information so that a message can arrive at the correct destination. Other segments or functions of the access path include a buffer process and an error control system. The buffer provides a means of saving incoming messages until the destination unit is free to process them and a means of holding outgoing messages until the physical transmission link is not busy. The error control system detects and, if possible, corrects any errors in the transmission. In addition, another major function of the access path is one of protocol conversion (called dialogue management), in which the formats and control signals of the transmitting device are converted so that they meet the requirements of the transmission link and then reconverted at the destination so that they meet the requirements of the receiving device. The layers of this simple access path model are shown in Figure 12.13. Most layer models include more detail than is shown in the figure.

The physical structure of the communication bus is another major segment of the protocol. That is, the actual wired communication link consists of several signals, and the definition of these signals specifies a standard. There are several of these communication standards, including the RS-232C, which we have already seen used for computer-terminal communication.

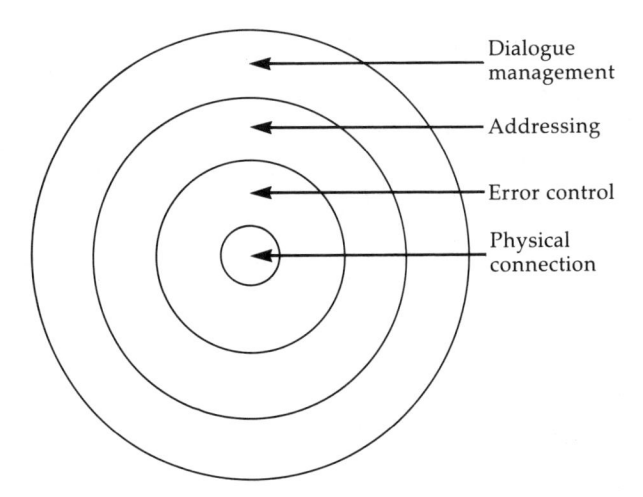

Figure 12.13 Layered model of communication

12.4 Packet Switching

The structure of the data transmitted between systems is another aspect of the communication protocol. One commonly used communication data structure is a **packet**. A packet is a part of a communication message that is organized as shown below.

MSG ID	Packet number	Total number of packets in the message	To	From	Text	...	Error control

Breaking a long message into packets may be helpful because some systems have difficulty processing long, variable-length messages. Also, continuous passing of long messages might prevent transmitting short but more important messages. A **packet-switching network** consists of transmission lines interconnected by packet switches, as shown in Figure 12.14. The packet switches break up each transmitted message into a set of independent packets, format a set of received packets back into a message for its host, and perform a store-and-forward function to transmit received packets to their destination. The store-and-forward function means that the packet switch serves as an intermediate memory for pack-

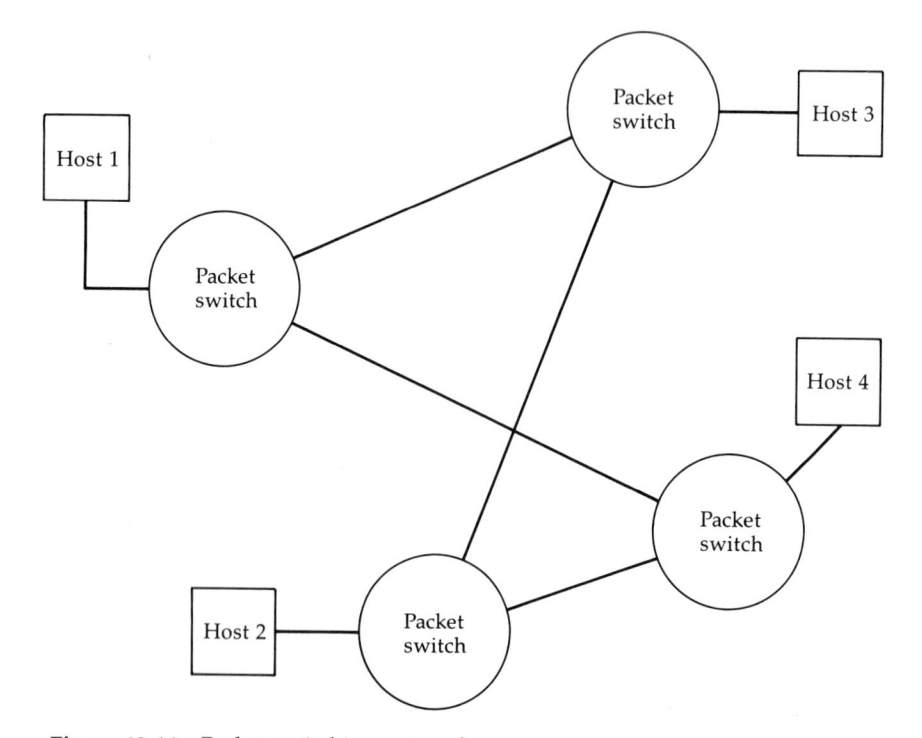

Figure 12.14 Packet-switching network

ets in transit. It will determine the destination of these in-transit packets and select a path along which to forward the packet. The store-and-forward function requires that the packet switch route any received packet along the best path to its destination. Three possible routing algorithms are the following:

1. Distributed flooding: a packet is retransmitted over every link connected to the packet except the one on which the packet was received.

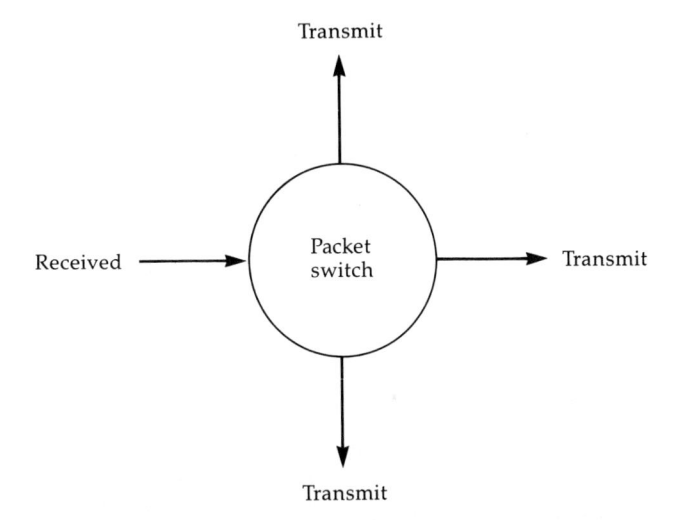

```
                    Transmit
                       ↑
                       |
                   ┌───────┐
  Received ──────▶ │ Packet│ ──────▶ Transmit
                   │ switch│
                   └───────┘
                       |
                       ↓
                    Transmit
```

2. Distributed random algorithm: the packet is retransmitted over a randomly selected link.
3. Fixed routing: each packet switch contains a directory that lists the best route to follow for any given destination.

The distributed flooding algorithm always results in the minimum delay in the transmission from the source to the destination. However, because multiple copies of the packet are created, it also generates excessive traffic on the network. Another problem is that the number of copies of a packet in circulation could grow without bounds. We can eliminate this growth by adding another field to the packet called the hop count. When the packet is created at its source, the hop count field is assigned a value such as the maximum number of communication links along any network path. A packet switch decrements this field by 1 each time it receives the packet. When the hop field is reduced to 0, the packet is not retransmitted.

DECnet Example

DEC provides a network structure for its computer systems called DECnet. We can construct a complete network of PDP-11s, VAXs, and other devices using DECnet. It is a packet-switching system where the packet size is variable and always equal to the message size (message-switching system). The physical connection between packet switches can be any communication standard, including RS-232C. The routing mechanism is a form of fixed routine where each node has a list of the best next hop to each destination.

12.5 Error Control

Error control is an important feature of the control layers for a communication system. When we transmit data over long distances or among several devices, there is a chance of error. An error in even a single bit of data (a 0 changing to a 1 or a 1 changing to a 0) could invalidate an entire computing process. Some method of detecting and possibly correcting an error in a communication is necessary. In this section we will consider the problem and develop some simple but powerful approaches to both error detection and error correction. The error control techniques that we discuss are also useful in protecting a computer against partial failure of both main and secondary memory and are frequently employed in these structures.

Error Detection

To provide error detection, we must supply **redundant information** (extra bits) with each transmitted word. For example, while characters are represented in ASCII using only seven bits, an eighth bit is often added to the transmitted character. This extra bit is called a **parity bit**. It represents the simplest method of error detection and is called parity checking. There are two types of parity.

1. Even parity: the extra bit is selected so that there is always an even number of ones in the word.
2. Odd parity: the extra bit is selected so that there is always an odd number of ones in the word.

Parity checking allows the system to detect a single error in the transmitted word. For example, if we want to transmit the ASCII code for the character A, which is 1000001, using odd parity, we would have to add an eighth bit with the value 1 so that an odd number, in this case three, of the bits would be 1. If there is an error in transmission—say, bit 5 is inverted—it could be detected by a parity check at the receiving end. The transmitted and received signals are as follows:

    Bit   6543210p
    Transmit— 10000011   odd parity
    Receive—   11000011   even parity

At the receiving end, the parity is checked and an even number of ones are found. It is determined that an error occurred. Although the receiving end can detect the error, it cannot determine which bit is wrong. In this case some systems request that the byte with the error be retransmitted. Note that if two bits are received incorrectly, neither one can be detected using this parity code. For example, say both bit 5 and bit 4 of the character A are inverted during the transmission, as shown below:

```
Bit           6543210p
Transmit—  10000011   odd parity
Receive—   11100011   odd parity
```

The receiving end determines that it received an odd parity word and assumes that there was no error during transmission. Thus, if there is a high probability of two or more errors in the same byte, a simple parity code is unacceptable for error control. Other, more sophisticated codes can detect and even correct multiple errors.

Error Correction

Once an error is detected, there are two major ways to recover. The first method, called **forward error correction (FEC)**, requires the use of additional redundant bits beyond the standard parity bits so that the byte with the error can be corrected. These extra bits could appear as a parity byte after a block of n bytes. For example, suppose that the block size is set at 4. After four characters are transmitted (each with a single parity bit), a parity byte is transmitted. Using even parity, transmission of a single block might look like the following:

```
Transmit   10100110
           10010101
           11000110
           01101010
           10011111   parity byte
```

Now if a single error occurs during transmission, it can be detected and corrected. For example, assume that the above transmission was received as follows:

```
Receive    10100110
           10110101   error in this row
           11000110
           01101010
           10011111
              ↑
           error in this column
```

The receiving device checks the parity of each column and row and discovers parity errors in the second row and third column. Thus the error is determined to be in bit 3 of word 2. The bit can be inverted to recover the correct transmission.

The second method, called **backward error correction (BEC)**, simply asks the transmitting end to retransmit any data in which an error has been detected. After several retransmit requests, if the receiving end still detects an error in transmission, the system stops the communication process, flags an error, and calls for a human operator to enter the process.

Generalized Parity Check Code (Hamming Code)

We can generalize the simple parity check code to provide multiple-error detection—error correction capability within a single word. This requires the addition of more than just one redundant parity bit. For example, building a single error-correcting code word with q data bits requires c additional parity check bits where c satisfies the inequality

$$2^c >= q + c + 1$$

Providing a single error-correcting capability for a 4-bit data word would require adding 3 additional parity bits. An 11-bit data word would require 4 parity bits.

We construct the coded word with the additional parity bits from the data bits in the following manner:

1. Assume q data bits.
2. Assume c parity check bits.
3. Transmit a $(q + c)$ bit word where the bits are given by: b_{q+c}, b_{q+c-1}, ..., b_2, b_1
4. Place the c parity bits at the following locations: b_2^0, b_2^1, b_2^2, ..., b_2^{c-1}

For example, suppose that we want to transmit four data bits at a time using this single error-correcting code. Because $2^3 >= 4 + 3 + 1$, we would have to add three parity check bits to each word, resulting in a 7-bit transmission. In this case the check bits will be placed in locations b_1, b_2, and b_4. A specific transmitted word such as 1101 would be rearranged as

b_7 b_6 b_5 b_4 b_3 b_2 b_1
 1   1   0   c   1   c   c

where c is a parity check bit.

So far we have only specified where the new bits should be placed in the data word but not what their value should be in order to provide an error-correcting capability. In order to determine their value, for $j = 1, \ldots, c$, we define the set P_j as those integers whose binary representations have c or fewer bits and have a 1 in the jth bit position. For $q = 4$ and $c = 3$, the following are the three P_j sets:

$P_1 = \{1, 3, 5, 7\}$
$P_2 = \{2, 3, 6, 7\}$
$P_3 = \{4, 5, 6, 7\}$.

These sets of integers are used to set up c equations whose solutions are the values of the c parity bits. The parity equations are given by

$\sum b_k = 0$ where k is in P_j for $j = 1, \ldots, c$

the sum is a mod 2 sum. For the $q = 4$ and $c = 3$ case, the three parity check equations are as follows:

$j = 1 \quad b_1 + b_3 + b_5 + b_7 = 0$
$j = 2 \quad b_2 + b_3 + b_6 + b_7 = 0$
$j = 3 \quad b_4 + b_5 + b_6 + b_7 = 0$

The location of the parity check bits were carefully chosen so that all but the first bit in each equation is known. For example, if we want to send the word 1101, the transmitted word is organized as

$b_7\ b_6\ b_5\ b_4\ b_3\ b_2\ b_1$
$1\ \ 1\ \ 0\ \ c\ \ 1\ \ c\ \ c$

so the equations become

$j = 1 \quad b_1 + 1 + 0 + 1 = 0$
$j = 2 \quad b_2 + 1 + 1 + 1 = 0$
$j = 3 \quad b_4 + 0 + 1 + 1 = 0$

The solutions to these equations (remember they use mod 2 sums) are

$b_1 = 0$
$b_2 = 1$
$b_4 = 0$

Now, the actual transmitted word is 1100110.

The next step is to detect and locate any errors at the receiving end. We can detect an error by applying the parity equations to the received word. If the sums of the left-hand side of all the parity equations are 0, the transmission is assumed to be error-free. These sums are called parity checksums. If some of the parity checksums are nonzero, the value of parity checksum points to the error as illustrated in the following example. Say we are transmitting the data word 1101. When the three parity bits are added to this word, the transmission consists of the seven bits 1100110. Now if the transmission is received as 1100010, an error clearly occurred in bit 3. Calculating the parity checksums for the received word, we find

$j = 1 \quad 0 + 0 + 0 + 1 = 1$

$j = 2 \quad 1 + 0 + 1 + 1 = 1$

$j = 3 \quad 0 + 0 + 1 + 1 = 0$

Because the parity checksums at the receiving end do not all equal zero, an error has been detected. Moreover, when the sums are arranged in reverse order, they form 011 or binary 3. In this way they identify the bit that was in error, bit 3. So the corrected word is 1100110.

Checksum Codes

A checksum code procedure is one of the least expensive approaches to error detection. We calculate the checksum for a block of data by adding together all the words in the data block modulo-n (the value for n is arbitrary). It is a very useful method for communication because the checksum for a message block can be calculated and sent along with the message. At the receiving end, the checksum can be recalculated and compared to the transmitted checksum. If the two agree, we assume that the transmission was error-free. For example, assume that the following block of eight-bit data is to be transmitted.

10101010
01110101
11110100
00000001

If n is selected to be decimal 110, the checksum for the block is

01011100

(the sum of the block is 532, which, when reduced mod 110, gives 92). So the checksum would be added to the block, and the five bytes would be transmitted to the destination. At the destination, the checksum would be determined from the first four bytes and compared to the fifth byte to detect a possible error.

Summary

In this chapter we have considered several of the important issues associated with establishing a communication link between computers and other devices. This has been only a brief look at a very complicated subject, and we covered only the major components of such a communication link. They include the nature of the physical communication link between systems, a survey of several common communication architectures, and a look at the protocol structure with an emphasis on the error control issue.

Exercises

1. Write an assembly language program that will encode any 11-bit binary input into a 16-bit generalized parity code word.

2. Write an assembly language program that will decode and correct any errors in a 16-bit word assuming that it has been encoded using your code from Exercise 1.

3. Given a communication system with nine interconnected units and the following characteristics:

   a. A link can transmit 10K bits per second
   b. There are four possible topologies: (1) direct connection, (2) loop (with the units connected in clockwise order 0 to 9), (3) bus, and (4) star.
   c. We want to transfer files of size 25K bits between units 1 and 4 and 6 and 7.

   For this case, fill in the following table:

Topology	Number of Links	Total Transmission Time (both files)
Direct		
Loop		
Bus		
Star		

4. Write an assembly language procedure that will perform the packet construction function for a packet switch. Assume that the host gives the packet switch (passes to your procedure) the size (in bytes) of the message; the destination of the message, which is a one-byte address; and the message, which is in ASCII. The text in a packet can be no longer than four bytes. Your source address is E5. The error control method is a checksum with $n = 117$ (decimal). The main program should pass the following messages to the procedure, and the procedure should output each packet.

   a. This is the first message, destination = F1.
   b. The second message is next, destination = 48.
   c. Now the problem is done, destination = 65.

5. Add an extra bit to the following words to make an odd parity code.

   a. 011101
   b. 1110101

6. Find the error in the following block of data, assuming even parity.

   101110101
   101011000
   000001101
   011100010
   001000010

7. Add the necessary bits to provide a single error-correcting capability to the following words.
   a. 10011100
   b. 11110101110
   c. 111000001010101
   d. 001011010111010

8. Find the checksum for the following block of data with $n = 57$.

   10100001

   11100011

   10001101

9. Assuming the use of a single error-correcting generalized parity code, determine if the following words are faulty. If so, correct them and list the actual data bits in the correct order (b_n to b_1).
   a. 1101101
   b. 110001000
   c. 1100000010011000
   d. 0101010010010101

10. If the probability of an error in a single bit during a transmission is 10^{-4}
    a. What is the probability of two errors in a 7-bit transmission?
    b. What is the probability of an uncorrected error in a transmission of seven data bits if the transmission process uses a generalized parity check code?
    c. Graph the probability of an uncorrected error in a received word that is protected by a generalized parity check code as a function of the number of data bits.

PART 5

ALTERNATIVE ARCHITECTURES

CHAPTER 13
Microprocessors

CHAPTER 14
Large System Architecture

CHAPTER 15
Fault-Tolerant Computer Architecture

CHAPTER CONTENTS

13.1 MICROPROCESSOR HISTORY

13.2 MICROPROCESSOR CHARACTERISTICS

    Microprocessor Construction
    General Microprocessor Architecture

13.3 THE MOTOROLA FAMILY

    The M6800
    The M68000

13.4 THE INTEL FAMILY

    The 8080
    The 8086

SUMMARY

EXERCISES

CHAPTER 13

Microprocessors

In this chapter we will explore the world of "computers on a chip," or microprocessors. These devices have come a long way since 1971, when the first commercial microprocessor was introduced. They opened the door to the computer revolution and today play a significant role in most computer applications. We briefly review the historical development (can anything less than 20 years old have a history?) of microprocessor systems in the first section of this chapter. We will discuss the general characteristics of microprocessor design and architecture and two specific microprocessor families in later sections.

What is a microprocessor and how is it different from a minicomputer such as the VAX? This is a difficult question, because any answer based on the absolute size of the computer would be wrong. A dozen years ago we might have said that a minicomputer is a 16-bit machine and a microprocessor is an 8-bit machine. Today we may claim that a minicomputer is a 32-bit machine and a microprocessor is a 16-bit machine. However, some new microprocessors are also 32-bit machines. The technology is changing so fast that a distinction between microprocessors, minicomputers, and even mainframes cannot be clearly drawn based just on word size. We must consider the complete environment of the machines, and even then the distinction can sometimes be hard to make. For now we will define a microprocessor as a small computer processing element and leave it to history to define what is "small."

13.1 Microprocessor History

The first commercial, "general-purpose" microprocessor was announced in an ad in the November 15, 1971, issue of *Electronic News*. Developed and marketed by Intel, it was a small 4-bit system called the 4004 CPU.

Intel designed this chip to serve as a calculator control system for a Japanese manufacturer. In its final form the 4004 CPU had about 2300 transistors on a single chip.

In 1972 Intel introduced the 8008, an 8-bit microprocessor that contained six 8-bit general-purpose registers and only 45 operations in its instruction set. It could address a whopping 16K of main memory. Rockwell and Fairchild also entered the microprocessor market in 1972.

In 1973 Intel introduced the 8080, which is still in use today. The 8-bit 8080 architecture provided a tenfold increase in throughput over the 8008. The 8080 has 74 operations in its instruction set and can directly address 64K of main memory. Its CPU is implemented on a 5000-transistor chip.

Based on the success of the 8080, Motorola announced the 6800 microprocessor in 1974. In fact, by the end of 1974, there were 19 microprocessors on the market.

In 1976 Zilog introduced the Z80, which is also still used today. This 8-bit machine has 158 instructions. More than 54 microprocessors became available during 1976. However, by then the 16-bit race was on. Fueled by the early (1974) announcement of the National Semiconductor IMP-16 and the Texas Instruments 9900 machines, the eventual move to 16-bit microprocessors was set.

In 1978 Intel entered the 16-bit arena with the 8086, which represented another tenfold increase in computing power over the 8080. The 8086 directly addresses one megabyte of main memory and consists of 29K transistors on a single chip. Other 16-bit chips include the Zilog Z8000, National Semiconductor's 16000, and Motorola's 68000.

The next generation of microprocessors, which appeared on the scene in 1985–1986, are the 32-bit machines. These include the VAX on a chip from DEC, the Motorola 68020, the NS32032, and the Intel iAPX 432. The Intel 32-bit machine is an amazing machine: it has a 16-megabyte address space, 2 million instructions-per-second execution rate, and consists of 200,000 transistors on two chips.

13.2 Microprocessor Characteristics

In this section we will outline some of the general characteristics of microprocessors, and in the following sections we will illustrate how these general principles have been used by different manufacturers in the construction of specific machines.

Microprocessor Construction

Microprocessors are feasible because of technology that allows the construction of complex circuits consisting of thousands of devices on a single silicon integrated circuit chip. There are several levels of complexity in integrated circuit design, based on the number of devices such as transistors on the chip, as shown below.

Device Count	Level
1–100	SSI (small-scale integrated)
100–1000	MSI (medium-scale integrated)
1000–10,000	LSI (large-scale integrated)
10,000–? (1,000,000)	VLSI (very large-scale integrated)

In 1985 the largest chips (other than memory chips) consisted of about 300,000 transistors or 70K logic gates. However, these numbers are constantly increasing, and by 1990 (or sooner) there will probably be chips with 1 million transistors. This improvement in the number of transistors per chip results from our ability to reduce the size of each individual wire on the silicon chip. For example, in 1978 the minimum "feature size" was 5 μm (a micrometer is 10^{-6} meters). By 1985, however, the minimum feature size was reduced to 1.5 μm.

Transistors implemented on silicon, using what is called MOS technology, basically consist of two different types of "doped" silicon layers that cross over each other. The top layer, called polysilicon, acts as a gate to control the current on the bottom diffusion layer. As shown in Figure 13.1, the channel blocks the connection between the source and drain on the diffusion layer. However, when voltage is applied to the gate on the poly layer, the gate creates an electrical field that changes the channel into the same type of material as the two separated diffusion layers, which results in a connection between the source and the drain, as shown in Figure 13.2.

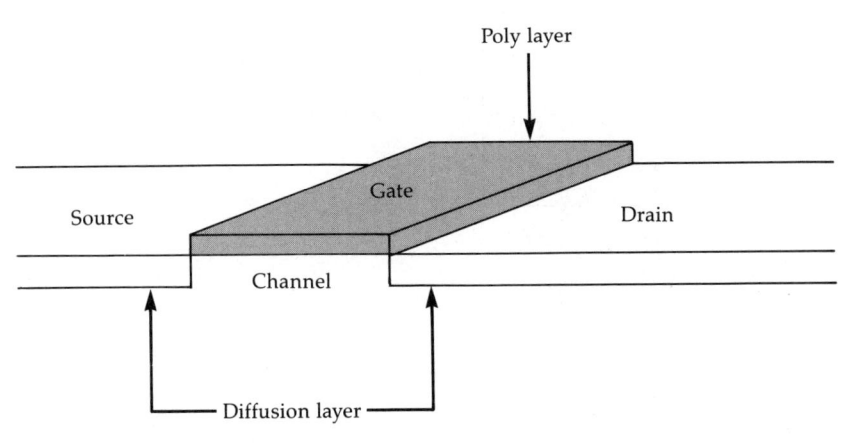

Figure 13.1 Open channel on silicon

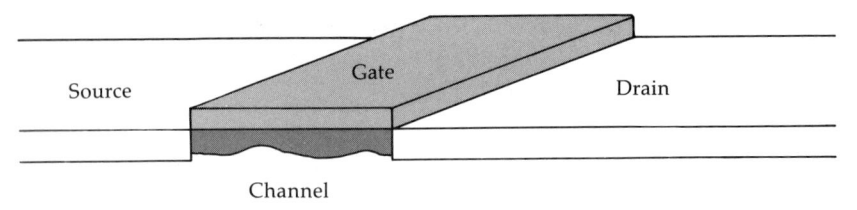

Figure 13.2 Closed channel on silicon

A typical inverter on a silicon chip looks like the device shown in Figure 13.3. When there is a voltage (or a 1) on the gate input, there is a connection between the source and the drain, so the source, which is connected to the output, is pulled to ground (or a 0). When there is no voltage (or a 0) on the gate input, the channel is open and there is no connection between the source and the drain, so the source is almost at +V (or a 1). So this device will output a 0 when there is a 1 in and output a 1 when there is a 0 in; in other words, it is a logic inverter.

The device shown in Figure 13.3 is also known as a metal oxide semiconductor field effect transistor (MOSFET). It is the basic unit with which

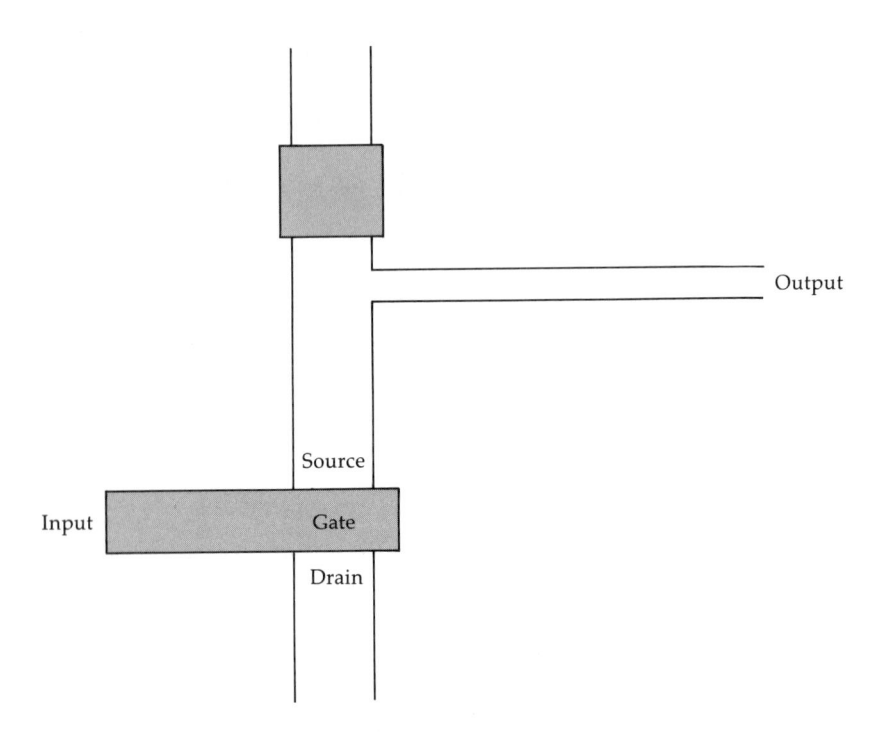

Figure 13.3 Inverter on a silicon chip

a microprocessor using this technology is constructed because the MOSFET can be modified and combined to form the AND and OR gates needed for logic circuits.

General Microprocessor Architecture

A typical microcomputer structure consists of four major components, as shown in Figure 13.4. These are the microprocessor itself; external memory in the form of RAM, ROM, or both; and I/O devices such as disk drives, tape units, keyboards, CRTs, and so on.

The internal architecture of a microprocessor is much like the structure of a general CPU. The usual difference between the two is in the size (number of bits/words) and the number of registers. However, this distinction is becoming blurred as microprocessors become more sophisticated. A typical microprocessor internal architecture is shown in Figure 13.5. This architecture is functionally quite similar to the single-bus architecture discussed in Chapter 4. It is given in the typical style for architecture drawings.

In the rest of this chapter we will consider several different microprocessors and examine how their specific architecture is similar to and different from the typical architecture shown in Figure 13.5. For each major family of microprocessors, we will examine the system architecture, the microinstruction set, and a sample program.

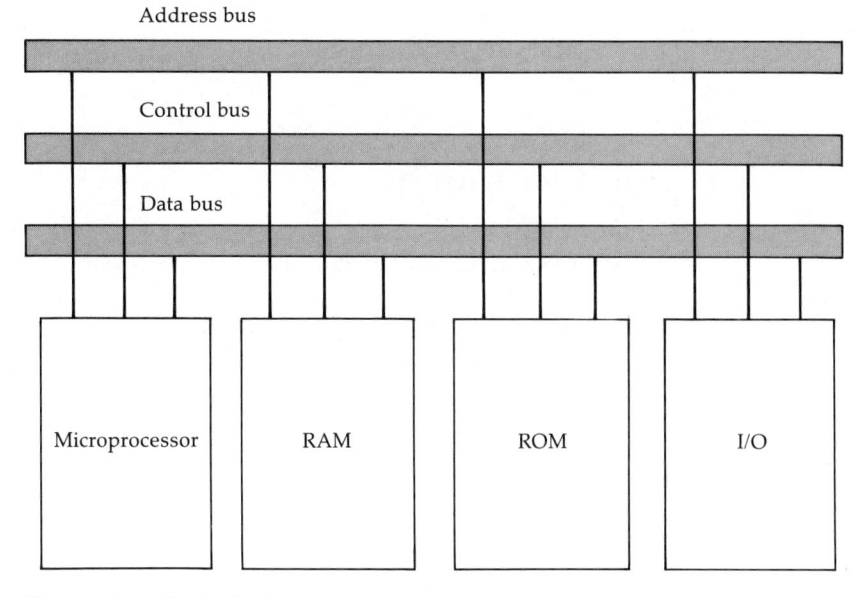

Figure 13.4 Typical microcomputer architecture

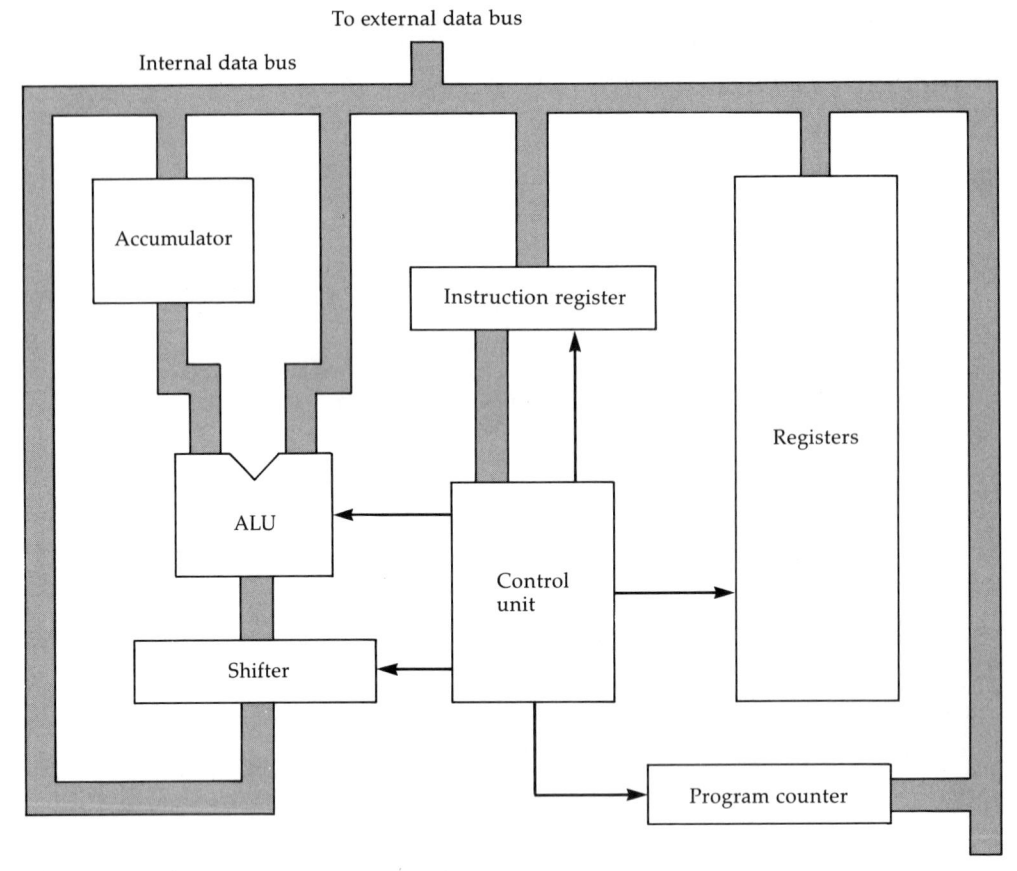

Figure 13.5 Typical microprocessor architecture

13.3 The Motorola Family

We will examine two of the Motorola series of microprocessors in this section: the older 6800 8-bit machine and the more recent 68000 series of 16/32-bit machines. Although the 68000 series really involves several machines, including the 68000, the 68010, and the 68020, we will cover only the details of the 68000.

The M6800

The M6800 is an 8-bit machine with only six user-accessible general-purpose registers. The internal architecture is shown in Figure 13.6 and is very similar to the architecture of Figure 13.5. In fact, for the most part, this machine looks like a reduced version of the VAX CPU in that

13.3 The Motorola Family

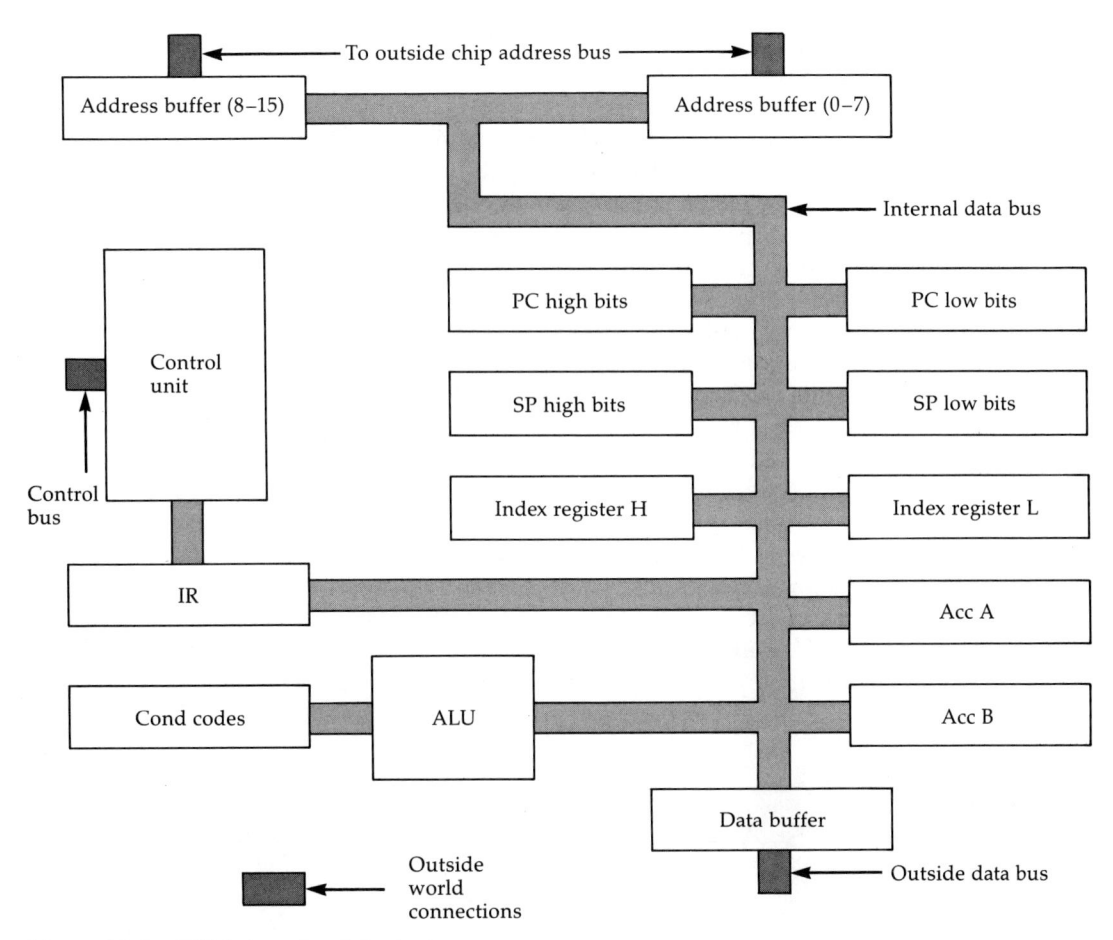

Figure 13.6 6800 internal architecture

it has registers (of course, fewer than the VAX), a program counter (PC), an IR, an ALU, and a control unit. However, remember that the VAX has a 32-bit internal data bus, while the 6800 has only an 8-bit data path, which means that it would take four bus cycles on the 6800 to transfer internally the same number of bits that the VAX can transfer in one bus cycle.

Note also that the 6800 only has six registers. Some of the registers are 16-bit registers, such as the PC, the SP (stack pointer), and the IX (index register), while the remaining registers (the two accumulators, A and B, and the condition code register, CCR) are 8-bit registers. The PC, SP, and IX registers all have 16 bits because the 6800 allows for 16-bit address information. However, the 6800 internally treats each of these registers as two 8-bit registers, so it still requires two 6800 bus cycles to transfer information from the 16-bit internal address registers to the 16-

bit address output buffer registers that are directly connected to the outside world. The 16-bit address registers allow the 6800 to directly address up to 64K of main memory. The condition code register is similar to the VAX PSW in that it includes the same set of condition bits: the carry (C), overflow (V), negative (N), and zero (Z) bits. There are two additional bits in the 6800 condition code register: H is used for decimal operations, and I is used for controlling interrupts. Data is passed between the outside world and the internal registers through three buses: the control, the address, and the data.

Externally, the 6800 chip alone is not enough to form a complete computer, just as the CPU of the VAX is of no use unless it is connected to the VAX memory and other circuits. To construct a working computer system using the 6800 microprocessor chip, it is necessary to wire the 6800 to a series of support chips, including ROM, RAM, and interface control systems. A minimal but complete 6800-based computer system is shown in the block diagram of Figure 13.7. Motorola provides all the support chips needed to complete the computer. Of course, a few additional components, such as a power supply, are needed. They all communicate along the three-system bus structure that is connected to the CPU internal buffers. Both the ROM and RAM chips serve as memory for the system. The ROM could be used to store the operating system and other system services permanently, while the RAM serves as the

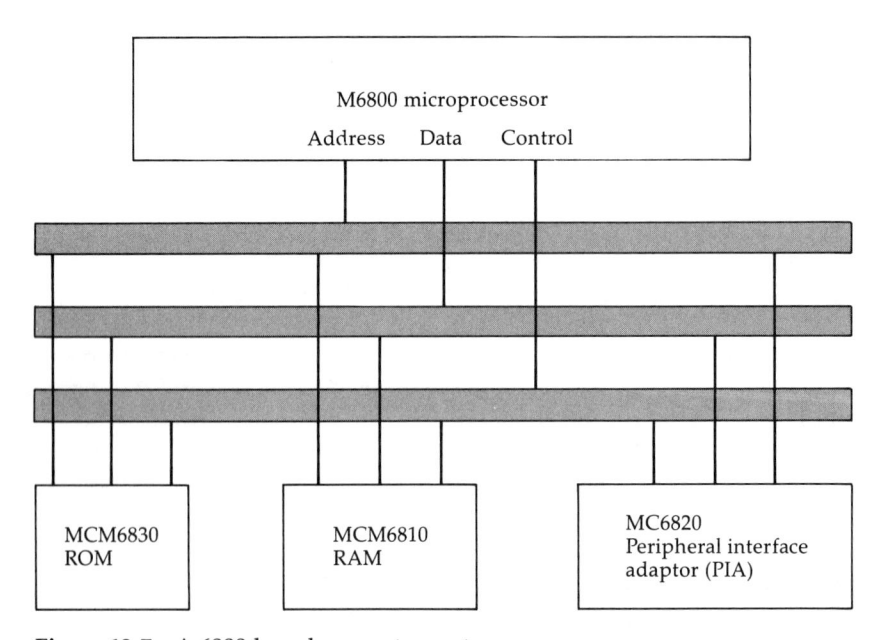

Figure 13.7 A 6800-based computer system

user memory unit. The peripheral interface adaptor chip is used to interface the chip with I/O devices.

The 6800 has 72 basic instructions that, when combined with the 5 available addressing modes, result in 197 different instructions. The 5 addressing modes are very similar to some of those available on the VAX.

1. **Direct addressing.** In this mode the instruction mnemonic is followed by the address of the data. The address is restricted to one byte, so this mode can be used to address only the first 256 memory locations.
2. **Extended addressing.** This is the same as direct addressing except that the two bytes following the opcode contain the address of the data. This allows the full 64K of memory to be used in the addressing mode.
3. **Immediate addressing.** In this mode the data is found in the location "immediately" following the opcode; that is, the data is pointed to by the PC.
4. **Index addressing.** A one-byte nonnegative offset is added to the index register to obtain the address of the data.
5. **Relative addressing.** This is used only in branching statements in which the byte following the opcode is added to the PC if the branch condition is satisfied.

Motorola defines one additional "addressing mode" called the implied mode. This is used in instructions such as ABA (add B to A), which don't require any additional addressing information. Direct and immediate modes are forms of absolute addressing because they give the address of the data.

The complete set of instructions for the 6800 is shown in Table 13.1. The table entries include the instruction mnemonic, the opcode, the number of bytes in the instruction (B), the number of basic machine cycles (T) it takes to complete the instruction, and the operation represented by the instruction. Based on your study of the VAX assembly language, most of the information in the table should be self-explanatory. A number of the instructions specify which accumulator is used. For example, PSHA will push the contents of accumulator A onto the system stack. Some instructions specify an accumulator and also require another memory address, such as ADDB, which will add the contents of accumulator B to a given memory location and save the result in accumulator B. The memory location is specified by the address that is supplied in the second byte or second and third bytes of the instruction. Still other instructions involve both accumulators, such as ABA, which will add the contents of accumulator A to the contents of accumulator B and save the result in accumulator A. There are also instructions for rotate and shift

Table 13.1 6800 Instruction Set

		\multicolumn{10}{c	}{**Address Mode**}	
		\multicolumn{2}{c}{*Immed*}	\multicolumn{2}{c}{*Direct*}	\multicolumn{2}{c}{*Absol*}	\multicolumn{2}{c}{*Index*}	\multicolumn{2}{c}{*Implied*}	
Operation	**Mnemonic**	B	T	B	T	B	T	B	T	B	T	**Operation**
Add	ADDA	2	2	2	3	3	4	2	5			A ← (A) + (M)
	ADDB	2	2	2	3	3	4	2	5			B ← (B) + (M)
Add A to B	ABA									1	2	A ← (A) + (B)
Add with carry	ADCA	2	2	2	3	3	4	2	5			A ← (A) + (M) + (C)
	ADCB	2	2	2	3	3	4	2	5			B ← (B) + (M) + (C)
AND	ANDA	2	2	2	3	3	4	2	5			A ← (A) (M)
	ANDB	2	2	2	3	3	4	2	5			B ← (B) (M)
Bit test	BITA	2	2	2	3	3	4	2	5			(A) (M)
	BITB	2	2	2	3	3	4	2	5			(B) (M)
Clear	CLR					3	6	2	7			M ← 0
Clear A or B	CLRA									1	2	A ← 0
	CLRB									1	2	B ← 0
Compare	CMPA	2	2	2	3	3	4	2	5			(A) − (M)
	CMPB	2	2	2	3	3	4	2	5			(B) − (M)
Compare A to B	CBA									1	2	(A) − (B)
Complement	COM					3	6	2	7			(M) ← (M)
	COMA									1	2	(A) ← (A)
	COMB									1	2	(B) ← (B)
Negate	NEG					3	6	2	7			M ← 0 − (M)
	NEGA									1	2	(A) ← 0 − (A)
	NEGB									1	2	(B) ← 0 − (B)
Decimal adj	DAA									1	2	
Decrement	DEC					3	6	2	7			M ← (M) − 1
	DECA									1	2	A − (A) − 1
	DECB									1	2	B ← (B) − 1
Exclusive-OR	EORA	2	2	2	3	4	3	2	5			A ← (A) (M)
	EORB	2	2	2	3	4	3	2	5			B ← (B) (M)
Increment	INC					3	6	2	7			M ← (M) + 1
	INCA									1	2	A ← (A) + 1
	INCB									1	2	B ← (B) + 1
Load ACC	LDA	2	2	2	3	3	4	2	5			A ← (M)
	LDB	2	2	2	3	3	4	2	5			B ← (M)
OR	ORA	2	2	2	3	3	4	2	5			A ← (A) (M)
	ORB	2	2	2	3	3	4	2	5			B ← (B) (M)

Table 13.1 (continued)

Operation	Mnemonic	Immed B T	Direct B T	Absol B T	Index B T	Implied B T	Operation
Push	PSHA					1 4	Push A on Stack
	PSHB					1 4	Push B on Stack
Pull	PULA					1 4	Pop A from Stack
	PULB					1 4	Pop B from Stack
Rotate left	ROL			3 6	2 7		Rotate memory
	ROLA					1 2	Rotate A
	ROLB					1 2	Rotate B
Rotate right	ROR			3 6	2 7		Rotate memory
	RORA					1 2	Rotate A
	RORB					1 2	Rotate B
Shift left	ASL			3 6	2 7		
	ASLA					1 2	
	ASLB					1 2	
Shift right	ASR			3 6	2 7		
	ASRA					1 2	
	ASRB					1 2	
Shift right (logic)	LSR			3 6	2 7		
	LSRA					1 2	
	LSRB					1 2	
Store ACC	STAA		2 4	3 5	2 6		M ← (A)
	STAB		2 4	3 5	2 6		M ← (B)
Subtract	SUBA	2 2	2 3	3 4	2 5		A ← (A) − (M)
	SUBB	2 2	2 3	3 4	2 5		B ← (B) − (M)
Subtract R/B	SBA∝					1 2	A ← (A) − (B)
Subtract with carry	SBCA	2 2	2 3	3 4	2 5		A ← (A) − (M) − (C)
	SBCB	2 2	2 3	3 4	2 5		B ← (B) − (M) − (C)
Transfer acc	TAB					1 2	B ← (A)
	TBA					1 2	A ← (B)
Test	TST			3 6	2 7		(M) − 0
	TSTA					1 2	(A) − 0
	TSTB					1 2	(B) − 0
Compare index register	CMX	3 3	2 4	3 5	2 6		

(continued)

Table 13.1 (continued)

Address Mode

Operation	Mnemonic	Immed B T	Direct B T	Absol B T	Index B T	Implied B T	Operation
Decrement index reg	DEX					1 4	IX ← (IX) − 1
Decrement stack pointer	DES					1 4	SP ← (SP) − 1
Increment index reg	IMX					1 4	IX ← (IX) + 1
Increment stack pointer	IMS					1 4	SP ← (SP) + 1
Load index reg	LDX	3 3	2 4	3 5	2 6		
Load stack pointer	LDS	3 3	2 4	3 5	2 6		
Store index reg	STX		2 5	3 6	2 7		
Store stack pointer	STS		2 5	3 6	2 7		
Move IX to stack pointer	TXS					1 4	SP ← (IX) − 1
Move SP to index reg	TSX					1 4	IX ← (SP) + 1
Clear carry	CLC					1 2	C ← 0
Clear interrupt mask	CLI					1 2	I ← 0
Clear overflow	CLV					1 2	V ← 0
Set carry	SEC					1 2	C ← 1
Set interrupt mask	SEI					1 2	C ← 1
Set overflow	SEV					1 2	V ← 1

Branch Instructions

Address Mode

Operation	Mnemonic	Rela B T	Absol B T	Index B T	Implied B T	Operation (test for)
Branch always	BRA	2 4				none
Branch if carry clear	BCC	2 4				(C) = 0

Table 13.1 (continued)

		Address Mode				
		Rela	Absol	Index	Implied	
Operation	**Mnemonic**	B T	B T	B T	B T	**Operation** (test for)
Branch if carry set	BCS	2 4				$(C) = 1$
Branch on zero	BEQ	2 4				$(Z) = 1$
Branch ≥ 0	BGE	2 4				$(N) \oplus (V) = 0$
Branch > 0	BGT	2 4				$(Z) + ((N) \oplus (V)) = 0$
Branch if higher	BHI	2 4				$(C) \vee (Z) = 0$
Branch ≤ 0	BLE	2 4				$(Z) \vee ((N) \oplus (V)) = 1$
Branch if lower or same	BLS	2 4				$(C) \vee (Z) = 1$
Branch < 0	BLT	2 4				$(N) \oplus (V) = 1$
Branch on minus	BMI	2 4				$(N) = 1$
Branch $\neq 0$	BNE	2 4				$(Z) = 0$
Branch overflow clear	BVC	2 4				$(V) = 0$
Branch overflow set	BVS	2 4				$(V) = 1$
Branch plus	BPL	2 4				$(N) = 0$
Branch to subroutine	BSR	2 8				
Jump	JMP		3 3	2 4		
Jump to subroutine	JSR		3 9	2 8		
No operation	NOP				1 2	
Return from interrupt	RTI				1 10	
Return from subroutine	RTS				1 5	
Software interrupt	SWO				1 12	
Wait for interrupt	WAI				1 9	

operations at the bit level, compare operations, and stack operations. For example, the simple program given below will add the top three numbers on the stack and save the sum on the stack.

Bytes	Cycles	Mnemonic	Operation
3	3	LDS STACK	Load the stack pointer with the address STACK
1	4	PULA	Load A with the top of the stack
1	4	PULB	Load B with the top of the stack
1	2	ABA	Add A and B—result in A
1	4	PULB	Load B with the top of the stack
1	2	ABA	Add A and B
1	4	PSHA	Save A on the top of the stack

The PULx instructions pull a value from the top of the stack (a pop stack operation). PSHx instructions push the specified register onto the stack. This program would require 9 bytes of memory and 23 machine cycles to execute. At a 1-MHz clock rate, that translates into 23 microseconds per execution or about 40,000 loops through the program in one second.

Because the 6800 does not have any multiply or divide instructions, software must carry out these operations. The next example is a simple subroutine designed to divide a nonnegative signed 8-bit number in accumulator A by another number in accumulator B, saving the result in memory location FFF0.

Bytes	Cycles		Code		
3	6	Ans:	CLR FFF0	;	Clear location FFF0
3	6	Step:	INC FFF0	;	Increment answer
1	2		SBA	;	Subtract B from A
2	4		BPL Step	;	Branch on plus
1	2		ABA	;	Restore A
3	4		LDB FFF0	;	Load answer into B
1	2		DECB	;	B was 1 too large
1	5		RTS	;	B has the result, A the
				;	remainder

According to Table 13.1, this subprogram would take a total of 31 cycles if it only required 1 cycle through the loop, plus 12 more cycles for each additional run through the loop. Because the 6800 can run at 1 MHz, this subprogram would take 31 microseconds to execute, plus 12 additional microseconds for each extra loop cycle.

It should come as no surprise that the VAX assembly language offers more functionality to the user than the 6800 assembly language. For example, the 6800 instruction set lacks the capability to work with different word sizes. Some operations that require a single instruction on the VAX require several instructions on the 6800. For example, the VAX has an instruction for bit manipulation called INS (INSert), which is used to insert a specific bit pattern into a segment of a word. The format of the instruction is

```
INSV    source, posn, size, base
```

where INSV inserts bits 0 to (size − 1) of the source into position posn of the base destination. The opcode for INSV is F0. An example of its use is

```
INSV  R3, #4, #4, R5
```

This instruction will take the first four bits of R3 and insert them into bit positions 4, 5, 6, and 7 of R5, as shown in Figure 13.8, leaving the other bits in R5 unchanged. A similar task on 6800 might be to copy the bits 0–3 of acc A into bits 4–7 of acc B. This becomes a very difficult task, as shown in the following code:

```
ASLA            ; Shift A left one bit
ASLA            ; Shift A again
ASLA            ; Shift A again
ASLA            ; Shift A a final time
                ; Now bits 0 to 3 are in position
                ;    4 to 7
ORA #15         ; Ensure that bits 0 to 3 of A are 1
STAA Temp       ; Save A at location Temp
ANDB Temp       ; AND B with Temp
ANDA #240       ; Ensure that bits 0 to 3 of A are 0
STAA Temp       ; Save new A at location Temp
ORB Temp        ; Now the transfer is complete
```

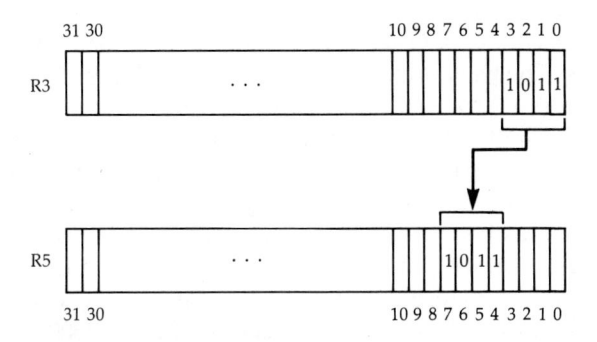

Figure 13.8 INSV Instruction operation

Figure 13.9

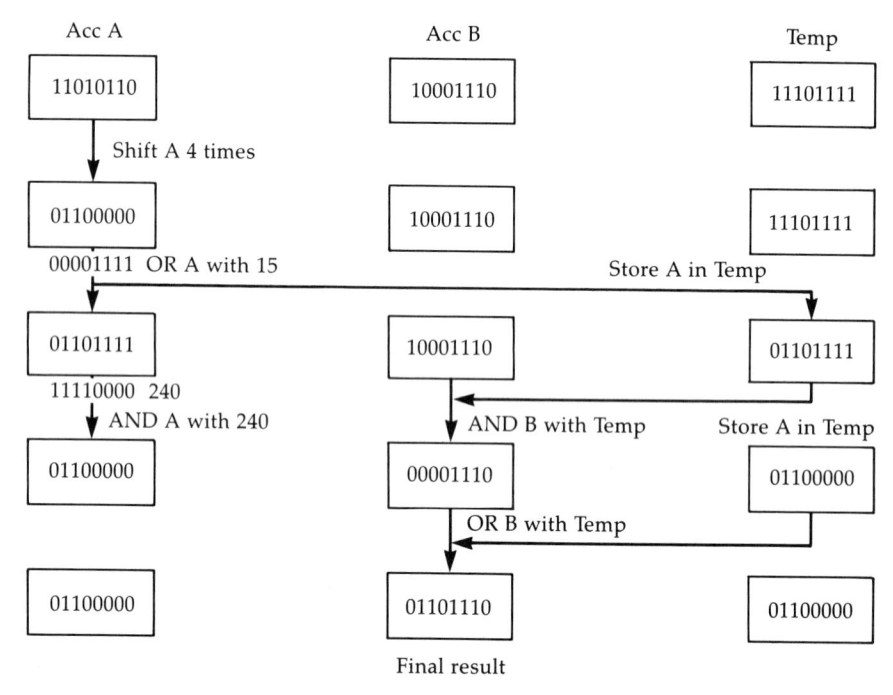

Acc A	Acc B	Temp
11010110	10001110	11101111

Shift A 4 times

| 01100000 | 10001110 | 11101111 |

00001111 OR A with 15   Store A in Temp

| 01101111 | 10001110 | 01101111 |

11110000 240
AND A with 240   AND B with Temp   Store A in Temp

| 01100000 | 00001110 | 01100000 |

OR B with Temp

| 01100000 | 01101110 | 01100000 |

Final result

Figure 13.9 Example run of 6800 bit insert routine

An example run of the above code is shown in Figure 13.9. In this case the 6800 required ten instructions to do what the VAX can do with one.

The M68000

The next step in the Motorola family of microprocessors is the 68000 chip, which has a 16-bit external bus and 32-bit internal registers. It is manufactured on a 64-pin chip that contains 68K transistors. Internally, it has 16 32-bit general-purpose registers, half of which are data registers (D0–D7) and half of which are address registers (A0–A7). There are actually two A7 registers (A7 and A7'), which are used as stack pointers. Both the address and data registers may be used for address or data manipulations. The basic architecture is shown in Figure 13.10. Although the 68000, like the VAX 11/780, has 16 32-bit registers, it still lacks the power of a VAX 11/780 because it has only 16-bit internal data and address buses and a 16-bit external data bus. As a result, it takes two clock pulses (or more) to transfer 32-bits of register data to the outside world. Note that the 68000 does have a 23-bit external address bus, which provides an addressable memory space of 2^{23} words (more than 8 million 16-bit words or 16 million bytes). The internal architecture is certainly more complicated than that of the 6800, so it is easier for a 68000 programmer to work with a simplified architecture in the form of the programming model shown in Figure 13.11.

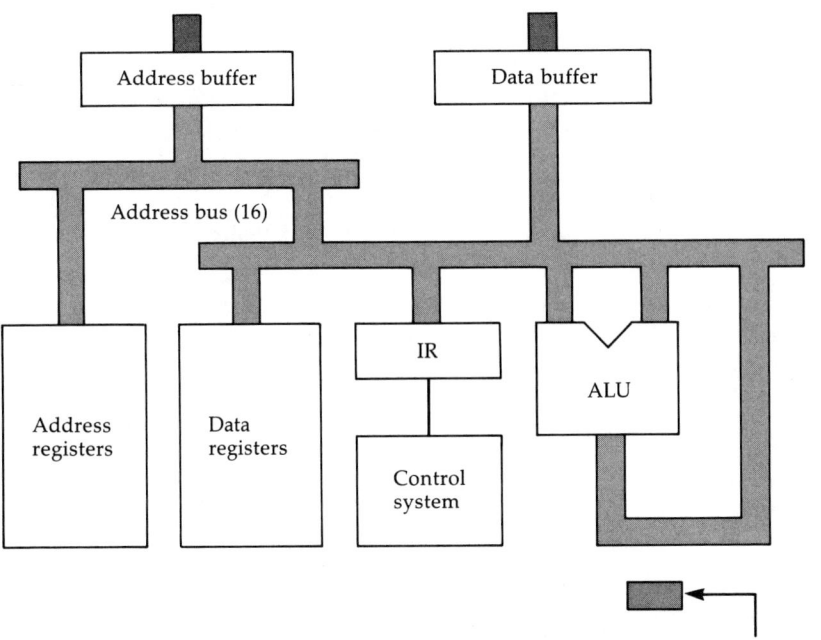

Figure 13.10 68000 architecture

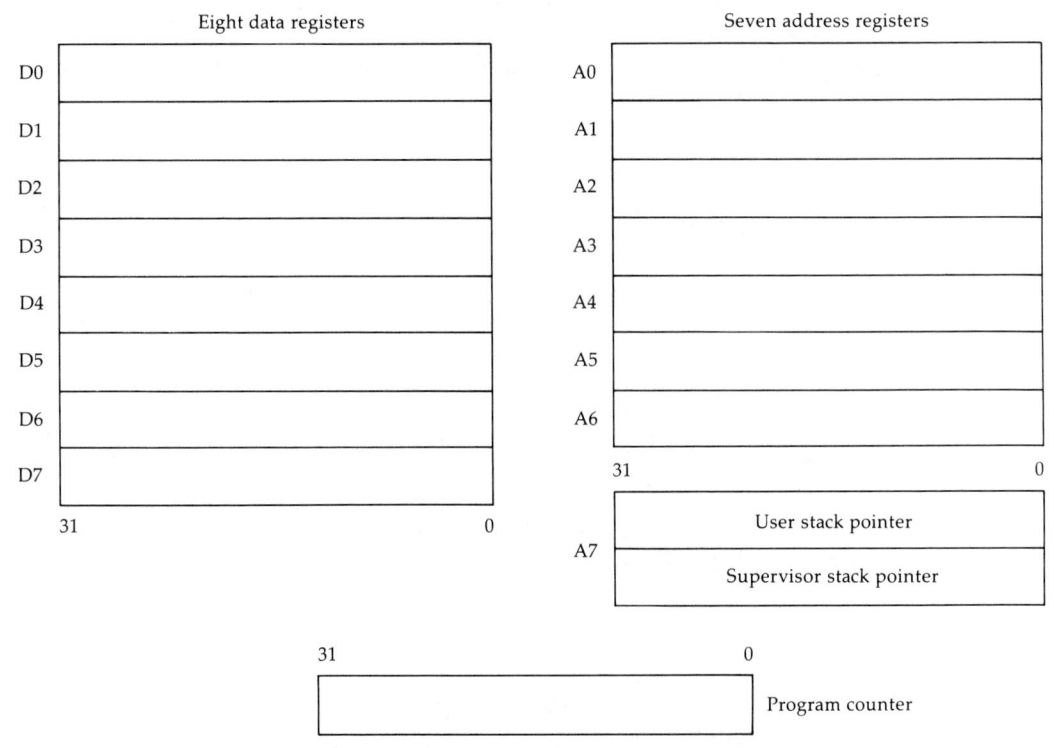

Figure 13.11 68000 programming model

The 68000 has two major operating modes. The user mode is the standard operating mode for running user programs. It uses A7 as the stack pointer. The supervisor mode is intended for running operating system routines. It uses A7' as the stack pointer. It has access to certain privileged instructions, such as the STOP command, which cannot be executed in the user mode.

The 68000 has a rich addressing mode structure, with 14 different methods of addressing data. Seven of these are summarized in the following list.

Mode	Action
Data register direct	Data is in the specified data register.
Address register direct	Data is in the specified address register.
Absolute short	Data is in the next instruction word.
Absolute long	Data is in the next two words.
Relative with offset	Data is located by the PC + offset.
Relative with index and offset	Data is at PC + index + offset.

As on the VAX, most 68000 instructions can use all the addressing modes, so the 68000 can get by with fewer general instructions than the 6800. In fact the 68000 has only 56 basic instructions. We will examine a few of them in this section.

One major group of 68000 operations is the set of data transfer instructions. These include MOVE, MOVEM (MOVE Multiple), EXG (EXchanGe), SWAP, and CLR (CleaR). For example, MOVE can be combined with the addressing modes to create eight different move operations. A simple register-to-register transfer such as MOVE D0,D1 will move the contents of data register D0 to data register D1. The move multiple instruction (MOVEM) allows for easy transfer of data between memory and a group of registers. The format of this instruction is

```
MOVEM   Reg-list, A
```

where Reg-list is a 16-bit word that contains 1 bit for each of the 16 data and address registers, much like a register mask on the VAX, and A is an effective base address in memory. For example, to save the contents of data registers 2, 4, and 6 and address registers 5 and 7 at the five memory locations beginning at 0078, the instruction would be

```
MOVEM   D2/D4/D6/A5/A7, $0078
```

This instruction could also be used to initialize a set of registers to values stored in consecutive memory locations using the following format:

```
MOVEM   A, Reg-list
```

A simple transfer of the data in one register to another can be done using the move instruction, as already mentioned, or a joint register-to-register transfer can also be accomplished using the exchange (EXG) instruction following the format

```
EXG   Ri,Rj
```

For example, EXG D3, A4 will move the data in address register A4 to data register D3 while also moving the current contents of D3 into A4. The exchange and swap instructions are easily confused. The swap instruction does not swap the data in two registers; instead it works on a single 32-bit register to swap the high-order 16-bits with the low-order 16-bits. For example, the instruction SWAP A2 will move bits 16–31 into positions 0–15 while also moving bits 0–15 into positions 16–31 to address register A2.

The 68000 has a complete set of arithmetic instructions, including addition, subtraction, multiplication, and division, as well as the logical operations AND, OR, NOT, and XOR. One thing missing from the 68000 instruction set is the standard increment instruction. In its place Motorola has provided an add quick instruction (ADDQ) that will add only the integers 1–8 to a source data item. Motorola has also provided a special decrement feature in the subtract quick (SUBQ) instruction.

It is easy to program loops on the 68000, which offers a full complement of jump and branch instructions. You can implement unconditional branches using the standard jump (JMP) instruction combined with an effective address. For example, JMP (A1) will load the contents of address register A1 into the PC, causing a branch to that address. Similar to the jump instruction is the branch always instruction (BRA), which initiates an unconditional branch. The difference between the jump and branch always instructions is the method of generating the jump address. For branch always, the branch address is given as an offset from the current position of the PC rather than a direct location as in the jump instruction. The 68000 also has 14 conditional branch instructions.

A special loop control instruction on the 68000 allows the system to specify several operations in a single instruction. This is the test condition, decrement, and branch (DBcc) instruction

```
DBcc   Dn, displacement
```

where cc specifies 1 of the 14 test conditions (that is, EQ = if equal, NE = if not equal, MI = if plus, GT = if greater than, and so on). In addition, 2 other test conditions may be used with the DB mnemonic: T for always true and F for always false. Dn specifies the data register that is used to maintain the loop count, and address is the branch location. This instruction operates as follows:

1. The test condition is evaluated; if it is true, the system continues on to the next instruction.
2. If the condition is false, the identified register is decremented by 1.
   a. If the register now contains a −1, then move on to the next instruction.
   b. If the register does not contain a −1, then branch to the location given by "address."

Several of the instructions mentioned above are included in the following example 68000 program. Given a set of ten numbers stored in consecutive memory locations, we would like to calculate their average.

```
        CLR   D0          ; D0 will contain the average
        LEA   List, A0    ; A0 will point to the list of numbers
        MOVE  #9, D1      ; D1 contains the count
Lp:     MOVE  (A0)+, D2   ; Move the next number into D2
        ADD   D2, D0      ; Find the current sum
        DBF   D1, Lp      ; Branch to LP if necessary
        DIVS  #10, D0     ; Divide by 10 to find the average
```

The first line contains a simple clear instruction to initialize the register that will contain the value Average. The second line is a load effective address (LEA) instruction, which in this case loads the address of the data LIST into address register A0. The third line moves the immediate value 9 into data register D1, which serves as the count register for the program. Notice the autoincrement indirect register addressing mode (A0)+ in line 4, which operates just as on the VAX. The data pointed to by address register A0 is moved into data register D2, and A0 is incremented to point at the next number in the data list. In line 5, the new data item in data register D2 is added to the current sum in data register D0, and the updated sum is saved in data register D0. Line 6 decrements the count register D1 and branches to location LP as long as D1 is greater than −1. Note that for this instruction the test condition is always false (F) because only the status of the count register is used to make the branch decision. The final line is executed after ten loops and calls for a signed divide by 10 operation, saving the result in data register D0.

13.4 The Intel Family

In this section we will examine the structure of the basic Intel microprocessors, the classic 8080 and the 8086. Both machines are quite similar to the microprocessors we have already studied, but they also display some distinct features that illustrate alternative approaches to the design and operation of microprocessor systems.

The 8080

The 8080 is an 8-bit microprocessor first introduced in December 1973. It is a powerful microprocessor, as evidenced by the fact that it is still being used in new system designs. The 8080 architecture has influenced many of the microprocessors designed and marketed since 1973.

The basic architecture of this machine is shown in Figure 13.12. As shown in the figure, this machine has two external bus connections; one to a 16-bit address bus and the other to an 8-bit data bus. However, it has only an 8-bit internal data bus. It has more registers than the 6800, including an 8-bit accumulator and six 8-bit general-purpose registers labeled B, C, D, E, H, and L. The six registers can form 16-bit pairs (BC, DE, and HL) to hold 16-bit addresses. It also has two 8-bit internal registers, W and Z, which are temporary storage registers used only by the CPU. A programmer cannot directly access registers W and Z. The 8080 also has a 16-bit program counter and a 16-bit stack pointer. The decimal adjust circuit allows the user to adjust the contents of the 8-bit accumulator to form a 4-bit binary-coded decimal (BCD).

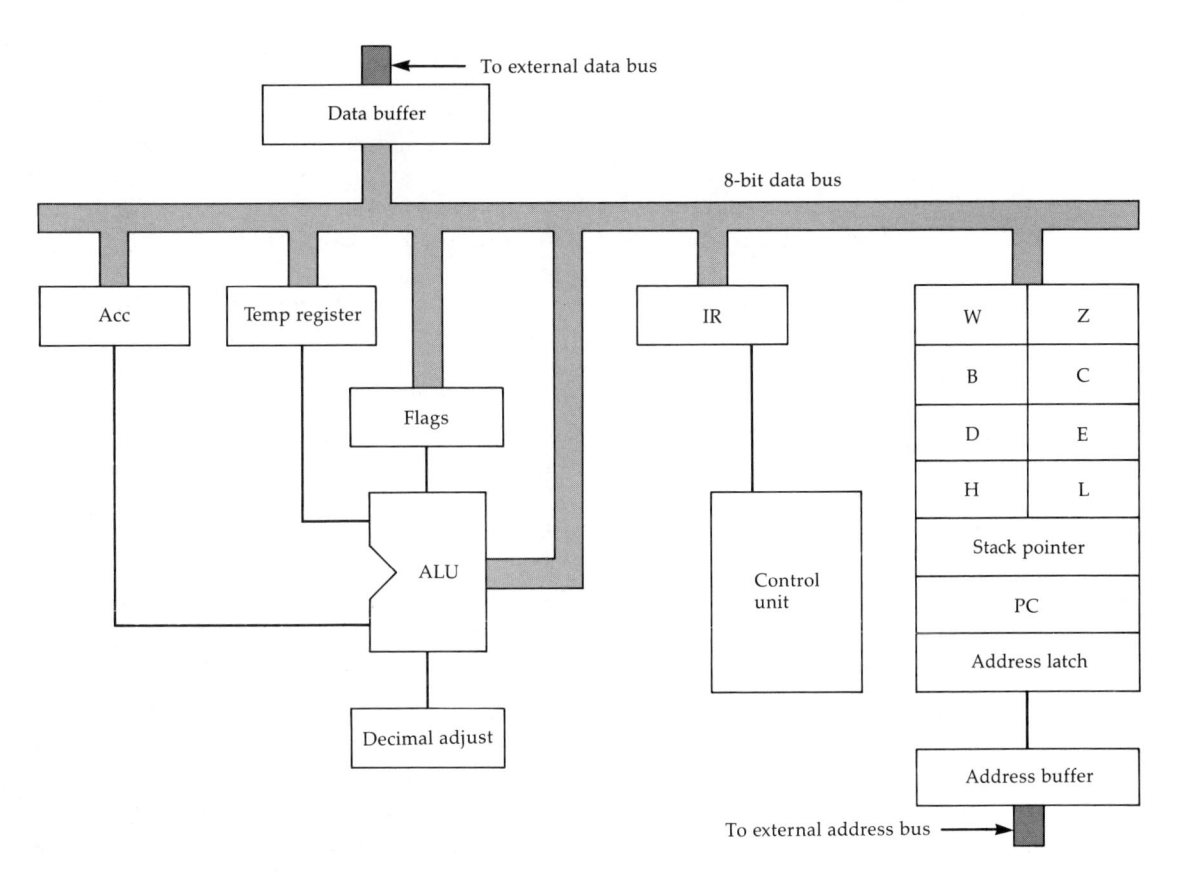

Figure 13.12 8080 architecture

The 8080 has a rich instruction set, with 74 basic instructions that, when combined with the addressing modes, result in 245 possible operations. The addressing modes include the following:

1. Direct (or absolute) addressing: the address is given in the two bytes following the opcode byte.
2. Register addressing: the data is contained in the identified register.
3. Register indirect addressing: a pair of 8-bit registers contains the address of the data.
4. Immediate addressing: the data is in the byte or two bytes that follow the opcode.

Some instructions use implied addressing; that is, the register used is implied by the instruction. One difficulty with the 8080 instruction set is that relatively few instructions allow direct addressing. In many cases it is necessary to load the data's address into a register and then use register indirect addressing. Branch instructions use absolute addresses instead of relative addresses. As a result, conditional branches require three bytes (one for the opcode and two for a 16-bit address) as compared to only two bytes on the VAX. The advantage for the 8080 is that conditional branches can jump to any location in memory.

Some of the 8080 instructions are shown in Table 13.2. They include a full set of data transfer, ALU, branching, and I/O instructions. Use of these instructions is illustrated in an example problem. We would like to add two 16-bit numbers stored in memory locations 0500–0503 and save the 16-bit results in the two memory locations starting at 0504 (all addresses are in hex). This can be done with the following code:

```
LXI   D, 0504     ; Load address for answer into DE
LXI   B, 0500     ; Load address of data into BC
LXI   H, 0502     ; Load address of data into HL
ANA   A           ; Clear carry
LDAX  B           ; Load data into accumulator
ADC   M           ; Add data pointed to by HL to acc
STAX  D           ; Save current result
INX   D           ; Increment result pointer in DE
INX   B           ; Increment data pointer in BC
INX   H           ; Increment data pointer in HL
LDAX  B           ; Load second part of data into acc
ADC   M           ; Add data with carry to acc
STAX  D           ; Save second part of answer
```

The LXI instruction will load the identified register pair with the data in the two bytes that follow the instruction opcode. In the first instruction it loads the 16 bits of address information (0504) into the register pair D-E. The ANA instruction will AND register A with itself and clear the carry bit; of course, in this case the only action the instruction is

Table 13.2 8080 Instruction Set

		\multicolumn{10}{c}{Address Mode}	
		Immed		Absol		Reg		Reg Ind		Implied		
Operation	Mnemonic	B	T	B	T	B	T	B	T	B	T	Operation
Add	ADD					1	4	1	7			$A \leftarrow (A) + (src)$
Add immediate	ADI	2	7									$A \leftarrow (A) + (byte)$
Add with carry	ADC					1	4	1	7			$A \leftarrow (A) + (src) + (C)$
Add immediate with carry	ACI	2	7									$A \leftarrow (A) + (src) + (byte)$
Add reg pair to H, L	DAD					1	10					$HL \leftarrow (HL) + (RP)$
AND	ANA					1	4	1	7			$A \leftarrow (A) \; (src)$
AND immediate	ANI	2	7									$A \leftarrow (A) \; (byte)$
Compare	CMP					1	4	1	7			$(A) - (src)$
Compare immediate	CPI	2	7									$(A) - (byte)$
Complement acc	CMA									1	4	$A \leftarrow (\overline{A})$
Complement carry	CMC									1	4	$C \leftarrow (\overline{C})$
Decrement	DCR					1	5	1	10			$src \leftarrow (src) - 1$
Decrement reg pair	DCX					1	5					$RP \leftarrow (RP) - 1$
Decimal adjust	DAA									1	4	
Disable interrupts	DI									1	4	
Exclusive-OR	XRA					1	4	1	7			$A \leftarrow (A) \; (src)$
Exclusive-OR immediate	XRI	2	7									$A \leftarrow (A) \; (byte)$
Exchange HL with DE	XCHG					1	4					
Exchange stack with HL	XTHL							1	18			
Enable interrupts	EI							1	4			
Halt	HLT							1	7			
Increment	INR					1	5	1	10			$src \leftarrow (src) + 1$
Increment reg pair	INX					1	5					$RP \leftarrow (RP) + 1$

(continued)

Table 13.2 (continued)

		\multicolumn{10}{c}{Address Mode}	
		Immed		Absol		Reg		Reg Ind		Implied		
Operation	Mnemonic	B	T	B	T	B	T	B	T	B	T	Operation
Input	IN			2	10							
Load RP immediate	LXI	3	10									RP ← (byte, byte)
Load acc direct	LDA			3	13							R ← ((byte, byte))
Load HL direct	LHLD			3	16							
Load acc indirect	LDRX							1	7			A ← ((RP))
Move	MOV					1	5	1	7			dst ← (src)
Move immediate	MVI					2	7	2	10			dst ← (byte)
Move HL to SP	SPHL					1	5					SP ← (HL)
No operation	NOP									1	4	
OR	ORA					1	4	1	7			A ← (A) (src)
OR immediate	ORI	2	7									A ← (A) (byte)
Output	OUT			2	10							
Push RP onto stack	PUSH					1	11					
Push PSW onto stack	PUSHPSW									1	11	
Pop reg pair	POP					1	10					
Pop PSW	POPPSW									1	10	
Rotate left	RLC									1	4	
Rotate right	RRC									1	4	
Rotate left carry	RAL									1	4	
Rotate right carry	RAR									1	4	
Set carry	STC									1	4	C ← 1
Store acc direct	STA			3	13							(byte, byte) ← (A)
Store acc indirect	STAX									1	7	(RP) ← (A)
Subtract	SUB					1	4	1	7			A ← (A) − (src)
Subtract immediate	SUI	2	7									A ← (A) − (byte)

Table 13.2 (continued)

		Address Mode										
		Immed		Absol		Reg		Reg Ind		Implied		
Operation	Mnemonic	B	T	B	T	B	T	B	T	B	T	Operation
Subtract with borrow	SBB					1	4	1	7			A ← (A) − (src) − (C)
Subtract with borrow immediate	SBI	2	7									A ← (A) − (byte) − (C)

Branch Instructions

		Address Mode				
		Absol		Implied		
Operation	Mnemonic	B	T	B	T	Operation (test for)
Jump unconditionally	JMP	3	10			none
Jump on carry	JC	3	10			C = 1
Jump on carry clear	JNC	3	10			C = 0
Jump on zero	JZ	3	10			Z = 1
Jump on not zero	JNZ	3	10			Z = 0
Jump on positive	JP	3	10			S = 0
Jump on minus	JM	3	10			S = 1
Jump on even parity	JPE	3	10			P = 1
Jump on odd parity	JPO	3	10			P = 0
Call unconditionally	CALL	3	17			none
Call on carry	CC	3	17			C = 1
Call on carry clear	CNC	3	17			C = 0
Call on zero	CZ	3	17			Z = 1
Call on not zero	CNZ	3	17			Z = 0
Call on positive	CP	3	17			S = 0

(continued)

Chapter 13 Microprocessors

Table 13.2 (continued)

		\multicolumn{4}{c	}{Address Mode}	
		\multicolumn{2}{c	}{Immed}	\multicolumn{2}{c	}{Implied}	
Operation	**Mnemonic**	B	T	B	T	**Operation**
Call on minus	CM	3	17			S = 1
Call on even parity	CPE	3	17			P = 1
Call on odd parity	CPO	3	17			P = 0
Return unconditionally	RET			1	10	none
Return on carry	RC			1	11	C = 1
Return on carry clear	RNC			1	11	C = 0
Return on zero	RZ			1	11	Z = 1
Return on not zero	RNZ			1	11	Z = 0
Return on positive	RP			1	11	S = 0
Return on minus	RM			1	11	S = 1
Return on even parity	RPE			1	11	P = 1
Return on odd parity	RPO			1	11	P = 0

performing is the carry clear. The LDAX instruction will load the accumulator with the contents pointed to by the register pair B-C or D-E. ADC M will add the contents of the accumulator, the carry bit, and the memory location pointed to by the H-L pair, saving the result in the accumulator. STAX D will store the accumulator in the memory location pointed to by the 16-bits in the register pair D-E. Finally, INX will increment the given register pair. Notice that even though the 8080 is an 8-bit machine, a number of instructions allow 16-bit operations on identified register pairs. This is certainly one reason that this machine has lasted as long as it has in the marketplace.

The 8086

The 8086, announced by Intel in 1978, was one of the first 16-bit microprocessors. It is on a single VLSI chip consisting of approximately 29,000 transistors. It is a true 16-bit machine, with both internal and external

13.4 The Intel Family

16-bit data buses. It also has a 20-bit address bus, allowing it to address 1M of main memory directly. Another member of the 8086 family is the 8088, which is very similar to the 8086 except that it has only an 8-bit external data bus. This chip is used in the IBM PC and IBM compatibles. The two chips share the same machine language and are identical to the assembly language programmer. In fact, the only real difference is the 8088's external bus size.

The basic internal architecture of the 8086 is shown in Figure 13.13, which illustrates several unique features of the microprocessor. For example, it is divided into two processing units, the bus interface unit (BIU) and the execution unit (EU). The BIU fetches instructions and handles I/O, while the EU executes instructions. These two units operate independently, so the instruction fetch and execution cycles occur in parallel, resulting in a net gain in processing speed. This is called a pipeline system, and we will discuss architectures that implement parallel operations such as this on a larger scale in Chapter 14. To ensure that the instructions fetched by the BIU are not lost before the EU can execute them, the 8086 has an instruction prefetch queue. The queue will save up to six bytes of instruction information (the 8088 has only four bytes in its instruction queue). The EU looks for the next instruction in the queue rather than in main memory. If there are at least two empty bytes

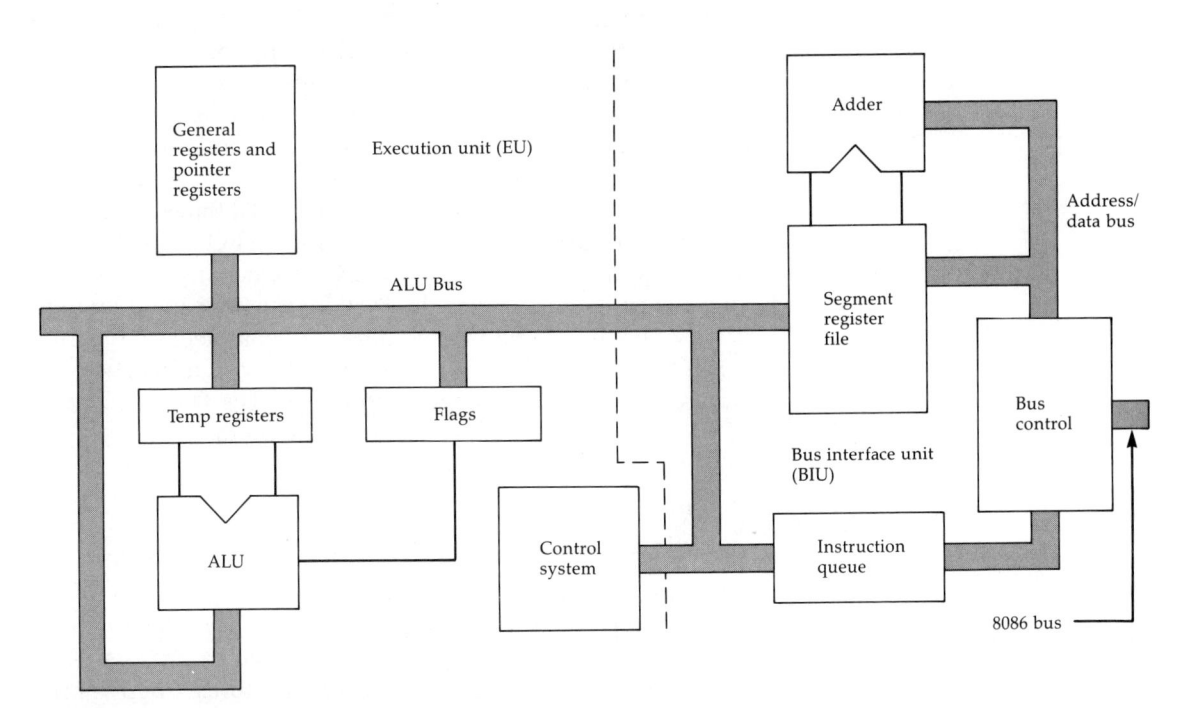

Figure 13.13 Basic 8086 architecture

in the queue and memory is idle, the BIU will fetch another instruction to put into the queue. As a result, the queue (sometimes called an instruction look-ahead queue) keeps the EU constantly supplied with instructions. The EU rarely has to wait for a fetch cycle before starting the next instruction except after a branch instruction, when the queue must be emptied and new instructions fetched.

The EU contains eight 16-bit registers. Four of them are data registers (A–D) that can also be used as eight 8-bit registers—a high (H) and low (L) part of A–D. Although these registers can be used as general-purpose registers, each has some special applications. For example, A serves as an accumulator and C is used as a counter in some operations. The other four are pointer and index registers. The EU also contains the 16-bit process status word (PSW).

The BIU contains four 16-bit registers that serve as segment registers. The 8086 addresses memory in 64K pages or segments, any four of which can be active at any one time. The base addresses of each active segment are contained in the BIU segment registers. This allows the 8086 to use 16-bit relative addresses in the code even though the machine uses 20-bit physical addresses. The contents of the 16-bit segment register are effectively multiplied by 16 (a 4-bit shift) and added to the 16-bit relative address used on the code to determine the actual 20-bit address. In addition to allowing shorter addresses within the code, this arrangement also makes it easy to handle code relocation. To relocate code, we need only change the segment register contents. The BIU also contains the 16-bit instruction pointer (IP), which we usually call the program counter. The programming model of the 8086 is shown in Figure 13.14.

Intel has developed a complete set of support chips for the 8086. One chip, the 8087, is a numeric processor. It executes special instructions involving complicated mathematical operations, such as square roots, trig functions, and floating-point arithmetic, up to 100 times faster than the 8086. Another support chip, the 8089, is a special I/O processor with two DMA channels that can handle all the I/O instructions.

The 8086 instruction set includes the 8080 instructions in addition to several new classes of instructions, including (1) a complete set of string manipulation instructions, (2) multiplication and division instructions, and (3) software-generated interrupt instructions. The 8086 also has a richer set of addressing modes than that available on the 8080.

Summary

In this chapter we introduced the basic features of several microprocessors. You should have noted the strong similarity between the architecture of the VAX series and those of the selected microprocessors. General-purpose machines tend to have similar architectures when viewed from the system level. But you should also have noted the differences

13.4 The Intel Family

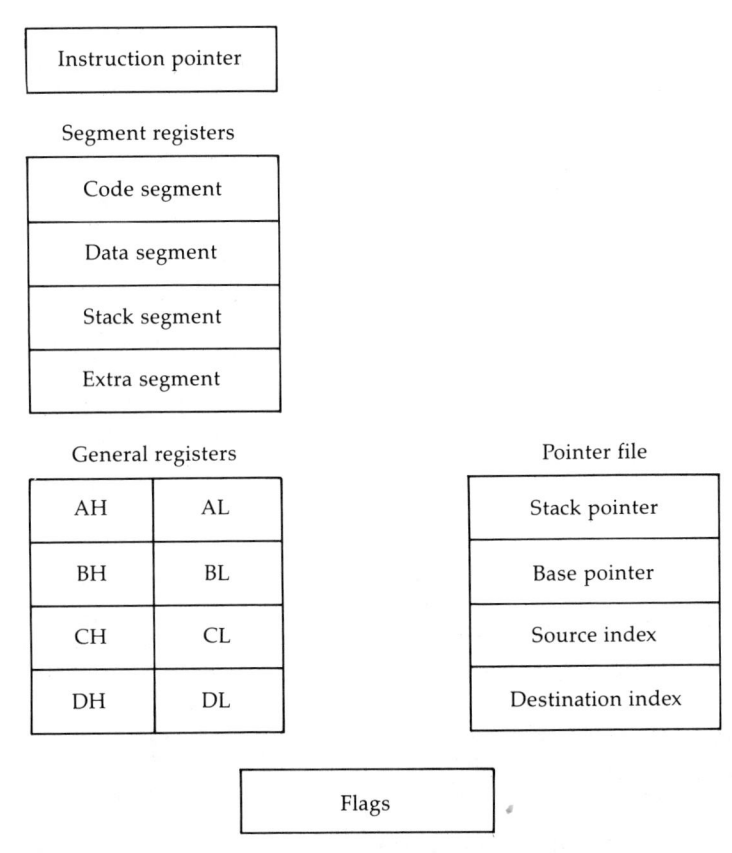

Figure 13.14 Programming model of the 8086

between the machines. They have different register sets, different bus sizes, different special-purpose registers, and different instruction sets. These all reflect different design philosophies and different performance requirements.

Exercises

For the following set of exercises, write an assembly language code segment for both the 6800 and the 8080.

1. Write an assembly language program that will find the average of ten 8-bit numbers stored in sequential memory locations where the location of the first number is 0020 (hex).
   a. Using a 6800, how many bytes does the program require? How fast will it run, assuming a 1-MHz clock?
   b. Using an 8080, how many bytes does the program require? How fast will it run, assuming a 2-MHz clock?

2. Write an assembly language program that will subtract the 16-bit number at location 0020 hex from the number at 0022 hex and save the result at location 0024 hex.
   a. Using a 6800, how many such subtractions could the 6800 do in a second? Note: 6800 machines typically store the high-order byte of a 16-bit number first; this is the reverse of the VAX's order.
   b. Using an 8080, how many such subtractions could the 8080 do in a second? Note: 8080 machines typically store the low-order byte first, like the VAX.
3. Write an assembly language program that will implement the Booth algorithm on signed 8-bit numbers where the data is stored at locations 20 and 42 hex. Store the answer starting at location 0024 hex.
   a. Using a 6800, how many such multiplications could the 6800 do in a second?
   b. Using an 8080, how many such multiplications could the 8080 do in a second?
4. Write an assembly language program that will search a 25-byte character string, starting at memory location 0020 hex, to find the character string "and." Stop when you get to the end of the string or the word "and," whichever comes first. Store the address of the "a" in "and" at location 200 if the word is found; store a 0 at location 200 if the word is not found.
   a. Use a 6800.
   b. Use an 8080.
5. Write an assembly language program that will encode data by shifting it by 3 characters. That is, A becomes D, B becomes E, . . . , W becomes Z, X becomes A, Y becomes B, and Z becomes C. Assume that the data is 20 characters long and starts at location 0020 hex. Store the encoded data beginning at location 0100 hex.
   a. Use a 6800.
   b. Use an 8080.
6. Count the number of times the letter "A" appears in an 80-hex-byte string starting at location 21A. Store the result in location 300.
   a. Use a 6800.
   b. Use an 8080.
7. Copy 30 hex bytes beginning at location 2A0 to the location beginning at 42A.
   a. Use a 6800.
   b. Use an 8080.
8. Implement the VAX instructions BISB #8,R3 on the 6800 where the data you want to operate on is in acc A.
9. How long will the example code for Figure 13.9 take to run assuming a 1-MHz clock? How many bytes will it take up in main memory?

Compare its size to the number of bytes required for the equivalent instruction on the VAX.

10. Write 6800 code that will move bits 0 and 2 in acc B to positions 5 and 7 in acc A without changing the other bits in A.

11. What are the advantages of the instruction prefetch queue on the 8086?

12. Observe that on the 6800 and the 8080, the addressing mode is specified as part of the opcode instead of part of the operand, as on the VAX. What are the advantages and disadvantages of this method? Why did the designers of these chips include the addressing mode in the opcode? Why did the VAX designers make the addressing mode part of the operands?

13. Consider the instruction set of the specified microprocessor. What type of instructions are missing? Are there any unnecessary instructions?

    a. On the 6800.
    b. On the 8080.

14. The action of the 8080 CALL instruction is

    $(SP) \leftarrow (PC)$

    $PC \leftarrow$ address from instruction

    $SP \leftarrow (SP) - 2$

    Which VAX instruction(s) correspond to this instruction? What are the implications of this instruction to assembly language programmers? In which direction does the 8080 stack grow?

15. The action of the 6800 BSR instruction is

    $(SP) \leftarrow (PC)$

    $SP \leftarrow SP - 2$

    $PC \leftarrow PC + \text{displacement}$

    Repeat Exercise 14 considering the 6800 BSR instruction.

CHAPTER CONTENTS

14.1 ARCHITECTURE CLASSIFICATION

14.2 PIPELINE STRUCTURES
   Pipeline Analysis
   The TI ASC

14.3 ARRAY STRUCTURES
   Complete Interconnection Network
   Permutation Networks

14.4 MULTIPROCESSORS

14.5 THE CRAY-1

   SUMMARY

   EXERCISES

CHAPTER 14

Large System Architecture

Up to this point we have considered the most common approach to computer structure—a single CPU connected to memory and I/O along some buslike path. Called von Neumann architecture, it has served as the major approach to computer structure since the 1940s and is used in most microcomputer, minicomputer, and mainframe systems. Other approaches to computer structure exist and are primarily used in what are called "supercomputers." These alternatives to von Neumann architecture have proven very useful and are now finding their way into new systems that we would not class as supercomputers. These approaches all involve some form of multiprocessor structure (that is, they have more than one CPU). We will explore several of the more common multiprocessor architectures in this chapter.

The development of computer architecture over the years has been characterized by major changes that represent new generations of machines. The first-generation machines, constructed prior to 1958, used vacuum tubes and relays. They include such machines as the IBM 701, which offered a mere 2K of main memory. To program some of these machines, the user actually had to rewire them. The second generation of machines, which appeared during 1958–1963, represented the first use of the transistor and high-level languages such as FORTRAN. Generation three, 1964–1975, saw the first use of integrated circuits and virtual memory. During this generation, some of the first alternatives to von Neumann architecture were designed, including the Texas Instruments Advanced Scientific Computer (TI ASC) and the Illiac IV. The present generation started around 1972. It is the generation of the supercomputer, which relies on multiprocessing and pipeline structures. The next generation is predicted to be the generation of artificial intelligence (AI), with machines capable of performing in the 100-gigaflop range (1 gigaflop is 10^9 floating-point operations per second).

14.1 Architecture Classification

Before we examine the specific details of the alternative architectures, we should classify them. One architectural classification scheme that has been widely used was suggested by Flynn* in 1972. It is based on the concept of a **stream**, which is a sequence of instructions or data that is executed or operated on by a processor. Given a system with both an instruction stream and a data stream, there are four possible interactions between them. Each interaction defines a new architecture type.

1. **Single instruction–single data (SISD).** This class includes most conventional computers, including the VAX 11/780 series. Each stream of instructions interacts with only one data stream, as shown in Figure 14.1.
2. **Single instruction–multiple data (SIMD).** This class consists of computers in which a single instruction is executed on several different data items in parallel, as shown in Figure 14.2. Note that such machines have more than one CPU. We will introduce array processors, which are primary examples of SIMD machines, in the next section.
3. **Multiple instruction–single data (MISD).** This class represents computers in which the same data item is operated on by a set of different instructions. The basic structure of such machines is shown in Figure 14.3. Sometimes these are called pipeline architectures,

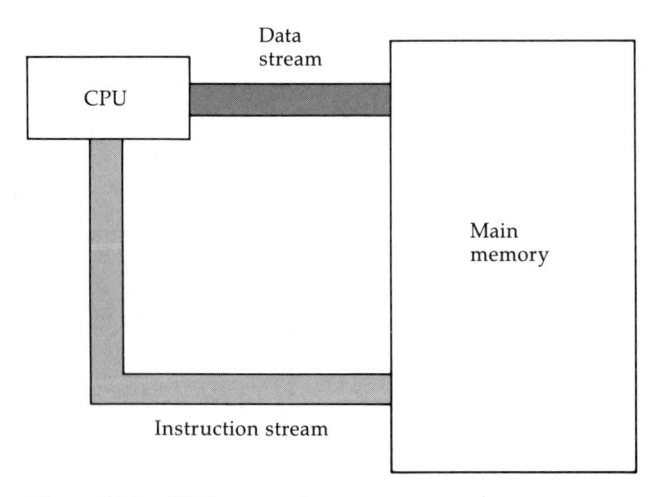

Figure 14.1 SISD computer

---

*M. J. Flynn, "Some Computer Organizations and Their Effectiveness," *IEEE Transaction on Computers,* September 1972: pp. 948–960.

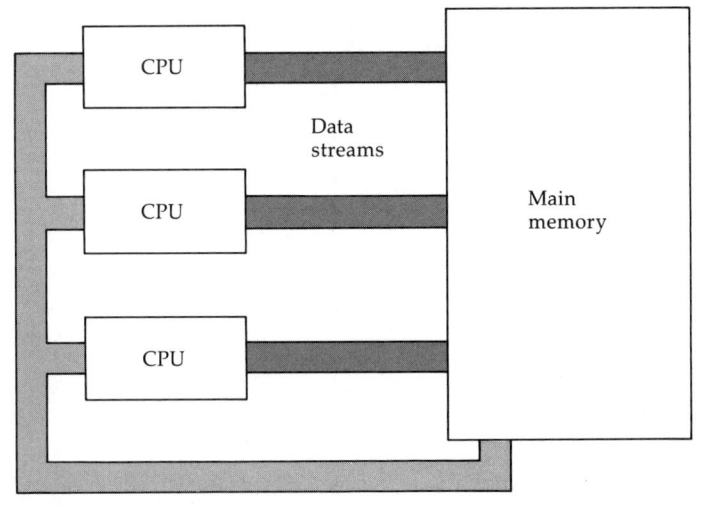

14.1 Architecture Classification 475

Figure 14.2 SIMD computer

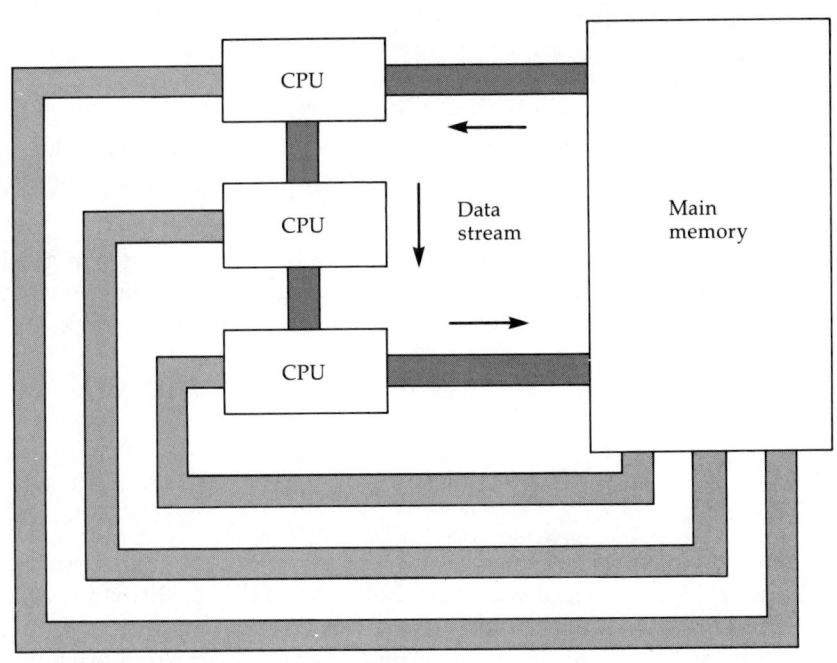

Figure 14.3 MISD computer

Figure 14.4 MIMD computer

although there is some controversy over the classification of pipeline structures in the MISD category.

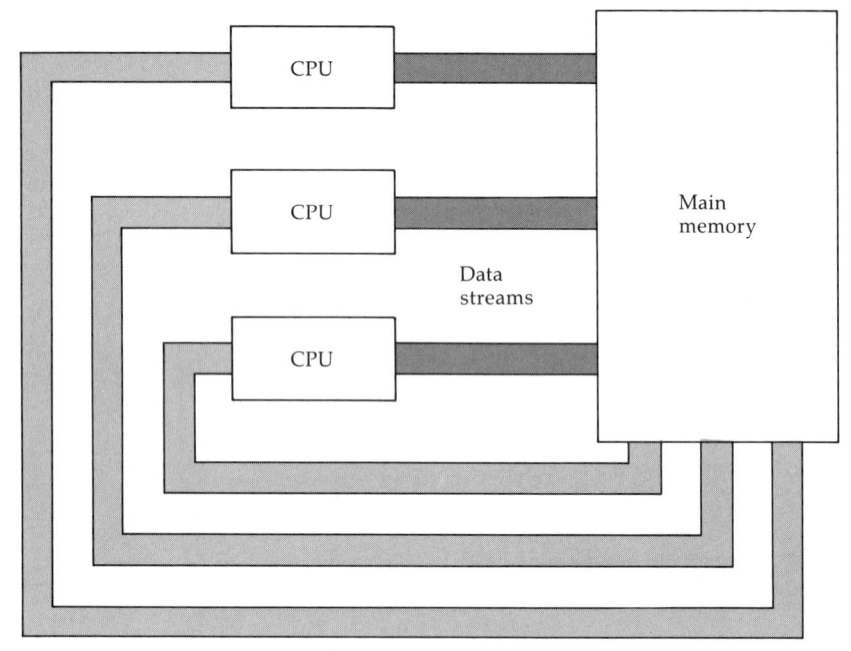

4. **Multiple instruction–multiple data (MIMD).** This class represents the set of multiprocessors as shown in the general structure of Figure 14.4.

In this text we have covered the structure of SISD machines in great detail. In the remaining sections of this chapter we will explore design issues associated with the other three classes of machine architecture.

14.2 Pipeline Structures

Pipelining is the technique of decomposing a repeated sequential process into subprocesses, each of which can be executed efficiently on a special dedicated module. Actually, pipelining is a simpler concept than this definition may indicate. Think of a pipeline as an industrial assembly line where each dedicated module is a separate station that performs some specialized task, as illustrated in Figure 14.5. Data enters into stage

14.2 Pipeline Structures

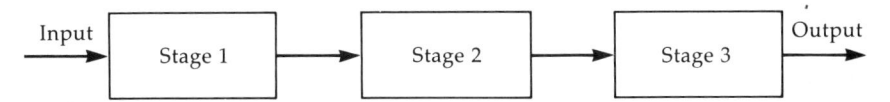

Figure 14.5 Pipeline structure

1. When this stage has completed its task, it passes the results on to stage 2. At this point stage 1 is available for a new data set. The process continues with each stage passing its results on to the next one and accepting a new set of data from the previous stage. Because the operations performed at each stage represent only a part of the total problem, each stage requires less time than a single stage executing the entire problem. Consequently, we can enter new data into the machine at a high rate of speed.

Consider the case of the basic instruction cycle in a computer. It can be broken up into four tasks: (1) instruction fetch, (2) instruction decode, (3) operand fetch, and (4) instruction execution. For simplicity, if we assume that each task can be accomplished in 1 time unit, it would take 4 time units to process each instruction and 16 time units to execute four instructions completely in a standard SISD machine. However, if the following four-stage instruction pipeline were used, four different stages could all be working at once. Consequently, it would take only 7 time units to execute four instructions, as shown in the operation diagram of Figure 14.6. The first instruction, (I1) starts in the instruction fetch (IF) stage at time 0. At time 1 the first instruction has been fetched, so it is sent on to stage 2 for an instruction decode (ID) operation, leaving stage 1 free to fetch instruction I2. So both the ID and IF stages are working during time 1. By time 7, the fourth instruction (I4) has left the instruction execution (IE) stage.

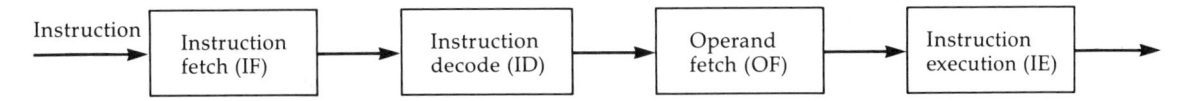

Pipeline Analysis

A pipeline system does not complete any single job faster than a non-pipeline system. After all, the job must still pass through each stage, and each stage must perform its task. Notice in Figure 14.6 that each instruction still took four time units to complete. However, a pipeline system reduces the amount of time a job must wait for a resource. In Figure 14.6 job 2 had to wait only one time unit before it could start, while it would have had to wait four time units (until instruction 1 was completed) in a nonpipeline system. In other words, a pipeline architecture will improve system throughput where throughput is defined as the number of jobs completed per unit time.

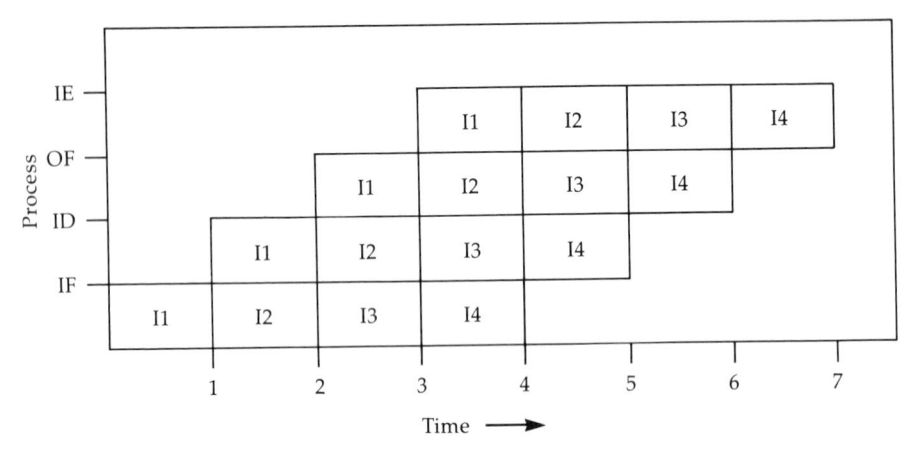

Figure 14.6 Pipeline operation diagram

For example, in a nonpipeline system say that four subprocesses must be completed for each job entering the system. If t_i is the time in seconds required by stage i to complete its processing task, the total time for one job to complete is

$$T = t_1 + t_2 + t_3 + t_4$$

In this case we can expect to see one job completed every T seconds. If the same system were implemented in a pipeline architecture, the time between job completions (when the pipeline is full) would be

$$T_p = \max\{t_1, t_2, t_3, t_4\}$$

T_p is sometimes called the clock period of the pipeline. Apply this analysis to the pipeline shown in Figure 14.7. The operation diagram for this pipeline is shown in Figure 14.8. Notice that the first job does not appear at the output until $t = 9$. However, at this point the pipeline becomes saturated (the pipeline is full). After $t = 9$, jobs appear at the output every four seconds, as shown in Figure 14.9, while for a standard system jobs would appear at the output every nine seconds. There are several other things that we can learn about this pipeline from Figure 14.8. Note that while processes 1 and 2 seem to be always busy as long as jobs are coming in, processes 3 and 4 seem to be unused most of the time. This is because process 2 is a bottleneck; it takes much longer to perform its task than any other process in the system. Process 3 must always wait

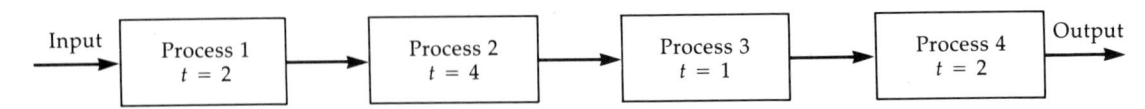

Figure 14.7 Example pipeline

14.2 Pipeline Structures

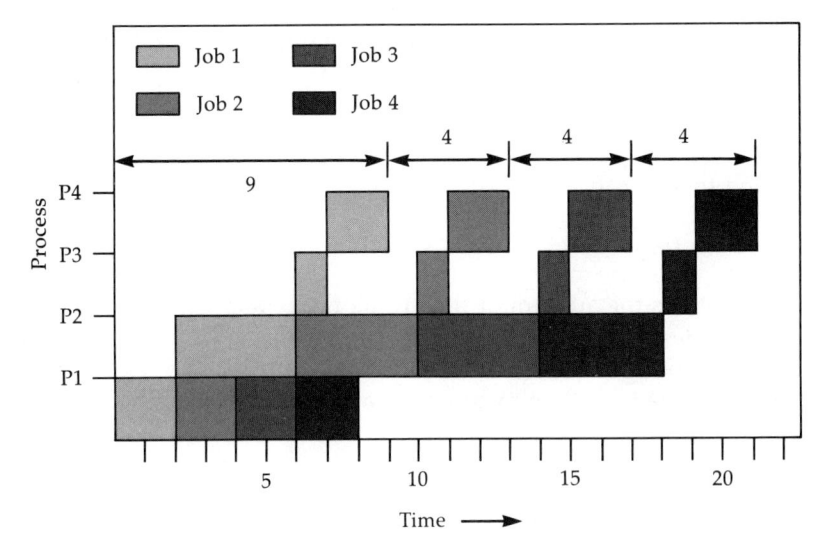

Figure 14.8 Example pipeline operation diagram

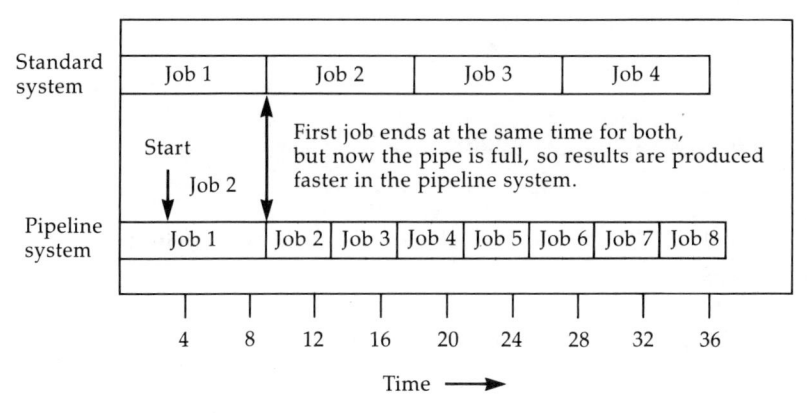

Figure 14.9 Pipeline versus standard architecture

for process 2 to complete its task. In fact, this process determines the time between outputs (in this case four time units).

Formally, throughput for a pipeline structure is defined as

Throughput = $1/T_p$

So, for a nonpipeline version of the above example, the throughput is $1/T$, or

Throughput = $1/9$ = .111 jobs/time unit

while for the pipeline version (after saturation), the throughput is

Throughput = $1/4$ = .25 jobs/time unit.

If the clock period of a pipeline is defined as time between job completions (T), that is, for a pipeline with k stages:

$$T_p = \max\{t_i\} \text{ for } i = 1, \ldots, k$$

then the pipeline can process n tasks in

$$T_k^{(n)} = k + (n-1)T_p$$

The first term is the amount of time to fill the pipeline and produce the output for the first job; the remaining $n - 1$ jobs appear at the output once every clock period. For the example, if four jobs are run through the pipeline, the total time to complete all four jobs would be

$$\begin{aligned}T_4^{(4)} &= 9 + (4-1)T_p \\ &= 9 + 3*4 \quad \text{(because one clock period for this pipeline is 4)} \\ &= 21\end{aligned}$$

This result is verified in Figure 14.8, where the fourth job leaves the pipeline at time $t = 21$. A nonpipeline structure required to complete the same n tasks would take

$$t_1^{(n)} = nT$$

which for the example would be

$$\begin{aligned}T_1^{(4)} &= 4*T \\ &= 4*9 \quad \text{(because one clock period for the nonpipeline is 9)} \\ &= 36\end{aligned}$$

The speedup ratio of a k-stage pipe is given by

$$S_k = T_1/T_k$$

All the terms still depend on n, the number of jobs. So the speedup of the example pipeline is

$$S_4 = 36/21 = 1.71$$

That is, the example pipeline will complete the four jobs 1.71 times faster than a similar nonpipeline architecture.

The efficiency of a pipeline is defined as the total amount of time the processors are busy divided by the total amount of time available for all the processors. For the example, there are four stages (or processors), each with 21 available time units, so the total time available to all the processors is 84 time units. The first processor is busy for 8 time units, the second for 16 time units, the third for only 4 time units, and the fourth for 8 time units. Overall the four processors are busy for 36 time units, so the efficiency of this pipeline over the four jobs is

36/84 = .43

In other words, the processors are idle more than half the time, as can be clearly seen in Figure 14.8.

The TI ASC

The Texas Instruments Advanced Scientific Computer (TI ASC) is one example of a pipeline architecture. This large pipeline system was designed in 1966, and the first unit was delivered in 1972. The basic structure is shown in Figure 14.10. The peripheral processor (PP) executes the operating system, while the central processor (CP) performs data analysis as a slave to the PP. All communication between the processors is through the central memory unit. The central processor has 48 registers, each with 32 bits, and has a pipeline unit such as the one shown in Figure 14.11. Each memory buffer unit (MBU) contains three buffers, each of which holds 32 bytes of data. The instruction-processing unit (IPU) is a four-stage instruction pipeline. The ALUs each contain an eight-stage pipeline, as shown in Figure 14.12. The pipeline can be configured differently for different operations. As a result of the pipeline structure, the TI ASC is a very fast machine. On one benchmark weather prediction program, an IBM 360/91 took 246 minutes to complete the calculations, while the TI ASC took only 30 minutes (we don't know if either one was accurate in predicting the weather, however).

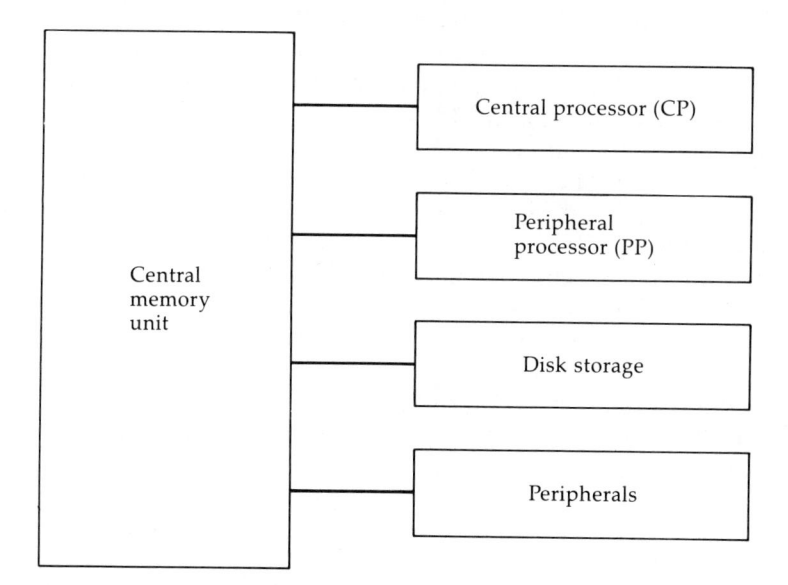

Figure 14.10 TI ASC Structure

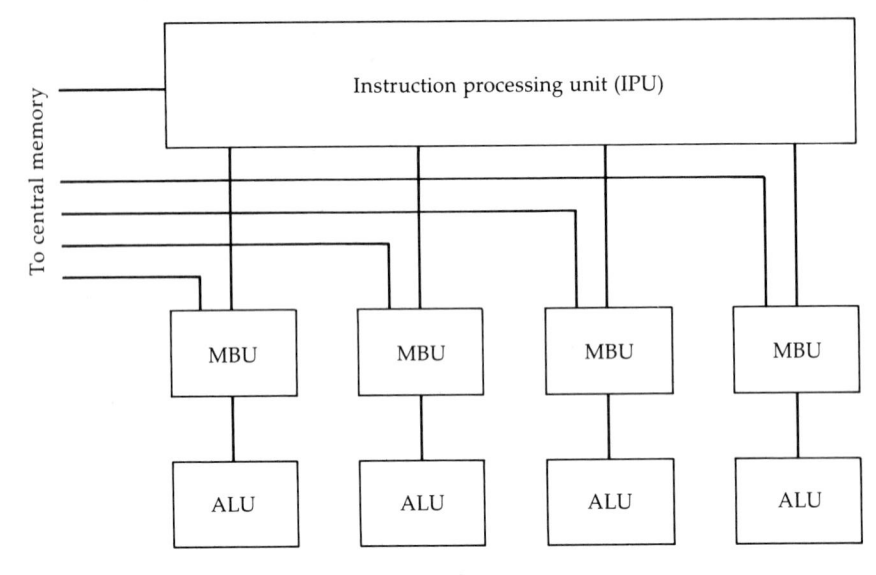

Figure 14.11 CP structure of the TI ASC

14.3 Array Structures

Array processors are SIMD machines used for solving large problems that typically involve vector operations such as air traffic control, signal processing, and pattern recognition. The general structure of such a machine is shown in Figure 14.13.

Such a structure can provide high throughput for problems that are solved with algorithms with a high degree of parallelism. For example, the sum of the column elements of an $N \times N$ matrix can be determined in N steps on an SIMD machine if each processor is assigned to one column. An SISD machine would require N^2 steps for the same calculation. The speedup occurs because each processor is doing its work in parallel. The characteristic of this structure is that each processor executes the same instruction at the same time on different data.

Because memory speed is slow compared to processor speed, rapid transfer of information from one processor to another is a significant problem. Thus the operation of the array structure is determined by the nature of the interconnection network that passes data between the processors. We will review several types of interconnection networks in this section.

Floating-point add configuration

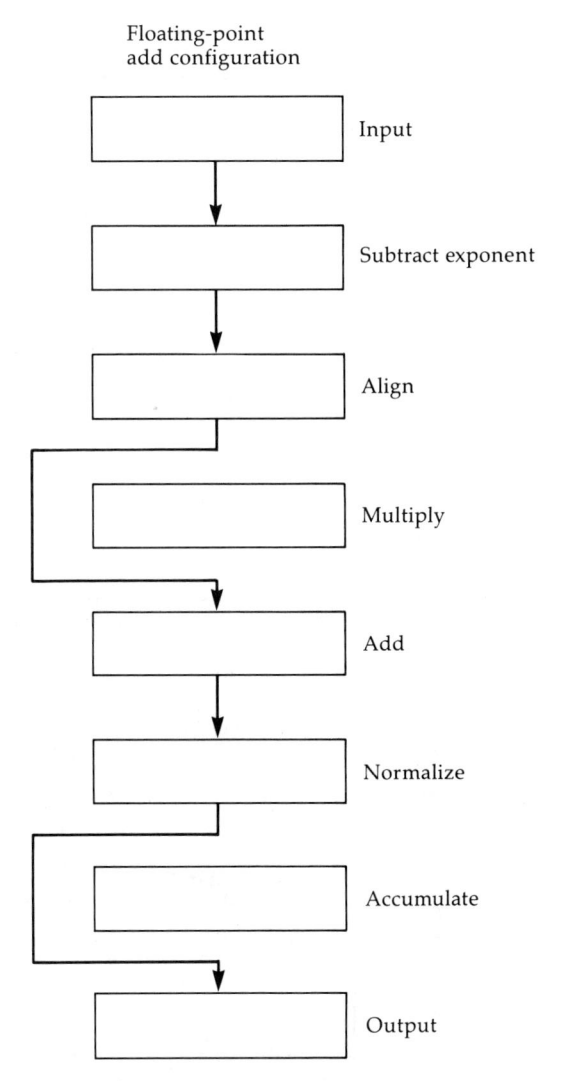

- Input
- Subtract exponent
- Align
- Multiply
- Add
- Normalize
- Accumulate
- Output

Figure 14.12 TI ASC Pipeline

Complete Interconnection Network

In this network every processor is directly connected to every other processor, as shown in Figure 14.14. If there are N processors, this method requires $N(N - 1)/2$ bidirectional links and $N(N - 1)$ switches. For the example in Figure 14.14, the four processing elements require twelve switching elements and six links. The major advantage of this network is that any two processors can transfer data in just one cycle. However, this method results in a very complex interconnection network, with

484   Chapter 14   Large System Architecture

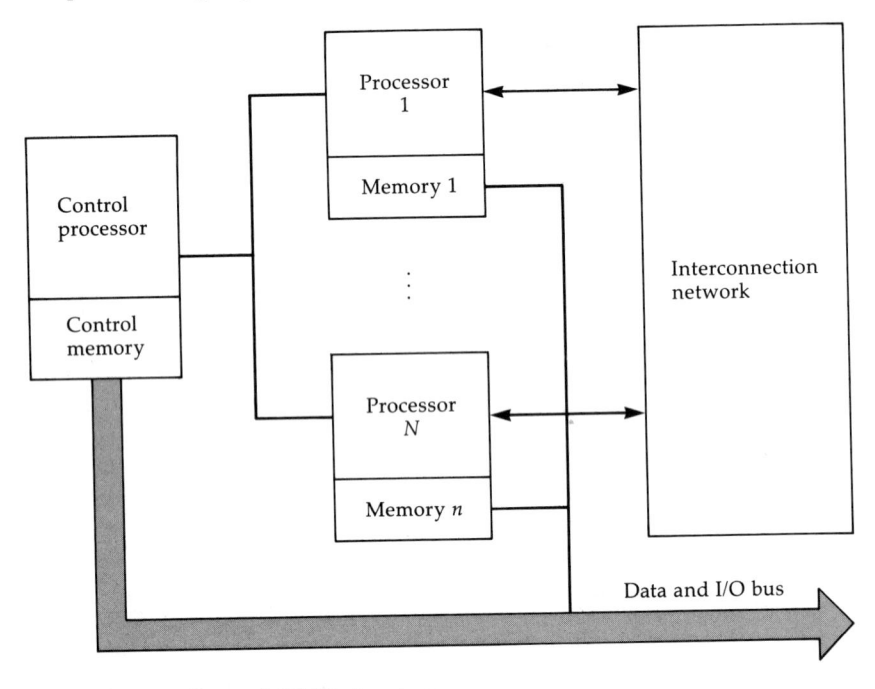

Figure 14.13   General SIMD structure

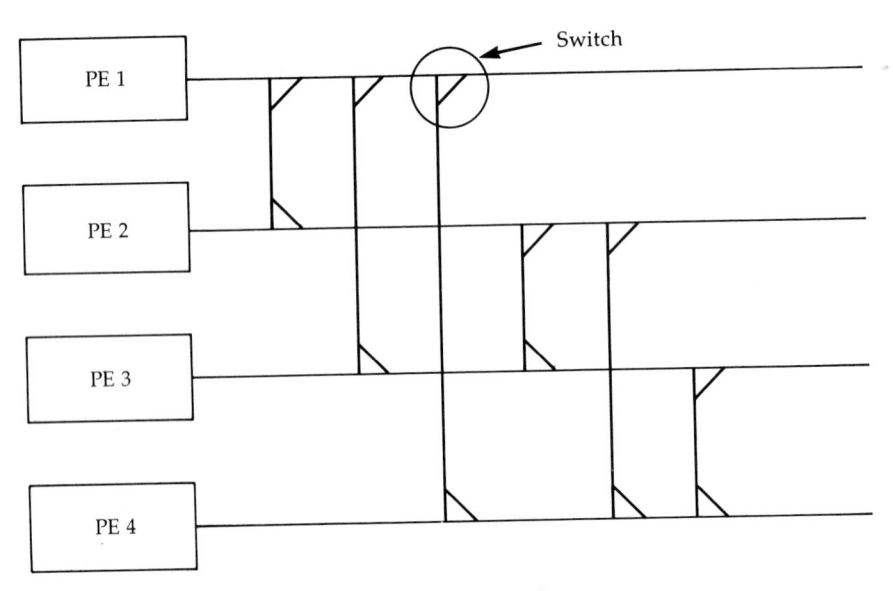

Figure 14.14   Complete interconnection network

more switches than are really necessary to meet the goal of providing a communication path between any two processors.

Permutation Networks

To reduce the number of switches required for complete data transfer, we can construct a permutation network. This network relies on the use of 2 × 2 crossbar switches such as the one shown in Figure 14.15. A crossbar switch will either pass the data straight through or switch the two input data lines. We can construct a network of these switches that will allow for any two processors connected at the inputs to transfer data. For example, Figure 14.16 illustrates a crossbar network for a six-processor system. If we set the switches in Figure 14.16 in an appropriate manner, any two processors can communicate. If it is necessary for processor 0 to send data to processor 3, we can set the switches as shown in Figure 14.17.

Notice that for the settings given in Figure 14.17, processor 1 can also send data to processor 5, and processor 2 can send data to processor 0. In other words, more than one data transfer can occur at a time within a permutation network. Note also that this permutation network requires only 15 switches, while a complete interconnection network for the same 6 processors would require 30 switches.

A more common permutation network structure is the Omega network. An 8 × 8 Omega network is shown in Figure 14.18. The crossbar switch has four positions: (1) straight, (2) exchange, (3) upper broadcast, and (4) lower broadcast. The upper broadcast sends the lower input to both the upper output and the lower output. As a result, the Omega network can perform one to many connections. For example, Figure 14.19 illustrates a broadcast of the data in processor 0 to all the processors.

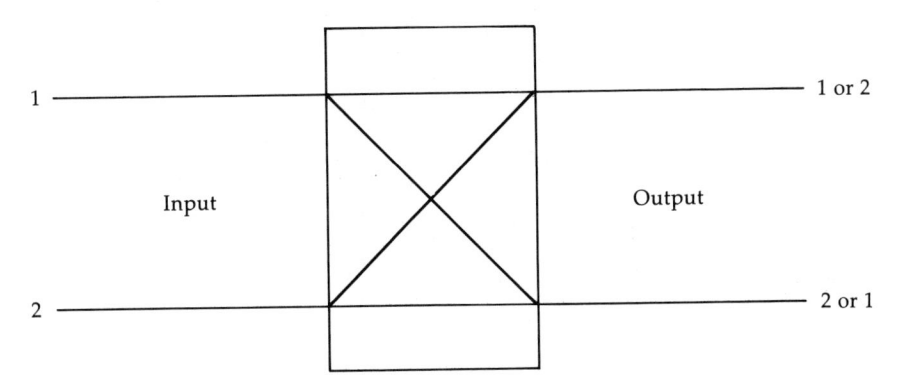

Figure 14.15 A 2 × 2 crossbar switch

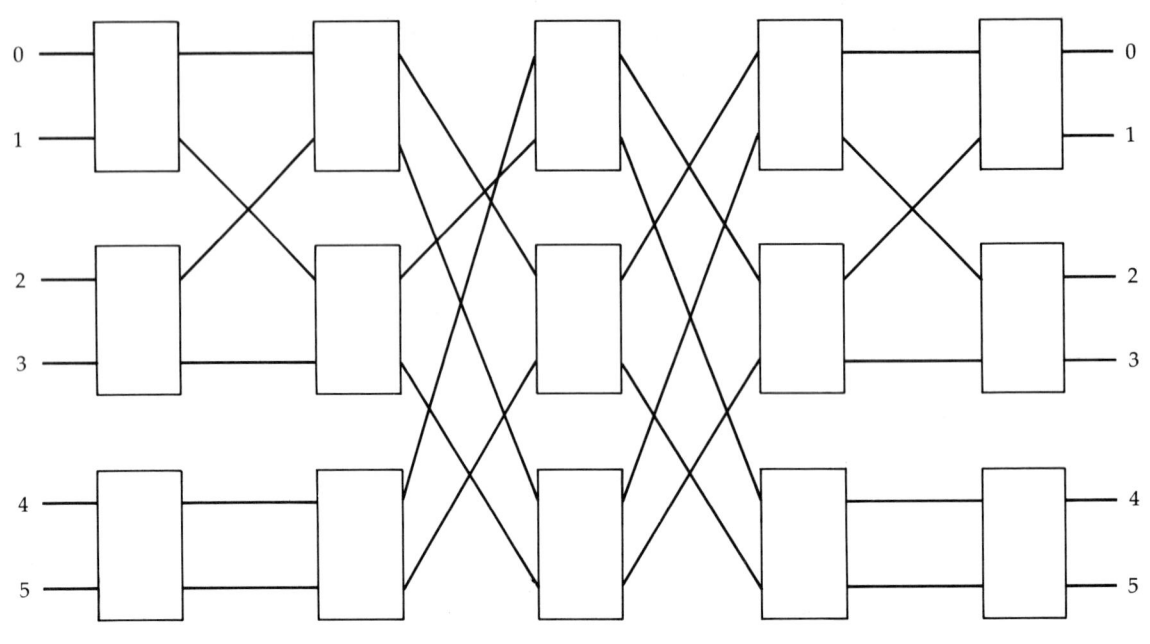

Figure 14.16 A six-processor permutation network

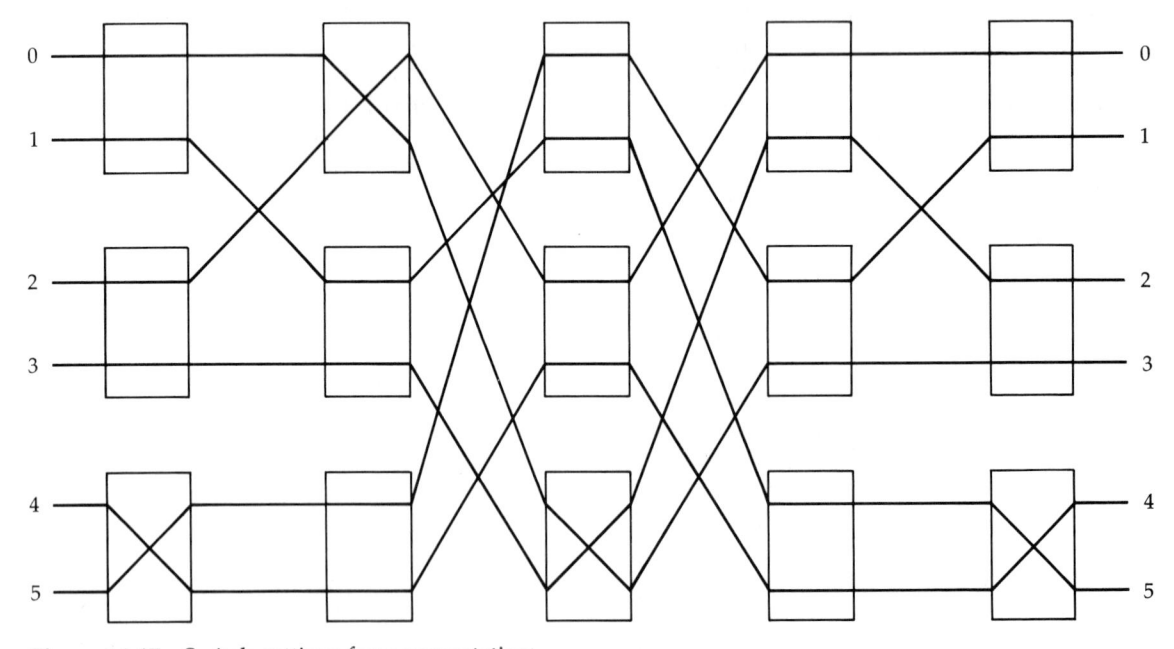

Figure 14.17 Switch settings for a permutation network

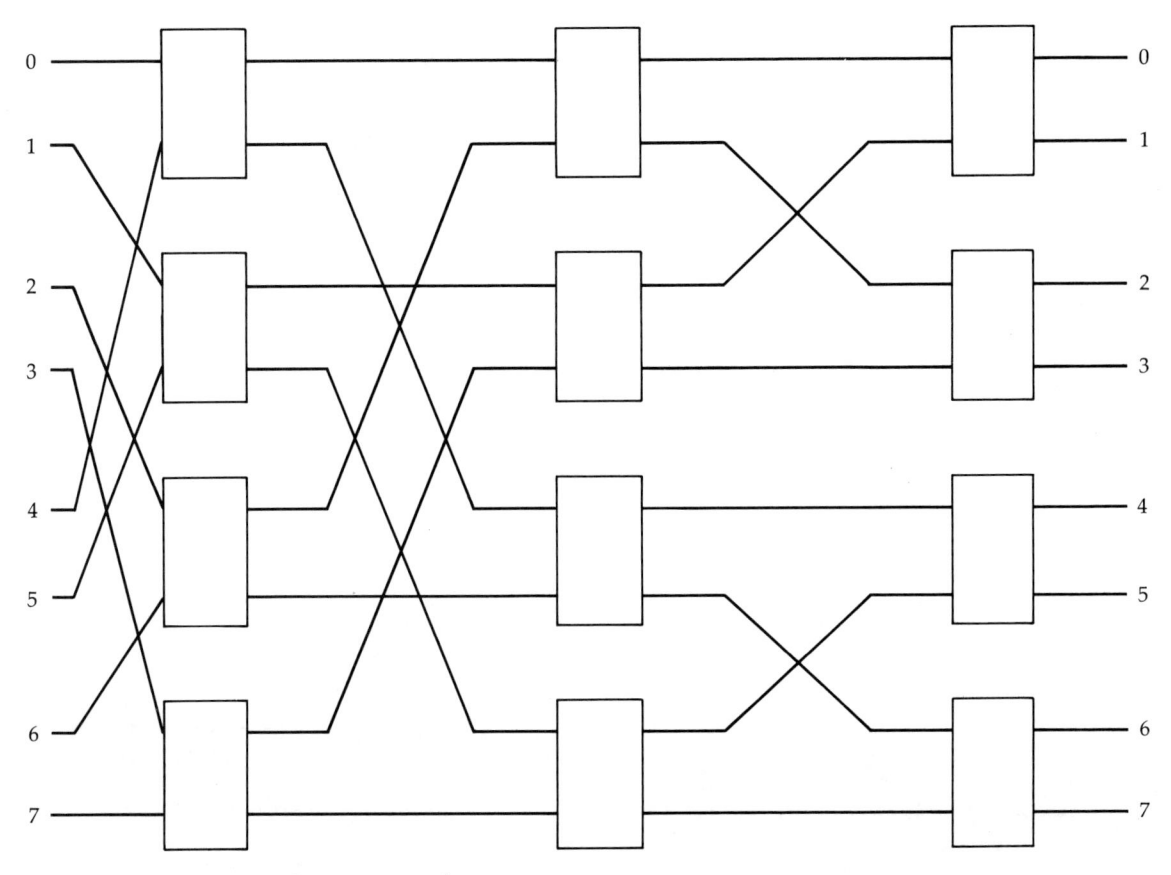

Figure 14.18 An 8 × 8 Omega network

The Illiac IV system, constructed at the University of Illinois in 1966, is the classic example of an array processor. The system was designed to consist of four processor quadrants, each with 64 processors. The quadrants are shown in Figure 14.20a. The processors in each quadrant were arranged in an 8 × 8 array, as shown in Figure 14.20b.

14.4 Multiprocessors

The MIMD structure is the most general multiprocessing architecture, as shown in Figure 14.21a for m memory units and p processors. The characteristics of an MIMD architecture are that

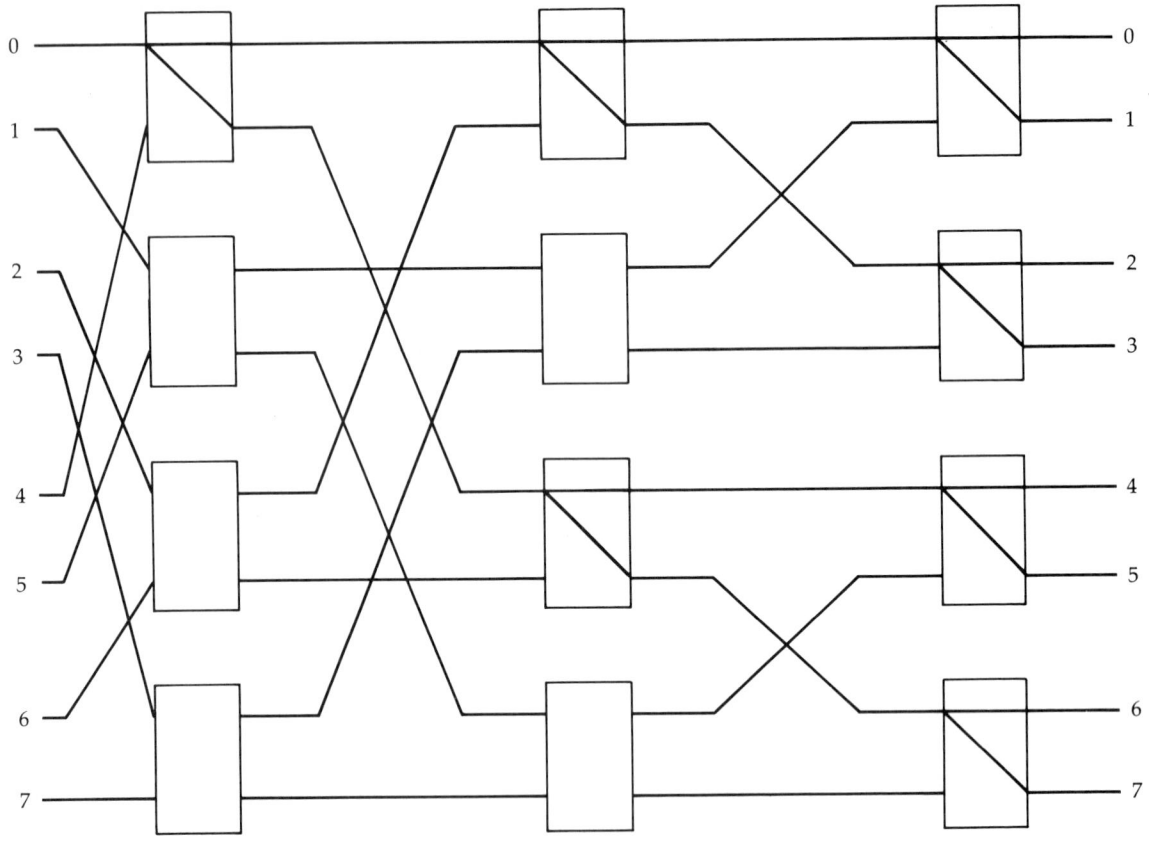

Figure 14.19 Broadcast of processor 0 to all the processors

1. It contains two or more processors of approximately equal capabilities.
2. All the processors have equal access to a common memory.
3. All the processors share access to I/O devices.

A classic example of an MIMD system is the Cm* architecture developed in 1972 at Carnegie Mellon University. The basic building block of Cm* is a Cm unit consisting of

1. An LSI-11 processor (P) (the LSI-11 is part of the DEC PDP-11 series)
2. A 4K–124K memory unit (M)
3. A switch unit (S) designed to connect the LSI-11 to the other Cm units

Up to 14 Cm building blocks are connected into a Cm cluster by a time-shared bus. The clusters communicate through an intercluster bus struc-

14.4 Multiprocessors

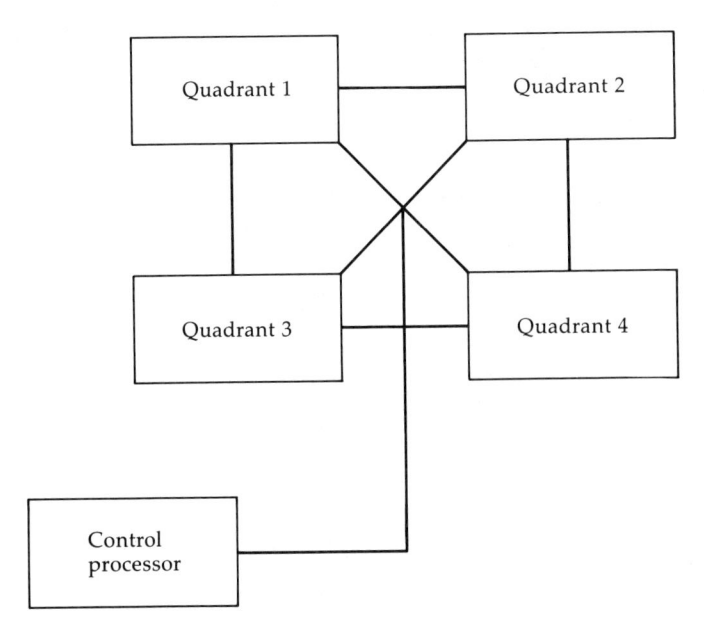

Figure 14.20a Illiac IV System structure

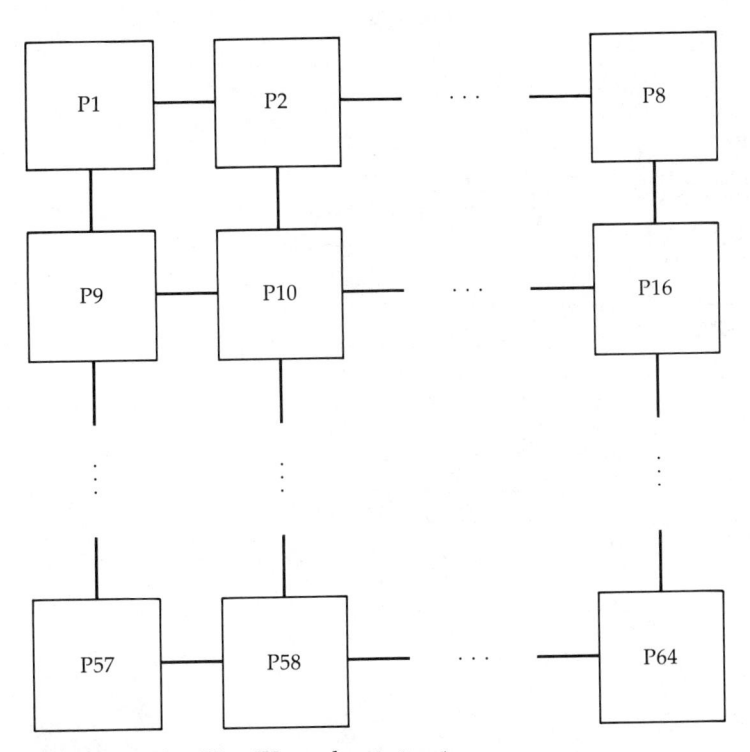

Figure 14.20b Illiac IV quadrant structure

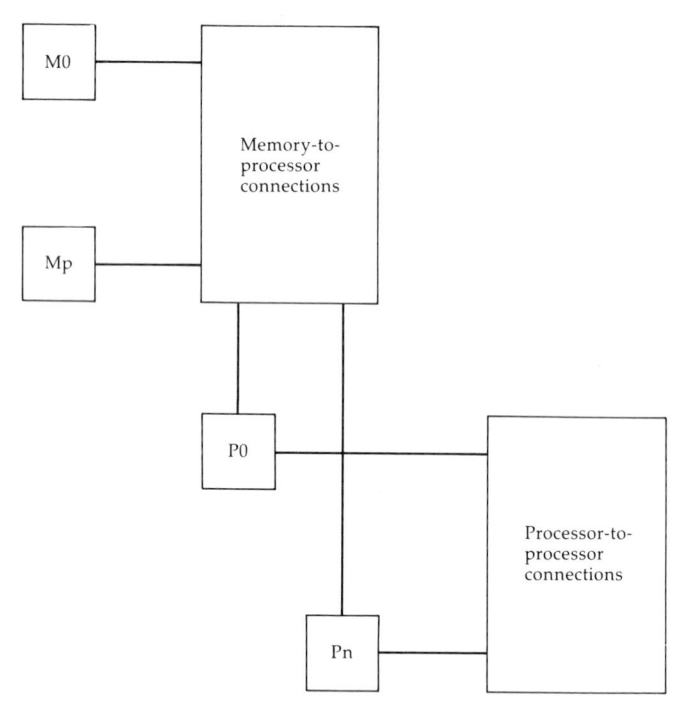

Figure 14.21a A MIMD structure

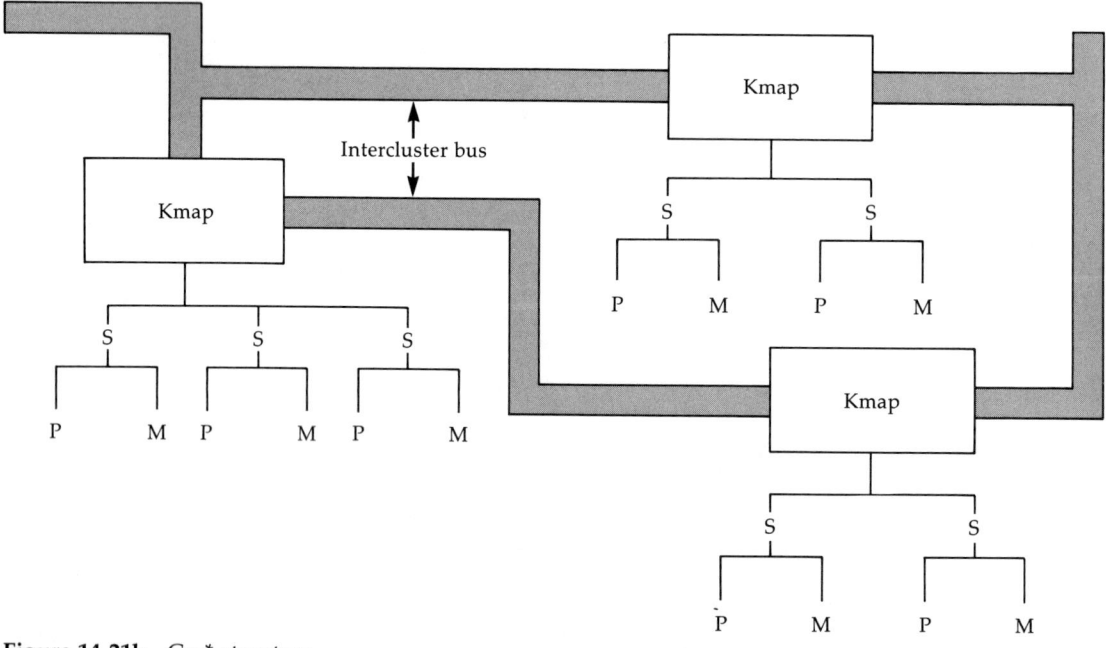

Figure 14.21b Cm* structure

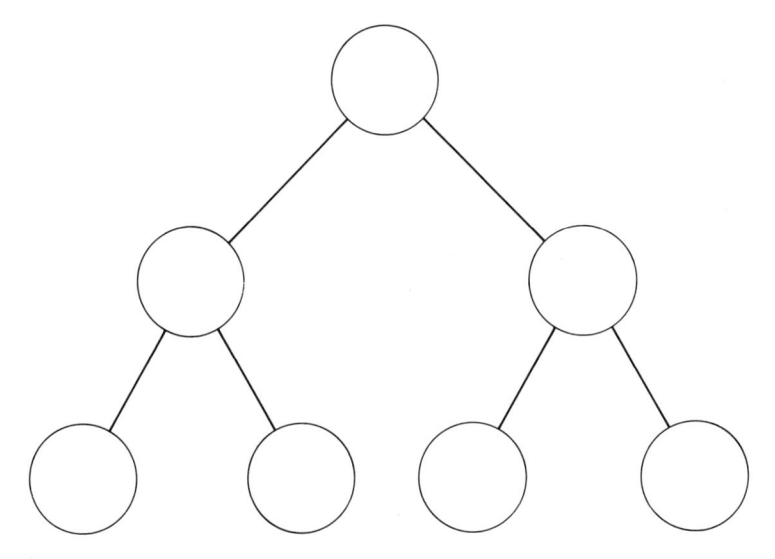

Figure 14.22 X-Tree structure

ture. The interface unit between a Cm cluster and the intercluster bus is called a Kmap. Each Kmap is connected to two intercluster buses. As a result, a single bus failure will not isolate a cluster. The full structure is shown in Figure 14.21b.

Another MIMD structure, which like Cm* is still in the experimental stage, is the X-Tree architecture developed at U.C. Berkeley. The structure consists of a full binary tree made up of VLSI microprocessors called X-nodes. An illustration of this architecture is given in Figure 14.22. The tree's topology guarantees that the average distance between nodes grows only logarithmically with the number of nodes; thus communication paths remain short for even large structures.

14.5 The CRAY-1

The CRAY-1 is a fourth-generation computer that utilizes several of the advanced architectural features discussed in this chapter. It was once considered to be the fastest computer in the world—able to process up to 138 million floating-point operations per second (Mflops), but it has since been replaced by the CRAY-2 and the CRAY-XP. A high-level block diagram is shown in Figure 14.23.

The memory unit consists of 1 million 64-bit words protected with a single error correction code. There are four instruction buffers, each with

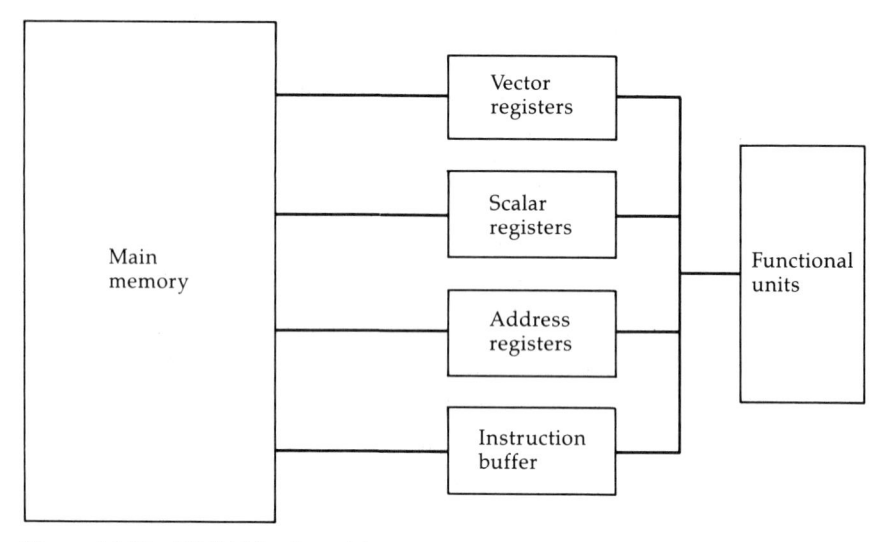

Figure 14.23 CRAY-1 basic architecture

64 16-bit registers. The system uses an instruction look-ahead feature, so most of the instructions needed during a fetch are found in one of the instruction buffers. If the system must go to memory for an instruction, it fetches 4 instructions and places them in the least recently used instruction buffer. The address register block contains eight 24-bit address registers that are used for memory access and index registers. Both the scalar and vector register blocks contain eight 64-bit registers for temporary data storage. The functional units block contains 12 independent functional units, including a vector functional unit that performs vector operations, a floating-point functional unit that performs floating-point arithmetic, a scalar functional unit that performs standard integer arithmetic and logic operations, and an address functional unit that performs address manipulations. All the units contain arithmetic pipelines, so they have a high throughput. In addition, the units may operate in parallel or in a chaining mode where the output of one unit serves as input to another, resulting in a large pipeline structure.

Summary

In this chapter we have briefly considered alternatives to the VAX architecture. We presented the four major classifications of computer architecture—SISD, SIMD, MISD, and MIMD—and we developed and analyzed examples of each class. We defined pipeline structures and offered the TI ASC as a working example of such a system. We also considered the nature of array processors and their interconnect structure. We also mentioned MIMD machines such as the Cm* and the X-Tree.

Exercises

1. Given the following pipeline

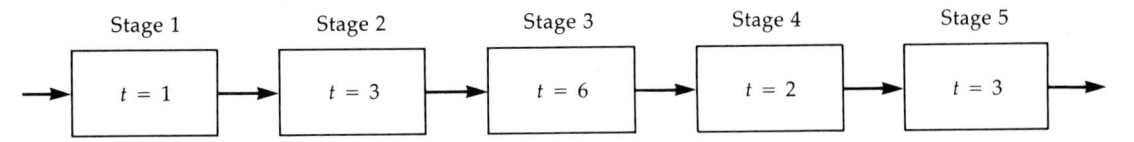

Stage 1	Stage 2	Stage 3	Stage 4	Stage 5
$t = 1$	$t = 3$	$t = 6$	$t = 2$	$t = 3$

   a. Draw the operational diagram showing the progress of three jobs through the pipeline.
   b. What is the throughput?
   c. Find the speedup ratio for this system.
   d. What is the efficiency of this pipeline?

2. Repeat Exercise 1 but now run six jobs through the pipeline. Note what happens to its efficiency. What generalization can you make about the number of jobs in a pipeline and its efficiency?

3. In Exercise 1 the bottleneck occurs at stage 3. Redo Exercise 1 on a new pipeline in which stage 3 is split into two substages, where substage 3a takes two time units and substage 3b takes four time units.

4. Redo Exercise 1 but now add an extra copy of stage 3 so that if one copy is busy, the other can take the output of stage 2 as shown below.

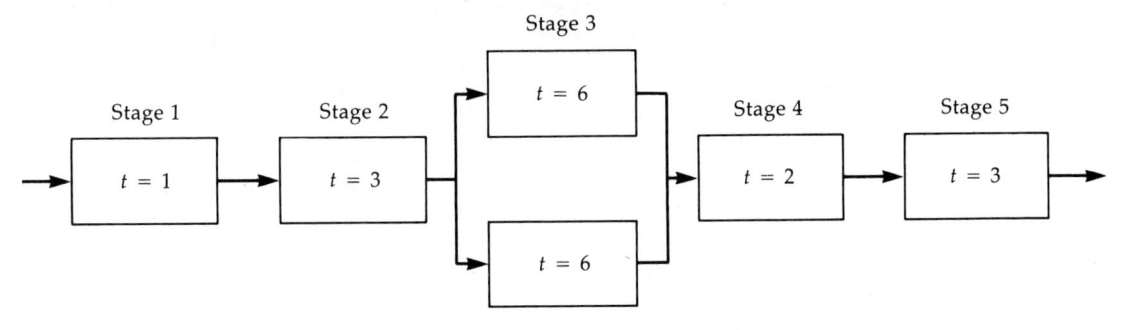

   Stage 1 ($t = 1$) → Stage 2 ($t = 3$) → Stage 3 ($t = 6$) / Stage 3 ($t = 6$) → Stage 4 ($t = 2$) → Stage 5 ($t = 3$)

   Which approach is best for reducing the bottleneck in this case (Exercise 3 or 4)?

5. Write an assembly language program that accepts as input a pipeline structure and outputs the speedup ratio, the efficiency, and the throughput.

6. Given a complete interconnection network for eight processing elements
   a. How many switches will it have?
   b. How many links will it have?

7. Show the switch pattern required on the following permutation network, which will allow processor 1 to transfer data to processor 5. Which other processors could communicate using this pattern?

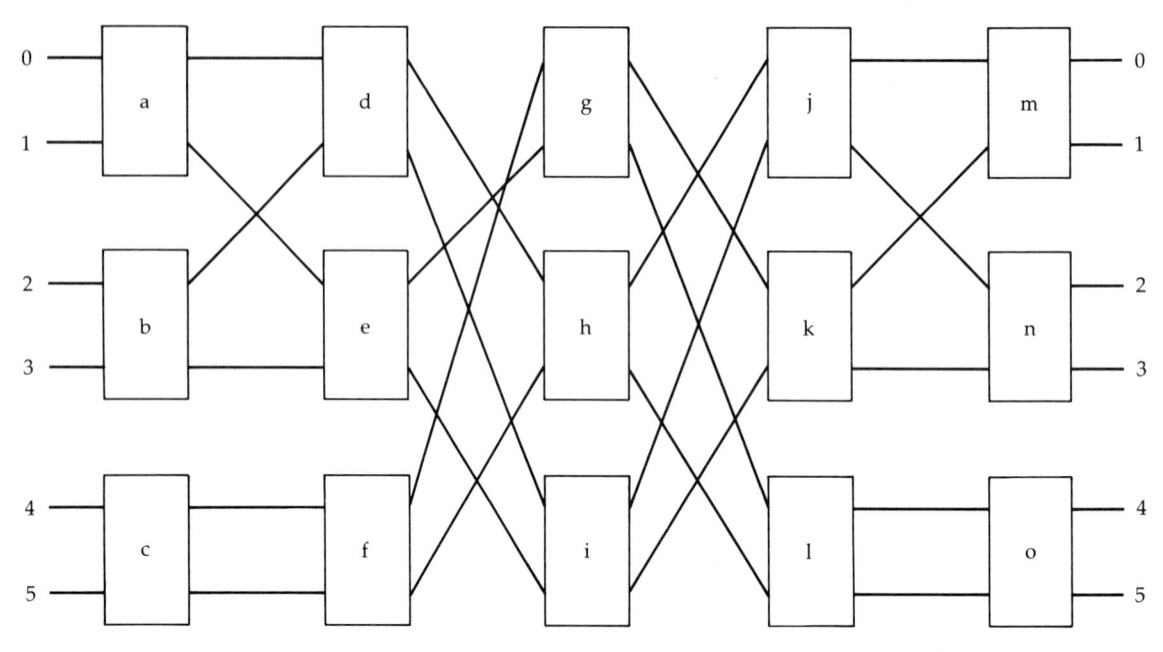

8. Each crossbar switch has an input control line where a 1 on the line causes the crossbar to flip the inputs, and a 0 allows the inputs to pass through. Assume that the permutation network of Exercise 7 has a control word of 15 bits, where bit 1 is the input control for switch a, bit 2 is the input control for switch b, ... , and bit 15 is the input control for switch 0. Find the sequence of control words that will allow

   Processor 1 to send data to processor 2, then

   Processor 2 to send data to processor 4, then

   Processor 4 to send data to processor 1.

9. Write an assembly language program that will determine the control word for any data transfer on the permutation network used in Exercise 8.

10. Suppose that you are designing a pipeline and must choose between three organizations. Which organization would you choose if throughput was the only objective? Justify your choice.

    a. Five stages with times 3, 2, 2, 6, 3.
    b. Six stages with times 3, 3, 2, 3, 2, 3.
    c. Three stages with times 6, 4, 6.

CHAPTER CONTENTS

15.1 RELIABILITY MEASURES

15.2 HARDWARE REDUNDANCY
   Static Redundancy
   Dynamic Redundancy
   Hybrid Redundancy

   SUMMARY

   EXERCISES

CHAPTER 15

Fault-Tolerant Computer Architecture

Since the early 1940s, when the first relay computers were developed, the question of how to ensure reliable computer operation has been an important one. Today, when computers are used in critical space missions, millions of miles from their human operators, and in biomedical systems where a human life depends on their correct operation, even a small computing error could result in the loss of a life or millions of dollars of equipment and years of research. Under such conditions, the design of computing systems that can operate correctly despite hardware or software failures is important. Such systems are called fault-tolerant systems. Specifically, fault-tolerant computing has been defined as the ability to execute specified algorithms correctly regardless of hardware and/or software failures. A **failure** occurs when a system does not perform as expected. A **fault** is a physical defect that may cause a failure. Faults include defective components, timing problems, shorts or breaks in signal lines, and so on.

The first step toward a fault-tolerant system is to build as much fault intolerance as possible into the system. Fault intolerance is the procedure whereby the reliability of the system is increased by avoiding the causes of system failures. After all, the fact that the final system will have some form of built-in fault tolerance is not an excuse for sloppy design and implementation. Fault intolerance is achieved in the design phase, before the final system is constructed. Designers select only the most reliable components, completely test software before it is released, and introduce fault detection and ease of repair considerations at the beginning of the design process and consider them at every succeeding step. Fault intolerance, however, can only postpone the occurrence of faults; it cannot eliminate them entirely. Thus the second step toward a fault-tolerant system requires protecting the system from faults.

There are several approaches to fault protection. Hardware redundancy involves introducing extra components into the system. Error-correcting codes such as parity checkers can protect memory and communication systems. Software fault-tolerant systems use special software procedures to recover from an error. In this chapter we will consider only the hardware redundancy approach because it impacts directly on the system architecture. Specifically, we will develop three redundancy techniques: static redundancy, dynamic redundancy, and hybrid redundancy.

15.1 Reliability Measures

Before we can evaluate a fault-tolerant approach, we must be able to at least estimate the effect of the approach on the overall reliability of the system. That is, we need some analytical measure of reliability.

We begin by defining reliability as the probability that at a given time (t), the system will still perform its tasks correctly, $R(t)$. From the definition, we know three things about reliability.

1. It is a function of time, $R(t)$
2. Because it is a probability, $0 \leq R(t) \leq 1$
3. $R(t)$ decreases over time

We will also assume that the reliability of the system when it begins its first task is 1; that is, $R(0) = 1$. We will also assume that if we ran the system long enough without any intervention, it would eventually fail; that is, $R(\infty) = 0$. We must determine the form of the reliability function for times between 0 and ∞. One assumption that has been shown experimentally to be very close to the truth is that during most of the life cycle of a system, its failure rate is a constant. In other words, the rate at which errors occur in a system does not change much over time. If we notice five failures in a computer product during its first month of operation, we will probably notice five failures per month throughout the lifetime of the product. In this case a good form for the reliability function is an exponential decay:

$$R(t) = e^{-\lambda t}$$

where λ is the failure rate. Figure 15.1 illustrates the behavior of this function over time. Notice that it has the correct behavior at $t = 0$ and $t = \infty$.

Another measure of system reliability is the **mean time between failures (MTBF)**, which is the average amount of time that a system can be

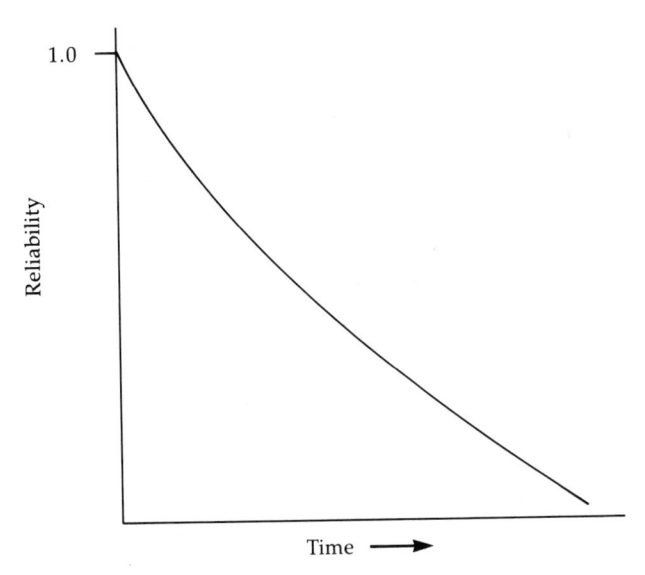

Figure 15.1 Graph of R(t) as a function of t

expected to run without a failure. We can find the MTBF directly from the reliability function using the relation

$$\text{MTBF} = \int_0^\infty R(t)\, dt$$

In fact, if the failure rate, λ, is a constant, then the MTBF is given by the value of the above integral which is

$$\text{MTBF} = 1/\lambda.$$

For example, if we have determined that the failure rate for a given system is 2×10^{-3} failures per hour, the MTBF for this system is 0.5×10^3 hours. In other words, on the average this system will operate for 500 hours between failures.

We will use both the reliability function and the MTBF in the following section to evaluate the improvements generated by the various fault-tolerant architectures.

15.2 Hardware Redundancy

We can overcome the effects of hardware errors through the use of protective redundancy. Hardware protective redundancy is the use of additional components that allow the system to continue to operate correctly in the presence of hardware faults. The cost of such extra components was once a strong argument against the use of redundancy. However, since the advent of LSI and MSI and the low cost of digital hardware, redundancy has become an important means of implementing fault-tolerant systems. There are three general classifications for the conventional redundancy techniques: static, dynamic, and hybrid. We will cover all three approaches in this section.

Static Redundancy

Static redundancy is sometimes called massive or masking redundancy. The term *masking* is applied to static redundancy because the fault-tolerant architecture instantaneously overcomes the effect of a failure so that it never appears at a system output.

In its simplest form, static redundancy is called **triple modular redundancy (TMR)**. We implement it by using three identical modules operating in parallel, as shown in Figure 15.2. The output of each module passes through a majority voting system whose output agrees with the majority of the module inputs. A truth table for the voter is shown in Figure 15.3. Notice, for example, if M1 and M2 produce an output of 0 and M3 produces an output of 1, the voter will produce an output of 0. The underlying assumption is that one module is more likely to fail (in this case M3) than two.

We can calculate the reliability of this architecture given the reliability of each of the modules and the voter. For example, say that the reliability of the voter is R_v and the reliability of a module is R (we will assume that

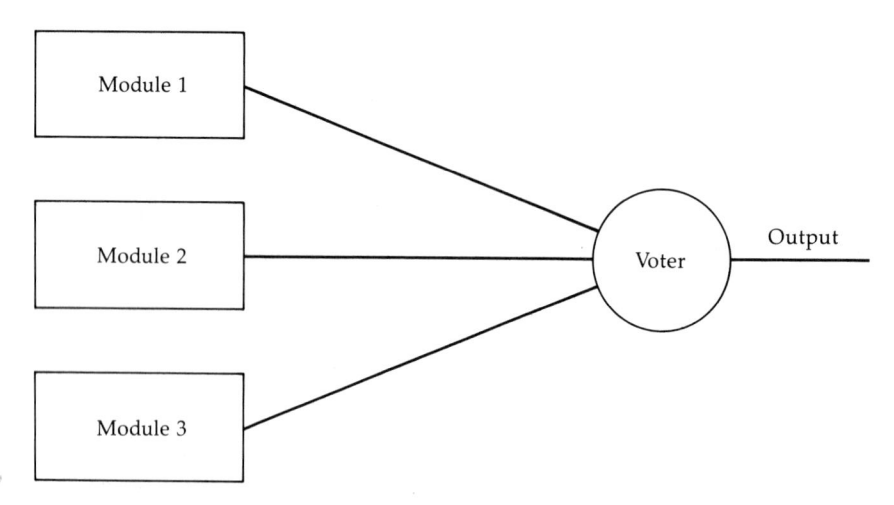

Figure 15.2 Triple modular redundancy (TMR) architecture

M1	M2	M3	Vote
0	0	0	0
0	0	1	0
0	1	0	0
0	1	1	1
1	0	0	0
1	0	1	1
1	1	0	1
1	1	1	1

Figure 15.3 Voter truth table

because all three modules are identical, their reliability is also identical). Now a TMR architecture will produce the correct output as long as

1. The voter is reliable (probability = R_v), and
2. Either (a) all three modules are reliable (probability = R^3), or (b) any two of the three modules are reliable. Now to find the probability of 2(b), we must consider all the ways that two modules could be fault-free and one could fail:
3. a. M1 and M2 could be fault-free and M3 could fail (probability = $R^2(1 - R)$),
   b. M1 and M3 could be fault-free and M2 could fail (probability = $R^2(1 - R)$), or
   c. M2 and M3 could be fault free and M1 could fail (probability = $R^2(1 - R)$.

Combining all these probabilities results in an expression for the reliability of a TMR system.

$$R_{TMR} = R_v(R^3 + 3R^2(1 - R))$$

If we assume that the voter reliability is very high compared to that of the individual module so that $R_V = 1$, the reliability of the TMR circuit is given by

$$R_{TMR} = 3R^2 - 2R^3$$

If we now assume that $R = e^{-\lambda t}$ and then graph the reliability of R_{TMR} over time, the result is shown in Figure 15.4, where R_M is the reliability of a single module.

Note that at some time T the reliability of an individual module is equal to the reliability of a TMR system. After time T, the reliability of the single module system is greater than the reliability of TMR because

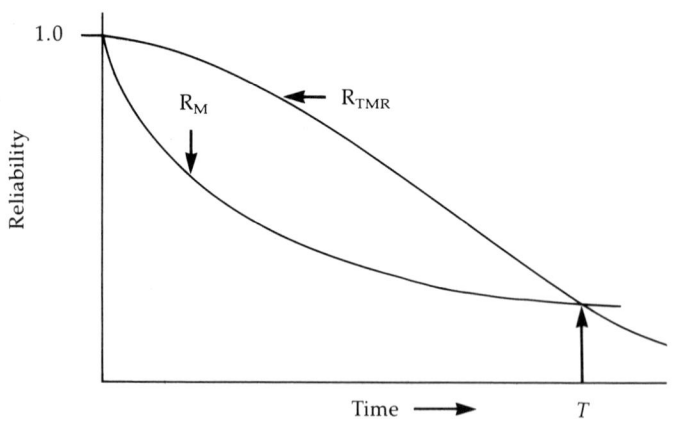

Figure 15.4 Reliability of TMR over time

the extra complexity of the TMR system begins to weigh against it. If we calculate the MTBF of the TMR system, we get another surprising result.

$$\text{MTBF}_{\text{TMR}} = \int_0^\infty R_{\text{TMR}} dt$$

$$= 5/(6\lambda)$$

The MTBF of the TMR system is smaller than the MTBF of the single-module system. Again, this result occurs because the TMR is more complicated and has at least three times the circuit elements of a single module, so there are more possible failures. As a result, the real advantage of the TMR architecture is that it offers a higher reliability over a set mission time, MT, as shown in Figure 15.5.

To account for this concept of a fixed mission time, the other measures of reliability have been suggested. The first is called the **reliability**

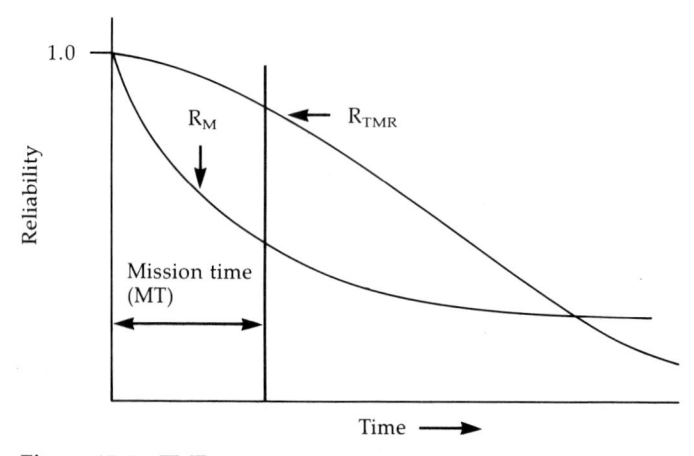

Figure 15.5 TMR mission time

improvement factor (RIF), which is the ratio of the probability of failure of the single-module system to the TMR system over a fixed mission time (T). Given the single-module reliability (R) its probability of failure is $1 - R$, and the probability of failure of a TMR systen is $1 - R_{TMR}$, so the RIF is given by

$$\text{RIF} = (1 - R)/(1 - R_{TMR})$$

For example, if failure rate for a module is 10^{-3} per hour, then over a 500-hour mission, the reliability of a single module is given by

$$R = e^{-\lambda t} = e^{-.5} = .61$$

where the reliability of a TMR system over the same 500-hour mission is

$$R_{TMR} = 3e^{-2\lambda t} - 2e^{-3\lambda t}$$
$$= 3e^{-1} - 2e^{-1.5} = .66$$

So the RIF is

$$\text{RIF} = (1 - .61)/(1 - .66) = 1.14.$$

The other measure of TMR performance is the **mission time improvement factor (MTIF)**, which is the ratio of the TMR mission time to the single-module mission time for a fixed level of reliability. That is, the MTIF tells us how long a TMR system can run with a reliability higher than some fixed value (say, .99) compared to how long a single-module system can run with the same high level of reliability. For the example above and a fixed level of reliability of .95, the two mission times are as follows:

Single module: find t such that $e^{-.001t} = .95$.

Take the ln of both sides to get $-.001t = \ln .95$, or $t = 51.29$ hours.

TMR system: find t such that $3e^{-.002t} - 2e^{-.003t} = .95$

This is more difficult to solve directly; however, we can solve it using a numerical technique called Newton's method. First, define the function, $F(t)$ to be

$$F(t) = 3e^{-.002t} - 2e^{-.003t} - .95$$

Now to solve for t such that $F(t) = 0$, we begin by guessing a value for t, the t_0 value, and then update our guess using

$$t_{i+1} = t_i - F(t_i)/F'(t_i)$$

where $F'(t_i)$ is the derivative of F. For this case, then, the updates are given by

$$t_{i+1} = t_i - (3e^{-.002t_i} - 2e^{-.003t_i} - .95)/(-.006e^{-.002t_i} + .006e^{-.003t_i})$$

We continue to update t_i until the difference between two values is less than some predetermined small positive number. For this case the starting guess for t is 100, and the small number used for stopping is .01. The result is the following table of values for t_i.

Step	t
1	100
2	142.10
3	142.10 so stop

In this case $t = 142.10$. Now the MTIF for this case is given by

MTIF = 142.10/51.29
     = 2.77

In other words, for this case the TMR system gives us almost three times the mission length of a single-module system.

If one module fails, the TMR system is no longer protected against a system failure. To provide protection against multiple module failures, a TMR architecture can be expanded to an NMR architecture where there are N identical modules for some odd number N. For example, a 5MR system is shown in Figure 15.6. In the NMR system up to $(N - 1)/2$

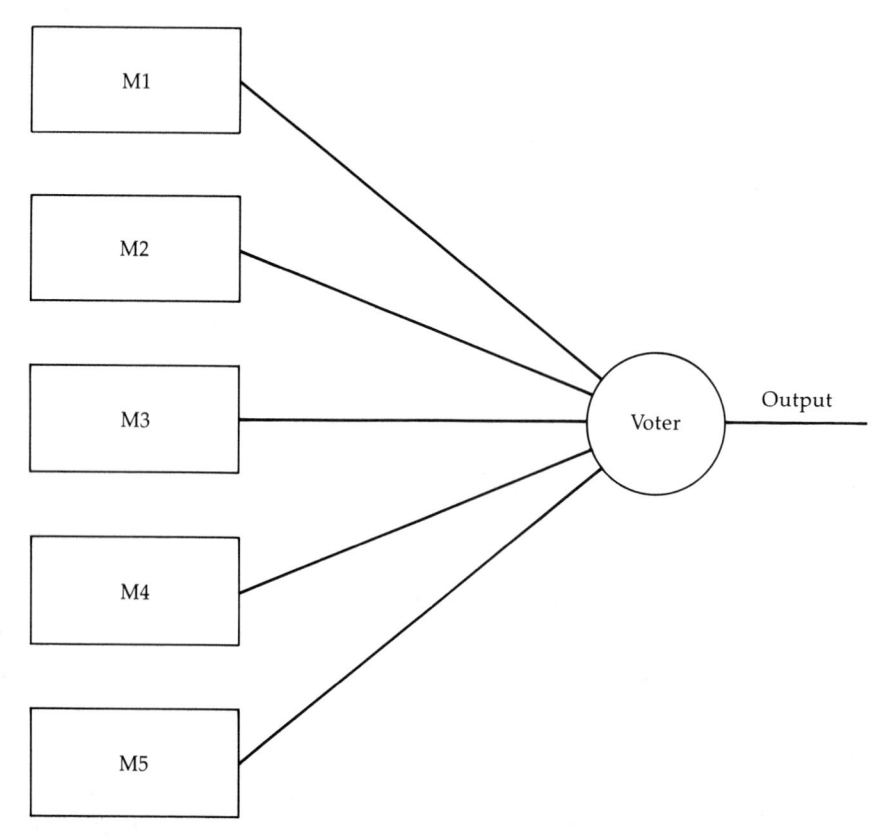

Figure 15.6 A SMR architecture

modules can fail and the voter will still produce the correct output. The reliability of an NMR system is given by

$$R_{NMR} = \sum_{i=0}^{n} \binom{N}{i} (1-R)^i R^{(N-i)}$$

where $n = (N-1)/2$ and $\binom{N}{i}$ is the number of ways to select i components out of N, which is given by:

$$\binom{N}{i} = \frac{N!}{(N-i)!\, i!}$$

We can verify that when $N = 3$, the above reliability equation reduces to that already given for the TMR case.

The advantages of static redundancy are as follows:

1. The corrective action is immediate, and the faulty module never affects the circuit.
2. There is no need for a fault detection procedure.
3. The conversion of a nonredundant system to a static redundant one is easily undertaken. For a TMR system, we simply construct two new copies of each nonredundant module.

Dynamic Redundancy

A system with **dynamic redundancy** consists of a single operating module with several spares, as shown in Figure 15.7. If a fault occurs in the operating module, it is automatically replaced with one of the spares. This system will continue to operate as long as there are spares available.

The reliability of a dynamic redundancy architecture with S spares is given by

$$R_D = 1 - (1-R)^{(S+1)}$$

where R is the reliability of an individual module and it is assumed that neither the switch nor the fault detection unit fail.

One problem with dynamic redundancy is that it requires some form of fault detection to determine when the single operating module has failed.

Hybrid Redundancy

If more than one module can fail over a given mission, TMR will not provide enough protection to the system. However, rather than relying on an NMR or a dynamic redundancy system, another approach involves the combination of TMR with spares. This approach attempts to imple-

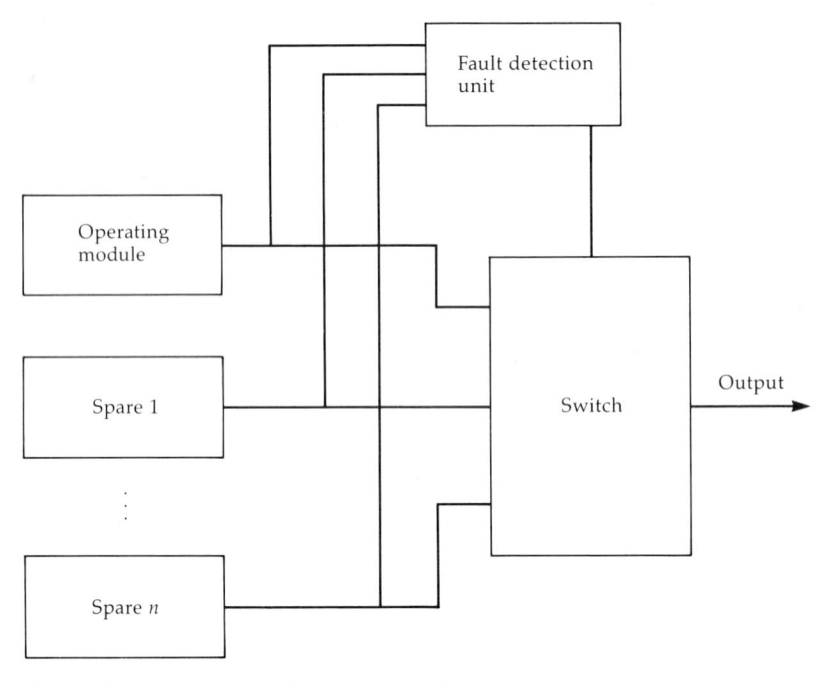

Figure 15.7 Dynamic redundancy architecture

ment the best of both TMR and dynamic redundancy in one architecture. It is called a **hybrid redundant system** and is illustrated in Figure 15.8.

The three operating modules send their signals through the switch to the voter. If one module fails, the detector notes the failure because the output of the failed module will not agree with the output of the voter. In the case of a module failure, the detector will instruct the switch to disconnect the defective active module and replace it with one of the spares. If S is the number of spares, the reliability of this system is given by

$$R(3, S) = 1 - \{\text{probability of all } (S + 3) \text{ modules failing} + \text{probability of all but one of the } (S + 3) \text{ modules failing}\}$$
$$= 1 - \{(1 - R)^{(S+3)} + (S + 3)R(1 - R)^{(S+2)}\}$$

A hybrid architecture with N modules ($N - 3$ spares and 3 active modules) can tolerate $N - 2$ failures. This is almost twice the number of failures that an equivalent NMR system will tolerate.

Summary

With the increasing use of computing systems in such critical areas as medicine and space, sophisticated computers must remain operational despite hardware failures. In this chapter we have outlined three major

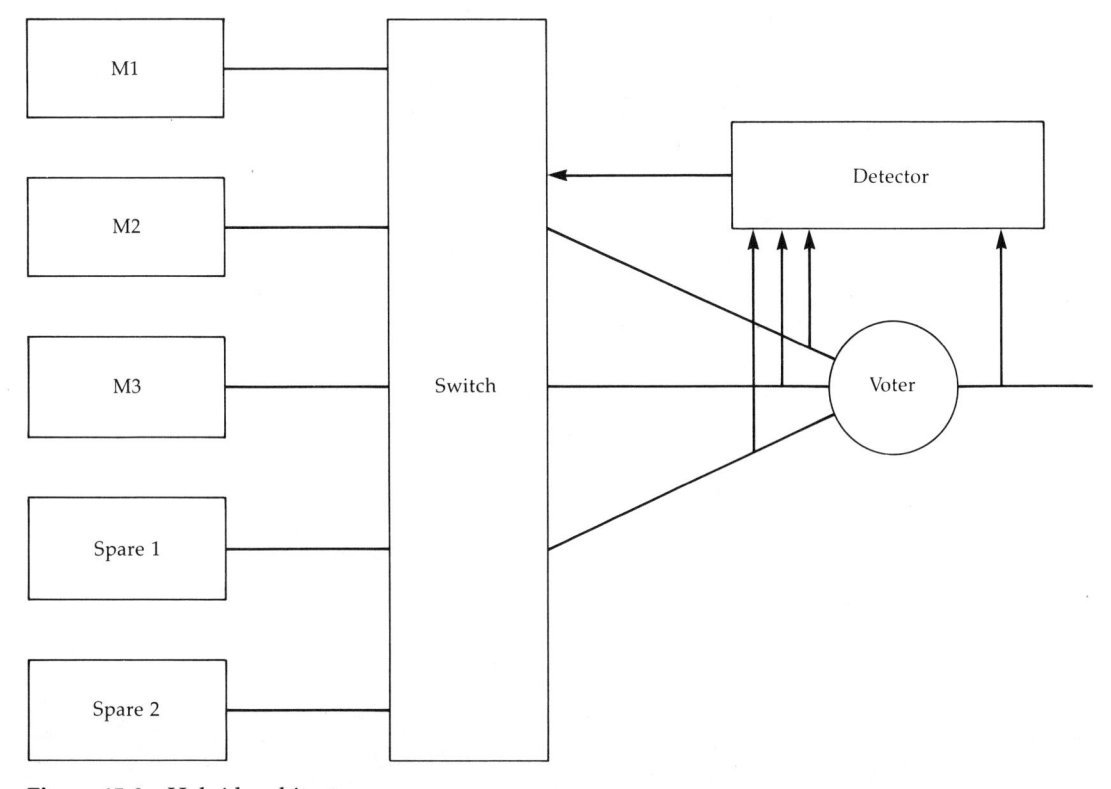

Figure 15.8 Hybrid architecture

approaches to fault tolerance: static redundancy, dynamic redundancy, and hybrid redundancy. We also developed several possible measures of reliability and reliability improvement.

Exercises

1. Graph the reliability over time of both a single-module system and a TMR architecture where the single-module failure rate is 10^{-3} failures per hour. Take the graph out to at least $t = 1000$.
2. Determine the MTBF, RIF, and MTIF (for a .95 reliability) for a TMR system with a single-module failure rate of 10^{-4} failures per hour and a 500-hour mission time.
3. Write an assembly language program that will calculate the MTBF and RIF for a TMR system given inputs of λ and the mission time.
4. Write an assembly language program that will find the MTIF for TMR assuming a .95 reliability level given the failure rate as an input.
5. Graph the reliability over time of a 5MR and a TMR (on the same

graph) where the single-module failure rate is 10^{-4}. Take the graph out to $t = 5000$.

6. What is the MTBF of a 5MR system given the single-module failure rate of 10^{-3}?

7. Find the RIF for a 5MR over a TMR with a single-module failure rate of 10^{-3}.

8. Graph the reliability over time of both a hybrid system with three spares and a TMR system (on the same graph) with a single-module failure rate of 10^{-3}.

9. Write an assembly language program that will find the reliability over time of a hybrid system. Your inputs will be the number of spares, the failure rate, the maximum time, and the time interval.

10. Prove algebraically that the reliability of a dynamic redundancy architecture with two spares is greater than the reliability of a TMR architecture. Assume that the required fault detection, switch, and voter circuits never fail.

APPENDIX A

Alphabetical List of VAX Instructions

Operand Specifier Notation

Operand specifiers are described in the following way:

<name>.<access type><data type>

where

1. Name is a suggestive name for the operand in the context of the instruction. The name is often abbreviated.
2. Access type is a letter denoting the operand specifier access type.

   a— Calculate the effective address of the specified operand. Address is returned in a longword that is the actual instruction operand. Context of address calculation is given by <data type>; that is, size to be used in autoincrement, autodecrement, and indexing.

   b— No operand reference. Operand specifier is a branch displacement. Size of branch displacement is given by <data type>.

   m—Operand is read, potentially modified, and written. Note that this it *not* an indivisible memory operation. Also note that if the operand is not actually modified, it may not be written back. However, modify-type operands are always checked for both read and write accessibility.

   r— Operand is read only.

   v— Calculate the effective address of the specified operand. If the effective address is in memory, the address is returned in a longword that is the actual instruction operand. Context of address calculation is given by <data type>. If the effective address is Rn, the operand is in Rn or R[n + 1]'Rn.

w—Operand is written only.

3. Data type is a letter denoting the data type of the operand.

  b—byte   o —octaword
  d—D_floating   q —quadword
  f —F_floating   w—word
  g—G_floating   x —first data type specified by instruction
  h—H_floating   y —second data type specified by instruction
  l —longword   * —multiple longwords (used only on implied operands)

4. Implied operands, that is, locations accessed by the instruction but not specified in an operand, are denoted in enclosing brackets [ ].

Condition Codes Legend

- · = conditionally cleared/set
- — = not affected
- 0 = cleared
- 1 = set

Instruction Set

OP	Mnemonic	Description	Arguments	Cond. Codes N Z V C
9D	ACBB	Add compare and branch byte	limit.rb, add.rb, index.mb, displ.bw	· · · —
6F	ACBD	Add compare and branch D_floating	limit.rd, add.rd, index.md, displ.bw	· · · —
4F	ACBF	Add compare and branch F_floating	limit.rf, add.rf, index.mf, displ.bw	· · · —
4FFD	ACBG	Add compare and branch G_floating	limit.rg, add.rg, index.mg, displ.bw	· · · —
6FFD	ACBH	Add compare and branch H_floating	limit.rh, add.rh, index.mh, displ.bw	· · · —
F1	ACBL	Add compare and branch long	limit.rl, add.rl, index.ml, displ.bw	· · · —
3D	ACBW	Add compare and branch word	limit.rw, add.rw, index.mw, displ.bw	· · · —

Instruction Set (continued)

OP	Mnemonic	Description	Arguments	Cond. Codes N Z V C
58	ADAWI	Add aligned word interlocked	add.rw, sum.mw	• • • •
80	ADDB2	Add byte 2-operand	add.rb, sum.mb	• • • •
81	ADDB3	Add byte 3-operand	add1.rb, add2.rb, sum.wb	• • • •
60	ADDD2	Add D_floating 2-operand	add.rd, sum.md	• • • 0
61	ADDD3	Add D_floating 3-operand	add1.rd, add2.rd, sum.wd	• • • 0
40	ADDF2	Add F_floating 2-operand	add.rf, sum.mf	• • • 0
41	ADDF3	Add F_floating 3-operand	add1.rf, add2.rf, sum.wf	• • • 0
40FD	ADDG2	Add G_floating 2-operand	add.rg, sum.mg	• • • 0
41FD	ADDG3	Add G_floating 3-operand	add1.rg, add2.rg, sum.wg	• • • 0
60FD	ADDH2	Add H_floating 2-operand	add.rh, sum.mh	• • • 0
61FD	ADDH3	Add H_floating 3-operand	add1.rh, add2.rh, sum.wh	• • • 0
C0	ADDL2	Add long 2-operand	add.rl, sum.ml	• • • •
C1	ADDL3	Add long 3-operand	add1.rl, add2.rl, sum.wl	• • • •
20	ADDP4	Add packed 4-operand	addlen.rw, addaddr.ab, sumlen.rw, sumaddr.ab, [R0-3.wl]	• • • 0
21	ADDP6	Add packed 6-operand	add1len.rw, add1addr.ab, add2len.rw, add2addr.ab, sumlen.rw, sumaddr.ab, [R0-5.wl]	• • • 0
A0	ADDW2	Add word 2-operand	add.rw, sum.mw	• • • •
A1	ADDW3	Add word 3-operand	add1.rw, add2.rw, sum.ww	• • • •
D8	ADWC	Add with carry	add.rl, sum.ml	• • • •
F3	AOBLEQ	Add one and branch on less or equal	limit.rl, index.ml, displ.bb	• • • —
F2	AOBLSS	Add one and branch on less	limit.rl, index.ml, displ.bb	• • • —
78	ASHL	Arithmetic shift long	count.rb, src.rl, dst.wl	• • • 0
F8	ASHP	Arithmetic shift and round packed	count.rb, srclen.rw, srcaddr.ab, round.rb, dstlen.rw, dstaddr.ab, [R0-3.wl]	• • • 0
79	ASHQ	Arithmetic shift quad	count.rb, src.rq, dst.wq	• • • 0
E1	BBC	Branch on bit clear	pos.rl, base.vb, displ.bb, [field.rv]	— — — —
E5	BBCC	Branch on bit clear and clear	pos.rl, base.vb, displ.bb, [field.mv]	— — — —

(continued)

Appendix A Alphabetical List of VAX Instructions

Instruction Set (continued)

OP	Mnemonic	Description	Arguments	Cond. Codes N Z V C
E7	BBCCI	Branch on bit clear and clear interlocked	pos.rl, base.vb, displ.bb, [field.mv]	— — — —
E3	BBCS	Branch on bit clear and set	pos.rl, base.vb, displ.bb, [field.mv]	— — — —
E0	BBS	Branch on bit set	pos.rl, base.vb, displ.bb, [field.rv]	— — — —
E4	BBSC	Branch on bit set and clear	pos.rl, base.vb, displ.bb, [field.mv]	— — — —
E2	BBSS	Branch on bit set and set	pos.rl, base.vb, displ.bb, [field.mv]	— — — —
E6	BBSSI	Branch on bit set and set interlocked	pos.rl, base.vb, displ.bb, [field mv]	— — — —
1E	BCC	Branch on carry clear	displ.bb	— — — —
1F	BCS	Branch on carry set	displ.bb	— — — —
13	BEQL	Branch on equal	displ.bb	— — — —
13	BEQLU	Branch on equal unsigned	displ.bb	— — — —
18	BGEQ	Branch on greater or equal	displ.bb	— — — —
1E	BGEQU	Branch on greater or equal unsigned	displ.bb	— — — —
14	BGTR	Branch on greater	displ.bb	— — — —
1A	BGTRU	Branch on greater unsigned	displ.bb	— — — —
8A	BICB2	Bit clear byte 2-operand	mask.rb, dst.mb	• • 0 —
8B	BICB3	Bit clear byte 3-operand	mask.rb, src.rb, dst.wb	• • 0 —
CA	BICL2	Bit clear long 2-operand	mask.rl, dst.ml	• • 0 —
CB	BICL3	Bit clear long 3-operand	mask.rl, src.rl, dst.wl	• • 0 —
B9	BICPSW	Bit clear processor status word	mask.rw	• • • •
AA	BICW2	Bit clear word 2-operand	mask.rw, dst.mw	• • 0 —
AB	BICW3	Bit clear word 3-operand	mask.rw, src.rw, dst.ww	• • 0 —
88	BISB2	Bit set byte 2-operand	mask.rb, dst.mb	• • 0 —
89	BISB3	Bit set byte 3-operand	mask.rb, src.rb, dst.wb	• • 0 —
C8	BISL2	Bit set long 2-operand	mask.rl, dst.ml	• • 0 —
C9	BISL3	Bit set long 3-operand	mask.rl, src.rl, dst.wl	• • 0 —
B8	BISPSW	Bit set processor status word	mask.rw	• • • •
A8	BISW2	Bit set word 2-operand	mask.rw, dst.mw	• • 0 —
A9	BISW3	Bit set word 3-operand	mask.rw, src.rw, dst.ww	• • 0 —
93	BITB	Bit test byte	mask.rb, src.rb	• • 0 —
D3	BITL	Bit test long	mask.rl, src.rl	• • 0 —
B3	BITW	Bit test word	mask.rw, src.rw	• • 0 —

Instruction Set (continued)

OP	Mnemonic	Description	Arguments	Cond. Codes N Z V C
E9	BLBC	Branch on low bit clear	src.rl, displ.bb	— — — —
E8	BLBS	Branch on low	src.rl, displ.bb	— — — —
15	BLEQ	Branch on less or equal	displ.bb	— — — —
1B	BLEQU	Branch on less or equal unsigned	displ.bb	— — — —
19	BLSS	Branch on less	displ.bb	— — — —
1F	BLSSU	Branch on less unsigned	displ.bb	— — — —
12	BNEQ	Branch on not equal	displ.bb	— — — —
12	BNEQU	Branch on not equal unsigned	displ.bb	— — — —
03	BPT	Break point fault	[—(KSP).w*]	0 0 0 0
11	BRB	Branch with byte displacement	displ.bb	— — — —
31	BRW	Branch with word displacement	displ.bw	— — — —
10	BSBB	Branch to subroutine with byte displacement	displ.bb, [—(SP).wl]	— — — —
30	BSBW	Branch to subroutine with word displacement	displ.bw, [—(SP).wl]	— — — —
FDFF	BUGL	VMS bugcheck		0 0 0 0
FEFF	BUGW	VMS bugcheck		0 0 0 0
1C	BVC	Branch on overflow clear	displ.bb	— — — —
1D	BVS	Branch on overflow set	displ.bb	— — — —
FA	CALLG	Call with general argument list	arglist.ab, dst.ab, [—(SP).w*]	0 0 0 0
FB	CALLS	Call with argument list on stack	numarg.rl, dst.ab, [—(SP).w*]	0 0 0 0
8F	CASEB	Case byte	selector.rb, base.rb, limit.rb, displ.bw-list	• • 0 •
CF	CASEL	Case long	selector.rl, base.rl, limit.rl, displ.bw-list	• • 0 •
AF	CASEW	Case word	selector.rw, base.rw, limit.rw, displ.bw-list	• • 0 •
BD	CHME	Change mode to executive	param.rw,[—(ySP).w*] y = MINU(E, PSL$current$-$mode$)	0 0 0 0
BC	CHMK	Change mode to kernel	param.rw,[—(KSP).w*]	0 0 0 0
BE	CHMS	Change mode to supervisor	param.rw,[—(ySP).w*] y = MINU(S, PSL$current$-$mode$)	0 0 0 0

(continued)

Appendix A Alphabetical List of VAX Instructions

Instruction Set (continued)

OP	Mnemonic	Description	Arguments	N	Z	V	C
BF	CHMU	Change mode to user	param.rw,[—(SP).w*]	0	0	0	0
94	CLRB	Clear byte	dst.wb	0	1	0	—
7C	CLRD	Clear D_floating	dst.wd	0	1	0	—
D4	CLRF	Clear F_floating	dst.wf	0	1	0	—
7C	CLRG	Clear G_floating	dst.wg	0	1	0	—
7CFD	CLRH	Clear H_floating	dst.wh	0	1	0	—
D4	CLRL	Clear long	dst.wl	0	1	0	—
7CFD	CLRO	Clear octaword	dst.wo	0	1	0	—
7C	CLRQ	Clear quad	dst.wq	0	1	0	—
B4	CLRW	Clear word	dst.ww	0	1	0	—
91	CMPB	Compare byte	src1.rb, src2.rb	•	•	0	•
29	CMPC3	Compare character 3-operand	len.rw, src1addr.ab, src2addr.ab, [R0-3.wl]	•	•	0	•
2D	CMPC5	Compare character 5-operand	src1len.rw, src1addr.ab, fill.rb, src2len.rw, src2addr.ab, [R0-3.wl]	•	•	0	•
71	CMPD	Compare D_floating	src1.rd, src2.rd	•	•	0	0
51	CMPF	Compare F_floating	src1.rf, src2.rf	•	•	0	0
51FD	CMPG	Compare G_floating	src1.rg, src2.rg	•	•	0	0
71FD	CMPH	Compare H_floating	src1.rh, src2.rh	•	•	0	0
D1	CMPL	Compare long	src1.rl, src2.rl	•	•	0	•
35	CMPP3	Compare packed 3-operand	len.rw, src1addr.ab, src2addr.ab, [R0-3.wl]	•	•	0	0
37	CMPP4	Compare packed 4-operand	src1len.rw, src1addr.ab, src2len.rw, src2addr.ab, [R0-3.wl]	•	•	0	0
EC	CMPV	Compare field	pos.rl, size.rb, base.vb, [field.rv], src.rl	•	•	0	•
B1	CMPW	Compare word	src1.rw, src2.rw	•	•	0	•
ED	CMPZV	Compare zero-extended field	pos.rl, size.rb, base.vb, [field.rv], src.rl	•	•	0	•
0B	CRC	Calculate cyclic redundancy check	tbl.ab, initialcrc.rl, strlen.rw, stream.ab, [R0-3.wl]	•	•	0	0
6C	CVTBD	Convert byte to D_floating	src.rb, dst.wd	•	•	•	0
4C	CVTBF	Convert byte to F_floating	src.rb, dst.wf	•	•	•	0
4CFD	CVTBG	Convert byte to G_floating	src.rb, dst.wg	•	•	•	0
6CFD	CVTBH	Convert byte to H_floating	src.rb, dst.wh	•	•	•	0
98	CVTBL	Convert byte to long	src.rb, dst.wl	•	•	•	0
99	CVTBW	Convert byte to word	src.rb, dst.ww	•	•	•	0
68	CVTDB	Convert D_floating to byte	src.rd, dst.wb	•	•	•	0

Instruction Set (continued)

OP	Mnemonic	Description	Arguments	Cond. Codes N Z V C
76	CVTDF	Convert D_floating to F_floating	src.rd, dst.wf	• • • 0
32FD	CVTDH	Convert D_floating to H_floating	src.rd, dst.wh	• • • 0
6A	CVTDL	Convert D_floating to long	src.rd, dst.wl	• • • 0
69	CVTDW	Convert D_floating to word	src.rd, dst.ww	• • • 0
48	CVTFB	Convert F_floating to byte	src.rf, dst.wb	• • • 0
56	CVTFD	Convert F_floating to D_floating	src.rf, dst.wd	• • • 0
99FD	CVTFG	Convert F_floating to G_floating	src.rf, dst.wg	• • • 0
98FD	CVTFH	Convert F_floating to H_floating	src.rf, dst.wh	• • • 0
4A	CVTFL	Convert F_floating to long	src.rf, dst.wl	• • • 0
49	CVTFW	Convert F_floating to word	src.rf, dst.ww	• • • 0
48FD	CVTGB	Convert G_floating to byte	src.rg, dst.wb	• • • 0
33FD	CVTGF	Convert G_floating to F_floating	src.rg, dst.wf	• • • 0
56FD	CVTGH	Convert G_floating to H_floating	src.rg, dst.wh	• • • 0
4AFD	CVTGL	Convert G_floating to longword	src.rg, dst.wl	• • • 0
49FD	CVTGW	Convert G_floating to word	src.rg, dst.ww	• • • 0
68FD	CVTHB	Convert H_floating to byte	src.rh, dst.wb	• • • 0
F7FD	CVTHD	Convert H_floating to D_floating	srd.rh, dst.wd	• • • 0
F6FD	CVTHF	Convert H_floating to F_floating	src.rh, dst.wf	• • • 0
76FD	CVTHG	Convert H_floating to G_floating	srd.rh, dst.wg	• • • 0
6AFD	CVTHL	Convert H_floating to longword	srd.rh, dst.wl	• • • 0
69FD	CVTHW	Convert H_floating to word	src.rh, dst.ww	• • • 0
F6	CVTLB	Convert long to byte	src.rl, dst.wb	• • • 0
6E	CVTLD	Convert long to D_floating	src.rl, dst.wd	• • • 0
4E	CVTLF	Convert long to F_floating	src.rl, dst.wf	• • • 0
4EFD	CVTLG	Convert longword to G_floating	src.rl, dst.wg	• • • 0

(continued)

Instruction Set (continued)

OP	Mnemonic	Description	Arguments	Cond. Codes N Z V C
6EFD	CVTLH	Convert longword to H_floating	src.rl, dst.wh	• • • 0
F9	CVTLP	Convert long to packed	src.rl, dstlen.rw, dstaddr.ab, [R0-3.wl]	• • • 0
F7	CVTLW	Convert long to word	src.rl, dst.ww	• • • 0
36	CVTPL	Convert packed to long	srclen.rw, srcaddr.ab, [R0-3.wl], dst.wl	• • • 0
08	CVTPS	Convert packed to leading separate	srclen.rw, srcaddr.ab, dstlen.rw, dstaddr.ab, [R0-3.wl]	• • • 0
24	CVTPT	Convert packed to trailing	srclen.rw, srcaddr.ab, tbladdr.ab, dstlen.rw, dstaddr.ab, [R0-3.wl]	• • • 0
6B	CVTRDL	Convert rounded D_floating to long	src.rd, dst.wl	• • • 0
4B	CVTRFL	Convert rounded F_floating to long	src.rf, dst.wl	• • • 0
4BFD	CVTRGL	Convert rounded G_floating to long	src.rg, dst.wl	• • • 0
6BFD	CVTRHL	Convert rounded H_floating to long	src.rh, dst.wl	• • • 0
09	CVTSP	Convert leading separate to packed	srclen.rw, srcaddr.ab, dstlen.rw, dstaddr.ab, [R0-3.wl]	• • • 0
26	CVTTP	Convert trailing to packed	srclen.rw, srcaddr.ab, tbladdr.ab, dstlen.rw, dstaddr.ab, [R0-3.wl]	• • • 0
33	CVTWB	Convert word to byte	src.rw, dst.wb	• • • 0
6D	CVTWD	Convert word to D_floating	src.rw, dst.wd	• • • 0
4D	CVTWF	Convert word to F_floating	src.rw, dst.wf	• • • 0
4DFD	CVTWG	Convert word to G_floating	src.rw, dst.wg	• • • 0
6DFD	CVTWH	Convert word to H_floating	src.rw, dst.wh	• • • 0
32	CVTWL	Convert word to long	src.rw, dst.wl	• • • 0
97	DECB	Decrement byte	dif.mb	• • • •
D7	DECL	Decrement long	dif.ml	• • • •
B7	DECW	Decrement word	dif.mw	• • • •
86	DIVB2	Divide byte 2-operand	divr.rb, quo.mb	• • • 0
87	DIVB3	Divide byte 3-operand	divr.rb, divd.rb, quo.wb	• • • 0

Instruction Set (continued)

OP	Mnemonic	Description	Arguments	Cond. Codes N Z V C
66	DIVD2	Divide D_floating 2-operand	divr.rd, quo.md	• • • 0
67	DIVD3	Divide D_floating 3-operand	divr.rd, divd.rd, quo.wd	• • • 0
46	DIVF2	Divide F_floating 2-operand	divr.rf, quo.mf	• • • 0
47	DIVF3	Divide F_floating 3-operand	divr.rf, divd.rf, quo.wf	• • • 0
46FD	DIVG2	Divide G_floating 2-operand	divr.rg, quo.mg	• • • 0
47FD	DIVG3	Divide G_floating 3-operand	divr.rg, divd.rg, quo.wg	• • • 0
66FD	DIVH2	Divide H_floating 2-operand	divr.rh, quo.mh	• • • 0
67FD	DIVH3	Divide H_floating 3-operand	divr.rh, divd.rh, quo.wh	• • • 0
C6	DIVL2	Divide long 2-operand	divr.rl, quo.ml	• • • 0
C7	DIVL3	Divide long 3-operand	divr.rl, divd.rl, quo.wl	• • • 0
27	DIVP	Divide packed	divrlen.rw, divraddr.ab, divdlen.rw, divdaddr.ab, quolen.rw, quoaddr.ab [R0-5.wl, −16(SP): −1(SP).wb]	• • • 0
A6	DIVW2	Divide word 2-operand	divr.rw, quo.mw	• • • 0
A7	DIVW3	Divide word 3-operand	divr.rw, divd.rw, quo.ww	• • • 0
38	EDITPC	Edit packed to character string	srclen.rw, srcaddr.ab, pattern.ab, dstaddr.ab, [R0-5.wl]	• • • •
7B	EDIV	Extended divide	divr.rl, divd.rq, quo.wl, rem.wl	• • • 0
74	EMODD	Extended modulus D_floating	mulr.rd, mulrx.rb, muld.rd, int.wl, fract.wd	• • • 0
54	EMODF	Extended modulus F_floating	mulr.rf, mulrx.rb, muld.rf, int.wl, fract.wf	• • • 0
54FD	EMODG	Extended modulus G_floating	mulr.rg, mulrx.rw, muld.rg, int.wl, fract.wg	• • • 0
74FD	EMODH	Extended modulus H_floating	mulr.rh, mulrx.rw, muld.rh, int.wl, fract.wh	• • • 0
7A	EMUL	Extended multiply	mulr.rl, muld.rl, add.rl, prod.wq	• • 0 0

(continued)

Appendix A Alphabetical List of VAX Instructions

Instruction Set (continued)

OP	Mnemonic	Description	Arguments	N	Z	V	C
FD	ESCD	Escape D		•	•	•	•
FE	ESCE	Escape E		•	•	•	•
FF	ESCF	Escape F		•	•	•	•
EE	EXTV	Extract field	pos.rl, size.rb, base.vb, [field.rv], dst.wl	•	•	0	—
EF	EXTZV	Extract zero-extended field	pos.rl, size.rb, base.vb, [field.rv], dst.wl	•	•	0	—
EB	FFC	Find first clear bit	startpos.rl, size.rb, base.vb, [field.rv], findpos.wl	0	•	0	0
EA	FFS	Find first set bit	startpos.rl, size.rb, base.vb, [field.rv], findpos.wl	0	•	0	0
00	HALT	Halt (kernel mode only)	[—(KSP).w*]	•	•	•	•
96	INCB	Increment byte	sum.mb	•	•	•	•
D6	INCL	Increment long	sum.ml	•	•	•	•
B6	INCW	Increment word	sum.mw	•	•	•	•
0A	INDEX	Index calculation	subscript.rl, low.rl, high.rl, size.rl, entry.rl, addr.wl	•	•	0	0
5C	INSQHI	Insert at head of queue, interlocked	entry.ab, header.aq	0	•	0	•
5D	INSQTI	Insert at tail of queue, interlocked	entry.ab, header.aq	0	•	0	•
0E	INSQUE	Insert into queue	entry.ab, addr.wl	•	•	0	•
F0	INSV	Insert field	src.rl, pos.rl, size.rb, base.vb, [field.wv]	—	—	—	—
17	JMP	Jump	dst.ab	—	—	—	—
16	JSB	Jump to subroutine	dst.ab, [—(SP) + .wl]	—	—	—	—
06	LDPCTX	Load process context (kernel mode only)	[PCB.r*. − (KSP).w*]	—	—	—	—
3A	LOCC	Locate character	char.rb, len.rw, addr.ab, [R0-1.wl]	0	•	0	0
39	MATCHC	Match characters	len1.rw, addr1.ab, len2.rw, addr2.ab, [R0-3.wl]	0	•	0	0
92	MCOMB	Move complemented byte	src.rb, dst.wb	•	•	0	—
D2	MCOML	Move complemented long	src.rl, dst.wl	•	•	0	—
B2	MCOMW	Move complemented word	src.rw, dst.ww	•	•	0	—
DB	MFPR	Move from processor register (kernel mode only)	procreg.rl, dst.wl	•	•	0	—
8E	MNEGB	Move negated byte	src.rb, dst.wb	•	•	•	•
72	MNEGD	Move negated D_floating	src.rd, dst.wd	•	•	0	0

Instruction Set (continued)

OP	Mnemonic	Description	Arguments	N	Z	V	C
52	MNEGF	Move negated F_floating	src.rf, dst.wf	•	•	0	0
52FD	MNEGG	Move negated G_floating	src.rg, dst.wg	•	•	0	0
72FD	MNEGH	Move negated H_floating	src.rh, dst.wh	•	•	0	0
CE	MNEGL	Move negated long	src.rl, dst.wl	•	•	•	•
AE	MNEGW	Move negated word	src.rw, dst.ww	•	•	•	•
9E	MOVAB	Move address of byte	src.ab, dst.wl	•	•	0	—
7E	MOVAD	Move address of D_floating	src.aq, dst.wl	•	•	0	—
DE	MOVAF	Move address of F_floating	src.al, dst.wl	•	•	0	—
7E	MOVAG	Move address of G_floating	src.aq, dst.wl	•	•	0	—
7EFD	MOVAH	Move address of H_floating	src.ao, dst.wl	•	•	0	—
DE	MOVAL	Move address of long	src.al, dst.wl	•	•	0	—
7EFD	MOVAO	Move address of octaword	src.ao, dst.wl	•	•	0	—
7E	MOVAQ	Move address of quad	src.aq, dst.wl	•	•	0	—
3E	MOVAW	Move address of word	src.aw, dst.wl	•	•	0	—
90	MOVB	Move byte	src.rb, dst.wb	•	•	0	—
28	MOVC3	Move character 3-operand	len.rw, srcaddr.ab, dstaddr.ab. [R0-5.wl]	0	1	0	0
2C	MOVC5	Move character 5-operand	srclen.rw, srcaddr.ab, fill.rb, dstlen.rw, dstaddr.ab, [R0-5.wl]	•	•	0	•
70	MOVD	Move D_floating	src.rd, dst.wd	•	•	0	—
50	MOVF	Move F_floating	src.rf, dst.wf	•	•	0	—
50FD	MOVG	Move G_floating	src.rg, dst.wg	•	•	0	—
70FD	MOVH	Move H_floating	src.rh, dst.wh	•	•	0	—
D0	MOVL	Move long	src.rl, dst.wl	•	•	0	—
7DFD	MOVO	Move octaword	src.ro, dst.wo	•	•	0	—
34	MOVP	Move packed	len.rw, srcaddr.ab, dstaddr.ab, [R0-3.wl]	•	•	0	—
DC	MOVPSL	Move processor status longword	dst.wl	—	—	—	—
7D	MOVQ	Move quad	src.rq, dst.wq	•	•	0	—
2E	MOVTC	Move translated characters	srclen.rw, srcaddr.ab, fill.rb, tbladdr.ab, dstlen.rw, dstaddr.ab, [R0-5.wl]	•	•	0	•

(continued)

Instruction Set (continued)

OP	Mnemonic	Description	Arguments	Cond. Codes N Z V C
2F	MOVTUC	Move translated until character	srclen.rw, srcaddr.ab, escape.rb, tbladdr.ab, dstlen.rw, dstaddr.ab, [R0-5.wl]	• • • •
B0	MOVW	Move word	src.rw, dst.ww	• • 0 —
9A	MOVZBL	Move zero-extended byte to long	src.rb, dst.wl	0 • 0 —
9B	MOVZBW	Move zero-extended byte to word	src.rb, dst.ww	0 • 0 —
3C	MOVZWL	Move zero-extended word to long	src.rw, dst.wl	0 • 0 —
DA	MTPR	Move to processor register (kernel mode only)	src.rl, procreg.wl	• • 0 —
84	MULB2	Multiply byte 2-operand	mulr.rb, prod.mb	• • • 0
85	MULB3	Multiply byte 3-operand	mulr.rb, muld.rb, prod.wb	• • • 0
64	MULD2	Multiply D_floating 2-operand	mulr.rd, prod.md	• • • 0
65	MULD3	Multiply D_floating 3-operand	mulr.rd, muld.rd, prod.wd	• • • 0
44	MULF2	Multiply F_floating 2-operand	mulr.rf, prod.mf	• • • 0
45	MULF3	Multiply F_floating 3-operand	mulr.rf, muld.rf, prod.wf	• • • 0
44FD	MULG2	Multiply G_floating 2-operand	mulr.rg, prod.mg	• • • 0
45FD	MULG3	Multiply G_floating 3-operand	mulr.rg, muld.rg, prod.wg	• • • 0
64FD	MULH2	Multiply H_floating 2-operand	mulr.rh, prod.mh	• • • 0
65FD	MULH3	Multiply H_floating 3-operand	mulr.rh, muld.rh, prod.wh	• • • 0
C4	MULL2	Multiply long 2-operand	mulr.rl, prod.ml	• • • 0
C5	MULL3	Multiply long 3-operand	mulr.rl, muld.rl, prod.wl	• • • 0
25	MULP	Multiply packed	mulrlen.rw, mulradr.ab, muldlen.rw, muldadr.ab, prodlen.rw, prodadr.ab, [R0-5.wl]	• • • 0
A4	MULW2	Multiply word 2-operand	mulr.rw, prod.mw	• • • 0
A5	MULW3	Multiply word 3-operand	mulr.rw, muld.rw, prod.ww	• • • 0
01	NOP	No operation		— — — —

Operand Specifier Notation   521

Instruction Set (continued)

OP	Mnemonic	Description	Arguments	Cond. Codes N Z V C
75	POLYD	Evaluate polynomial D_floating	arg.rd, degree.rw, tbladdr.ab, [R0-5.wl]	• • • 0
55	POLYF	Evaluate polynomial F_floating	arg.rf, degree.rw, tbladdr.ab, [R0-3.wl]	• • • 0
55FD	POLYG	Evaluate polynomial G_floating	arg.rg, degree.rw, tbladdr.ab, [R0-5.wl]	• • • 0
75FD	POLYH	Evaluate polynomial H_floating	arg.rh, degree.rw, tbladdr.ab, [R0-5.wl, −16(SP): −1(SP).wl]	• • • 0
BA	POPR	Pop registers	mask.rw, [(SP) + .r*]	— — — —
0C	PROBER	Probe read access	mode.rb, len.rw, base.ab	0 • 0 —
0D	PROBEW	Probe write access	mode.rb, len.rw, base.ab	0 • 0 —
9F	PUSHAB	Push address of byte	src.ab, [−(SP).wl]	• • 0 —
7F	PUSHAD	Push address of D_floating	src.aq, [−(SP).wl]	• • 0 —
DF	PUSHAF	Push address of F_floating	src.al, [−(SP).wl]	• • 0 —
7F	PUSHAG	Push address of G_floating	src.aq, [−(SP).wl]	• • 0 —
7FFD	PUSHAH	Push address of H_floating	src.ao, [−(SP).wl]	• • 0 —
DF	PUSHAL	Push address of long	src.al, [−(SP).wl]	• • 0 —
7FFD	PUSHAO	Push address of octaword	src.ao, [−(SP).wl]	• • 0 —
7F	PUSHAQ	Push address of quad	src.aq, [−(SP).wl]	• • 0 —
3F	PUSHAW	Push address of word	src.aw, [−(SP).wl]	• • 0 —
DD	PUSHL	Push long	src.rl, [−(SP).wl]	• • 0 —
BB	PUSHR	Push registers	mask.rw, [−(SP).w*]	— — — —
02	REI	Return from exception or interrupt	[(SP) + .r*]	• • • •
5E	REMQHI	Remove from head of queue, interlocked	header.aq, addr.wl	0 • • •
5F	REMQTI	Remove from tail of queue, interlocked	header.aq, addr.wl	0 • • •
0F	REMQUE	Remove from queue	entry.ab, addr.wl	• • • •
04	RET	Return from procedure	[(SP) + .r*]	• • • •
9C	ROTL	Rotate long	count.rb, src.rl, dst.wl	• • 0 —
05	RSB	Return from subroutine	[(SP) + .rl]	— — — —
57	Reserved	Reserved		
5A	Reserved	Reserved		
5B	Reserved	Reserved		
77	Reserved	Reserved		
FE	Reserved	Reserved		

(continued)

Instruction Set (continued)

OP	Mnemonic	Description	Arguments	Cond. Codes N Z V C
FF	Reserved	Reserved		
D9	SBWC	Subtract with carry	sub.rl, dif.ml	• • • •
2A	SCANC	Scan for character	len.rw, addr.ab, tbladdr.ab, mask.rb, [R0-3.wl]	0 • 0 0
3B	SKPC	Skip character	char.rb, len.rw, addr.ab, [R0-1.wl]	0 • 0 0
F4	SOBGEQ	Subtract one and branch on greater or equal	index.ml, displ.bb	• • • —
F5	SOBGTR	Subtract one and branch on greater	index.ml, displ.bb	• • • —
2B	SPANC	Span characters	len.rw, addr.ab, tbladdr.ab, mask.rb, [R0-3.wl]	0 • 0 0
82	SUBB2	Subtract byte 2-operand	sub.rb, dif.mb	• • • •
83	SUBB3	Subtract byte 3-operand	sub.rb, min.rb, dif.wb	• • • •
62	SUBD2	Subtract D_floating 2-operand	sub.rd, dif.md	• • • 0
63	SUBD3	Subtract D_floating 3-operand	sub.rd, min.rd, dif.wd	• • • 0
42	SUBF2	Subtract F_floating 2-operand	sub.rf, dif.mf	• • • 0
43	SUBF3	Subtract F_floating 3-operand	sub.rf, min.rf, dif.wf	• • • 0
42FD	SUBG2	Subtract G_floating 2-operand	sub.rg, dif.mg	• • • 0
43FD	SUBG3	Subtract G_floating 3-operand	sub.rg, min.rg, dif.wg	• • • 0
62FD	SUBH2	Subtract H_floating 2-operand	sub.rh, dif.mh	• • • 0
63FD	SUBH3	Subtract H_floating 3-operand	sub.rh, min.rh, dif.wh	• • • 0
C2	SUBL2	Subtract long 2-operand	sub.rl, dif.ml	• • • •
C3	SUBL3	Subtract long 3-operand	sub.rl, min.rl, dif.wl	• • • •
22	SUBP4	Subtract packed 4-operand	sublen.rw, subaddr.ab, diflen.rw, difaddr.ab, [R0-3.wl]	• • • 0
23	SUBP6	Subtract packed 6-operand	sublen.rw, subaddr.ab, minlen.rw, minaddr.ab, diflen.rw, difaddr.ab, [R0-5.wl]	• • • 0
A2	SUBW2	Subtract word 2-operand	sub.rw, dif.mw	• • • •
A3	SUBW3	Subtract word 3-operand	sub.rw, min.rw, dif.ww	• • • •

Instruction Set (continued)

OP	Mnemonic	Description	Arguments	Cond. Codes N Z V C
07	SVPCTX	Save process context (kernel mode only)	[(SP) + .r* , −(KSP).w*]	— — — —
95	TSTB	Test byte	src.rb	• • 0 0
73	TSTD	Test D_floating	src.rd	• • 0 0
53	TSTF	Test F_floating	src.rf	• • 0 0
53FD	TSTG	Test G_floating	src.rg	• • 0 0
73FD	TSTH	Test H_floating	src.rh	• • 0 0
D5	TSTL	Test long	src.rl	• • 0 0
B5	TSTW	Test word	src.rw	• • 0 0
FC	XFC	Extended function call	user defined operands	0 0 0 0
8C	XORB2	Exclusive or byte 2-operand	mask.rb, dst.mb	• • 0 —
8D	XORB3	Exclusive or byte 3-operand	mask.rb, src.rb, dst.wb	• • 0 —
CC	XORL2	Exclusive or long 2-operand	mask.rl, dst.ml	• • 0 —
CD	XORL3	Exclusive or long 3-operand	mask.rl, src.rl, dst.wl	• • 0 —
AC	XORW2	Exclusive or word 2-operand	mask.rw, dst.mw	• • 0 —
AD	XORW3	Exclusive or word 3-operand	mask.rw, src.rw, dst.ww	• • 0 —

Source: *VAX-11 Programming Card.* Maynard, Mass.: Digital Equipment Corporation, 1984. Copyright, Digital Equipment Corporation, 1984. All rights reserved. Reprinted by permission.

APPENDIX B

VAX Instructions in Numerical Order

Instructions

Numerical Order

00	HALT	13	BEQL	24	CVTPT	36	CVTPL
01	NOP	13	BEQLU	25	MULP	37	CMPP4
02	REI	14	BGTR	26	CVTTP	38	EDITPC
03	BPT	15	BLEQ	27	DIVP	39	MATCHC
04	RET	16	JSB	28	MOVC3	3A	LOCC
05	RSB	17	JMP	29	CMPC3	3B	SKPC
06	LDPCTX	18	BGEQ	2A	SCANC	3C	MOVZWL
07	SVPCTX	19	BLSS	2B	SPANC	3D	ACBW
08	CVTPS	1A	BGTRU	2C	MOVC5	3E	MOVAW
09	CVTSP	1B	BLEQU	2D	CMPC5	3F	PUSHAW
0A	INDEX	1C	BVC	2E	MOVTC	40	ADDF2
0B	CRC	1D	BVS	2F	MOVTUC	40FD	ADDG2
0C	PROBER	1E	BCC	30	BSBW	41	ADDF3
0D	PROBEW	1E	BGEQU	31	BRW	41FD	ADDG3
0E	INSQUE	1F	BCS	32	CVTWL	42	SUBF2
0F	REMQUE	1F	BLSSU	32FD	CVTDH	42FD	SUBG2
10	BSBB	20	ADDP4	33	CVTWB	43	SUBF3
11	BRB	21	ADDP6	33FD	CVTGF	43FD	SUBG3
12	BNEQ	22	SUBP4	34	MOVP	44	MULF2
12	BNEQU	23	SUBP6	35	CMPP3	44FD	MULG2

Instructions (continued)

Numerical Order

45	MULF3	5F	REMQTI	75	POLYD	91	CMPB
45FD	MULG3	60	ADDD2	75FD	POLYH	92	MCOMB
46	DIVF2	60FD	ADDH2	76	CVTDF	93	BITB
46FD	DIVG2	61	ADDD3	76FD	CVTHG	94	CLRB
47	DIVF3	61FD	ADDH3	77	Reserved	95	TSTB
47FD	DIVG3	62	SUBD2	78	ASHL	96	INCB
48	CVTFB	62FD	SUBH2	79	ASHQ	97	DECB
48FD	CVTGB	63	SUBD3	7A	EMUL	98	CVTBL
49	CVTFW	63FD	SUBH3	7B	EDIV	98FD	CVTFH
49FD	CVTGW	64	MULD2	7C	CLRD	99	CVTBW
4A	CVTFL	64FD	MULH2	7C	CLRG	99FD	CVTFG
4AFD	CVTGL	65	MULD3	7C	CLRQ	9A	MOVZBL
4B	CVTRFL	65FD	MULH3	7CFD	CLRH	9B	MOVZBW
4BFD	CVTRGL	66	DIVD2	7CFD	CLRO	9C	ROTL
4C	CVTBF	66FD	DIVH2	7D	MOVQ	9D	ACBB
4CFD	CVTBG	67	DIVD3	7DFD	MOVO	9E	MOVAB
4D	CVTWF	67FD	DIVH3	7E	MOVAD	9F	PUSHAB
4DFD	CVTWG	68	CVTDB	7E	MOVAG	A0	ADDW2
4E	CVTLF	68FD	CVTHB	7E	MOVAQ	A1	ADDW3
4EFD	CVTLG	69	CVTDW	7EFD	MOVAH	A2	SUBW2
4F	ACBF	69FD	CVTHW	7EFD	MOVAO	A3	SUBW3
4FFD	ACBG	6A	CVTDL	7F	PUSHAD	A4	MULW2
50	MOVF	6AFD	CVTHL	7F	PUSHAG	A5	MULW3
50FD	MOVG	6B	CVTRDL	7F	PUSHAQ	A6	DIVW2
51	CMPF	6BFD	CVTRHL	7FFD	PUSHAH	A7	DIVW3
51FD	CMPG	6C	CVTBD	7FFD	PUSHAO	A8	BISW2
52	MNEGF	6CFD	CVTBH	80	ADDB2	A9	BISW3
52FD	MNEGG	6D	CVTWD	81	ADDB3	AA	BICW2
53	TSTF	6DFD	CVTWH	82	SUBB2	AB	BICW3
53FD	TSTG	6E	CVTLD	83	SUBB3	AC	XORW2
54	EMODF	6EFD	CVTLH	84	MULB2	AD	XORW3
54FD	EMODG	6F	ACBD	85	MULB3	AE	MNEGW
55	POLYF	6FFD	ACBH	86	DIVB2	AF	CASEW
55FD	POLYG	70	MOVD	87	DIVB3	B0	MOVW
56	CVTFD	70FD	MOVH	88	BISB2	B1	CMPW
56FD	CVTGH	71	CMPD	89	BISB3	B2	MCOMW
57	Reserved	71FD	CMPH	8A	BICB2	B3	BITW
58	ADAWI	72	MNEGD	8B	BICB3	B4	CLRW
59	Reserved	72	MNEGD	8B	BICB3	B4	CLRW
5A	Reserved	72FD	MNEGH	8C	XORB2	B5	TSTW
5B	Reserved	73	TSTD	8D	XORB3	B6	INCW
5C	INSQHI	73FD	TSTH	8E	MNEGB	B7	DECW
5D	INSQTI	74	EMODD	8F	CASEB	B8	BISPSW
5E	REMQHI	74FD	EMODH	90	MOVB	B9	BICPSW

(continued)

Instructions (continued)

Numerical Order

BA	POPR	CE	MNEGL	DF	PUSHAL	F3	AOBLEQ		
BB	PUSHR	CF	CASEL	E0	BBS	F4	SOBGEQ		
BC	CHMK	D0	MOVL	E1	BBC	F5	SOBGTR		
BD	CHME	D1	CMPL	E2	BBSS	F6	CVTLB		
BE	CHMS	D2	MCOML	E3	BBCS	F6FD	CVTHF		
BF	CHMU	D3	BITL	E4	BBSC	F7	CVTLW		
C0	ADDL2	D4	CLRF	E5	BBCC	F7FD	CVTHD		
C1	ADDL3	D4	CLRL	E6	BBSSI	F8	ASHP		
C2	SUBL2	D5	TSTL	E7	BBCCI	F9	CVTLP		
C3	SUBL3	D6	INCL	E8	BLBS	FA	CALLG		
C4	MULL2	D7	DECL	E9	BLBC	FB	CALLS		
C5	MULL3	D8	ADWC	EA	FFS	FC	XFC		
C6	DIVL2	D9	SBWC	EB	FFC	FD	ESCD		
C7	DIVL3	DA	MTPR	EC	CMPV	FDFF	BUGL		
C8	BISL2	DB	MFPR	ED	CMPZV	FE	ESCE		
C9	BISL3	DC	MOVPSL	EE	EXTV	FE	Reserved		
CA	BICL2	DD	PUSHL	EF	EXTZV	FEFF	BUGW		
CB	BICL3	DE	MOVAF	F0	INSV	FF	ESCF		
CC	XORL2	DE	MOVAL	F1	ACBL	FF	Reserved		
CD	XORL3	DF	PUSHAF	F2	AOBLSS				

Source: *VAX-11 Programming Card*. Maynard, Mass.: Digital Equipment Corporation, 1984. Copyright, Digital Equipment Corporation, 1984. All rights reserved. Reprinted by permission.

APPENDIX C

ASCII Table

Control Codes

Dec	Hex	Code	Meaning	Dec	Hex	Code	Meaning
0	00	NUL	Null	16	10	DLE	Data link escape
1	01	SOH	Start of heading	17	11	DC1	Device control 1 (XON)
2	02	STX	Start of text	18	12	DC2	Device control 2
3	03	ETX	End of text	19	13	DC3	Device control 3 (XOFF)
4	04	EOT	End of transmission	20	14	DC4	Device control 4
5	05	ENQ	Enquiry	21	15	NAK	Negative acknowledge
6	06	ACK	Acknowledge	22	16	SYN	Synchronous idle
7	07	BEL	Bell	23	17	ETB	End of transmission block
8	08	BS	Backspace	24	18	CAN	Cancel
9	09	HT	Horizontal tab	25	19	EM	End of medium
10	0A	LF	Line feed	26	1A	SUB	Substitute
11	0B	VT	Vertical tab	27	1B	ESC	Escape
12	0C	FF	Form feed	28	1C	FS	File separator
13	0D	CR	Carriage return	29	1D	GS	Group separator
14	0E	SO	Shift out	30	1E	RS	Record separator
15	0F	SI	Shift in	31	1F	US	Unit separator

Dec	Hex	Code	Meaning
127	7F	DEL	Delete

Appendix C ASCII Table

Printable Characters

Dec	Hex	Code	Dec	Hex	Code	Dec	Hex	Code	Dec	Hex	Code	Dec	Hex	Code	Dec	Hex	Code
32	20		48	30	0	64	40	@	80	50	P	96	60	`	112	70	p
33	21	!	49	31	1	65	41	A	81	51	Q	97	61	a	113	71	q
34	22	"	50	32	2	66	42	B	82	52	R	98	62	b	114	72	r
35	23	#	51	33	3	67	43	C	83	53	S	99	63	c	115	73	s
36	24	&	52	34	4	68	44	D	84	54	T	100	64	d	116	74	t
37	25	%	53	35	5	69	45	E	85	55	U	101	65	e	117	75	u
38	26	$	54	36	6	70	46	F	86	56	V	102	66	f	118	76	v
39	27	'	55	37	7	71	47	G	87	57	W	103	67	g	119	77	w
40	28	(	56	38	8	72	48	H	88	58	X	104	68	h	120	78	x
41	29	)	57	39	9	73	49	I	89	59	Y	105	69	i	121	79	y
42	2A	*	58	3A	:	74	4A	J	90	5A	Z	106	6A	j	122	7A	z
43	2B	+	59	3B	;	75	4B	K	91	5B	[	107	6B	k	123	7B	{
44	2C	,	60	3C	<	76	4C	L	92	5C	\	108	6C	l	124	7C	|
45	2D	—	61	3D	=	77	4D	M	93	5D	]	109	6D	m	125	7D	}
46	2E	.	62	3E	>	78	4E	N	94	5E	^	110	6E	n	126	7E	~
47	2F	/	63	3F	?	79	4F	O	95	5F	_	111	6F	o			

APPENDIX D

Preparing and Running MACRO Programs Under VMS

In this appendix we will discuss procedures for running MACRO programs on a VAX using virtual memory system (VMS). We assume that the programmer is using a terminal and has some familiarity with the computer and a text editor. If necessary, the reader should refer to the various manuals on the VAX, including the *Command Language User's Guide** and the *EDT Editor Manual*.**

D.1 File Types

Before looking at the process of running an assembly language program, we will review file-naming conventions under VMS. Within a particular directory, filenames have the format

    filename.type;version

Thus EXAMPLE.MAR;2 is a legal filename.

**Command Language User's Guide.* Maynard, Mass.: Digital Equipment Corporation, 1984.
***EDT Editor Manual.* Maynard, Mass.: Digital Equipment Corporation, 1984.

The "filename" may consist of any alphanumeric characters.

The "type" has up to three characters. Some file types that might be useful when processing MACRO programs and procedures include the following:

MAR	A MACRO source file
OBJ	The object code
EXE	The executable image that is run
LIS	A list file that is suitable for printing
LOG	A log file that logs processes as they happen
FOR	A FORTRAN source file
PAS	A Pascal source file
C	A C source file

The "version" is a number representing the revision number of the file. VMS automatically increments the version number each time a new copy of the file is created. Because VMS automatically uses the highest version of the file, we normally do not need to specify a file's version number (except when using the operating system's DELETE command).

In many cases it is unnecessary to specify the complete filename. As described above, the VAX normally assumes the highest version of a file if the version is omitted. In some cases the operating system will also select the appropriate type. For example, the default file type for the RUN command is EXE, and the default for MACRO is MAR.

D.2 Developing MACRO Programs on the VAX

The procedure for developing MACRO programs is similar to the edit, compile, link, and run process used with high-level languages such as Pascal and FORTRAN. In general, the steps used to develop a program called "example" would be as follows:

Step 1. Create a source program using a text editor.

For example, to use the EDT text editor to create and correct the source program, we would use the system command

```
$ EDIT example.MAR
```

The capital letters indicate required wording, while the lower-case letters indicate names chosen by the user. Underlines indicate information typed by the user.

If desired, we can print the source file using

```
$ PRINT /QUEUE = printerqueue example.MAR
```

after returning to the operating system. If needed, consult with your instructor or computer center about the printer queues available on your system.

Step 2. Assemble the MACRO program.

We can assemble the program with the command

```
$ MACRO example
```

The output from this step is an object file example.OBJ. If errors are discovered in this step, we would return to the edit step to correct them.

Several options may be useful, and we will discuss three of them. We can request an assembler listing of the program by adding /LIST to the MACRO command. When requested, the assembler saves the listing in a file having the same name but with the LIS type. We can type the list file on our terminal with the command

```
$ TYPE example.LIS
```

or print it using

```
$ PRINT /QUEUE = printerqueue example.LIS
```

as desired. (.LIS is the default file type on these instructions, so we can omit it if we wish.)

The symbolic debugger is often used to provide simple input and output for MACRO programs as well as aid in the debugging process. To use it most effectively, we should use the /DEBUG option in the MACRO command.

If we use both options, the command becomes

```
$ MACRO /DEBUG /LIST example
```

If the program uses macros in a library, the /LIBRARY qualifier (often abbreviated /LIB) is used after the library's name. For example, we might use

```
$ MACRO example+macrolibrary/LIBRARY
```

Observe the plus sign joining the filename and the library name.

Step 3. Link the program.

We must link the program before it can be run. We do this with

$ LINK example

If we need to use the debugger, we would use the command

$ LINK /DEBUG example

instead.

The output of this step is the executable image with the file type EXE. The object file may no longer be needed after the link step. If not, we can delete it with

$ DELETE example.OBJ;*

where the wildcard "*" indicates that all versions are to be deleted.

We can combine separately assembled or compiled program segments into one executable program when we link. After the main program and the various functions and procedures are assembled or compiled with different filenames, we can link the various object files together by simply including the various names in the link command, separated by commas. For example, if we are calling a subroutine stored in a file with the name sub from the main program "example", the link statement would be

$ LINK example,sub

The debugger can be specified, if desired. When different object files are linked together in this manner, the resulting EXE file receives the name of the first object file mentioned. Thus, in our example, the executable file would be called example.EXE.

Step 4. Run the program.

To execute this program, we would simply type

$ RUN example

The program will run in the normal fashion unless we specified the debug option during the link step. In that case control will be turned over to the debugger. Use of the debugger is described in Appendix E.

Should an error be discovered while testing the program, we must return to the edit step to correct the problem.

Customizing VMS Commands

If desired, you can create your own abbreviations for system commands when using VMS. You do this by typing

```
$ your abbreviation :== normal command
```

For example, suppose you type

```
$ E      :== EDIT example.MAR
$ MACDEB :== MACRO /DEBUG example
$ LDEB   :== LINK  /DEBUG example
$ R      :== RUN example
```

For the rest of your terminal session, you need only type E after the system prompt to use the editor, MACDEB to macro your program, and likewise with the other abbreviations.

You may want to check into the use of .COM files to further automate command generation.

D.3 An Assembly Listing

A program listing generated by the /LIST option of the MACRO command is shown in Listing D.1. The program is a slightly modified version of a sample program from Chapter 2. We have added two labels to make the use of the debugger more convenient and have introduced an error to illustrate error messages.

The main portion of the assembly listing is divided into four parts. The right-hand side contains a copy of the source file, while the left-hand side shows the machine code generated by the assembler. The quantities in the machine code are organized by opcodes, addressing modes, offsets, and values. VAX machine code listings are unusual in that the bytes are ordered right to left. Why? Remember that the VAX stores numbers backward, with the least significant byte first. The assembler prints the machine code backward to show how it is stored in memory. As a result of the two reversals, integers are printed in their normal order. However, the bytes in character strings are listed in reverse order because they are stored in normal order but printed backward.

The left center column contains the next relative memory location available for an instruction or data value. Observe that some lines do not change this number because they do not generate any machine code. The memory locations shown are relative to the beginning of the program and are in hexadecimal. The actual memory locations used at run time are determined by the linker and the operating system.

Listing D.1 A MACRO listing

```
                                   1 ; This program will calculate the value
                                   2 ; of the function F(x) = 2x + 512x^2 for
                                   3 ; integer inputs
                                   4
                    0000           5 X:      .LONG   ^D15        ; Input is decimal 15
         0000000F   0000           6
                    0004           7        .ENTRY  Function, 0
      52 F6 AF 02   0004           8 Begin: MULL3   #2, X, R2   ; R2 now has 2x
   53 F0 AF F2 AF   0006           9        MULL3   X, X, R3    ; R3 now has x*x
   53 00000200 8F   000B          10        MULL2   #512, R3    ; R3 now has 3x*x
%MACRO-E-OPRNDSYNX, Operand syntax error
                    0018
         53 52 C0   0018          11        ADDL2   R2, R3      ; R3 has the value
                    001B          12 Done:  $EXIT_S
                    0024          13        .end    Function
   ↑                  ↑            ↑                ↑
 Machine           Relative       Line           Source
  code             memory        number           code
                  location
```

The right center column is the assembler's line count of the source program's statements.

For example, consider line 8.

```
Begin:    MULL3     #2,  X,  R2
```

The machine code that begins at relative location 0006 is

```
52    F6 AF    02    C5
```

The first value (52) is the addressing mode for the third operand (R2). The final value (C5) is the opcode. In this book, we would normally write and comment this code in a top-down manner as follows:

Code	Meaning
C5	MULL3
02	Short literal mode, #2
AF	Byte relative mode
F6	Offset of -10
52	Register direct, R2

We should make some comments about the listing of the machine code. The assembler normally does not print the machine code for macros like $EXIT_S. However, we know that some code was generated if the relative memory location changes. For example, $EXIT_S takes $(24)_{16} - (1B)_{16} = 9$ bytes of code.

Sometimes the assembler cannot determine the final address of a label. In this case it marks the spot in the machine code with an apostrophe, which indicates that the linker will have to calculate the value.

Any errors in the source program are flagged in the listing. The assembler inserts an exclamation point to mark the location that it thinks is in error. The listing shows shows an operand syntax error on line 10. The error marker points to the field following R3 because the semicolon indicating the beginning of the comment field was omitted.

APPENDIX E

Using the Symbolic Debugger

The symbolic debugger, a part of the VAX's virtual memory system (VMS), serves two very useful purposes for MACRO programmers. First, it provides a powerful tool to aid in debugging programs by allowing the programmer to monitor the contents of various registers or memory locations while instructing the computer to step through the program line by line or section by section. Second, its capacity to examine memory locations allows the programmer to write simple programs illustrating assembly language features without getting involved with difficult I/O coding.

The debugger allows you to

1. Examine the contents of memory locations and registers. Output formats include binary, hexadecimal, decimal, ASCII, and even one that disassembles machine language instruction code into assembler format.
2. Change the contents of memory locations and registers by depositing new values in them. Any of the formats mentioned above can be used.
3. Step through the program one instruction at a time.
4. Execute sections of the program one at a time. You arrange this by setting breakpoints at certain instructions. While executing the code, the debugger will suspend execution and return control to you just before processing an instruction marked as a breakpoint. If desired, you can specify debugger commands to be carried out automatically before giving you the debugger prompt.

5. Set watchpoints at variable locations. When the program is executed, the debugger will return control to you immediately after the variable's value is changed, allowing you to determine which instructions cause the variable to be modified.
6. Specify instruction addresses in the program called tracepoints and debugger commands to be carried out every time the specified instructions are executed while the program is running.
7. Calculate arithmetic expressions.

If you are using one of DEC's standard video terminals, such as a VT100, VT220, or an equivalent, and version 4.0 or higher of the operating system, you can instruct the debugger to display specified registers and memory locations on the screen automatically while running or stepping through the program.

The debugger is designed to be used with the standard VAX languages such as FORTRAN and Pascal as well as with MACRO. However, we will confine our discussion to its use with assembly language. For details on using the debugger with high-level languages, consult the *VAX-11 Symbolic Debugger Reference Manual* or the user's guide for that language.

E.1 Preparing to Use the Debugger

In this section we will use capital letters to indicate the required portions of commands and small letters to indicate words picked by the user. You can use either case. Underlines indicate information that you would type.

When writing MACRO programs that will be run using the debugger, it is useful to include labels on several key instructions even if the labels are not required by the program logic. In particular, labels on the first and last statements in the program are especially helpful. This will allow you to refer to the instructions by name when working with the debugger.

If the debugger is to understand the symbolic names for variables and instructions, you must provide it with a symbol table prepared by the assembler. Consequently, if you plan to use the debugger, you should indicate this when you assemble and link. The required procedure is illustrated by the following commands, which would be used to prepare a program stored in example.MAR.

```
$ MACRO /DEBUG /LIST example
$ LINK /DEBUG example
```

The /LIST qualifier on the MACRO command is optional, but a listing is sometimes helpful while debugging.

The program is now ready to run. The normal run command

```
$ RUN example
```

is used, but the computer will respond with something like the following:

```
VAX-11 DEBUG Version 4.2-2
```

```
%DEBUG-I-INITIAL, language is MACRO, module set to 'EXAMPLE'
DBG>
```

At this point you can issue debugger commands as desired. Before telling the computer to GO run the program, it is often desirable to issue some commands to set breakpoints, watchpoints, tracepoints, or the radix for input and output. We will discuss some useful commands in the next section. In Section E.3 we will show an example of the normal mode of operation. In Section E.4 we will look at the alternate screen mode.

E.2 Some Debugger Commands

We will discuss a few of the symbolic debugger commands and options.

GO

This command tells the debugger to start or continue execution of your program. The program will continue to run until it reaches a breakpoint, a watchpoint, a run-time error, or the end of the program. At this point the debugger regains control and asks you for further commands. If desired, you can tell the debugger to start execution at a given label using

```
GO label
```

STEP

This command tells the debugger to execute one or more instructions. Then the debugger will regain control, print the *next* instruction, and issue a prompt after completing its duties. The format is as follows:

STEP	Execute the next program instruction
STEP n	Execute the next *n* program instructions

EXAMINE Address

EXAMINE instructs the debugger to display the contents of the specified address or addresses. Unless you direct otherwise, the output is a longword expressed in hexadecimal. Some qualifiers that can be used to modify the output include the following:

Interpretation of Data	Length of Data
/DECIMAL	/BYTE
/HEX (default)	/WORD
/OCTAL	/LONG (default)
/ASCII:n	/QUADWORD
/INSTRUCTION	
/FLOAT	
/BINARY	
/PACKED:n	

You can abbreviate the EXAMINE instruction by its first letter (E) or by its first few letters, if desired. You must list qualifiers immediately after the keyword EXAMINE. For example:

EXAMINE x	Print the value of x using the default settings.
EXAMINE /DECIMAL /BYTE y	Print the value of byte y in decimal.
E /OCTAL /WORD val, k	Print the values of the words val and k in octal.
E	Print contents of next item.
E /ASCII:20 name	Print the ASCII value of the 20-byte string called "name".
E /INSTRUCTION begin:done	Disassemble (convert machine instructions into assembly language) starting at the label "begin" and continuing until the label "done".
E /INST @PC	Disassemble the instruction pointed to by the program counter.
E R0:R11	Print the contents of registers R0–R11.
EXAM 2B5	Print contents of memory location 2B5.
EXAMINE x:x+20	Print contents of the memory locations from x to 20 bytes beyond x.

DEPOSIT Address = Expression

This instruction tells the debugger to deposit the value of the expression at the given address. Some of the available qualifiers include /BYTE, /WORD, /LONG, /QUADWORD, /FLOAT, /INSTRUCTION, /ASCII:n, and /PACKED:n. Beware that the debugger will assume deposited values are in hex even when /FLOAT or /PACKED:n is specified unless you have issued the SET RADIX DECIMAL command. For example:

`DEPOSIT R2 = 0A13A7`	Deposit the hexadecimal number A13A7 in R2.
`DEPOSIT /WORD k = 1A, 20`	Deposit the numbers 1A and 20 in the words at k and $k + 2$.
`D /ASCII:5 x = "abcde"`	Deposit the characters "abcde" in five bytes starting at x.
`D /INSTRUCTION loop = "BLSS repeat"`	Deposit the given instruction at the address "loop".
`D PC = begin`	Deposit the address of "begin" in the PC.

When you replace data or instructions, the new values must have the same length in bytes of storage as the old values to ensure that the modified program is valid. You must precede hexadecimal values beginning with a letter A through F with 0; that is, we would say deposit 0ABC instead of ABC.

EVALUATE Expression

The expression that may contain program labels is evaluated and its value is printed. For example:

`EVALUATE /DEC 100`	Convert hex 100 to decimal (assuming radix = hex).
`EVAL x+50`	Evaluate the *address* of the location 50 past x.

EXIT

This instruction terminates the debugging session and returns control to the operating system. You must spell out EXIT completely.

SET BREAK Address

This instruction sets a breakpoint at the address of the specified instruction. When the program is running after a GO command, execution will stop and the debugger will return control to you just before the instruction would otherwise be carried out.

If desired, you can instruct the debugger to carry out some commands when it stops. For example,

```
SET BREAK loop DO (EXAMINE x,y; EXAMINE/BYTE z)
```

will cause the debugger to stop and display the values of x, y, and z just before it would have executed the instruction at "loop".

SET TRACE Address DO (Debugger Commands)

A tracepoint is similar to a breakpoint except that program execution continues after the specified instructions are carried out. For example:

```
SET TRACE repeat DO (EXAMINE /DECIMAL x, R2)
```

Just before executing the instruction at "repeat", the values of x and R2 will be printed in decimal, and the program will continue running without further interruption.

SET WATCH Address

This instruction sets a watchpoint at the address of the specified data item. While a program is running, execution will stop whenever the program writes a value into that address. When this happens, the new value and the address of the instruction that changed the value are displayed, and you are prompted for a debugger command. If desired, you can include a DO clause in the same manner as in the SET BREAK command.

SET RADIX Keyword

This command, introduced with version 4.0 of the operating system, is used to determine the base in which integers including addresses are input and displayed. The possible keywords include BINARY, DECIMAL, OCTAL, and HEXADECIMAL. Consider the following sequence of instructions.

```
SET RADIX DECIMAL
DEPOSIT x = 11          Convert decimal number 11 to binary and
                        store in x.
EXAMINE y               Examine the contents of y in decimal.
```

You can use the qualifiers /INPUT and /OUTPUT if you need different radixes for input and output.

SET TYPE Keyword

This command controls the default variable type. It is often useful when your program works with a data size different than a longword. Options include the following:

```
SET TYPE ASCII:n      SET TYPE ASCID
SET TYPE BYTE         SET TYPE WORD
SET TYPE LONG         SET TYPE FLOAT
```

SET MODULE Modulename

Module names are determined by the .TITLE directive in a program segment. You can use this command when more than one program segment has been combined into a single program. It tells the debugger which module's list of symbols are to be used during the debug run.

SET LANGUAGE Languagename

This instruction is used when program segments written in different languages have been combined into one program. It tells the debugger which language to use when interpreting machine instructions. For example, if we call a MACRO procedure containing .TITLE Proc from a Pascal program and want to use the debugger to study the macro portion of the program, we would type

```
SET LANGUAGE MACRO
SET MODULE Proc
```

There are many other set commands. See the references for further details.

SHOW Item

You can request the status of various items. Some of the show commands are as follows:

SHOW BREAK	Show the current breakpoints.
SHOW TRACE	Show the current tracepoints.
SHOW WATCH	Show the current watchpoints.
SHOW RADIX	Show the current radix.
SHOW TYPE	Show the current type.
SHOW MODE	Show several modes including radix.

CANCEL Item

Some of the cancel commands include the following:

CANCEL BREAK address	Cancel the given breakpoint.
CANCEL TRACE address	Cancel the given tracepoint.
CANCEL WATCH address	Cancel the given watchpoint.

If desired, you can cancel all breakpoints, tracepoints, or watchpoints at once using /ALL. For example:

CANCEL BREAK /ALL   Cancel all breakpoints.

HELP

The debugger provides information about its commands.

SET OUTPUT LOG

The debugger will copy all subsequent input and output to the file DEBUG.LOG, which can be printed after the run to obtain a hard-copy transcript of debugger operations.

E.3 An Example Using the Symbolic Debugger

We will use the sample program from Chapter 2, but we will add some labels to the first and last instructions to make it more convenient to use the debugger. The modified program is as follows:

```
        .TITLE  Example

;   This program will calculate the value of the
;      function F(X) = 2*X + 512*X*X for integer inputs

;   Variable list:
X:      .LONG   15              ; Input is decimal 15

        .ENTRY  Function, 0
Begin:  MULL3   #2, X, R2       ; R2 now has 2*X
        MULL3   X, X, R3        ; R3 now has X*X
        MULL2   #512, R3        ; R3 now has 512*X*X
        ADDL2   R2, R3          ; R3 has the result
Done:   EXIT_S
        .END    Function
```

In the following discussion, exclamation marks denote comments added to explain the listing.

Let us suppose that the program is stored in FUNCTION.MAR. The required VMS commands to assemble, link, and run the file are as follows:

```
$ MACRO /DEBUG FUNCTION
$ LINK  /DEBUG FUNCTION
$ RUN FUNCTION
```

The computer would respond with

```
        VAX DEBUG Version 4.2-2

%DEBUG-I-INITIAL, language is MACRO, module set to 'EXAMPLE'
DBG>
```

EXAMPLE is the name of our program module found in the .TITLE statement. We will begin by setting a breakpoint at Done. (This is very important in versions 4.1 and 4.2-2 of the debugger because it is difficult to reset the PC after executing the $EXIT_S macro. Future versions of the debugger may correct this problem.)

```
    DBG>SET BREAK Done
```

Now we can run the program and examine R3.

```
DBG>GO
break at EXAMPLE\DONE:  PUSHL    S^#01    ! PUSHL is part of the
                                          !    way MACRO translates EXIT_S
DBG>EXAMINE R3
0\%R3:   0001C21E                         ! Debug prints the hex value R3
```

Suppose that we want to test the function with X equal to hexadecimal 10. Because X is a longword, we will not have to specify its length.

```
DBG>DEPOSIT X=10
DBG>GO Begin                              ! Tell the debugger to start at Begin
break at EXAMPLE\DONE:  PUSHL    S^#01
DBG>EXAM X, R3                            ! Examine the values in X and R3
EXAMPLE\X:       00000010
0\%R3:   00020020
```

To simplify matters, we might want to have the debugger print the values of X and R3 automatically when it gets to Done.

E.3 An Example Using the Symbolic Debugger

```
DBG>SET BREAK Done DO (EXAM X, R3)
DBG>GO Begin
break at EXAMPLE\DONE:  PUSHL      S^#01
EXAMPLE\X:        00000010          ! The debugger prints these
0\%R3:   00020020                   ! automatically when stopping at Done
```

This time we will step through the program, examining the registers as we go. We will have to reset the program counter to the beginning of the program where we want to start. Observe that when the debugger disassembles a statement, the output is more formal than in our program. For example, the module name is added to variable names. The debugger is not given a copy of our MACRO program. It must try to figure out what we wrote by looking at the machine code and the symbol table. You should understand that after each step, the debugger prints out the next statement to be executed, not the statement that it just processed.

```
DBG>DEPOSIT PC = Begin              ! Reset the PC to the address of Begin
DBG>STEP                            ! Execute one instruction
stepped to EXAMPLE\BEGIN+5:  MULL3  B^EXAMPLE\X, B^EXAMPLE\X, R3
DBG>E R2                            ! Examine R2 before executing
                                    !   the instruction listed above

0\%R2:   00000020
DBG>STEP
stepped to EXAMPLE\BEGIN+OB: MULL2  I^#00000200, R3
DBG>E R3
0\%R3:   00000100
DBG>STEP
stepped to EXAMPLE\BEGIN+12: ADDL2  R2, R3
DBG>E R3
0\%R3:   00020000
DBG>S                               ! Step
stepped to EXAMPLE\DONE:  PUSHL     S^#01
break at EXAMPLE\DONE:  PUSHL       S^#01 ! We stepped to the
                                          !   breakpoint
EXAMPLE\X:        00000010
0\%R3:   00020020
```

Suppose that we would like the computer to print the values of R2 and R3 automatically after executing the second instruction. We will set a tracepoint at the third instruction, whose address we found while stepping through the program. (We did not put a label on this statement.)

```
DBG>SET TRACE Begin+0B DO (E R2, R3)
DBG>GO Begin                                  ! Execute the program
trace at EXAMPLE\BEGIN+0B: MULL2    I^#00000200,R3
0\%R2:    00000020                            ! Output from tracepoint
0\%R3:    00000100                            ! Shows R3 before MULL2
break at EXAMPLE\DONE: PUSHL      S^#01
EXAMPLE\X:           00000010
0\%R3:    00020020
```

We would like to be able to use decimal values in our I/O. We will use the SET RADIX command.

```
DBG>SET RADIX DECIMAL                         ! Request decimal values
DBG>DEPOSIT X = 16                            ! Assign decimal 16 to X
DBG>GO Begin
trace at EXAMPLE\BEGIN+0B: MULL2    I^#512,R3
0\%R2:    32                                  ! Output from tracepoint
0\%R3:    256
break at EXAMPLE\DONE: PUSHL      S^#01
EXAMPLE\X:           16
0\%R3:    131104
```

We have investigated this program quite carefully, so we can terminate the debugger session.

```
DBG>EXIT                                      ! Back to the operating system
```

In the next section we will look at an alternate mode of operation.

E.4 The Screen Mode

Versions 4.0 and above of the symbolic debugger have a screen mode that is particularly suited for use on DEC's VT100, VT220, or equivalent terminals. This mode also works on VT52 or compatible terminals but requires repeated rewriting of the screen, significantly slowing its operation. The screen mode allows us to see "what is happening inside the computer." In this mode the screen of a video terminal is divided into different parts called windows. These windows allow us to view the code being executed, output from the program or the debugger, and, optionally, contents of registers and memory locations. You can use each window to display different types of data. For exanple, the standard screen for MACRO programs has three parts, as shown in Figure E.1. The top window, called INST, provides a view of a portion of the program

```
--INST---instruction-scroll----------------------------------------
   00000203:  HALT
   00000204:  entry mask ^M<>
->00000206:   MULW3     S^#02,B^EXAMPLE\X,R2
   0000020B:  MULW3     B^EXAMPLE\X,B^EXAMPLE\X,R3
   00000211:  MULW2     S^#20,R3
   00000214:  ADDW3     R2,R3,B^EXAMPLE\Y
   00000219:  PUSHL     S^#01
   0000021B:  CALLS     S^#01,@#SYS$EXIT

--OUT---output-----------------------------------------------------




-------------------------------------------------------------------
DBG>  SET BREAK Done
DBG>  SET MODE SCREEN
DBG>
```

Figure E.1 Initial screen windows

being executed. (Actually, we see a disassembled version of the machine code.) An arrow points to the instruction whose address is in the PC. The middle section, called OUT, provides a view of a display containing the output from the debugger. In the figure this section is empty because there has been no output since we entered the screen mode. The bottom portion is used for input to the debugger. If desired, you can create new windows and delete or reshape existing ones.

(In this appendix we describe the screen mode as available in version 4.2-2 of the debugger.* Version 4.1 displayed a window called REG on the top of the screen instead of the INST window, which was not yet available for MACRO users. We will describe the REG window later in this appendix.)

A window may provide only a partial view of the display behind it. Because the OUT display can contain up to 100 lines, we can view only a small portion at one time. Normally the last few lines of output are exhibited. The window is scrolled downward as new output is added at the bottom of the display. You can ask the debugger to scroll the window over the text in a display, allowing you to inspect output that disappeared from view earlier.

We now will look at a simple example illustrating the screen mode using a slightly modified version of the program in the previous section.

*The instructor's guide describes the screen mode as found in VMS version 4.4.

Appendix E Using the Symbolic Debugger

We have added a location Y to store the result of the function evaluation and have reduced the data length to "word" to demonstrate how different data types are processed. We also reduced the coefficient of X * X to help prevent overflow.

```
               .TITLE   EXAMPLE

        ;   This program will calculate the value of the
        ;      function F(X) = 2*X + 32*X*X for integer inputs

        ;   Variable list:
X:          .WORD    15          ; Input is decimal 15
Y:          .BLKW    1           ; Provide storage for the result

            .ENTRY   Function, 0
Begin:  MULW3    #2, X, R2       ; R2 now has 2*X
        MULW3    X, X, R3        ; R3 now has X*X
        MULW2    #32, R3         ; R3 now has 32*X*X
        ADDW3    R2, R3, Y       ; Y has the value
Done:   $EXIT_S
        .END     Function
```

Assuming that the program is stored in CALCULATE.MAR, we can use the following steps to execute the program in the screen mode.

```
$ MACRO /DEBUG CALCULATE
$ LINK /DEBUG CALCULATE
$ RUN CALCULATE
DBG>SET BREAK Done
DBG>SET MODE SCREEN
```

We set a breakpoint at the last statement in the program as suggested in the previous section.

At this point the display looks like that shown in Figure E.1. The arrow in the INST window points to the first instruction in the program.

We can execute the program and examine the contents of variables X and Y and registers R2 and R3.

```
DBG>GO
DBG>EXAMINE /WORD X, Y, R2, R3
```

The resulting screen is shown in Figure E.2.

We could continue to issue more debugger commands to test the program, but instead let us create a new display for the important data values and arrange to have it automatically updated as we run or step through the program. First we will create a display called VARIABLE and

```
--INST---instruction-scroll------------------------------------------
   00000203:  HALT
   00000204:  entry mask ^M<>
   00000206:  MULW3    S^#02,B^EXAMPLE\X,R2
   0000020B:  MULW3    B^EXAMPLE\X,B^EXAMPLE\X,R3
   00000211:  MULW2    S^#20,R3
   00000214:  ADDW3    R2,R3,B^EXAMPLE\Y
->00000219:  PUSHL    S^#01
   0000021B:  CALLS    S^#01,@#SYS$EXIT

--OUT---output------------------------------------------------------
break at EXAMPLE\DONE:  PUSHL      S^#01
EXAMPLE\X:          000F
EXAMPLE\Y:          1C3E
0\%R2:    001E
0\%R3:    1C20



--------------------------------------------------------------------
DBG> GO
DBG> EXAMINE /WORD X, Y, R2, R3
DBG>
```

Figure E.2 The standard screen after execution

request to see those values in it. We use the SET DISPLAY command for this purpose.

```
DBG>SET DISPLAY /MARK_CHANGE VARIABLE AT Q1
                        DO (EXAMINE /WORD X,Y,R2,R3)
```

This command can be interpreted in the following manner. Create a new display. If the terminal permits, displayed values are to be highlighted after they are changed. Call the display VARIABLE. The window for this display is to be located in the top (first) quarter (Q1) of the screen. The values of the words X, Y, R2, and R3 are to be displayed in the window and updated each time the debugger takes control. The four values fit into this window exactly. We will discuss how to get larger windows later.

After we issue this command, observe that the first few lines of the INST display are hidden beneath the new window. However, they are not forgotten. We might assume that the VARIABLE display was pasted over the top of the older display. To avoid hiding part of INST, we will change its position and size to fit below the new window using the display command.

```
DBG>DISPLAY INST AT Q2
```

We use the display command to alter existing displays. Though several options are possible, we need only tell the computer to use the second quarter (Q2) of the screen for this window. The resulting screen is shown in Figure E.3.

Before we test our program again, we would like to add a predefined display that is particularly helpful to assembly language coders. A display called REG contains the values of the registers and the values of the four condition codes. In addition, it holds the four values at the beginning of the argument list (@AP) and at the top of the stack (@SP). Because this display is predefined, we need only specify its location on the screen. To put it in the third quarter of the screen, we can say

```
DBG>DISPLAY REG AT Q3
```

```
--VARIABLE----------------------------------------------------
EXAMPLE\X:         000F
EXAMPLE\Y:         1C3E
0\%R2:    001E
0\%R3:    1C20
  --INST---instruction-scroll--------------------------------
    00000206:  MULW3    S^#02, B^EXAMPLE\X, R2
    0000020B:  MULW3    B^EXAMPLE\X, B^EXAMPLE\X, R3
    00000211:  MULW2    S^#20, R3
    00000214:  ADDW3    R2, R3, B^EXAMPLE\Y
--OUT---output-----------------------------------------------
break at EXAMPLE\DONE:  PUSHL     S^#01
EXAMPLE\X:         000F
EXAMPLE\Y:         1C3E
0\%R2:    001E
0\%R3:    1C20


-------------------------------------------------------------
DBG> SET DISPLAY /MARK_CHANGE VARIABLE AT Q1 DO (EXAMINE /WORD X, Y, R2, R3)
DBG> DISPLAY INST AT Q2
DBG>
```

Figure E.3 A user-defined display

Of course this will cover up the top half of the OUT window. We can reduce the size of its window with

```
DBG>DISPLAY OUT AT Q4
```

To test our program with a new X value, we deposit hexadecimal 10 into this variable using

```
DBG>DEPOSIT /WORD X = 10
```

We would like to step through the program so that we deposit the address of Begin into the program counter and make four steps.

```
DBG>DEPOSIT PC = Begin
DBG>STEP
DBG>S
DBG>S
DBG>S
```

The resulting display is shown in Figure E.4.

```
--VARIABLE-------------------------------------------------------------
EXAMPLE\X:        0010
EXAMPLE\Y:        2020
0\%R2:    0020
0\%R3:    2000
--INST---instruction-scroll-------------------------------------------
  00000211:  MULW2    S^#20,R3
  00000214:  ADDW3    R2,R3,B^EXAMPLE\Y
->00000219:  PUSHL    S^#01
  0000021B:  CALLS    S^#01,@#SYS$EXIT
--REG-----------------------------------------------------------------
R0: 00000000 R4: 00000000 R8:  7FFED052 AP: 7FF709CC   @AP: 00000006 @SP: 00000000   N: 0
R1: 00000000 R5: 00000000 R9:  7FFED25A FP: 7FF70984    +4: 7FFE6440  +4: 00000000   Z: 0
R2: 00000020 R6: 7FF70649 R10: 7FFEDDD4 SP: 7FF70984    +8: 7FFA8EAD  +8: 7FF709CC   V: 0
R3: 7FF72000 R7: 8001E4DD R11: 7FFE33DC PC: 00000219   +12: 7FFE640C +12: 7FF709B8   C: 0
--OUT---output--------------------------------------------------------
stepped to EXAMPLE\BEGIN+0B: MULW2     S^#20,R3
stepped to EXAMPLE\BEGIN+0E: ADDW3     R2,R3,B^EXAMPLE\Y
stepped to EXAMPLE\DONE: PUSHL    S^#01
break   at EXAMPLE\DONE: PUSHL    S^#01
----------------------------------------------------------------------
DBG> S
DBG> S
DBG>
```

Figure E.4 User-defined display after stepping to the program

We conclude this section by looking at some commands that can be used to set up or manipulate displays.

SET MODE SCREEN
SET MODE NOSCREEN

These commands turn the screen mode on or off.

SET DISPLAY /Qualifiers Name AT Position DO (Commands)

This SET command establishes *new* displays. An interesting qualifier is /MARK_CHANGE, which causes new values to be displayed in reverse video if the terminal permits. "Name" is the name that we will use to refer to this display. We can use several predefined positions; among them are the following:

FS	full screen	T1	top third	Q1	top quarter
H1	top half	T2	2nd third	Q2	2nd quarter
H2	bottom half	T3	bottom third	Q3	3rd quarter
Q23	middle half	T12	top 2/3rds	Q4	4th quarter
		T23	bottom 2/3rds		

The most common command in the DO clause is EXAMINE. However, other instructions may sometimes be helpful. The qualifiers and the AT and DO clauses are optional.

DISPLAY /Qualifiers Name AT Position DO (Commands)

We use this display command to modify *existing* displays. We can use it to modify the original definition of a display made at its creation. Again, the qualifiers and the AT and DO clauses are optional. We could break up the long set display command used in the sample run in the following manner:

```
DBG>SET DISPLAY VARIABLE
DBG>DISPLAY VARIABLE AT Q1
DBG>DISPLAY VARIABLE DO (EXAMINE /WORD X, Y, R2, R3)
DBG>DISPLAY /MARK_CHANGE VARIABLE
```

Some other useful qualifiers include

/REMOVE

Remove the contents of the display from the screen but not from the computer's memory. We can recall the display later by specifying its location and size.

> /GENERATE

Recalculate the display.

SCROLL /Qualifier Name

We use this instruction to move the window of the named screen over the text in the display. The qualifiers include /UP, /DOWN, /LEFT, /RIGHT, /TOP, and /BOTTOM. If desired, you can specify the number of lines or spaces moved by adding a colon and the number to the direction qualifier. For example:

> SCROLL /DOWN: 5 OUT

If the name of the display is omitted, the display marked–scroll–is used. You can use the keypad to move the window quickly.

SELECT /SCROLL Name

This instruction changes the default–scroll–display to the one named. If the name is omitted, the command rotates the default for the scroll commands to the next display.

CANCEL DISPLAY Name

This instruction completely removes the display from the computer's memory and the screen.

SHOW DISPLAY

This command shows information about any displays that have been defined.

SHOW WINDOW

This command shows a number of predefined (and any user-defined) windows that can be used as part of an AT clause in a SET DISPLAY or DISPLAY command.

<CTRL W>

This command refreshes the terminal's screen.

The *VAX-11 Symbolic Debugger Reference Manual* contains much more information about the screen mode.

E.5 The Keypad on VT100 and VT220 Terminals

The debugger programs the keypad of a VT100 or VT220 so that many debugger commands can be given with only a few keystrokes. The interpretation of the keys is shown in Figure E.5.

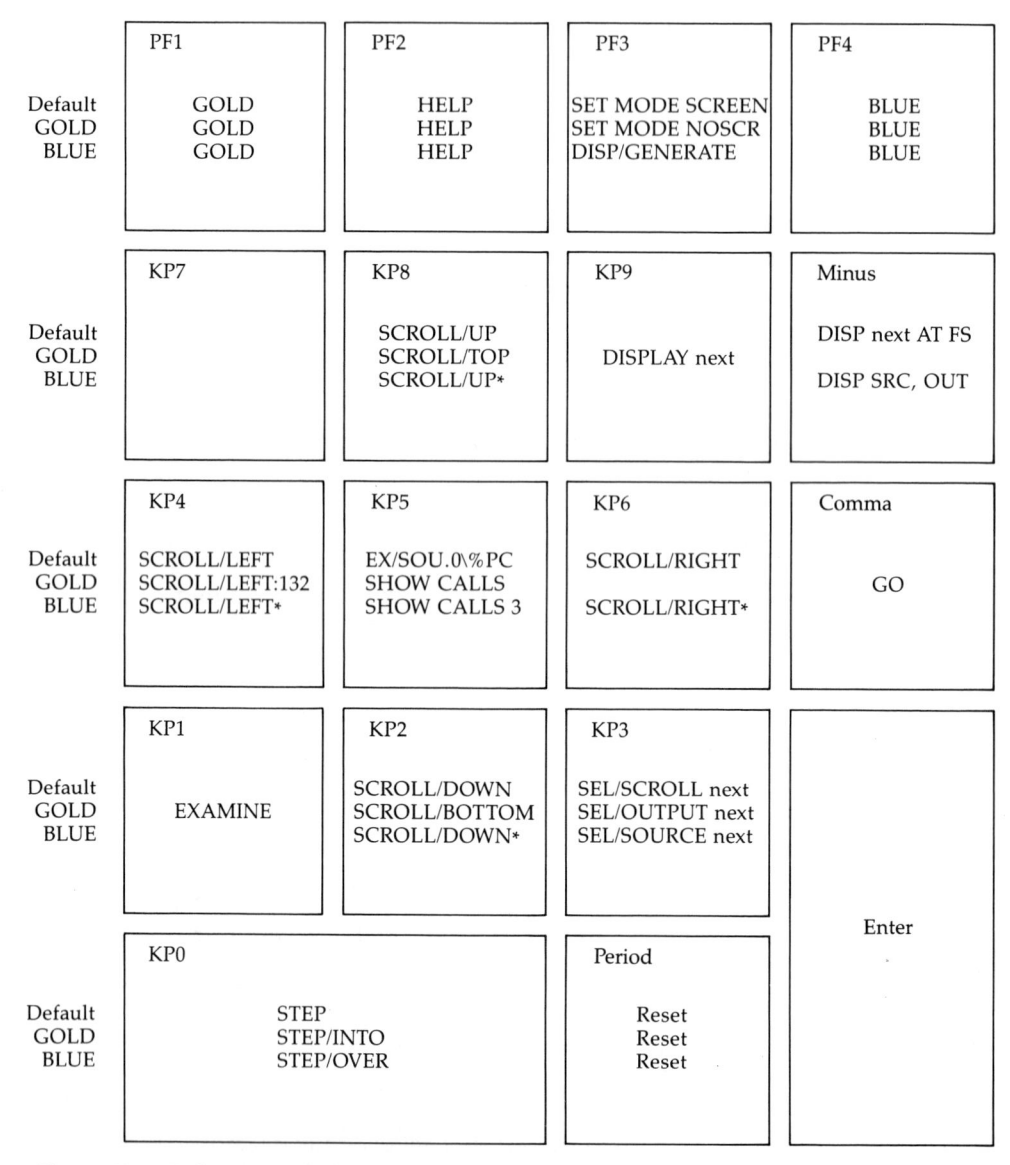

	PF1	PF2	PF3	PF4
Default	GOLD	HELP	SET MODE SCREEN	BLUE
GOLD	GOLD	HELP	SET MODE NOSCR	BLUE
BLUE	GOLD	HELP	DISP/GENERATE	BLUE

	KP7	KP8	KP9	Minus
Default		SCROLL/UP		DISP next AT FS
GOLD		SCROLL/TOP	DISPLAY next	
BLUE		SCROLL/UP*		DISP SRC, OUT

	KP4	KP5	KP6	Comma
Default	SCROLL/LEFT	EX/SOU.0\%PC	SCROLL/RIGHT	
GOLD	SCROLL/LEFT:132	SHOW CALLS		GO
BLUE	SCROLL/LEFT*	SHOW CALLS 3	SCROLL/RIGHT*	

	KP1	KP2	KP3	
Default		SCROLL/DOWN	SEL/SCROLL next	
GOLD	EXAMINE	SCROLL/BOTTOM	SEL/OUTPUT next	
BLUE		SCROLL/DOWN*	SEL/SOURCE next	Enter

	KP0		Period	
Default	STEP		Reset	
GOLD	STEP/INTO		Reset	
BLUE	STEP/OVER		Reset	

Figure E.5 Debugger-defined keypad key functions
Source: *VAX-11 Symbolic Debugger Reference Manual.* Copyright, Digital Equipment Corporation, 1984. All rights reserved. Reprinted by permission.

Many keys have three interpretations. If the key is preceded by the PF1 key, the "gold" interpretation is used. If it is preceded by the PF4 key, the "blue" interpretation is used. Otherwise the default interpretation is used.

Many key definitions include a carriage return so that pressing the key is all that is needed. However, a few "blue" interpretations allow you to add additional text before pressing the carriage return. These keys are marked with an asterisk in the figure.

We have not discussed some of the lesser-used commands in this appendix. Refer to the reference manual or use HELP to get information on such instructions.

APPENDIX F

Input/Output Macros

This appendix includes listings of two macros, called Input and Output, that provide easy I/O for MACRO programs. Each can process byte, word, longword, and floating values in decimal, characters and strings in ASCII, and longword data in hex. Input provides for prompts and Output allows labeling lines. They restore all the registers they use to the registers' original values. Both process one data value per call.

Typical calls to these macros have the following format:

```
Input    <prompt>, datatype = location
Output   <message>, datatype = location
```

The <prompt> is optional for Input. If it is included, it must be the first argument and be enclosed in corner brackets. You must specify the value to be input using the "datatype = location" clause. The possible data types include the following:

Byte   Word   Long
Float   ASCII   Hex

Values for Byte, Word, Long, and Float are input in decimal. The number may optionally have a plus or minus sign. Floating input may include a decimal (for example, 16.8) and/or an E exponent (for example, 3.8E17). By default, ASCII can be used to input a single character. To input a string, we need an optional argument Length, which will be discussed later. Hex indicates that a longword will be input in a hexadecimal format. The location is a memory location or, for numerical values, one of the registers R8–R11. You specify the location using one of the normal addressing modes. However, you should not use registers R0–R7 in an Input macro call.

Output works in a similar way except that both the <message> and the data value specified by the "datatype = location" clause are optional. Thus this macro can be used to print a blank line, a heading, a value, or a value with a label. The location can be a memory address or, for numerical output, any one of the registers or even an immediate or short literal operand. The Float output is in exponential form, including seven decimal places and an E exponent.

To process an ASCII string of more than one character, you must include an additional argument specifying its length. The formats are as follows:

```
Input     <prompt>, ASCII = location, -
                Length = numberbytes
Output    <message>, ASCII = location, -
                Length = numberbytes
```

The default for Length is 1 byte. The number of bytes specified by ASCII should be less than or equal to 20. If larger strings are specified, only the first 20 characters are processed. On input, additional characters will be blank filled.

Some sample input and output statements include the following:

```
Input     <Enter GPA: >, Float = GPA
Input     ASCII = Letter
Input     <Enter name - >, ASCII = Name, Length = #12
Output                              ; print a blank line
Output    <The student is>
Output    <Name:    >, ASCII = Name, Length = NumChar
Output    <GPA:     >, Float = GPA
Output    ASCII = Letter
```

The sixth statement assumes that NumChar is a word (or longword). A sample run (the user's input is underlined) might look like this:

```
Enter GPA: 3.143
B
Enter name - Dale

The student is
Name:    Dale
GPA:     0.3143000E+01
 B
```

We have adapted the following program from Chapter 2 by adding the Input and Output macros. We have changed the directive reserving space for variable X from .LONG to .BLKL because the variable's value will be supplied at run time.

```
        .TITLE  Example

;   This program will calculate the value of the
;       function F(X) = 2*X + 512*X*X for integer inputs

;   Variable list:
X:      .BLKL    1                           ; Reserve room for X

        .ENTRY   Function, 0
        Input    <Enter x value :>, Long = X
        MULL3    #2, X, R2                   ; R2 now has 2*X
        MULL3    X, X, R3                    ; R3 now has X*X
        MULL2    #512, R3                    ; R3 now has 512*X*X
        ADDL2    R2, R3                      ; R3 has the result
        Output   <X       :>, Long = X
        Output   <Result :>, Long = R3
        $EXIT_S
        .END     Function
```

A sample run is shown below.

```
Enter x value : 10
X       : +0000000010
Result : +0000051220
```

We need to make some comments about the operation of these macros. Input saves and restores the registers R0–R7, which should not be used in a call to this macro. Output saves and restores the registers R0–R5. Numerical values can occur in any register or memory location. You can use any appropriate addressing mode with either macro with two restrictions: (1) the addressing mode should not change any of the saved registers, and (2) the stack pointer should not be changed.

The following type of code is suggested for processing arrays.

```
         Output  <The list of values>  ; Print heading
         MOVL    #Number, R10          ; R10 <-- element count
         MOVAB   List, R11             ; R11 <-- address List
Loop:    Output  Byte = (R11)+         ; Output next element
         SOBGTR  R10, Loop             ; Decrement count and
                                       ;   repeat if needed.
         Output                        ; Print blank line
```

Observe that we carefully chose R11 to be outside the range of those registers that are saved and restored.

There are several ways in which these macros can be assembled with your code. If desired, you could use the INCLUDE statement in the editor to add the macros to the beginning of your program, but it is better to place them in a library. In this case the system command

```
$ MACRO   programname+libraryname/LIB
```

would assemble the program (note the plus sign). In case of difficulty with the macro calls, it may help to get a listing showing the macro expansions. You can use the command

```
$ MACRO   /LIST  /SHOW=MEB   programname+libraryname/LIB
```

(The ME option for SHOW is not recommended because of the macros' length.)

To create a library to hold these macros, use the instruction

```
$ LIBRARY  /MACRO  /CREATE  /LOG  libraryname macrofilename
```

To update the code in the libraries, use the command

```
$ LIBRARY  /MACRO  /REPLACE  /LOG  libraryname macrofilename
```

The file macrofilename.MAR should hold only the macros. All users on the system can share the resulting library if the protection is set properly with

```
$ SET PROTECTION = W:R libraryname.MLB
```

The input comes from the logical device SYS$INPUT, and output is sent to SYS$OUTPUT. These logical names are normally assigned to the user's terminal in interactive runs. If desired, you can reassign them to files or other devices before the run. For example:

```
$ ASSIGN   Indata.DAT   SYS$INPUT
```

If that is done, you should deassign the names after the run with

```
$ DEASSIGN SYS$INPUT
```

Several bytes of code are added to the program every time these macros are called. You should use word offsets to branch around the macro calls (that is, use BRW, not BRB or conditional branches).

These macros have the undesirable characteristic of storing the I/O buffer and data in the instruction code. Thus you cannot use them in a program section (.PSECT) marked NOWRT. Consequently, while they

Appendix F Input/Output Macros

are suitable for simple programs, they are not recommended for serious coding efforts.

You should be able to understand the code in the macros after studying Chapters 8 and 9. They carry out their own conversions for decimal integers. Procedures supplied in the run-time library are used to convert floating-point and hex values. The procedure FOR$CVT_D_TE is the standard FORTRAN output routine for numbers printed with the E format code. OTS$CVT_T_D is the system standard input routine for double-precision real numbers, which can then be converted to floating. OTS$CVT_TZ_L converts hexadecimal text to longwords, and OTS$CVT_L_TZ reverses that process. The descriptor ValueDesc in OUTPUT is used to tell these conversion routines where the character form of the number is to be stored in the Message that will be printed.

The .WARN macro and following .PRINT lines print a warning during assembly time if the user includes both a prompt or message and a location but forgets to specify the data type in the argument list. The underline (___) has been added to symbols created in the macros to help prevent conflicts with programmer-defined symbols.

```
;
;                       * * * * * * * * * * *
;                       *    INPUT MACRO    *
;                       * * * * * * * * * * *

        .MACRO     Input    Prompt, Byte, Word, Long, Float, -
                   ASCII, Length=#1, Hex, ?PromptBuf, -
                   ?Cont, ?Message, ?TempBuf, ?HasSign

        .EXTERNAL  Lib$Get_Input, Lib$Put_Output
        .EXTERNAL  OTS$CVT_T_D, OTS$CVT_TZ_L

;   Inputs various types of data

;   Registers R0 through R7 are saved and restored.  They cannot
;       be changed by a call to this macro.

;                       * * * * * * * * * * *

        .NARG      NumArg___              ; *** Check for too many
        .IF GT NumArg___-1                ;     positional arguments
          .WARN    1  ; Missing argument name in Input macro
          .PRINT   1  ; Remember to use the format
          .PRINT   1  ;     Input    <YourPrompt>, VariableType = Location
        .ENDC

;                       * * * * * * * * * * *

        BRB        Cont                   ; *** Skip past buffers
```

```
Message:                                  ; *** Room for buffers
        .ASCID    "                    "  ; 20-character buffer
MessageLength___ = . - Message - 8
        .BLKB     1                       ;    allows room for shift
PromptBuf:
        .ASCID    "Prompt"
TempBuf:
        .BLKB     8

;                         * * * * * * * * * *

Cont:                                     ; *** Initialize
        PUSHR     #^M<R0, R1, R2, R3, R4, R5, R6, R7>


        PUSHAW    PromptBuf               ; *** Input string
        PUSHAW    Message
        CALLS     #2, G^Lib$Get_Input

        .IF NB Byte'Word'Long             ; *** Convert Integer
            SKPC   #^A" ", #MessageLength___, @Message+4
                                          ; Find leading sign
            MOVW   R0, R6                 ; Save remaining bytes
            MOVL   R1, R7                 ; Save address of sign
            CMPB   (R1), #^A"-"           ; Does it begin with "-"?
            BEQL   HasSign                ;    then HasSign
            CMPB   (R1), #^A"+"           ; Does it begin with "+"?
            BEQL   HasSign                ;    then HasSign
            MOVC3  R0, (R1), 1(R1)        ; Make room for sign
            MOVB   #^A"+", (R7)           ;    and insert + sign
            INCW   R6                     ; Increment char count
HasSign:    LOCC   #^A" ", R6, (R7)       ; Find end of number
            SUBW   R0, R6                 ; Find number of bytes
            DECW   R6                     ; Find number of digits
            CVTSP  R6, (R7), R6, TempBuf  ; Convert to packed
            CVTPL  R6, TempBuf, R0        ; Convert to longword
        .ENDC

        .IIF NB, Byte, CVTLB R0, Byte; *** Store Byte

        .IIF NB, Word, CVTLW R0, Word; *** Store Word

        .IIF NB, Long, MOVL  R0, Long; *** Store Long

        .IF NB ASCII
            MOVC5 Message, @Message+4, #^A" ", Length, ASCII
        .ENDC

        .IF NB Float                      ; *** Read floating value
            PUSHL  #1                     ; Push flag to ignore blanks
```

```
        PUSHL   #0                      ; Push scale factor
        PUSHL   #0                      ; Push digits in assumed fraction
        PUSHAQ  TempBuf                 ; Push address of quad buffer
        PUSHAL  Message                 ; Push address of descriptor
        CALLS   #5, G^OTS$CVT_T_D       ; Call conversion routine
        CVTDF   TempBuf, Float          ; Convert and store value
    .ENDC

    .IF NB Hex                          ; *** Read hex value into longword
        PUSHL   #1                      ; Push flag to ignore blanks
        PUSHL   #4                      ; Push number of bytes in value
        PUSHAL  TempBuf                 ; Push address of temp buffer
        PUSHAL  Message                 ; Push address descriptor
        CALLS   #4, G^OTS$CVT_TZ_L      ; Call conversion routine
        MOVL    TempBuf, Hex            ; Store longword
    .ENDC

        POPR    #^M<R0, R1, R2, R3, R4, R5, R6, R7>
    .ENDM   Input

;                       * * * * * * * * * *
;                       *   OUTPUT MACRO   *
;                       * * * * * * * * * *

    .MACRO  Output  Label, Byte, Word, Long, Float, -
                    ASCII, Length=#1, Hex, -
                    ?Cont, ?Message, ?TempBuf, ?ValueDesc

    .EXTERNAL Lib$Put_Output
    .EXTERNAL FOR$CVT_D_TE, OTS$CVT_L_TZ

;       Outputs various types of data

;       Registers R0 through R5 are saved and restored.  They cannot
;           be changed by a call to this macro.

;                       * * * * * * * * * *

    .NARG   NumArg___               ; *** Check for too many
    .IF  GT NumArg___-1             ;     positional arguments
        .WARN   2 ; Missing argument name on Output macro
        .PRINT  2 ; Remember to use the format
        .PRINT  2 ;     Output <YourLabel>, VariableType = Location
    .ENDC

;                       * * * * * * * * * *

        BRB     Cont                    ; *** Skip past buffers

    .NCHR   NumChar___, <Label>     ; *** Determine label length
```

```
Message:                            ; *** Room for buffers
        .ASCID    "Label                    "; label + 21 blanks
MessageLength___ = . - Message - 8

TempBuf:
        .BLKB     8
                                    ; *** Floating and Hex conversions
        .IIF NB, Float, ValueLength___ = 15   ; # characters floating
        .IIF NB, Hex,   ValueLength___ = 9    ; # characters hex
        .IF NB Float'Hex
ValueDesc:                          ; Descriptor for string value
        .WORD     ValueLength___    ;   Length of string
        .BYTE     14                ;   Character string
        .BYTE     1                 ;   Mode 1
        .ADDRESS  Message+8+NumChar___ ; Address of string in Message
        .ENDC

;                       * * * * * * * * * *

Cont:   PUSHR     #^M<R0, R1, R2, R3, R4, R5>; *** Initialize
        Digits___ = 0

        .IF NB Byte                 ; *** Process bytes
          Digits___ = 3
          CVTBL    Byte, R0
        .ENDC

        .IF NB Word                 ; *** Process words
          Digits___ = 5
          CVTWL    Word, R0
        .ENDC

        .IF NB Long                 ; *** Process longwords
          Digits___ = 10
          MOVL     Long, R0
        .ENDC

        .IF NE Digits___            ; *** Convert integers
          CVTLP    R0, #Digits___, TempBuf
          CVTPS    #Digits___, TempBuf, #Digits___, -
                   Message+NumChar___+9
        .ENDC

        .IF NB ASCII                ; *** Process ASCII strings
          MOVC5    Length, ASCII, #^A" ", #MessageLength___ - 1, -
                   Message+NumChar___+9
        .ENDC

        .IF NB Float                ; *** Output Floating
          CVTFD    Float, TempBuf   ;   Convert to double
```

```
        PUSHL       #7                          ;   7 decimal places
        PUSHAL      ValueDesc                   ;   Push address of descriptor
        PUSHAD      TempBuf                     ;   Location of quad value
        CALLS       #3, G^FOR$CVT_D_TE          ;   Convert to exponential
    .ENDC

    .IF NB Hex                                  ; *** Output longword in hex
        MOVL        Hex, TempBuf                ;   Move value to TempBuf
        PUSHL       #8                          ;   Push (min) number digits
        PUSHAL      ValueDesc                   ;   Push address of descriptor
        PUSHAL      TempBuf                     ;   Push address of TempBuf
        CALLS       #3, G^OTS$CVT_L_TZ          ;   Convert value to text
    .ENDC

        PUSHAB      Message                     ; *** Output the message
        CALLS       #1, G^Lib$Put_Output
        POPR        #^M<R0, R1, R2, R3, R4, R5>
    .ENDM       Output
```

Trademarks

8080, 8086, 8088, and Intel are trademarks of Intel Corporation.
Amdahl 470 and Amdahl are trademarks of Amdahl Corporation.
CDC is a trademark of Control Data Corporation.
IBM is a registered trademark of International Business Machines, Inc.
DEC, VAX, PDP, VMS, DECnet, UNIBUS, SBI, MASSBUS, and MicroVAX
    are trademarks of Digital Equipment Corporation.
6800, 68000, and Motorola are trademarks of Motorola Corporation.

The 6800 instruction set is courtesy of Motorola Corporation.
The VAX instruction set is courtesy of Digital Equipment Corporation.
The 8080 instruction set is reprinted by permission of Intel Corporation.
    Copyright Intel Corporation, 1984.
All 8080 and 8086 mnemonics copyright Intel Corporation, 1986.

INDEX

4004, 441
6502, 11
6800, 11, 442, 446–456
  ABA, 449
  ADDB, 449
  addressing modes, 449
  PSHA, 449
  registers, 447
8008, 442
8080, 11, 442, 461–466
  addressing modes, 462
  ANA, 462
  LDAX, 466
  LXI, 462
  registers, 461
8086, 11, 466–468
  registers, 467–468
8087, 167, 468
8088, 11, 167
68000, 442, 456–460
  addressing modes, 458
  DBcc, 459
  EXG, 458
  MOVEM, 458
  registers, 456
  SWAP, 458
68020, 442

access path, 429
accumulator, 8, 44, 106
ADD instruction, 49

addition
  floating point, 170
  multiple-word, 141–142
  signed numbers, 137–139
ADDP4, 323
ADDP5, 323
addressing
  absolute, 83
  autodecrement, 76
  autoincrement, 72
  autoincrement deferred, 74
  displacement, 76
  displacement deferred, 79
  immediate, 61
  index, 83–85
  literal, 80
  register deferred, 55
  register direct, 54
  relative, 58
  relative deferred, 82
ADWC, 142
ancillary control program (ACP), 407
AND, 129, 130
answer register, 106
AP, 233
argument list, 233
argument pointer, 233
arithmetic and logic unit (ALU), 7, 127
arithmetic shift, 157
ASCII, 18, 300
ASHL, 157

Index

ASHQ, 157
assembler, 40
assembly language, 5
ASSIGN, 395
associative mapping, 357–359

backward error correction, 434
BBS, 164
BCD, 300
biased, 31
BIC, 161
BICPSW, 162
binary adders, 131
BIS, 161
BISPSW, 162
bistable, 20
BIT, 160
bit string, 164
BLBC, 161
BLBS, 161
block-set associative mapping, 358
Boolean algebra, 128
Booth algorithm, 148–151
branch instructions, 89
BRB instruction, 92
BRW instruction, 92
BSBB, 227
BSBW, 227
bus, 11

C functions, 241
C bit, 88
cache memory, 353
call by descriptor, 225
call by reference, 225
call by value, 225
call frame, 235
CALLG, 233
CALLS, 233
CDC 6600, 8, 169
central processing unit (CPU), 7
channel, 385
channel control block, 385
checksum code, 436
CLR instruction, 47
Cm*, 488
CMP instruction, 90
CMPC3, 305–306, 309, 312

CMPC5, 312, 314
CMPP3, 323
CMPP4, 323
COBOL, 325
communication
  full duplex, 421
  half duplex, 421
  layers, 429
  simplex, 421
compatibility mode, 112
compiler, 39
complete interconnection network, 483–485
complex instruction set computer (CISC), 119
concatenation, 283
condition select field, 198
conditional assembly, 286–288
conditional branch, 88–91
control memory, 180
control signals, 183–198
control unit, 7
control word, 180, 186
CPU bus, 105
Cray-1, 491–492
Cray-2, 491
Cray-XP, 491
crossbar switch, 485
CVT instruction, 326–329

D floating, 30, 31, 32
daisy chain, 380
debugger, 466, 485
DEC instruction, 93
DECnet, 431
decoder, 186–187
device controller, 12
device data register, 372
device status register, 372
diffusion layer, 443
direct dedicated complete network, 425
direct memory access, 375
direct shared bus, 426
directive
  .ADDRESS, 230
  .ALIGN LONG, 397
  .ASCIC, 301
  .ASCID, 302, 307

Index

.ASCII, 301
.ASCIZ, 301
.BLK, 64
.DISABLE, 244
.END, 64, 66, 246
.ENDC, 287
.ENDM, 270
.ENDR, 289
.ENTRY, 64, 234, 245, 249
.EXTERNAL, 244
.GLOBAL, 245, 249
.IF, 286
.IFF, 288
.IF_FALSE, 287
.IRP, 289
.LONG, 63
.MACRO, 269, 270
.NARG, 285
.NCHR, 286
.NOSHOW, 273
.PSECT, 216, 222–224
.REPEAT, 288
.SHOW, 273
.TITLE, 64
.WORD, 64
directives, 5
displacement, 58
distributed control loop, 425
distributive rule, 129
DIV instruction, 51
division
   floating point, 171
   nonrestoring, 153
   restoring, 152
   signed integers, 151–154
DIVP, 323
dynamic memory, 349
dynamic redundancy, 505

EBCDIC, 300
EDITPC, 329
EDIV, 156
effective address, 58
EMUL, 156
end-around carry, 137
entry mask, 234
Ethernet, 427
excess 128, 31
Exclusive-OR, 129, 130

exponent, 30
external subprograms, 251
EXTZV, 164

F floating, 30, 31, 32
FAB, 394
failure, 492
fan-in, 136
fan-out, 136
fast adder, 134
fault, 492
Fetch Cycle, 109
file access block, 394
flag select field, 203
floating point, 30
floating point accelerator, 168
FORTRAN, 252–253
forward error correction, 433
FP, 236
frame pointer, 236

G floating, 32
generate function, 133

H floating, 32
Hamming code, 434–436
Horner's method, 17
hybrid redundancy, 505–506

I/O unit, 8
iAPX 432, 442
IBM 360, 481
IBM 370, 11, 154, 169, 170
IBM 701, 473
Illiac IV, 473
INC instruction, 85
instruction buffer, 118
instruction cycle, 8
instruction decoder, 106
instruction processing unit, 481
instruction queue, 118
instruction register, 8, 105
INSV, 455
interblock gaps, 407
interleaved memory, 352
internal subprograms, 251

interrecord gaps, 406
interrupt acknowledge, 379
interrupt disable, 379
IO$M_CvtLow, 393
IO$_ReadPrompt, 393
IO$_ReadVBlk, 389, 391
IO$_WriteVBlk, 389
IOSB, 389

JMP instruction, 92
JSB, 227

label, 63
latency, 407
least recently used algorithm, 358
LED, 420
Lib$Get_Input, 306, 319
Lib$Put_Output, 306, 319
LIFO, 216
linker, 247–250
LOCC, 319
logic gates, 129–130

machine language, 4
macro, 5
   $ASSIGN_S, 384
   $CLOSE, 394, 398
   $CONNECT, 394, 398
   $CREATE, 394, 398
   $DASSGN_S, 384
   $EXIT_S, 65
   $FAB, 394, 395
   $GET, 394, 399
   $OPEN, 394, 398
   $PUT, 394, 399
   $QIO, 389
   $QIOW_S, 384, 388, 390
   $QIO_S, 388
   $RAB, 394, 396
   arguments, 272
   default values, 275–276
   definition, 269
   labels, 274
mantissa, 30
mapping function, 355
masking redundancy, 500
massbus, 13

MCOM, 163
MDR, 347
memory access time, 8, 355
memory address register (MAR), 106, 347
memory bank, 351
memory control circuit, 354
memory data register (MDR), 106
memory function complete (MFC), 107
memory interface, 13
memory mapped IO, 372
microinstructions, 180
microprogram counter, 180
microprogramming
   horizontal, 187
   vertical, 187
MicroVAX, 11
MIMD, 476
minuend, 139
MISD, 474
MNEG, 141
mnemonic, 39
modem, 421
MOS, 443–444
MOSFET, 444
MOV instruction, 48
MOVA instruction, 73
MOVC3, 304–305, 312
MOVC5, 312–313
MOVP, 323
MOVTC, 339
MP-1, 188–198
MTBF, 498
MUL instruction, 51
MULP, 323
multiplication
   floating point, 169
   signed integers, 146–151
   unsigned integers, 143–146

N bit, 88
NAND, 130
next address field, 199
NMR, 504–505
NOR, 130
NOT, 130
NS16000, 442
NS32032, 442

Index

Omega network, 485
one's complement, 22, 24, 137
OR, 129, 130
OTS$CVT_L_TI, 330
OutASCII, 330–336
OutFloat, 330–336
OutLong, 330–336

packed decimal, 321, 323–325
packet switch, 430
page table, 361
page table entries, 362
parity
   bit, 432
   byte, 433
   even, 432
   generalized code, 434
   odd, 432
Pascal, 253–254
PDP 8, 11
PDP 10, 11
PDP 11, 10, 11, 13, 27, 112, 115
peripheral processor, 481
permutation network, 485–487
photodiode, 420
pipeline, 120, 476–481
   clock period, 478
   efficiency, 480
   throughput, 479
polling, 378
poly layer, 443
POPL, 218
POPR, 218
priority arbitration circuit, 380
procedure call, 226
processor status longword (PSL), 105
processor status register (PSR), 8, 105
processor status word (PSW), 87–88
program counter (PC), 8, 104
program-controlled IO, 374–375
programmable read-only memory, 348
propagate function, 134
protocol, 420
PUSHA instruction, 218
PUSHL, 218
PUSHR, 218

QIO, 370, 382

RAB, 394
random access memory (RAM), 9, 348
read-only memory (ROM), 9, 348
record access block, 394
records, 393
recursion, 256–260
reduced instruction set, 118
redundant information, 432
refresh cycle, 349
register mask, 220
reliability
   function, 498
   improvement factor, 503
   mission time improvement, 503
repeat blocks, 288–290
replacement algorithm, 355
RET, 233
ripple carry adder, 133
RMS, 370, 382, 393
rotation, 157
ROTL, 157
RS 232C, 422–423
RSB, 227

SBWC, 142
seek time, 407
serial access memory (SAM), 348
sign and magnitude, 22, 137
sign extension, 146
SIMD, 474
single-bus 1 (SB-1), 104
SISD, 474
SKPC, 315
SOBGEQ, 174
SOBGTR, 262
source register, 106
spooling, 406
stack pointer, 218
star network, 427
starting address generator, 181
static memory, 349
static redundancy, 500
stream concept, 474–475
streaming, 407
SUB instruction, 50
SUBP4, 323
SUBP6, 323
subprogram, 224
subroutine call, 226

subtrahend, 139
subtraction, 139–141, 171
super rotator, 157
symbolic constant, 95
synchronous backplane interconnect, 13
synthetic division, 17
SYS$EXIT, 371

TI 9900, 442
TI Advanced Scientific Computer (TI ASC), 473, 481
TMR, 500–504
transfer time, 407, 408
tri-state logic, 185
TST instruction, 91
twos complement, 22, 23, 25–26, 138

unconditional branch, 92
UNIBUS, 13
UNIX, 5
user stack, 218

V bit, 88
VAX 11/750, 11, 183, 353, 355
VAX 11/780, 11, 13

VAX 11/785, 13, 355
VAX 8200, 13
VAX 8300, 14
VAX 8600, 14, 105, 120
VAX 8650, 14
VAX 8800, 14
VAX C, 254–255
VAX page table, 362–363
VAXBI, 14
vector interrupts, 378
virtual memory, 10, 359–363
VMS, 5
von Neumann architecture, 6, 7, 10, 473
voter, 500

word length, 11
write-through, 359

X-Tree, 491
XOFF, 423
XON, 423
XOR, 161

Z bit, 88
Z80, 442
Z8000, 442